DRAMA
IN THE WESTERN WORLD

samuel a. weiss
university of illinois, chicago circle

DRAMA
IN THE WESTERN WORLD

9 PLAYS WITH ESSAYS

d. c. heath
and
company

Acknowledgments are to be found on page 505.

Printed in the United States of America
Library of Congress Number 68-17700

contents

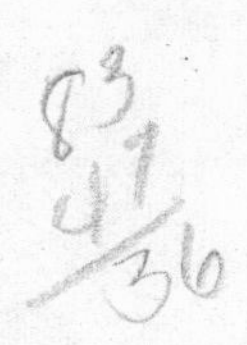

sophocles 496–406 b.c.

oedipus the king

translated by Kenneth Cavander

Sophocles, the most prolific and favored of the Greek tragic writers, stands midway between Aeschylus and Euripides in the development of Greek drama. Born of a prosperous family at the beginning of Athenian democracy, Sophocles witnessed the triumph of Athens over Persia, the succeeding fifty years of comparative peace, and the prolonged struggle with Sparta which sapped Athenian material and moral vigor and led to Athens' defeat shortly after his death. Of reputed elegance and charm, Sophocles was not only a highly honored artist—winning many competitions at the dramatic festivals—but a public figure. Of his more than one hundred plays, seven remain. The most famous of the seven are *Antigone* (c. 441 B. C.), *Oedipus the King* (c. 430 B. C.), *Electra* (c. 410 B. C.), *Philoctetes* (409 B. C.), and *Oedipus at Colonus* (406 B. C.). By adding a third actor and deepening characterization, Sophocles developed the drama far beyond its origins in choral ritual. His tragedies project man's heroic struggle with divine and human forces in an irresistible moral order whose violation, willing or unwilling, leads to disaster.

the characters

OEDIPUS, *King of Thebes*
PRIEST
CREON, *brother of* JOCASTA
TEIRESIAS, *an old, blind prophet*
JOCASTA, *wife of* OEDIPUS

MESSENGER, SHEPHERD, SERVANT

(In front of the palace of OEDIPUS *at Thebes. Near the altar stands the* PRIEST *with a large crowd of supplicants.)*
(Enter OEDIPUS.*)*

OEDIPUS My children, why do you crowd and wait at my altars?
Olive branches . . . and wreathes of sacred flowers—
Why do you bring these, my people of Thebes? Your streets
Are heavy with incense, solemn with prayers for healing,
And when I heard your voices, I would not let
My messengers tell me what you said. I came

To be your messenger myself, Oedipus, whose name
Is greatest known and greatest feared.
(to PRIEST*)* Will you tell me, then? You have dignity enough
To speak for them all—is it fear that makes you kneel
Before me, or do you need my help? I am ready,
Whatever you ask will be done . . . Come, I am not cold
Or dead to feeling—I will have pity on you.

PRIEST King Oedipus, our master in Thebes, if you will look
At your altars, and at the ages of those who kneel there,
You will see children, too small to fly far from home;
You will see old men, slow with the years they carry,
And priests—I am a priest of Zeus; and you will see
The finest warriors you have; the rest of your people
Kneel, praying, in the open city, in the temples
Of Athene, and in the shrine where we keep a flame
Always alive and the ash whispers the future.
Look about you. The whole city drowns
And cannot lift its hand from the storm of death
In which it sinks: the green corn withers
In the fields, cattle die in the meadows,
Our wives weep in agony, and never give birth!
Apollo brings his fire like a drover and herds us
Into death, and nature is at war with herself.
Thebes is sick, every house deserted, and the blind
Prison of the dead grows rich with mourning
And our dying cries.
Eternal powers control our lives, and we do not
Think you are their equal; yet we pray to you, as your children,
Believing that you, more than any man, may direct
Events, and come to terms with the powers beyond us.
When the savage riddle of the Sphinx enslaved
Thebes, you came to set us free.[1] We
Were powerless, we could not tell you how to answer her.
And now they say, and it is believed, that you
Were close to God when you raised our city from the dead.
Oedipus, we pray to your power, which can overcome
Sufferings we do not understand; guard us
From this evil. In heaven and earth there must
Be some answer to our prayer, and you may know it.
You have struggled once with the powers above us and been
Victorious; we trust that strength and believe your words.

[1]The Sphinx was a monster with the head of a woman, body of a lion, tail of a serpent, and the wings of an eagle who had been devouring all those in Thebes who could not solve her riddle. Laius had been on his way to consult the Oracle at Delphi concerning the Sphinx when Oedipus accidentally killed him on the road. Oedipus subsequently arrived in Thebes, solved the riddle, and was made King by the grateful populace. *(Translator's notes.)*

Oedipus, you are the royal glory of Thebes—
Give us life; Oedipus—think. Because
You overpowered the evil in the Sphinx
We call you saviour still. Must we remember
Your reign for the greatness in which you began, and the sorrow
In which you ended? The country is sick, and you
Must heal us. You were once our luck, our furtune, the augury
Of good we looked for in the world outside. Fulfill
That augury now. You are king of Thebes, but consider:
Which is it better to rule—a kingdom? Or a desert?
What is a castle or a ship if there are
No men to give it life? Emptiness! Nothing!

OEDIPUS My children, I know your sorrows, I know why
You have come, and what you ask of me. I see
The pain of sickness in you all, and yet in all
That sickness, who is so sick as I? Each
Of you has one sorrow, his grief is his own—
But I must feel for my country, for myself,
And for you. That is why you did not find me
Deaf or indifferent to your prayers. No,
I have spent many tears, and in my thoughts
Travelled long journeys. And then I saw
That we could be saved in one way only;
I took that way and sent Creon, my brother-
In-law, to the Oracle of Apollo; there
The god will tell him how I can save the city—
The price may be an act of sacrifice, or perhaps
A vow, a prayer, will be enough . . . But the days
Run on and the measure of time keeps pace with them
And I begin to fear. What is he doing?
I did not think he would stay so long—he should not
Stay so long! . . . But when he comes I will do
Whatever the god commands; if I disobeyed
It would be a sin.

PRIEST Heaven listened then;
This messenger says that Creon is returning.

OEDIPUS My lord Apollo, let his news be the shining sun
That answers our prayers and guides us out of death!

PRIEST I can see him now . . . the news must be good
Look, there is a crown of bay thick with flowers
Covering his hair.

OEDIPUS At last we shall know the truth.
If I shout, he will hear me . . . Creon!
My brother, son of Menoeceus, Lord of Thebes,
What answer does Apollo send to us? Do you bring
An answer?
(Enter CREON.*)*

CREON Our danger is gone. This load of sorrow

Will be lifted if we follow the way
Where Apollo points.

OEDIPUS What does this mean? I expected
Hope, or fear, but your answer gives me neither.

CREON I am ready to tell you my message now, if you wish;
But they can hear us, and if we go inside . . .

OEDIPUS Tell me now and let them hear! I must not think
Of myself; I grieve only when my people suffer.

CREON Then this is what I was told at Delphi:
Our land is tainted. We carry the guilt in our midst.
A foul disease, which will not be healed unless
We drive it out and deny it life.

OEDIPUS But how
Shall we be clean? How did this happen to us?

CREON The crime of murder is followed by a storm.
Banish the murder and you banish the storm, kill
Again and you kill the storm.

OEDIPUS But Apollo means
One man—who is this man?

CREON My lord,
There was once a king of Thebes; he was our master
Before you came to rule our broken city.

OEDIPUS I have heard of him . . . I never saw your king.

CREON Now that he is dead your mission from the god
Is clear: take vengeance on his murderers!

OEDIPUS But where are they now? The crime is old,
And time is stubborn with its secrets. How
Can you ask me to find these men?

CREON The god said
You must search in Thebes; what is hunted can
Be caught, only what we ignore escapes.

OEDIPUS Where was the murder? Was Laius killed in the city?
Or did this happen in another country?

CREON He was travelling
To Delphi, he said. But he never returned to the palace
He left that day.

OEDIPUS Did no one see this?
A messenger? The guard who watched his journey? You could
Have questioned them.

CREON They were all killed, except
One. He ran home in terror, and could only
Repeat one thing.

OEDIPUS What did he repeat?
Once we have learnt one thing, we may learn the rest.
This hope is the beginning of other hopes.

CREON He said they met some robbers who killed the king.
He talked of an army, too strong for the servants of Laius.

OEDIPUS Robbers would not dare to kill a king—unless

They had bribes. They must have had bribes from the city!
CREON We suspected that, but with Laius dead
We were defenceless against our troubles.
OEDIPUS Were
Your troubles so great that they prevented you
From knowing the truth? Your king had been murdered . . . !
CREON But the Sphinx
Had a riddle to which there was no answer, and we thought
Of our closest sorrows. We had no time for other
Mysteries.
OEDIPUS But I will begin again, and make your mysteries
Plain. Apollo was right, and you were right,
To turn my thoughts to the king who dies. Now
You will see the measure of my power; I come to defend you,
Avenging your country and the god Apollo.
(aside) If I can drive out this corruption and make the city
Whole, I shall do more than save my people,
Who are my friends, but still my subjects—I shall save
Myself. For the knife that murdered Laius may yet
Drink from my heart, and the debt I pay to him
Lies to my own credit.
My children, quickly, leave this altar and take
Your branches. I will have the people of Thebes assembled
To hear that I shall do all the god commands.
And in the end we shall see my fortune smiling
From heaven, or my fall. *(Exit* OEDIPUS.*)*
PRIEST Let us go, my sons; our king has given the order
We came to hear. May Apollo, who sent this answer
From his oracle, come to lay our sickness
To rest, and give us life.
(Exeunt PRIEST, CREON, *and some of the elders.)*

■■■

(Enter CHORUS.*)*
CHORUS From golden Delphi Apollo replies to Thebes
And the words of heaven send a warning.
As a lyre is strung and tightened, so we
Are tightened by fear.
As a lyre trembles, so we tremble at the touch of fear.
Apollo, god of healing, god of newness,
We fear you, and the commands you send to humble us.
Do you ask a new submission? Or is your command
The same as we hear in every wind, and every season, and every
year?
Only the child of golden hope, whose voice
Will never die, only the spirit of truth can tell us.
First in my prayers is the goddess Athene, the daughter of Zeus;
Second, her sister Artemis, who is queen in Thebes,

For she sits at our country's heart, pure and honoured,
In a temple like the sun. And third in our prayer
Is Phoebus Apollo, whose arm reaches over all the world.
Come three times to drive our wrongs before you!
If ever in the past, when evil and blindness
Rose like a wave, when grief was burning in our city,
If ever you banished that grief,
Come now to help us.

There is no numbering our sorrows;
The whole country is sick, and mortal will and human mind
Are no weapons to defend us.
The great earth whom we call our mother
Is barren and dead; women weep in the pain of childbirth
But they fall sick and die.
Look, can you see the dying go following each other,
Gliding like gentle birds, quicker
Then the restless flash of fire that will never sleep,
The dying on their flight to the shore
Where evening sits like a goddess?
The city of the dying goes countless away
And the children of life fall to the earth,
The toys of death,
With no pity and no remembering tears.

In the rest of our city wives and mothers
Stand grey at the altars,
Which tell us of a certainty resisting the seas of doubt;
They weep, pray, plead for release
From the harsh revenge which heaven brings.
A cry for healing rises and burns above the still crowd
That mourns in the city.
Send us strength that will look kindly on us,
Golden daughter of Zeus.
Ares, the god of war, confronts us, bitter in his cruelty,
And his shout burns like fire;
But his war is fought with no armour, and Ares
Carries no shield, for he brings his conflict
Into the moment of our birth and death.
Oh turn him flying down the winds, turn him
Back and dash him from our country
Into the wide chambers where Amphitrite sleeps,
Or to the lonely cliffs of Thrace where the seas
Allow no guests. For Ares comes to finish
The deadly work left undone by the night.
Zeus, you are the lord of lightning, lord of fire,
Destroy him with your thunder, crush our enemy!

Lord Apollo, god in the sun, we pray for your light;
Strike with your golden spears and your hands of fire,
Strike to protect us.
We pray for Artemis to bring her chaste fires,
Which we see her carry like a shining torch across
The mountains where the wolf runs.
I call you, the god with the golden crown,
Born in our country, Bacchus,
With the fire of wine in your cheek,
And the voice of wine in your shout,
Come with your pine branch burning, and your Maenads
Following the light, the fire of heaven's madness
In their eyes, come to guard us against the treacherous power
Who goes to war with justice and the harmony of heaven!

(Enter OEDIPUS.*)*

OEDIPUS You have told me of your need. Are you content
To hear me speak, obey my words, and work
To humour the sickness? . . . Then you will thrust away
The weight with which you struggle, and fulfil
Your need. I am a stranger to this story,
And to the crime; I have no signs to guide me,
And so if I am to trap this murderer, my hunt
Must follow every hope. I am speaking, then,
To every citizen of Thebes, and I shall not
Exempt myself, although I am a citizen only
In name, and not in blood.
Whoever knows the murderer of Laius, son
Of Labdacus, must make his knowledge mine.
It is the king's command! And if he is afraid,
Or thinks he will escape, I say to him, "Speak!
You will go into exile, but you will go unharmed—
Banishment is all you have to fear."
Or if you know the assassin comes from another
Country, you must not be silent. I shall pay
The value of your knowledge, and your reward
Will be more than gratitude.
But if I find only silence, if you are afraid
To betray a friend or reveal yourself, and lock
The truth away, listen, this is my decree:
This murderer, no matter who he is, is banished
From the country where my power and my throne
Are supreme. No one must shelter him or speak to him;
When you pray to heaven, he must not pray with you;
When you sacrifice, drive him away, do not
Give him holy water, beat him from your doors!
He carries the taint of corruption with him—for so

The god Apollo has revealed to me . . . You see
How I serve the god and revenge the king who died!
I curse that murderer; if he is alone, I curse him!
If he shares his guilt with others, I curse him! May
His evil heart beat out its years in sorrow,
Throughout his life may he breathe the air of death!
If I give him shelter, knowing who
He is, and let him feel the warmth of my fire,
I ask this punishment for myself.
This must de done! In every word I speak
I command obedience, and so does the god Apollo,
And so does your country, which a barren sickness
And an angry heaven drag to death. But even
If it is not a god that comes to punish you
It would be shame to leave your land impure.
Your king was killed—he was a royal and noble
Man; hunt his murderer down!
I live in Laius' palace, my queen was once
The queen of Laius, and if his line had prospered
His children would have shared my love.
But now time has struck his head to earth
And in revenge I will fight for him as I
Would fight for my own father. My search will never
End until I take in chains the murderer
Of Laius, son of Labdacus. I pray heaven
That those who will not help me may watch the soil
They have ploughed crumble and turn black, let them see
Their women barren, let them be destroyed by the fury
That scourges us, but may it rage more cruelly!
And for all the Thebans who will obey me gladly
I ask the strength of justice, and the power of heaven.
So we shall live in peace; so we shall be healed.

CHORUS Your curse menaces me, my lord, if I lie.
I swear I did not kill him, nor can I tell
Who did. Apollo sent the reply, and Apollo
Should find the murderer.

OEDIPUS Yes, we believe
It is Apollo's task—but we cannot make
The gods our slaves; we must act for ourselves.

CHORUS Our next
Hope then, must be . . .

OEDIPUS And every hope
You have. When I search, nothing escapes.

CHORUS We know a lord who sees as clearly as the lord
Apollo—Teiresias; we could ask Teiresias, my king,
And be given the truth.

OEDIPUS Creon told me, and his advice
Did not lie idle for want of action. I have sent

Two servants . . . It is strange they are not here.
CHORUS And there are the old rumours—but they tell us nothing . . .
OEDIPUS What do these rumours say? I must know
Everything.
CHORUS They say some travellers killed him.
OEDIPUS I have heard that too. But the man who saw those travelers
Was never seen himself.
CHORUS The murderer will leave our country;
There is a part of every man that is ruled
By fear, and when he hears your curse . . .
OEDIPUS A sentence
Holds no terror for the man who is not afraid
To kill.
CHORUS But now he will be convicted. Look,
They are leading your priest to you; Teiresias comes.
When he speaks, it is the voice of heaven
That we hear.
(Enter TEIRESIAS, *guided by a boy.)*
OEDIPUS Teiresias, all things lie
In your power, for you have harnessed all
Knowledge and all mysteries; you know what heaven
Hides, and what runs in the earth below, and you
Must know, though you cannot see,[2] the sickness with which
Our country struggles. Defend us, my lord, and save us—
We shall find no other defence or safety.
For Apollo—and yet you must hae heard the message—
Apollo, whom we asked in our doubt, promised release—
But on one condition: that we find the murderers
Of Laius, and banish them, or repay the murder.
Teiresias, the singing birds will tell you of the future,
You have many ways of knowing the truth. Do not grudge
Your knowledge, but save yourself and your city, save me,
For murder defiles us all. Think of us
As your prisoners, whose lives belong to you!
To have the power and use that power for good
Is work to bring you honour.
TEIRESIAS When truth cannot help
The man who knows, then it brings terror. I knew
That truth, but I stifled it. I should not have come.
OEDIPUS What is it? You come as sadly as despair.
TEIRESIAS Send me away, I tell you! Then it will be easy
For you to play the king, and I the priest.
OEDIPUS This is no reply. You cannot love Thebes—your own

[2]Athena, who was supposed to have blinded Teiresias for having inadvertently seen her bathing, was later moved to endow him with prophetic insight.

Country, Teiresias—if you hide what tde gods tell you.
TEIRESIAS I see your words guiding you on the wrong
Path; I pray for my own escape.
OEDIPUS Teiresias!
You do not turn away if you know the truth; we all
Come like slaves to a king with our prayers to you.
TEIRESIAS But you come without the truth, and I can never
Reveal my own sorrows, lest they become
Yours.
OEDIPUS You cannot? Then you know and will not tell us!
Instead, you plan treason and the city's death.
TEIRESIAS I mean to protect us both from pain. You search
And probe, and it is all wasted. I will not tell you!
OEDIPUS You demon! You soul of evil! You would goad
A thing of stone to fury. Will you never speak?
Can you feel, can you suffer? Answer me, and end this!
TEIRESIAS You see wrong in my mood, you call me evil—blind
To the mood that settles in you and rages there.
OEDIPUS Rages! Yes, that is what your words
Have done, when they shout your contempt for Thebes.
TEIRESIAS The truth will come; my silence cannot hide it.
OEDIPUS And what must come is what you must tell me.
TEIRESIAS I can tell you no more, and on this answer let
Your fury caper like a beast.
OEDIPUS It is
A fury that will never leave me. Listen, I know
What you are. I see now that you conspired to plan
This murder, and you committed it—all but the stroke
That killed him. If you had eyes, I would have said
The crime was yours alone.
TEIRESIAS Oedipus, I warn you!
Obey your own decree and the oath you swore.
Never from this day speak to me, or to these nobles;
Your are our corruption, the unholiness in our land.
OEDIPUS How you must despise me to flaunt your scorn like this,
Thinking you will escape. How?
TEIRESIAS I have escaped.
I carry the truth; it is my child, and guards me.
OEDIPUS Truth! Who taught you? Heaven never taught you!
TEIRESIAS You taught me; you forced me to the point of speech.
OEDIPUS Repeat your words, I do not remember this speech.
TEIRESIAS You did not understand? Or do you try to trap me?
OEDIPUS I know nothing! Repeat your truth!
TEIRESIAS I said, you are the murderer you are searching for.
OEDIPUS Again you attack me, but I will not forgive you again!
TEIRESIAS Shall I say more to make your anger sprawl?
OEDIPUS All you have breath for—it will all be useless.
TEIRESIAS Then . . . you live with your dearest one in burning

Shame, and do not know it- nor can you see
The evil that surrounds you.

OEDIPUS Do you think
You will always smile in freedom if you talk like this?

TEIRESIAS If truth can give strength, I will.

OEDIPUS It can—
But not to you; you have no truth. Your senses
Have died in you—ears: deaf! eyes: blind!

TEIRESIAS Yes, be bitter, mock at me, poor Oedipus.
Soon they will all mock as bitterly at you.

OEDIPUS You live in perpetual night; you cannot harm
Me, nor anyone who moves in the light.

TEIRESIAS Your downfall
Will come, but I will not be the cause. Apollo
Is a great power; he watches over the end.

OEDIPUS Did you or Creon plan this?

TEIRESIAS Creon is not
Your enemy; you carry your enemy with you—in your soul.

OEDIPUS We have wealth and power, the mind reaches higher, grows,
Breaks its own fetters, our lives are great and envied,
And the world rewards us—with spitefulness and hate!
Consider my power—I did not come begging, the city
Laid its submission in my hands as a gift.
Yet, for this power, Creon, my trusted, my first
Friend, goes like a thief behind my back,
Tries to exile me, and sends this wizard,
This patcher of threadbare stories, this cunning peddler
Of the future, with no eyes except
For money, and certainly no eyes for mysteries.
Tell me, tell me, when did you ever foretell the truth?
When the Sphinx howled her mockeries and riddles
Why could you find no answer to free the city?
Her question was too hard for the simple man,
The humble man; only heaven's wisdom could find
A reply. But you found none!Neither your birds
Above you, nor the secret voice of your inspiration
Sent you knowledge—then we saw what you were!
But I came, ignorant Oedipus, and silenced her,
And my only weapon was in my mind and my will;
I had no omens to teach me. And this is the man
You would usurp! You think, when Creon is king
You will sit close to the throne; but I think
Your plans to drive the accursed away will return
To defeat you, and to defeat their architect.
You are old, Teiresias, or else your prophetic wisdom
Would have been your death.

CHORUS Your majesty, what he has said

And your reply—they were both born in anger.
We do not need this wildness; we ask the best
Fulfillment of Apollo's commands. This must be the search.

TEIRESIAS *(to* OEDIPUS*)* Your flourish your power; but you must give me the right
To make my reply, and that will have equal power.
I have not lived to be your servant, but Apollo's;
Nor am I found in the list of those whom Creon
Protects. You call me blind, you jeer at me—
I say your sight is not clear enough to see
Who shares your palace, nor the rooms in which you walk,
Nor the sorrow about you. Do you know who gave you birth?
You are the enemy of the dead, and of the living,
And do not know it. The curse is a two-edged sword,
From your mother, from your father; the curse will hunt you,
Like a destruction, from your country. Now
You have sight, but then you will go in blindness;
When you know the truth of your wedding night
All the world will bear your crying to rest,
Every hill a Cithaeron to echo you.
You thought that night was peace, like a gentle harbour—
But there was no harbour for that voyage, only grief.
Evil crowds upon you; you do not see
How it will level you with your children and reveal
Yourself as you truly are. Howl your abuse
At Creon and at me . . . All men must suffer,
Oedipus, but none will find suffering more terrible
Than you.

OEDIPUS Must I bear this? Must I be silent?
Die! Go to your death! Leave my palace now!
Get away from me!

TEIRESIAS Yet you called me here, or I would not have come.

OEDIPUS If I had known you would talk in the raving language
Of a madman, I would never have sent for you.

TEIRESIAS I am no more than you see. You see a madman,
The parents who gave you life saw a prophet.

OEDIPUS My parents? Wait! Who were my parents?

TEIRESIAS Today will be your parent, and your murderer.

OEDIPUS Always riddles, always lies and riddles!

TEIRESIAS You were best at solving riddles, were you not?

OEDIPUS When you think of my greatness, it inspires your mockery.

TEIRESIAS That greatness has conspired to be your traitor.

OEDIPUS I saved this country, I care for nothing else.

TEIRESIAS Then I shall go . . . *(to his guide)* Boy, lead me away.

OEDIPUS Yes lead him . . . You come and trouble me—you are nothing
But hindrance to my plans. Go, and I shall be safe.

TEIRESIAS I came to speak, and I shall not leave until I speak.
I need not cower at your frown, you cannot
Harm me. This man for whom you search,
Whom you threaten,and to the people call "the murderer
Of Laius," this man is here, a stranger, a foreigner;
But he will see his Theban blood, though he will not
Have any joy at the discovery.
He will be blind—though now he sees; a beggar—
Though now he is rich, and he will go feeling
Strange ground before him with a stick.
He is a father to children—then he will
Be called their brother; he is his mother's son—
Then he will be called her husband, then
He will be called his father's murderer.
Consider this when you walk between your palace walls;
If you find I have been false to you, then say
That all my prophetic wisdom is a lie.
(Exeunt all but the CHORUS*)*

■■■

CHORUS In the rock at Delphi there is a cave
Which is the mouth of heaven; now
The cave warns us of one man, whose hands are red
With murder, and whose actions
Break the unspoken laws that shackle us.
Time tells him now to escape,
Faster than the jostling horses of the storm,
For Apollo, the son of Zeus, leaps down on him,
Armed with lightning, dressed in fire,
And the terrible avengers follow where he goes,
The Furies who never mistake and are never cheated.
From the snow of Parnassus over Delphi the message
Gleamed and came shining to Thebes.
We must all hunt the murderer
Who hides from justice. Like a lonely bull
He crosses and crosses our country, through the harsh
forests,
The hollows of the mountains, and the rocks.
Sadly thinking and alone,
Sadly trying to escape
The words that came from Delphi, the heart of the world.
But their wings are always beating in his head.

The wisdom of the priest sets fear, fear, beating in
our blood;
Truth or lies, nothing comforts, nothing denies.
The world is built out of our beliefs,
And when we lose those beliefs in doubt,

Our world is destroyed, and the present and the past
Vanish into night.
We must have proof, a certainty that we can touch
And feel, before we turn against Oedipus.
The land is peopled with rumours and whispers—
They cannot make us avenge King Laius,
Whose death is guarded by such mystery.

All that men may do is watched and remembered
By Zeus, and by Apollo. But they are gods;
Can any man, even the prophet, the priest,
Can even he know more than us?
And if he can, who will be judge of him, and say he lied
Or spoke the truth.
Yet wisdom may come to us, not the wisdom that sees
How the world is ruled, but the wisdom that guides
The modest life. In this alone we may excel.
But the proof must be clear and certain,
Before I can accuse Oedipus.
Remember that the Sphinx came flying
To meet him, evil beyond our comprehension,
And we saw his wisdom then, we knew and felt
The goodness of his heart towards our country.
Thoughts cannot be guilty traitors to such a man.

(Enter CREON.*)*

CREON Lords of Thebes, this message has called me here
In terror . . . These crimes of which our king accuses me—
No one would dare to think of them! If he
Believes I could wrong him, or even speak of wrong,
At such a time, when we are in such sorrow,
Let me die! I have no wish to live out my years
If I must live them suspected and despised.
I will not bear this slander, which is no trifle
To forget, but the greatest injury—the name
Of traitor. The people will call me that, even
You will call me that!

CHORUS His fury mastered him;
Perhaps he did not mean the charge.

CREON He said
To you all—you all heard—that the priest
Had been told to lie, and that I had planned the answer?

CHORUS He said that, but I know he did not mean it.

CREON And when he
Accused me, he seemed master of his thoughts, and there was
Reason in his voice?

CHORUS I cannot remember,
I do not observe my king so closely . . . But here

He comes from the palace himself to meet you.
(Enter OEDIPUS.*)*

OEDIPUS So,
My citizen, you have come to your king? Your eyes have great
Courage—they can look on my palace out of a murderer's
Face, a robber's face! Yes, I know you;
You blaze, you thief of power . . . In heaven's name
Tell me: when you planned to kill me, did you think I had
Become a coward or a fool? Did you think I would not
Notice your treason stalking me? Or were you sure
That if I knew, I would not dare defence?
See your insane attempt! You try to capture
Power, which must be hunted with armies and gold;
But no one will follow you, no one will make
You rich!

CREON Wait! You have accused,but you must not judge
Until you have heard my defence; I can reply.

OEDIPUS You talk with the fangs of cleverness; but how
Can I understand? I understand only
That you are my enemy, and dangerous.

CREON There is one thing I must say; hear it first.

OEDIPUS One thing you must not say: "I am innocent."

CREON You are stubborn, Oedipus, your will is too hard;
It is nothing to treasure, and you are wrong to think it is.

OEDIPUS Treason, crimes against a brother, will not
Escape justice: you are wrong to think they will.

CREON I do not quarrel with your talk of justice.
But tell me how I have harmed you: what is my crime?

OEDIPUS Did you persuade me—perhaps you did not—to send for
The priest whom we used to worship for his wisdom?

CREON And I still have faith in that advice.

OEDIPUS How long
Is it since Laius . . .

CREON What has Laius to do
With this? I do not see . . .

OEDIPUS Since he was hidden
From the living sun, since he was attacked and killed?

CREON The years are old and the time is long since then.

OEDIPUS Was Teiresias already a priest and prophet then?

CREON As wise as now, and no less honoured and obeyed.

OEDIPUS But at the time he did not mention me?

CREON I did not hear him . . .

OEDIPUS But surely you tried to find
The murderer?

CREON We searched, of course, we could discover
Nothing.

OEDIPUS
If I was guilty, why did Teiresias

Not accuse me then? He must have known, for he is wise.
CREON I do not know. If I cannot know the truth
I would rather be silent.
OEDIPUS But there is one truth
You will confess to; none knows it better . . .?
CREON What is that? I shall deny nothing . . .
OEDIPUS That only by some insidious plan of yours
Could Teiresias ever say I murdered Laius!
CREON If he says that, I cannot unsay it for him;
But give me an answer in return for mine.
OEDIPUS Question till you have no questions left;
You cannot prove me a murderer.
CREON Now,
You have married my sister?
OEDIPUS I do not deny it; the truth
Was in your question.
CREON You and she rule
This country, you are equal?
OEDIPUS If she has a wish
I grant it all to her.
CREON And am I not
Considered equal to you both?
OEDIPUS Yes, there your friendship
Shows the face of evil it concealed.
CREON No, reason to yourself as I have reasoned.
First, imagine two ways of ruling, each
Bringing equal power. With one of these fear
Never leaves you, but with the other you sleep
Calm in the night. Who do you think
Would not choose the second? I feel no ambition
To be the king, when I have the power of a king.
For I have my place in the world, I know it, and will not
Overreach myself. Now, you give me all
I wish, and no fear comes with the gift;
But if I were king myself, much more would be forced
Upon me. Why should I love the throne better
Than a throne's power and a throne's majesty
Without the terrors of a throne? Now,
I may smile to all, and all will bow to me;
Those who need you petition me,
For I am their hopes of success. Is this such a worthless
Life that I should exchange it for yours? Treason
Is for those who cannot value what they have.
I have never had longing thoughts about your power,
Nor would I help a man who had. Send
To Delphi, make a test of me, ask the god
Whether my message was true, and if you find
I have plotted with your priest, then you may kill me—

I will be your authority, I will assent
When you decree my death. But do not accuse me
Yet, when you know nothing. You wrong your friends
To think them enemies, as much as you do wrong
To take enemies for friends. Think, be sure!
You banish life from your body—and life you love
Most dearly—by banishing a good friend.
Time will set this knowledge safely in your heart;
Time alone shows the goodness in a man—
One day is enough to tell you all his evil.

CHORUS My king, a cautious man would listen; beware
Of being convinced too quickly. Suddenness is not safety.

OEDIPUS When the attack is quick and sudden, and the plot
Runs in the darkness, my thoughts must be sudden
In reply. If I wait, sitting in silence,
He will have done his work, and I lost
My chance to begin.

CREON Your decision then! Will you
Banish me?

OEDIPUS No, not banishment; I
Will have your life! You must teach men the rewards
That I keep for the envious and the cruel.

CREON Will you not listen to persuasion and the truth?

OEDIPUS You will never persuade me that you speak the truth.

CREON No, I can see you are blind to truth.

OEDIPUS I see
Enough to guard my life.

CREON My life is as precious
To me.

OEDIPUS But you are a traitor!

CREON You know nothing!

OEDIPUS Yet the king must rule.

CREON Not when the king is evil.

OEDIPUS My city! My city!

CREON It is my city too, do not forget that!

CHORUS Stop, my lords! Look, here is Jocasta coming to you
From the palace, at the moment when she may help you
To bring this quarrel to rest.

(Enter JOCASTA.*)*

JOCASTA My lords, it is pitiful to hear your senseless voices
Shouting and wrangling. Have you no shame? Our country
Is sick, and you go bustling about your private
Quarrels. My king, you must go inside, and you,
Creon, go to the palace. At this time
We have no troubles except the plague; all
Others are pretence.

CREON My sister, your sovereign, Oedipus,
Condemns me cruelly in his efforts to be just.

He will banish me, or murder me; in both he does wrong.
OEDIPUS No, I have found a traitor, my queen, who plots
Against my life.
CREON Never let me breathe
In freedom again, let me die under your curse,
If I am guilty of those crimes!
JOCASTA Oh, Oedipus,
Believe him. Believe him for the sake of those words
That heaven witnessed; you have a duty to that oath,
And to me, and to your people.
CHORUS Obey her, my lord, I beg you; do not be harsh,
Be wise.
OEDIPUS Must I be ruled by you?
CHORUS Creon was always wise and faithful in the past; his oath
was great
And you must respect it.
OEDIPUS You know what you are asking?
CHORUS I know.
OEDIPUS Tell me, what do you advise?
CHORUS He is your friend—that is a truth
As simple as the light of day;
But only confused and uncertain rumours call him traitor;
No cause to rob him of his honour.
OEDIPUS But listen, in asking this, you ask
For my banishment, or for my death.
CHORUS No! By the sun who is prince of the sky!
If that was ever my intention,
I pray for death, without friends on earth
Without love in heaven,
Death in pain and misery.
Now, now, when the decaying earth eats our lives
Away, will you add your quarrels to all
That we already suffer?
OEDIPUS Let him go then; I shall die, I do not care;
I shall be driven into banishment and disgrace.
I do this for love and pity of you. For him, I feel none;
Wherever he goes, he cannot escape my hatred.
CREON For you submission is a torment—you do not hide it.
And when you force your way against the world
You crush us all beneath you. Such natures
Find their own company most terrible to bear.
It is their punishment.
OEDIPUS Leave my sight, then! Leave me to myself!
CREON I shall leave you. In all the time you knew me,
You never understood me . . . They see my innocence. *(Exit* CREON.*)*
CHORUS My queen, take our king to the palace now.
JOCASTA I must know what has happened.
CHORUS Doubt and suspicion. Oedipus spoke without thinking;

He was unjust, and Creon cannot bear injustice.
JOCASTA Both were to blame?
CHORUS Yes.
JOCASTA What was said?
CHORUS The country is weary with sickness already;
I am content, content to go no further
And let the evil rest.
OEDIPUS You see what you have done, you good,
Good adviser? My temper was a spear
And you have turned the edge and blunted it.
CHORUS Your majesty, I have repeated many times–
But I tell you again;
I would have been robbed of all my senses,
Emptied of all my reason,
If I caused your death.
You came like the wind we pray for in danger,
When the storm was conquering us with sorrows,
And carried our country into safety. Again
You may bring a spirit to guide us.
JOCASTA But I still do not know why you were quarrelling, my king,
And I must know, for they talked of your death.
OEDIPUS Jocasta,
You may command me when even my people may not,
And I let Creon go. But he had conspired
Against me . . .
JOCASTA Treason! Is this true? Can you prove it?
OEDIPUS He says I am Laius' murderer.
JOCASTA How
Can he know? Has he always known, or has someone told him?
OEDIPUS He sent that priest Teiresias, the wicked Teiresias.
Creon's lips do not commit themselves to words!
JOCASTA Then set all this talk aside and listen. I
Will teach you that no priest, no holy magic
Can know your future or your destiny. And my proof
Is as short as the stroke of a knife. Once, an oracle
Came to Laius–I will not say it was from
Apollo–but from Apollo's priests. It told him
He was destined to be murdered by the son that I
Would bear to him. But Laius, so they say,
Was murdered by robbers from another country at a place
Where three roads meet. A son was born
To us, but lived no more than three days. Yes,
Laius pinned his ankles together and sent him
Away to die on a distant, lonely mountain.
Once he was there, no power could make him a murderer,
Nor make Laius die at the hands of his son–
And he feared that above anything in the world.

You see how you may rely upon priests and their talk
Of the future. Never notice them! When god wishes
The truth discovered, he will easily work his will.

OEDIPUS As I listened, my queen, my thoughts went reaching out
And touched on memories that make me shudder . . .

JOCASTA What memories? You stare as if you were trapped.

OEDIPUS You said—I heard you say—that Laius' blood
Was spilt at a place where three roads meet.

JOCASTA We were all told that, and no one has denied it.

OEDIPUS And where is the place where this happened?

JOCASTA The country
Is called Phocis; the road splits, to Delphi
And to Daulia.

OEDIPUS When did all this happen?

JOCASTA The city was given the news a little before
You became king of Thebes.

OEDIPUS God,
What do you hold prepared for me?

JOCASTA Oedipus!
What made you frown when I talked of your becoming king?

OEDIPUS Do not ask me yet . . . Laius—what was he like?
His appearance, his age, describe them to me.

JOCASTA He was tall, his hair beginning to be flecked with a down
Of white; he was built like you . . .

OEDIPUS Stop! You torture me!
I have hurled myself blindly against unthinking
Fury and destruction!

JOCASTA How? I cannot bear
To watch you, my lord.

OEDIPUS So little hope is frightening.
Listen, Teiresias the priest was not blind!
But one more answer, one more, will be better proof.

JOCASTA I dare not answer; but if my answers help you,
Ask.

OEDIPUS When he left Thebes, was he alone,
Or did he have a company of men at arms
So that all could recognize he was a king?

JOCASTA No, five were all the travellers, and one
Was a herald. A single chariot carried Laius . . .

OEDIPUS Yes! Now I see the truth . . . Who told you this?

JOCASTA A servant, the only man who returned alive.

OEDIPUS Is he still in the palace with us?

JOCASTA No, after
He escaped, and found that you were king, and Laius
Dead, he implored me by my duty to a suppliant
To send him away. To the country, he said, herding
Sheep on the hillsides, where he could never see
The city he had left . . . And I let him go; he was

A good servant, deserving more than this
Small favour.

OEDIPUS He must be found at once;
Can this be done?

JOCASTA Yes, but why do you want him?

OEDIPUS My queen, as I look into myself I begin to fear;
I had no right to say those things, and so
I must see this man.

JOCASTA He will come. But I
Expect to be told your sorrows, my king, when they weigh
So heavily.

OEDIPUS And I will not refuse you, Jocasta.
I have come to face such thoughts, and who should hear
Of them before you? I walk among
Great menaces.
My father is king of Corinth – Polybus; my mother –
Merope from Doris. In Corinth I was called
Their prince, their greatest noble, until
This happened to me – it was strange, yet not
So strange as to deserve my thoughts so much.
A man, stuffed with wine at a feast, called out
To me as he drank. He said I was a son only
In the imagination of my father. Anger
And pain would not let me rest that day; the next
I went to my parents and questioned them. They answered
The drunkard harshly for his insulting story,
And for their sakes I was glad he lied. Yet I always
Felt the wound, and the story spread in whispers.
At last I went to Delphi – my parents did not know –
But Apollo thought me unworthy of an answer
To that question. Instead he foretold many trials,
Many dangers, many sorrows. I was to be
My mother's husband, I was to murder my own
Father, my children would carry the guilt and none
Would dare look on them. When I heard this
I ran from my home and afterwards knew the land
Only by the stars that stood above it.
Never must I see the shame of that evil prophecy
Acted out by me in Corinth. I travelled
Until I came to this place where you say your king
Was killed . . . My wife, this is the truth . . . I will tell you . . .
My journey brought me to the meeting of three roads;
And there a herald, and an old man who rode
A chariot drawn by mares, came towards me . . .
Jocasta, the rider was like the man you described!
He and the herald, who went in front, tried
To force me out of their path. In a rage I struck
The one who touched me, the servant at the wheel.

The old man watched me, and waited till I was passing;
Then from the chariot he aimed at the crown of my head
With the twin prongs of his goad. It was a costly
Action! Slashing with my stick I cut at him
And my blow tumbled him backwards out of the chariot—
Then I killed them all! If this man I met may be said
To resemble Laius, to be, perhaps, Laius,
I stand condemned to more sorrow than any man,
More cursed by an evil power than any man.
No one in Thebes, no stranger, may shelter me
Or speak to me; they must hunt me from their doors.
And I, it was I, who cursed myself, cursed myself!
And the dead king's pillow is fouled by the touch
Of my murdering hands. Is the evil in my soul?
Is my whole nature tainted? Must I go into exile,
Never see my people again, nor turn home
And set foot in Corinth?—for if I do, I must wed
My mother, and kill my father—Polybus, who gave me
Life and youth. Can you see this happen, and then
Deny that a cruel power has come to torture me?
No! You heavens, you pure light and holiness!
Let me die before that day, hide me before
I feel that black corruption in my soul!

CHORUS My king, this is a frightening story. But hope,
Until you hear from the man who saw what happened.

OEDIPUS Yes, that is all the hope I have. Oedipus
Waits for one man, and he is a shepherd.

JOCASTA What makes you so eager for him to come?

OEDIPUS I reason like this. We may find that his story
Matches yours. Then I shall be as free
As if this had never happened.

JOCASTA Was there anything in what
I said that could have such power?

OEDIPUS You said
He told you robbers murdered Laius. If he still
Says "robbers" and not "a robber," I am innocent.
One man cannot be taken for many.
But if he says a murderer, alone,
The guilt comes to rest on me.

JOCASTA But we all
Heard him say "robbers"; that is certain. He cannot
Unsay it. I am not alone, for the whole city heard.
But even if he swerves a little from his old account,
That will not prove you Laius' murderer,
Not in truth, not in justice. For Apollo said
He was to be killed by a son that was born to me . . .
And yet my son, poor child, could not have killed him,
For he died first . . . but that shows the deceit

Of prophecies. They beckon at you, but I
Would fix my eyes ahead, and never look at them!

OEDIPUS You are right. Nevertheless send someone
To bring me that servant; do not forget.

JOCASTA Yes,
I will send now. Let us go to the palace;
I would do nothing that could harm or anger you.
(Exeunt all but the CHORUS.*)*

■■■

CHORUS All actions must beware of the powers beyond us, and each word
Must speak our fear of heaven. I pray
That I may live every hour in obedience.
The laws that hold us in subjection
Have always stood beyond our reach, conceived
In the high air of heaven. Olympus
Was their sire, and no woman on earth
Gave them life. They are laws
That will never be lured to sleep in the arms of oblivion,
And in their strength heaven is great and cannot grow old.
Yet man desires to be more than man, to rule
His world for himself.
This desire, blown to immensity
On the rich empty food of its ambition,
Out of place, out of time,
Clambers to the crown of the rock, and stands there,
Tottering; then comes the steepling plunge down to earth,
To the earth where we are caged and mastered.
But this desire may work for good
When it fights to save a country, and I pray
That heaven will not weaken it then.
For then it comes like a god to be our warrior
And we shall never turn it back.

Justice holds the balance of all things,
And we must fear her.
Do not despise the frontiers in which we must live,
Do not cross them, do not talk of them,
But bow before the places where the gods are throned.
Time will come with cruel vengeance on the man
Who disobeys; that is the punishment
For those who are proud and are more than men—
They are humbled.
If a man grows rich in defiance of this law,
If his actions trespass on a world that he should fear,
If he reaches after mysteries that no man should know,
No prayer can plead for him when the sword of heaven is raised.

If he were to glory in success
All worship would fall dumb.

Delphi is the heart of the world and holds its secrets;
The temple of Zeus, and Olympia, command our prayers;
But we shall never believe again
Until the truth of this murder is known.
Let us be sure of our beliefs, give us proof.
Zeus, you may do your will; do not forget that you are immortal,
Your empire cannot die; hear our prayers.
For the oracle given to Laius in the years of the long past
Is dying and forgotten, wiped from the memory,
Apollo's glory turns to shadows,
And all divinity to ruin.

(Enter JOCASTA.*)*

JOCASTA My lords, I have been summoned by my thoughts
To the temples of the gods, and I have brought
These garlands and this incense for an offering.
Oedipus is like a lonely bird among
The terrors that flock about his mind. He forgets
His wisdom, and no longer thinks the past will guide him
When he tries to foresee the future. Instead, he is
The slave of any word that talks of fear.
I try to reach him, to make him see that there is hope,
But it is useless; I have failed. And so I turn
To you, Apollo, nearest to us in Thebes,
A suppliant with prayers and gifts. Resolve this doubt
By sending the truth. He is the guide and master
Of our ship. What shall we do when even he
Is struck into bewilderment?
(Enter MESSENGER.*)*

MESSENGER I do not know this country. Will you show me the palace
Of King Oedipus? I must find King Oedipus . . .
Do you know where he is?

CHORUS This is his palace, sir.
He is inside, and you see his queen before you.

MESSENGER Heaven give her and all she loves riches
And happiness if she is the queen of such a king.

JOCASTA I return your greeting. You have spoken well and deserve
Well wishing. But what do you want with Oedipus?
Or do you bring a message for us?

MESSENGER A message
Of good, for your palace and your husband, my queen.

JOCASTA What is it? Who sent you here?

MESSENGER I come from Corinth.
My story may be quickly told. You will be glad, of course,

For the news is glad, and yet . . . yet you may grieve.
JOCASTA Well, what is this story with a double meaning?
MESSENGER The people of Corinth—it was already announced
There—will make Oedipus their king.
JOCASTA But why?
Your king is Polybus. He is wise, revered . . .
MESSENGER But no longer our king. Death hugs him to the earth.
JOCASTA Is this true? Polybus is dead?
MESSENGER By my hopes of living out my years, it is true.
JOCASTA Servant, go, tell this to your master. Run!
(Exit SERVANT.*)*
Where are the prophecies of heaven now? Always
Oedipus dreaded to kill this man, and hid
From him. But look, Polybus has been murdered
By the careless touch of time, and not by Oedipus.
(Enter OEDIPUS.*)*
OEDIPUS Dear Jocasta, dear wife, why have you called me
Here from the palace?
JOCASTA This man brings a message;
Listen, and then ask yourself what comes
Of the oracles from heaven that used to frighten us.
OEDIPUS Who is this man? What has he to say to me?
JOCASTA He comes from Corinth, and his message is the death
Of Polybus. You will never see Polybus again!
OEDIPUS You said that, stranger? Let me hear you say that plainly.
MESSENGER Since you force me to give that part of my message first,
I repeat, he walks among the dead.
OEDIPUS A plot?
Or did sickness conspire to kill him?
MESSENGER A small
Touch on the balance sends old lives to sleep.
OEDIPUS So, my poor father, sickness murdered you.
MESSENGER And many years had measured out his life.
OEDIPUS Oh look, look, who would listen to Apollo
Talking in his shrine at Delphi, or notice birds
That clamour to the air? They were the signs
That told me—and I believed—that I would kill
My father. But now he has the grave to protect him,
While I stand here, and I never touched a sword . . .
Unless he died of longing to see me—
Then perhaps he died because of me. No!
Polybus lies in darkness, and all those prophecies
Lie with him, chained and powerless.
JOCASTA I told you long ago how it would happen . . .
OEDIPUS Yes, but I was led astray by fears.
JOCASTA Then think no more of them; forget them all.
OEDIPUS Not all. The marriage with my mother—I think of it.

JOCASTA But is there anything a man need fear, if he knows
That chance is supreme throughout the world, and he cannot
See what is to come? Give way to the power
Of events and live as they allow! It is best.
Do not fear this marriage with your mother. Many
Men have dreams, and in those dreams they wed
Their mothers. Life is easiest, if you do not try
To oppose these things that seem to threaten us.
OEDIPUS You are right, and I would agree with all
You say, if my mother were not alive. And though
You are right, I must fear. She is alive.
JOCASTA Think of your father, and his grave.
There is a light to guide you.
OEDIPUS It does guide me!
I know he . . . But she is alive and I am afraid.
MESSENGER You are afraid of a woman, my lord?
OEDIPUS Yes,
Merope—Polybus was her husband.
MESSENGER How can you be afraid of her?
OEDIPUS A prophecy warned me
To beware of sorrow . . .
MESSENGER Can you speak of it, or are you
Forbidden to talk of these things to others?
OEDIPUS No,
I am not forbidden. The Oracle at Delphi
Has told me my destiny—to be my mother's husband
And my father's murderer. And so I left
Corinth, many years ago and many
Miles behind me. The word has rewarded me richly,
And yet all those riches are less than the sight
Of a parent's face.
MESSENGER And you went into exile because
You feared this marriage?
OEDIPUS And to save myself from becoming
My father's murderer.
MESSENGER Then, my king,
I ought to have freed you from that fear since I
Wished to be thought your friend.
OEDIPUS Your reward
Will be measured by my gratitude.
MESSENGER I had hoped for reward
When you returned as king of your palace in Corinth.
OEDIPUS I must never go where my parents are.
MESSENGER My son,
You do not know what you say; I see you do not.
OEDIPUS How, sir? Tell me quickly.
MESSENGER . . . If you live in exile
Because of Polybus and Merope.

OEDIPUS Yes, and I live
In fear that Apollo will prove he spoke the truth.
MESSENGER And it is from your parents that the guilt is to come?
OEDIPUS Yes, stranger, the fear never leaves my side.
MESSENGER You have no cause to be afraid—do you know that?
OEDIPUS No cause? But they were my parents—that is the cause!
MESSENGER No cause, because they were not your parents, Oedipus.
OEDIPUS What do you mean? Polybus was not my father?
MESSENGER As much as I, and yet no more than I am.
OEDIPUS How could my father be no more than nothing?
MESSENGER But Polybus did not give you life, nor did I.
OEDIPUS Then why did he call me son?
MESSENGER Listen, you were
A gift that he took from my hands.
OEDIPUS A child
Given him by a stranger? But he loved me
Dearly.
MESSENGER He had no children, and so consented.
OEDIPUS So you gave me to . . . Had you bought me for your slave?
Where did you find me?
MESSENGER You were lying beneath the trees
In a glade upon Cithaeron.
OEDIPUS What were you doing on Cithaeron?
MESSENGER My flocks were grazing in the mountains;
I was guarding them.
OEDIPUS Guarding your flocks—you were
A shepherd, a servant!
MESSENGER It was in that service that I saved
Your life, my child.
OEDIPUS Why? Was I hurt or sick
When you took me home?
MESSENGER Your ankles will be my witness
That you would not have lived.
OEDIPUS Why do you talk
Of that? The pain is forgotten!
MESSENGER Your feet were pierced
And clamped together. I set you free.
OEDIPUS The child
In the cradle had a scar—I still carry
The shame of it.
MESSENGER You were named in remembrance
Of that scar.
OEDIPUS In heaven's name, who did this?
My mother? My father?
MESSENGER I do not know. The man
Who gave you to me knows more of the truth.
OEDIPUS But you said you found me! Then it was not true . . .

You had me from someone else?

MESSENGER Yes, another
Shepherd gave me the child.

OEDIPUS Who? Can you
Describe him?

MESSENGER They said he was a servant of Laius.

OEDIPUS Laius, who was once king of Thebes?

MESSENGER Yes,
This man was one of his shepherds.

OEDIPUS Is he still
Alive; could I see him?

MESSENGER Your people here
Will know that best.

OEDIPUS Do any of you,
My friends, know the shepherd he means? Has he
Been seen in the fields, or in the palace? Tell me,
Now! It is time these things were known!

CHORUS I think
He must be the man you were searching for, the one
Who left the palace after Laius was killed.
But Jocasta will know as well as I.

OEDIPUS My wife, you remember the man we sent for a little
Time ago? Is he the one this person means?

JOCASTA Perhaps . . . But why should he . . . Think nothing of
this!
Do not idle with memories and stories . . .

OEDIPUS No, I have been given these signs, and I must
Follow them, until I know who gave me birth.

JOCASTA No! Give up this search! I am tortured and sick
Enough. By the love of heaven, if you value life . . .

OEDIPUS Courage! You are still a queen, though I discover
That I am three times three generations a slave.

JOCASTA No, listen to me, I implore you! You must stop!

OEDIPUS I cannot listen when you tell me to ignore the truth.

JOCASTA But I know the truth, and I only ask you to save
Yourself.

OEDIPUS I have always hated that way to safety!

JOCASTA But evil lies in wait for you . . . Oh, do not let him
Find the truth!

OEDIPUS Bring this shepherd to me,
And let her gloat over the riches of her ancestry.

JOCASTA My poor child! Those are the only words
I shall ever have for you . . . I can speak no others! *(Exit* JOCASTA.*)*

CHORUS What is the torment that drives your queen so wildly
Into the palace, Oedipus? Her silence threatens
A storm. I fear some wrong . . .

OEDIPUS Let the storm
Come if it will. I must know my birth,

I must know it, however humble. Perhaps she,
For she is a queen, and proud, is ashamed
That I was born so meanly. But I consider
Myself a child of Fortune, and while she brings me
Gifts, I shall not lack honour. For she has given me
Life itself; and my cousins, the months, have marked me
Small and great as they marched by. Such
Is my ancestry, and I shall be none other—
And I will know my birth!

CHORUS There are signs
Of what is to come, and we may read them,
Casting our thoughts into the future,
And drawing in new knowledge.
For we have seen how the world goes
And we have seen the laws it obeys.
Cithaeron, mountain of Oedipus, the moon
Will not rise in tomorrow's evening sky
Before our king calls you his true father,
His only nurse and mother—and then
You will have your greatest glory.
You will be honoured with dances and choirs
For your gentle kindness to our king—Hail
To the god Apollo! May he be content
With all our words.

Pan walks among the mountains, and one
Of the immortal nymphs could have lain with him;
Who was the goddess who became your mother, Oedipus?
Or was she the wife of Apollo, for he loves
The wild meadows and the long grass.
Or was it the prince of Cyllene, Hermes?
Or, Bacchus, whose palace is the mountain top?
Did he take you as a gift from the nymphs of Helicon,
With whom he plays through all his immortal years?

OEDIPUS I never knew the shepherd or encountered him,
My people, but the man I see there must be
The one we have been seeking. His age answers
My riddle for me; it holds as many years
As our messenger's. And now I see that those
Who lead him are my servants. But you have known him
Before, you can tell me whether I am right.

CHORUS Yes, we recognise him—the most faithful
Of Laius' shepherds.

OEDIPUS And you, Corinthian,
You must tell me first. Is this the man you mean?

MESSENGER It is; you see him there.

(Enter SHEPHERD.*)*

OEDIPUS You, sir, come to me,

Look me in the eyes, and answer all my questions!
Did you once serve Laius?

SHEPHERD Yes, and I was born
In his palace; I was not brought from another country . . .

OEDIPUS Your life? How were you employed?

SHEPHERD Most
Of my life I watched his flocks.

OEDIPUS And where
Was their pasture? They had a favourite meadow?

SHEPHERD Sometimes Cithaeron, sometimes the places near.

OEDIPUS Do you recognise this man? Did you see him on Cithaeron?

SHEPHERD Why should anyone go there? Whom do you mean?

OEDIPUS Here! Standing beside me. Have you ever met him?

SHEPHERD I do not think so . . . My memory is not quick.

MESSENGER We should not wonder at this, your majesty;
But I shall remind him of all he has forgotten.
I know that he remembers when for three
Whole years I used to meet him near Cithaeron,
Six months, from each spring to the rising of the Bear;
I had a single flock and he had two.
Then, in the winters, I would take my sheep to their pens
While he went to the fields of Laius . . . Did this happen?
Have I told it as it happened, or have I not?

SHEPHERD The time is long since then . . . yes, it is the truth.

MESSENGER Good; now, tell me: you know the child you gave me . . . ?

SHEPHERD What is happening? What do these questions mean?

MESSENGER Here is the child, my friend, who was so little then.

SHEPHERD Damnation seize you! Can you not keep your secret?

OEDIPUS Wait, Shepherd? Do not find fault; as I listened
I found more fault in you than in him.

SHEPHERD What
Have I done wrong, most mighty king?

OEDIPUS You will not
Admit the truth about that child.

SHEPHERD He wastes
His time. He talks, but it is all lies.

OEDIPUS When it would please me, you will not speak; but you will
When I make you cry for mercy . . .

SHEPHERD No, my king,
I am an old man—do not hurt me!

OEDIPUS *(to guards)* Take his arms and tie them quickly!

SHEPHERD But why,
Poor child? What more do you want to know?

OEDIPUS You gave
The boy to this Corinthian?

SHEPHERD Yes, I did . . .
And I should have prayed for death that day.
OEDIPUS Your prayer will be answered now if you lie to me!
SHEPHERD But you will surely kill me if I tell the truth.
OEDIPUS He will drive my patience to exhaustion!
SHEPHERD No!
I told you now, I did give him the child.
OEDIPUS Where did it come from? Your home? Another's?
SHEPHERD It was not mine, it was given to me.
OEDIPUS By someone
In the city? . . . I want to know the house!
SHEPHERD By all that is holy,
No more, your majesty, no more questions!
OEDIPUS You die
If I have to ask again!
SHEPHERD The child was born
In the palace of King Laius.
OEDIPUS By one of his slaves?
Or was it a son of his own blood?
SHEPHERD My king,
How shall I tell a story of such horror?
OEDIPUS And how shall I hear it? And yet I must, must hear.
SHEPHERD The child was called his son. But your queen in the palace
May tell you the truth of that most surely.
OEDIPUS Jocasta gave you the child?
SHEPHERD Yes, my king.
OEDIPUS Why? What were you to do?
SHEPHERD I was to destroy him.
OEDIPUS The poor mother asked that?
SHEPHERD She was afraid.
A terrible prophecy . . .
OEDIPUS What?
SHEPHERD There was a story
That he would kill his parents.
OEDIPUS Why did you give
The child away to this stranger?
SHEPHERD I pitied it,
My lord, and I thought he would take it to the far land
Where he lived. But he saved its life only for
Great sorrows. For if you are the man he says,
You must know your birth was watched by evil powers.
OEDIPUS All that was foretold will be made true! Light,
Now turn black and die; I must not look on you!
See, this is what I am; son of parents
I should not have known, I lived with those
I should not have touched, and murdered those

A man must not kill! *(Exit* OEDIPUS.*)*

■■■

CHORUS Every man who has ever lived
Is numbered with the dead; they fought with the world
For happiness, yet all they won
Was a shadow that slipped away to die.
And you, Oedipus, are all those men. I think of the power
Which carried you to such victories and such misery
And I know there is no joy or triumph in the world.

Oedipus aimed beyond the reach of man
And fixed with his arrowing mind
Perfection and rich happiness.
The Sphinx's talons were sharp with evil, she spoke in the mysteries
Of eternal riddles, and he came to destroy her,
To overcome death, to be a citadel
Of strength in our country.
He was called our king, and was
The greatest noble in great Thebes.
And now his story ends in agony.
Death and madness hunt him,
Destruction and sorrow haunt him.
Now his life turns and brings the reward of his greatness . . .
Glorious Oedipus, son, and then father,
In the same chamber, in the same silent room,
Son and father in the same destruction;
Your marriage was the harvesting of wrong.
How could it hold you where your father lay,
And bear you in such silence for such an end?

Child of Laius, I wish, I wish I had never known you,
For now there is only mourning, sorrow flowing
From our lips.
And yet we must not forget the truth;
If we were given hope and life, it was your work.

(Enter SERVANT.*)*

SERVANT My lords of Thebes, on whom rest all the honours
Of our country, when you hear what has happened,
When you witness it, how will you bear your grief
In silence? Weep, if you have ever loved
The royal house of Thebes. For I do not think
The great streams of the Phasis or the Ister
Could ever wash these walls to purity. But all
The crimes they hide must glare out to the light,
Crimes deliberate and considered. The sorrows

We choose ourselves bring the fiercest pain!

CHORUS We have seen great wrongs already, and they were frightening.
Do you bring new disasters?

SERVANT I bring a message
That I may tell, and you may hear, in a few
Swift words. Jocasta is dead.

CHORUS Then she died in grief. What caused her death?

SERVANT It was her own will. Of that terrible act
The worst must remain untold, for I did not watch it.
Yet you will hear what happened to our poor queen
As far as memory guides me. When she went
Into the domed hall of the palace, whirled
On the torrent of her grief, she ran straight
To her marriage chamber, both hands clutched at her hair,
Tearing like claws. Inside, she crashed shut the door
And shrieked the name Laius, Laius who died
So long ago. She talked to herself of the son
She once bore, and of Laius murdered by that son;
Of the mother who was left a widow, and became
Wife and mother again in shame and sorrow.
She wept for her marriage, in which her husband gave
To her a husband, and her children, children.
How her death followed I cannot tell you . . .
We heard a shout, and now Oedipus blazed
And thundered through the door. I could not see
How her sorrow ended, because he was there,
Circling in great mad strides, and we watched
Him. He went round begging to each
Of us; he asked for a sword, he asked to go
To his wife who was more than a wife, to his mother in whom
His birth and his children's birth, like two harvests
From the same field, had been sown and gathered. His grief
Was a raging madness, and some power must have guided him—
It was none of us who were standing there. He gave
A cry full of fear and anguish, then, as if
A ghost was leading him, he leaped against the double
Doors of Jocasta's room. The hinges tilted
Full out of their sockets, and shattered inside
The chamber—and there we saw his wife, hanging
By her throat in the grip of a tall rope. And when
He saw her, he shrieked like a wounded beast, wrenched loose
The knot that held her, and laid her on the ground.
What followed was terrible to watch. He ripped
The gold-worked brooches from her robes—she wore them
As jewels—and raised them above his head. Then he plunged them

Deep into the sockets of his eyes, shouting
That he would never look upon the wrongs
He had committed and had suffered. Now
In his blackness he must see such shapes as he deserved
And never look on those he loved. Repeating
This like a chant, he lifted his hands and stabbed
His eyes, again and again. We saw his eyeballs
Fill with tears of blood that dyed his cheeks,
And a red stream pouring from his veins, dark
As the blood of life, thick as storming hail.
Yes, this is a storm that has broken, a storm
That holds the queen and the king in its embrace.
They were rich and fortunate, and they were so
As we should wish to be. Now, in one day,
See how we must mourn them. The blind rush
To death, the shame, all the evils that we
Have names for—they have escaped none!

CHORUS Has our poor king found ease for his sorrow yet?

SERVANT He shouts at us to open the doors and show
To all Thebes the murderer of his father
And his mother's . . . his words are blasphemous,
I dare not speak them . . . He will be driven from Thebes,
Will not stay beneath this curse that he called upon
Himself. Yet he needs help and a guide. No one
Could bear that agony . . . But he comes himself to show you;
The great doors of the palace open, and what you will see
Will turn you away in horror—yet will ask for pity.
(Enter OEDIPUS.*)*

CHORUS This suffering turns a face of terror to the world.
There is no story told, no knowledge born
That tells of greater sorrow.
Madness came striding upon you, Oedipus,
The black, annihilating power that broods
And waits in the hand of time . . .
I cannot look!
We have much to ask and learn and see.
But you blind us with an icy sword of terror.

OEDIPUS Where will you send this wreckage and despair of man?
Where will my voice be heard, like the wind drifting emptily
On the air. Oh you powers, why do you drive me on?

CHORUS They drive you to the place of horror,
That only the blind may see,
And only the dead hear of.

OEDIPUS Here in my cloud of darkness there is no escape,
A cloud, thick in my soul, and there it dumbly clings;
That cloud is my own spirit
That now wins its fiercest battle and turns back
To trample me . . . The memory of evil can tear

Like goads of molten fire, and go deep,
Infinity could not be so deep.

CHORUS More than mortal in your acts of evil.
More than mortal in your suffering, Oedipus.

OEDIPUS You are my last friend, my only help; you have
Waited for me, and will care for the eyeless body
Of Oedipus. I know you are there . . . I know . . .
Through this darkness I can hear your voice.

CHORUS Oedipus, all that you do
Makes us draw back in fear. How could you take
Such vivid vengeance on your eyes? What power lashed you on?

OEDIPUS Apollo, my lords, Apollo sent this evil on me.
I was the murderer; I struck the blow. Why should I
Keep my sight? If I had eyes, what could delight them?

CHORUS It is so; it is as you say.

OEDIPUS No, I can look on nothing . . .
And I can love nothing—for love has lost
Its sweetness, I can hear no voice—for words
Are sour with hate . . . Take stones and beat me
From your country. I am the living curse, the source
Of sickness and death!

CHORUS Your own mind, reaching after the secrets
Of the gods, condemned you to your fate.
If only you had never come to Thebes . . .

OEDIPUS But when my feet were ground by iron teeth
That bolted me in the meadow grass,
A man set me free and ransomed me from death.
May hell curse him for that murderous kindness!
I should have died then
And never drawn this sorrow on those I love
And on myself . . .

CHORUS Our prayers echo yours.

OEDIPUS Nor killed my father,
Nor led my mother to the room where she gave me life.
But now the gods desert me, for I am
Born of impurity, and my blood
Mingles with those who gave me birth.
If evil can grow with time to be a giant
That masters and usurps our world,
That evil lords its way through Oedipus.

CHORUS How can we say that you have acted wisely?
Is death not better than a life in blindness?

OEDIPUS Do not teach me that this punishment is wrong—
I will have no advisers to tell me it is wrong!
Why choke my breath and go among the dead
If I keep my eyes? For there I know I could not
Look upon my father or my poor mother . . .
My crimes have been too great for such a death.

Or should I love my sight because it let me
See my children? No, for then I would
Remember who their father was. My eyes
Would never let me love them, nor my city,
Nor my towers, nor the sacred images
Of gods. I was the noblest lord in Thebes,
But I have stripped myself of Thebes, and become
The owner of all miseries. For I commanded
My people to drive out the unclean thing, the man
Heaven had shown to be impure in the house
Of Laius.
I found such corruption in me—could I see
My people and not turn blind for shame? . . .
My ears are a spring, and send a river
Of sound through me; if I could have dammed that river
I would have made my poor body into a bolted prison
In which there would be neither light nor sound.
Peace can only come if we shut the mind
Away from the sorrow in the world outside.
Cithaeron, why did you let me live? Why
Did you not kill me as I lay there? I would
Have been forgotten, and never revealed the secret
Of my birth. Polybus, Corinth, the palace
They told me was my father's, you watched over
My youth, but beneath that youth's nobility lay
Corruption—you see it in my acts, in my blood!
There are three roads, a hidden valley, trees,
And a narrow place where the roads meet—they
Drink my blood, the blood I draw from my father—
Do they remember me, do they remember what I did?
Do they know what next I did? . . . The room, the marriage
Room—it was there I was given life, and now
It is there I give the same life to my children.
The blood of brothers, fathers, sons, the race
Of daughters, wives, mothers, all the blackest
Shame a man may commit . . . But I must not name
Such ugly crimes. Oh, you heavens, take me
From the world and hide me, drown me in oceans
Where I can be seen no more! Come, do not fear
To touch a single unhappy man. Yes, a man,
No more. Be brave, for my sufferings can fall to no one
But myself to bear!

CHORUS Oedipus, Creon came
While you were praying; he brings advice and help.
You can protect us no more, and we turn to him.

OEDIPUS What can I say to Creon? I have given him
No cause to trust me or to listen. In all I said
Before, he has seen that I was wrong.

(Enter CREON *with* ANTIGONE *and* ISMENE.*)*

CREON I have not come scorning or insulting you, Oedipus,
For those wrongs. *(To servants)* Have you no shame before
Your countrymen? At least show reverence to the sun's
Flame that sends us life, and do not let
This curse lie open to disfigure heaven.
Neither earth, nor the pure falling rain, nor light
May come near it. Take him to the palace now!
When evil grows in the family, only the family
May hear of it and look without pollution.

OEDIPUS Creon, I thought . . . but now you have struck those fears
Away—you will be a gentle king.
But I ask one thing, and I ask it to help you,
Not myself, for I am hated by powers too strong
For us.

CREON What do you ask so eagerly?

OEDIPUS Banish me from the country now. I must go
Where no one can see or welcome me again.

CREON I would have done so, Oedipus, but first
I must know from Apollo what he commands.

OEDIPUS But we have heard all his answer—destroy the
Parricide, the unholiness, destroy me!

CREON So it was said . . . And yet we are in such danger;
It is better to hear what we must do.

OEDIPUS Why need you
Go to Delphi for my poor body?

CREON Delphi will never deceive us; you know it speaks
The truth.

OEDIPUS But Creon, I command you! . . . I will kneel
And pray to you . . . Bury my queen as you wish
In her royal tomb; she is your sister and
And it is her right. But as for myself, I
Must never think of entering my father's city
Again, so long as its people live. Let me
Have no home but the mountains, where the hill
They call Cithaeron, my Cithaeron, stands.
There my mother and my father, while
They lived, decreed I should have my grave.
My death will be a gift from them, for they
Have destroyed me . . . And yet I know that sickness
Cannot break in and take my life, nothing
May touch me. I am sure of this, for each moment
Is a death, and I am kept alive only
For the final punishment . . . But let it go,
Let it go, I do not care what is done with me.
Creon, my sons will ask nothing more from you;
They are men, wherever they go they will take what they need

From life. But pity my two daughters, who will have
No love. All that was owned by me, they shared,
And when I banqueted, they were always beside me.
You must become their father . . . But let me touch them
And talk to them of our sorrows. Come, my lord,
Come, my noble kinsman, let me feel them
In my arms and believe they are as much my own
As when I saw . . . I cannot think . . . Their weeping,
Their dear voices are near. Creon has pitied me
And given me my children. Is this true?

CREON I sent for them; I know what joy they would give you
And how you loved them once. Yes, it is true.

OEDIPUS May heaven bless your life, and may the power
Watching us, guard you more safely on the throne
Than me. My children, where are you? Come near, come
To my hands; they are your brother's hands and they
Went searching out and took your father's seeing
Eyes to darkness. I did not know my children,
And did not ask, but now the world may see
That I gave you life from the source that gave me mine.
Why is there no light? I cannot see you! . . . And tears
Come when I think of the years you will have to live
In a cruel world. In the city they will shun you,
Fear your presence; when they feast and dance in the streets
You will not be allowed to watch, and they
Will send you weeping home. And when you come
To the years of marriage, children, who will there be
So careless of his pride as to accept the shame
That glares on my birth and on yours? "Your father
Killed his father!" "Your father gave life where he
Was given life, you are children where he was once
A child." That will be your humiliation!
And who will wed you?
No one, my daughters, there will be no one, and I see
You must pine to death in lonely childlessness.
Creon, you are their father, you alone.
For they have lost their parents. Do not let them go
Into beggary and solitude—their blood is yours.
I have nothing, but do not afflict them with
My poverty. Have pity on them. See, so young
And robbed of all except your kindliness.
Touch me once, my lord, and give your consent.
My children, I would have said much to comfort
And advise you—but how could you understand?
But pray, you must pray to live as the world allows
And find a better life than the father whom you follow.

CREON No more now. Go inside the palace.

OEDIPUS It is hard, but I must obey.

CREON All things are healed
By time.
OEDIPUS But Creon, I demand one thing before
I go.
CREON What do you demand?
OEDIPUS Banishment!
CREON Only heaven can answer your prayer. When Apollo . . .
OEDIPUS But Apollo can only detest me.
CREON Then your prayer will be
The sooner heard.
OEDIPUS You mean what you say?
CREON I cannot
Promise, when I see nothing certain.
OEDIPUS Now!
Exile me now!
CREON Go then, and leave your children.
OEDIPUS You must not take them from me!
CREON You give
Commands as if you were king. You must remember
Your rule is over, and it could not save your life.
CHORUS Men of Thebes, look at the king who ruled
Your country; there is Oedipus.
He knew how to answer the mystery
Of evil in the Sphinx, and was our greatest lord.
We saw him move the world with his will, and we envied him.
But look, the storm destroys him, the sea
Has come to defeat him.
Remember that death alone can end all suffering;
Go towards death, and ask for no greater
Happiness than a life
In which there has been no anger and no pain.

francis fergusson

oedipus, myth and play

When Sophocles came to write his play he had the myth of Oedipus to start with. Laius and Jocasta, King and Queen of Thebes, are told by the oracle that their son will grow up to kill his father and marry his mother. The infant, his feet pierced, is left on Mount Kitharon to die. But a shepherd finds him and takes care of him; at last gives him to another shepherd, who takes him to Corinth, and there the King and Queen bring him up as their own son. But Oedipus—"Clubfoot"—is plagued in his turn by the oracle; he hears that he is fated to kill his father and marry his mother; and to escape that fate he leaves Corinth never to return. On his journey he meets an old man with his servants; gets into a dispute with him, and kills him and all his followers. He comes to Thebes at the time when the Sphinx is preying upon that City; solves the riddle which the Sphinx propounds, and saves the City. He marries the widowed Queen, Jocasta; has several children by her; rules prosperously for many years. But, when Thebes is suffering under a plague and a drought, the oracle reports that the gods are angry because Laius' slayer is unpunished. Oedipus, as King, undertakes to find him; discovers that he is himself the culprit and that Jocasta is his own mother. He blinds himself and goes into exile. From this time forth he becomes a sort of sacred relic, like the bones of a saint; perilous, but "good medicine" for the community that possesses him. He dies, at last, at Athens, in a grove sacred to the Eumenides, female spirits of fertility and night.

It is obvious, even from this sketch, that the myth, which covers several generations, has as much narrative material as *Gone with the Wind.* We do not know what versions of the story Sophocles used. It is the way of myths that they generate whole progenies of elaborations and varying versions. They are so suggestive, seem to say so much, yet so mysteriously, that the mind cannot rest content with any single form, but must add, or interpret, or simplify—reduce to terms which the reason can accept. Mr. William Troy suggests that "what is possibly most in order at the moment is a thoroughgoing refurbishment of the medieval fourfold method of interpretation, which was first developed, it will be recalled, for just such a purpose—to make at least partially available to the reason that complex of human problems which are embedded, deep and imponderable, in the Myth."[1] It appears that Sophocles, in his play, succeeded in preserving the suggestive mystery of the Oedipus myth, while presenting it in a wonderfully unified dramatic form; and this drama has all the dimensions which the fourfold method was intended to explore.

Everyone knows that when Sophocles planned the plot of the play itself, he started almost at the end of the story, when the plague descends upon the City of Thebes which Oedipus and Jocasta had been ruling with great success for a number of years. The action of the play takes less than a day, and consists of Oedipus' quest for Laius' slayer—his consulting the Oracle of Apollo, his examination of the Prophet, Tiresias, and of a series of witnesses, ending with the old Shepherd who gave him to the King and Queen of Corinth. The play ends when Oedipus is unmistakably revealed as himself the culprit.

At this literal level, the play is intelligible as a murder mystery. Oedipus takes the role of District Attorney; and when he at last convicts himself, we have a twist, a *coup de théâtre,* of unparalleled excitement. But no one who sees or reads the play can rest content with its literal coher-

[1]"Myth, Method and the Future," by William Troy. *Chimera,* spring, 1946.

ence. Questions as to its meaning arise at once: Is Oedipus really guilty, or simply a victim of the gods, or his famous complex, of fate, of original sin? How much did he know, all along? How much did Jocasta know? The first, and most deeply instinctive effort of the mind, when confronted with this play, is to endeavor to reduce its meanings to some set of rational categories.

The critics of the Age of Reason tried to understand it as a fable of the enlightened moral will, in accordance with the philosophy of that time. Voltaire's version of the play, following Corneille, and his comments upon it, may be taken as typical. He sees it as essentially a struggle between a strong and righteous Oedipus, and the malicious and very human gods, aided and abetted by the corrupt priest Tiresias; he makes it an antireligious tract, with an unmistakable moral to satisfy the needs of the discursive intellect. In order to make Oedipus "sympathetic" to his audience, he elides, as much as possible, the incest motif; and he adds an irrelevant love story. He was aware that his version and interpretation were not those of Sophocles but, with the complacent provinciality of his period, he attributes the difference to the darkness of the age in which *Sophocles* lived.

Other attempts to rationalize *Oedipus Rex* are subtler than Voltaire's, and take us further toward an understanding of the play. Freud's reduction of the play to the concepts of his psychology reveals a great deal, opens up perspectives which we are still exploring. If one reads *Oedipus* in the light of Fustel de Coulanges' *The Ancient City*, one may see it as the expression of the ancient patriarchal religion of the Greeks. And other interpretations of the play, theological, philosophical, historical, are available, none of them wrong, but all partial, all reductions of Sophocles' masterpiece to an alien set of categories. For the peculiar virtue of Sophocles' presentation of the myth is that it preserves the ultimate mystery by focusing upon the tragic human at a level beneath, or prior to any rationalization whatever. The plot is so arranged that we see the action, as it were, illumined from many sides at once.

By starting the play at the end of the story, and showing on stage only the last crucial episode in Oedipus' life, the past and present action of the protagonist are revealed together; and, in each other's light, are at last felt as one. Oedipus' quest for the slayer of Laius becomes a quest for the hidden reality of his own past; and as that slowly comes into focus, like repressed material under psychoanalysis—with sensory and emotional immediacy, yet in the light of acceptance and understanding—his immediate quest also reaches its end: he comes to see himself (the Savior of the City) and the guilty one, the plague of Thebes, at once and at one.

This presentation of the myth of Oedipus constitutes, in one sense, an "interpretation" of it. What Sophocles saw as the essence of Oedipus' nature and destiny, is not what Seneca or Dryden or Cocteau saw; and one may grant that even Sophocles did not exhaust the possibilities in the materials of the myth. But Sophocles' version of the myth does not constitute a "reduction" in the same sense as the rest.

I have said that the action which Sophocles shows is a quest, the quest for Laius' slayer; and that as Oedipus' past is unrolled before us his whole life is seen as a kind of quest for his true nature and destiny. But since the object of this quest is not clear until the end, the seeking action takes many forms, as its object appears in different lights. The object, indeed, the final perception, the "truth," looks so different at the end from what it did at the beginning that Oedipus' action itself may seem not a quest, but its opposite, a flight. Thus it would be hard to say, simply, that Oedipus either succeeds or fails. He succeeds; but his success is his undoing. He fails to find what, in one way, he sought; yet from another point of view his search is brilliantly successful. The same ambiguities surround his effort to discover who and what he is. He seems to find that he is nothing; yet thereby finds himself. And what of his relation to the gods? His quest may be regarded as a heroic attempt to escape their decrees, or as an attempt, based upon some deep natural faith, to discover what their wishes are, and what true obedience would be. In one sense Oedipus suffers forces he can neither control nor understand, the puppet of fate; yet at the same time he wills and intelligently intends his every move.

The meaning, or spiritual content of the play, is not to be sought by trying to resolve such ambiguities as these. The spiritual content of the play is the tragic action which Sophocles directly presents; and this action is in its essence *zweideutig:* triumph and destruction, darkness and enlightenment, mourning and rejoicing, at any moment we care to consider it. But this action has also a shape: a beginning, middle, and end, in time. It starts with the reasoned purpose of finding Laius' slayer. But this aim meets unforeseen difficulties, evidences which do not fit, and therefore shake the purpose as it was first understood; and so the characters suffer the piteous and terrible sense of the mystery of the human situation. From this suffering or passion, with its shifting visions, a new perception of the situation emerges; and on that basis the purpose of the action is redefined, and a new movement starts. This movement, or *tragic rhythm of action,* constitutes the shape of the play as a whole; it is also the shape of each episode, each discussion between principals with the chorus following. Mr. Kenneth Burke has studied the tragic rhythm in his *Philosophy of Literary Form*, and also in *A Grammar of Motives*, where he gives the three moments traditional designations which are very suggestive: *Poiema, Pathema, Mathema.* They may also be called, for convenience, Purpose, Passion (or Suffering) and Perception. It is this tragic rhythm of action which is the substance or spiritual content of the play, and the clue to its extraordinarily comprehensive form.

In order to illustrate these points in more detail, it is convenient to examine the scene between Oedipus and Tiresias with the chorus following it. This episode, being early in the play (the first big agon), presents, as it were, a preview of the whole action and constitutes a clear and complete example of action in the tragic rhythm. . . .

OEDIPUS: RITUAL AND PLAY

The Cambridge School of Classical Anthropologists has shown in great detail that the form of Greek tragedy follows the form of a very ancient ritual, that of the *Enniautos-Daimon,* or seasonal god.[2] This was one of the most influential discoveries of the last few generations, and it gives us new insights into *Oedipus* which I think are not yet completely explored. The clue to Sophocles' dramatizing of the myth of Oedipus is to be found in this ancient ritual, which had a similar form and meaning—that is, it also moved in the "tragic rhythm."

Experts in classical anthropology, like experts in other fields, dispute innumerable questions of fact and of interpretation which the layman can only pass over in respectful silence. One of the thornier questions seems to be whether myth or ritual came first. Is the ancient ceremony merely an enactment of the Ur-Myth of the year-god—Attis, or Adonis, or Osiris, or the "Fisher-King"—in any case that Hero-King-Father-High-Priest who fights with his rival, is slain and dismembered, then rises anew with the spring season? Or did the innumerable myths of this kind arise to "explain" a ritual which was perhaps mimed or danced or sung to celebrate the annual change of seasons?

For the purpose of understanding the form and meaning of *Oedipus,* it is not necessary to worry about the answer to this question of historic fact. The figure of Oedipus himself fulfills all the requirements of the scapegoat, the dismembered king or god-figure. The situation in which Thebes is presented at the beginning of the play—in peril of its life; its crops, its herds, its women mysteriously infertile, signs of a mortal disease of the City, and the disfavor of the gods—is like the withering which winter brings, and calls, in the same way, for struggle, dismemberment, death, and renewal. And this tragic sequence is the substance of the play. It is enough to know that myth and ritual are close together in their genesis, two direct imitations of the perennial experience of the race.

But when one considers *Oedipus* as a ritual one understands it in ways which one cannot by thinking of it merely as a dramatization of a story, even that story. Harrison has shown that the Festival of Dionysos, based ultimately upon the yearly vegetation ceremonies, included *rites de passage,* like that celebrating the assumption of adulthood—celebrations of the mystery of individual growth and development. At the same time, it was a prayer for the welfare of the whole City; and this welfare was understood not only as material prosperity, but also as the natural order of the family, the ancestors, the present members, and the generations still to come, and, by the same token, obedience to the gods who were jealous, each in his own province, of this natural and divinely sanctioned order and proportion.

[2]See especially Jane Ellen Harrison's *Ancient Art and Ritual,* and her *Themis* which contains an "Excursus on the ritual forms preserved in Greek Tragedy" by Professor Gilbert Murray.

We must suppose that Sophocles' audience (the whole population of the City) came early, prepared to spend the day in the bleachers. At their feet was the semicircular dancing-ground for the chorus, and the thrones for the priests, and the altar. Behind that was the raised platform for the principal actors, backed by the all-purpose, emblematic façade, which would presently be taken to represent Oedipus' palace in Thebes. The actors were not professionals in our sense, but citizens selected for a religious office, and Sophocles himself had trained them and the chorus.

This crowd must have had as much appetite for thrills and diversion as the crowds who assemble in our day for football games and musical comedies, and Sophocles certainly holds the attention with an exciting show. At the same time his audience must have been alert for the fine points of poetry and dramaturgy, for *Oedipus* is being offered in competition with other plays on the same bill. But the element which distinguishes this theater, giving it its unique directness and depth, is the *ritual expectancy* which Sophocles assumed in his audience. The nearest thing we have to this ritual sense of theater is, I suppose, to be found at an Easter performance of the *Mattias Passion.* We also can observe something similar in the dances and ritual mummery of the Pueblo Indians. Sophocles' audience must have been prepared, like the Indians standing around their plaza, to consider the playing, the make-believe it was about to see—the choral invocations, with dancing and chanting; the reasoned discourses and the terrible combats of the protagonists; the mourning, the rejoicing, and the contemplation of the final stage-picture of epiphany—as imitating and celebrating the mystery of human nature and destiny. And this mystery was at once that of individual growth and development, and that of the precarious life of the human City.

I have indicated how Sophocles presents the life of the mythic Oedipus in the tragic rhythm, the mysterious quest of life. Oedipus is shown seeking his own true being; but at the same time and by the same token, the welfare of the City. When one considers the ritual form of the whole play, it becomes evident that it presents the tragic but perennial, even normal, quest of the whole City for its well-being. In this larger action, Oedipus is only the protagonist, the first and most important champion. This tragic quest is realized by all the characters in their various ways; but in the development of the action as a whole it is the chorus alone that plays a part as important as that of Oedipus; its counterpart, in fact. The chorus holds the balance between Oedipus and his antagonists, marks the progress of their struggles, and restates the main theme, and its new variation, after each dialogue or agon. The ancient ritual was probably performed by a chorus alone without individual developments and variations, and the chorus, in *Oedipus,* is still the element that throws most light on the ritual form of the play as a whole.

The chorus consists of twelve or fifteen "Elders of Thebes." This group is not intended to represent literally all of the citizens either of Thebes or of Athens. The play opens with a large delegation of Theban citizens before Oedipus' palace, and the chorus proper does not enter until after the prologue. Nor does the chorus speak directly for the Athenian audience;

we are asked throughout to make-believe that the theater is the agora at Thebes; and at the same time Sophocles' audience is witnessing a ritual. It would, I think, be more accurate to say that the chorus represents the point of view and the faith of Thebes as a whole, and, by analogy, of the Athenian audience. Their errand before Oedipus' palace is like that of Sophocles' audience in the theater: they are watching a sacred combat, in the issue of which they have an all-important and official stake. Thus they represent the audience and the citizens in a particular way—not as a mob formed in response to some momentary feeling, but rather as an organ of a highly self-conscious community: something closer to the "conscience of the race" than to the overheated affectivity of a mob.

According to Aristotle, a Sophoclean chorus is a character that takes an important role in the action of the play, instead of merely making incidental music between the scenes, as in the plays of Euripides. The chorus may be described as a group personality, like an old Parliament. It has its own traditions, habits of thought and feeling, and mode of being. It exists, in a sense, as a living entity, but not with the sharp actuality of an individual. It perceives; but its perception is at once wider and vaguer than that of a single man. It shares, in its way, the seeking action of the play as a whole; but it cannot act in all the modes; it depends upon the chief agonists to invent and try out the detail of policy, just as a rather helpless but critical Parliament depends upon the Prime Minister to act but, in its less specific form of life, survives his destruction.

When the chorus enters after the prologue, with its questions, its invocation of the various gods, and its focus upon the hidden and jeopardized welfare of the City—Athens or Thebes—the list of essential *dramatis personae*, as well as the elements needed to celebrate the ritual, is complete, and the main action can begin. It is the function of the chorus to mark the stages of this action, and to perform the suffering and perceiving part of the tragic rhythm. The protagonist and his antagonists develop the "purpose" with which the tragic sequence begins; the chorus, with its less than individual being, broods over the agons, marks their stages with a word (like that of the chorus leader in the middle of the Tiresias scene), and (expressing its emotions and visions in song and dance) suffers the results, and the new perception at the end of the fight.

The choral odes are lyrics but they are not to be understood as poetry, the art of words, only, for they are intended also to be danced and sung. And though each chorus has its own shape, like that of a discrete lyric—its beginning, middle, and end—it represents also one passion or pathos in the changing action of the whole. This passion, like the other moments in the tragic rhythm, is felt at so general or, rather, so deep a level that it seems to contain both the mob ferocity that Nietzsche felt in it and, at the other extreme, the patience of prayer. It is informed by faith in the unseen order of nature and the gods, and moves through a sequence of modes of suffering. This may be illustrated from the chorus I have quoted at the end of the Tiresias scene.

It begins (close to the savage emotion of the end of the fight) with images suggesting that cruel "Bacchic frenzy" which is supposed to be the common root of tragedy and of the "old" comedy: "In panoply of fire and lightning / The son of Zeus now springs upon him." In the first antistrophe these images come together more clearly as we relish the chase; and the fleeing culprit, as we imagine him, begins to resemble Oedipus, who is lame, and always associated with the rough wilderness of Kitharon. But in the second strophe, as though appalled by its ambivalent feelings and the imagined possibilities, the chorus sinks back into a more dark and patient posture of suffering, "in awe," "hovering in hope." In the second antistrophe this is developed into something like the orthodox Christian attitude of prayer, based on faith, and assuming the possibility of a hitherto unimaginable truth and answer: "Zeus and Apollo are wise," etc. The whole chorus then ends with a new vision of Oedipus, of the culprit, and of the direction in which the welfare of the City is to be sought. This vision is still colored by the chorus's human love of Oedipus as Hero, for the chorus has still its own purgation to complete, cannot as yet accept completely either the suffering in store for it, or Oedipus as scapegoat. But it marks the end of the first complete "purpose-passion-perception" unit, and lays the basis for the new purpose which will begin the next unit.

It is also to be noted that the chorus changes the scene which we, as audience, are to imagine. During the agon between Oedipus and Tiresias, our attention is fixed upon their clash, and the scene is literal, close, and immediate: before Oedipus' palace. When the fighters depart and the choral music starts, the focus suddenly widens, as though we had been removed to a distance. We become aware of the interested City around the bright arena; and beyond that, still more dimly, of Nature, sacred to the hidden gods. Mr. Burke has expounded the fertile notion that human action may be understood in terms of the scene in which it occurs, and vice versa: the scene is defined by the mode of action. The chorus's action is not limited by the sharp, rationalized purposes of the protagonist; its mode of action, more patient, less sharply realized, is cognate with a wider, if less accurate, awareness of the scene of human life. But the chorus's action, as I have remarked, is not that of passion itself (Nietzsche's cosmic void of night) but suffering informed by the faith of the tribe in a human and a divinely sanctioned natural order: "If such deeds as these are honored," the chorus asks after Jocasta's impiety, "why should I dance and sing?" (lines 894, 895). Thus it is one of the most important functions of the chorus to reveal, in its widest and most mysterious extent, the theater of human life which the play, and indeed the whole Festival of Dionysos, assumed. Even when the chorus does not speak, but only watches, it maintains this theme and this perspective—ready to take the whole stage when the fighters depart.

If one thinks of the movement of the play, it appears that the tragic rhythm analyzes human action temporally into successive modes, as a crystal analyzes a white beam of light spatially into the colored bands of the spectrum. The chorus, always present, represents one of these modes, and at the recurrent moments when reasoned purpose is gone, it takes the stage with its faith-informed passion, moving through an ordered succession of modes of suffering, to a new perception of the immediate situation.

aristophanes 450–385 b.c.

lysistrata

translated by Jack Lindsay

Greek Old Comedy, derived from ancient fertility and phallic rites, survives in the eleven extant plays of Aristophanes. Using invented fantasy, lyrical choruses, and social, political, and literary satire, Aristophanic comedy was festival entertainment for a predominantly male audience, and it freely exploited bawdry and farce. Nevertheless, it was penetrated with wit, imagination, conviction, and poetry. Aristophanes, born into the landowning class, was a staunch conservative and a lively critic of the democratic State which had led Athens to ruin in war with Sparta. His satire attacked new schemes in education (*Clouds*, 423 B.C.) and in literature, (*Frogs*, 405 B.C.) as well as the folly of war (*Acharnians*, 425 B.C., *Knights*, 424 B.C., *Peace*, 421 B.C., and *Lysistrata*, 411 B.C.). *Birds* (414 B.C.) is more purely fantasy, but generally Aristophanic comedy is based on local issues and personalities. With the defeat of Athens, political and social satire declined, and Old Comedy, through Middle Comedy, gave way to New Comedy, which dealt with stock types involved with love, marriage, intrigue, hidden identities, and happy reversals.

the characters

LYSISTRATA
CALONICE
MYRRHINE
LAMPITO
STRATYLLIS
CINESIAS

HERALD OF THE LACEDAEMONIANS
CHORUS OF OLD WOMEN
CHORUS OF OLD MEN
ATHENIANS, SPARTANS, MAGISTRATE, LOUNGER

(Athens; a public square; early morning.)

(LYSISTRATA *stands alone with the Propylaea at her back.*)

LYSISTRATA If they were trysting for a Bacchanal,

A feast of Pan or Colias or Genetyllis,[1]
The tambourines would block the rowdy streets.
But now there's not a woman to be seen
Except—ah, yes—this neighbor of mine yonder.
(Enter CALONICE.*)*
Good day, Calonice.

CALONICE Good day, Lysistrata.
But what has vexed you so? Tell me, child.
What are these black looks for? It doesn't suit you
To knit your eyebrows up glumly like that.

LYSISTRATA Calonice, it's more than I can bear,
I am hot all over with blushes for our sex.
Men say we're slippery rogues—

CALONICE And aren't they right?

LYSISTRATA Yet summoned on the most tremendous business
For deliberation, still they snuggle in bed.

CALONICE My dear, they'll come. It's hard for women, you know,
To get away. There's so much to do.
Husbands to be patted and put in good tempers;
Servants to be poked out; children washed
Or soothed with lullays or fed with mouthfuls of pap.

LYSISTRATA But I tell you, here's a far more weighty object.

CALONICE What is it all about, dear Lysistrata,
That you've called the women hither in a troop?
What kind of an object is it?

LYSISTRATA A very large one!

CALONICE Is it long too?

LYSISTRATA Both large and long to handle—

CALONICE And yet they're not all here!

LYSISTRATA O I didn't mean that.
If that was the prize, they'd soon come fluttering along.
No, no, it concerns an object I've felt over
And turned this way and that for sleepless nights.

CALONICE It must be fine to stand such long attention.

LYSISTRATA So fine it comes to this—Greece saved by Woman!

CALONICE By Woman! Wretched thin, I'm sorry for it.

LYSISTRATA Our country's fate is henceforth in our hands:
To destroy the Peloponnesians root and branch—

CALONICE What could be nobler!

LYSISTRATA Wipe out the Boeotians—

CALONICE Not utterly. Have mercy on the eels![2]

LYSISTRATA But with regard to Athens, note I'm careful
Not to say any of these nasty things;
Still, thought is free. . . . But if the women join us

[1]The dieties of love and wine. *(Translator's notes.)*
[2]Boeotia was noted for its eels.

From Peloponnesus and Boeotia, then
Hand in hand we'll rescue Greece.

CALONICE How could we do
Such a big wise deed? We women who dwell
Quietly adorning ourselves in a back room
With gowns of lucid gold and gawdy toilets
Of stately silk and dainty little slippers. . . .

LYSISTRATA These are the very armaments of the rescue.
These crocus gowns, this outlay of the best myrrh,
Slippers, cosmetics dusting beauty, and robes
With rippling creases of light.

CALONICE Yes, but how?

LYSISTRATA No man will lift a lance against another–

CALONICE I'll run to have my tunic dyed crocus.

LYSISTRATA Or take a shield–

CALONICE I'll get a stately gown.

LYSISTRATA Or unscabbard a sword–

CALONICE Let me buy a pair of slippers.

LYSISTRATA Now, tell me, are the women right to lag?

CALONICE They should have turned birds, they should have grown wings and flown.

LYSISTRATA My friend, you'll see that they are true Athenians:
Always too late. Why, there's not a woman
From the shoreward demes arrived, not one from Salamis.

CALONICE I know for certain they were up at dawn,
Rocking aboard their husbands if not the skiffs.

LYSISTRATA And I'd have staked my life the Acharnian dames
Would be here first, yet they haven't come either!

CALONICE Well anyhow there is Theagenes' wife
We can expect–she consulted Hecate.[3]
But look, here are some at last, and more behind them.
See . . . where are they from?

LYSISTRATA From Anagyra they come.

CALONICE Yes, they generally manage to come first.
(Enter MYRRHINE.*)*

MYRRHINE Are we late, Lysistrata? . . . What is that?
Nothing to say?

LYSISTRATA I've not much to say for you,
Myrrhine, dawdling on so vast an affair.

MYRRHINE I couldn't find my girdle in the dark.
But if the affair's so wonderful, tell us, what is it?

LYSISTRATA No, let us stay a little longer till
The Peloponnesian girls and the girls of Boeotia
Are here to listen.

MYRRHINE That's the best advice.

[3]Theagenes never left home without consulting Hecate; here this superstition is transfered to his wife.

Ah, there comes Lampito.
(Enter LAMPITO.*)*

LYSISTRATA Welcome Lampito!
Dear Spartan girl with a delightful face,
Washed with the rosy spring, how fresh you look
In the easy stride of your sleek slenderness,
Why you could strangle a bull!

LAMPITO I think I could.
It's frae exercise and kicking at my arse.[4]

LYSISTRATA What lovely breasts to own!

LAMPITO Oo . . . your fingers
Assess them, ye tickler, wi' such tender chucks
I feel as if I were an altar victim.

LYSISTRATA Who is this youngster?

LAMPITO A Boeotian lady.

LYSISTRATA There never was much undergrowth in Boeotia,
Such a smooth place, and this girl takes after it.

CALONICE Yes, I never saw a lawn so primly kept.

LYSISTRATA This girl?

LAMPITO A sonsie open-looking jinker!
She's a Corinthian.

LYSISTRATA Yes, isn't she?
Very open, in some parts particularly.

LAMPITO But who's garred this Council o' Women to meet here?

LYSISTRATA I have.

LAMPITO Propound then what you want o' us.

MYRRHINE What is the amazing news you have to tell?

LYSISTRATA I'll tell you, but first answer one small question.

MYRRHINE As you like.

LYSISTRATA Are you not sad your children's fathers
Go endlessly off soldiering afar
In this plodding war? I am willing to wager
There's not one here whose husband is at home.

CALONICE Mine's been in Thrace, keeping an eye on Eucrates[5]
For five months past.

MYRRHINE And mine left me for Pylos
Seven months ago at least.

LAMPITO And as for mine
No sooner has he slipped out frae the line
He straps his shield and he's snickt off again.

LYSISTRATA And not the slightest glitter of a lover!
And since the Milesians betrayed us, I've not seen
An eight-inch toy to give a proper grip
And be a leathern consolation to us.

[4]One of the dances frequently enjoyed by Greek girls where the girl kicked her buttocks with her heels.
[5]A certain general about whom little is known.

Now will you help me, if I find a means
To stamp the war out.

MYRRHINE By the two Goddesses, Yes!
I will though I've to pawn this very dress
And drink the barter money the same day.

CALONICE And I too though I'm split up like a turbot
And half is hackt off as the price of peace.

LAMPITO And I too! Why, to get a peep at the shy thing
I'd clamber up to the tip-top o' Taygetus.[6]

LYSISTRATA Then I'll expose my mighty mystery.
O women, if we would compel the men
To bow to Peace, we must refrain—

MYRRHINE From what?
O tell us!

LYSISTRATA Will you truly do it then?

MYRRHINE We will, we will, if we must die for it.

LYSISTRATA We must refrain from all touch of baubled love. . . .
Why do you turn your backs? Where are you going?
Why do you bite your lips and shake your heads?
Why are your faces blanched? Why do you weep?
Will you or won't you, or what do you mean?

MYRRHINE No, I won't do it. Let the war proceed.

CALONICE No, I won't do it. Let the war proceed.

LYSISTRATA You too, dear turbot, you that said just now
You didn't mind being split right up in the least?

CALONICE Anything else! O bid me walk in fire
But do not rob us of that darling pet.
What else is like it, dearest Lysistrata?

LYSISTRATA And you?

MYRRHINE O please give me the fire instead.

LYSISTRATA Lewd to the least drop in the tiniest vein,
Our sex is fitly food for Tragic Poets,
Our whole life's but a pile of kisses and babies.
But, hardy Spartan, if you join with me
All may be righted yet. O help me, help me.

LAMPITO It's a sair, sair thing to ask of us, by the Twa,[7]
A lass to sleep her lane and never fill
Love's gap except wi' makeshifts. . . . But let it be.
Peace maun be thought of first.

LYSISTRATA My friend, my friend!
The only one amid this herd of weaklings.

CALONICE But if—which heaven forbid—we should refrain
As you would have us, how is Peace induced?

LYSISTRATA By the two Goddesses, now can't you see
All we have to do is idly sit indoors

[6]A rugged mountain range in the Peloponnesus.
[7]The two goddesses, Demeter and Persephone.

With smooth roses powdered on our cheeks,
Our bodies burning naked through the folds
Of shining Amorgos' silk, and meet the men
With our dear Venus plats plucked trim and neat.
Their stirring love will rise up furiously,
They'll beg our knees to open. That's our time!
We'll disregard their knocking, beat them off—
And they will soon be rabid for a Peace.
I'm sure of it.

LAMPITO Just as Menelaus, they say,
Seeing the breasties of his naked Helen
Flang down the sword.

CALONICE But we'll be tearful fools
If our husbands take us at our word and leave us.

LYSISTRATA There's only left then, in Pherecrates' phrase,
To flay a skinned dog—flay further our flayed toys.

CALONICE Bah, proverbs are no satisfaction in bed.
But what avail will your scheme be if the men
Drag us for all our kicking on to the couch?

LYSISTRATA Cling to the doorposts.

CALONICE But if they should rape us?

LYSISTRATA Yield then, but with a sluggish, cold indifference.
There's no pleasure for them if they rasp it in.
Besides we have other ways to madden them;
They cannot stand up long, and they've no delight
Unless we fit their aim with merry succor.

CALONICE Well if you must have it so, we'll all agree.

LAMPITO For us I ha' no doubt. We can persuade
Our men to strike a fair an' decent Peace,
But how will ye pitch out the battle frenzy
O' the Athenian populace?

LYSISTRATA I promise you
We'll wither up that curse.

LAMPITO I don't believe it.
Not while they own ane trireme oared an' rigged,
Or a' those stacks an' stacks an' stacks o' siller.

LYSISTRATA I've thought the whole thing out till there's no flaw.
We shall surprise the Acropolis today:
That is the duty set the older dames.
While we sit here talking, they are to go
And under pretense of sacrificing, seize it.

LAMPITO Certie, that's fine; all's warking for the best.

LYSISTRATA Now quickly, Lampito, let us tie ourselves
To this high purpose as tightly as the hemp of words
Can knot together.

LAMPITO Set out the terms in detail
And we'll a' swear to them.

LYSISTRATA Of course. . . . Well then

Where is our Scythianess? Why are you staring?
First lay the shield, boss downward, on the floor
And bring the victim's innards.

CALONICE But, Lysistrata,
What is this oath that we're to swear?

LYSISTRATA What oath!
In Aeschylus[8] they take a slaughtered sheep
And swear upon a buckler. Why not we?

CALONICE O Lysistrata, Peace sworn on a buckler!

LYSISTRATA What oath would suit us then?

CALONICE Something we could ride
Would be our best insignia. . . . A white horse!
Let's swear upon its entrails.

LYSISTRATA A horse indeed!

CALONICE Then what will symbolize us?

LYSISTRATA This, as I tell you—
First set a great dark bowl upon the ground
And disembowel a skin of Thasian wine,
Then swear that we'll not add a drop of water.

LAMPITO Ah, what aith could clink pleasanter than that!

LYSISTRATA Bring me a bowl then and a skin of wine.

CALONICE My dears, see what a splendid bowl it is;
I'd not say No if asked to sip it off.

LYSISTRATA Put down the bowl. Lay hands, all, on the victim.
Skiey Queen who givest the last word in arguments,
And thee, O Bowl, dear comrade, we beseech:
Accept our oblation and be propitious to us.

CALONICE What healthy blood, la, how it gushes out!

LAMPITO An' what a leesome fragrance through the air.

LYSISTRATA Now, dears, if you will let me, I'll speak first.

CALONICE Only if you draw the lot, by Aphrodite!

LYSISTRATA So, grasp the brim, you, Lampito, and all.
You, Calonice, repeat for the rest
Each word I say. Then you must all take oath
And pledge your legs to the same stern conditions—
To husband or lover I'll not open thighs

CALONICE *To husband or lover I'll not open thighs*

LYSISTRATA Though he bring proof-of-love of monstrous size

CALONICE *Though he bring proof-of-love of monstrous size*
O, O, my knees are failing me, Lysistrata.

LYSISTRATA But still at home, ignoring him, I'll stay

CALONICE *But still at home, ignoring him, I'll stay*

LYSISTRATA Beautiful, clad in saffron silks all day

CALONICE *Beautiful, clad in saffron silks all day*

LYSISTRATA That so his passion I may swell and pinch

CALONICE *That so his passion I may swell and pinch*

[8]In his play, *Seven Against Thebes*

LYSISTRATA I'll fight him to the very latest inch
CALONICE *I'll fight him to the very latest inch*
LYSISTRATA If, spite of hostile knees, he rapes me there
CALONICE *If, spite of hostile knees, he rapes me there*
LYSISTRATA I'll put him out, so frigid and aloof
CALONICE *I'll put him out, so frigid and aloof*
LYSISTRATA Nor wriggle with my toes stretched at the roof
CALONICE *Nor wriggle with my toes stretched at the roof*
LYSISTRATA Nor crouch like carven lions with arse in air
CALONICE *Nor crouch like carven lions with arse in air*
LYSISTRATA If I keep faith, then bounteous cups be mine
CALONICE *If I keep faith, then bounteous cups be mine*
LYSISTRATA If not, to nauseous water change this wine.
CALONICE *If not, to nauseous water change this wine.*
LYSISTRATA Do you all swear to this?
MYRRHINE We do, we do.
LYSISTRATA Then I shall immolate the victim thus. *(she drinks.)*
CALONICE Here now, share fair, haven't we made a pact?
Let's all quaff down that friendship in our turn.
LAMPITO Hark, what caterwauling hubbub's that?
LYSISTRATA As I told you,
The women have appropriated the citadel.
So Lampito, dash off to your own land
And raise the rebels there. These will serve as hostages,
While we ourselves take our places in the ranks
And drive the bolts right home.
CALONICE But won't the men
March straight against us?
LYSISTRATA And what if they do?
No threat shall creak our hinges wide, no torch
Shall light a fear in us; we will come out
To Peace alone.
CALONICE That's it, by Aphrodite!
As of old let us seem hard and obdurate.
*(*LAMPITO *and some go off, the others go up into the Acropolis.)*

■■■

*(*CHORUS OF OLD MEN *enter to attack the captured Acropolis.)*
CHORUS OF OLD MEN Make room, Draces, move ahead;
why your shoulder's chafed, I see,
With lugging uphill these lopped branches of the olive tree.
How upside-down and wrong-way-round a long life sees
things grow.
Ah, Strymodorus, who'd have thought affairs could tangle so?

The women whom at home we fed,
Like witless fools, with fostering bread,

Have impiously come to this—
They've stolen the Acropolis,
With bolts and bars our orders flout
And shut us out.

Come Philurgus, bustle thither; lay our faggots on the ground,
In neat stacks beleaguering the insurgents all around;
And the vile conspiratresses, plotters of such mischief dire,
Pile and burn them all together in one vast and righteous pyre:
Fling with our own hands Lycon's wife[9] to fry in the thickest fire.

By Demeter, they'll get no brag while I've a vein to beat!
Cleomenes himself was hurtled out in sore defeat.[10]
His stiff-backed Spartan pride was bent.
Out, stripped of all his arms, he went:
A pygmy cloak that would not stretch
To hide his rump (the draggled wretch),
Six sprouting years of beard, the spilth
Of six years' filth.

That was a siege! Our men were ranged in lines of seventeen deep
Before the gates, and never left their posts there, even to sleep.
Shall I not smite the rash presumption then of foes like these,
Detested both of all the gods and of Euripides—
Else, may the Marathon plain not boast my trophied victories!

Ah, now, there's but a little space
To reach the place!
A deadly climb it is, a tricky road
With all this bumping load:
A pack-ass soon would tire. . . .
How these logs bruise my shoulders; farther still
Jog up the hill,
And puff the fire inside,
Or just as we reach the top we'll find it's died.
Ough, phew!
I choke with the smoke.

Lord Heracles, how acrid-hot
Out of the pot
This mad-dog smoke leaps, worrying me
And biting angrily. . . .
'Tis Lemnian fire that smokes,
Or else it would not sting my eyelids thus. . . .

[9]A famous beauty
[10]The Spartan king, Cleomenes, had barricaded himself in the Athenian Acropolis a century earlier, but had eventually been ignominiously starved out.

Haste, all of us;
Athene invokes our aid.
Laches, now or never the assult must be made!
Ough, phew!
I choke with the smoke.

Thanked be the gods! The fire peeps up and crackles as it should.
Now why not first slide off our backs these weary loads of wood
And dip a vine branch in the brazier till it glows, then straight
Hurl it at the battering-ram against the stubborn gate?
If they refuse to draw the bolts in immediate compliance,
We'll set fire to the wood, and smoke will strangle their defiance.
Phew, what a spluttering drench of smoke! Come, now from
off my back. . . .
Is there no Samos general to help me to unpack?
Ah there, that's over! For the last time now it's galled my shoulder.
Flare up thine embers, brazier, and dutifully smolder,
To kindle a brand, that I the first may strike the citadel.
Aid me, Lady Victory, that a triumph trophy may tell
How we did anciently this insane audacity quell!

CHORUS OF WOMEN What's that rising yonder? That ruddy
glare, that smoky skurry?
O is it something in a blaze? Quick, quick, my comrades, hurry!

Nicodice, helter-skelter!
Or poor Calyce's in flames
And Cratylla's stifled in the welter.
O these dreadful old men
And their dark laws of hate!
There, I'm all of a tremble lest I turn out to be too late.
I could scarcely get near to the spring though I rose before dawn.
What with tattling of tongues and rattling of pitchers in
one jostling din
With slaves pushing in! . . .

Still here at last the water's drawn
And with it eagerly I run
To help those of my friends who stand
In danger of being burned alive.
For I am told a dribbling band
Of graybeards hobble to the field,
Great fagots in each palsied hand,
As if a hot bath to prepare,
And threatening that out they'll drive
These wicked women or soon leave them charring into ashes there.
O Goddess, suffer not, I pray, this harsh deed to be done,
But show us Greece and Athens with their warlike acts repealed!

For this alone, in this thy hold,
Thou Goddess with the helm of gold,
We laid hands on thy sanctuary,
Athene. . . . Then our ally be
And where they cast their fires of slaughter
Direct our water!

STRATYLLIS *(caught)* Let me go!

WOMEN You villainous old men, what's this you do?
No honest man, no pious man, could do such things as you.

MEN Ah ha, here's something most original, I have no doubt:
A swarm of women-sentinels to man the walls without.

WOMEN So then we scare you, do we? Do we seem a fearful host?
You only see the smallest fraction mustered at this post.

MEN Ho, Phaedrias, shall we put a stop to all these chattering tricks?
Suppose that now upon their backs we splintered these our sticks.

WOMEN Let us lay down the pitchers, so our bodies will be free,
In case these lumping fellows try to cause some injury.

MEN O hit them hard and hit again and hit until they run away
And perhaps they'll learn, like Bupalus, not to have too much to say.

WOMEN Come on then, do it! I won't budge, but like a bitch I'll snap
Till you can show no more than I myself beneath the lap.

MEN Be quiet, or I'll pash you out of any years to come.

WOMEN Now you just touch Stratyllis with the top joint of your thumb.

MEN What vengeance can you take if with my fists your face I beat?

WOMEN I'll rip you with my teeth and strew your entrails at your feet.

MEN Now I appreciate Euripides' strange subtlety:
Woman is the most shameless beast of all the beasts that be.

WOMEN Rhodippe, come and let's pick up our water-jars once more.

MEN Ah cursed drab, what have you brought this water hither for?

WOMEN What is your fire for then, you smelly corpse? Yourself to burn?

MEN To build a pyre and make your comrades ready for the urn.

WOMEN And I've the water to put out your fire immediately.

MEN What, you put out my fire?

WOMEN Yes, sirrah, as you soon will see.

MEN I don't know why I hesitate to roast you with this flame.

WOMEN If you have any soap you'll go off cleaner than you came.

MEN Cleaner, you dirty slut?

WOMEN A nuptial bath in which to lie!

MEN Did you hear that insolence?

WOMEN I'm a free woman, I.

MEN I'll make you hold your tongue.

WOMEN Henceforth you'll serve in no more juries.

MEN Burn off her hair for her.

WOMEN Now forward, water, quench their furies!

MEN O dear, O dear!

WOMEN So . . . was it hot?

MEN Hot! . . . Enough, O hold.

WOMEN Watered, perhaps you'll bloom again—why not?
MEN Brrr, I'm wrinkled up from shivering with cold.
WOMEN Next time you've fire you'll warm yourself and leave
us to our lot.

(MAGISTRATE *enters with attendant Scythians.)*
MAGISTRATE Have the luxurious rites of the women glittered
Their libertine show, their drumming tapped out crowds,
The Sabazian Mysteries summoned their mob,
Adonis been wept to death on the terraces,[11]
As I could hear the last day in the Assembly?
For Demostratus[12]—let bad luck befoul him—
Was roaring, *We must sail for Sicily*,
While a woman, throwing herself about in a dance
Lopsided with drink, was shrilling out *Adonis,*
Woe for Adonis. Then Demostratus shouted,
We must levy hoplites at Zacynthus,
And there the woman, up to the ears in wine,
Was screaming *Weep for Adonis* on the house top,
The scoundrelly politician, that lunatic ox,
Bellowing bad advice through tipsy shrieks:
Such are the follies wantoning in them.
MEN O if you knew their full effrontery!
All of the insults they've done, besides sousing us
With water from their pots to our public disgrace
For we stand here wringing our clothes as though we'd pissed' em.
MAGISTRATE By Poseidon, justly done! For in part with us
The blame must lie for dissolute behavior
And for the pampered appetites they learn.
Thus grows the seedling lust to blossoming:
We go into a shop and say, "Here, goldsmith,
You remember the necklace that you wrought my wife;
Well, the other night in fervor of a dance
Her clasp broke open. Now I'm off for Salamis;
If you've the leisure, would you go tonight
And stick a bolt pin into her opened clasp."
Another goes to a cobbler, a soldierly fellow,
Always standing up erect, and says to him,
"Cobbler, a sandal strap of my wife's pinches her,
Hurts her little toe in a place where she's sensitive.
Come at noon and see if you can stretch out wider
This thing that troubles her, loosen its tightness."
And so you view the result. Observe my case—
I, a magistrate, come here to draw

[11]The passage refers to the women's frenzied celebration of the feast of Adonis, which supposedly helped egg the men on to the disastrous decision to invade Sicily four years earlier.
[12]A famous demagogue who urged troops for Sicily.

Money to buy oar blades, and what happens?
The women slam the door full in my face.
But standing still's no use. Bring me a crowbar,
And I'll chastise this their impertinence.
What do you gape at, wretch, with dazzled eyes?
Peering for a tavern, I suppose.
Come, force the gates with crowbars, prise them apart!
I'll prise away myself too. . . .
(LYSISTRATA *appears.*)

LYSISTRATA Stop this banging.
I'm coming of my own accord. . . . Why bars?
It is not bars we need but common sense.

MAGISTRATE Indeed, you slut! Where is the archer now?
Arrest this woman, tie her hands behind.

LYSISTRATA If he brushes me with a finger, by Artemis,
The public menial, he'll be sorry for it.

MAGISTRATE Are you afraid? Grab her about the middle.
Two of you then, lay hands on her and end it.

CALONICE By Pandrosos! if your hand touches her
I'll spread you out and trample on your guts.

MAGISTRATE My guts! Where is the other archer gone?
Bind that minx there who talks so prettily.

MYRRHINE By Phosphor, if your hand moves out her way
You'd better have a surgeon somewhere handy.

MAGISTRATE You too! Where is that archer? Take that woman.
I'll put a stop to these surprise parties.

STRATYLLIS By the Tauric Artemis, one inch nearer
My fingers, and it's a bald man that'll be yelling.

MAGISTRATE Tut tut, what's here? Deserted by my archers. . . .
But surely women never can defeat us;
Close up your ranks, my Scythians.[13] Forward at them.

LYSISTRATA By the Goddesses, you'll find that here await you
Four companies of most pugnacious women
Armed cap-a-pie from the topmost louring curl
To the lowest angry dimple.

MAGISTRATE On, Scythians, bind them.

LYSISTRATA On, gallant allies of our high design,
Vendors of grain-eggs-pulse-and-vegetables,
Ye garlic-tavern-keepers of bakeries,
Strike, batter, knock, hit, slap, and scratch our foes,
Be finely imprudent, say what you think of them. . . .
Enough! retire and do not rob the dead.

MAGISTRATE How basely did my archer force come off.

LYSISTRATA Ah, ha, you thought it was a herd of slaves
You had to tackle, and you didn't guess
The thirst for glory ardent in our blood.

[13]Athens' most skillful archers.

MAGISTRATE By Apollo, I know well the thirst that heats you—
Especially when a wineskin's close.
MEN You waste your breath, dear magistrate, I fear, in answering back.
What's the good of argument with such a rampageous pack?
Remember how they washed us down (these very clothes I wore)
With water that looked nasty and that smelt so even more.
WOMEN What else to do, since you advanced too dangerously nigh.
If you should do the same again, I'll punch you in the eye.
Though I'm a stay-at-home and most a quiet life enjoy,
Polite to all and every (for I'm naturally coy),
Still if you wake a wasps' nest then of wasps you must beware.
MEN How may this ferocity be tamed? It grows too great to bear.
Let us question them and find if they'll perchance declare
The reason why they strangely dare
To seize on Cranaos' citadel,
This eyrie inaccessible,
This shrine above the precipice,
The Acropolis.
Probe them and find what they mean with this idle talk; listen, but watch they don't try to deceive.
You'd be neglecting your duty most certainly if now this mystery unplumbed you leave.
MAGISTRATE Women there! Tell what I ask you, directly. . . .
Come, without rambling, I wish you to state
What's your rebellious intention in barring up thus on our noses our own temple gate.
LYSISTRATA To take first the treasury out of your management, and so stop the war through the absence of gold.
MAGISTRATE Is gold then the cause of the war?
LYSISTRATA Yes, gold caused it and miseries more, too many to be told.
'Twas for money, and money alone, that Pisander[14] with all of the army of mob agitators
Raised up revolutions. But, as for the future, it won't be worth while to set up to be traitors.
Not an obol they'll get as their loot, not an obol! while we have the treasure chest in our command.
MAGISTRATE What then is that you propose?
LYSISTRATA Just this—merely to take the exchequer henceforth in hand.
MAGISTRATE The exchequer!
LYSISTRATA Yes, why not? Of our capabilities you have had various clear evidences.
Firstly remember we have always administered soundly the budget of all home expenses.

[14]A political intriguer who, at the time of this play, was plotting the overthrow of Athenian democracy.

MAGISTRATE But this matter's different.

LYSISTRATA How is it different?

MAGISTRATE Why, it deals chiefly with wartime supplies.

LYSISTRATA But we abolish war straight by our policy.

MAGISTRATE What will you do if emergencies arise?

LYSISTRATA Face them our own way.

MAGISTRATE What, *you* will?

LYSISTRATA Yes, *we* will!

MAGISTRATE Then there's no help for it; we're all destroyed.

LYSISTRATA No, willy-nilly you must be safeguarded.

MAGISTRATE What madness is this?

LYSISTRATA Why, it seems you're annoyed.
It must be done, that's all.

MAGISTRATE Such awful oppression never, O never in the past yet I bore.

LYSISTRATA You must be saved, sirrah—that's all there is to it.

MAGISTRATE If we don't want to be saved?

LYSISTRATA All the more.

MAGISTRATE Why do women come prying and meddling in matters of state touching wartime and peace?

LYSISTRATA That I will tell you.

MAGISTRATE O tell me or quickly I'll—

LYSISTRATA Hearken awhile and from threatening cease.

MAGISTRATE I cannot, I cannot; it's growing too insolent.

WOMEN Come on; you've far more than we have to dread.

MAGISTRATE Stop from your croaking, old carrion crow there. . . .
Continue.

LYSISTRATA Be calm then and I'll go ahead.
All the long years when the hopeless war dragged along, we, unassuming, forgotten in quiet,
Endured without question, endured in our loneliness all your incessant child's antics and riot.
Our lips we kept tied, though aching with silence, though well all the while in our silence we knew
How wretchedly everything still was progressing by listening dumbly the day long to you.
For always at home you continued discussing the war and its politics loudly, and we
Sometimes would ask you, our hearts deep with sorrowing, though we spoke lightly, though happy to see,
"What's to be inscribed on the side of the Treaty-stone?
What, dear, was said in the Assembly today?"
"Mind your own business," he'd answer me growlingly, "hold your tongue, woman, or else go away."
And so I would hold it.

WOMEN I'd not be silent for any man living on earth, no, not I!

MAGISTRATE Not for a staff?

LYSISTRATA Well, so I did nothing but sit in the house, feeling dreary, and sigh,
While ever arrived some fresh tale of decisions more foolish by far and presaging disaster.
Then I would say to him, "O my dear husband, why still do they rush on destruction the faster?"
At which he would look at me sideways, exclaiming, "Keep for your web and your shuttle your care,
Or for some hours hence your cheeks will be sore and hot; leave this alone, war is Man's sole affair!"

MAGISTRATE By Zeus, but a man of fine sense, he.

LYSISTRATA How sensible? You dotard, because he at no time had lent
His intractable ears to absorb from our counsel one temperate word of advice, kindly meant?
But when at the last in the streets we heard shouted (everywhere ringing the ominous cry)
"Is there no one to help us, no savior in Athens?" and, "No, there is no one," come back in reply.
At once a convention of all wives through Hellas here for a serious purpose was held,
To determine how husbands might yet back to wisdom despite their reluctance in time be compelled.
Why then delay any longer? It's settled. For the future you'll take up our old occupation.
Now in turn you're to hold tongue, as we did, and listen while we show the way to recover the nation.

MAGISTRATE *You* talk to *us!* Why, you're mad. I'll not stand it.

LYSISTRATA Cease babbling, you fool; till I end, hold your tongue.

MAGISTRATE If I should take orders from one who wears veils, may my neck straightaway be deservedly wrung.

LYSISTRATA O if that keeps pestering you,
I've a veil here for your hair,
I'll fit you out in everything
As is only fair.

CALONICE Here's a spindle that will do.

MYRRHINE I'll add a wool basket too.

LYSISTRATA Girdled now sit humbly at home,
Munching beans, while you card wool and comb.
For war from now on is the Women's affair.

WOMEN Come then, down pitchers, all,
And on, courageous of heart,
In our comradely venture
Each taking her due part.

I could dance, dance, dance, and be fresher after,
I could dance away numberless suns,
To no weariness let my knees bend.

Earth I could brave with laughter,
Having such wonderful girls here to friend.
O the daring, the gracious, the beautiful ones!
Their courage unswerving and witty
Will rescue our city.

O sprung from the seed of most valiant-wombed grandmothers, scions of savage and dangerous nettles!
Prepare for the battle, all. Gird up your angers.
Our way the wind of sweet victory settles.

LYSISTRATA O tender Eros and Lady of Cyprus,
some flush of beauty I pray you devise
To smooth twixt our nipples and O Aphrodite
prettily slip twixt our valorous thighs!
Joy will raise up its head through the legions warring
and all of the far-serried ranks of mad love
Bristle the earth to the pillared horizon,
pointing in vain to the heavens above.
I think that perhaps then they'll give us our title—
Peacemakers.

MAGISTRATE What do you mean? Please explain.

LYSISTRATA First, we'll not see you now flourishing arms about into the Marketing-place clang again.

WOMEN No, by the Paphian.

LYSISTRATA Still I can conjure them
as past where the herbs stand or crockery's sold
Like Corybants[15] jingling (poor sots) fully armored, they
noisily round on their promenade strolled.

MAGISTRATE And rightly; that's discipline, they—

LYSISTRATA But what's sillier
than to go on an errand of buying a fish
Carrying along an immense Gorgon buckler
instead of the usual platter or dish?
A phylarch I lately saw, mounted on horseback,
dressed for the part with long ringlets and all,
Stow in his helmet the omelet bought steaming
from an old woman who kept a food stall.
Nearby a soldier, a Thracian, was shaking
wildly his spear, like Tereus in the play,
To frighten a fig girl while unseen the ruffian
filched from her fruit trays the ripest away.

MAGISTRATE How, may I ask, will your rule re-establish
order and justice in lands so tormented?

LYSISTRATA Nothing is easier.

MAGISTRATE Out with it speedily—
what is this plan that you boast you've invented?

[15]Frenzied mythical dancers.

LYSISTRATA If, when yarn we are winding, it chances to tangle,
then, as perchance you may know, through the skein
This way and that still the spool we keep passing
till it is finally clear all again:
So to untangle the War and its errors,
ambassadors out on all sides we will send
This way and that, here, there and round about—
soon you will find that the War has an end.

MAGISTRATE So with these trivial tricks of the household,
domestic analogies of threads, skeins, and spools,
You think that you'll solve such a bitter complexity,
unwind such political problems, you fools!

LYSISTRATA Well, first as we wash dirty wool so's to cleanse it,
so with a pitiless zeal we will scrub
Through the whole city for all greasy fellows;
burrs too, the parasites, off we will rub.
That verminous plague of insensate place seekers
soon between thumb and forefinger we'll crack.
All who inside Athens' walls have their dwelling
into one great common basket we'll pack.
Disenfranchised or citizens, allies or aliens,
pell-mell the lot of them in we will squeeze
Till they discover humanity's meaning. . . .
As for disjointed and far colonies,
Them you must never from this time imagine as
scattered about just like lost hanks of wool.
Each portion we'll take and wind in to this center,
inward to Athens each loyalty pull,
Till from the vast heap where all's piled together
at last can be woven a strong Cloak of State.

MAGISTRATE How terrible is it to stand here and watch them
carding and winding at will with our fate,
Witless in war as they are.

LYSISTRATA What of us then,
who ever in vain for our children must weep
Borne but to perish afar and in vain?

MAGISTRATE Not that, O let that one memory sleep!

LYSISTRATA Then while we should be companioned still merrily, happy
as brides may, the livelong night,
Kissing youth by, we are forced to lie single. . . .
But leave for a moment our pitiful plight,
It hurts even more to behold the poor maidens
helplessly wrinkling in staler virginity.

MAGISTRATE Does not a man age?

LYSISTRATA Not in the same way.
Not as a woman grows withered, grows he.
He, when returned from the war, though gray-headed,
yet if he wishes can choose out a wife.

But she has no solace save peering for omens,
wretched and lonely the rest of her life.

MAGISTRATE But the old man who still can erect—

LYSISTRATA O why not finish and die?
A bier is easy to buy,
A honey cake I'll knead you with joy,
This garland will see you are decked.

CALONICE I've a wreath for you too.

MYRRHINE I also will fillet you.

LYSISTRATA What more is lacking? Step aboard the boat.
See, Charon shouts ahoy.
You're keeping him, he wants to shove afloat.

MAGISTRATE Outrageous insults! Thus my place to flout!
Now to my fellow magistrates I'll go
And what you've perpetrated on me show.

LYSISTRATA Why are you blaming us for laying you out?
Assure yourself we'll not forget to make
The third day offering early for your sake.
(MAGISTRATE retires, LYSISTRATA returns within.)

■■■

MEN All men who call your loins your own, awake at last, arise
And strip to stand in readiness. For as it seems to me
Some more perilous offensive in their heads they now devise.

I'm sure a Tyranny
Like that of Hippias[16]
In this I detect. . . .
They mean to put us under
Themselves I suspect,
And that Laconians assembling
At Cleisthenes' house have played
A trick-of-war and provoked them
Madly to raid
The Treasury, in which term I include
The pay for my food.

For is it not preposterous
They should talk this way to us
On a subject such as battle!
And, women as they are, about bronze bucklers dare to prattle—
Make alliance with the Spartans—people I for one
Like very hungry wolves would always most sincerely shun. . . .
Some dirty game is up their sleeve,
I believe.
A Tyranny, no doubt . . . but they won't catch me, that I know.

[16]The last of the Athenian tyrants.

Henceforth on my guard I'll go,
A sword with myrtle branches wreathed forever in my hand,
And under arms in the Public Place I'll take my watchful stand,
Shoulder to shoulder with Aristogeiton. Now my staff I'll draw
And start at once by knocking
that shocking
Hag upon the jaw.

WOMEN Your own mother will not know you when you get back to the town.
But first, my friends and allies, let us lay these garments down,
And all ye fellow-citizens, hark to me while I tell
What will aid Athens well.
Just as is right, for I
Have been a sharer
In all the lavish splendor
Of the proud city.
I bore the holy vessels
At seven, then
I pounded barley
At the age of ten,
And clad in yellow robes,
Soon after this,
I was Little Bear to
Brauronian Artemis;[17]
Then neckleted with figs,
Grown tall and pretty,
I was a Basket bearer.
And so it's obvious I should
Give you advice that I think good,
The very best I can.
It should not prejudice my voice that I'm not born a man,
If I say something advantageous to the present situation.
For I'm taxed too, and as a toll provide men for the nation.
While, miserable graybeards, you,
It is true,
Contribute nothing of any importance whatever to our needs;
But the treasure raised against the Medes
You've squandered, and no nothing in return, save that you make
Our lives and persons hazardous by some imbecile mistake.
What can you answer? Now be careful, don't arouse my spite,
Or with my slipper I'll take you napping,
faces slapping
Left and right.

MEN What villainies they contrive!
Come, let vengeance fall,

[17]A ceremony for Artemis in which a young girl impersonated a bear was usually held in the town of Brauron.

You that below the waist are still alive,
Off with your tunics at my call—
Naked, all.
For a man must surely savor of a man.
No quaking, brave steps taking, careless what protrudes, white-shoeed,
In the nude, onward bold,
All ye who garrisoned Leipsidrion of old. . . .
Let each one wag
As youthfully as he can,
And if he has the cause at heart
Rise at least a span.

We must take a stand and keep to it,
For if we yield the smallest bit
To their importunity,
Then nowhere from their inroads will be left to us immunity.
But they'll be building ships and soon their navies will attack us,
As Artemisia did, and seek to fight us and to sack us.
And if they mount, the Knights they'll rob
Of a job.
For everyone knows how talented they all are in the saddle,
Having long practiced how to straddle;
No matter how they're jogged there up and down, they're never thrown.
Then think of Myron's painting, and each horsebackéd Amazon
In combat hand-to-hand with men. . . . Come, on these women fall,
And in pierced wood-collars let's stick
quick
The necks of one and all.

WOMEN Don't cross me or I'll loose
The Beast that's kenneled here. . . .
And soon you will be howling for a truce,
Howling out with fear.
But my dear,
Strip also, that women may savor of woman's passion. . . .
But you, you'll be too sore to eat garlic more, or one black bean, I really
mean, so great's my spleen, to kick you black and blue
With these my dangerous legs.
I'll hatch the lot of you,
If my rage you dash on,
The way the relentless Beetle
Hatched the Eagle's eggs.

Scornfully aside I set
Every silly old-man threat
While Lampito's with me.
Or dear Ismenia, the noble Theban girl. Then let decree
Be hotly piled upon decree; in vain will be your labors,
You futile rogue abominated by your suffering neighbors.

To Hecate's feast I yesterday went—
Off I sent
To our neighbors in Boeotia, asking as a gift to me
For them to pack immediately
That darling dainty thing . . . a good fat eel I meant of course;
But they refused because some idiotic old decree's in force.
O this strange passion for decrees nothing on earth can check,
Till someone puts a foot out tripping you,
and slipping you
Break your neck.

■■■

(The scene shifts to a court within the Acropolis. Re-enter LYSISTRATA.*)*

WOMEN Dear Mistress of our martial enterprise,
Why do you come with sorrow in your eyes?

LYSISTRATA O 'tis our naughty femininity,
So weak in one spot, that hath saddened me.

WOMEN What's this? Please speak.

LYSISTRATA Poor women, O so weak!

WOMEN What can it be? Surely your friends may know.

LYSISTRATA Yea, I must speak it though it hurt me so.

WOMEN Speak; can we help? Don't stand there mute in need.

LYSISTRATA I'll blurt it out then—our wombs, our wombs have mutinied.

WOMEN O Zeus!

LYSISTRATA What use is Zeus to our anatomy?
Here is the gaping calamity I meant:
I cannot shut their ravenous appetites
A moment more now. They are all deserting.
The first I caught was sidling through the postern
Close by the Cave of Pan:[18] the next hoisting herself
With rope and pulley down: a third on the point
Of slipping past: while a fourth malcontent seated
For instant flight to Orsilochus' brothel
On bird-back I dragged off by the hair in time. . . .
They are all snatching excuses to sneak home.
Look, there goes one. . . . Hey, what's the hurry?

FIRST WOMAN I must get home. I've some Milesian wool
Packed wasting away, and moths are pushing through it.

LYSISTRATA Fine moths indeed, I know. Get back within.

FIRST WOMAN By the Goddesses, I'll return instantly.
I only want to stretch it on my bed.

LYSISTRATA You shall stretch nothing and go nowhere either.

FIRST WOMAN Must I never use my wool then?

LYSISTRATA If needs be.

SECOND WOMAN How unfortunate I am. O my poor flax!
It's left at home unstript.

[18]A cave near the Acropolis.

LYSISTRATA So here's another
That wishes to go home and strip her flax.
Inside again!
SECOND WOMAN No, by the Goddess of Light,
I'll be back as soon as I have flayed it properly.
LYSISTRATA You'll not flay anything. For if you begin
There'll not be one here but has a patch to be flayed.
THIRD WOMAN O holy Eilithyia, stay this birth
Till I have left the precincts of the place![19]
LYSISTRATA What nonsense is this?
THIRD WOMAN I'll drop it any minute.
LYSISTRATA Yesterday you weren't with child.
THIRD WOMAN But I am today.
O let me find a midwife, Lysistrata.
O quickly!
LYSISTRATA Now what story is this you tell?
What is this hard lump here?
THIRD WOMAN It's a male child.
LYSISTRATA By Aphrodite, it isn't. Your belly's hollow,
And it has the feel of metal. . . . Well, I soon can see.
You hussy, it's Athene's sacred helm,
And you said you were with child.
THIRD WOMAN And so I am.
LYSISTRATA Then why the helm?
THIRD WOMAN So if the throes should take me
Still in these grounds I could use it like a dove
As a laying nest in which to drop the child.
LYSISTRATA More pretexts! You can't hide your clear intent,
And anyway why not wait till the tenth day
Meditating a brazen name for your brass brat?
FOURTH WOMAN And I can't sleep a wink. My nerve is gone
Since I saw that snake sentinel of the shrine.[20]
FIFTH WOMAN And all those dreadful owls with their weird hooting!
Though I'm wearied out, I can't close an eye.
LYSISTRATA You wicked women, cease from juggling lies.
You want your men. But what of them as well?
They toss as sleepless in the lustful night.
I'm sure of it. Hold out awhile, hold out,
But persevere a teeny-weeny longer.
An oracle has promised Victory
If we don't wrangle. Would you hear the words?
WOMEN Yes, yes, what is it?
LYSISTRATA Silence then, your chatterboxes.
Here—
"Whenas the swallows flocking in one place from the hoopoes

[19]It was unlawful to give birth in a sacred place.
[20]The sacred snake of the Acropolis which was thought to guard the holy ground.

Deny their legs love's gambols any more,
All woes shall then have ending and great Zeus the Thunderer
Shall put above what was below before."

WOMEN Are the men then always to be underneath?

LYSISTRATA "But if the swallows squabble among themselves and fly away
Out of the temple, refusing to agree,
Then The Most Lascivious Birds in all the World
They shall be named forever." That's his decree.

WOMEN It's obvious what it means.

LYSISTRATA Now by all the gods
We must let no agony deter from duty.
Back to your quarters. For we are base indeed.
My friends, if we betray the oracle. *(She goes out.)*

OLD MEN I'd like to remind you of a fable they used to employ,
When I was a little boy:
How once through fear of the marriage bed a young man,
Melanion[21] by name, to the wilderness ran,
And there on the hills he dwelt.
For hares he wove a net
Which with his dog he set—
Most likely he's there yet.
For he never came back home, so great was the fear he felt.
I loathe the sex as much as he,
And therefore I no less shall be
As chaste as was Melanion.

MAN Grann'am, do you much mind rape?

WOMAN Onions you won't need, to cry.

MAN From my foot you shan't escape.

WOMAN What thick forests I espy.

MEN So Myronides' fierce beard[22]
And ponderous black arse were feared,
That the foe fled when they were shown—
Brave he as Phormion.

WOMEN Well, I'll relate a rival fable just to show to you
A different point of view:
There was a rough-hewn fellow, Timon, with a face[23]
That glowered as through a thorn-bush in a wild, bleak place.
He too decided on flight,
This very Furies' son,
All the world's ways to shun
And hide from everyone,

[21]Here, the legend of Atalanta, who hated men, and her suitor, Melanion, has been reversed.
[22]A famous Athenian general.
[23]A well-known misanthrope.

Spitting out curses on all knavish men to left and right.
But though for men he reared this hate,
With women still he loved to mate
And never thought them enemies.
WOMAN O your jaw I'd like to break.
MAN That I fear do you suppose?
WOMAN Learn what kicks my legs can make.
MAN Hair and more than hair expose.
WOMAN Nay, you'll see there, I engage,
All is well kept despite my age,
And tended smoothly so's to please,
Scorched for emergencies.
(LYSISTRATA *appears.*)
LYSISTRATA Hollo, there, hasten hither to me.
Skip fast along.
WOMAN What is this? Why the noise?
LYSISTRATA A man, a man! I spy a frenzied man!
He carries Love before him like a staff.
O Lady of Cyprus, and Cythera, and Paphos,
I beseech you, keep our minds and hands to the oath.
WOMAN Where is he, whoever he is?
LYSISTRATA By the Temple of Chloe.
WOMAN Yes, now I see him, but who can he be?
LYSISTRATA Look at him. Does anyone recognise his face?
MYRRHINE I do. He is my husband, Cinesias.
LYSISTRATA You know how to work. Play with him, lead him on,
Seduce him to the cozening point—kiss him, kiss him,
Then slip your mouth aside just as he's sure of it,
Ungirdle every caress his mouth feels at
Save that the oath upon the bowl has locked.
MYRRHINE You can rely on me.
LYSISTRATA I'll stay here to help
In stroking up his passion to its height
Of vain magnificence. . . . The rest to their quarters.
(*Enter* CINESIAS.)
Who is this that stands within our lines?
CINESIAS I.
LYSISTRATA A man?
CINESIAS Too much a man!
LYSISTRATA Then be off at once.
CINESIAS Who are you that thus eject me?
LYSISTRATA Guard for the day.
CINESIAS By all the gods, then call Myrrhine hither.
LYSISTRATA So, call Myrrhine hither! Who are you?
CINESIAS I am her husband, Cinesias, son of Penis.
LYSISTRATA Welcome dear friend. That glorious name of yours
Is quite familiar in our ranks. Your wife
Continually has it in her mouth.

She cannot touch an apple or an egg
But she must say, *This to Cinesias!*
CINESIAS O is that true?
LYSISTRATA By Aphrodite, it is.
If the conversation strikes on men, your wife
Cuts in with, "All are boobies by Cinesias."
CINESIAS Then call her here.
LYSISTRATA And what am I to get?
CINESIAS This, if you want it. . . . See, what I have here.
I'll give it you to dandle.
LYSISTRATA Then I'll call her.
CINESIAS Be quick, be quick. All grace is wiped from life
Since she went away. O sad, sad am I
When there I enter on that loneliness,
And wine is unvintaged of the sun's flavor,
And food tasteless, since I've grown this extra limb.
MYRRHINE *(above)* I love him O so much! but he won't have it.
Don't call me down to him.
CINESIAS Sweet little Myrrhine!
What do you mean? Come here.
MYRRHINE O no I won't.
Why are you calling me? You don't want me.
CINESIAS Not want you! with this week's old length of love.
MYRRHINE Farewell.
CINESIAS Don't go, please don't go, Myrrhine.
At least you'll hear our child. Call your mother, lad.
CHILD Mummy . . . mummy . . . mummy!
CINESIAS There now, don't you feel pity for the child
He's not been fed or washed now for six days.
MYRRHINE I certainly pity him with so heartless a father.
CINESIAS Come down, my sweetest, come for the child's sake.
MYRRHINE A trying life it is to be a mother!
I suppose I'd better go.
(She comes down.)
CINESIAS How much younger she looks,
How fresher and how prettier! Myrrhine,
Lift up your lovely face, your disdainful face;
And your ankle . . . let your scorn step out its worst;
It only rubs me to more passion here.
MYRRHINE *(playing with the child)* You're as innocent as he's iniquitous.
Let me kiss you, honey petling, mother's darling.
CINESIAS How wrong to follow other women's counsel
And let loose all these throbbing voids in yourself
As well as in me. Don't you go throb-throb?
MYRRHINE Take away your hands.
CINESIAS Everything in the house
Is being ruined.
MYRRHINE I don't care at all.

CINESIAS The roosters are picking all your web to rags.
Do you mind that?
MYRRHINE Not I.
CINESIAS What time we've wasted
We might have drenched with Paphian laughter, flung
On Aphrodite's Mysteries. O come here.
MYRRHINE Not till a treaty finishes the war.
CINESIAS If you must have it, then we'll get it done.
MYRRHINE Do it and I'll come home. Till then I am bound.
CINESIAS Well, let us have a quick one on the ground.
MYRRHINE No . . . no . . . still I'll not say that I don't love you.
CINESIAS You love me! Then, dear girl, let me get above you.
MYRRHINE You must be joking. The boy's looking on.
CINESIAS Here, Manes, take the child home. . . . There, he's gone.
There's nothing in the way now. Come, lie down.
MYRRHINE But, villain, where shall we do it?
CINESIAS In Pan's cave.
A splendid place!
MYRRHINE Where shall I make my ablutions
Before returning to the citadel?
CINESIAS You can easily wash yourself in the Clepsydra.
MYRRHINE But how can I break my oath?
CINESIAS Leave that to me,
I'll take all risk.
MYRRHINE Well, I'll get you a small couch.
CINESIAS Don't worry. I'd as soon lie on the ground.
MYRRHINE No, by Apollo, in spite of all your faults
I won't have you lying on the nasty earth.
(From here MYRRHINE *keeps on going off to fetch things.)*
CINESIAS Ah, how she loves me.
MYRRHINE Get into the bed,
While I take off my clothes. O what a nuisance,
I must find a mattress first.
CINESIAS Why a mattress?
Please don't get one!
MYRRHINE Lie on crude sacking!
Never, by Artemis! That would be too vulgar.
CINESIAS Open your legs.
MYRRHINE No. Wait a second.
CINESIAS O . . .
Then hurry back again.
MYRRHINE Here's a mattress, now
Lie down while I undress. But what a shame,
You have no pillow.
CINESIAS I don't want one, dear.
MYRRHINE But I do.
CINESIAS Miserable Comrade mine,
They treat you just like Heracles at a feast

With cheats of dainties, O disappointing legs!

MYRRHINE Raise up your head.

CINESIAS There, that's everything at last.

MYRRHINE Yes, all.

CINESIAS Then run to my arms, you golden girl.

MYRRHINE I'm undoing my girdle now. But you've not forgotten?
You're not deceiving me about the Treaty?

CINESIAS No, by my life, I'm not.

MYRRHINE Why, you've no blanket.

CINESIAS It's not the blanket but you I want to ravish.

MYRRHINE Never mind. You'll do that soon. I'll come straight back

CINESIAS The woman will choke me with her coverlets.

MYRRHINE Get up a moment.

CINESIAS Something else is up.

MYRRHINE Would you like me to perfume you?

CINESIAS By Apollo, no!

MYRRHINE By Aphrodite, I'll do it anway.

CINESIAS Lord Zeus, may she soon use up all the myrrh.

MYRRHINE Stretch out your hand. Take it and rub it in.

CINESIAS Hmm, it's not as fragrant as might be; that is,
Not before it's smeared. It doesn't smell of kisses.

MYRRHINE How silly I am: I've brought you Rhodian scents.

CINESIAS It's good enough, leave it, love.

MYRRHINE You must be jesting.

CINESIAS Plague rack the man who first compounded scent!

MYRRHINE Here, take this flask.

CINESIAS I've a far better one.
Don't tease me, lie down, and get nothing more.

MYRRHINE I'm coming . . . I'm just drawing off my shoes. . . .
You're sure you will vote for Peace?

CINESIAS I'll think about it.
(She runs off.)
I'm dead: the woman's worn me all away.
She's gone and left me with an anguished pulse.
What shall I put thee in (O woe!)
Since into something thou must go,
Poor little lad . . . he pines and peeks.
Our lovely girl has proved a curse.
(Where's Cynalopex?)
A nurse to cherish him, a nurse!

MEN Balked in your amorous delight
How melancholy is your plight.
With sympathy your case I view!
What loins, I ask, what liver too,
What cods, what buttocks, could sustain
This awful stretch and stiffening strain,
And not a single trace
Of lewd-thighed wenches in the place!

CINESIAS O Zeus, what sinewy suffering!
MEN She did it all, the harlot, she
With her atrocious harlotry.
WOMEN Nay, rather call her darling sweet.
MEN What, sweet? She's a rude, wicked thing.
CINESIAS A wicked thing, as I repeat.
O Zeus, O Zeus,
Canst thou not suddenly let loose
Some twirling hurricane to tear
Her flapping up along the air
And drop her, when she's whirled around,
Here to the ground
Neatly impaled upon this stake
That rises only for her sake. *(He goes out.)*

■■■

(Enter Spartan HERALD. *The* MAGISTRATE *comes forward.)*
HERALD Where gabs the Senate an' the Prytanes?
I've fetched dispatches for them.
MAGISTRATE Are you a man
Or a Priapus, pray?
HERALD My scrimp-brained lad,
I'm a herald, as ye see, who hae come frae Sparta
Anent a Peace.
MAGISTRATE Then why do you hide that lance
That sticks out under your arms?
HERALD I've brought no lance.
MAGISTRATE Then why do you turn aside and hold your cloak
So far out from your body? Is your groin swollen
With stress of traveling?
HERALD By Castor, I'll swear
The man is wud.
MAGISTRATE Why, look, it stands right out,
My rascal fellow.
HERALD But I tell ye No!
Enow o' fleering!
MAGISTRATE Well, what is it then?
HERALD It's my dispatch cane.
MAGISTRATE Of course—a Spartan cane!
But speak right out. I know all this too well.
Are new privations springing up in Sparta?
HERALD Och, hard as could be: in lofty lusty columns
Our allies stand united. We maun get Pellene.
MAGISTRATE Whence has this evil come? Is it from Pan?
HERALD No. Lampito first ran asklent, then the ithers
Sprinted after her example, and blocked, the hizzies,
Their wames unskaithed against our every fleech.
MAGISTRATE What did you do?

HERALD We are broken, and bent double
Limp like men carrying lanthorns in great winds
About the city. They winna let us even
Wi' lightest neif skim their primsie howes
Till we've concluded Peace-terms wi' a' Hellas.
MAGISTRATE So the conspiracy is universal;
This proves it. Then return to Sparta, bid them
Send envoys with full powers to treat of Peace;
And I will urge the Senate here to choose
Plenipotentiary ambassadors,
As argument adducing this erection.
HERALD I'm off. Your wisdom nane could contravert.
(They retire.)

■■■

MEN There is no beast, no rush of fire, like woman so untamed.
She calmly goes her way where even panthers would be shamed.
WOMEN And yet you are fool enough, it seems, to dare to war with me,
When for your faithful ally you might win me easily.
MEN Never could the hate I feel for womankind grow less.
WOMEN Then have your will. But I'll take pity on your nakedness.
For I can see just how ridiculous you look, and so
Will help you with your tunic if close up I now may go.
MEN Well, that, by Zeus, is no scoundrel deed, I frankly will admit.
I only took them off myself in a scoundrel raging fit.
WOMEN Now you look sensible, and that you're men no one could doubt.
If you were but good friends again, I'd take the insect out
That hurts your eye.
MEN Is that what's wrong? That nasty bitie thing.
Please squeeze it out, and show me what it is that makes this sting.
It's been paining me a long while now.
WOMEN Well I'll agree to that,
Although you're most unmannerly. O what a giant gnat.
Here, look! It comes from marshy Tricorysus, I can tell.
MEN O thank you. It was digging out a veritable well.
Now that it's gone, I can't hold back my tears. See how they fall.
WOMEN I'll wipe them off, bad as you are, and kiss you after all.
MEN I won't be kissed.
WOMEN O yes, you will. Your wishes do not matter.
MEN O botheration take you all! How you cajole and flatter.
A hell it is to live with you; to live without, a hell:
How truly was that said. But come, these enmities let's quell.
You stop from giving orders and I'll stop from doing wrong.
So let's join ranks and seal our bargain with a choric song.
CHORUS (MEN *and* WOMEN *form joint* CHORUS.)
Athenians, it's not our intention
To sow political dissension
By giving any scandal mention;

But on the contrary to promote good feeling in the state
By word and deed. We've had enough calamities of late.
So let a man or woman but divulge
They need a trifle, say,
Two minas, three or four,
I've purses here that bulge.
There's only one condition made
(Indulge my whim in this I pray)—
When Peace is signed once more,
On no account am I to be repaid.

And I'm making preparation
For a gay select collation
With some youths of reputation.
I've managed to produce some soup and they're slaughtering for me
A sucking pig: its flesh should taste as tender as could be.
I shall expect you at my house today.
To the baths make an early visit,
And bring your children along;
Don't dawdle on the way.
Ask no one; enter as if the place
Was all your own—yours henceforth is it.
If nothing chances wrong,
The door will then be shut bang in your face.

(The SPARTAN AMBASSADORS *approach.)*

CHORUS Here come the Spartan envoys with long, worried beards.
What's there?
That contraption like a wattled pig-sty jumbled twixt their thighs?
Hail, Spartans how do you fare?
Did anything new arise?

SPARTAN No need for a clutter o' words. Do ye see our condition?

CHORUS The situation swells to greater tension.
Something will explode soon.

SPARTAN It's awfu' truly.
But come, let us wi' the best speed we may
Scribble a Peace.

CHORUS I notice that our men
Like wrestlers poised for contest, hold their clothes
Out from their bellies. An athlete's malady!
Since exercise alone can bring relief.

ATHENIAN Can anyone tell us where Lysistrata is?
There is no need to describe our men's condition,
It shows up plainly enough.

CHORUS It's the same disease.
Do you feel a jerking throb there in the morning?

ATHENIAN By Zeus, yes! In these straits I'm racked all through.
Unless Peace is soon declared, we shall be driven

In the void of women to try Cleisthenes.
CHORUS Be wise and put your tunics on; who knows,
One of the Hermes castrators may perceive you.
ATHENIAN By Zeus, you're right.
SPARTAN By the Twa Goddesses,
Indeed ye are. Let's put our tunics on.
ATHENIAN Hail O my fellow sufferers, hail Spartans.
SPARTAN O hinnie darling, what a waefu' thing
If they had seen us wi' our lunging waddies!
ATHENIAN Tell us then, Spartans, what has brought you here?
SPARTAN We come to treat o' Peace.
ATHENIAN Well spoken there!
And we the same. Let us call out Lysistrata
Since she alone can settle the Peace terms.
SPARTAN Call out Lysistrata too if ye don't mind.
CHORUS No indeed. She hears your voices and she comes.
(Enter LYSISTRATA.*)*
Hail, Wonder of all women! Now you must be in turn
Hard, shifting, clear, deceitful, noble, crafty, sweet, and stern.
The foremost men of Hellas, smitten by your fascination,
Have brought their tangled quarrels here for your sole arbitration.
LYSISTRATA An easy task if their love's raging homesickness
Doesn't start trying out how well each other
Will serve instead of us. But I'll know at once
If they do. O where's that girl, Reconciliation?
Bring first before me the Spartan delegates,
And see you lift no rude or violent hands—
None of the churlish ways our husbands used.
But lead them courteously, as women should.
And if they grudge fingers, catch what's a better handle.
And introduce them with ready tact. The Athenians
Draw by whatever offers you a grip.
Now, Spartans, stay here facing me. Here you,
Athenians. Both hearken to my words.
I am a woman, but I'm not a fool.
And what of natural intelligence I own
Has been filled out with the remembered precepts
My father and the city elders taught me.
First I reproach you both sides equally
That when at Pylae and Olympia,
At Pytho and the many other shrines
That I could name, you sprinkle from one cup
The altars common to all Hellenes, yet
You wrack Hellenic cities, bloody Hellas
With deaths of her own sons, while yonder clangs
The gathering menace of barbarians.
ATHENIAN I cannot hold it in much longer now.
LYSISTRATA Now unto you, O Spartans, do I speak.

Do you forget how your own countryman,
Pericleidas, once came hither suppliant
Before our altars, pale in his purple robes,
Praying for an army when in Messenia
Danger growled, and the Sea god made earth quaver.
Then with four thousand hoplites Cimon marched
And saved all Sparta. Yet base ingrates now,
You are ravaging the soil of your preservers.

ATHENIAN By Zeus, they do great wrong, Lysistrata.

SPARTAN Great wrang, indeed. O what a pretty arse.

LYSISTRATA And now I turn to the Athenians.
Have you forgotten too how once the Spartans
In days when you wore slavish tunics, came
And with their spears broke a Thessalian host
And all the partisans of Hippias?
They alone stood by your shoulder on that day.
They freed you, so that for the slave's short skirt
You should wear the trailing cloak of liberty.

SPARTAN I've never seen a nobler woman anywhere.

ATHENIAN Nor I one with such prettily jointing hips.

LYSISTRATA Now, brethren twined with mutual benefactions,
Can you still war, can you suffer such disgrace?
Why not be friends? What is there to prevent you?

SPARTAN We're agreed, gin that we get this tempting Mole,

LYSISTRATA Which one?

SPARTAN That ane we've wanted to get into,
O for sae lang. . . . Pylos, of course.

ATHENIAN By Poseidon,
Never!

LYSISTRATA Give it up.

ATHENIAN Then what will we do?
We need some ticklish place united to us—

LYSISTRATA Ask for some other lurking-hole in return.

ATHENIAN Then, ah, we'll choose this snug thing here, Echinus,
Shall we call the nestling spot? And this backside haven,
These desirable twin promontories, the Maliac,
And then of course these Megarean Legs.

SPARTAN Not that, O surely not that, never that.

LYSISTRATA Agree! Now what are two legs more or less?

ATHENIAN I want to strip at once and plow my land.

SPARTAN And I too—but I want to dung it first.

LYSISTRATA And so you can, when Peace is once declared.
If you mean it, get your allies' heads together
And come to some decision.

ATHENIAN What allies?
There's no distinction in our politics:
We've risen as one man to this conclusion;
Every ally is jumping-mad to drive it home.

SPARTAN And ours the same, for sure.
ATHENIAN The Carystians first!
I'll bet on that.
LYSISTRATA I agree with all of you.
Now off and cleanse yourselves for the Acropolis,
For we invite you all in to a supper
From our commissariat-baskets. There at table
You will pledge your good behavior to our loins;
Then each man's wife is his to hustle home.
ATHENIAN Come, as quickly as possible.
SPARTAN As quick as ye like.
Lead on.
ATHENIAN O Zeus, quick, quick, lead quickly on. *(They hurry off.)*
CHORUS Broidered stuffs on high I'm heaping,
Fashionable cloaks and sweeping
Trains, not even gold gawds keeping.
Take them all, I pray you, take them all (I do not care)
And deck your children—your daughter, if the Basket she's to bear,
Come, everyone of you, come in and take
Of this rich hoard a share.
Nought's tied so skillfully
But you its seal can break
And plunder all you spy inside.
I've laid out all that I can spare,
And therefore you will see
Nothing unless than I you're sharper-eyed.
If lacking corn a man should be
While his slaves clamor hungrily
And his excessive progeny,
Then I've a handful of grain at home which is always to be had,
And to which in fact a more-than-life-size loaf I'd gladly add.
Then let the poor bring with them bag or sack
And take this store of food.
Manes, my man, I'll tell
To help them all to pack
Their wallets full. But O take care.
I had forgotten; don't intrude,
Or terrified you'll yell.
My dog is hungry too, and bites—beware!

■■■

(Some LOUNGERS *from the Market with torches approach the Banqueting hall. The* PORTER *bars their entrance.)*
FIRST LOUNGER Open the door.
PORTER Here, move along.
FIRST LOUNGER What's this?
You're sitting down. Shall I singe you with my torch?
That's vulgar! O I couldn't do it . . . yet

If it would gratify the audience,
I'll mortify myself.

SECOND LOUNGER And I will too.
We'll both be crude and vulgar, yes we will.

PORTER Be off at once now or you'll be wailing
Dirges for your hair. Get off at once,
And see you don't disturb the Spartan envoys
Just coming out from the splendid feast they've had.
(The banqueters begin to come out.)

FIRST ATHENIAN I've never known such a pleasant banquet before,
And what delightful fellows the Spartans are.
When we are warm with wine, how wise we grow.

SECOND ATHENIAN That's only fair, since sober we're such fools.
This is the advice I'd give the Athenians—
See our ambassadors are always drunk.
For when we visit Sparta sober, then
We're on the alert for trickery all the while
So that we miss half of the things they say,
And misinterpret things that were never said,
And then report the muddle back to Athens.
But now we're charmed with each other. They might cap
With the Telamon-catch instead of the Cleitagora,
And we'd applaud and praise them just the same;
We're not too scrupulous in weighing words.

PORTER Why, here the rascals come again to plague me.
Won't you move on, you sorry loafers there!

LOUNGER Yes, by Zeus, they're already coming out.

SPARTAN Now hinnie dearest, please tak' up your pipe
That I may try a spring an' sing my best
In honor o' the Athenians an' oursels.

ATHENIAN Aye, take your pipe. By all the gods, there's nothing
Could glad my heart more than to watch you dance.

SPARTANS Mnemosyne,[24]
Let thy fire storm these younkers,
O tongue wi' stormy ecstasy
  My Muse that knows
Our deeds and theirs, how when at sea
Their navies swooped upon
The Medes at Artemision—[25]
Gods for their courage, did they strike
Wrenching a triumph frae their foes;
  While at Thermopylae
Leonidas' army stood: wild boars they were like,
  Wild boars that wi' fierce threat

[24]The Goddess of Memory.

[25]Sixty-nine years earlier the Athenian fleet defeated the Persians at Artemision at the same time as the Spartans were making their famous stand at Thermoplae.

Their terrible tusks whet;
The sweat ran streaming down each twisted face,
Faem blossoming i' strange petals o' death
Panted frae mortal breath,
The sweat drenched a' their bodies i' that place,
For the hurlyburly o' Persians glittered more
Than the sands on the shore.
Come, Hunting Girl, an' hear my prayer—
You whose arrows whizz in woodlands, come an' bless
This Peace we swear.
Let us be fenced wi' agelong amity,
O let this bond stick ever firm through thee
In friendly happiness.
Henceforth no guilefu' perjury be seen!
O hither, hither O
Thou wildwood queen.

LYSISTRATA Earth is delighted now, peace is the voice of earth.
Spartans, sort out your wives: Athenians, yours.
Let each catch hands with his wife and dance his joy,
Dance out his thanks, be grateful in music,
And promise reformation with his heels.

ATHENIANS O Dancers, forward. Lead out the Graces,
Call Artemis out;
Then her brother, the Dancer of Skies,
That gracious Apollo.
Invoke with a shout
Dionysus out of whose eyes
Breaks fire on the maenads that follow;
And Zeus with his flares of quick lightning, and call
Happy Hera, Queen of all,
And all the Daimons summon hither to be
Witnesses of our revelry
And of the noble Peace we have made,
Aphrodite our aid.
Io Paieon, Io, cry—
For victory, leap!
Attained by me, leap!
Euoi Euoi Euai Euai.

SPARTAN Piper, gie us the music for a new sang.

SPARTANS Leaving again lovely lofty Taygetus
Hither O Spartan Muse, hither to greet us,
And wi' our choric voice to raise
To Amyclean Apollo praise,
And Tyndareus' gallant sons whose days
Alang Eurotas' banks merrily pass,
An' Athene o' the House o' Brass.

Now the dance begin;

Dance, making swirl your fringe o' woolly skin,
 While we join voices
To hymn dear Sparta that rejoices
 I' a beautifu' sang,
 An' loves to see
Dancers tangled beautifully,
For the girls i' tumbled ranks
 Alang Eurotas' banks
 Like wanton fillies thrang,
 Frolicking there
An' like Bacchantes shaking the wild air
 To comb a giddy laughter through the hair,
Bacchantes that clench thyrsi as they sweep
 To the ecstatic leap.

 An' Helen, Child o' Leda, come
Thou holy, nimble, gracefu' Queen,
Lead thou the dance, gather thy joyous tresses up i' bands
An' play like a fawn. To madden them, clap thy hands,
And sing praise to the warrior goddess templed i' our lands,
 Her o' the House o' Brass.[26]
(Exeunt.)

c. h. whitman

war between the sexes

As often, Aristophanes' mind is overfertile in the invention of fantastic devices, which quite overwhelm literal consistency. Lysistrata's basic plan, for women to refuse intercourse with their husbands until peace is made, is based on the sound and ancient observation that Aphrodite subdues every creature, even Zeus, with the exception, of course, of her three virgin sisters, Athena, Artemis, and Hestia. Actually, the plan involves a practical dilemma: the thing which is troubling Lysistrata and her friends is precisely the fact that their husbands are never at home, but always at war, so that there is no sex anyway—not even with an adulterer. But practical dilemmas never obstruct a comic plot, and often they further it. What Aristophanes wants is the confrontation of the symbols of war and peace as embodied in the two sexes, on the theory that the bosom is mightier than the sword. As the Spartan woman puts it:

[26]A famous Spartan temple.

> When Menelaus cast an eye upon
> Bare Helen's apples, he threw down his sword.

Accordingly, the men are to be enticed out of their wits by seeing their wives parading beautifully but untouchably about the house, adorned by every cosmetic wile known to woman, but maddeningly chaste. We are not told how, with the men away, this is to happen; and as a matter of fact, it does not happen. What happens is rather the opposite; the women secure their position by seizing the Acropolis and barricading themselves within, where they are anon besieged by the men. This might seem clashingly inconsistent with the plan as stated; yet in the symbolic terms of drama it finds justification in that it fulfills the given situation of the plot, that the act of war has supplanted the act of love. Certainly it motivates with skill the fighting parodos and the agon which follows.

The proposed tactics of enticement and refusal at home, which could scarcely have been presented en masse, are carried out only in the scene between Myrrhine and Cinesias. The major effort occurs at the Acropolis, in the struggle between the mocking women and the helpless warmongers who curse, threaten, and appeal, but all in vain. And yet the two schemes are not wholly divorced from each other. As Lysistrata follows her friends into the Propylaea, she swears that

> The men will come with neither fire nor threats
> Such as to make us open up these gates
> Again, save on the conditions we have said.

In view of what had been said, it is hardly farfetched to see in the gates of the citadel an anlogue to the gates of love; and it should not be forgotten that the Acropolis was the shrine of virgin Athena, goddess of war, indeed, but one of the three who resist Aphrodite. Athena and her rock thus become a complex motif, embodying generally the women's position; and it becomes a question, later in the play, whether they can maintain that position with Athena-like restraint, or whether they will prove weaker than the men and yield to their own desires. Somehow, the total symbol of the Acropolis is felicitously expressive of feminine sexual attitudes.

The other two goddesses who resist Aphrodite are not without notice in the play. As the Proboulos orders his archers to arrest Lysistrata, and one starts to do so, she swears by Artemis that he will get the worst of it. Her oath must be a little more than casually chosen, for three of her followers similarly threaten the other three archers, invoking, in turn, Pandrosos, Phosphorus, and Tauropolus. Phosphorus and Tauropolus are certainly epithets of Artemis; whether or not Pandrosos is also, as has been suggested, is perhaps not crucial, for it could be equally appropriate to invoke the virgin heroine Pandrosos, daughter of Cecrops, whose precinct lay near the north edge of the Acropolis. The point is inviolable chastity. As for the third goddess, Hestia, she is not in fact mentioned, but as little more than the personification of the home and the sacred hearth, her presence, or at least her meaning, makes itself felt throughout the play in the abundant images of domestic life, especially the domestic life of women. Hestia, the sanctity of the hearth as the center of the home, is really more important to the *Lysistrata* than either Athena or Artemis; even Aphrodite is in alliance with her, for the nonce, for the chief antinomy to war in the play is not simply sex, but domesticity, including sex. Aristophanes had dramatized the war between the generations in the *Wasps* and *Clouds;* he dramatizes here the war between the sexes, the male painted in its extremest colors of belligerence, bull-headedness, and the will to victory, the female with equal extremity identified with security, harmony, and the centripetal life of the home. Both, of course, are characterized by comically exaggerated carnal drives, and this in the end unites them. But the women's action unfolds through two simultaneous efforts: first, to recover Aphrodite, as Trygaeus struggled to recover Peace; and second, to recover Hestia, domestic integrity, for which purpose Aphrodite must be temporarily sequestered behind the ramparts of virgin goddesses.

This statement may appear like an overrational explanation of comic incongruence and farce. But it consists, at least, with the feminine inconsistencies revealed in the characters, and it explains why in the symbolic world of comedy love and peace can be recovered by means of warlike hostilities. More important, it offers a clue to why the *Lysistrata,* despite its evident bawdry and the coarseness of numerous episodes, possesses a delicacy of charm very difficult to convey in translation, but pervasively felt in the Greek. Far from being a pornographic orgy, as if often supposed, the play is a celebration of the life-giving properties of love, a fertility rite, not a witches' sabbath. Aristophanes was, of course, quite capable of writing uninhibitedly about any kind of sexual practice, and did so in many a play; but in this one, despite passing references to adultery and other makeshifts, he wrote about marriage, the marriage of men and women, and, in the end, the marriage of Athens and Sparta.

The play abounds in images of home life. When the women do not appear at Lysistrata's summons, Calonice explains why:

> They'll come; it's hard for women to get out.
> One of us, you know, is fussing with her husband,
> One's waking the hired man, one's tucking in
> The baby, one's bathing, another feeding him.

Lysistrata herself is a part of this existence, or had been. She had been a good wife, and she makes it clear that her present revolt has been thrust upon her only after long-suffering and patience:

> We bore as we could your earlier war, a long time bravely enduring,
> Because of our patient restraint, in the face of whatever you menfolk were doing.
> Anyway, you didn't let us complain, however little you pleased us;
> But we were aware of your antics throughout, and often at home in our houses,
> We'd hear of the miserable mess that you'd made of a really imperative business;
> And then in our sorrow, but smiling in any case (indoor creatures!), we'd ask you:
> "Well, what was decided today about peace, to write on a public inscription,

In the people's assembly?" And what do you think my husband said? He said, "Shut up!
What's that to you?" So I shut up.

Here, the note of war, entering and damaging domestic harmony, leads on to even wintrier images of husbands and sons sent to the campaigns, while the young girl sits at home, losing her bloom, and becoming a day-dreaming spinster. The cessation of the life of the home somewhat recalls the frozen stoppage throughout the earth described in the Babylonian poem where the goddess Inanna descends into the underworld: "The ox goes not to the plough, the maiden lies on her side." Of all the so-called "peace" plays, the *Lysistrata* has the saddest and tenderest imagery, for it is drawn not from the proliferations of a gigantic and preposterous metaphor, but simply and directly from life, the life of Athenian women who tend their families, and girls who fetch water from the fountain houses, "jostled by slaves, in the crowd and noise and rattle of pots," the girls whom the city reared "in luxuriant pride," each taking her part in the festivals and liturgies, as an *arrhephoros,* a mill girl for the sacred meal, a Brauronian "bear," a stately basket bearer at the Panathenaea.

The image of the young girl unmarried and hopeless is balanced and countered by the image of the baby quoted earlier. As loud and vigorous proof of regenerate life, and the natural opposite of the imagery of war, a baby is a domestic focal point, and as such he appears in the scene between Cinesias and Myrrhine. Even here, where the action comes close to the traditional strip tease of burlesque, the symbol of the household is present, and the quarrel between the male and the female takes the well-known familial form of each parent telling the child it is the other's fault. Again, in the scene where Lysistrata is having trouble with her troops, the basic antinomy of the play involves at least an imaginary baby. One of the women claims that she is pregnant and must go home to avoid giving birth on the sacred Acropolis. Yesterday she had not been pregnant, but today she tells her leader, showing her distended belly, that she is having a "male child"; male indeed, for the bulge turns out to be a helmet, in fact Athena's own helmet. It is, one might say, the image of the non-baby, the "hollow, brass thing" of war, at once the cause of the trouble, and the symbol of the city's total plight.

More important than the baby, however, is the image of wool. Cinesias accuses Myrrhine of neglecting her household:

Myrrh.: I care little for that.
Cines.: You care little as well for your yarn, all pulled
Apart by the chickens?
Myrrh.: That's right, by Zeus.

From earliest times the spinning and weaving of wool marks the good wife; "lanam fecit" says an early Roman tombstone, and no more need be said. It is true, Cinesias has not come primarily out of concern for the wool, and he passes immediately to the "rites of Aphrodite" which Myrrhine has also been neglecting. This juxtaposition of the two, marking the balance of woman's married life, has also occurred before, in the scene where the women are trying to desert the cause:

> Woman: I have a lot of Milesian wool at home,
> All being chomped up by the moths.
> Lysis.: Moths, eh?
> Come back here!
> Woman: By the two goddesses, I'll come back
> Immediately! Just let me spread it on the bed—
> Lysis.: Don't spread anything.

And with similar sexual innuendo, the next woman protests that she must peel the hackles off some flax from Amorgos.

These are, of course, mere pretexts, for the women's real motives do not differ from that of the girl whom Lysistrata pulled back by the hair as she was headed on sparrow-back for the brothel of Orsilochus. But the neglected wool, or flax, keeps before us the image of the wasted home nonetheless. If Eros has suffered from the war, it is part of Lysistrata's therapy that wool shall suffer too, and she is no longer ready to submit as she did formerly, when her husband told her to leave public matters alone, and "spin her thread, or get a whack in the face." All this finds its positive converse in the agon, where the heroine argues with the Proboulos. The Proboulos demands to know how Lysistrata proposes to solve the tangled problems of the city, and she replies in a magnificent simile, the reverse of Demosthenes' image in the *Knights* of politics as hash:

> Why, in the way that we loosen our wool, when it gets all tangled; we take it
> And picking out single threads with our spindles, we lead them this way or that way,
> Just so too we will loosen this war from the mess that it's in, if you let us.

And she continues the analogue for nearly twenty lines more, concluding that when the yarn is washed clean—of dirty politicians—she will make "a big skein and weave from it a cloak for the people." The Proboulos is naturally not impressed by this vision of the body politic wrapped in the homespun cloak of peace and harmony. Yet, as the action moves on the image achieves dramatic form when the chorus of old women coaxingly make up to the chorus of old men, and help them put on their cloaks, which they had thrown off in their rage. It is the turning point of the play, for the Spartan herald has just entered to offer peace.

The running imagery of domestic life is not, perhaps, the first thing which attracts attention in the *Lysistrata*, nor is it, perhaps, meant to be. But it is there, however implicitly, throughout the texture, to emerge with clear and tender simplicity in Lysistrata's two last speeches:

> Now purify yourselves
> That we women may entertain you all
> In the citadel, on what our stores afford.
> And there you will exchange good faith, and oaths,
> And afterward, take each of you his own
> Wife, and depart.

And later: "Let husband stand by wife,/And wife by husband." It is the cluster of domestic images which constitutes the heart of the play, the real antitype of war, the warm, woolly cloak versus the hollow, brass helmet. And it is surely this undercurrent which gives the rampant bawdry of the play its charm. Aristophanes has offered a whole vision, not a half. Sex is not viewed through any distorting lenses of unreal glamour or inhibited wish, but directly and realistically in the context of that institution which G. B. Shaw said combined the maximum of temptation with the maximum of opportunity. Nor is domestic life romanticized, as in the Menandrian world of stereotyped lovers ending up in a stereotype of happy union. Aristophanes' family picture includes a full measure of humdrum homeliness, bickerings, and ear-boxing. But the keynote is love. "Yes, I love my husband," says Myrrhine, "but he does not want to be loved by me," an odd thing to say when Cinesias is on his knees begging for her return. All that she means is that her husband, merely by being male, stands with the belligerents as a violator of the total vision, peace-love-home. If he will not settle for the whole, he can do without the part.

But if domesticity and marriage form a delicate inner symbolism of the play which determines the character of its denouement, the more evident imagery throughout presents, by contrast, a cheerful and compelling indelicacy. The chief controlling image of the play's action is, of course, the phallus. Whatever be the answer to the controversy over whether or not comic actors wore a leather phallus, it is hard to see how it is dispensable in this particular play. Old Comedy dealt so freely in what we call obscenity, that one wonders why such antics do not strike us as simply jejune and immature. Part of the answer may be in the fact that there is never any question of "daring," that lurid word which today sells so many mildly suggestive novels and movies. The adolescent, or the novelist who writes to appeal to the adolescent mentality, tries to show how far he dares to go in transgressing taboos. But the Old Comic poet did not have to dare to smash taboos; he was supposed to smash them, and his challenge lay in trying to discover how ingeniously he could smash them. For there were taboos, of course, and the place to smash them was the comic stage. There were in Greek, for instance, proper and improper words for the reproductive organs. The proper words occur with reasonable frequency from Homer to Aristotle, and quite frequently in the scholiasts of comedy, but they never occur in comedy; they would have been as out of place there as the improper words would have been in Homer. The absence of the element of daring, therefore, threw the poet totally onto his own competitive genius, whether for subtle innuendo of gargantuan breadth, and Aristophanes is a master of both. Nor was there any limit as to how far one could go; the *Lysistrata* is one of the best examples of the comic power of putting shame to shame by the sheer limitlessness of its freedom. Yet all the licentiousness of its speech and action does not contradict the motifs of domesticity, or even contrast with them, for as yet marrying and burning had not been thought of as opposites; they all fit together in the harmonious lyrical tension of Aristophanes' work at its best. Titania with the ass's head of Bottom in her lap gives something of the perspective.

molière 1622–1673

the misanthrope

translated by Richard Wilbur

Drama, influenced by the classical revival, developed in France under the royal patronage of Louis XIV, notably in the work of Racine and Molière. Jean Baptiste Poquelin, born of solid middle-class stock and respectably educated, was early lured to the dubious calling of actor, taking the stage-name of Molière. Success as a playwright was delayed for Molière through twelve years of touring the provinces until his troupe returned to Paris to produce his comedy of manners, *The Precious Young Ladies* (1659). Many works followed, constructed around key satiric ideas and portraits, exposing social folly and abuse of good sense in marital and parental relations, piety, social climbing, learning, and medicine. Those included *The School for Wives* (1662), *Tartuffe,* or the *Imposter* (1664), banned as irreligious, *The Misanthrope* (1666), *The Doctor in Spite of Himself* (1666), *The Miser* (1668), *The Bourgeois Gentleman* (1670), and *The Learned Ladies* (1672). Meanwhile, Molière had married an actress much younger than himself (probably the daughter of his former mistress), a mismating that may have fed his ironic portraits of unsuited couples. In 1673, while acting the lead in his *The Imaginary Invalid,* Molière was stricken and died shortly after.

the characters

ALCESTE, *in love with* CÉLIMÈNE
PHILINTE, ALCESTE'S *friend*
ORONTE, *in love with* CÉLIMÈNE
CÉLIMÈNE, ALCESTE'S *beloved*
ELIANTE, CÉLIMÈNE'S *cousin*
ARSINOE, *a friend of* CÉLIMÈNE'S
ACASTE } *marquesses*
CLITANDRE } *marquesses*

BASQUE, CÉLIMÈNE'S *servant;*
A GUARD *of the Marshalsea;*
DUBOIS, ALCESTE'S *valet*

(The setting throughout is in CÉLIMÈNE'S *house at Paris.)*

act I

scene 1

PHILINTE Now, what's got into you?
ALCESTE *(seated)* Kindly leave me alone.
PHILINTE Come, come, what is it? This lugubrious tone . . .
ALCESTE Leave me, I said; you spoil my solitude.
PHILINTE Oh, listen to me, now, and don't be rude.
ALCESTE I choose to be rude, Sir, and to be hard of hearing.
PHILINTE These ugly moods of yours are not endearing;
Friends though we are, I really must insist . . .
ALCESTE *(Abruptly rising)* Friends? Friends, you say? Well, cross me off your list.
I've been your friend till now, as you well know;
But after what I saw a moment ago
I tell you flatly that our ways must part.
I wish no place in a dishonest heart.
PHILINTE Why, what have I done, Alceste? Is this quite just?
ALCESTE My God, you ought to die of self-disgust.
I call your conduct inexcusable, Sir,
And every man of honor will concur.
I see you almost hug a man to death,
Exclaim for joy until you're out of breath,
And supplement these loving demonstrations
With endless offers, vows, and protestations;
Then when I ask you "Who was that?," I find
That you can barely bring his name to mind!
Once the man's back is turned, you cease to love him,
And speak with absolute indifference of him!
By God, I say it's base and scandalous
To falsify the heart's affections thus;
If I caught myself behaving in such a way,
I'd hang myself for shame, without delay.
PHILINTE It hardly seems a hanging matter to me;
I hope that you will take it graciously
If I extend myself a slight reprieve,
And live a little longer, by your leave.
ALCESTE How dare you joke about a crime so grave?
PHILINTE What crime? How else are people to behave?
ALCESTE I'd have them be sincere, and never part
With any word that isn't from the heart.
PHILINTE When someone greets us with a show of pleasure,
It's but polite to give him equal measure,
Return his love the best that we know how,
And trade him offer for offer, vow for vow.
ALCESTE No, no, this formula you'd have me follow,
However fashionable, is false and hollow,

And I despise the frenzied operations
Of all these barterers of protestations,
These lavishers of meaningless embraces,
These utterers of obliging commonplaces,
Who court and flatter everyone on earth
And praise the fool no less than the man of worth.
Should you rejoice that someone fondles you,
Offers his love and service, swears to be true,
And fills your ears with praises of your name,
When to the first damned fop he'll say the same?
No, no: no self-respecting heart would dream
Of prizing so promiscuous an esteem;
However high the praise, there's nothing worse
Than sharing honors with the universe.
Esteem is founded on comparison:
To honor all men is to honor none.
Since you embrace this indiscriminate vice,
Your friendship comes at far too cheap a price;
I spurn the easy tribute of a heart
Which will not set the worthy man apart:
I choose, Sir, to be chosen; and in fine,
The friend of mankind is no friend of mine.

PHILINTE But in polite society, custom decrees
That we show certain outward courtesies. . . .

ALCESTE Ah, no! we should condemn with all our force
Such false and artificial intercourse.
Let men behave like men; let them display
Their inmost hearts in everything they say;
Let the heart speak, and let our sentiments
Not mask themselves in silly compliments.

PHILINTE In certain cases it would be uncouth
And most absurd to speak the naked truth;
With all respect for your exalted notions,
It's often best to veil one's true emotions.
Wouldn't the social fabric come undone
If we were wholly frank with everyone?
Suppose you met with someone you couldn't bear;
Would you inform him of it then and there?

ALCESTE Yes.

PHILINTE Then you'd tell old Emilie it's pathetic
The way she daubs her features with cosmetic
And plays the gay coquette at sixty-four?

ALCESTE I would.

PHILINTE And you'd call Dorilas a bore,
And tell him every ear at court is lame
From hearing him brag about his noble name?

ALCESTE Precisely.

PHILINTE Ah, you're joking.
ALCESTE *Au contraire:*
In this regard there's none I'd choose to spare.
All are corrupt; there's nothing to be seen
In court or town but aggravates my spleen.
I fall into deep gloom and melancholy
When I survey the scene of human folly,
Finding on every hand base flattery,
Injustice, fraud, self-interest, treachery. . . .
Ah, it's too much; mankind has grown so base,
I mean to break with the whole human race.
PHILINTE This philosophic rage is a bit extreme;
You've no idea how comical you seem;
Indeed, we're like those brothers in the play
Called *School for Husbands*,[1] one of whom was prey . . .
ALCESTE Enough, now! None of your stupid similes.
PHILINTE Then let's have no more tirades, if you please.
The world won't change, whatever you say or do;
And since plain speaking means so much to you,
I'll tell you plainly that by being frank
You've earned the reputation of a crank,
And that you're thought ridiculous when you rage
And rant against the manners of the age.
ALCESTE So much the better; just what I wish to hear.
No news could be more grateful to my ear.
All men are so detestable in my eyes,
I should be sorry if they thought me wise.
PHILINTE Your hatred's very sweeping, is it not?
ALCESTE Quite right: I hate the whole degraded lot.
PHILINTE Must all poor human creatures be embraced,
Without distinction, by your vast distaste?
Even in these bad times, there are surely a few . . .
ALCESTE No, I include all men in one dim view:
Some men I hate for being rogues; the others
I hate because they treat the rogues like brothers,
And, lacking a virtuous scorn for what is vile,
Receive the villain with a complaisant smile.
Notice how tolerant people choose to be
Toward that bold rascal who's at law with me.
His social polish can't conceal his nature;
One sees at once that he's a treacherous creature;
No one could possibly be taken in
By those soft speeches and that sugary grin.
The whole world knows the shady means by which
The low-brow's grown so powerful and rich,
And risen to a rank so bright and high

[1]A play by Molière. *(Translator's notes.)*

That virtue can but blush, and merit sigh.
Whenever his name comes up in conversation,
None will defend his wretched reputation;
Call him knave, liar, scoundrel, and all the rest,
Each head will not, and no one will protest.
And yet his smirk is seen in every house,
He's greeted everywhere with smiles and bows,
And when there's any honor that can be got
By pulling strings, he'll get it, like as not.
My God! It chills my heart to see the ways
Men come to terms with evil nowadays;
Sometimes, I swear, I'm moved to flee and find
Some desert land unfouled by humankind.

PHILINTE Come, let's forget the follies of the times
And pardon mankind for its petty crimes;
Let's have an end of rantings and of railings,
And show some leniency toward human failings.
This world requires a pliant rectitude;
Too stern a virtue makes one stiff and rude;
Good sense views all extremes with detestation,
And bids us to be noble in moderation.
The rigid virtues of the ancient days
Are not for us; they jar with all our ways
And ask of us too lofty a perfection.
Wise men accept their times without objection,
And there's no greater folly, if you ask me,
Than trying to reform society.
Like you, I see each day a hundred and one
Unhandsome deeds that might be better done,
But still, for all the faults that meet my view,
I'm never known to storm and rave like you.
I take men as they are, or let them be,
And teach my soul to bear their frailty;
And whether in court or town, whatever the scene,
My phlegm's as philosophic as your spleen.[2]

ALCESTE The phlegm which you so eloquently commend,
Does nothing ever rile it up, my friend?
Suppose some man you trust should treacherously
Conspire to rob you of your property,
And do his best to wreck your reputation?
Wouldn't you feel a certain indignation?

PHILINTE Why, no. These faults of which you so complain
Are part of human nature, I maintain,
And it's no more a matter for disgust

[2] A reference to opposing "humours" in the old physiology. A preponderance of phlegm produced an apathetic temperament; a preponderance of bile a splenetic temperament.

That men are knavish, selfish and unjust,
Than that the vulture dines upon the dead,
And wolves are furious, and apes ill-bred.

ALCESTE Shall I see myself betrayed, robbed, torn to bits,
And not . . . Oh, let's be still and rest our wits.
Enough of reasoning, now. I've had my fill.

PHILINTE Indeed, you would do well, Sir, to be still.
Rage less at your opponent, and give some thought
To how you'll win this lawsuit that he's brought.

ALCESTE I assure you I'll do nothing of the sort.

PHILINTE Then who will plead your case before the court?

ALCESTE Reason and right and justice will plead for me.

PHILINTE Oh, Lord. What judges do you plan to see?[3]

ALCESTE Why, none. The justice of my cause is clear.

PHILINTE Of course, man; but there's politics to fear. . . .

ALCESTE No, I refuse to lift a hand. That's flat.
I'm either right, or wrong.

PHILINTE Don't count on that.

ALCESTE No, I'll do nothing.

PHILINTE Your enemy's influence
Is great you know . . .

ALCESTE That makes no difference.

PHILINTE It will; you'll see.

ALCESTE Must honor bow to guile?
If so, I shall be proud to lose the trial.

PHILINTE Oh, really . . .

ALCESTE I'll discover by this case
Whether or not men are sufficiently base
And impudent and villainous and perverse
To do me wrong before the universe.

PHILINTE What a man!

ALCESTE Oh, I could wish, whatever the cost,
Just for the beauty of it, that my trial were lost.

PHILINTE If people heard you talking so, Alceste,
They'd split their sides. Your name would be a jest.

ALCESTE So much the worse for jesters.

PHILINTE May I enquire
Whether this rectitude you so admire,
And these hard virtues you're enamored of
Are qualities of the lady whom you love?
It much surprises me that you, who seem
To view mankind with furious disesteem,
Have yet found something to enchant your eyes
Amidst a species which you so despise.
And what is more amazing, I'm afraid,

[3]It was customary to try to influence judges before a trial.

Is the most curious choice your heart has made.
The honest Eliante is fond of you,
Arsinoé, the prude, admires you too;
And yet your spirit's been perversely led
To choose the flighty Célimène instead,
Whose brittle malice and coquettish ways
So typify the manners of our days.
How is it that the traits you most abhor
Are bearable in this lady you adore?
Are you so blind with love that you can't find them?
Or do you contrive, in her case, not to mind them?

ALCESTE My love for that young widow's not the kind
That can't perceive defects; no, I'm not blind.
I see her faults, despite my ardent love,
And all I see I fervently reprove.
And yet I'm weak; for all her falsity,
That woman knows the art of pleasing me,
And though I never cease complaining of her,
I swear I cannot manage not to love her.
Her charm outweighs her faults; I can but aim
To cleanse her spirit in my love's pure flame.

PHILINTE That's no small task; I wish you all success.
You think then that she loves you?

ALCESTE Heavens, yes!
I wouldn't love her did she not love me.

PHILINTE Well, if her taste for you is plain to see,
Why do these rivals cause you such despair?

ALCESTE True love, Sir, is possessive, and cannot bear
To share with all the world. I'm here today
To tell her she must send that mob away.

PHILINTE If I were you, and had your choice to make,
Eliante, her cousin, would be the one I'd take;
That honest heart, which cares for you alone,
Would harmonize far better with your own.

ALCESTE True, true: each day my reason tells me so;
But reason doesn't rule in love, you know.

PHILINTE I fear some bitter sorrow is in store;
This love . . .

scene 2

(Enter ORONTE.*)*

ORONTE *(To* ALCESTE*)* The servants told me at the door
That Eliante and Célimène were out,
But when I heard, dear Sir, that you were about,
I came to say, without exaggeration,
That I hold you in the vastest admiration,
And that it's always been my dearest desire

To be the friend of one I so admire.
I hope to see my love of merit requited,
And you and I in friendship's bond united.
I'm sure you won't refuse—if I may be frank—
A friend of my devotedness—and rank.
(During this speech of ORONTE'S, ALCESTE *is abstracted, and seems unaware that he is being spoken to. He only breaks off his reverie when* ORONTE *says)*
It was for you, if you please, that my words were intended.

ALCESTE For me, Sir?
ORONTE Yes, for you. You're not offended?
ALCESTE By no means. But this much surprises me. . . .
The honor comes most unexpectedly. . . .
ORONTE My high regard should not astonish you;
The whole world feels the same. It is your due.
ALCESTE Sir . . .
ORONTE Why, in all the State there isn't one
Can match your merits; they shine, Sir, like the sun.
ALCESTE Sir . . .
ORONTE You are higher in my estimation
Than all that's most illustrious in the nation.
ALCESTE Sir . . .
ORONTE If I lie, may heaven strike me dead!
To show you that I mean what I have said,
Permit me, Sir, to embrace you most sincerely,
And swear that I will prize our friendship dearly.
Give me your hand. And now, Sir, if you choose,
We'll make our vows.
ALCESTE Sir . . .
ORONTE What! You refuse?
ALCESTE Sir, it's a very great honor you extend:
But friendship is a sacred thing, my friend;
It would be profanation to bestow
The name of friend on one you hardly know.
All parts are better played when well-rehearsed;
Let's put off friendship, and get acquainted first.
We may discover it would be unwise
To try to make our natures harmonize.
ORONTE By heaven! You're sagacious to the core;
This speech has made me admire you even more.
Let time, then, bring us closer day by day;
Meanwhile, I shall be yours in every way.
If, for example, there should be anything
You wish at court, I'll mention it to the King.
I have his ear, of course; it's quite well known
That I am much in favor with the throne.
In short, I am your servant. And now, dear friend,
Since you have such fine judgment, I intend

To please you, if I can, with a small sonnet
I wrote not long ago. Please comment on it,
And tell me whether I ought to publish it.

ALCESTE You must excuse me, Sir; I'm hardly fit
To judge such matters.

ORONTE Why not?

ALCESTE I am, I fear,
Inclined to be unfashionably sincere.

ORONTE Just what I ask; I'd take no satisfaction
In anything but your sincere reaction.
I beg you not to dream of being kind.

ALCESTE Since you desire it, Sir, I'll speak my mind.

ORONTE *Sonnet.* It's a sonnet. . . . *Hope* . . . The poem's addressed
To a lady who wakened hopes within my breast.
Hope . . . this is not the pompous sort of thing,
Just modest little verses, with a tender ring.

ALCESTE Well, we shall see.

ORONTE *Hope* . . . I'm anxious to hear
Whether the style seems properly smooth and clear,
And whether the choice of words is good or bad.

ALCESTE We'll see, we'll see.

ORONTE Perhaps I ought to add
That it took me only a quarter-hour to write it.

ALCESTE The time's irrelevant, Sir: kindly recite it.

ORONTE *(reading)* Hope comforts us awhile, t'is true,
Lulling our cares with careless laughter,
And yet such joy is full of rue,
My Phyllis, if nothing follows after.

PHILINTE I'm charmed by this already; the style's delightful.

ALCESTE *(sotto voce to* PHILINTE*)* How can you say that? Why, the thing is frightful.

ORONTE Your fair face smiled on me awhile,
But was it kindness so to enchant me?
'Twould have been fairer not to smile,
If hope was all you meant to grant me.

PHILINTE What a clever thought! How handsomely you phrase it!

ALCESTE *(sotto voce to* PHILINTE*)* You know the thing is trash. How dare you praise it?

ORONTE If it's to be my passion's fate
Thus everlastingly to wait,
Then death will come to set me free:
For death is fairer than the fair;
Phyllis, to hope is to despair
When one must hope eternally.

PHILINTE The close is exquisite—full of feeling and grace.

ALCESTE *(sotto voce, aside)* Oh, blast the close; you'd better close your face
Before you send your lying soul to hell.

PHILINTE I can't remember a poem I've liked so well.
ALCESTE *(sotto voce, aside)* Good Lord!
ORONTE *(to* PHILINTE*)* I fear you're flattering me a bit.
PHILINTE Oh, no!
ALCESTE *(sotto voce, aside)* What else d'you call it, you hypocrite?
ORONTE *(to* ALCESTE*)* But you, Sir, keep your promise now: don't shrink
From telling me sincerely what you think.
ALCESTE Sir, these are delicate matters; we all desire
To be told that we've the true poetic fire.
But once, to one whose name I shall not mention,
I said, regarding some verse of his invention,
That gentlemen should rigorously control
That itch to write which often afflicts the soul;
That one should curb the heady inclination
To publicize one's little avocation;
And that in showing off one's works of art
One often plays a very clownish part.
ORONTE Are you suggesting in a devious way
That I ought not . . .
ALCESTE Oh, that I do not say.
Further, I told him that no fault is worse
Than that of writing frigid, lifeless verse,
And that the merest whisper of such a shame
Suffices to destroy a man's good name.
ORONTE D'you mean to say my sonnet's dull and trite?
ALCESTE I don't say that. But I went on to cite
Numerous cases of once-respected men
Who came to grief by taking up the pen.
ORONTE And am I like them? Do I write so poorly?
ALCESTE I don't say that. But I told this person, "Surely
You're under no necessity to compose;
Why you should wish to publish, heaven knows.
There's no excuse for printing tedious rot
Unless one writes for bread, as you do not.
Resist temptation, then, I beg of you;
Conceal your pastimes from the public view;
And don't give up, on any provocation,
Your present high and courtly reputation,
To purchase at a greedy printer's shop
The name of silly author and scribbling fop."
These were the points I tried to make him see.
ORONTE I sense that they are also aimed at me;
But now—about my sonnet—I'd like to be told . . .
ALCESTE Frankly, that sonnet should be pigeonholed.
You've chosen the worst models to imitate.
The style's unnatural. Let me illustrate:

Followed by, *'Twould have been fairer not to smile!*

For example, *Your fair face smiled on me awhile,*
Or this: *such joy is full of rue;*
Or this: *For death is fairer than the fair;*
Or, *Phyllis, to hope is to despair*
When one must hope eternally!

This artificial style, that's all the fashion,
Has neither taste, nor honesty, nor passion;
It's nothing but a sort of wordy play,
And nature never spoke in such a way.
What, in this shallow age, is not debased?
Our fathers, though less refined, had better taste;
I'd barter all that men admire today
For one old love-song I shall try to say:

If the King had given me for my own
Paris, his citadel,
And I for that must leave alone
Her whom I love so well,
I'd say then to the Crown,
Take back your glittering town;
My darling is more fair, I swear,
My darling is more fair.

The rhyme's not rich, the style is rough and old,
But don't you see that it's the purest gold
Beside the tinsel nonsense now preferred,
And that there's passion in its every word?

If the King had given me for my own
Paris, his citadel,
And I for that must leave alone
Her whom I love so well,
I'd say then to the Crown,
Take back your glittering town;
My darling is more fair, I swear,
My darling is more fair.

There speaks a loving heart. *(to* PHILINTE*)* You're laughing, eh?
Laugh on, my precious wit. Whatever you say,
I hold that song's worth all the bibelots
That people hail today with ah's and oh's.
ORONTE And I maintain my sonnet's very good.
ALCESTE It's not at all surprising that you should.
You have your reasons; permit me to have mine
For thinking that you cannot write a line.
ORONTE Others have praised my sonnet to the skies.
ALCESTE I lack their art of telling pleasant lies.

ORONTE You seem to think you've got no end of wit.
ALCESTE To praise your verse, I'd need still more of it.
ORONTE I'm not in need of your approval, Sir.
ALCESTE That's good; you couldn't have it if you were.
ORONTE Come now, I'll lend you the subject of my sonnet;
I'd like to see you try to improve upon it.
ALCESTE I might, by chance, write something just as shoddy;
But then I wouldn't show it to everybody.
ORONTE You're most opinionated and conceited.
ALCESTE Go find your flatterers, and be better treated.
ORONTE Look here, my little fellow, pray watch your tone.
ALCESTE My great big fellow, you'd better watch your own.
PHILINTE *(stepping between them)* Oh, please, please, gentlemen! This will never do.
ORONTE The fault is mine, and I leave the field to you.
I am your servant, Sir, in every way.
ALCESTE And I, Sir, am your most abject valet.
(Exit ORONTE.*)*

scene 3

PHILINTE Well, as you see, sincerity in excess
Can get you into a very pretty mess;
Oronte was hungry for appreciation. . . .
ALCESTE Don't speak to me.
PHILINTE What?
ALCESTE No more conversation.
PHILINTE Really, now . . .
ALCESTE Leave me alone.
PHILINTE If I . . .
ALCESTE Out of my sight!
PHILINTE But what . . .
ALCESTE I won't listen.
PHILINTE But . . .
ALCESTE Silence!
PHILINTE Now, is it polite . . .
ALCESTE By heaven, I've had enough. Don't follow me.
PHILINTE Ah, you're just joking. I'll keep you company.

act II

scene 1

ALCESTE Shall I speak plainly, Madam? I confess
Your conduct gives me infinite distress,
And my resentment's grown too hot to smother.
Soon, I foresee, we'll break with one another.
If I said otherwise, I should deceive you;
Sooner or later, I shall be forced to leave you,

And if I swore that we shall never part,
I should misread the omens of my heart.

CELIMENE You kindly saw me home, it would appear,
So as to pour invectives in my ear.

ALCESTE I've no desire to quarrel. But I deplore
Your inability to shut the door
On all these suitors who beset you so.
There's what annoys me, if you care to know.

CELIMENE Is it my fault that all these men pursue me?
Am I to blame if they're attracted to me?
And when they gently beg an audience,
Ought I to take a stick and drive them hence?

ALCESTE Madam, there's no necessity for a stick;
A less responsive heart would do the trick.
Of your attractiveness I don't complain;
But those your charms attract, you then detain
By a most melting and receptive manner,
And so enlist their hearts beneath your banner.
It's the agreeable hopes which you excite
That keep these lovers round you day and night;
Were they less liberally smiled upon,
That sighing troop would very soon be gone.
But tell me, Madam, why it is that lately
This man Clitandre interests you so greatly?
Because of what high merits do you deem
Him worthy of the honor of your esteem?
Is it that your admiring glances linger
On the splendidly long nail of his little finger?
Or do you share the general deep respect
For the blond wig he chooses to affect?
Are you in love with his embroidered hose?
Do you adore his ribbons and his bows?
Or is it that this paragon bewitches
Your tasteful eye with his vast German breeches?
Perhaps his giggle, or his falsetto voice,
Makes him the latest gallant of your choice?[4]

CELIMENE You're much mistaken to resent him so.
Why I put up with him you surely know:
My lawsuit's very shortly to be tried,
And I must have influence on my side.

ALCESTE Then lose your lawsuit, Madam, or let it drop;
Don't torture me by humoring such a fop.

CELIMENE You're jealous of the whole world, Sir.

ALCESTE That's true,
Since the whole world is well-received by you.

[4]Molière frequently ridicules the fashionable fops of the day.

CELIMENE That my good nature is so unconfined
Should serve to pacify your jealous mind;
Were I to smile on one, and scorn the rest,
Then you might have some cause to be distressed.
ALCESTE Well, if I mustn't be jealous, tell me, then,
Just how I'm better treated than other men.
CELIMENE You know you have my love. Will that not do?
ALCESTE What proof have I that what you say is true?
CELIMENE I would expect, Sir, that my having said it
Might give the statement a sufficient credit.
ALCESTE But how can I be sure that you don't tell
The selfsame thing to other men as well?
CELIMENE What a gallant speech! How flattering to me!
What a sweet creature you make me out to be!
Well then, to save you from the pangs of doubt,
All that I've said I hereby cancel out;
Now, none but yourself shall make a monkey of you:
Are you content?
ALCESTE Why, why am I doomed to love you?
I swear that I shall bless the blissful hour
When this poor heart's no longer in your power!
I make no secret of it: I've done my best
To exorcise this passion from my breast;
But thus far all in vain; it will not go;
It's for my sins that I must love you so.
CELIMENE Your love for me is matchless, Sir; that's clear.
ALCESTE Indeed, in all the world it has no peer;
Words can't describe the nature of my passion,
And no man ever loved in such a fashion.
CELIMENE Yes, it's a brand-new fashion, I agree:
You show your love by castigating me,
And all your speeches are enraged and rude.
I've never been so furiously wooed.
ALCESTE Yet you could calm that fury, if you chose.
Come, shall we bring our quarrels to a close?
Let's speak with open hearts, then, and begin . . .

scene 2

(Enter BASQUE.*)*
CELIMENE What is it?
BASQUE Acaste is here.
CELIMENE Well, send him in.
(Exit BASQUE.*)*

scene 3

ALCESTE What! Shall we never be alone at all?
You're always ready to receive a call,

And you can't bear, for ten ticks of the clock,
Not to keep open house for all who knock.
CELIMENE I couldn't refuse him: he'd be most put out.
ALCESTE Surely that's not worth worrying about.
CELIMENE Acaste would never forgive me if he guessed
That I consider him a dreadful pest.
ALCESTE If he's a pest, why bother with him then?
CELIMENE Heavens! One can't antagonize such men;
Why, they're the chartered gossips of the court,
And have a say in things of every sort.
One must receive them, and be full of charm;
They're no great help, but they can do you harm,
And though your influence be ever so great,
They're hardly the best people to alienate.
ALCESTE I see, dear lady, that you could make a case
For putting up with the whole human race;
These friendships that you calculate so nicely . . .

scene 4

(Enter BASQUE.*)*
BASQUE Madam, Clitandre is here as well.
ALCESTE Precisely.
CELIMENE Where are you going?
ALCESTE Elsewhere.
CELIMENE Stay.
ALCESTE No, no.
CELIMENE Stay, Sir.
ALCESTE I can't.
CELIMENE I wish it.
ALCESTE No, I must go.
I beg you, Madam, not to press the matter;
You know I have no taste for idle chatter.
CELIMENE Stay: I command you.
ALCESTE No, I cannot stay.
CELIMENE Very well; you have my leave to go away.

scene 5

(Enter ELIANTE, PHILINTE, ACASTE, CLITANDRE.*)*
ELIANTE *(To* CELIMENE*)* The Marquesses have kindly come to call.
Were they announced?
CELIMENE Yes. Basque, bring chairs for all.
*(*BASQUE *provides the chairs, and exits.)*
(To ALCESTE*)* You haven't gone?
ALCESTE No; and I shan't depart
Till you decide who's foremost in your heart.
CELIMENE Oh, hush.
ALCESTE It's time to choose; take them, or me.

CELIMENE You're mad.
ALCESTE I'm not, as you shall shortly see.
CELIMENE Oh?
ALCESTE You'll decide.
CELIMENE You're joking now, dear friend.
ALCESTE No, no; you'll choose; my patience is at an end.
CLITANDRE Madam, I come from court, where poor Cléonte
Behaved like a perfect fool, as is his wont.
Has he no friend to counsel him, I wonder,
And teach him less unerringly to blunder?
CELIMENE It's true, the man's a most accomplished dunce;
His gauche behavior strikes the eye at once;
And every time one sees him, on my word,
His manner's grown a trifle more absurd.
ACASTE Speaking of dunces, I've just now conversed
With old Damon, who's one of the very worst;
I stood a lifetime in the broiling sun
Before his dreary monologue was done.
CELIMENE Oh, he's a wondrous talker, and has the power
To tell you nothing hour after hour:
If, by mistake, he ever came to the point,
The shock would put his jawbone out of joint.
ELIANTE *(to* PHILINTE*)* The conversation takes its usual turn,
And all our dear friends' ears will shortly burn.
CLITANDRE Timante's a character, Madam.
CELIMENE Isn't he, though?
A man of mystery from top to toe,
Who moves about in a romantic mist
On secret missions which do not exist.
His talk is full of eyebrows and grimaces;
How tired one gets of his momentous faces;
He's always whispering something confidential
Which turns out to be quite inconsequential;
Nothing's too slight for him to mystify;
He even whispers when he says "good-by."
ACASTE Tell us about Géralde.
CELIMENE That tiresome ass.
He mixes only with the titled class,
And fawns on dukes and princes, and is bored
With anyone who's not at least a lord.
The man's obsessed with rank, and his discourses
Are all of hounds and carriages and horses;
He uses Christian names with all the great,
And the word Milord, with him, is out of date.
CLITANDRE He's very taken with Bélise, I hear.
CELIMENE She is the dreariest company, poor dear.
Whenever she comes to call, I grope about
To find some topic which will draw her out,

But, owing to her dry and faint replies,
The conversation wilts, and droops, and dies.
In vain one hopes to animate her face
By mentioning the ultimate commonplace;
But sun or shower, even hail or frost
Are matters she can instantly exhaust.
Meanwhile her visit, painful though it is,
Drags on and on through mute eternities,
And though you ask the time, and yawn, and yawn,
She sits there like a stone and won't be gone.

ACASTE Now for Adraste.

CELIMENE Oh, that conceited elf
Has a gigantic passion for himself;
He rails against the court, and cannot bear it
That none will recognize his hidden merit;
All honors given to others give offense
To his imaginary excellence.

CLITANDRE What about young Cléon? His house, they say,
Is full of the best society, night and day.

CELIMENE His cook has made him popular, not he:
It's Cléon's table that people come to see.

ELIANTE He gives a splendid dinner, you must admit.

CELIMENE But must he serve himself along with it?
For my taste, he's a most insipid dish
Whose presence sours the wine and spoils the fish.

PHILINTE Damis, his uncle, is admired no end.
What's your opinion, Madam?

CELIMENE Why, he's my friend.

PHILINTE He seems a decent fellow, and rather clever.

CELIMENE He works too hard at cleverness, however.
I hate to see him sweat and struggle so
To fill his conversation with bon mots.
Since he's decided to become a wit
His taste's so pure that nothing pleases it;
He scolds at all the latest books and plays,
Thinking that wit must never stoop to praise,
That finding fault's a sign of intellect,
That all appreciation is abject,
And that by damning everything in sight
One shows oneself in a distinguished light.
He's scornful even of our conversations:
Their trivial nature sorely tries his patience;
He folds his arms, and stands above the battle,
And listens sadly to our childish prattle.

ACASTE Wonderful, Madam! You've hit him off precisely.

CLITANDRE No one can sketch a character so nicely.

ALCESTE How bravely, Sirs, you cut and thrust at all.
These absent fools, till one by one they fall:

But let one come in sight, and you'll at once
Embrace the man you lately called a dunce,
Telling him in a tone sincere and fervent
How proud you are to be his humble servant.

CLITANDRE Why pick on us? Madame's been speaking, Sir,
And you should quarrel, if you must, with her.

ALCESTE No, no, by God, the fault is yours, because
You lead her on with laughter and applause,
And make her think that she's the more delightful
The more her talk is scandalous and spiteful.
Oh, she would stoop to malice far, far less
If no such claque approved her cleverness.
It's flatterers like you whose foolish praise
Nourishes all the vices of these days.

PHILINTE But why protest when someone ridicules
Those you'd condemn, yourself, as knaves or fools?

CELIMENE Why, Sir? Because he loves to make a fuss.
You don't expect him to agree with us,
When there's an opportunity to express
His heaven-sent spirit of contrariness?
What other people think, he can't abide;
Whatever they say, he's on the other side;
He lives in deadly terror of agreeing;
'Twould make him seem an ordinary being.
Indeed, he's so in love with contradiction,
He'll turn against his most profound conviction
And with a furious eloquence deplore it,
If only someone else is speaking for it.

ALCESTE Go on, dear lady, mock me as you please;
You have your audience in ecstasies.

PHILINTE But what she says is true: you have a way
Of bridling at whatever people say;
Whether they praise or blame, your angry spirit
Is equally unsatisfied to hear it.

ALCESTE Men, Sir, are always wrong, and that's the reason
That righteous anger's never out of season;
All that I hear in all their conversation
Is flattering praise or reckless condemnation.

CELIMENE But . . .

ALCESTE No, no, Madam, I am forced to state
That you have pleasures which I deprecate,
And that these others, here, are much to blame
For nourishing the faults which are your shame.

CLITANDRE I shan't defend myself, Sir; but I vow
I'd thought this lady faultless until now.

ACASTE I see her charms and graces, which are many;
But as for faults, I've never noticed any.

ALCESTE I see them, Sir; and rather than ignore them,

I strenuously criticize her for them.
The more one loves, the more one should object
To every blemish, every least defect.
Were I this lady, I would soon get rid
Of lovers who approved of all I did,
And by their slack indulgence and applause
Endorsed my follies and excused my flaws.

CELIMENE If all hearts beat according to your measure,
The dawn of love would be the end of pleasure;
And love would find its perfect consummation
In ecstasies of rage and reprobation.

ELIANTE Love, as a rule, affects men otherwise,
And lovers rarely love to criticize.
They see their lady as a charming blur,
And find all things commendable in her.
If she has any blemish, fault, or shame,
They will redeem it by a pleasing name.
The pale-faced lady's lily-white, perforce;
The swarthy one's a sweet brunette, of course;
The spindly lady has a slender grace;
The fat one has a most majestic pace;
The plain one, with her dress in disarray,
They classify as *beauté négligée;*
The hulking one's a goddess in their eyes,
The dwarf, a concentrate of Paradise;
The haughty lady has a noble mind;
The mean one's witty, and the dull one's kind;
The chatterbox has liveliness and verve,
The mute one has a virtuous reserve.
So lovers manage, in their passion's cause,
To love their ladies even for their flaws.[5]

ALCESTE But I still say . . .

CELIMENE I think it would be nice.
To stroll around the gallery once or twice.
What! You're not going, Sirs?

CLITANDRE AND ACASTE No, Madam, no.

ALCESTE You seem to be in terror lest they go.
Do what you will, Sirs; leave, or linger on,
But I shan't go till after you are gone.

ACASTE I'm free to linger, unless I should perceive
Madame is tired, and wishes me to leave.

CLITANDRE And as for me, I needn't go today
Until the hour of the King's *coucher*.

CELIMENE *(to* ALCESTE*)* You're joking, surely?

ALCESTE Not in the least; we'll see

[5]A paraphrase of a passage from Lucretius, *De Rerum Natura,* Book IV. Molière is said to have translated Lucretius' poem as a student.

Whether you'd rather part with them, or me.

scene 6

(Enter BASQUE.*)*
BASQUE *(to* ALCESTE*)* Sir, there's a fellow here who bids me state
That he must see you, and that it can't wait.
ALCESTE Tell him that I have no such pressing affairs.
BASQUE It's a long tailcoat that this fellow wears,
With gold all over.
CELIMENE *(to* ALCESTE*)* You'd best go down and see.
Or—have him enter.
(Exit BASQUE.*)*

scene 7

(Enter GUARD.*)*
ALCESTE *(confronting the* GUARD*)* Well, what do you want with me?
Come in, Sir.
GUARD I've a word, Sir, for your ear.
ALCESTE Speak it aloud, Sir; I shall strive to hear.
GUARD The Marshals have instructed me to say
You must report to them without delay.
ALCESTE Who? Me, Sir?
GUARD Yes, Sir; you.
ALCESTE But what do they want?
PHILINTE *(to* ALCESTE*)* To scotch your silly quarrel with Oronte.
CELIMENE *(to* PHILINTE*)* What quarrel?
PHILINTE Oronte and he have fallen out
Over some verse he spoke his mind about;
The Marshals wish to arbitrate the matter.[6]
ALCESTE Never shall I equivocate or flatter!
PHILINTE You'd best obey their summons; come, let's go.
ALCESTE How can they mend our quarrel, I'd like to know?
Am I to make a cowardly retraction,
And praise those jingles to his satisfaction?
I'll not recant; I've judged that sonnet rightly.
It's bad.
PHILINTE But you might say so more politely. . . .
ALCESTE I'll not back down; his verses make me sick.
PHILINTE If only you could be more politic!
But come, let's go.
ALCESTE I'll go, but I won't unsay
A single word.
PHILINTE Well, let's be on our way.
ALCESTE Till I am ordered by my lord the King
To praise that poem, I shall say the thing

[6]The Marshalls were charged with preventing duels, which, though against the law, were frequent.

Is scandalous, by God, and that the poet
Ought to be hanged for having the nerve to show it.
(to CLITANDRE *and* ACASTE, *who are laughing)*
By heaven, Sirs, I really didn't know
That I was being humorous.

CELIMENE Go, Sir, go;
Settle your business.

ALCESTE I shall, and when I'm through,
I shall return to settle things with you.

act III

scene 1

CLITANDRE Dear Marquess, how contented you appear;
All things delight you, nothing mars your cheer.
Can you, in perfect honesty, declare
That you've a right to be so debonair?

ACASTE By Jove, when I survey myself, I find
No cause whatever for distress of mind.
I'm young and rich; I can in modesty
Lay claim to an exalted pedigree;
And owing to my name and my condition
I shall not want for honors and position.
Then as to courage, that most precious trait,
I seem to have it, as was proved of late
Upon the field of honor, where my bearing,
They say, was very cool and rather daring.
I've wit, of course; and taste in such perfection
That I can judge without the least reflection,
And at the theater, which is my delight,
Can make or break a play on opening night,
And lead the crowd in hisses or bravos,
And generally be known as one who knows.
I'm clever, handsome, gracefully polite;
My waist is small, my teeth are strong and white;
As for my dress, the world's astonished eyes
Assure me that I bear away the prize.
I find myself in favor everywhere,
Honored by men, and worshiped by the fair;
And since these things are so, it seems to me
I'm justified in my complacency.

CLITANDRE Well, if so many ladies hold you dear,
Why do you press a hopeless courtship here?

ACASTE Hopeless, you say? I'm not the sort of fool
That likes his ladies difficult and cool.
Men who are awkward, shy, and peasantish
May pine for heartless beauties, if they wish,

Grovel before them, bear their cruelties,
Woo them with tears and sighs and bended knees,
And hope by dogged faithfulness to gain
What their poor merits never could obtain.
For men like me, however, it makes no sense
To love on trust, and foot the whole expense.
Whatever any lady's merits be,
I think, thank God, that I'm as choice as she;
That if my heart is kind enough to burn
For her, she owes me something in return;
And that in any proper love affair
The partners must invest an equal share.

CLITANDRE You think, then, that our hostess favors you?
ACASTE I've reason to believe that that is true.
CLITANDRE How did you come to such a mad conclusion?
You're blind, dear fellow. This is sheer delusion.
ACASTE All right, then: I'm deluded and I'm blind.
CLITANDRE Whatever put the notion in your mind?
ACASTE Delusion.
CLITANDRE What persuades you that you're right?
ACASTE I'm blind.
CLITANDRE But have you any proofs to cite?
ACASTE I tell you I'm deluded.
CLITANDRE Have you, then,
Received some secret pledge from Célimène?
ACASTE Oh, no: she scorns me.
CLITANDRE Tell me the truth, I beg.
ACASTE She just can't bear me.
CLITANDRE Ah, don't pull my leg.
Tell me what hope she's given you, I pray.
ACASTE I'm hopeless, and it's you who win the day,
She hates me thoroughly, and I'm so vexed
I mean to hang myself on Tuesday next.
CLITANDRE Dear Marquess, let us have an armistice
And make a treaty. What do you say to this?
If ever one of us can plainly prove
That Célimène encourages his love,
The other must abandon hope, and yield,
And leave him in possession of the field.
ACASTE Now, there's a bargain that appeals to me;
With all my heart, dear Marquess, I agree.
But hush.

scene 2

(Enter CELIMENE.*)*

CELIMENE Still here?
CLITANDRE T'was love that stayed our feet.
CELIMENE I think I heard a carriage in the street.

Whose is it? D'you know?

scene 3

(Enter BASQUE.*)*
BASQUE Arsinoé is here,
Madame.
CELIMENE Arsinoé, you say? Oh, dear.
BASQUE Eliante is entertaining her below.
CELIMENE What brings the creature here, I'd like to know?
ACASTE They say she's dreadfully prudish, but in fact
I think her piety . . .
CELIMENE It's all an act.
At heart she's worldly, and her poor success
In snaring men explains her prudishness.
It breaks her heart to see the beaux and gallants
Engrossed by other women's charms and talents,
And so she's always in a jealous rage
Against the faulty standards of the age.
She lets the world believe that she's a prude
To justify her loveless solitude,
And strives to put a brand of moral shame
On all the graces that she cannot claim.
But still she'd love a lover; and Alceste
Appears to be the one she'd love the best.
His visits here are poison to her pride;
She seems to think I've lured him from her side;
And everywhere, at court or in the town,
The spiteful, envious woman runs me down.
In short, she's just as stupid as can be,
Vicious and arrogant in the last degree,
And . . .

scene 4

(Enter ARSINOE.*)*
CELIMENE Ah! What happy chance has brought you here?
I've thought about you ever so much, my dear.
ARSINOE I've come to tell you something you should know.
CELIMENE How good of you to think of doing so!
(CLITANDRE *and* ACASTE *go out, laughing)*

scene 5

ARSINOE It's just as well those gentlemen didn't tarry.
CELIMENE Shall we sit down?
ARSINOE That won't be necessary.
Madam, the flame of friendship ought to burn
Brightest in matters of the most concern,
And as there's nothing which concerns us more
Than honor, I have hastened to your door

To bring you, as your friend, some information
About the status of your reputation.
I visited, last night, some virtuous folk,
And, quite by chance, it was of you they spoke;
There was, I fear, no tendency to praise
Your light behavior and your dashing ways.
The quantity of gentlemen you see
And your by now notorious coquetry
Were both so vehemently criticized
By everyone, that I was much surprised.
Of course, I needn't tell you where I stood;
I came to your defense as best I could,
Assured them you were harmless, and declared
Your soul was absolutely unimpaired.
But there are some things, you must realize,
One can't excuse, however hard one tries,
And I was forced at last into conceding
That your behavior, Madam, is misleading,
That it makes a bad impression, giving rise
To ugly gossip and obscene surmise,
And that if you were more *overtly* good,
You wouldn't be so much misunderstood.
Not that I think you've been unchaste—no! no!
The saints preserve me from a thought so low!
But mere good conscience never did suffice:
One must avoid the outward show of vice.
Madam, you're too intelligent, I'm sure,
To think my motives anything but pure
In offering you this counsel—which I do
Out of a zealous interest in you.

CELIMENE Madam, I haven't taken you amiss;
I'm very much obliged to you for this;
And I'll at once discharge the obligation
By telling you about *your* reputation.
You've been so friendly as to let me know
What certain people say of me, and so
I mean to follow your benign example
By offering you a somewhat similar sample.
The other day, I went to an affair
And found some most distinguished people there
Discussing piety, both false and true.
The conversation soon came round to you.
Alas! Your prudery and bustling zeal
Appeared to have a very slight appeal.
Your affectation of a grave demeanor,
Your endless talk of virtue and of honor,
The aptitude of your suspicious mind
For finding sin where there is none to find,

Your towering self-esteem, that pitying face
With which you contemplate the human race,
Your sermonizings and your sharp aspersions
On people's pure and innocent diversions—
All these were mentioned, Madam, and, in fact,
Were roundly and concertedly attacked.
"What good," they said, "are all these outward shows,
When everything belies her pious pose?
She prays incessantly; but then, they say,
She beats her maids and cheats them of their pay;
She shows her zeal in every holy place,
But still she's vain enough to paint her face;
She holds that naked statues are immoral,
But with a naked *man* she'd have no quarrel."
Of course, I said to everybody there
That they were being viciously unfair;
But still they were disposed to criticize you,
And all agreed that someone should advise you
To leave the morals of the world alone,
And worry rather more about your own.
They felt that one's self-knowledge should be great
Before one thinks of setting others straight;
That one should learn the art of living well
Before one threatens other men with hell,
And that the Church is best equipped, no doubt,
To guide our souls and root our vices out.
Madam, you're too intelligent, I'm sure,
To think my motives anything but pure
In offering you this counsel—which I do
Out of a zealous interest in you.

ARSINOE I dared not hope for gratitude, but I
Did not expect so acid a reply;
I judge, since you've been so extremely tart,
That my good counsel pierced you to the heart.

CELIMENE Far from it, Madam. Indeed, it seems to me
We ought to trade advice more frequently.
One's vision of oneself is so defective
That it would be an excellent corrective.
If you are willing, Madam, let's arrange
Shortly to have another frank exchange
In which we'll tell each other, *entre nous*,
What you've heard tell of me, and I of you.

ARSINOE Oh, people never censure you, my dear;
It's me they criticize. Or so I hear.

CELIMENE Madam, I think we either blame or praise
According to our taste and length of days.
There is a time of life for coquetry,
And there's a season, too, for prudery.

When all one's charms are gone, it is, I'm sure,
Good strategy to be devout and pure:
It makes one seem a little less forsaken.
Some day, perhaps, I'll take the road you've taken:
Time brings all things. But I have time aplenty,
And see no cause to be a prude at twenty.

ARSINOE You give your age in such a gloating tone
That one would think I was an ancient crone;
We're not so far apart, in sober truth,
That you can mock me with a boast of youth!
Madam, you baffle me. I wish I knew
What moves you to provoke me as you do.

CELIMENE For my part, Madam, I should like to know
Why you abuse me everywhere you go.
Is it my fault, dear lady, that your hand
Is not, alas, in very great demand?
If men admire me, if they pay me court
And daily make me offers of the sort
You'd dearly love to have them make to you,
How can I help it? What would you have me do?
If what you want is lovers, please feel free
To take as many as you can from me.

ARSINOE Oh, come. D'you think the world is losing sleep
Over that flock of lovers which you keep,
Or that we find it difficult to guess
What price you pay for their devotedness?
Surely you don't expect us to suppose
Mere merit could attract so many beaux?
It's not your virtue that they're dazzled by;
Nor is it virtuous love for which they sigh.
You're fooling no one, Madam; the world's not blind;
There's many a lady heaven has designed
To call men's noblest, tenderest feelings out,
Who has no lovers dogging her about;
From which it's plain that lovers nowadays
Must be acquired in bold and shameless ways,
And only pay one court for such reward
As modesty and virtue can't afford.
Then don't be quite so puffed up, if you please,
About your tawdry little victories;
Try, if you can, to be a shade less vain,
And treat the world with somewhat less disdain.
If one were envious of your amours,
One soon could have a following like yours;
Lovers are no great trouble to collect
If one prefers them to one's self-respect.

CELIMENE Collect them then, my dear; I'd love to see
You demonstrate that charming theory;

Who knows, you might . . .

ARSINOE Now, Madam, that will do;
It's time to end this trying interview.
My coach is late in coming to your door,
Or I'd have taken leave of you before.

CELIMENE Oh, please don't feel that you must rush away;
I'd be delighted, Madam, if you'd stay.
However, lest my conversation bore you,
Let me provide some better company for you;
This gentleman, who comes most apropos,
Will please you more than I could do, I know.

scene 6

(Enter ALCESTE.*)*

CELIMENE Alceste, I have a little note to write
Which simply must go out before tonight;
Please entertain *Madame;* I'm sure that she
Will overlook my incivility.
(Exit CELIMENE.*)*

scene 7

ARSINOE Well, Sir, our hostess graciously contrives
For us to chat until my coach arrives;
And I shall be forever in her debt
For granting me this little tête-à-tête.
We women very rightly give our hearts
To men of noble character and parts,
And your especial merits, dear Alceste,
Have roused the deepest sympathy in my breast.
Oh, how I wish they had sufficient sense
At court, to recognize your excellence!
They wrong you greatly, Sir. How it must hurt you
Never to be rewarded for your virtue!

ALCESTE Why, Madam, what cause have I to feel aggrieved?
What great and brilliant thing have I achieved?
What service have I rendered to the King
That I should look to him for anything?

ARSINOE Not everyone who's honored by the State
Has done great services. A man must wait
Till time and fortune offer him the chance.
Your merit, Sir, is obvious at a glance,
And . . .

ALCESTE Ah, forget my merit; I'm not neglected.
The court, I think, can hardly be expected
To mine men's souls for merit, and unearth
Our hidden virtues and our secret worth.

ARSINOE *Some* virtues, though, are far too bright to hide;
Yours are acknowledged, Sir, on every side.

Indeed, I've heard you warmly praised of late
By persons of considerable weight.

ALCESTE This fawning age has praise for everyone,
And all distinctions, Madam, are undone.
All things have equal honor nowadays,
And no one should be gratified by praise.
To be admired, one only need exist,
And every lackey's on the honors list.

ARSINOE I only wish, Sir, that you had your eye
On some position at court, however high;
You'd only have to hint at such a notion
For me to set the proper wheels in motion;
I've certain friendships I'd be glad to use
To get you any office you might choose.

ALCESTE Madam, I fear that any such ambition
Is wholly foreign to my disposition.
The soul God gave me isn't of the sort
That prospers in the weather of a court.
It's all too obvious that I don't possess
The virtues necessary for success.
My one great talent is for speaking plain;
I've never learned to flatter or to feign;
And anyone so stupidly sincere
Had best not seek a courtier's career.
Outside the court, I know, one must dispense
With honors, privilege, and influence;
But still one gains the right, foregoing these,
Not to be tortured by the wish to please.
One needn't live in dread of snubs and slights,
Nor praise the verse that every idiot writes,
Nor humor silly Marquesses, nor bestow
Politic sighs on Madam So-and-So.

ARSINOE Forget the court, then; let the matter rest.
But I've another cause to be distressed
About your present situation, Sir.
It's to your love affair that I refer.
She whom you love, and who pretends to love you,
Is, I regret to say, unworthy of you.

ALCESTE Why, Madam! Can you seriously intend
To make so grave a charge against your friend?

ARSINOE Alas, I must. I've stood aside too long
And let that lady do you grievous wrong;
But now my debt to conscience shall be paid:
I tell you that your love has been betrayed.

ALCESTE I thank you, Madam; you're extremely kind.
Such words are soothing to a lover's mind.

ARSINOE Yes, though she *is* my friend, I say again
You're very much too good for Célimène.

She's wantonly misled you from the start.

ALCESTE You may be right; who knows another's heart?
But ask yourself if it's the part of charity
To shake my soul with doubts of her sincerity.

ARSINOE Well, if you'd rather be a dupe than doubt her,
That's your affair. I'll say no more about her.

ALCESTE Madam, you know that doubt and vague suspicion
Are painful to a man in my position;
It's most unkind to worry me this way
Unless you've some real proof of what you say.

ARSINOE Sir, say no more: all doubt shall be removed,
And all that I've been saying shall be proved.
You've only to escort me home, and there
We'll look into the heart of this affair.
I've ocular evidence which will persuade you
Beyond a doubt, that Célimène's betrayed you.
Then, if you're saddened by that revelation,
Perhaps I can provide some consolation.

act IV

scene 1

PHILINTE Madam, he acted like a stubborn child;
I thought they never would be reconciled;
In vain we reasoned, threatened, and appealed;
He stood his ground and simply would not yield.
The Marshals, I feel sure, have never heard
An argument so splendidly absurd.
"No, gentlemen," said he, "I'll not retract.
His verse is bad: extremely bad, in fact.
Surely it does the man no harm to know it.
Does it disgrace him, not to be a poet?
A gentleman may be respected still,
Whether he writes a sonnet well or ill.
That I dislike his verse should not offend him;
In all that touches honor, I commend him;
He's noble, brave, and virtuous—but I fear
He can't in truth be called a sonneteer.
I'll gladly praise his wardrobe; I'll endorse
His dancing, or the way he sits a horse;
But, gentlemen, I cannot praise his rhyme.
In fact, it ought to be a capital crime
For anyone so sadly unendowed
To write a sonnet, and read the thing aloud."
At length he fell into a gentler mood
And, striking a concessive attitude,
He paid Oronte the following courtesies:

"Sir, I regret that I'm so hard to please,
And I'm profoundly sorry that your lyric
Failed to provoke me to a panegyric."
After these curious words, the two embraced,
And then the hearing was adjourned—in haste.

ELIANTE His conduct has been very singular lately;
Still, I confess that I respect him greatly.
The honesty in which he takes such pride
Has—to my mind—its noble, heroic side.
In this false age, such candor seems outrageous;
But I could wish that it were more contagious.

PHILINTE What most intrigues me in our friend Alceste
Is the grand passion that rages in his breast.
The sullen humors he's compounded of
Should not, I think, dispose his heart to love;
But since they do, it puzzles me still more
That he should choose your cousin to adore.

ELIANTE It does, indeed, belie the theory
That love is born of gentle sympathy,
And that the tender passion must be based
On sweet accords of temper and of taste.

PHILINTE Does she return his love, do you suppose?

ELIANTE Ah, that's a difficult question, Sir. Who knows?
How can we judge the truth of her devotion?
Her heart's a stranger to its own emotion.
Sometimes it thinks it loves, when no love's there;
At other times it loves quite unaware.

PHILINTE I rather think Alceste is in for more
Distress and sorrow than he's bargained for;
Were he of my mind, Madam, his affection
Would turn in quite a different direction,
And we would see him more responsive to
The kind regard which he receives from you.

ELIANTE Sir, I believe in frankness, and I'm inclined,
In matters of the heart, to speak my mind.
I don't oppose his love for her; indeed,
I hope with all my heart that he'll succeed,
And were it in my power, I'd rejoice
In giving him the lady of his choice.
But if, as happens frequently enough
In love affairs, he meets with a rebuff—
If Célimène should grant some rival's suit—
I'd gladly play the role of substitute;
Nor would his tender speeches please me less
Because they'd once been made without success.

PHILINTE Well, Madam, as for me, I don't oppose
Your hopes in this affair; and heavens knows
That in my conversations with the man

I plead your cause as often as I can.
But if those two should marry, and so remove
All chance that he will offer you his love,
Then I'll declare my own, and hope to see
Your gracious favor pass from him to me.
In short, should you be cheated of Alceste,
I'd be most happy to be second best.

ELIANTE Philinte, you're teasing.

PHILINTE Ah, Madam, never fear;
No words of mine were ever so sincere,
And I shall live in fretful expectation
Till I can make a fuller declaration.

scene 2

(Enter ALCESTE.*)*

ALCESTE Avenge me, Madam! I must have satisfaction,
Or this great wrong will drive me to distraction!

ELIANTE Why, what's the matter? What's upset you so?

ALCESTE Madam, I've had a mortal, mortal blow.
If Chaos repossessed the universe,
I swear I'd not be shaken any worse.
I'm ruined. . . . I can say no more. . . . My soul . . .

ELIANTE Do try, Sir, to regain your self-control.

ALCESTE Just heaven! Why were so much beauty and grace
Bestowed on one so vicious and so base?

ELIANTE Once more, Sir, tell us. . . .

ALCESTE My world has gone to wrack;
I'm—I'm betrayed; she's stabbed me in the back:
Yes, Célimène (who would have thought it of her?)
Is false to me, and has another lover.

ELIANTE Are you quite certain? Can you prove these things?

PHILINTE Lovers are prey to wild imaginings
And jealous fancies. No doubt there's some mistake. . . .

ALCESTE Mind your own business, Sir, for heaven's sake.
(To ELIANTE*)* Madam, I have the proof that you demand
Here in my pocket, penned by her own hand.
Yes, all the shameful evidence one could want
Lies in this letter written to Oronte—
Oronte! whom I felt sure she couldn't love,
And hardly bothered to be jealous of.

PHILINTE Still, in a letter, appearances may deceive;
This may not be so bad as you believe.

ALCESTE Once more I beg you, Sir, to let me be;
Tend to your own affairs; leave mine to me.

ELIANTE Compose yourself; this anguish that you feel . . .

ALCESTE Is something, Madam, you alone can heal.
My outraged heart, beside itself with grief,
Appeals to you for comfort and relief.

Avenge me on your cousin, whose unjust
And faithless nature has deceived my trust;
Avenge a crime your pure soul must detest.

ELIANTE But how, Sir?

ALCESTE Madam, this heart within my breast
Is yours; pray take it; redeem my heart from her,
And so avenge me on my torturer.
Let her be punished by the fond emotion,
The ardent love, the bottomless devotion,
The faithful worship which this heart of mine
Will offer up to yours as to a shrine.

ELIANTE You have my sympathy, Sir, in all you suffer;
Nor do I scorn the noble heart you offer;
But I suspect you'll soon be mollified,
And this desire for vengeance will subside.
When some beloved hand has done us wrong
We thirst for retribution—but not for long;
However dark the deed that she's committed,
A lovely culprit's very soon acquitted.
Nothing's so stormy as an injured lover,
And yet no storm so quickly passes over.

ALCESTE No, Madam, no—this is no lovers' spat;
I'll not forgive her; it's gone too far for that;
My mind's made up; I'll kill myself before
I waste my hopes upon her any more.
Ah, here she is. My wrath intensifies.
I shall confront her with her tricks and lies,
And crush her utterly, and bring you then
A heart no longer slave to Célimène.
(Exit ELIANTE.*)*

scene 3

ALCESTE *(aside)* Sweet heaven, help me to control my passion.

CELIMENE *(aside)*
(to ALCESTE*)* Oh, Lord. Why stand there staring in that fashion?
And what d'you mean by those dramatic sighs,
And that malignant glitter in your eyes?

ALCESTE I mean that sins which cause the blood to freeze
Look innocent beside your treacheries;
That nothing Hell's or Heaven's wrath could do
Ever produced so bad a thing as you.

CELIMENE Your compliments were always sweet and pretty.

ALCESTE Madam, it's not the moment to be witty.
No, blush and hang your head; you've ample reason,
Since I've the fullest evidence of your treason.
Ah, this is what my sad heart prophesied;
Now all my anxious fears are verified;
My dark suspicion and my gloomy doubt

Divined the truth, and now the truth is out.
For all your trickery, I was not deceived;
It was my bitter stars that I believed.
But don't imagine that you'll go scot-free;
You shan't misuse me with impunity.
I know that love's irrational and blind;
I know the heart's not subject to the mind,
And can't be reasoned into beating faster;
I know each soul is free to choose its master;
Therefore had you but spoken from the heart,
Rejecting my attentions from the start,
I'd have no grievance, or at any rate
I could complain of nothing but my fate.
Ah, but so falsely to encourage me—
That was a treason and a treachery
For which you cannot suffer too severely,
And you shall pay for that behavior dearly.
Yes, now I have no pity, not a shred;
My temper's out of hand; I've lost my head;
Shocked by the knowledge of your double-dealings,
My reason can't restrain my savage feelings;
A righteous wrath deprives me of my senses,
And I won't answer for the consequences.

CELIMENE What does this outburst mean? Will you please explain?
Have you, by any chance, gone quite insane?

ALCESTE Yes, yes, I went insane the day I fell
A victim to your black and fatal spell,
Thinking to meet with some sincerity
Among the treacherous charms that beckoned me.

CELIMENE Pooh. Of what treachery can you complain?

ALCESTE How sly you are, how cleverly you feign!
But you'll not victimize me any more.
Look: here's a document you've seen before.
This evidence, which I acquired today,
Leaves you, I think, without a thing to say.

CELIMENE Is this what sent you into such a fit?

ALCESTE You should be blushing at the sight of it.

CELIMENE Ought I to blush? I truly don't see why.

ALCESTE Ah, now you're being bold as well as sly;
Since there's no signature, perhaps you'll claim . . .

CELIMENE I wrote it, whether or not it bears my name.

ALCESTE And you can view with equanimity
This proof of your disloyalty to me!

CELIMENE Oh, don't be so outrageous and extreme.

ALCESTE You take this matter lightly, it would seem.
Was it no wrong to me, no shame to you,
That you should send Oronte this billet-doux?

CELIMENE Oronte! Who said it was for him?

ALCESTE Why, those
Who brought me this example of your prose.
But what's the difference? If you wrote the letter
To someone else, it pleases me no better.
My grievance and your guilt remain the same.

CELIMENE But need you rage, and need I blush for shame,
If this was written to a *woman* friend?

ALCESTE Ah! Most ingenious. I'm impressed no end;
And after that incredible evasion
Your guilt is clear. I need no more persuasion.
How dare you try so clumsy a deception?
D'you think I'm wholly wanting in perception?
Come, come, let's see how brazenly you'll try
To bolster up so palpable a lie:
Kindly construe this ardent closing section
As nothing more than sisterly affection!
Here, let me read it. Tell me, if you dare to,
That this is for a woman . . .

CELIMENE I don't care to.
What right have you to badger and berate me,
And so highhandedly interrogate me?

ALCESTE Now, don't be angry; all I ask of you
Is that you justify a phrase or two . . .

CELIMENE No, I shall not. I utterly refuse,
And you may take those phrases as you choose.

ALCESTE Just show me how this letter could be meant
For a woman's eyes, and I shall be content.

CELIMENE No, no, it's for Oronte; you're perfectly right.
I welcome his attentions with delight,
I prize his character and his intellect,
And everything is just as you suspect.
Come, do your worst now; give your rage free rein;
But kindly cease to bicker and complain.

ALCESTE *(aside)* Good God! Could anything be more inhuman?
Was ever a heart so mangled by a woman?
When I complain of how she has betrayed me,
She bridles, and commences to upbraid me!
She tries my tortured patience to the limit;
She won't deny her guilt; she glories in it!
And yet my heart's too faint and cowardly
To break these chains of passion, and be free,
To scorn her as it should, and rise above
This unrewarded, mad, and bitter love.
(to CELIMENE*)* Ah, traitress, in how confident a fashion
You take advantage of my helpless passion,
And use my weakness for your faithless charms
To make me once again throw down my arms!
But do at least deny this black transgression;

Take back that mocking and perverse confession;
Defend this letter and your innocence,
And I, poor fool, will aid in your defense.
Pretend, pretend, that you are just and true,
And I shall make myself believe in you.
CELIMENE Oh, stop it. Don't be such a jealous dunce,
Or I shall leave off loving you at once.
Just why should I *pretend?* What could impel me
To stoop so low as that? And kindly tell me
Why, if I loved another, I shouldn't merely
Inform you of it, simply and sincerely!
I've told you where you stand, and that admission
Should altogether clear me of suspicion;
After so generous a guarantee,
What right have you to harbor doubts of me?
Since women are (from natural reticence)
Reluctant to declare their sentiments,
And since the honor of our sex requires
That we conceal our amorous desires,
Ought any man for whom such laws are broken
To question what the oracle has spoken?
Should he not rather feel an obligation
To trust that most obliging declaration?
Enough, now, Your suspicions quite disgust me;
Why should I love a man who doesn't trust me?
I cannot understand why I continue,
Fool that I am, to take an interest in you.
I ought to choose a man less prone to doubt,
And give you something to be vexed about.
LCESTE Ah, what a poor enchanted fool I am;
These gentle words, no doubt, were all a sham;
But destiny requires me to entrust
My happiness to you, and so I must.
I'll love you to the bitter end, and see
How false and treacherous you dare to be.
ELIMENE No, you don't really love me as you ought.
LCESTE I love you more than can be said or thought;
Indeed, I wish you were in such distress
That I might show my deep devotedness.
Yes, I could wish that you were wretchedly poor,
Unloved, uncherished, utterly obscure;
That fate had set you down upon the earth
Without possessions, rank, or gentle birth;
Then, by the offer of my heart, I might
Repair the great injustice of your plight;
I'd raise you from the dust, and proudly prove
The purity and vastness of my love.
ELIMENE This is a strange benevolence indeed!

God grant that I may never be in need. . . .
Ah, here's Monsieur Dubois, in quaint disguise.

scene 4

(Enter DUBOIS.*)*

ALCESTE Well, why this costume? Why those frightened eyes?
What ails you?
DUBOIS Well, Sir, things are most mysterious.
ALCESTE What do you mean?
DUBOIS I fear they're very serious.
ALCESTE What?
DUBOIS Shall I speak more loudly?
ALCESTE Yes; speak out.
DUBOIS Isn't there someone here, Sir?
ALCESTE Speak, you lout!
Stop wasting time.
DUBOIS Sir, we must slip away.
ALCESTE How's that?
DUBOIS We must decamp without delay.
ALCESTE Explain yourself.
DUBOIS I tell you we must fly.
ALCESTE What for?
DUBOIS We mustn't pause to say good-by.
ALCESTE Now what d'you mean by all of this, you clown?
DUBOIS I mean, Sir, that we've got to leave this town.
ALCESTE I'll tear you limb from limb and joint from joint
If you don't come more quickly to the point.
DUBOIS Well, Sir, today a man in a black suit,
Who wore a black and ugly scowl to boot,
Left us a document scrawled in such a hand
As even Satan couldn't understand.
It bears upon your lawsuit, I don't doubt;
But all hell's devils couldn't make it out.
ALCESTE Well, well, go on. What then? I fail to see
How this event obliges us to flee.
DUBOIS Well, Sir: an hour later, hardly more,
A gentleman who's often called before
Came looking for you in an anxious way.
Not finding you, he asked me to convey
(Knowing I could be trusted with the same)
The following message. . . . Now, what *was* his name?
ALCESTE Forget his name, you idiot. What did he say?
DUBOIS Well, it was one of your friends, Sir, anyway.
He warned you to begone, and he suggested
That if you stay, you may well be arrested.
ALCESTE What? Nothing more specific? Think, man, think!
DUBOIS No, Sir. He had me bring him pen and ink,
And dashed you off a letter which, I'm sure,

Will render things distinctly less obscure.
ALCESTE Well—let me have it!
CELIMENE What *is* this all about?
ALCESTE God knows; but I have hopes of finding out.
How long am I to wait, you blitherer?
DUBOIS *(after a protracted search for the letter)* I must have left it on your table, Sir.
ALCESTE I ought to . . .
CELIMENE No, no, keep your self-control;
Go find out what's behind his rigmarole.
ALCESTE It seems that fate, no matter what I do,
Has sworn that I may not converse with you;
But, Madam, pray permit your faithful lover
To try once more before the day is over.

act V

scene 1

ALCESTE No, it's too much. My mind's made up, I tell you.
PHILINTE Why should this blow, however hard, compel you . . .
ALCESTE No, no, don't waste your breath in argument;
Nothing you say will alter my intent;
This age is vile, and I've made up my mind
To have no further commerce with mankind.
Did not truth, honor, decency, and the laws
Oppose my enemy and approve my cause?
My claims were justified in all men's sight;
I put my trust in equity and right;
Yet, to my horror and the world's disgrace,
Justice is mocked, and I have lost my case!
A scoundrel whose dishonesty is notorious
Emerges from another lie victorious!
Honor and right condone his brazen fraud,
While rectitude and decency applaud!
Before his smirking face, the truth stands charmed,
And virtue conquered, and the law disarmed!
His crime is sanctioned by a court decree!
And not content with what he's done to me,
The dog now seeks to ruin me by stating
That I composed a book now circulating,
A book so wholly criminal and vicious
That even to speak its title is seditious!
Meanwhile Oronte, my rival, lends his credit
To the same libelous tale, and helps to spread it!
Oronte! a man of honor and of rank,
With whom I've been entirely fair and frank;
Who sought me out and forced me, willy-nilly,

To judge some verse I found extremely silly;
And who, because I properly refused
To flatter him, or see the truth abused,
Abets my enemy in a rotten slander!
There's the reward of honesty and candor!
The man will hate me to the end of time
For failing to commend his wretched rhyme!
And not this man alone, but all humanity
Do what they do from interest and vanity;
They prate of honor, truth, and righteousness,
But lie, betray, and swindle nonetheless.
Come then: man's villainy is too much to bear;
Let's leave this jungle and this jackal's lair.
Yes! treacherous and savage race of men,
You shall not look upon my face again.

PHILINTE Oh, don't rush into exile prematurely;
Things aren't as dreadful as you make them, surely.
It's rather obvious, since you're still at large,
That people don't believe your enemy's charge.
Indeed, his tale's so patently untrue
That it may do more harm to him than you.

ALCESTE Nothing could do that scoundrel any harm:
His frank corruption is his greatest charm,
And, far from hurting him, a further shame
Would only serve to magnify his name.

PHILINTE In any case, his bald prevarication
Has done no injury to your reputation,
And you may feel secure in that regard.
As for your lawsuit, it should not be hard
To have the case reopened, and contest
This judgment . . .

ALCESTE No, no, let the verdict rest.
Whatever cruel penalty it may bring,
I wouldn't have it changed for anything.
It shows the times' injustice with such clarity
That I shall pass it down to our posterity
As a great proof and signal demonstration
Of the black wickedness of this generation.
It may cost twenty thousand francs; but I
Shall pay their twenty thousand, and gain thereby
The right to storm and rage at human evil,
And send the race of mankind to the devil.

PHILINTE Listen to me. . . .

ALCESTE Why? What can you possibly say?
Don't argue, Sir; your labor's thrown away.
Do you propose to offer lame excuses
For men's behavior and the times' abuses?

PHILINTE No, all you say I'll readily concede:

This is a low, conniving age indeed;
Nothing but trickery prospers nowadays,
And people ought to mend their shabby ways.
Yes, man's a beastly creature; but must we then
Abandon the society of men?
Here in the world, each human frailty
Provides occasion for philosophy,
And that is virtue's noblest exercise;
If honesty shone forth from all men's eyes,
If every heart were frank and kind and just,
What could our virtues do but gather dust
(Since their employment is to help us bear
The villainies of men without despair)?
A heart well-armed with virtue can endure. . . .

ALCESTE Sir, you're a matchless reasoner, to be sure;
Your words are fine and full of cogency;
But don't waste time and eloquence on me.
My reason bids me go, for my own good.
My tongue won't lie and flatter as it should;
God knows what frankness it might next commit,
And what I'd suffer on account of it.
Pray let me wait for Célimène's return
In peace and quiet. I shall shortly learn,
By her response to what I have in view,
Whether her love for me is feigned or true.

PHILINTE Till then, let's visit Eliante upstairs.

ALCESTE No, I am too weighed down with somber cares.
Go to her, do; and leave me with my gloom
Here in the darkened corner of this room.

PHILINTE Why, that's no sort of company, my friend;
I'll see if Eliante will not descend.
(Exit PHILINTE.*)*

scene 2

(Enter CELIMENE, ORONTE.*)*

ORONTE Yes, Madam, if you wish me to remain
Your true and ardent lover, you must deign
To give me some more positive assurance.
All this suspense is quite beyond endurance.
If your heart shares the sweet desires of mine,
Show me as much by some convincing sign;
And here's the sign I urgently suggest:
That you no longer tolerate Alceste,
But sacrifice him to my love, and sever
All your relations with the man forever.

CELIMENE Why do you suddenly dislike him so?
You praised him to the skies not long ago.

ORONTE Madam, that's not the point. I'm here to find

Which way your tender feelings are inclined.
Choose, if you please, between Alceste and me,
And I shall stay or go accordingly.

ALCESTE *(emerging from the corner)* Yes, Madam, choose; this gentleman's demand
Is wholly just, and I support his stand.
I too am true and ardent; I too am here
To ask you that you make your feelings clear.
No more delays, now; no equivocation;
The time has come to make your declaration.

ORONTE Sir, I've no wish in any way to be
An obstacle to your felicity.

ALCESTE Sir, I've no wish to share her heart with you;
That may sound jealous, but at least it's true.

ORONTE If, weighing us, she leans in your direction . . .

ALCESTE If she regards you with the least affection . . .

ORONTE I swear I'll yield her to you there and then.

ALCESTE I swear I'll never see her face again.

ORONTE Now, Madam, tell us what we've come to hear.

ALCESTE Madam, speak openly and have no fear.

ORONTE Just say which one is to remain your lover.

ALCESTE Just name one name, and it will all be over.

ORONTE What! Is it possible that you're undecided?

ALCESTE What! Can your feelings possibly be divided?

CELIMENE Enough: this inquisition's gone too far:
How utterly unreasonable you are!
Not that I couldn't make the choice with ease;
My heart has no conflicting sympathies;
I know full well which one of you I favor,
And you'd not see me hesitate or waver.
But how can you expect me to reveal
So cruelly and bluntly what I feel?
I think it altogether too unpleasant
To choose between two men when both are present;
One's heart has means more subtle and more kind
Of letting its affections be divined,
Nor need one be uncharitably plain
To let a lover know he loves in vain.

ORONTE No, no, speak plainly; I for one can stand it.
I beg you to be frank.

ALCESTE And I demand it.
The simple truth is what I wish to know,
And there's no need for softening the blow.
You've made an art of pleasing everyone,
But now your days of coquetry are done:
You have no choice now, Madam, but to choose,
For I'll know what to think if you refuse;
I'll take your silence for a clear admission

That I'm entitled to my worst suspicion.
ORONTE I thank you for this ultimatum, Sir,
And I may say I heartily concur.
CELIMENE Really, this foolishness is very wearing:
Must you be so unjust and overbearing?
Haven't I told you why I must demur?
Ah, here's Eliante; I'll put the case to her.

scene 3

(Enter PHILINTE *and* ELIANTE.*)*
CELIMENE Cousin, I'm being persecuted here
By these two persons, who, it would appear,
Will not be satisfied till I confess
Which one I love the more, and which the less,
And tell the latter to his face that he
Is henceforth banished from my company.
Tell me, has ever such a thing been done?
ELIANTE You'd best not turn to me; I'm not the one
To back you in a matter of this kind:
I'm all for those who frankly speak their mind.
ORONTE Madam, you'll search in vain for a defender.
ALCESTE You're beaten, Madam, and may as well surrender.
ORONTE Speak, speak, you must; and end this awful strain.
ALCESTE Or don't, and your position will be plain.
ORONTE A single word will close this painful scene.
ALCESTE But if you're silent, I'll know what you mean.

scene 4

(Enter ACASTE, CLITANDRE, ARSINOE.*)*
ACASTE *(to* CELIMENE*)* Madam, with all due deference, we two
Have come to pick a little bone with you.
CLITANDRE *(to* ORONTE *and* ALCESTE*)* I'm glad you're present, Sirs; as you'll soon learn,
Our business here is also your concern.
ARSINOE *(to* CELIMENE*)* Madam, I visit you so soon again
Only because of these two gentlemen,
Who came to me indignant and aggrieved
About a crime too base to be believed.
Knowing your virtue, having such confidence in it,
I couldn't think you guilty for a minute,
In spite of all their telling evidence;
And, rising above our little difference,
I've hastened here in friendship's name to see
You clear yourself of this great calumny.
ACASTE Yes, Madam, let us see with what composure
You'll manage to respond to this disclosure.
You lately sent Clitandre this tender note.
CLITANDRE And this one, for Acaste, you also wrote.

ACASTE *(to* ORONTE *and* ALCASTE*)* You'll recognize this writing, Sirs, I think;
The lady is so free with pen and ink
That you must know it all too well, I fear.
But listen: this is something you should hear.
"How absurd you are to condemn my lightheartedness in society, and to accuse me of being happiest in the company of others. Nothing could be more unjust; and if you do not come to me instantly and beg pardon for saying such a thing, I shall never forgive you as long as I live. Our big bumbling friend the Viscount . . ."
What a shame that he's not here.
"Our big bumbling friend the Viscount, whose name stands first in your complaint, is hardly a man to my taste; and ever since the day I watched him spend three-quarters of an hour spitting into a well, so as to make circles in the water, I have been unable to think highly of him. As for the little Marquess . . ."
In all modesty, gentlemen, that is I.
"As for the little Marquess, who sat squeezing my hand for such a long while yesterday, I find him in all respects the most trifling creature alive; and the only things of value about him are his cape and his sword. As for the man with the green ribbons . . ."
(to ALCESTE*)* It's your turn now, Sir.
"As for the man with the green ribbons, he amuses me now and then with his bluntness and his bearish ill-humor; but there are many times indeed when I think him the greatest bore in the world. And as for the sonneteer . . ."
(to ORONTE*)* Here's your helping.
"And as for the sonneteer, who has taken it into his head to be witty, and insists on being an author in the teeth of opinion, I simply cannot be bothered to listen to him, and his prose wearies me quite as much as his poetry. Be assured that I am not always so well-entertained as you suppose; that I long for your company, more than I dare to say, at all these entertainments to which people drag me; and that the presence of those one loves is the true and perfect seasoning to all one's pleasures."

CLITANDRE And now for me.
"Clitandre, whom you mention, and who so pesters me with his saccharine speeches, is the last man on earth for whom I could feel any affection. He is quite mad to suppose that I love him, and so are you, to doubt that you are loved. Do come to your senses; exchange your suppositions for his; and visit me as often as possible, to help me bear the annoyance of his unwelcome attentions."
It's a sweet character that these letters show,
And what to call it, Madam, you well know.
Enough. We're off to make the world acquainted
With this sublime self-portrait that you've painted.

ACASTE Madam, I'll make you no farewell oration;
No, you're not worthy of my indignation.
Far choicer hearts than yours, as you'll discover,

Would like this little Marquess for a lover.
(Exit ACASTE *and* CLITANDRE.*)*

scene 5

ORONTE So! After all those loving letters you wrote,
You turn on me like this, and cut my throat!
And your dissembling, faithless heart, I find,
Has pledged itself by turns to all mankind!
How blind I've been! But now I clearly see;
I thank you, Madam, for enlightening me.
My heart is mine once more, and I'm content;
The loss of it shall be your punishment.
(to ALCESTE*)* Sir, she is yours; I'll seek no more to stand
Between your wishes and this lady's hand.
(Exit ORONTE.*)*

scene 6

ARSINOE *(to* CELIMENE*)* Madam, I'm forced to speak. I'm far too stirred
To keep my counsel, after what I've heard.
I'm shocked and staggered by your want of morals.
It's not my way to mix in others' quarrels;
But really, when this fine and noble spirit,
This man of honor and surpassing merit,
Laid down the offering of his heart before you,
How *could* you . . .
ALCESTE Madam, permit me, I implore you,
To represent myself in this debate.
Don't bother, please, to be my advocate.
My heart, in any case, could not afford
To give your services their due reward;
And if I chose, for consolation's sake,
Some other lady, t'would not be you I'd take.
ARSINOE What makes you think you could, Sir? And how dare you
Imply that I've been trying to ensnare you?
If you can for a moment entertain
Such flattering fancies, you're extremely vain.
I'm not so interested as you suppose
In Célimène's discarded gigolos.
Get rid of that absurd illusion, do.
Women like me are not for such as you.
Stay with this creature, to whom you're so attached;
I've never seen two people better matched.
(Exit ARSINOE.*)*

scene 7

ALCESTE *(to* CELIMENE*)* Well, I've been still throughout this exposé,
Till everyone but me has said his say.
Come, have I shown sufficient self-restraint?

And may I now . . .

CELIMENE Yes, make your just complaint.
Reproach me freely, call me what you will;
You've every right to say I've used you ill.
I've wronged you, I confess it; and in my shame
I'll make no effort to escape the blame.
The anger of those others I could despise;
My guilt toward you I sadly recognize.
Your wrath is wholly justified, I fear;
I know how culpable I must appear,
I know all things bespeak my treachery,
And that, in short, you've grounds for hating me.
Do so; I give you leave.

ALCESTE Ah, traitress—how,
How should I cease to love you, even now?
Though mind and will were passionately bent
On hating you, my heart would not consent.
(To ELIANTE *and* PHILINTE*)* Be witness to my madness, both of you;
See what infatuation drives one to;
But wait; my folly's only just begun,
And I shall prove to you before I'm done
How strange the human heart is, and how far
From rational we sorry creatures are.
(To CELIMENE*)* Woman, I'm willing to forget your shame,
And clothe your treacheries in a sweeter name;
I'll call them youthful errors, instead of crimes,
And lay the blame on these corrupting times.
My one condition is that you agree
To share my chosen fate, and fly with me
To that wild, trackless, solitary place
In which I shall forget the human race.
Only by such a course can you atone
For those atrocious letters; by that alone
Can you remove my present horror of you,
And make it possible for me to love you.

CELIMENE What! *I* renounce the world at my young age,
And die of boredom in some hermitage?

ALCESTE Ah, if you really loved me as you ought,
You wouldn't give the world a moment's thought;
Must you have me, and all the world beside?

CELIMENE Alas, at twenty one is terrified
Of solitude. I fear I lack the force
And depth of soul to take so stern a course.
But if my hand in marriage will content you,
Why, there's a plan which I might well consent to,
And . . .

ALCESTE No, I detest you now. I could excuse
Everything else, but since you thus refuse

To love me wholly, as a wife should do,
And see the world in me, as I in you,
Go! I reject your hand, and disenthrall
My heart from your enchantments, once for all.
(Exit CELIMENE.*)*

scene 8

ALCESTE *(to* ELIANTE*)* Madam, your virtuous beauty has no peer;
Of all this world, you only are sincere;
I've long esteemed you highly, as you know;
Permit me ever to esteem you so,
And if I do not now request your hand,
Forgive me, Madam, and try to understand.
I feel unworthy of it; I sense that fate
Does not intend me for the married state,
That I should do you wrong by offering you
My shattered heart's unhappy residue,
And that in short . . .

ELIANTE Your argument's well taken:
Nor need you fear that I shall feel forsaken.
Were I to offer him this hand of mine,
Your friend Philinte, I think, would not decline.

PHILINTE Ah, Madam, that's my heart's most cherished goal,
For which I'd gladly give my life and soul.

ALCESTE *(To* ELIANTE *and* PHILINTE*)* May you be true to all you now profess,
And so deserve unending happiness.
Meanwhile, betrayed and wronged in everything,
I'll flee this bitter world where vice is king,
And seek some spot unpeopled and apart
Where I'll be free to have an honest heart.

PHILINTE Come, Madam, let's do everything we can
To change the mind of this unhappy man.

robert j. nelson

the unreconstructed heroes of molière

There are, as Bailly has said, no conversions in Molière.[1] To the end, Arnolphe remains a bigot, Harpagon a miser, Jourdain a parvenu, Argan a hypochondriac. Thus Molière remains true to a rule of comedy far more important than the conventions of time, place, and unity considered the hallmarks of classical dramaturgy: the rule of the unity of character. For conversion would take the spectator into affective and moral regions where the satiric purpose—laughter—might be compromised. A repentant Arnolphe, a disabused Jourdain, an enlightened Argan might satisfy our sense of the pathetic or the propitious, but only at the expense of our pleasure. In fact, to make us feel sorry for such characters at the end of the play or to make them share our superior view of their previous conduct would come dangerously close to identifying us with them in that previous conduct as well. In leaving these characters "unreconstructed" Molière earns our gratitude as well as our applause.

Yet, this "non-conversion" disturbs us in three of his greatest comedies: *Le Tartuffe,* in which the hypocrite remains a hypocrite; *Dom Juan,* in which the "sinner" refuses to repent; *Le Misanthrope,* in which the hater of men hates them more at the end of the play than at the beginning. Holding a similar place in the Molière canon to *All's Well, Troilus and Cressida,* and *Measure for Measure* in the Shakespeare canon, these plays might be described as Molière's "bitter comedies." In them, as Borgerhoff has observed, Molière has reversed his usual dramaturgy, unsettling the categories into which we have cast his work: triumph of the golden mean, the importance of common sense, the essentially bourgeois outlook, etc.[2] Usually, the "hero" (in the purely structural sense of the major role) is a monomaniac, a person lacking what Ramon Fernandez has called "la vision double"[3] or the capacity for what I have described in an earlier essay as "the deliberate multiplication of the self."[4] In a Molière play, the "others" have this capacity: the Agnèses, the Toinettes, the Scapins who use it to check the effects of the principal character's monomania. "The true hero of a comedy," I wrote in that essay, "is, in fact, the 'others' and their view ought more appropriately be compared with that of the tragic hero in any discussion of the tragic and the comic. . . . The

[1]Auguste Bailly, *L'École classique française* (Paris, n.d.), p. 53.
[2]*The Freedom of French Classicism* (Princeton, 1950), pp. 149–160.
[3]*La Vie de Molière* (Paris, 1929), p. 136. Fernandez defines the concept in slightly different terms, pp. 74–77.
[4]*Play Within a Play: The Dramatist's Conception of His Art: Shakespeare to Anouilh* (New Haven, 1958), p. 69.

comic 'others' are ready to assume a mask, they are willing to play a double game. The central figure (an Argan, an Harpagon) simply cannot play such a game, for he does not know of its possibility. Ironically, the tragic hero yearns for the singleness of vision of the comic figure, for whom appearance and reality coincide. However, if the tragic figure and the comic 'others' are alike in their doubleness of vision, they differ in the very essence of that vision: where the tragic hero sees discrepancy and even duplicity, the comic 'others' see combination and complementarity: of the social and the natural, of the logical and the illogical, of the conditioned and the instinctive, of the material and the spiritual."[5] Through the use of mask or ruse the "others" usually get the upper hand over the monomaniacal figure. However, in *Le Tartuffe* the unscrupulous Tartuffe also possesses the usually commendable "double vision." Indeed, short of the King's intervention, his wiles prove more effective than those of the "others" (Elmire, Dorine). In *Dom Juan,* throughout much of the play, the relationship between the "hero" and the "others" is turned completely inside out: aware of the doubleness of vision of the "others," Dom Juan asserts the moral superiority of his single vision and, in spite of a complex departure from it himself, succeeds in imposing it upon the spectator if not upon the "others." Finally, in *Le Misanthrope* as in *Dom Juan,* the monomaniac, though fully aware of doubleness, tries to impose his single vision upon the double vision of the "others." However, unlike Dom Juan, Alceste does not find ultimate victory in the very face of defeat.

These three plays are marked by a questioning and at times aggressive outlook and their dates suggest that the outlook was an enduring one: *Le Tartuffe* in its first version during the festivities at Versailles) dates from May 1664; *Dom Juan* from February 1665; *Le Misanthrope* from June 1666. Only *L'Amour médecin* (September 1665) interrupts this mood, a fact to which I shall return. Whatever causes account for this mood (professional bitterness at the prudish criticism of *L'École des femmes;* personal unhappiness because of marriage difficulties, etc.) the outlook itself, the patent reversal of dramaturgy, and the chronology of the plays suggest that at this stage of his career Molière sees in a different light the relationship between appearance and reality, the theme which Lionel Trilling has described as the essential theme of all literature. I should now like to look at Molière's "review" of this theme in some detail, in order to assess its meaning for Molière's art in particular and for comic theory in general. . . .

LE MISANTHROPE

If Tartuffe is the only hypocrite in a world of innocents, Alceste is the only innocent in a world of hypocrites. In describing the most controversial of Molière's characters as "innocent" I am not implying that he is naïve nor in stressing his uniqueness do I mean to forget Philinte and Eliante. Like Dom Juan, Alceste knows only too well the duplicity of human behavior. He himself compromises his integrity in his behavior

[5]Nelson, p. 74.

with the writer of the sonnet and with Célimène. Nevertheless, to the contrary of the "others" of this play, at the moment of ultimate decisions he upholds the ideal of absolute integrity; his deeds then match his intentions. In his readiness to pay the supreme price "selon les lois constitutives de l'univers de la pièce"[6] Alceste differs from Philinte and Eliante. The latter are but relatively innocent, set apart by the "virtue" of their tolerance from the rigid Alceste, cast very much in their relationship to him as Le Pauvre to Dom Juan.

Isolated from the "others" of this play, Alceste is a kind of Dom Juan *raté*, one seen in the distorting mirror of "la vie mondaine," one who salvages nothing from his defeat at the end of the play. The implicit lessons of *Le Tartuffe* and *Dom Juan,* obscured in the triumphant accents of the final scenes, become explicit in the final scenes of *Le Misanthrope.* The absence of a Guarantor has been remarked and Alceste does not banish himself to his "désert" with the *éclat* of Dom Juan sublimely proffering his hand to his destroyer. The anarchy of hypocrisy has reached man not in his relations with the invisible but in his relations with his fellow man. In *Le Misanthrope* Molière questions the root idea of society: the good faith of its members upon which the social contract is based. The denouement offers us two symbols of the most somber significance: Célimène telling us that society is committed to doubleness, to a discrepancy between appearance and reality, between intention and deed; Alceste telling us that the correspondence of intention and deed is possible only in a social void.

Alceste's *désert* is, of course, only metaphorical. "On le dit . . . d'un homme qui, aimant la solitude, a fait bâtir quelque jolie maison hors des grands chemins et éloignée du commerce du monde, pour s'y retirer[7] [It is used . . . for a man who, loving solitude, had some pretty house built away from the highways and far from the business of the world, in which to withdraw]." Yet, given Alceste's quasi-religious fervor, the term re-acquires some of its literal meaning, evoking for us those early Christian saints who monastically retreated to the desert in their search for purity. In announcing his intention Alceste is only making explicit what we assume about the other great monomaniacs of Molière comedy: they too go to a desert at the end of the play. Not that the denouement of *Le Misanthrope* simply repeats the lessons of the other plays. We should remember that Alceste willingly banishes himself to his desert; the Harpagons and the Arnolphes are banished unwillingly. Or more precisely, unwittingly. In fact, they have been living psychologically in a desert from the very beginning of the play: the desert of their particular obsessions. Monomania prevents them from effectively participating in society, the arena of compromise, self-criticism, and, to a certain degree, self-sacrifice. What makes Alceste unique among these monomaniacs is his

[6]A concept I borrow from Lucien Goldmann, *Jean Racine: dramaturge* (Paris, 1956), p. 13.

[7]A. Furetière, *Dictionnaire universel* (edition of 1690), quoted by Gaston Cayrou, *Le Français classique* (Paris, 1948), p. 260.

awareness of the compromise upon which society is based. Thus, his self-exile constitutes a powerful doubt as to the value of self-sacrifice for the sake of society. For the first time the self is posited as an equal and possibly superior value to society. Alceste represents that bifurcation of the personality into public and private selves which characterizes man in society and which creates the tensions of "civilization and its discontents." As the demands of society become greater, molding the self to acceptable "norms," the self is forced into its own recesses, into its own "désert."

Of course, in the ideal world of the *généreux*, Alceste would have no problems—were he not so single-minded, paradoxically enough, in his *générosité*. For, in spite of a basic similarity, Alceste differs from Dom Juan in one essential aspect: he is incapable of that esthetic hypocrisy which justifies, from a moral point of view, Dom Juan's behavior toward women. If Alceste is right in his condemnation of many of the forms of society, he is wrong in his failure to recognize the value of the esthetic in the domain of love. There, his integrity dehumanizes him and renders him ridiculous. Does this mean that Célimène's behavior is implicitly justified? Hardly, for her estheticism is only an opposite extreme to Alceste's integrity. She is an artificial character: Half Dom Juan, half Tartuffe. Like the former she plays a role, but like the latter she plays the role everywhere. In Dom Juan, the esthetics of courtship led to sensual satisfaction; in Célimène they are subverted to the purely social: satisfaction is frustrated in order that the game might go on. Her sociability exacts as high a price as Alceste's sincerity. Her "tartuffism" is not thoroughgoing, of course: she accepts exposure, admits to wrongdoing. But in the very admission she remains unconverted: looking forward to the spirit of Marivaux comedy, she believes that everything can be arranged after the damage is done in the simple admission that her intentions were not after all vicious, that it was all only a kind of game—a cruel one, to be sure, but a game.

Le Misanthrope ends in a moral stalemate. It is a comedy without a happy ending, a tragedy without a tragic illumination. Both Célimène and Alceste are presented to us with strong reservations; each is the object of Molière's satire. The play is, in fact, Molière's supreme achievement in the satiric mode. In this mode he invites us to laugh at man's foibles, to delight in the depiction of man's obsessions and pretensions and so to rise above such "vices" in ourselves. Now, it is in this self-protective laughter that we usually locate the essence of Molière's "comic view of life." Yet, it is debatable whether the definition of comedy as self-protective or dissociative laughter is a valid one—at least in contradistinction to tragedy. Satire points up the discrepancy between ideals and performance, between reality and appearance; it emphasizes man's limitations. Indeed, to the extent that in the "non-conversion" of the comic figure a given limitation is shown to be ineradicable, Molière's satirical comedy repeats the lesson of tragedy without offering the paradoxical victory of tragedy: in the very act of perceiving the limitation which is inherent in the scheme of things (fate) man transcends his limitation.

Seen in this perspective, the happy endings of the satiric plays are "smoke screens" to cover up the negative, depressing view of the unreconstructed comic figure who has just been taught a lesson whose point he cannot see. In the euphoria of Horace's union with Agnès, for example, we lose sight of the fact that Arnolphe has been left "holding the bag," we are spared the uncomfortable reminder of his humanity. Traditionally, criticism has tried to escape this bitter lesson by locating the real lesson of the play somewhere in between convention and obsession—in the moderateness of the Chrysaldes and the Philintes. Thus, with Philinte's marriage to Eliante, *Le Misanthrope* seems a typical Molière play, one teaching a familiar lesson: society, the marriage of different wills and temperaments, depends on a spirit of compromise. But is it not indeed a watered-down euphoria which this marriage creates? Eliante, we remember, takes Philinte as a sort of consolation prize. Moreover, far from seeing Molière's position in Philinte's moderation, we might see in it only a dramatic foil which casts the extremes on either side of it in a stronger light. Even so, whether dramatic principle or lesson of the play, this moderation accepts the basically tragic notion of man as a limited creature, ultimately frustrated in his fondest ambitions and his highest aspirations.

Indeed, a professional psychiatrist, Ludwig Jekels, has seen in the climate of comedy the same preoccupation with Oedipal guilt which we have become accustomed to find in tragedy. He reads the ascension of the young in comedy as a "doing away with the father" so that the son can fulfill his wish to take the father's place sexually. In such a reading, the son is the true monomaniac, but he transfers his monomaniacal love rivalry and its attendant guilt feeling onto the father figure. "This withdrawal of the super-ego and its meaning in the ego are all in complete conformity with the phenomenon of mania . . . In each we find the ego, which has liberated itself from the tyrant, uninhibitedly venturing its humor, wit and every sort of comic manifestation in a very ecstasy of freedom."[8] Frankly admitting the Bergsonian echoes of his theory, Jekels says that "comedy represents an esthetic correlate of mania." Yet, such a theory of comedy fails to account for those comedies in which the father figure remains dominant, or in which the pattern of relationships cannot be fitted into the Oedipal scheme. But its very premises, of course, the psychoanalytical interpretation must regard the former types as tragedies and the latter type as nonexistent. Thus, Jekels reads into *Le Tartuffe* a disguised Oedipal relationship: Tartuffe is the son who displaces his guilt onto Orgon. Yet, what would Jekels make of *Dom Juan,* where the "mania" is not displaced but is steadily defended by the son-figure? Indeed, the whole point of *Dom Juan* in Freudian terms is that the son refuses to accept as blameworthy his desire to replace the father and, as I have shown, successfully defies both father figures of the play (his biological father and the statue). Or to take a Molière play in which the father figure remains dominant, in *Amphitryon* we might read the pattern of relationships between father and son figures in two ways, but in each the father-figure remains dominant: (1) Jupiter, without being a clear rival of his

[8]"On the Psychology of Comedy," *Tulane Drama Review,* II, No. 3 (May 1958), 60.

"son" Mercure, keeps the latter in his place—a pattern repeated in the Amphitryon-Sosie relationship; or in a truer Freudian parallel (2) Jupiter and Mercure play father figures to Amphitryon and Sosie respectively, displacing their "sons" in the love intrigues of the play. Yet these plays, like the Oedipal comedies Jekel cites, also end in a "very ecstasy of freedom." Obviously, comedy in which this is true is an "esthetic correlate" of something different from mania.

Thus, we can define Molière's "comic view of life" in the Jekelian sense only by dismissing that part of his work in which a different sense of the comic prevails. This is in the so-called "court work," the series of *comédies-ballets* which makes up nearly one-half the canon, but which has been treated as "minor" by the main current of Molière criticism since the early nineteenth century. Essentially liberal-bourgeois in ethos, this criticism has found it difficult to assimilate these poetic plays, created to please Molière's royal patron, into its portrait of the "scourge" of the *ancien régime*, the unmasker of social hypocrisy in a class-structured society, the enemy of all absolutisms in the very heyday of absolutism. Yet, however convenient, the division of the canon into major and minor, satire and poetry, is ill-founded. The entire canon expresses a single, consistent "comic view of life." Like the first *Le Tartuffe*, the satiric plays reflect an aristocratic bias negatively. This negative bias reached its peak in *Le Tartuffe*, *Dom Juan*, and *Le Misanthrope*, in the period of approximately one year between the first version of *Le Tartuffe* (May 1664) and the completion of *Dom Juan* (February 1665). . . . All three bitter comedies are enclosed between two *comédies-ballets: La Princesse d'Élide* of May 1664 and *L'Amour médecin* of September 1665. *Le Misanthrope*, with its unhappy ending, is "negative" only in the sense that the positive faith on which it is based is implicit. The absence of a Guarantor of truth in the play does not mean that one does not exist: he is in the audience in the person of Molière's royal patron. Or was to have been, the play having been first shown to the "town" due to the unforeseen departure of the king and much of the court just before the scheduled premiere. Like the plays which immediately surround it, the play was written with the court in mind, Molière actually having read it before its production to members of the court and accepting minor revisions. Rousseau notwithstanding, the stalemate with which the play ends is thus no more of a tragic defeat for man than was the triumph of the hypocrite at the end of the three-act *Le Tartuffe*. In the negativism of this great satiric play we see only the underside of Molière's "comic view of life."

henrik ibsen 1828–1906

ghosts

translated by Farquharson Sharp

Ibsen's early years in Norway were spent in narrow provincialism and poverty. At fifteen he left his family for an apprenticeship in pharmacy. Rebelling against small-town conformity, he turned from medical studies to the literary world and began to write poetry. In 1848 he wrote his first play, *Cataline,* a revolutionary drama in verse. Shortly thereafter, Ibsen became stage manager at the state theatre in Bergen, and until 1862 he worked as a producer, director, and writer in Bergen and Christiana. In 1864, disturbed by Norway's backwardness, he left for Italy and did not resettle in Norway until 1891. Abroad, he wrote his poetic dramas, *Brand* (1866) and *Peer Gynt* (1867). He is most remembered, however, for his realistic prose plays which struck out against stultifying conformism in favor of self-realization: *A Doll's House* (1879), *Ghosts* (1881), *An Enemy of the People* (1882). Yet Ibsen knew the limits of his iconoclasm and in such subtle studies as *The Wild Duck* (1884), *Rosmersholm* (1886), and *Hedda Gabler* (1890), he exposed neurotic idealists and pseudo-Ibsenites. With *The Master Builder* (1892), Ibsen turned to the tragedy of the aging artist. A note of frustration and futility entered his work which, toward the end of his life, became more symbolic: *Little Eyolf* (1894), and *When We Dead Awaken* (1899). Ibsen's works have had a profound influence on modern playwrights.

the characters

MRS. ALVING, *a widow*
OSWALD ALVING, *her son, an artist*
MANDERS, *the Pastor of the parish*
ENGSTRAND, *a carpenter*
REGINA ENGSTRAND, *his daughter, in Mrs. Alving's service*

(The action takes place at Mrs. Alving's house on one of the larger fjords of western Norway.)

act 1

(A large room looking upon a garden. A door in the left-hand wall, and two in the right. In the middle of the room, a round table with chairs set about it, and books, magazines and newspapers upon it. In the foreground on the

left, a window, by which is a small sofa with a work-table in front of it. At the back the room opens into a conservatory rather smaller than the room. From the right-hand side of this a door leads to the garden. Through the large panes of glass that form the outer wall of the conservatory, a gloomy fjord landscape can be discerned, half obscured by steady rain.

ENGSTRAND *is standing close up to the garden door. His left leg is slightly deformed, and he wears a boot with a clump of wood under the sole.* REGINA, *with an empty garden-syringe in her hand, is trying to prevent his coming in.)*

REGINA *(below her breath)* What is it you want? Stay where you are. The rain is dripping off you.

ENGSTRAND God's good rain, my girl.

REGINA The Devil's own rain, that's what it is!

ENGSTRAND Lord, how you talk, Regina. *(Takes a few limping steps forward)* What I wanted to tell you was this–

REGINA Don't clump about like that, stupid! The young master is lying asleep upstairs.

ENGSTRAND Asleep still? In the middle of the day?

REGINA Well, it's no business of yours.

ENGSTRAND I was out on the spree last night–

REGINA I don't doubt it.

ENGSTRAND Yes, we are poor weak mortals, my girl–

REGINA We are indeed.

ENGSTRAND –and the temptations of the world are manifold, you know–but, for all that, here I was at my work at half-past five this morning.

REGINA Yes, yes, but make yourself scarce now. I am not going to stand here as if I had a *rendez-vous* with you.

ENGSTRAND As if you had a what?

REGINA I am not going to have any one find you here; so now you know, and you can go.

ENGSTRAND *(coming a few steps nearer)* Not a bit of it! Not before we have had a little chat. This afternoon I shall have finished my job down at the school house, and I shall be off home to town by to-night's boat.

REGINA *(mutters)* Pleasant journey to you!

ENGSTRAND Thanks, my girl. Tomorrow is the opening of the Orphanage, and I expect there will be a fine kick-up here and plenty of good strong drink, don't you know. And no one shall say of Jacob Engstrand that he can't hold off when temptation comes in his way.

REGINA Oho!

ENGSTRAND Yes, because there will be a lot of fine folk here tomorrow. Parson Manders is expected from town, too.

REGINA What is more, he's coming today.

ENGSTRAND There you are! And I'm going to be precious careful he doesn't have anything to say against me, do you see?

REGINA Oh, that's your game, is it?

ENGSTRAND What do you mean?

REGINA *(with a significant look at him)* What is it you want to humbug Mr. Manders out of, this time?

ENGSTRAND Sh! Sh! Are you crazy? Do you suppose *I* would want to humbug Mr. Manders? No, no—Mr. Manders has always been too kind a friend for me to do that. But what I wanted to talk to you about, was my going back home tonight.

REGINA The sooner you go, the better I shall be pleased.

ENGSTRAND Yes, only I want to take you with me, Regina.

REGINA *(open-mouthed)* You want to take me—? What did you say?

ENGSTRAND I want to take you home with me, I said.

REGINA *(contemptuously)* You will never get me home with you.

ENGSTRAND Ah, we shall see about that.

REGINA Yes, you can be quite certain we *shall* see about that. I, who have been brought up by a lady like Mrs. Alving? —I, who have been treated almost as if I were her own child?—do you suppose I am going home with *you?*—to such a house as yours? Not likely!

ENGSTRAND What the devil do you mean? Are you setting yourself up against your father, you hussy?

REGINA *(mutters, without looking at him)* You have often told me I was none of yours.

ENGSTRAND Bah!—why do you want to pay any attention to that?

REGINA Haven't you many and many a time abused me and called me a—? For shame!

ENGSTRAND I'll swear I never used such an ugly word.

REGINA Oh, it doesn't matter what word you used.

ENGSTRAND Besides, that was only when I was a bit fuddled—hm! Temptations are manifold in this world, Regina.

REGINA Ugh!

ENGSTRAND And it was when your mother was in a nasty temper. I had to find some way of getting my knife into her, my girl. She was always so precious genteel. *(Mimicking her)* "Let go, Jacob! Let me be! Please to remember that I was three years with the Alvings at Rosenvold, and they were people who went to Court!" *(Laughs)* Bless my soul, she never could forget that Captain Alving got a Court appointment while she was in service here.

REGINA Poor mother—you worried her into her grave pretty soon.

ENGSTRAND *(shrugging his shoulders)* Of course, of course; I have got to take the blame for everything.

REGINA *(beneath her breath, as she turns away)* Ugh—that leg, too!

ENGSTRAND What are you saying, my girl?

REGINA *Pied de mouton.*

ENGSTRAND Is that English?

REGINA Yes.

ENGSTRAND You have had a good education out here, and no mistake; and it may stand you in good stead now, Regina.

REGINA *(after a short silence)* And what was it you wanted me to come to town for?

ENGSTRAND Need you ask why a father wants his only child? Ain't I a poor lonely widower?

REGINA Oh, don't come to me with that tale. Why do you want me to go?

ENGSTRAND Well, I must tell you I am thinking of taking up a new line now.

REGINA *(whistles)* You have tried that so often—but it has always proved a fool's errand.

ENGSTRAND Ah, but this time you will just see, Regina! Strike me dead if—

REGINA *(stamping her foot)* Stop swearing!

ENGSTRAND Sh! Sh!—you're quite right, my girl, quite right! What I wanted to say was only this, that I have put by a tidy penny out of what I have made by working at this new Orphanage up here.

REGINA Have you? All the better for you.

ENGSTRAND What is there for a man to spend his money on, out here in the country?

REGINA Well, what then?

ENGSTRAND Well, you see, I thought of putting the money into something that would pay. I thought of some kind of an eating-house for seafaring folk—

REGINA Heavens!

ENGSTRAND Oh, a high-class eating-house, of course,—not a pigsty for common sailors. Damn it, no; it would be a place ships' captains and first mates would come to; really good sort of people, you know.

REGINA And what should I—?

ENGSTRAND You would help there. But only to make a show, you know. You wouldn't find it hard work, I can promise you, my girl. You should do exactly as you liked.

REGINA Oh, yes, quite so!

ENGSTRAND But we must have some women in the house; that is as clear as daylight. Because in the evening we must make the place a little attractive—some singing and dancing, and that sort of thing. Remember they are seafolk—wayfarers on the waters of life! *(Coming nearer to her)* Now don't be a fool and stand in your own way, Regina. What good are you going to do here? Will this education, that your mistress has paid for, be of any use? You are to look after the children in the new Home, I hear. Is that the sort of work for you? Are you so frightfully anxious to go and wear out your health and strength for the sake of these dirty brats?

REGINA No, if things were to go as I want them to, then—. Well, it may happen; who knows? It may happen!

ENGSTRAND What may happen?

REGINA Never you mind. Is it much that you have put by, up here?

ENGSTRAND Taking it all round, I should say about forty or fifty pounds.

REGINA That's not so bad.

ENGSTRAND It's enough to make a start with, my girl.

REGINA Don't you mean to give me any of the money?

ENGSTRAND No, I'm hanged if I do.

REGINA Don't you mean to send me as much as a dresslength of stuff, just for once?

ENGSTRAND Come and live in the town with me and you shall have plenty of dresses.

REGINA Pooh!—I can get that much for myself, if I have a mind to.

ENGSTRAND But it's far better to have a father's guiding hand, Regina. Just now I can get a nice house in Little Harbour Street. They don't want much money down for it—and we could make it like a sort of seamen's home, don't you know.

REGINA But I have no intention of living with you! I have nothing whatever to do with you. So now, be off!

ENGSTRAND You wouldn't be living with me long, my girl. No such luck—not if you knew how to play your cards. Such a fine wench as you have grown this last year or two—

REGINA Well—?

ENGSTRAND It wouldn't be very long before some first mate came along—or perhaps a captain.

REGINA I don't mean to marry a man of that sort. Sailors have no *savoir-vivre.*

ENGSTRAND What haven't they got?

REGINA I know what sailors are, I tell you. They aren't the sort of people to marry.

ENGSTRAND Well, don't bother about marrying them. You can make it pay just as well. *(More confidentially)* That fellow—the Englishman—the one with the yacht—he gave seventy pounds, he did; and she wasn't a bit prettier than you.

REGINA *(advancing towards him)* Get out!

ENGSTRAND *(stepping back)* Here! here!—you're not going to hit me, I suppose?

REGINA Yes! If you talk like that of mother, I will hit you. Get out, I tell you! *(Pushes him up to the garden door.)* And don't bang the doors. Young Mr. Alving—

ENGSTRAND Is asleep—I know. It's funny how anxious you are about young Mr. Alving. *(In a lower tone)* Oho! is it possible that it is *he* that—?

REGINA Get out, and be quick about it! Your wits are wandering, my good man. No, don't go that way; Mr. Manders is just coming along. Be off down the kitchen stairs.

ENGSTRAND *(moving towards the right)* Yes, yes—all right. But have a bit of a chat with him that's coming along. He's the chap to tell you what a child owes to its father. For I am your father, anyway, you know. I can prove it by the Register. *(He goes out through the farther door which* REGINA *has opened. She shuts it after him, looks hastily at herself in the mirror, fans herself with her handkerchief and sets her collar straight; then busies herself with the flowers.* MANDERS *enters the conservatory through the garden door. He wears an overcoat, carries an umbrella, and has a small travelling-bag slung over his shoulder on a strap.)*

MANDERS Good morning, Miss Engstrand.

REGINA *(turning round with a look of pleased surprise)* Oh, Mr. Manders, good morning. The boat is in, then?

MANDERS Just in. *(Comes into the room)* It is most tiresome, this rain every day.

REGINA *(following him in)* It's a splendid rain for the farmers, Mr. Manders.

MANDERS Yes, you are quite right. We town-folk think so little about that. *(Begins to take off his overcoat)*

REGINA Oh, let me help you. That's it. Why, how wet it is! I will hang it up in the hall. Give me your umbrella, too; I will leave it open, so that it will dry.

(She goes out with the things by the farther door on the right. MANDERS *lays his bag and his hat down on a chair.* REGINA *re-enters.)*

MANDERS Ah, it's very pleasant to get indoors. Well, is everything going on well here?

REGINA Yes, thanks.

MANDERS Properly busy, though, I expect, getting ready for tomorrow?

REGINA Oh, yes, there is plenty to do.

MANDERS And Mrs. Alving is at home, I hope?

REGINA Yes, she is. She has just gone upstairs to take the young master his chocolate.

MANDERS Tell me—I heard down at the pier that Oswald had come back.

REGINA Yes, he came the day before yesterday. We didn't expect him till today.

MANDERS Strong and well, I hope?

REGINA Yes, thank you, well enough. But dreadfully tired after his journey. He came straight from Paris without a stop—I mean, he came all the way without breaking his journey. I fancy he is having a sleep now, so we must talk a little bit more quietly, if you don't mind.

MANDERS All right, we will be very quiet.

REGINA *(while she moves an armchair up to the table)* Please sit down, Mr. Manders, and make yourself at home. *(He sits down; she puts a footstool under his feet.)* There! Is that comfortable?

MANDERS Thank you, thank you. That is most comfortable. *(Looks at her)* I'll tell you what, Miss Engstrand, I certainly think you have grown up since I saw you last.

REGINA Do you think so? Mrs. Alving says, too, that I have developed.

MANDERS Developed? Well, perhaps a little—just suitably. *(A short pause)*

REGINA Shall I tell Mrs. Alving you are here?

MANDERS Thanks, there is no hurry, my dear child.—Now tell me, Regina, my dear, how has your father been getting on here?

REGINA Thank you, Mr. Manders, he is getting on pretty well.

MANDERS He came to see me, the last time he was in town.

REGINA Did he? He is always so glad when he can have a chat with you.

MANDERS And I suppose you have seen him pretty regularly every day?

REGINA I? Oh, yes, I do—whenever I have time, that is to say.

MANDERS Your father has not a very strong character, Miss Engstrand. He sadly needs a guiding hand.

REGINA Yes, I can quite believe that.

MANDERS He needs someone with him that he can cling to, someone whose judgment he can rely on. He acknowledged that freely himself, the last time he came up to see me.

REGINA Yes, he has said something of the same sort to me. But I don't know whether Mrs. Alving could do without me—most of all just now, when we have the new Orphanage to see about. And I should be dreadfully unwilling to leave Mrs. Alving, too; she has always been so good to me.

MANDERS But a daughter's duty, my good child—. Naturally we should have to get your mistress' consent first.

REGINA Still I don't know whether it would be quite the thing, at my age, to keep house for a single man.

MANDERS What! My dear Miss Engstrand, it is your own father we are speaking of!

REGINA Yes, I dare say, but still—. Now, if it were in a good house and with a real gentleman—

MANDERS But, my dear Regina—

REGINA —one whom I could feel an affection for, and really feel in the position of a daughter to—

MANDERS Come, come—my dear good child—

REGINA I should like very much to live in town. Out here it is terribly lonely; and you know yourself, Mr. Manders, what it is to be alone in the world. And, though I say it, I really am both capable and willing. Don't you know any place that would be suitable for me, Mr. Manders?

MANDERS I? No, indeed I don't.

REGINA But, dear Mr. Manders—at any rate don't forget me, in case—

MANDERS *(getting up)* No, I won't forget you, Miss Engstrand.

REGINA Because, if I—

MANDERS Perhaps you will be so kind as to let Mrs. Alving know I am here?

REGINA I will fetch her at once, Mr. Manders. *(Goes out to the left.* MANDERS *walks up and down the room once or twice, stands for a moment at the farther end of the room with his hands behind his back and looks out into the garden. Then he comes back to the table, takes up a book and looks at the title page, gives a start, and looks at some of the others.)*

MANDERS Hm!—Really!

*(*MRS. ALVING *comes in by the door on the left. She is followed by* REGINA, *who goes out again at once through the nearer door on the right.)*

MRS. ALVING *(holding out her hand)* I am very glad to see you, Mr. Manders.

MANDERS How do you do, Mrs. Alving. Here I am, as I promised.

MRS. ALVING Always punctual!

MANDERS Indeed, I was hard put to it to get away. What with vestry meetings and committees—

MRS. ALVING It was all the kinder of you to come in such good time; we can settle our business before dinner. But where is your luggage?

MANDERS *(quickly)* My things are down at the village shop. I am going to sleep there tonight.

MRS. ALVING *(repressing a smile)* Can't I really persuade you to stay the night here this time?

MANDERS No, no; many thanks all the same; I will put up there, as usual. It is so handy for getting on board the boat again.

MRS. ALVING Of course you shall do as you please. But it seems to me quite another thing, now we are two old people—

MANDERS Ha! ha! You will have your joke! And it's natural you should be in high spirits today—first of all there is the great event tomorrow, and also you have got Oswald home.

MRS. ALVING Yes, am I not a lucky woman! It is more than two years since he was home last, and he has promised to stay the whole winter with me.

MANDERS Has he, really? That is very nice and filial of him; because there must be many more attractions in his life in Rome or in Paris, I should think.

MRS. ALVING Yes, but he has his mother here, you see. Bless the dear boy, he has got a corner in his heart for his mother still.

MANDERS Oh, it would be very sad if absence and preoccupation with such a thing as Art were to dull the natural affections.

MRS. ALVING It would, indeed. But there is no fear of that with him, I am glad to say. I am quite curious to see if you recognise him again. He will be down directly; he is just lying down for a little on the sofa upstairs. But do sit down, my dear friend.

MANDERS Thank you. You are sure I am not disturbing you?

MRS. ALVING Of course not. *(She sits down at the table.)*

MANDERS Good. Then I will show you—. *(He goes to the chair where his bag is lying and takes a packet of papers from it; then sits down at the opposite side of the table and looks for a clear space to put the papers down.)* Now first of all, here is—*(breaks off)*. Tell me, Mrs. Alving, what are these books doing here?

MRS. ALVING These books? I am reading them.

MANDERS Do you read this sort of thing?

MRS. ALVING Certainly I do.

MANDERS Do you feel any the better or the happier for reading books of this kind?

MRS. ALVING I think it makes me, as it were, more self-reliant.

MANDERS That is remarkable. But why?

MRS. ALVING Well, they give me an explanation or a confirmation of lots of different ideas that have come into my own mind. But what surprises me, Mr. Manders, is that, properly speaking, there is nothing at all new in these books. There is nothing more in them than what most people think and believe. The only thing is, that most people either take no account of it or won't admit it to themselves.

MANDERS But, good heavens, do you seriously think that most people—?

MRS. ALVING Yes, indeed, I do.

MANDERS But not here in the country at any rate? Not here amongst people like ourselves?

MRS. ALVING Yes, amongst people like ourselves too.

MANDERS Well, really, I must say—!

MRS. ALVING But what is the particular objection that you have to these books?

MANDERS What objection? You surely don't suppose that I take any particular interest in such productions?

MRS. ALVING In fact, you don't know anything about what you are denouncing?

MANDERS I have read quite enough about these books to disapprove of them.

MRS. ALVING Yes, but your own opinion—

MANDERS My dear Mrs. Alving, there are many occasions in life when one has to rely on the opinion of others. That is the way in this world, and it is quite right that it should be so. What would become of society, otherwise?

MRS. ALVING Well, you may be right.

MANDERS Apart from that, naturally I don't deny that literature of this kind may have a considerable attraction. And I cannot blame you, either, for wishing to make yourself acquainted with the intellectual tendencies which I am told are at work in the wider world in which you have allowed your son to wander for so long. But—

MRS. ALVING But—?

MANDERS *(lowering his voice)* But one doesn't talk about it, Mrs. Alving. One certainly is not called upon to account to every one for what one reads or thinks in the privacy of one's own room.

MRS. ALVING Certainly not. I quite agree with you.

MANDERS Just think of the consideration you owe to this Orphanage, which you decided to build at a time when your thoughts on such subjects were very different from what they are now—as far as I am able to judge.

MRS. ALVING Yes, I freely admit that. But it was about the Orphanage—

MANDERS It was about the Orphanage we were going to talk; quite so. Well—walk warily, dear Mrs. Alving! And now let us turn to the business in hand. *(Opens an envelope and takes out some papers)* You see these?

MRS. ALVING The deeds?

MANDERS Yes, the whole lot—and everything in order. I can tell you it has been no easy matter to get them in time. I had positively to put pressure on the authorities; they are almost painfully conscientious when it is a question of settling property. But here they are at last. *(Turns over the papers)* Here is the deed of conveyance of that part of the Rosenvold estate known as the Solvik property, together with the buildings newly erected thereon—the school, the masters' houses and the chapel. And here is the legal sanction for the statutes of the institution. Here, you see—*(reads)* "Statutes for the Captain Alving Orphanage."

MRS. ALVING *(after a long look at the papers)* That seems all in order.

MANDERS I thought "Captain" was the better title to use, rather than your husband's Court title of "Chamberlain." "Captain" seems less ostentatious.

MRS. ALVING Yes, yes; just as you think best.

MANDERS And here is the certificate for the investment of the capital in the bank, the interest being earmarked for the current expenses of the Orphanage.

MRS. ALVING Many thanks; but I think it will be most convenient if you will kindly take charge of them.

MANDERS With pleasure. I think it will be best to leave the money in the bank for the present. The interest is not very high, it is true; four per cent at six months' call. Later on, if we can find some good mortgage—of course it must be a first mortgage and on unexceptionable security—we can consider the matter further.

MRS. ALVING Yes, yes, my dear Mr. Manders, you know best about all that.

MANDERS I will keep my eye on it, anyway. But there is one thing in connection with it that I have often meant to ask you about.

MRS. ALVING What is that?

MANDERS Shall we insure the buildings, or not?

MRS. ALVING Of course we must insure them.

MANDERS Ah, but wait a moment, dear lady. Let us look into the matter a little more closely.

MRS. ALVING Everything of mine is insured—the house and its contents, my livestock—everything.

MANDERS Naturally. They are your own property. I do exactly the same, of course. But this, you see, is quite a different case. The Orphanage is, so to speak, dedicated to higher uses.

MRS. ALVING Certainly, but—

MANDERS As far as I am personally concerned, I can conscientiously say that I don't see the smallest objection to our insuring ourselves against all risks.

MRS. ALVING That is exactly what I think.

MANDERS But what about the opinion of the people hereabouts?

MRS. ALVING Their opinion—?

MANDERS Is there any considerable body of opinion here—opinion of some account, I mean—that might take exception to it?

MRS. ALVING What, exactly, do you mean by opinion of some account?

MANDERS Well, I was thinking particularly of persons of such independent and influential position that one could hardly refuse to attach weight to their opinion.

MRS. ALVING There are a certain number of such people here, who might perhaps take exception to it if we—

MANDERS That's just it, you see. In town there are lots of them. All my fellow-clergymen's congregations, for instance! It would be so extremely easy for them to interpret it as meaning that neither you nor I had a proper reliance on Divine protection.

MRS. ALVING But as far as you are concerned, my dear friend, you have at all events the consciousness that—

MANDERS Yes I know, I know; my own mind is quite easy about it, it is true. But we should not be able to prevent a wrong and injurious interpretation of our action. And that sort of thing, moreover, might very easily end in exercising a hampering influence on the work of the Orphanage.

MRS. ALVING Oh, well, if that is likely to be the effect of it—

MANDERS Nor can I entirely overlook the difficult—indeed, I may say, painful—position I might possibly be placed in. In the best circles in town the matter of this Orphanage is attracting a great deal of attention. Indeed the Orphanage is to some extent built for the benefit of the town too, and it is to be hoped that it may result in the lowering of our poor-rate by a considerable amount. But as I have been your adviser in the matter and have taken charge of the business side of it, I should be afraid that it would be I that spiteful persons would attack first of all—

MRS. ALVING Yes, you ought not to expose yourself to that.

MANDERS Not to mention the attacks that would undoubtedly be made upon me in certain newspapers and reviews—

MRS. ALVING Say no more about it, dear Mr. Manders; that quite decides it.

MANDERS Then you don't wish it to be insured?

MRS. ALVING No, we will give up the idea.

MANDERS *(leaning back in his chair)* But suppose, now, that some accident happened?—one can never tell—would you be prepared to make good the damage?

MRS. ALVING No; I tell you quite plainly I would not do so under any circumstances.

MANDERS Still, you know, Mrs. Alving—after all, it is a serious responsibility that we are taking upon ourselves.

MRS. ALVING But do you think we can do otherwise?

MANDERS No, that's just it. We really can't do otherwise. We ought not to expose ourselves to a mistaken judgment; and we have no right to do anything that will scandalise the community.

MRS. ALVING You ought not to, as a clergyman, at any rate.

MANDERS And, what is more, I certainly think that we may count upon our enterprise being attended by good fortune—indeed, that it will be under a special protection.

MRS. ALVING Let us hope so, Mr. Manders.

MANDERS Then we will leave it alone?

MRS. ALVING Certainly.

MANDERS Very good. As you wish. *(Makes a note)* No insurance, then.

MRS. ALVING It's a funny thing that you should just have happened to speak about that today—

MANDERS I have often meant to ask you about it—

MRS. ALVING —because yesterday we very nearly had a fire up there.

MANDERS Do you mean it!

MRS. ALVING Oh, as a matter of fact it was nothing of any consequence. Some shavings in the carpenter's shop caught fire.

MANDERS Where Engstrand works?

MRS. ALVING Yes. They say he is often so careless with matches.

MANDERS He has so many things on his mind, poor fellow—so many anxieties. Heaven be thanked, I am told he is really making an effort to live a blameless life.

MRS. ALVING Really? Who told you so?

MANDERS He assured me himself that it is so. He's a good workman, too.

MRS. ALVING Oh, yes, when he is sober.

MANDERS Ah, that sad weakness of his! But the pain in his poor leg often drives him to it, he tells me. The last time he was in town, I was really quite touched by him. He came to my house and thanked me so gratefully for getting him work here, where he could have the chance of being with Regina.

MRS. ALVING He doesn't see very much of her.

MANDERS But he assured me that he saw her every day.

MRS. ALVING Oh well, perhaps he does.

MANDERS He feels so strongly that he needs some one who can keep a hold on him when temptations assail him. That is the most winning thing about Jacob Engstrand; he comes to one like a helpless child and accuses himself and confesses his frailty. The last time he came and had a talk with me—. Suppose now, Mrs. Alving, that it were really a necessity of his existence to have Regina at home with him again—

MRS. ALVING *(standing up suddenly)* Regina!

MANDERS —you ought not to set yourself against him.

MRS. ALVING Indeed, I set myself very definitely against that. And, besides, you know Regina is to have a post in the Orphanage.

MANDERS But consider, after all he is her father—

MRS. ALVING I know best what sort of a father he has been to her. No, she shall never go to him with my consent.

MANDERS *(getting up)* My dear lady, don't judge so hastily. It is very sad how you misjudge poor Engstrand. One would really think you were afraid—

MRS. ALVING *(more calmly)* That is not the question. I have taken Regina into my charge, and in my charge she remains. *(Listens)* Hush, dear Mr. Manders, don't say any more about it. *(Her face brightens with pleasure)* Listen! Oswald is coming downstairs. We will only think about him now.

*(*OSWALD ALVING, *in a light overcoat, hat in hand and smoking a big meerschaum pipe, comes in by the door on the left.)*

OSWALD *(standing in the doorway)* Oh, I beg your pardon, I thought you were in the office. *(Comes in)* Good morning, Mr. Manders.

MANDERS *(staring at him)* Well! It's most extraordinary—

MRS. ALVING Yes, what do you think of him, Mr. Manders?

MANDERS I—I— no, can it possibly be—?

OSWALD Yes, it really is the prodigal son, Mr. Manders.

MANDERS Oh, my dear young friend—

OSWALD Well, the son come home, then.

MRS. ALVING Oswald is thinking of the time when you were so opposed to the idea of his being a painter.

MANDERS We are only fallible, and many steps seem to us hazardous at first, that afterwards—*(grasps his hand)*. Welcome, welcome! Really, my dear Oswald—may I still call you Oswald?

OSWALD What else would you think of calling me?

MANDERS Thank you. What I mean, my dear Oswald, is that you must not imagine that I have any unqualified disapproval of the artist's life. I admit that there are many who, even in that career, can keep the inner man free from harm.

OSWALD Let us hope so.

MRS. ALVING *(beaming with pleasure)* I know one who has kept both the inner and the outer man free from harm. Just take a look at him, Mr. Manders.

OSWALD *(walks across the room)* Yes, yes, mother dear, of course.

MANDERS Undoubtedly—no one can deny it. And I hear you have begun to make a name for yourself. I have often seen mention of you in the papers—and extremely favourable mention, too. Although, I must admit, latterly I have not seen your name so often.

OSWALD *(going towards the conservatory)* I haven't done so much painting just lately.

MRS. ALVING An artist must take a rest sometimes, like other people.

MANDERS Of course, of course. At those times the artist is preparing and strengthening himself for a greater effort.

OSWALD Yes. Mother, will dinner soon be ready?

MRS. ALVING In half an hour. He has a fine appetite, thank goodness.

MANDERS And a liking for tobacco too.

OSWALD I found father's pipe in the room upstairs, and—

MANDERS Ah, that is what it was!

MRS. ALVING What?

MANDERS When Oswald came in at that door with the pipe in his mouth, I thought for the moment it was his father in the flesh.

OSWALD Really?

MRS. ALVING How can you say so! Oswald takes after me.

MANDERS Yes, but there is an expression about the corners of his mouth—something about the lips—that reminds me so exactly of Mr. Alving—especially when he smokes.

MRS. ALVING I don't think so at all. To my mind, Oswald has much more of a clergyman's mouth.

MANDERS Well, yes—a good many of my colleagues in the church have a similar expression.

MRS. ALVING But put your pipe down, my dear boy. I don't allow any smoking in here.

OSWALD *(puts down his pipe)* All right, I only wanted to try it, because I smoked it once when I was a child.

MRS. ALVING You?

OSWALD Yes; it was when I was quite a little chap. And I can remember going upstairs to father's room one evening when he was in very good spirits.

MRS. ALVING Oh, you can't remember anything about those days.

OSWALD Yes, I remember plainly that he took me on his knee and let me smoke his pipe. "Smoke, my boy," he said, "have a good smoke, boy!"

And I smoked as hard as I could, until I felt I was turning quite pale and the perspiration was standing in great drops on my forehead. Then he laughed—such a hearty laugh—

MANDERS It was an extremely odd thing to do.

MRS. ALVING Dear Mr. Manders, Oswald only dreamt it.

OSWALD No indeed, mother, it was no dream. Because—don't you remember—you came into the room and carried me off to the nursery, where I was sick, and I saw that you were crying. Did father often play such tricks?

MANDERS In his young days he was full of fun—

OSWALD And, for all that, he did so much with his life—so much that was good and useful, I mean—short as his life was.

MANDERS Yes, my dear Oswald Alving, you have inherited the name of a man who undoubtedly was both energetic and worthy. Let us hope it will be a spur to your energies—

OSWALD It ought to be, certainly.

MANDERS In any case it was nice of you to come home for the day that is to honour his memory.

OSWALD I could do no less for my father.

MRS. ALVING And to let me keep him so long here—that's the nicest part of what he has done.

MANDERS Yes, I hear you are going to spend the winter at home.

OSWALD I am here for an indefinite time, Mr. Manders. —Oh, it's good to be at home again!

MRS. ALVING *(beaming)* Yes, isn't it?

MANDERS *(looking sympathetically at him)* You went out into the world very young, my dear Oswald.

OSWALD I did. Sometimes I wonder if I wasn't too young.

MRS. ALVING Not a bit of it. It is the best thing for an active boy, and especially for an only child. It's a pity when they are kept at home with their parents and get spoilt.

MANDERS That is a very debatable question, Mrs. Alving. A child's own home is, and always must be, his proper place.

OSWALD There I agree entirely with Mr. Manders.

MANDERS Take the case of your own son. Oh yes, we can talk about it before him. What has the result been in his case? He is six or seven and twenty, and has never yet had the opportunity of learning what a well-regulated home means.

OSWALD Excuse me, Mr. Manders, you are quite wrong there.

MANDERS Indeed? I imagined that your life abroad had practically been spent entirely in artistic circles.

OSWALD So it has.

MANDERS And chiefly amongst the younger artists.

OSWALD Certainly.

MANDERS But I imagined that those gentry, as a rule, had not the means necessary for family life and the support of a home.

OSWALD There are a considerable number of them who have not the means to marry, Mr. Manders.

MANDERS That is exactly my point.

OSWALD But they can have a home of their own, all the same; a good many of them have. And they are very well-regulated and very comfortable homes, too.

(MRS. ALVING, *who has listened to him attentively, nods assent, but says nothing.)*

MANDERS Oh, but I am not talking of bachelor establishments. By a home I mean family life—the life a man lives with his wife and children.

OSWALD Exactly, or with his children and his children's mother.

MANDERS *(starts and clasps his hands)* Good heavens!

OSWALD What is the matter?

MANDERS Lives with—with—his children's mother!

OSWALD Well, would you rather he should repudiate his children's mother?

MANDERS Then what you are speaking of are those unprincipled conditions known as irregular unions!

OSWALD I have never noticed anything particularly unprincipled about these people's lives.

MANDERS But do you mean to say that it is possible for a man of any sort of bringing up, and a young woman, to reconcile themselves to such a way of living—and to make no secret of it, either!

OSWALD What else are they to do? A poor artist, and a poor girl—it costs a good deal to get married. What else are they to do?

MANDERS What are they to do? Well, Mr. Alving, I will tell you what they ought to do. They ought to keep away from each other from the very beginning—that is what they ought to do!

OSWALD That advice wouldn't have much effect upon hot-blooded young folk who are in love.

MRS. ALVING No, indeed it wouldn't.

MANDERS *(persistently)* And to think that the authorities tolerate such things! That they are allowed to go on, openly! *(Turns to* MRS. ALVING*)* Had I so little reason, then, to be sadly concerned about your son? In circles where open immorality is rampant—where, one may say, it is honoured—

OSWALD Let me tell you this, Mr. Manders. I have been a constant Sunday guest at one or two of these "irregular" households—

MANDERS On Sunday, too!

OSWALD Yes, that is the day of leisure. But never have I heard one objectionable word there, still less have I ever seen anything that could be called immoral. No; but do you know when and where I *have* met with immorality in artists' circles?

MANDERS No, thank heaven, I don't!

OSWALD Well, then, I shall have the pleasure of telling you. I have met with it when some one or other of your model husbands and fathers have come out there to have a bit of a look round on their own account, and have done the artists the honour of looking them up in their humble quarters. Then we had a chance of learning something, I can tell you. These gentlemen were able to instruct us about places and things that we had never so much as dreamt of.

MANDERS What? Do you want me to believe that honourable men when they get away from home will—

OSWALD Have you never, when these same honourable men come home again, heard them deliver themselves on the subject of the prevalence of immorality abroad?

MANDERS Yes, of course, but—

MRS. ALVING I have heard them, too.

OSWALD Well, you can take their word for it, unhesitatingly. Some of them are experts in the matter. *(Putting his hands to his head.)* To think that the glorious freedom of the beautiful life over there should be so besmirched!

MRS. ALVING You mustn't get too heated, Oswald; you gain nothing by that.

OSWALD No, you are quite right, mother. Besides, it isn't good for me. It's because I am so infernally tired, you know. I will go out and take a turn before dinner. I beg your pardon, Mr. Manders. It is impossible for you to realise the feeling; but it takes me that way. *(Goes out by the farther door on the right)*

MRS. ALVING My poor boy!

MANDERS You may well say so. This is what it has brought him to! *(*MRS. ALVING *looks at him, but does not speak.)* He called himself the prodigal son. It's only too true, alas—only too true! *(*MRS. ALVING *looks steadily at him.)* And what do you say to all this?

MRS. ALVING I say that Oswald was right in every single word he said.

MANDERS Right? Right? To hold such principles as that?

MRS. ALVING In my loneliness here I have come to just the same opinions as he, Mr. Manders. But I have never presumed to venture upon such topics in conversation. Now there is no need; my boy shall speak for me.

MANDERS You deserve the deepest pity, Mrs. Alving. It is my duty to say an earnest word to you. It is no longer your business man and adviser, no longer your old friend and your dead husband's old friend, that stands before you now. It is your priest that stands before you, just as he did once at the most critical moment of your life.

MRS. ALVING And what is it that my priest has to say to me?

MANDERS First of all I must stir your memory. The moment is well chosen. Tomorrow is the tenth anniversary of your husband's death; tomorrow the memorial to the departed will be unveiled; tomorrow I shall speak to the whole assembly that will be met together. But today I want to speak to you alone.

MRS. ALVING Very well, Mr. Manders, speak!

MANDERS Have you forgotten that after barely a year of married life you were standing at the very edge of a precipice?—that you forsook your house and home?—that you ran away from your husband—yes, Mrs. Alving, ran away, ran away—and refused to return to him in spite of his requests and entreaties?

MRS. ALVING Have you forgotten how unspeakably unhappy I was during that first year?

MANDERS To crave for happiness in this world is simply to be possessed by a spirit of revolt. What right have we to happiness? No! we must do our duty, Mrs. Alving. And your duty was to cleave to the man you had chosen and to whom you were bound by a sacred bond.

MRS. ALVING You know quite well what sort of a life my husband was living at that time—what excesses he was guilty of.

MANDERS I know only too well what rumour used to say of him; and I should be the last person to approve of his conduct as a young man, supposing that rumour spoke the truth. But it is not a wife's part to be her husband's judge. You should have considered it your bounden duty humbly to have borne the cross that a higher will had laid upon you. But, instead of that, you rebelliously cast off your cross, you deserted the man whose stumbling footsteps you should have supported, you did what was bound to imperil your good name and reputation, and came very near to imperilling the reputation of others into the bargain.

MRS. ALVING Of others? Of one other, you mean.

MANDERS It was the height of imprudence, your seeking refuge with me.

MRS. ALVING With our priest? With our intimate friend?

MANDERS All the more on that account. You should thank God that I possessed the necessary strength of mind—that I was able to turn you from your outrageous intention, and that it was vouchsafed to me to succeed in leading you back into the path of duty and back to your lawful husband.

MRS. ALVING Yes, Mr. Manders, that certainly was your doing.

MANDERS I was but the humble instrument of a higher power. And is it not true that my having been able to bring you again under the yoke of duty and obedience sowed the seeds of a rich blessing on all the rest of your life? Did things not turn out as I foretold to you? Did not your husband turn from straying in the wrong path, as a man should? Did he not, after that, live a life of love and good report with you all his days? Did he not become a benefactor to the neighbourhood? Did he not so raise you up to his level, so that by degrees you became his fellow-worker in all his undertakings—and a noble fellow-worker, too, I know, Mrs. Alving; that praise I will give you.—But now I come to the second serious false step in your life.

MRS. ALVING What do you mean?

MANDERS Just as once you forsook your duty as a wife, so, since then, you have forsaken your duty as a mother.

MRS. ALVING Oh—!

MANDERS You have been overmastered all your life by a disastrous spirit of wilfulness. All your impulses have led you towards what is undisciplined and lawless. You have never been willing to submit to any restraint. Anything in life that has seemed irksome to you, you have thrown aside recklessly and unscrupulously, as if it were a burden that you were free to rid yourself of if you would. It did not please you to be a wife any longer, and so you left your husband. Your duties as a mother were irksome to you, so you sent your child away among strangers.

MRS. ALVING Yes, that is true; I did that.

MANDERS And that is why you have become a stranger to him.

MRS. ALVING No, no, I am not that!

MANDERS You are; you must be. And what sort of a son is it that you have got back? Think over it seriously, Mrs. Alving. You erred grievously in your husband's case—you acknowledge as much, by erecting this memorial to him. Now you are bound to acknowledge how much you have erred in your son's case; possibly there may still be time to reclaim him from the paths of wickedness. Turn over a new leaf, and set yourself to reform what there may still be that is capable of reformation in him. Because *(with uplifted forefinger)* in very truth, Mrs. Alving, you are a guilty mother!—That is what I have thought it my duty to say to you.

(A short silence)

MRS. ALVING *(speaking slowly and with self-control)* You have had your say, Mr. Manders, and tomorrow you will be making a public speech in memory of my husband. I shall not speak tomorrow. But now I wish to speak to you for a little, just as you have been speaking to me.

MANDERS By all means; no doubt you wish to bring forward some excuses for your behaviour—

MRS. ALVING No. I only want to tell you something.

MANDERS Well?

MRS. ALVING In all that you said just now about me and my husband, and about our life together after you had, as you put it, led me back into the path of duty—there was nothing that you knew at first hand. From that moment you never again set foot in our house—you, who had been our daily companion before that.

MANDERS Remember that you and your husband moved out of town immediately afterwards.

MRS. ALVING Yes, and you never once came out here to see us in my husband's lifetime. It was only the business in connection with the Orphanage that obliged you to come and see me.

MANDERS *(in a low and uncertain voice)* Helen—if that is a reproach, I can only beg you to consider—

MRS. ALVING —the respect you owed to your calling?—yes. All the more as I was a wife who had tried to run away from her husband. One can never be too careful to have nothing to do with such reckless women.

MANDERS My dear—Mrs. Alving, you are exaggerating dreadfully—

MRS. ALVING Yes, yes,—very well. What I mean is this, that when you condemn my conduct as a wife you have nothing more to go upon than ordinary public opinion.

MANDERS I admit it. What then?

MRS. ALVING Well—now, Mr. Manders, now I am going to tell you the truth. I had sworn to myself that you should know it one day—you, and you only!

MANDERS And what may the truth be?

MRS. ALVING The truth is this, that my husband died just as great a profligate as he had been all his life.

MANDERS *(feeling for a chair)* What are you saying?

MRS. ALVING After nineteen years of married life, just as profligate—in his desires at all events—as he was before you married us.

MANDERS And can you talk of his youthful indiscretions—his irregularities—his excesses, if you like—as a profligate life!

MRS. ALVING That was what the doctor who attended him called it.

MANDERS I don't understand what you mean.

MRS. ALVING It is not necessary you should.

MANDERS It makes my brain reel. To think that your marriage—all the years of wedded life you spent with your husband—were nothing but a hidden abyss of misery.

MRS. ALVING That and nothing else. Now you know.

MANDERS This—this bewilders me. I can't understand it! I can't grasp it! How in the world was it possible—? How could such a state of things remain concealed?

MRS. ALVING That was just what I had to fight for incessantly, day after day. When Oswald was born, I thought I saw a slight improvement. But it didn't last long. And after that I had to fight doubly hard—fight a desperate fight so that no one should know what sort of a man my child's father was. You know quite well what an attractive manner he had; it seemed as if people could believe nothing but good of him. He was one of those men whose mode of life seems to have no effect upon their reputations. But at last, Mr. Manders—you must hear this too—at last something happened more abominable than everything else.

MANDERS More abominable than what you have told me!

MRS. ALVING I had borne with it all, though I knew only too well what he indulged in in secret, when he was out of the house. But when it came to the point of the scandal coming within our four walls—

MANDERS Can you mean it! Here?

MRS. ALVING Yes, here, in our own home. It was in there *(pointing to the nearer door on the right)* in the dining-room that I got the first hint of it. I had something to do in there and the door was standing ajar. I heard our maid come up from the garden with water for the flowers in the conservatory.

MANDERS Well—?

MRS. ALVING Shortly afterwards I heard my husband come in too. I heard him say something to her in a low voice. And then I heard—*(with a short laugh)*—oh, it rings in my ears still, with its mixture of what was heart-breaking and what was so ridiculous—I heard my own servant whisper: "Let me go, Mr. Alving! Let me be!"

MANDERS What unseemly levity on his part! But surely nothing more than levity, Mrs. Alving, believe me.

MRS. ALVING I soon knew what to believe. My husband had his will of the girl—and that intimacy had consequences, Mr. Manders.

MANDERS *(as if turned to stone)* And all that in this house! In this house!

MRS. ALVING I have suffered a good deal in this house. To keep him at home in the evening—and at night—I have had to play the part of boon companion in his secret drinking-bouts in his room up there. I have had to sit there alone with him, have had to hobnob and drink with him, have had to listen to his ribald senseless talk, have had to fight with brute force to get him to bed—

MANDERS *(trembling)* And you were able to endure all this!

MRS. ALVING I had my little boy, and endured it for his sake. But when the crowning insult came—when my own servant—then I made up my mind that there should be an end of it. I took the upper hand in the house, absolutely—both with him and all the others. I had a weapon to use against him, you see; he didn't dare to speak. It was then that Oswald was sent away. He was about seven then, and was beginning to notice things and ask questions as children will. I could endure all that, my friend. It seemed to me that the child would be poisoned if he breathed the air of this polluted house. That was why I sent him away. And now you understand, too, why he never set foot here as long as his father was alive. No one knows what it meant to me.

MANDERS You have indeed had a pitiable experience.

MRS. ALVING I could never have gone through with it, if I had not had my work. Indeed, I can boast that I have worked. All the increase in the value of the property, all the improvements, all the useful arrangements that my husband got the honour and glory of—do you suppose that he troubled himself about any of them? He, who used to lie the whole day on the sofa reading old Official Lists! No, you may as well know that too. It was I that kept him up to the mark when he had his lucid intervals; it was I that had to bear the whole burden of it when he began his excesses again or took to whining about his miserable condition.

MANDERS And this is the man you are building a memorial to!

MRS. ALVING There you see the power of an uneasy conscience.

MANDERS An uneasy conscience? What do you mean?

MRS. ALVING I had always before me the fear that it was impossible that the truth should not come out and be believed. That is why the Orphanage is to exist, to silence all rumours and clear away all doubt.

MANDERS You certainly have not fallen short of the mark in that, Mrs. Alving.

MRS. ALVING I had another very good reason. I did not wish Oswald, my own son, to inherit a penny that belonged to his father.

MANDERS Then it is with Mr. Alving's property—

MRS. ALVING Yes. The sums of money that, year after year, I have given towards this Orphanage, make up the amount of property—I have reckoned it carefully—which in the old days made Lieutenant Alving a catch.

MANDERS I understand.

MRS. ALVING That was my purchase money. I don't wish it to pass into Oswald's hands. My son shall have everything from me, I am determined.

*(*OSWALD *comes in by the farther door on the right. He has left his hat and coat outside.)*

MRS. ALVING Back again, my own dear boy?

OSWALD Yes, what can one do outside in this everlasting rain? I hear dinner is nearly ready. That's good!

(REGINA *comes in from the dining-room, carrying a parcel.)*

REGINA This parcel has come for you, ma'am. *(Gives it to her)*

MRS. ALVING *(glancing at* MANDERS*)* The ode to be sung tomorrow, I expect.

MANDERS Hm—!

REGINA And dinner is ready.

MRS. ALVING Good. We will come in a moment. I will just—*(begins to open the parcel).*

REGINA *(to* OSWALD*)* Will you drink white or red wine, sir?

OSWALD Both, Miss Engstrand.

REGINA *Bien*—very good, Mr. Alving. *(Goes into the dining-room)*

OSWALD I may as well help you to uncork it—. *(Follows her into the dining-room, leaving the door ajar after him)*

MRS. ALVING Yes, I thought so. Here is the ode, Mr. Manders.

MANDERS *(clasping his hands)* How shall I ever have the courage tomorrow to speak the address that—

MRS. ALVING Oh, you will get through it.

MANDERS *(in a low voice, fearing to be heard in the dining-room)* Yes, we must raise no suspicions.

MRS. ALVING *(quietly but firmly)* No; and then this long dreadful comedy will be at an end. After tomorrow, I shall feel as if my dead husband had never lived in this house. There will be no one else here then but my boy and his mother.

(From the dining-room is heard the noise of a chair falling; then REGINA'S *voice is heard in a loud whisper:* Oswald! Are you mad? Let me go!*)*

MRS. ALVING *(starting in horror)* Oh—! *(She stares wildly at the half-open door.* OSWALD *is heard coughing and humming, then the sound of a bottle being uncorked.)*

MANDERS *(in an agitated manner)* What's the matter? What is it, Mrs. Alving?

MRS. ALVING *(hoarsely)* Ghosts. The couple in the conservatory—over again.

MANDERS What are you saying! Regina—? Is *she*—?

MRS. ALVING Yes. Come. Not a word! *(Grips* MANDERS *by the arm and walks unsteadily with him into the dining-room)*

act II

(The same scene. The landscape is still obscured by mist. MANDERS *and* MRS. ALVING *come in from the dining-room.)*

MRS. ALVING *(calls into the dining-room from the doorway)* Aren't you coming in here, Oswald?

OSWALD No, thanks; I think I will go out for a bit.

MRS. ALVING Yes, do; the weather is clearing a little. *(She shuts the dining-room door, then goes to the hall door and calls.)* Regina!

REGINA *(from without)* Yes, ma'am?

MRS. ALVING Go down into the laundry and help with the garlands.
REGINA Yes, ma'am.
(MRS. ALVING *satisfies herself that she has gone, then shuts the door.)*
MANDERS I suppose he can't hear us?
MRS. ALVING Not when the door is shut. Besides, he is going out.
MANDERS I am still quite bewildered. I don't know how I managed to swallow a mouthful of your excellent dinner.
MRS. ALVING *(walking up and down, and trying to control her agitation)* Nor I. But what are we to do?
MANDERS Yes, what are we to do? Upon my word I don't know; I am so completely unaccustomed to things of this kind.
MRS. ALVING I am convinced that nothing serious has happened yet.
MANDERS Heaven forbid! But it is most unseemly behaviour, for all that.
MRS. ALVING It is nothing more than a foolish jest of Oswald's, you may be sure.
MANDERS Well, of course, as I said, I am quite inexperienced in such matters; but it certainly seems to me—
MRS. ALVING Out of the house she shall go—and at once. That part of it is as clear as daylight—
MANDERS Yes, that is quite clear.
MRS. ALVING But where is she to go? We should not be justified in—
MANDERS Where to? Home to her father, of course.
MRS. ALVING To whom, did you say?
MANDERS To her—. No, of course Engstrand isn't—. But, great heavens, Mrs. Alving, how is such a thing possible? You surely may have been mistaken, in spite of everything.
MRS. ALVING There was no chance of mistake, more's the pity. Joanna was obliged to confess it to me—and my husband couldn't deny it. So there was nothing else to do but to hush it up.
MANDERS No, that was the only thing to do.
MRS. ALVING The girl was sent away at once, and was given a tolerably liberal sum to hold her tongue. She looked after the rest herself when she got to town. She renewed an old acquaintance with the carpenter Engstrand; gave him a hint, I suppose, of how much money she had got, and told him some fairy tale about a foreigner who had been here in his yacht in the summer. So she and Engstrand were married in a great hurry. Why, you married them yourself!
MANDERS I can't understand it—. I remember clearly Engstrand's coming to arrange about the marriage. He was full of contrition, and accused himself bitterly for the light conduct he and his fiancée had been guilty of.
MRS. ALVING Of course he had to take the blame on himself.
MANDERS But the deceitfulness of it! And with me, too! I positively would not have believed it of Jacob Engstrand. I shall most certainly give him a serious talking to.—And the immorality of such a marriage! Simply for the sake of the money—! What sum was it that the girl had?
MRS. ALVING It was seventy pounds.
MANDERS Just think of it—for a paltry seventy pounds to let yourself be

bound in marriage to a fallen woman!

MRS. ALVING What about myself, then?—I let myself be bound in marriage to a fallen man.

MANDERS Heaven forgive you! what are you saying? A fallen man?

MRS. ALVING Do you suppose my husband was any purer, when I went with him to the altar, than Joanna was when Engstrand agreed to marry her?

MANDERS The two cases are as different as day from night—

MRS. ALVING Not so very different, after all. It is true there was a great difference in the price paid, between a paltry seventy pounds and a whole fortune.

MANDERS How can you compare such totally different things! I presume you consulted your own heart—and your relations.

MRS. ALVING *(looking away from him)* I thought you understood where what you call my heart had strayed to at that time.

MANDERS *(in a constrained voice)* If I had understood anything of the kind, I would not have been a daily guest in your husband's house.

MRS. ALVING Well, at any rate this much is certain, that I didn't consult myself in the matter at all.

MANDERS Still you consulted those nearest to you, as was only right—your mother, your two aunts.

MRS. ALVING Yes, that is true. The three of them settled the whole matter for me. It seems incredible to me now, how clearly they made out that it would be sheer folly to reject such an offer. If my mother could only see what all that fine prospect has led to!

MANDERS No one can be responsible for the result of it. Anyway there is this to be said, that the match was made in complete conformity with law and order.

MRS. ALVING *(going to the window)* Oh, law and order! I often think it is that that is at the bottom of all the misery in the world.

MANDERS Mrs. Alving, it is very wicked of you to say that.

MRS. ALVING That may be so; but I don't attach importance to those obligations and considerations any longer. I cannot! I must struggle for my freedom.

MANDERS What do you mean?

MRS. ALVING *(tapping on the window panes)* I ought never to have concealed what sort of a life my husband led. But I had not the courage to do otherwise then—for my own sake, either. I was too much of a coward.

MANDERS A coward?

MRS. ALVING If others had known anything of what happened, they would have said: "Poor man, it is natural enough that he should go astray, when he has a wife that has run away from him."

MANDERS They would have had a certain amount of justification for saying so.

MRS. ALVING *(looking fixedly at him)* If I had been the woman I ought, I would have taken Oswald into my confidence and said to him: "Listen, my son, your father was a dissolute man"—

MANDERS Miserable woman—

MRS. ALVING —and I would have told him all I have told you, from beginning to end.

MANDERS I am almost shocked at you, Mrs. Alving.

MRS. ALVING I know. I know quite well! I am shocked at myself when I think of it. *(Comes away from the window)* I am coward enough for that.

MANDERS Can you call it cowardice that you simply did your duty! Have you forgotten that a child should love and honour his father and mother?

MRS. ALVING Don't let us talk in such general terms. Suppose we say: "Ought Oswald to love and honour Mr. Alving?"

MANDERS You are a mother—isn't there a voice in your heart that forbids you to shatter your son's ideals?

MRS. ALVING And what about the truth?

MANDERS What about his ideals?

MRS. ALVING Oh—ideals, ideals! If only I were not such a coward as I am!

MANDERS Do not spurn ideals, Mrs. Alving—they have a way of avenging themselves cruelly. Take Oswald's own case, now. He hasn't many ideals, more's the pity. But this much I have seen, that his father is something of an ideal to him.

MRS. ALVING You are right there.

MANDERS And his conception of his father is what you inspired and encouraged by your letters.

MRS. ALVING Yes, I was swayed by duty and consideration for others; that was why I lied to my son, year in and year out. Oh, what a coward—what a coward I have been!

MANDERS You have built up a happy illusion in your son's mind, Mrs. Alving—and that is a thing you certainly ought not to undervalue.

MRS. ALVING Ah, who knows if that is such a desirable thing after all! —But anyway I don't intend to put up with any goings on with Regina. I am not going to let him get the poor girl into trouble.

MANDERS Good heavens, no—that would be a frightful thing!

MRS. ALVING If only I knew whether he meant it seriously, and whether it would mean happiness for him—

MANDERS In what way? I don't understand.

MRS. ALVING But that is impossible; Regina is not equal to it, unfortunately.

MANDERS I don't understand. What do you mean?

MRS. ALVING If I were not such a miserable coward, I would say to him: "Marry her, or make any arrangements you like with her—only let there be no deceit in the matter."

MANDERS Heaven forgive you! Are you actually suggesting anything so abominable, so unheard of, as a marriage between them!

MRS. ALVING Unheard of, do you call it? Tell me honestly, Mr. Manders, don't you suppose there are plenty of married couples out here in the country that are just as nearly related as they are?

MANDERS I am sure I don't understand you.

MRS. ALVING Indeed you do.

MANDERS I suppose you are thinking of cases where possibly—. It is only too true, unfortunately, that family life is not always as stainless as it should be. But as for the sort of thing you hint at—well, it's impossible to tell, at all events with any certainty. Here, on the other hand—for you, a mother, to be willing to allow your—

MRS. ALVING But I am not willing to allow it. I would not allow it for anything in the world; that is just what I was saying.

MANDERS No, because you are a coward, as you put it. But, supposing you were not a coward—! Great heavens—such a revolting union!

MRS. ALVING Well, for the matter of that, we are all descended from a union of that description, so we are told. And who was it that was responsible for this state of things, Mr. Manders?

MANDERS I can't discuss such questions with you, Mrs. Alving; you are by no means in the right frame of mind for that. But for you to dare to say that it is cowardly of you—!

MRS. ALVING I will tell you what I mean by that. I am frightened and timid, because I am obsessed by the presence of ghosts that I never can get rid of.

MANDERS The presence of what?

MRS. ALVING Ghosts. When I heard Regina and Oswald in there, it was just like seeing ghosts before my eyes. I am half inclined to think we are all ghosts, Mr. Manders. It is not only what we have inherited from our fathers and mothers that exists again in us, but all sorts of old dead ideas and all kinds of old dead beliefs and things of that kind. They are not actually alive in us; but there they are dormant, all the same, and we can never be rid of them. Whenever I take up a newspaper and read it, I fancy I see ghosts creeping between the lines. There must be ghosts all over the world. They must be as countless as the grains of the sands, it seems to be. And we are so miserably afraid of the light, all of us.

MANDERS Ah!—there we have the outcome of your reading. Fine fruit it has borne—this abominable, subversive, free-thinking literature!

MRS. ALVING You are wrong there, my friend. You are the one who made me begin to think; and I owe you my best thanks for it.

MANDERS I!

MRS. ALVING Yes, by forcing me to submit to what you called my duty and my obligations; by praising as right and just what my whole soul revolted against, as it would against something abominable. That was what led me to examine your teachings critically. I only wanted to unravel one point in them; but as soon as I had got that unravelled, the whole fabric came to pieces. And then I realised that it was only machine-made.

MANDERS *(softly, and with emotion)* Is that all I accomplished by the hardest struggle of my life?

MRS. ALVING Call it rather the most ignominious defeat of your life.

MANDERS It was the greatest victory of my life, Helen; victory over myself.

MRS. ALVING It was a wrong done to both of us.

MANDERS A wrong?—wrong for me to entreat you as a wife to go back to your lawful husband, when you came to me half distracted and crying: "Here I am, take me!" Was that a wrong?

MRS. ALVING I think it was.
MANDERS We two do not understand one another.
MRS. ALVING Not now, at all events.
MANDERS Never—even in my most secret thoughts—have I for a moment regarded you as anything but the wife of another.
MRS. ALVING Do you believe what you say?
MANDERS Helen—!
MRS. ALVING One so easily forgets one's own feelings.
MANDERS Not I. I am the same as I always was.
MRS. ALVING Yes, yes—don't let us talk any more about the old days. You are buried up to your eyes now in committees and all sorts of business; and I am here, fighting with ghosts both without and within me.
MANDERS I can at all events help you to get the better of those without you. After all that I have been horrified to hear from you today, I cannot conscientiously allow a young defenceless girl to remain in your house.
MRS. ALVING Don't you think it would be best if we could get her settled? —by some suitable marriage, I mean.
MANDERS Undoubtedly. I think, in any case, it would have been desirable for her. Regina is at an age now that—well, I don't know much about these things, but—
MRS. ALVING Regina developed very early.
MANDERS Yes, didn't she. I fancy I remember thinking she was remarkably well developed, bodily, at the time I prepared her for Confirmation. But, for the time being, she must in any case go home. Under her father's care—no, but of course Engstrand is not—. To think that he, of all men, could so conceal the truth from me!
(A knock is heard at the hall door.)
MRS. ALVING Who can that be? Come in!
(ENGSTRAND, *dressed in his Sunday clothes, appears in the doorway.)*
ENGSTRAND I humbly beg pardon, but—
MANDERS Aha! Hm!—
MRS. ALVING Oh, it's you, Engstrand!
ENGSTRAND There were none of the maids about, so I took the great liberty of knocking.
MRS. ALVING That's all right. Come in. Do you want to speak to me?
ENGSTRAND *(coming in)* No, thank you very much, ma'am. It was Mr. Manders I wanted to speak to for a moment.
MANDERS *(walking up and down)* Hm!—do you. You want to speak to me, do you?
ENGSTRAND Yes, sir, I wanted so very much to—
MANDERS *(stopping in front of him)* Well, may I ask what it is you want?
ENGSTRAND It's this way, Mr. Manders. We are being paid off now. And many thanks to you, Mrs. Alving. And now the work is quite finished, I thought it would be so nice and suitable if all of us, who have worked so honestly together all this time, were to finish up with a few prayers this evening.
MANDERS Prayers? Up at the Orphanage?

ENGSTRAND Yes, sir, but if it isn't agreeable to you, then—

MANDERS Oh, certainly—but—hm!—

ENGSTRAND I have made a practice of saying a few prayers there myself each evening—

MRS. ALVING Have you?

ENGSTRAND Yes, ma'am, now and then—just as a little edification, so to speak. But I am only a poor common man, and haven't rightly the gift, alas—and so I thought that as Mr. Manders happened to be here, perhaps—

MANDERS Look here, Engstrand. First of all I must ask you a question. Are you in a proper frame of mind for such a thing? Is your conscience free and untroubled?

ENGSTRAND Heaven have mercy on me a sinner! My conscience isn't worth our speaking about, Mr. Manders.

MANDERS But it is just what we must speak about. What do you say to my question?

ENGSTRAND My conscience? Well—it's uneasy sometimes, of course.

MANDERS Ah, you admit that at all events. Now will you tell me, without any concealment—what is your relationship to Regina?

MRS. ALVING *(hastily)* Mr. Manders!

MANDERS *(calming her)* —Leave it to me!

ENGSTRAND With Regina? Good Lord, how you frightened me! *(Looks at* MRS. ALVING.*)* There is nothing wrong with Regina, is there?

MANDERS Let us hope not. What I want to know is, what is your relationship to her? You pass as her father, don't you?

ENGSTRAND *(unsteadily)* Well—hm!—you know, sir, what happened between me and my poor Joanna.

MANDERS No more distortion of the truth! Your late wife made a full confession to Mrs. Alving, before she left her service.

ENGSTRAND What!—do you mean to say—? Did she do that after all?

MANDERS You see it has all come out, Engstrand.

ENGSTRAND Do you mean to say that she, who gave me her promise and solemn oath—

MANDERS Did she take an oath?

ENGSTRAND Well, no—she only gave me her word, but as seriously as a woman could.

MANDERS And all these years you have been hiding the truth from me—from me, who have had such complete and absolute faith in you.

ENGSTRAND I am sorry to say I have, sir.

MANDERS Did I deserve that from you, Engstrand? Haven't I been always ready to help you in word and deed as far as lay in my power? Answer me! Is it not so?

ENGSTRAND Indeed there's many a time I should have been very badly off without you, sir.

MANDERS And this is the way you repay me—by causing me to make false entries in the church registers, and afterwards keeping back from me for years the information which you owed it both to me and to your sense of the truth to divulge. Your conduct has been absolutely inexcusable,

Engstrand, and from today everything is at an end between us.

ENGSTRAND *(with a sigh)* Yes, I can see that's what it means.

MANDERS Yes, because how can you possibly justify what you did?

ENGSTRAND Was the poor girl to go and increase her load of shame by talking about it? Just suppose, sir, for a moment that your reverence was in the same predicament as my poor Joanna—

MANDERS I!

ENGSTRAND Good Lord, sir, I don't mean the same predicament. I mean, suppose there were something your reverence were ashamed of in the eyes of the world, so to speak. We men oughtn't to judge a poor woman too hardly, Mr. Manders.

MANDERS But I am not doing so at all. It is you I am blaming.

ENGSTRAND Will your reverence grant me leave to ask you a small question?

MANDERS Ask away.

ENGSTRAND Shouldn't you say it was right for a man to raise up the fallen?

MANDERS Of course it is.

ENGSTRAND And isn't a man bound to keep his word of honour?

MANDERS Certainly he is; but—

ENGSTRAND At the time when Joanna had her misfortune with this Englishman—or maybe he was an American or a Russian, as they call 'em—well, sir, then she came to town. Poor thing, she had refused me once or twice before; she only had eyes for good-looking men in those days, and I had this crooked leg then. Your reverence will remember how I had ventured up into a dancing-saloon where seafaring men were revelling in drunkenness and intoxication, as they say. And when I tried to exhort them to turn from their evil ways—

MRS. ALVING *(coughs from the window)* Ahem!

MANDERS I know, Engstrand, I know—the rough brutes threw you downstairs. You have told me about that incident before. The affliction to your leg is a credit to you.

ENGSTRAND I don't want to claim credit for it, your reverence. But what I wanted to tell you was that she came then and confided in me with tears and gnashing of teeth. I can tell you, sir, it went to my heart to hear her.

MANDERS Did it, indeed, Engstrand? Well, what then?

ENGSTRAND Well, then I said to her: "The American is roaming about on the high seas, he is. And you, Joanna," I said, "you have committed a sin and are a fallen woman. But here stands Jacob Engstrand," I said, "on two strong legs"—of course that was only speaking in a kind of metaphor, as it were, your reverence.

MANDERS I quite understand. Go on.

ENGSTRAND Well, sir, that was how I rescued her and made her my lawful wife, so that no one should know how recklessly she had carried on with the stranger.

MANDERS That was all very kindly done. The only thing I cannot justify was your bringing yourself to accept the money—

ENGSTRAND Money? I? Not a farthing.

MANDERS *(to* MRS. ALVING, *in a questioning tone)* But–

ENGSTRAND Ah, yes!–wait a bit; I remember now. Joanna did have a trifle of money, you are quite right. But I didn't want to know anything about that. "Fie," I said, "on the mammon of unrighteousness, it's the price of your sin; as for this tainted gold"–or notes, or whatever it was –"we will throw it back in the American's face," I said. But he had gone away and disappeared on the stormy seas, your reverence.

MANDERS Was that how it was, my good fellow?

ENGSTRAND It was, sir. So then Joanna and I decided that the money should go towards the child's bringing-up, and that's what became of it; and I can give a faithful account of every single penny of it.

MANDERS This alters the complexion of the affair very considerably.

ENGSTRAND That's how it was, your reverence. And I make bold to say that I have been a good father to Regina–as far as was in my power –for I am a poor erring mortal, alas!

MANDERS There, there, my dear Engstrand–

ENGSTRAND Yes, I do make bold to say that I brought up the child, and made my poor Joanna a loving and careful husband, as the Bible says we ought. But it never occurred to me to go to your reverence and claim credit for it or boast about it because I had done one good deed in this world. No; when Jacob Engstrand does a thing like that, he holds his tongue about it. Unfortunately it doesn't often happen, I know that only too well. And whenever I do come to see your reverence, I never seem to have anything but trouble and wickedness to talk about. Because, as I said just now–and I say it again–conscience can be very hard on us sometimes.

MANDERS Give me your hand, Jacob Engstrand.

ENGSTRAND Oh, sir, I don't like–

MANDERS No nonsense. *(Grasps his hand)* That's it!

ENGSTRAND And may I make bold humbly to beg your reverence's pardon–

MANDERS You? On the contrary it is for me to beg your pardon–

ENGSTRAND Oh no, sir.

MANDERS Yes, certainly it is, and I do it with my whole heart. Forgive me for having so much misjudged you. And I assure you that if I can do anything for you to prove my sincere regret and my goodwill towards you–

ENGSTRAND Do you mean it, sir?

MANDERS It would give me the greatest pleasure.

ENGSTRAND As a matter of fact, sir, you could do it now. I am thinking of using the honest money I have put away out of my wages up here, in establishing a sort of Sailors' Home in the town.

MRS. ALVING You?

ENGSTRAND Yes, to be a sort of Refuge, as it were. There are such manifold temptations lying in wait for sailor men when they are roaming about on shore. But my idea is that in this house of mine they should have a sort of parental care looking after them.

MANDERS What do you say to that, Mrs. Alving!

ENGSTRAND I haven't much to begin such a work with, I know; but Heaven might prosper it, and if I found any helping hand stretched out to me, then–

MANDERS Quite so; we will talk over the matter further. Your project attracts me enormously. But in the meantime go back to the Orphanage and put everything tidy and light the lights, so that the occasion may seem a little solemn. And then we will spend a little edifying time together, my dear Engstrand, for now I am sure you are in a suitable frame of mind.

ENGSTRAND I believe I am, sir, truly. Good-bye, then, Mrs. Alving, and thank you for all your kindness; and take good care of Regina for me. *(Wipes a tear from his eye)* Poor Joanna's child–it is an extraordinary thing, but she seems to have grown into my life and to hold me by the heartstrings. That's how I feel about it, truly. *(Bows, and goes out)*

MANDERS Now, then, what do you think of him, Mrs. Alving! That was quite another explanation that he gave us.

MRS. ALVING It was, indeed.

MANDERS There, you see how exceedingly careful we ought to be in condemning our fellow-men. But at the same time it gives one genuine pleasure to find that one was mistaken. Don't you think so?

MRS. ALVING What I think is that you are, and always will remain, a big baby, Mr. Manders.

MANDERS I?

MRS. ALVING *(laying her hands on his shoulders)* And I think that I should like very much to give you a good hug.

MANDERS *(drawing back hastily)* No, no, good gracious! What an idea!

MRS. ALVING *(with a smile)* Oh, you needn't be afraid of me.

MANDERS *(standing by the table)* You choose such an extravagant way of expressing yourself sometimes. Now I must get these papers together and put them in my bag. *(Does so)* That's it. And now good-bye, for the present. Keep your eyes open when Oswald comes back. I will come back and see you again presently. *(He takes his hat and goes out by the hall door.* MRS. ALVING *sighs, glances out of the window, puts one or two things tidy in the room and turns to go into the dining-room. She stops in the doorway with a stifled cry.)*

MRS. ALVING Oswald, are you still sitting at table!

OSWALD *(from the dining-room)* I am only finishing my cigar.

MRS. ALVING I thought you had gone out for a little turn.

OSWALD *(from within the room)* In weather like this? *(A glass is heard clinking.* MRS. ALVING *leaves the door open and sits down with her knitting on the couch by the window.)* Wasn't that Mr. Manders that went out just now?

MRS. ALVING Yes, he has gone over to the Orphanage.

OSWALD Oh. *(The clink of a bottle on a glass is heard again.)*

MRS. ALVING *(with an uneasy expression)* Oswald, dear, you should be careful with that liqueur. It is strong.

OSWALD It's a good protective against the damp.

MRS. ALVING Wouldn't you rather come in here?

OSWALD You know you don't like smoking in there.
MRS. ALVING You may smoke a cigar in here, certainly.
OSWALD All right; I will come in, then. Just one drop more. There! *(Comes in, smoking a cigar, and shuts the door after him. A short silence)* Where has the parson gone?
MRS. ALVING I told you he had gone over to the Orphanage.
OSWALD Oh, so you did.
MRS. ALVING You shouldn't sit so long at table, Oswald.
OSWALD *(holding his cigar behind his back)* But it's so nice and cosy, mother dear. *(Caresses her with one hand)* Think what it means to me —to have come home; to sit at my mother's own table, in my mother's own room, and to enjoy the charming meals she gives me.
MRS. ALVING My dear, dear boy!
OSWALD *(a little impatiently, as he walks up and down smoking)* And what else is there for me to do here? I have no occupation—
MRS. ALVING No occupation?
OSWALD Not in this ghastly weather, when there isn't a blink of sunshine all day long. *(Walks up and down the floor)* Not to be able to work, it's—!
MRS. ALVING I don't believe you were wise to come home.
OSWALD Yes, mother; I had to.
MRS. ALVING Because I would ten times rather give up the happiness of having you with me, sooner than that you should—
OSWALD *(standing still by the table)* Tell me, mother—is it really such a great happiness for you to have me at home?
MRS. ALVING Can you ask?
OSWALD *(crumpling up a newspaper)* I should have thought it would have been pretty much the same to you whether I were here or away.
MRS. ALVING Have you the heart to say that to your mother, Oswald?
OSWALD But you have been quite happy living without me so far.
MRS. ALVING Yes, I have lived without you—that is true.
(A silence. The dusk falls by degrees. OSWALD *walks restlessly up and down. He has laid aside his cigar.)*
OSWALD *(stopping beside* MRS. ALVING*)* Mother, may I sit on the couch beside you?
MRS. ALVING Of course, my dear boy.
OSWALD *(sitting down)* Now I must tell you something, mother.
MRS. ALVING *(anxiously)* What?
OSWALD *(staring in front of him)* I can't bear it any longer.
MRS. ALVING Bear what? What do you mean?
OSWALD *(as before)* I couldn't bring myself to write to you about it; and since I have been at home—
MRS. ALVING *(catching him by the arm)* Oswald, what is it?
OSWALD Both yesterday and today I have tried to push my thoughts away from me—to free myself from them. But I can't.
MRS. ALVING *(getting up)* You must speak plainly, Oswald!
OSWALD *(drawing her down to her seat again)* Sit still, and I will try and tell you. I have made a great deal of the fatigue I felt after my journey—
MRS. ALVING Well, what of that?

OSWALD But that isn't what is the matter. It is no ordinary fatigue—

MRS. ALVING *(trying to get up)* You are not ill, Oswald!

OSWALD *(pulling her down again)* Sit still, mother. Do take it quietly. I am not exactly ill—not ill in the usual sense. *(Takes his head in his hands)* Mother, it's my mind that has broken down—gone to pieces—I shall never be able to work any more! *(Buries his face in his hands and throws himself at her knees in an outburst of sobs)*

MRS. ALVING *(pale and trembling)* Oswald! Look at me! No, no, it isn't true!

OSWALD *(looking up with a distracted expression)* Never to be able to work any more! Never—never! A living death! Mother, can you imagine anything so horrible!

MRS. ALVING My poor unhappy boy! How has this terrible thing happened?

OSWALD *(sitting up again)* That is just what I cannot possibly understand. I have never lived recklessly, in any sense. You must believe that of me, mother! I have never done that.

MRS. ALVING I haven't a doubt of it, Oswald.

OSWALD And yet this comes upon me all the same!—this terrible disaster!

MRS. ALVING Oh, but it will all come right again, my dear precious boy. It is nothing but overwork. Believe me, that is so.

OSWALD *(dully)* I thought so too, at first; but it isn't so.

MRS. ALVING Tell me all about it.

OSWALD Yes, I will.

MRS. ALVING When did you first feel anything?

OSWALD It was just after I had been home last time and had got back to Paris. I began to feel the most violent pains in my head—mostly at the back, I think. It was as if a tight band of iron was pressing on me from my neck upwards.

MRS. ALVING And then?

OSWALD At first I thought it was nothing but the headaches I always used to be so much troubled with while I was growing.

MRS. ALVING Yes, yes—

OSWALD But it wasn't; I soon saw that. I couldn't work any longer. I would try and start some big new picture; but it seemed as if all my faculties had forsaken me, as if all my strength were paralysed. I couldn't manage to collect my thoughts; my head seemed to swim—everything went round and round. It was a horrible feeling! At last I sent for a doctor—and from him I learnt the truth.

MRS. ALVING In what way, do you mean?

OSWALD He was one of the best doctors there. He made me describe what I felt, and then he began to ask me a whole heap of questions which seemed to me to have nothing to do with the matter. I couldn't see what he was driving at—

MRS. ALVING Well?

OSWALD At last he said: "You have had the canker of disease in you practically from your birth"—the actual word he used was *"vermoulu."*

MRS. ALVING *(anxiously)* What did he mean by that?

OSWALD I couldn't understand, either—and I asked him for a clearer explanation. And then the old cynic said—*(clenching his fist)* Oh!—

MRS. ALVING What did he say?

OSWALD He said: "The sins of the fathers are visited on the children."

MRS. ALVING *(getting up slowly)* The sins of the fathers—.

OSWALD I nearly struck him in the face—

MRS. ALVING *(walking across the room)* The sins of the fathers—!

OSWALD *(smiling sadly)* Yes, just imagine! Naturally I assured him that what he thought was impossible. But do you think he paid any heed to me? No, he persisted in his opinion; and it was only when I got out your letters and translated to him all the passages that referred to my father—

MRS. ALVING Well, and then?

OSWALD Well, then of course he had to admit that he was on the wrong tack; and then I learnt the truth—the incomprehensible truth! I ought to have had nothing to do with the joyous happy life I had lived with my comrades. It had been too much for my strength. So it was my own fault!

MRS. ALVING No, no, Oswald! Don't believe that!

OSWALD There was no other explanation of it possible, he said. That is the most horrible part of it. My whole life incurably ruined—just because of my own imprudence. All that I wanted to do in the world—not to dare to think of it any more—not to be *able* to think of it! Oh! if only I could live my life over again—if only I could undo what I have done! *(Throws himself on his face on the couch.* MRS. ALVING *wrings her hands, and walks up and down silently fighting with herself.)*

OSWALD *(looks up after a while, raising himself on his elbows)* If only it had been something I had inherited—something I could not help. But, instead of that, to have disgracefully, stupidly, thoughtlessly thrown away one's happiness, one's health, everything in the world—one's future, one's life—

MRS. ALVING No, no, my darling boy; that is impossible! *(Bending over him)* Things are not so desperate as you think.

OSWALD Ah, you don't know—. *(Springs up)* And to think, mother, that I should bring all this sorrow upon you! Many a time I have almost wished and hoped that you really did not care so very much for me.

MRS. ALVING I, Oswald? My only son! All that I have in the world! The only thing I care about!

OSWALD *(taking hold of her hands and kissing them)* Yes, yes, I know that is so. When I am at home I know that is true. And that is one of the hardest parts of it to me. But now you know all about it; and now we won't talk any more about it today. I can't stand thinking about it long at a time. *(Walks across the room)* Let me have something to drink, mother!

MRS. ALVING To drink? What do you want?

OSWALD Oh, anything you like. I suppose you have got some punch in the house.

MRS. ALVING Yes, but my dear Oswald—!

OSWALD Don't tell me I mustn't, mother. Do be nice! I must have something to drown these gnawing thoughts. *(Goes into the conservatory)* And how—how gloomy it is here! (MRS. ALVING *rings the bell)* And this incessant rain. It may go on week after week—a whole month. Never a ray of sunshine. I don't remember ever having seen the sun shine once when I have been at home.

MRS. ALVING Oswald—you are thinking of going away from me!

OSWALD Hm!—*(sighs deeply)* I am not thinking about anything. I *can't* think about anything! *(In a low voice)* I have to let that alone.

REGINA *(coming from the dining-room)* Did you ring, ma'am?

MRS. ALVING Yes, let us have the lamp in.

REGINA In a moment, ma'am; it is all ready lit. *(Goes out.)*

MRS. ALVING *(going up to* OSWALD*)* Oswald, don't keep anything back from me.

OSWALD I don't, mother. *(Goes to the table)* It seems to me I have told you a good loc.

(REGINA *brings the lamp and puts it upon the table)*

MRS. ALVING Regina, you might bring us a small bottle of champagne.

REGINA Yes, ma'am. *(Goes out)*

OSWALD *(taking hold of his mother's face)* That's right. I knew my mother wouldn't let her son go thirsty.

MRS. ALVING My poor dear boy, how could I refuse you anything now?

OSWALD *(eagerly)* Is that true, mother? Do you mean it?

MRS. ALVING Mean what?

OSWALD That you couldn't deny me anything?

MRS. ALVING My dear Oswald—

OSWALD Hush!

(REGINA *brings in a tray with a small bottle of champagne and two glasses, which she puts on the table)*

REGINA Shall I open the bottle?

OSWALD No, thank you, I will do it.

(REGINA *goes out)*

MRS. ALVING *(sitting down at the table)* What did you mean, when you asked if I could refuse you nothing?

OSWALD *(busy opening the bottle)* Let us have a glass first—or two. *(He draws the cork, fills one glass and is going to fill the other.)*

MRS. ALVING *(holding her hand over the second glass)* No, thanks—not for me.

OSWALD Oh, well, for me then! *(He empties his glass, fills it again and empties it; then sits down at the table.)*

MRS. ALVING *(expectantly)* Now, tell me.

OSWALD *(without looking at her)* Tell me this; I thought you and Mr. Manders seemed so strange—so quiet—at dinner.

MRS. ALVING Did you notice that?

OSWALD Yes. Ahem! *(After a short pause)* Tell me—what do you think of Regina?

MRS. ALVING What do I think of her?

OSWALD Yes, isn't she splendid!

MRS. ALVING Dear Oswald, you don't know her as well as I do—
OSWALD What of that?
MRS. ALVING Regina was too long at home, unfortunately. I ought to have taken her under my charge sooner.
OSWALD Yes, but isn't she splendid to look at, mother? *(Fills his glass)*
MRS. ALVING Regina has many serious faults—
OSWALD Yes, but what of that? *(Drinks)*
MRS. ALVING But I am fond of her, all the same; and I have made myself responsible for her. I wouldn't for the world she should come to any harm.
OSWALD *(jumping up)* Mother, Regina is my only hope of salvation!
MRS. ALVING *(getting up)* What do you mean?
OSWALD I can't go on bearing all this agony of mind alone.
MRS. ALVING Haven't you your mother to help you to bear it?
OSWALD Yes, I thought so; that was why I came home to you. But it is no use; I see that it isn't. I cannot spend my life here.
MRS. ALVING Oswald!
OSWALD I must live a different sort of life, mother; so I shall have to go away from you. I don't want you watching it.
MRS. ALVING My unhappy boy! But, Oswald, as long as you are ill like this—
OSWALD If it was only a matter of feeling ill, I would stay with you, mother. You are the best friend I have in the world.
MRS. ALVING Yes, I am that, Oswald, am I not?
OSWALD *(walking restlessly about)* But all this torment—the regret, the remorse—and the deadly fear. Oh—this horrible fear!
MRS. ALVING *(following him)* Fear? Fear of what? What do you mean?
OSWALD Oh, don't ask me any more about it. I don't know what it is. I can't put it into words. *(*MRS. ALVING *crosses the room and rings the bell)* What do you want?
MRS. ALVING I want my boy to be happy, that's what I want. He mustn't brood over anything. *(To* REGINA, *who has come to the door.)* More champagne—a large bottle.
OSWALD Mother!
MRS. ALVING Do you think we country people don't know how to live?
OSWALD Isn't she splendid to look at! What a figure! And the picture of health!
MRS. ALVING *(sitting down at the table)* Sit down, Oswald, and let us have a quiet talk.
OSWALD *(sitting down)* You don't know, mother, that I owe Regina a little reparation.
MRS. ALVING You!
OSWALD Oh, it was only a little thoughtlessness—call it what you like. Something quite innocent, anyway. The last time I was home—
MRS. ALVING Yes?
OSWALD —she used often to ask me questions about Paris, and I told her one thing and another about the life there. And I remember saying one day: "Wouldn't you like to go there yourself?"

MRS. ALVING Well?

OSWALD I saw her blush, and she said: "Yes, I should like to very much." "All right," I said, "I daresay it might be managed"—or something of that sort.

MRS. ALVING And then?

OSWALD I naturally had forgotten all about it; but the day before yesterday I happened to ask her if she was glad I was to be so long at home—

MRS. ALVING Well?

OSWALD —and she looked so queerly at me, and asked: "But what is to become of my trip to Paris?"

MRS. ALVING Her trip!

OSWALD And then I got it out of her that she had taken the thing seriously, and had been thinking about me all the time, and had set herself to learn French—

MRS. ALVING So that was why—

OSWALD Mother—when I saw this fine, splendid, handsome girl standing there in front of me—I had never paid any attention to her before then—but now, when she stood there as if with open arms ready for me to take her to myself—

MRS. ALVING Oswald!

OSWALD —then I realised that my salvation lay in her, for I saw the joy of life in her.

MRS. ALVING *(starting back)* The joy of life—? Is there salvation in that?

REGINA *(coming in from the dining-room with a bottle of champagne)* Excuse me for being so long; but I had to go to the cellar. *(Puts the bottle down on the table)*

OSWALD Bring another glass, too.

REGINA *(looking at him in astonishment)* The mistress's glass is there, sir.

OSWALD Yes, but fetch one for yourself, Regina. *(*REGINA *starts, and gives a quick shy glance at* MRS. ALVING*)* Well?

REGINA *(in a low and hesitating voice)* Do you wish me to, ma'am?

MRS. ALVING Fetch the glass, Regina. *(*REGINA *goes into the dining-room)*

OSWALD *(looking after her)* Have you noticed how well she walks?—so firmly and confidently!

MRS. ALVING It cannot be, Oswald.

OSWALD It is settled. You must see that. It is no use forbidding it. *(*REGINA *comes in with a glass, which she holds in her hand.)* Sit down, Regina. *(*REGINA *looks questioningly at* MRS. ALVING.*)*

MRS. ALVING Sit down. *(*REGINA *sits down on a chair near the dining-room door, still holding the glass in her hand.)* Oswald, what was it you were saying about the joy of life?

OSWALD Ah, mother—the joy of life! You don't know very much about that at home here. I shall never realise it here.

MRS. ALVING Not even when you are with me?

OSWALD Never at home. But you can't understand that.

MRS. ALVING Yes, indeed I almost think I do understand you—now.

OSWALD That—and the joy of work. They are really the same thing at bottom. But you don't know anything about that either.

MRS. ALVING Perhaps you are right. Tell me some more about it, Oswald.

OSWALD Well, all I mean is that here people are brought up to believe that work is a curse and a punishment for sin, and that life is a state of wretchedness and that the sooner we can get out of it the better.

MRS. ALVING A vale of tears, yes. And we quite conscientiously make it so.

OSWALD But the people over there will have none of that. There is no one there who really believes doctrines of that kind any longer. Over there the mere fact of being alive is thought to be a matter for exultant happiness. Mother, have you noticed that everything I have painted has turned upon the joy of life?—always upon the joy of life, unfailingly. There is light there, and sunshine, and a holiday feeling—and people's faces beaming with happiness. That is why I am afraid to stay at home here with you.

MRS. ALVING Afraid? What are you afraid of here, with me?

OSWALD I am afraid that all these feelings that are so strong in me would degenerate into something ugly here.

MRS. ALVING *(looking steadily at him)* Do you think that is what would happen?

OSWALD I am certain it would. Even if one lived the same life at home here, as over there—it would never really be the same life.

MRS. ALVING *(who has listened anxiously to him, gets up with a thoughtful expression and says:)* Now I see clearly how it all happened.

OSWALD What do you see?

MRS. ALVING I see it now for the first time. And now I can speak.

OSWALD *(getting up)* Mother, I don't understand you.

REGINA *(who has got up also)* Perhaps I had better go.

MRS. ALVING No, stay here. Now I can speak. Now, my son, you shall know the whole truth. Oswald! Regina!

OSWALD Hush!—here is the parson—

(MANDERS comes in by the hall door.)

MANDERS Well, my friends, we have been spending an edifying time over there.

OSWALD So have we.

MANDERS Engstrand must have help with his Sailors' Home. Regina must go home with him and give him her assistance.

REGINA No, thank you, Mr. Manders.

MANDERS *(perceiving her for the first time)* What—? You in here?—and with a wineglass in your hand!

REGINA *(putting down the glass hastily)* I beg your pardon—!

OSWALD Regina is going away with me, Mr. Manders.

MANDERS Going away! With you!

OSWALD Yes, as my wife—if she insists on that.

MANDERS But, good heavens—!

REGINA It is not my fault, Mr. Manders.

OSWALD Or else she stays here if I stay.

REGINA *(involuntarily)* Here!

MANDERS I am amazed at you, Mrs. Alving.

MRS. ALVING Neither of those things will happen, for now I can speak openly.

MANDERS But you won't do that! No, no, no!

MRS. ALVING Yes, I can and I will. And without destroying any one's ideals.

OSWALD Mother, what is it that is being concealed from me?

REGINA *(listening)* Mrs. Alving! Listen! They are shouting outside. *(Goes into the conservatory and looks out.)*

OSWALD *(going to the window on the left)* What can be the matter? Where does that glare come from?

REGINA *(calls out)* The Orphanage is on fire!

MRS. ALVING *(going to the window)* On fire?

MANDERS On fire? Impossible. I was there just a moment ago.

OSWALD Where is my hat? Oh, never mind that. Father's Orphanage—! *(Runs out through the garden door)*

MRS. ALVING My shawl, Regina! The whole place is in flames.

MANDERS How terrible! Mrs. Alving, That fire is a judgment on this house of sin!

MRS. ALVING Quite so. Come, Regina. *(She and* REGINA *hurry out.)*

MANDERS *(clasping his hands)* And no insurance! *(Follows them out.)*

act III

(The same scene. All the doors are standing open. The lamp is still burning on the table. It is dark outside, except for a faint glimmer of light seen through the windows at the back.

MRS. ALVING, *with a shawl over her head, is standing in the conservatory, looking out.* REGINA, *also wrapped in a shawl, is standing a little behind her.)*

MRS. ALVING Everything burnt—down to the ground.

REGINA It is burning still in the basement.

MRS. ALVING I can't think why Oswald doesn't come back. There is no chance of saving anything.

REGINA Shall I go and take his hat to him?

MRS. ALVING Hasn't he even got his hat?

REGINA *(pointing to the hall)* No, there it is, hanging up.

MRS. ALVING Never mind. He is sure to come back soon. I will go and see what he is doing. *(Goes out by the garden door.* MANDERS *comes in from the hall.)*

MANDERS Isn't Mrs. Alving here?

REGINA She has just this moment gone down into the garden.

MANDERS I have never spent such a terrible night in my life.

REGINA Isn't it a shocking misfortune, sir!

MANDERS Oh, don't speak about it. I scarcely dare to think about it.

REGINA But how can it have happened?

MANDERS Don't ask me, Miss Engstrand! How should I know! Are you going to suggest too—? Isn't it enough that your father—?

REGINA What has he done?

MANDERS He has nearly driven me crazy.

ENGSTRAND *(coming in from the hall)* Mr. Manders—!

MANDERS *(turning round with a start)* Have you even followed me here!

ENGSTRAND Yes, God help us all—! Great heavens! What a dreadful thing, your reverence!

MANDERS *(walking up and down)* Oh dear, oh dear!

REGINA What do you mean?

ENGSTRAND Our little prayer-meeting was the cause of it all, don't you see? *(Aside, to* REGINA*)* Now we've got the old fool, my girl. *(Aloud.)* And to think it is my fault that Mr. Manders should be the cause of such a thing!

MANDERS I assure you, Engstrand—

ENGSTRAND But there was no one else carrying a light there except you, sir.

MANDERS *(standing still)* Yes, so you say. But I have no clear recollection of having had a light in my hand.

ENGSTRAND But I saw quite distinctly your reverence take a candle and snuff it with your fingers and throw away the burning bit of wick among the shavings.

MANDERS Did you see that?

ENGSTRAND Yes, distinctly.

MANDERS I can't understand it at all. It is never my habit to snuff a candle with my fingers.

ENGSTRAND Yes, it wasn't like you to do that, sir. But who would have thought it could be such a dangerous thing to do?

MANDERS *(walking restlessly backwards and forwards)* Oh, don't ask me!

ENGSTRAND *(following him about)* And you hadn't insured it either, had you, sir?

MANDERS No, no, no; you heard me say so.

ENGSTRAND You hadn't insured it—and then went and set light to the whole place! Good Lord, what bad luck!

MANDERS *(wiping the perspiration from his forehead)* You may well say so, Engstrand.

ENGSTRAND And that it should happen to a charitable institution that would have been of service both to the town and the country, so to speak! The newspapers won't be very kind to your reverence, I expect.

MANDERS No, that is just what I am thinking of. It is almost the worst part of the whole thing. The spiteful attacks and accusations—it is horrible to think of!

MRS. ALVING *(coming in from the garden)* I can't get him away from the fire.

MANDERS Oh, there you are, Mrs. Alving.

MRS. ALVING You will escape having to make your inaugural address now, at all events, Mr. Manders.

MANDERS Oh, I would so gladly have—

MRS. ALVING *(in a dull voice)* It is just as well it has happened. This Orphanage would never have come to any good.

MANDERS Don't you think so?
MRS. ALVING Do you?
MANDERS But it is none the less an extraordinary piece of ill luck.
MRS. ALVING We will discuss it simply as a business matter.—Are you waiting for Mr. Manders, Engstrand?
ENGSTRAND *(at the hall door)* Yes, I am.
MRS. ALVING Sit down then, while you are waiting.
ENGSTRAND Thank you, I would rather stand.
MRS. ALVING *(to* MANDERS*)* I suppose you are going by the boat?
MANDERS Yes. It goes in about an hour.
MRS. ALVING Please take all the documents back with you. I don't want to hear another word about the matter. I have something else to think about now—
MANDERS Mrs. Alving—
MRS. ALVING Later on I will send you a power of attorney to deal with it exactly as you please.
MANDERS I shall be most happy to undertake that. I am afraid the original intention of the bequest will have to be entirely altered now.
MRS. ALVING Of course.
MANDERS Provisionally, I should suggest this way of disposing of it. Make over the Solvik property to the parish. The land is undoubtedly not without a certain value; it will always be useful for some purpose or another. And as for the interest on the remaining capital that is on deposit in the bank, possibly I might make suitable use of that in support of some undertaking that promises to be of use to the town.
MRS. ALVING Do exactly as you please. The whole thing is a matter of indifference to me now.
ENGSTRAND You will think of my Sailors' Home, Mr. Manders?
MANDERS Yes, certainly, that is a suggestion. But we must consider the matter carefully.
ENGSTRAND *(aside)* Consider!—devil take it! Oh Lord.
MANDERS *(sighing)* And unfortunately I can't tell how much longer I may have anything to do with the matter—whether public opinion may not force me to retire from it altogether. That depends entirely upon the result of the enquiry into the cause of the fire.
MRS. ALVING What do you say?
MANDERS And one cannot in any way reckon upon the result beforehand.
ENGSTRAND *(going nearer to him)* Yes, indeed one can; because here stand I, Jacob Engstrand.
MANDERS Quite so, but—
ENGSTRAND *(lowering his voice)* And Jacob Engstrand isn't the man to desert a worthy benefactor in the hour of need, as the saying is.
MANDERS Yes, but, my dear fellow—how—?
ENGSTRAND You might say Jacob Engstrand is an angel of salvation, so to speak, your reverence.
MANDERS No, no, I couldn't possibly accept that.
ENGSTRAND That's how it will be, all the same. I know someone who has taken the blame for someone else on his shoulders before now, I do.

MANDERS Jacob! *(Grasps his hand.)* You are one in a thousand! You shall have assistance in the matter of your Sailors' Home, you may rely upon that.

(ENGSTRAND *tries to thank him, but is prevented by emotion.)*

MANDERS *(hanging his wallet over his shoulder)* Now we must be off. We will travel together.

ENGSTRAND *(by the dining-room, says aside to* REGINA*)* Come with me, you hussy! You shall be as cosy as the yolk in an egg!

REGINA *(tossing her head) Merci! (She goes out into the hall and brings back* MANDERS' *luggage.)*

MANDERS Good-bye, Mrs. Alving! And may the spirit of order and of what is lawful speedily enter into this house.

MRS. ALVING Good-bye, Mr. Manders. *(She goes into the conservatory, as she sees* OSWALD *coming in by the garden door.)*

ENGSTRAND *(as he and* REGINA *are helping* MANDERS *on with his coat).* Good-bye, my child. And if anything should happen to you, you know where Jacob Engstrand is to be found. *(Lowering his voice.)* Little Harbour Street, ahem—! *(To* MRS. ALVING *and* OSWALD*)* And my house for poor seafaring men shall be called the "Alving Home," it shall. And, if I can carry out my own ideas about it, I shall make bold to hope that it may be worthy of bearing the late Mr. Alving's name.

MANDERS *(at the door)* Ahem—ahem! Come along, my dear Engstrand. Good-bye—good-bye!

(He and ENGSTRAND *go out by the hall door.)*

OSWALD *(going to the table)* What house was he speaking about?

MRS. ALVING I believe it is some sort of a Home that he and Mr. Manders want to start.

OSWALD It will be burnt up just like this one.

MRS. ALVING What makes you think that?

OSWALD Everything will be burnt up; nothing will be left that is in memory of my father. Here am I being burnt up, too.

(REGINA *looks at him in alarm.)*

MRS. ALVING Oswald! You should not have stayed so long over there, my poor boy.

OSWALD *(sitting down at the table)* I almost believe you are right.

MRS. ALVING Let me dry your face, Oswald; you are all wet. *(Wipes his face with her handkerchief.)*

OSWALD *(looking straight before him, with no expression in his eyes)* Thank you, mother.

MRS. ALVING And aren't you tired, Oswald? Don't you want to go to sleep?

OSWALD *(uneasily)* No, no—not to sleep! I never sleep; I only pretend to. *(Gloomily.)* That will come soon enough.

MRS. ALVING *(looking at him anxiously)* Anyhow you are really ill, my darling boy.

REGINA *(intently)* Is Mr. Alving ill?

OSWALD *(impatiently)* And do shut all the doors! This deadly fear—

MRS. ALVING Shut the doors, Regina. (REGINA *shuts the doors and remains standing by the hall door.* MRS. ALVING *takes off her shawl;* REGINA *does the same.* MRS. ALVING *draws up a chair near to* OSWALD'S *and sits down beside him.)* That's it! Now I will sit beside you—

OSWALD Yes, do. And Regina must stay in here too. Regina must always be near me. You must give me a helping hand, you know, Regina. Won't you do that?

REGINA I don't understand—

MRS. ALVING A helping hand?

OSWALD Yes—when there is need for it.

MRS. ALVING Oswald, have you not your mother to give you a helping hand?

OSWALD You? *(Smiles.)* No, mother, you will never give me the kind of helping hand I mean. *(Laughs grimly.)* You! Ha, ha! *(Looks gravely at her)* After all, you have the best right. *(Impetuously)* Why don't you call me by my Christian name, Regina? Why don't you say Oswald?

REGINA *(in a low voice)* I did not think Mrs. Alving would like it.

MRS. ALVING It will not be long before you have the right to do it. Sit down here now beside us, too. (REGINA *sits down quietly and hesitatingly at the other side of the table.)* And now, my poor tortured boy, I am going to take the burden off your mind —

OSWALD You, mother?

MRS. ALVING —all that you call remorse and regret and self-reproach.

OSWALD And you think you can do that?

MRS. ALVING Yes, now I can, Oswald. A little while ago you were talking about the joy of life, and what you said seemed to shed a new light upon everything in my whole life.

OSWALD *(shaking his head)* I don't in the least understand what you mean.

MRS. ALVING You should have known your father in his young days in the army. He was full of the joy of life, I can tell you.

OSWALD Yes, I know.

MRS. ALVING It gave me a holiday feeling only to look at him, full of irrepressible energy and exuberant spirits.

OSWALD What then?

MRS. ALVING Well, then this boy, full of the joy of life—for he was just like a boy, then—had to make his home in a second-rate town which had none of the joy of life to offer him, but only dissipations. He had to come out here and live an aimless life; he had only an official post. He had no work worth devoting his whole mind to; he had nothing more than official routine to attend to. He had not a single companion capable of appreciating what the joy of life meant; nothing but idlers and tipplers—

OSWALD Mother—!

MRS. ALVING And so the inevitable happened!

OSWALD What was the inevitable?

MRS. ALVING You said yourself this evening what would happen in your case if you stayed at home.

OSWALD Do you mean by that, that father—?

MRS. ALVING Your poor father never found any outlet for the overmastering joy of life that was in him. And I brought no holiday spirit into his home, either.

OSWALD You didn't, either?

MRS. ALVING I had been taught about duty, and the sort of thing that I believed in so long here. Everything seemed to turn upon duty—my duty, or his duty—and I am afraid I made your poor father's home unbearable to him, Oswald.

OSWALD Why did you never say anything about it to me in your letters?

MRS. ALVING I never looked at it as a thing I could speak of to you, who were his son.

OSWALD What way did you look at it, then?

MRS. ALVING I only saw the one fact, that your father was a lost man before you were born.

OSWALD *(in a choking voice)* Ah—! *(He gets up and goes to the window.)*

MRS. ALVING And then I had the one thought in my mind, day and night, that Regina in fact has as good a right in this house—as my own boy had.

OSWALD *(turns round suddenly)* Regina—?

REGINA *(gets up and asks in choking tones)* I—?

MRS. ALVING Yes, now you both know it.

OSWALD Regina!

REGINA *(to herself)* So mother was one of that sort too.

MRS. ALVING Your mother had many good qualities, Regina.

REGINA Yes, but she was one of that sort too, all the same. I have even thought so myself, sometimes, but—. Then, if you please, Mrs. Alving, may I have permission to leave at once?

MRS. ALVING Do you really wish to, Regina?

REGINA Yes, indeed, I certainly wish to.

MRS. ALVING Of course you shall do as you like, but—

OSWALD *(going up to* REGINA*)* Leave now? This is your home.

REGINA *Merci,* Mr. Alving—oh, of course, I may say Oswald now, but that is not the way I thought it would become allowable.

MRS. ALVING Regina, I have not been open with you—

REGINA No, I can't say you have! If I had known Oswald was ill—. And now that there can never be anything serious between us—. No, I really can't stay here in the country and wear myself out looking after invalids.

OSWALD Not even for the sake of one who has so near a claim on you?

REGINA No, indeed I can't. A poor girl must make some use of her youth, otherwise she may easily find herself out in the cold before she knows where she is. And I have got the joy of life in me too, Mrs. Alving!

MRS. ALVING Yes, unfortunately; but don't throw yourself away, Regina.

REGINA Oh, what's going to happen will happen. If Oswald takes after his father, it is just as likely I take after my mother, I expect.—May I ask, Mrs. Alving, whether Mr. Manders knows this about me?

MRS. ALVING Mr. Manders knows everything.

REGINA *(putting on her shawl)* Oh, well then, the best thing I can do is to get away by the boat as soon as I can. Mr. Manders is such a nice gentleman to deal with; and it certainly seems to me that I have just as much right to some of that money as he—as that horrid carpenter.

MRS. ALVING You are quite welcome to it, Regina.

REGINA *(looking at her fixedly)* You might as well have brought me up like a gentleman's daughter; it would have been more suitable. *(Tosses her head)* Oh, well—never mind! *(With a bitter glance at the unopened bottle)* I daresay some day I shall be drinking champagne with gentlefolk, after all.

MRS. ALVING If ever you need a home, Regina, come to me.

REGINA No, thank you, Mrs. Alving. Mr. Manders takes an interest in me, I know. And if things should go very badly with me, I know one house at any rate where I shall feel at home.

MRS. ALVING Where is that?

REGINA In the "Alving Home."

MRS. ALVING Regina—I can see quite well—you are going to your ruin!

REGINA Pooh!—good-bye.

(She bows to them and goes out through the hall.)

OSWALD *(standing by the window and looking out)* Has she gone?

MRS. ALVING Yes.

OSWALD *(muttering to himself)* I think it's all wrong.

MRS. ALVING *(going up to him from behind and putting her hands on his shoulders)* Oswald, my dear boy—has it been a great shock to you?

OSWALD *(turning his face towards her)* All this about father, do you mean?

MRS. ALVING Yes, about your unhappy father. I am so afraid it may have been too much for you.

OSWALD What makes you think that? Naturally it has taken me entirely by surprise; but, after all, I don't know that it matters much to me.

MRS. ALVING *(drawing back her hands)* Doesn't matter!—that your father's life was such a terrible failure!

OSWALD Of course I can feel sympathy for him, just as I would for anyone else, but—

MRS. ALVING No more than that! For your own father!

OSWALD *(impatiently)* Father—father! I never knew anything of my father. I don't remember anything else about him except that he once made me sick.

MRS. ALVING It is dreadful to think of!—But surely a child should feel some affection for his father, whatever happens?

OSWALD When the child has nothing to thank his father for? When he has never known him? Do you really cling to that antiquated superstition—you, who are so broad-minded in other things?

MRS. ALVING You call it nothing but a superstition!

OSWALD Yes, and you can see that for yourself quite well, mother. It is one of those beliefs that are put into circulation in the world, and—

MRS. ALVING Ghosts of beliefs!

OSWALD *(walking across the room)* Yes, you might call them ghosts.

MRS. ALVING *(with an outburst of feeling)* Oswald—then you don't love me either!

OSWALD You I know, at any rate—

MRS. ALVING You know me, yes; but is that all?

OSWALD And I know how fond you are of me, and I ought to be grateful to you for that. Besides, you can be so tremendously useful to me, now that I am ill.

MRS. ALVING Yes, can't I, Oswald! I could almost bless your illness, as it has driven you home to me. For I see quite well that you are not my very own yet; you must be won.

OSWALD *(impatiently)* Yes, yes, yes; all that is just a way of talking. You must remember I am a sick man, mother. I can't concern myself much with anyone else; I have enough to do, thinking about myself.

MRS. ALVING *(gently)* I will be very good and patient.

OSWALD And cheerful too, mother!

MRS. ALVING Yes, my dear boy, you are quite right. *(Goes up to him)* Now have I taken away all your remorse and self-reproach?

OSWALD Yes, you have done that. But who will take away the fear?

MRS. ALVING The fear?

OSWALD *(crossing the room)* Regina would have done it for one kind word.

MRS. ALVING I don't understand you. What fear do you mean—and what has Regina to do with it?

OSWALD Is it very late, mother?

MRS. ALVING It is early morning. *(Looks out through the conservatory windows)* The dawn is breaking already on the heights. And the sky is clear, Oswald. In a little while you will see the sun.

OSWALD I am glad of that. After all, there may be many things yet for me to be glad of and to live for—

MRS. ALVING I should hope so!

OSWALD Even if I am not able to work—

MRS. ALVING You will soon find you are able to work again now, my dear boy. You have no longer all those painful depressing thoughts to brood over.

OSWALD No, it is a good thing that you have been able to rid me of those fancies. If only, now, I could overcome this one thing—. *(Sits down on the couch)* Let us have a little chat, mother.

MRS. ALVING Yes, let us. *(Pushes an armchair near to the couch and sits down beside him)*

OSWALD The sun is rising—and you know all about it; so I don't feel the fear any longer.

MRS. ALVING I know all about what?

OSWALD *(without listening to her)* Mother, isn't it the case that you said this evening there was nothing in the world you would not do for me if I asked you?

MRS. ALVING Yes, certainly I said so.

OSWALD And will you be as good as your word, mother?

MRS. ALVING You may rely upon that, my own dear boy. I have nothing else to live for, but you.

OSWALD Yes, yes; well, listen to me, mother. You are very strong-minded, I know. I want you to sit quite quiet when you hear what I am going to tell you.

MRS. ALVING But what is this dreadful thing—?

OSWALD You mustn't scream. Do you hear? Will you promise me that?

We are going to sit and talk it over quite quietly. Will you promise me that, mother?

MRS. ALVING Yes, yes, I promise—only tell me what it is.

OSWALD Well, then, you must know that this fatigue of mine—and my not being able to think about my work—all that is not really the illness itself—

MRS. ALVING What is the illness itself?

OSWALD What I am suffering from is hereditary; it—*(touches his forehead, and speaks very quietly)*—it lies here.

MRS. ALVING *(almost speechless)* Oswald! No—no!

OSWALD Don't scream; I can't stand it. Yes, I tell you, it lies here, waiting. And any time, any moment, it may break out.

MRS. ALVING How horrible—!

OSWALD Do keep quiet. That is the state I am in—

MRS. ALVING *(springing up)* It isn't true, Oswald! It is impossible! It can't be that!

OSWALD I had one attack while I was abroad. It passed off quickly. But when I learnt the condition I had been in, then this dreadful haunting fear took possession of me.

MRS. ALVING That was the fear, then—

OSWALD Yes, it is so indescribably horrible, you know. If only it had been an ordinary mortal disease—. I am not so much afraid of dying; though, of course, I should like to live as long as I can.

MRS. ALVING Yes, yes, Oswald, you must!

OSWALD But this is so appallingly horrible. To become like a helpless child again—to have to be fed, to have to be—. Oh, it's unspeakable!

MRS. ALVING My child has his mother to tend him.

OSWALD *(jumping up)* No, never; that is just what I won't endure! I dare not think what it would mean to linger on like that for years—to get old and grey like that. And you might die before I did. *(Sits down in* MRS. ALVING'S *chair)* Because it doesn't necessarily have a fatal end quickly, the doctor said. He called it a kind of softening of the brain—or something of that sort. *(Smiles mournfully)* I think that expression sounds so nice. It always makes me think of cherry-coloured velvet curtains—something that is soft to stroke.

MRS. ALVING *(with a scream)* Oswald!

OSWALD *(jumps up and walks about the room)* And now you have taken Regina from me! If I had only had her. She would have given me a helping hand, I know.

MRS. ALVING *(going up to him)* What do you mean, my darling boy? Is there any help in the world I would not be willing to give you?

OSWALD When I had recovered from the attack I had abroad, the doctor told me that when it recurred—and it will recur—there would be no more hope.

MRS. ALVING And he was heartless enough to—

OSWALD I insisted on knowing. I told him I had arrangements to make—. *(Smiles cunningly)* And so I had. *(Takes a small box from his inner breast-pocket.)* Mother, do you see this?

MRS. ALVING What is it?
OSWALD Morphia powders.
MRS. ALVING *(looking at him in terror)* Oswald—my boy!
OSWALD I have twelve of them saved up—
MRS. ALVING *(snatching at it)* Give me the box, Oswald!
OSWALD Not yet, mother. *(Puts it back in his pocket.)*
MRS. ALVING I shall never get over this!
OSWALD You must. If I had had Regina here now, I would have told her quietly how things stand with me—and asked her to give me this last helping hand. She would have helped me, I am certain.
MRS. ALVING Never!
OSWALD If this horrible thing had come upon me and she had seen me lying helpless, like a baby, past help, past saving, past hope—with no chance of recovering—
MRS. ALVING Never in the world would Regina have done it.
OSWALD Regina would have done it. Regina was so splendidly light-hearted. And she would very soon have tired of looking after an invalid like me.
MRS. ALVING Then thank heaven Regina is not here!
OSWALD Well, now you have got to give me that helping hand, mother.
MRS. ALVING *(with a loud scream)* I!
OSWALD Who has a better right than you?
MRS. ALVING I! Your mother!
OSWALD Just for that reason.
MRS. ALVING I, who gave you your life!
OSWALD I never asked you for life. And what kind of a life was it that you gave me? I don't want it! You shall take it back!
MRS. ALVING Help! Help! *(Runs into the hall.)*
OSWALD *(following her)* Don't leave me! Where are you going?
MRS. ALVING *(in the hall)* To fetch the doctor to you, Oswald! Let me out!
OSWALD *(going into the hall)* You shan't go out. And no one shall come in. *(Turns the key in the lock)*
MRS. ALVING *(coming in again)* Oswald! Oswald!—my child!
OSWALD *(following her)* Have you a mother's heart—and can bear to see me suffering this unspeakable terror?
MRS. ALVING *(controlling herself, after a moment's silence)* There is my hand on it.
OSWALD Will you—?
MRS. ALVING If it becomes necessary. But it shan't become necessary. No, no—it is impossible it should!
OSWALD Let us hope so. And let us live together as long as we can. Thank you, mother. *(He sits down in the armchair, which* MRS. ALVING *had moved beside the couch. Day is breaking; the lamp is still burning on the table.)*
MRS. ALVING *(coming cautiously nearer)* Do you feel calmer now?
OSWALD Yes.
MRS. ALVING *(bending over him)* It has only been a dreadful fancy of yours, Oswald. Nothing but fancy. All this upset has been bad for you.

But now you will get some rest, at home with your own mother, my darling boy. You shall have everything you want, just as you did when you were a little child.—There, now. The attack is over. You see how easily it passed off! I knew it would.—And look, Oswald, what a lovely day we are going to have! Brilliant sunshine. Now you will be able to see your home properly. *(She goes to the table and puts out the lamp. It is sunrise. The glaciers and peaks in the distance are seen bathed in bright morning light.)*

OSWALD *(who has been sitting motionless in the armchair, with his back to the scene outside, suddenly says:)* Mother, give me the sun.

MRS. ALVING *(standing at the table, and looking at him in amazement)* What do you say?

OSWALD *(repeats in a dull, toneless voice)* The sun—the sun.

MRS. ALVING *(going up to him)* Oswald, what is the matter with you? *(*OSWALD *seems to shrink up in the chair; all his muscles relax; his face loses its expression, and his eyes stare stupidly.* MRS. ALVING *is trembling with terror)* What is it! *(Screams.)* Oswald! What is the matter with you! *(Throws herself on her knees beside him and shakes him)* Oswald! Oswald! Look at me! Don't you know me!

OSWALD *(in an expressionless voice, as before)* The sun—the sun.

MRS. ALVING *(jumps up despairingly, beats her head with her hands, and screams)* I can't bear it! *(Whispers as though paralysed with fear)* I can't bear it! Never! *(Suddenly.)* Where has he got it? *(Passes her hand quickly over his coat.)* Here! *(Draws back a little way and cries:)* No, no, no!—Yes!—no, no! *(She stands a few steps from him, her hands thrust into her hair, and stares at him in speechless terror.)*

OSWALD *(sitting motionless, as before)* The sun—the sun.

eric bentley

henrik ibsen

A PERSONAL STATEMENT

The world's attitude to Ibsen has gone through two phases and is now, as I see it, entering upon a third. The first phase was that of the late nineteenth century, at which time one either expressed one's detestation of the dramatist's iconoclasm or one's enthusiastic acceptance of it. Either way, the Ibsen under consideration was the revolutionary; and one accepted or rejected him according as one was oneself a revolutionary or not.

The second phase of opinion came with the acceptance of Ibsen in the early twentieth century by society at large. A gain of this sort is always, at the same time, a loss. For general acceptance implies only a cessation of hostilities, not an active interest in an author; to be accepted is the first step towards being ignored. When the rear guard accepts an author, moreover, the advance guard drops him. Necessarily so, as the advance guard's function has been to scold the rear guard for paying no attention. Not so necessary, but quite natural, is the advance guard's tendency to turn against those it used to champion, perhaps even reviving arguments against them that had first been formulated by the rear guard. . . . In the nineteenth century, playwrights were warned against Ibsen by the die-hard, older critics; in the twentieth century they began to be warned against him by the advanced young spirits. Bertolt Brecht's Epic Theatre, beginning in the nineteen twenties, was, on the technical side, mainly a revolt against Ibsen, whose forms Brecht has described as rigid and narrow.

More important than technique, perhaps, was ideology. As the only fully elaborated Marxist theory of drama, Brecht's Epic Theatre is the purest example of collectivism in twentieth-century dramatic writing, and the extreme statement of his thought is to be found in the play *Die Massnahme* (published in English as *The Measures Taken* in *The Colorado Review*, Winter 1956–7) which celebrates the sacrifice of the individual to the group. In her book *Stalin and German Communism*, Ruth Fischer intimates that this play was suggested by the experiences of Gerhart Eisler as a Communist agent in China, and, by anticipation, it dramatizes the deaths of Radek and Bukharin, Rajk and Slansky, though not the subsequent admission, in 1956, that the confessions these men made were a pack of lies.

During the phase of history that produced Epic Theatre, collectivistic thought spread far beyond the confines of the Communist movement, and, when I was in college in the nineteen thirties, the standard opinion was that Henrik Ibsen was *borné* and *petit bourgeois*—that he represented the end of individualism and not the beginning of the great new order. Only later did I learn that this view had been first expressed by Friedrich Engels himself and thereafter had been echoed by all Marxist critics from Mehring on.

And Marx and Engels were right, if their philosophy as a whole was right; it is a matter of that; while, equally, Ibsen will cease to seem *borné* and *petit bourgeois*, will become important again, to those who wish to stand *for* the individual and *against* what seems to them the hideous monolith of Soviet collectivism. To these the great individualists of the nineteenth century are still great, Ibsen among them. Great and exemplary—for they possess what we have lost but must at all costs recover.

They possessed, first and foremost, what Lionel Trilling and others have been calling the *mystique* of the self: their self-respect, and their belief in self-respect, went beyond opinion to sentiment, and beyond sentiment to faith. For them, there existed no Radeks and Bukharins—no people, that is, who could be asked to lie their lives away for an alleged collective good. In some much-quoted lines of verse, Henrik Ibsen once said that to live was to fight with the devils that infest the head and heart and to hold a Last Judgment over the self. The *mystique* of the self never found more pithy expression, nor the subject-matter of Ibsen's plays more precise definition. Even where Ibsen criticizes an individualist—as in *Brand* and *The Wild Duck*—he does so, not from any standpoint acceptable to a Marxist, but from that of another individualism. Brand's flaw, after all, is a defect in self-knowledge. Instead of living in harmony with his own nature, he attempts to live according to an abstract law which he must constantly foist on himself and others by arbitrary violence. This individualist becomes less of an individual all the time. By a supposed attachment to the *super*human, he has become *in*human.

Consider Mrs. Alving, the individualist as woman. We know that she reads the right books, though Ibsen leaves them unnamed so that each spectator can supply the titles of his own favorites. She belongs to the nineteenth-century Enlightenment. But we find out that she achieves enlightenment in general while keeping herself ignorant in particular of precisely those two or three things which it would do her most good to know: above all, of her complicity in the tragedy of Captain Alving. When she tells Oswald—at the end—that she shared the blame, because, in her prudishness, her fear of sexuality, she had not welcomed Alving's joy of life, she is also telling herself. Catastrophe in this story plays, as it were, the role of psychoanalysis, bringing to consciousness the guilty facts which the protagonist has so zealously kept under. Mrs. Alving, reader of books, has come to know many things; she has not come to know herself. She is not too much an individual, as Manders thinks, but too little.

My generation of undergraduates—that of the nineteen thirties—reserved its greatest contempt for the person who was "only interested in saving his soul" and was therefore neglecting the real task, that of changing the world. We didn't realize to what an appalling extent the motive force of our reforming zeal was fear of the self, a failure to face the self. We scoffed at the escapism of certain individualistic poets, and did not see that social collectivism could be the supreme escape, and conversely that there can be no healthy altruism which is not grounded in self-respect. Yet, if we hadn't been tipped off that Ibsen was *petit bourgeois,* we might have learned our lesson from him. For he saw that the altruism of a Gregers Werle was the outgrowth of a sick conscience; Gregers persecutes Hedwig because he is running away from himself.

With the disrespect for the self that has been so prevalent in our time goes, naturally, a disrespect for the whole inner life of man, as witness the overtone that the word *subjective* now carries. The *objective* is real, the *subjective* is unreal—in other words, you get at the truth by getting away from yourself. If anyone remarked of Neville Chamberlain in 1938 that at least his motives were good, there was always a young Marxist on hand to remark that we must not judge by motives but by objective facts. Here again, Ibsen belongs to the earlier tradition. He believes the motive itself to be an objective fact, and, in a strict sense, the primary fact—the one to start from. He would never have written a play about the rightness or wrongness of Chamberlain's policy, but he might well have written one about whether the man did indeed have good motives, whether his conscience was healthy. His plays are studies in *un*healthy conscience. Naturally, then, he seems not only old-fashioned but even wrongheaded to those who assume that life begins after integrity has been surrendered to a party, a class, or a state.

But I do not wish to focus my whole argument upon Communism because, in the present connection, Communism is only the extreme instance of a universal phenomenon—conformism parading as virtue. And in the West we encounter the danger less in the form of Communism than as a new attitude to life which David Riesman calls other-directedness, i.e., being oriented toward other people, not just in external matters, not just, as it were, when other people are looking, but in one's most intimate mental activity. Modern civilization lives under the sign of Mrs. Grundy.

Allowing for the inaccuracy of all such generalizations we may say that the spiky, individualistic Victorians were inner-directed. Trained under strong fathers in the discipline of self-reliance, they hearkened to the inner voice, and went their independent way. Whether we can ever get back to anything of the sort is a question going far beyond the scope of the present statement. But even Mr. Riesman (who seems to be a fatalist) permits himself some unmistakably nostalgic admiration, and, certainly, the stock of all the Victorian individualists has been rising as men have come to realize what a frightful mess the anti-individualists have been making of the world. Ibsen is a great exemplar of the inner-directed culture. *Peer Gynt*, though not quite a prophecy of other-directedness, is about the danger of self-disrespect, of having no sense of identity, of being a human onion, all layers and no center. . . .

By this time, I may have given the impression that what Ibsen means to me is Conservatism, the Nineteenth Century, Darby and Joan, or even Songs My Mother Taught Me. Assuredly we have come to the point where Victorianism no longer suggests a narrow and enervating stuffiness but manliness, free intellect, abundant individuality—men like Henrik Ibsen rather than Parson Manders. The great Victorians were rebels against Victorian*ism*, non-conformists one and all. In political theory, Henrik Ibsen leaned towards anarchism—of all *isms* the most remote from totalitarianism. His first audiences, as I have said, regarded him as primarily a rebel; and in the future, I think, he will be regarded as a rebel again.

Ibsen's plays are *about* rebels—from Catiline to Brand and Julian, and from Lona Hessel and Nora Helmer to Hedda Gabler and John Gabriel Borkman—and we should not need to be told by Ibsen himself (as we were) that he wrote only of what he had lived through, for rebelliousness is not only the subject of the plays but the motive force. Anti-clericalism (as in the portrait of Manders and of the Dean in *Brand*) and political satire (as in *The League of Youth* or the characterization of the Mayor in *Brand*) are merely the most obtrusive signs of a mentality that was critical through and through. As we retreat in horror, disgust, or mere boredom from the idea of the writer as Official Mouthpiece, we come back to the old liberal conception, most signally represented in this century by André Gide: the writer as questioner, dissenter, challenger, troublemaker, at war with his age, yet by that token standing for the best in his age and helping the age to understand itself. In Ibsen, as in Gide, we who live in a time of fake radicalism are confronted by a real radical.

In speaking of fake radicalism, I again have more than Communism in mind—more even than politics. I am thinking, for example, of all playwrights who are considered daring, and whose courage is rather lightheartedly connected by critics with that of Ibsen and Strindberg. As people these playwrights are often much more Bohemian than Ibsen, and something much more quickly identifiable as Daring is smeared over the whole surface of their plays, which deal with assorted neuroses not even mentionable in the theatre of Ibsen's day. But Ibsen is supposed to have given Daring its start in *Ghosts*.

The mistake here is to imagine that the subject of *Ghosts* is syphilis. Lucky for Ibsen that it isn't, as the medical science of the play is now quite obsolete! His daring was not a matter of bringing up repellent subjects, though it included that. It consisted in his genuinely radical attitude to life in general. It is at the heart of his writing, not merely on its surface.

What is true in the sexual sphere applies also to politics. In our political plays today, we are given what is conventionally regarded as daring but what actually takes no courage at all to say—it is at best what used to be daring and is now calculated to produce cheers from a clique, class, or party rather than bad reviews in the press and rotten eggs from the gallery. An instance, oddly enough, is *An Enemy of the People* as freely adapted to the American stage in the mid-twentieth century by Arthur Miller. Ibsen's original, by contrast, though no profound piece of thought, and in my view one of his least vital plays, is genuinely daring, especially in its blunt challenge to the idea of majority rule. The reason the newer version is dull is that Mr. Miller was himself offended by Ibsen's daring, made excuses for him in a preface, and proceeded to censor offensive passages. The dangerous thoughts of the latter-day quasi-radical are all completely safe; Ibsen's plays were so subversive they frightened, at times, even their author.

One difference between the old radical and the new is that the former explored life while the latter lays down the law about it. *Die Massnahme* perfectly represents the newer procedure. Such a play is not drama of discussion or ideas, for the author isn't talking it over with you, he is telling you. Still less is it drama of exploration, for it is but an exemplification of an idea the author started out with.

Gerhart Hauptmann remarked once that the playwright must never reword thoughts which he or his character has already thought: dramatic dialogue must only present thoughts in the process of being thought. Which is another way of saying that the playwright must not be directly didactic, for it is the didactic writer, out not to learn but to teach, who concentrates on finding effective form for thinking that was finished long ago. Didacticism seems not to have been a besetting temptation for Ibsen as it was for Brecht. It is an irony that the man considered the father of the drama of ideas makes so few explicit references to ideas in his plays.

Incidentally, *An Enemy of the People* is inferior Ibsen just because it is one of the few plays in which this author seems simply to be "telling us"—with upraised finger and an inclination to be very angry if we aren't good and do as we're "told." Generally, with Ibsen, we feel we are his companions in a search and therefore, in line with Hauptmann's principle, are not given summaries of what has been thought already but are present at the thinking. Mere summaries of experience (intellectual experience or otherwise) are without dramatic life. The pulse of the drama begins to beat at the moment the playwright begins to struggle with his experience. There is no better evidence for this truth than the life-work of Henrik Ibsen.

The principle invoked by Hauptmann enables us to understand the radical differences not only between Ibsen and Brecht but between Ibsen and the Ibsenites. The more the Ibsenites agreed with the Master, the worse the result was bound to be: for they were starting where he ended, namely, with his findings. It is of course open to writers who do this to improve on their Master in all the external qualities of literature—elegance, concision, clarity, and so on. For they are only paraphrasing. And it makes one realize that one values literature, ultimately, for other qualities than these. One will indeed suffer inelegance, inconcision, even unclarity with a good grace if only there is also a degree of inner movement, action, energy, conflict. . . .

There is a lesson in Ibsen for our so-called profession of playwrights today. The profession—by definition, perhaps—acquires a certain craft and then uses it. In other words, the professional writer works within the resources he has found himself to possess. Such-and-such worked very well last time; the presumption that it may work well again is enough to prompt a second use, and a third, and so on. Hence his youth is the professional writer's only creative period; there can indeed, on the terms just stated, be no development, but at best an increasing facility. Ibsen chose the path of constant development, accepting the risks, paying the price, and reaping the reward. The price is the foregoing of small perfection and easy success. Professional dramatic critics, out of something more than fellow feeling, will always tend to prefer the professional craftsman to the real artist: the merits of what the former has to offer are more easily recognized and measured, while the latter undoubtedly makes far more mistakes, and is not always improving. The pay-off comes at the end when the "mistake"—about which the critics have "rightly" been merciless—reveals itself as a needed part of a pattern. It has been said that all Shakespeare's plays taken together form one long play. Something of the kind can be said of the collected work of any real artist. Not the smallest fascination of Ibsen is the unity of his work, the profound meaning in the relation of play to play. To write both *Brand* and *Peer Gynt* is not just twice the job of writing one of the two; it is to force the reader to read the plays as thesis and antithesis in an artist's effort at synthesis. To follow up *Ghosts* with *An Enemy of the People* was more than an act of moral reprisal, and to follow up *An Enemy* with *The Wild Duck* was more than an act of self-correction: one thing leads to another in a drama which has *Catiline* for prologue and *When We Dead Awaken* for epilogue, the drama of Ibsen's whole *œuvre*.

Henrik Ibsen meant a lot to me when I first encountered theatre, literature, and adult life, and I return to him a couple of decades later when trying, as we do, to come to terms with the theatre, the literature, and the life around us, trying to locate the essential problems, discard impeding prejudices, correct obstructive errors, see through the facts to the meaning of the facts and, in all this, to accept the self that does the locating, discarding, correcting, and seeing, for, while the Bible tells us to love our neighbor as ourselves, Henrik Ibsen seems to remind us how unhelpful that injunction would be to people who did *not* love themselves.

george bernard shaw 1856–1950

caesar and cleopatra

A HISTORY

Shaw grew up in a family of Protestant Dubliners with an unhappy alcoholic father and a cheerfully indifferent mother who eventually departed for a musical career in London. Shaw, joining her at the age of twenty, was for nearly ten years an erratic London dilettante: he studied, wrote unsuccessful novels, became a socialist, a pamphleteer, and public speaker. Finally, in 1885 he began reviewing books and subsequently became a distinguished music and drama critic. He championed Wagner and Ibsen, and in 1892 launched his playwright's career with *Widower's Houses,* an attack on slum-landlordism. A fierce iconoclast, Shaw had a sure theatrical sense, versatile comic gifts, eloquence, brilliant intellect, and deep moral sensibility. Among his subjects were sex and marriage (*Mrs. Warren's Profession,* 1893, *Candida,* 1894, and *Man and Superman,* 1903); economics, poverty, and war (*Major Barbara,* 1905 and *Heartbreak House,* 1913–16); the great man (*Caesar and Cleopatra,* 1898 and *Sain Joan,* 1923); and religion (*Androcles and the Lion,* 1912 and *Back to Methuselah,* 1921). In 1926 Shaw won the Nobel Prize for literature. Shy of intimacy, Shaw fought his nature and donned a mask of cockiness and clowning. Despite his keen awareness of human shortcomings, he never surrendered to misanthropy or despair.

the characters

JULIUS CÆSAR
CLEOPATRA
RUFIO, CÆSAR'S *lieutenant*
BRITANNUS, CÆSAR'S *secretary*
APOLLODORUS, *the Sicilian*
PTOLEMY XII, CLEOPATRA'S *brother*
POTHINUS, PTOLEMY'S *guardian*
FTATATEETA, CLEOPATRA'S *nurse*
LUCIUS SEPTIMIUS, *Military Tribune in Alexandria*

THEODOTUS, PTOLEMY'S *tutor;* ACHILLAS, PTOLEMY'S *chief general;* BELZANOR, *captain of* CLEOPATRA'S *guard;* BEL AFFRIS, *military novice from the Temple of Ra in Memphis;* A PERSIAN GUARDSMAN; CHARMIAN *and* IRAS, *ladies of* CLEOPATRA'S *retinue;* A CENTURION; A WOUNDED

SOLDIER; THREE ROMAN SENTINELS; A BOATMAN; A PROFESSOR OF MUSIC; FOUR MARKET PORTERS; A HARP PLAYER; A MAJOR-DOMO; A PRIEST; A NUBIAN SENTINEL; A NUBIAN SLAVE; OFFICIALS; COURTIERS; SOLDIERS

prologue

(In the doorway of the temple of Ra[1] in Memphis.[2] Deep gloom. An august personage with a hawk's head is mysteriously visible by his own light in the darkness within the temple. He surveys the modern audience with great contempt; and finally speaks the following words to them.)

Peace! Be silent and hearken unto me, ye quaint little islanders. Give ear, ye men with white paper on your breasts and nothing written thereon (to signify the innocency of your minds). Hear me, ye women who adorn yourselves alluringly and conceal your thoughts from your men, leading them to believe that ye deem them wondrous strong and masterful whilst in truth ye hold them in your hearts as children without judgment. Look upon my hawk's head; and know that I am Ra, who was once in Egypt a mighty god. Ye cannot kneel nor prostrate yourselves; for ye are packed in rows without freedom to move, obstructing one another's vision; neither do any of ye regard it as seemly to do ought until ye see all the rest do so too; wherefore it commonly happens that in great emergencies ye do nothing, though each telleth his fellow that something must be done. I ask you not for worship, but for silence. Let not your men speak nor your women cough; for I am come to draw you back two thousand years over the graves of sixty generations. Ye poor posterity, think not that ye are the first. Other fools before ye have seen the sun rise and set, and the moon change her shape and her hour. As they were so ye are; and yet not so great; for the pyramids my people built stand to this day; whilst the dustheaps on which ye slave, and which ye call empires, scatter in the wind even as ye pile your dead sons' bodies on them to make yet more dust.

Hearken to me then, oh ye compulsorily educated ones. Know that even as there is an old England and a new, and ye stand perplexed between the twain; so in the days when I was worshipped was there an old Rome and a new, and men standing perplexed between them. And the old Rome was poor and little, and greedy and fierce, and evil in many ways; but because its mind was little and its work was simple, it knew its own mind and did its own work; and the gods pitied it and helped it and strengthened it and shielded it; for the gods are patient with littleness. Then the old Rome, like the beggar on horseback,[3] presumed on the favor of the gods, and said, "Lo! there is neither riches nor greatness in our littleness: the road to riches and greatness is through robbery of the poor and

[1]Sun-god, and one of the most important gods in ancient Egypt.
[2]Ancient city in lower Egypt. Traditionally the capitol of Menes and of most of the rulers of the Old Kingdom of ancient Egypt. At the time of the play, it had lost its prominence to Alexandria.
[3]Referring to the proverb "set a beggar on horseback and he'll ride to the devil."

slaughter of the weak." So they robbed their own poor until they became great masters of that art, and knew by what laws it could be made to appear seemly and honest. And when they had squeezed their own poor dry, they robbed the poor of other lands, and added those lands to Rome until there came a new Rome, rich and huge. And I, Ra, laughed; for the minds of the Romans remained the same size whilst their dominion spread over the earth.

Now mark me, that ye may understand what ye are presently to see. Whilst the Romans still stood between the old Rome and the new, there arose among them a mighty soldier: Pompey the Great. And the way of the soldier is the way of death; but the way of the gods is the way of life; and so it comes that a god at the end of his way is wise and a soldier at the end of his way is a fool. So Pompey held by the old Rome, in which only soldiers could become great; but the gods turned to the new Rome, in which any man with wit enough could become what he would. And Pompey's friend Julius Cæsar was on the side of the gods; for he saw that Rome had passed beyond the control of the little old Romans. This Cæsar was a great talker and a politician: he bought men with words and with gold, even as ye are bought. And when they would not be satisfied with words and gold, and demanded also the glories of war, Cæsar in his middle age turned his hand to that trade; and they that were against him when he sought their welfare, bowed down before him when he became a slayer and a conqueror; for such is the nature of you mortals. And as for Pompey, the gods grew tired of his triumphs and his airs of being himself a god; for he talked of law and duty and other matters that concerned not a mere human worm. And the gods smiled on Cæsar; for he lived the life they had given him boldly, and was not forever rebuking us for our indecent ways of creation, and hiding our handiwork as a shameful thing. Ye know well what I mean; for this is one of your own sins.

And thus it fell out between the old Rome and the new, that Cæsar said, "Unless I break the law of old Rome, I cannot take my share in ruling her; and the gift of ruling that the gods gave me will perish without fruit." But Pompey said, "The law is above all; and if thou break it thou shalt die." Then said Cæsar, "I will break it: kill me who can." And he broke it. And Pompey went for him, as ye say, with a great army to slay him and uphold the old Rome. So Cæsar fled across the Adriatic sea; for the high gods had a lesson to teach him, which lesson they shall also teach you in due time if ye continue to forget them and to worship that cad among gods, Mammon. Therefore before they raised Cæsar to be master of the world, they were minded to throw him down into the dust, even beneath the feet of Pompey, and blacken his face before the nations. And Pompey they raised higher than ever, he and his laws and his high mind that aped the gods, so that his fall might be the more terrible. And Pompey followed Cæsar, and overcame him with all the majesty of old Rome, and stood over him and over the whole world even as ye stand over it with your fleet that covers thirty miles of the sea. And when Cæsar was brought down to utter nothingness, he made a last stand to die honorably, and did not despair; for he said, "Against me there is Pompey, and the old Rome, and the law and the legions: all against me; but high above these are the gods; and Pompey is a fool." And the gods laughed and approved; and on the field of Pharsalia the impossible came to pass; the blood and iron ye pin your faith on fell before the spirit of man; for the spirit of man is the will of the gods; and Pompey's power crumbled in his hand, even as the power of imperial Spain crumbled when it was set against your fathers in the days when England was little, and knew her own mind, and had a mind to know instead of a circulation of newspapers. Wherefore look to it, lest some little people whom ye would enslave rise up and become in the hand of God the scourge of your boastings and your injustices and your lusts and stupidities.

And now, would ye know the end of Pompey, or will ye sleep while a god speaks? Heed my words well; for Pompey went where ye have gone, even to Egypt, where there was a Roman occupation even as there was but now a British one. And Cæsar pursued Pompey to Egypt; a Roman fleeing, and a Roman pursuing: dog eating dog. And the Egyptians said, "Lo: these Romans which have lent money to our kings and levied a distraint upon us with their arms, call for ever upon us to be loyal to them by betraying our own country to them. But now behold two Romes! Pompey's Rome and Cæsar's Rome! To which of the twain shall we pretend to be loyal?" So they turned in their perplexity to a soldier that had once served Pompey, and that knew the ways of Rome and was full of her lusts. And they said to him, "Lo: in thy country dog eats dog; and both dogs are coming to eat us: what counsel hast thou to give us?" And this soldier, whose name was Lucius Septimius, and whom ye shall presently see before ye, replied, "Ye shall diligently consider which is the bigger dog of the two; and ye shall kill the other dog for his sake and thereby earn his favor." And the Egyptians said, "Thy counsel is expedient; but if we kill a man outside the law we set ourselves in the place of the gods; and this we dare not do. But thou, being a Roman, art accustomed to this kind of killing; for thou hast imperial instincts. Wilt thou therefore kill the lesser dog for us?" And he said, "I will; for I have made my home in Egypt; and I desire consideration and influence among you." And they said, "We knew well thou wouldst not do it for nothing: thou shalt have thy reward." Now when Pompey came, he came alone in a little galley, putting his trust in the law and the constitution. And it was plain to the people of Egypt that Pompey was now but a very small dog. So when he set his foot on the shore he was greeted by his old comrade Lucius Septimius, who welcomed him with one hand and with the other smote off his head, and kept it as it were a pickled cabbage to make a present to Cæsar. And mankind shuddered; but the gods laughed; for Septimius was but a knife that Pompey had sharpened; and when it turned against his own throat they said that Pompey had better have made Septimius a ploughman than so brave and readyhanded a slayer. Therefore again I bid you beware, ye who would all be Pompeys if ye dared; for war is a wolf that may come to your own door.

Are ye impatient with me? Do ye crave for a story of an unchaste woman? Hath the name of Cleopatra tempted ye hither? Ye foolish ones; Cleopatra is as yet but a child that is whipped by her nurse. And what I am about to shew you for the good of your souls is how Cæsar, seeking Pompey in Egypt, found Cleopatra; and how he received that present of a pickled cabbage that was once the head of Pompey; and what things happened between the old Cæsar and the child queen before he left Egypt and battled his way back to Rome to be slain there as Pompey was slain, by men in whom the spirit of Pompey still lived. All this ye shall see; and ye shall marvel, after your ignorant manner, that men twenty centuries ago were already just such as you, and spoke and lived as ye speak and live, no worse and no better, no wiser and no sillier. And the two thousand years that have past are to me, the god Ra, but a moment; nor is this day any other than the day in which Cæsar set foot in the land of my people. And now I leave you; for ye are a dull folk, and instruction is wasted on you; and I had not spoken so much but that it is in the nature of a god to struggle for ever with the dust and the darkness, and to drag from them, by the force of his longing for the divine, more life and more light. Settle ye therefore in your seats and keep silent; for ye are about to hear a man speak, and a great man he was, as ye count greatness. And fear not that I shall speak to you again: the rest of the story must ye learn from them that lived it. Farewell; and do not presume to applaud me. *(The temple vanishes in utter darkness).*

an alternative to the prologue

An October night on the Syrian border of Egypt towards the end of the XXXIII Dynasty, in the year 706 by Roman computation, afterwards reckoned by Christian computation as 48 B.C. *A great radiance of silver fire, the dawn of a moonlit night, is rising in the east. The stars and the cloudless sky are our own contemporaries, nineteen and a half centuries younger than we know them; but you would not guess that from their appearance. Below them are two notable drawbacks of civilization: a palace, and soldiers. The palace, an old, low, Syrian building of whitened mud, is not so ugly as Buckingham Palace; and the officers in the courtyard are more highly civilized than modern English officers: for example, they do not dig up the corpses of their dead enemies and mutilate them, as we dug up Cromwell and the Mahdi. They are in two groups: one intent on the gambling of their captain Belzanor, a warrior of fifty, who, with his spear on the ground beside his knee, is stooping to throw dice with a sly-looking young Persian recruit; the other gathered about a guardsman who has just finished telling a naughty story (still current in English barracks) at which they are laughing uproariously. They are about a dozen in number, all highly aristocratic young Egyptian guardsmen, handsomely equipped with weapons and armor, very unEnglish in point of not being ashamed of and uncomfortable in their professional dress; on the contrary, rather ostentatiously and arrogantly warlike, as valuing themselves on their military caste.*

Belzanor is a typical veteran, tough and wilful; prompt, capable and crafty where brute force will serve; helpless and boyish when it will not: an effective sergeant, an incompetent general, a deplorable dictator. Would, if influentially connected, be employed in the two last capacities by a modern European State on the strength of his success in the first. Is rather to be pitied just now in view of the fact that Julius Cæsar is invading his country. Not knowing this, is intent on his game with the Persian, whom, as a foreigner, he considers quite capable of cheating him.

His subalterns are mostly handsome young fellows whose interest in the game and the story symbolize with tolerable completeness the main interests in life of which they are conscious. Their spears are leaning against the walls, or lying on the ground ready to their hands. The corner of the courtyard forms a triangle of which one side is the front of the palace, with a doorway, the other a wall with a gateway. The storytellers are on the palace side: the gamblers, on the gateway side. Close to the gateway, against the wall, is a stone block high enough to enable a Nubian sentinel, standing on it, to look over the wall. The yard is lighted by a torch stuck in the wall. As the laughter from the group round the storyteller dies away, the kneeling Persian, winning the throw, snatches up the stake from the ground.

BELZANOR By Apis, Persian, thy gods are good to thee.

THE PERSIAN Try yet again, O captain. Double or quits!

BELZANOR No more. I am not in the vein.

THE SENTINEL *(poising his javelin as he peers over the wall)* Stand. Who goes there?

(They all start, listening. A strange voice replies from without.)

VOICE The bearer of evil tidings.

BELZANOR *(calling to the sentry)* Pass him.

THE SENTINEL *(grounding his javelin)* Draw near, O bearer of evil tidings.

BELZANOR *(pocketing the dice and picking up his spear)* Let us receive this man with honor. He bears evil tidings.

(The guardsmen seize their spears and gather about the gate, leaving a way through for the new comer.)

PERSIAN *(rising from his knee)* Are evil tidings, then, so honorable?

BELZANOR O barbarous Persian, hear my instruction. In Egypt the bearer of good tidings is sacrificed to the gods as a thank offering; but no god will accept the blood of the messenger of evil. When we have good tidings, we are careful to send them in the mouth of the cheapest slave we can find. Evil tidings are borne by young noblemen who desire to bring themselves into notice. *(They join the rest at the gate.)*

THE SENTINEL Pass, O young captain; and bow the head in the House of the Queen.

VOICE Go anoint thy javelin with fat of swine, O Blackamoor; for before morning the Romans will make thee eat it to the very butt.

(The owner of the voice, a fairhaired dandy, dressed in a different fashion from that affected by the guardmen, but no less extravagantly, comes through the gateway laughing. He is somewhat battlestained; and his left forearm, bandaged, comes through a torn sleeve. In his right hand

he carries a Roman sword in its sheath. He swaggers down the courtyard, the PERSIAN *on his right,* BELZANOR *on his left, and the guardsmen crowding down behind him.)*

BELZANOR Who are thou that laughest in the House of Cleopatra the Queen, and in the teeth of Belzanor, the captain of her guard?

THE NEW COMER I am Bel Affris, descended from the gods.

BELZANOR *(ceremoniously)* Hail, cousin!

ALL *(except the* PERSIAN*)* Hail, cousin!

PERSIAN All the Queen's guards are descended from the gods, O stranger, save myself. I am Persian, and descended from many kings.

BEL AFFRIS *(to the guardsmen)* Hail, cousins! *(to the* PERSIAN, *condescendingly)* Hail, mortal!

BELZANOR You have been in battle, Bel Affris; and you are a soldier among soldiers. You will not let the Queen's women have the first of your tidings.

BEL AFFRIS I have no tidings, except that we shall have our throats cut presently, women, soldiers, and all.

PERSIAN *(to* BELZANOR*)* I told you so.

THE SENTINEL *(who has been listening)* Woe, alas!

BEL AFFRIS *(calling to him)* Peace, peace, poor Ethiop: destiny is with the gods who painted thee black. *(to* BELZANOR*)* What has this mortal *(indicating the* PERSIAN*)* told you?

BELZANOR He says that the Roman Julius Cæsar, who has landed on our shores with a handful of followers, will make himself master of Egypt. He is afraid of the Roman soldiers. *(The guardsmen laugh with boisterous scorn).* Peasants, brought up to scare crows and follow the plough! Sons of smiths and millers and tanners! And we nobles, consecrated to arms, descended from the gods!

PERSIAN Belzanor: the gods are not always good to their poor relations.

BELZANOR *(hotly, to the* PERSIAN*)* Man to man, are we worse than the slaves of Cæsar?

BEL AFFRIS *(stepping between them)* Listen, cousin. Man to man, we Egyptians are as gods above the Romans.

THE GUARDSMEN *(exultantly)* Aha!

BEL AFFRIS But this Cæsar does not pit man against man: he throws a legion at you where you are weakest as he throws a stone from a catapult; and that legion is as a man with one head, a thousand arms, and no religion. I have fought against them; and I know.

BELZANOR *(derisively)* Were you frightened, cousin?

(The guardsmen roar with laughter, their eyes sparkling at the wit of their captain.)

BEL AFFRIS No, cousin; but I was beaten. They were frightened (perhaps); but they scattered us like chaff.

(The guardsmen, much damped, utter a growl of contemptuous disgust.)

BELZANOR Could you not die?

BEL AFFRIS No: that was too easy to be worthy of a descendant of the gods. Besides, there was no time: all was over in a moment. The attack came just where we least expected it.

BELZANOR That shews that the Romans are cowards.

BEL AFFRIS They care nothing about cowardice, these Romans: they fight to win. The pride and honor of war are nothing to them.

PERSIAN Tell us the tale of the battle. What befell?

THE GUARDSMEN *(gathering eagerly round* BEL AFFRIS*)* Ay: the tale of the battle.

BEL AFFRIS Know then, that I am a novice in the guard of the temple of Ra in Memphis, serving neither Cleopatra nor her brother Ptolemy, but only the high gods. We went a journey to inquire of Ptolemy why he had driven Cleopatra into Syria, and how we of Egypt should deal with the Roman Pompey, newly come to our shores after his defeat by Cæsar at Pharsalia. What, think ye, did we learn? Even that Cæsar is coming also in hot pursuit of his foe, and that Ptolemy has slain Pompey, whose severed head he holds in readiness to present to the conqueror. *(sensation among the guardsmen)* Nay, more: we found that Cæsar is already come; for we had not made half a day's journey on our way back when we came upon a city rabble flying from his legions, whose landing they had gone out to withstand.

BELZANOR And ye, the temple guard! did ye not withstand these legions?

BEL AFFRIS What man could, that we did. But there came the sound of a trumpet whose voice was as the cursing of a black mountain. Then saw we a moving wall of shields coming towards us. You know how the heart burns when you charge a fortified wall; but how if the fortified wall were to charge you?

THE PERSIAN *(exulting in having told them so)* Did I not say it?

BEL AFFRIS When the wall came nigh, it changed into a line of men—common fellows enough, with helmets, leather tunics, and breastplates. Every man of them flung his javelin: the one that came my way drove through my shield as through a papyrus—lo there! *(he points to the bandage on his left arm)* and would have gone through my neck had I not stooped. They were charging at the double then, and were upon us with short swords almost as soon as their javelins. When a man is close to you with such a sword, you can do nothing with our weapons: they are all too long.

THE PERSIAN What did you do?

BEL AFFRIS Doubled my fist and smote my Roman on the sharpness of his jaw. He was but mortal after all: he lay down in a stupor; and I took his sword and laid it on. *(drawing the sword)* Lo! a Roman sword with Roman blood on it!

THE GUARDSMEN *(approvingly)* Good! *(They take the sword and hand it round, examining it curiously.)*

THE PERSIAN And your men?

BEL AFFRIS Fled. Scattered like sheep.

BELZANOR *(furiously)* The cowardly slaves! Leaving the descendants of the gods to be butchered!

BEL AFFRIS *(with acid coolness)* The descendants of the gods did not stay to be butchered, cousin. The battle was not to the strong; but the race was to the swift. The Romans, who have no chariots, sent a cloud of horsemen in pursuit, and slew multitudes. Then our high priest's captain rallied a dozen descendants of the gods and exhorted us to die fighting. I said to myself: surely it is safer to stand than to lose my breath and be stabbed in the back; so I joined our captain and stood. Then the Romans treated us with respect; for no man attacks a lion when the field is full of sheep, except for the pride and honor of war, of which these Romans know nothing. So we escaped with our lives; and I am come to warn you that you must open your gates to Cæsar; for his advance guard is scarce an hour behind me; and not an Egyptian warrior is left standing between you and his legions.

THE SENTINEL Woe, alas! *(He throws down his javelin and flies into the palace.)*

BELZANOR Nail him to the door, quick! *(The guardsmen rush for him with their spears; but he is too quick for them.)* Now this news will run through the palace like fire through stubble.

BEL AFFRIS What shall we do to save the women from the Romans?

BELZANOR Why not kill them?

PERSIAN Because we should have to pay blood money for some of them. Better let the Romans kill them: it is cheaper.

BELZANOR *(awestruck at his brain power)* O subtle one! O serpent!

BELL AFFRIS But your Queen?

BELZANOR True: we must carry off Cleopatra.

BEL AFFRIS Will ye not await her command?

BELZANOR Command! a girl of sixteen! Not we. At Memphis ye deem her a Queen: here we know better. I will take her on the crupper of my horse. When we soldiers have carried her out of Cæsar's reach, then the priests and the nurses and the rest of them can pretend she is a queen again, and put their commands into her mouth.

PERSIAN Listen to me, Belzanor.

BELZANOR Speak, O subtle beyond thy years.

THE PERSIAN Cleopatra's brother Ptolemy is at war with her. Let us sell her to him.

THE GUARDSMEN O subtle one! O serpent!

BELZANOR We dare not. We are descended from the gods; but Cleopatra is descended from the river Nile; and the lands of our fathers will grow no grain if the Nile rises not to water them. Without our father's gifts we should live the lives of dogs.

PERSIAN It is true: the Queen's guard cannot live on its pay. But hear me further, O ye kinsmen of Osiris.

THE GUARDSMEN Speak, O subtle one. Hear the serpent begotten!

PERSIAN Have I heretofore spoken truly to you of Cæsar, when you thought I mocked you?

GUARDSMEN Truly, truly.

BELZANOR *(reluctantly admitting it)* So Bel Affris says.

PERSIAN Hear more of him, then. This Cæsar is a great lover of women: he makes them his friends and counsellors.

BELZANOR Faugh! This rule of women will be the ruin of Egypt.

THE PERSIAN Let it rather be the ruin of Rome! Cæsar grows old now: he is past fifty and full of labors and battles. He is too old for the young women; and the old women are too wise to worship him.

BEL AFFRIS Take heed, Persian. Cæsar is by this time almost within earshot.

PERSIAN Cleopatra is not yet a woman: neither is she wise. But she already troubles men's wisdom.

BELZANOR Ay: that is because she is descended from the river Nile and a black kitten of the sacred White Cat. What then?

PERSIAN Why, sell her secretly to Ptolemy, and then offer ourselves to Cæsar as volunteers to fight for the overthrow of her brother and the rescue of our Queen, the Great Granddaughter of the Nile.

THE GUARDSMEN O serpent!

PERSIAN He will listen to us if we come with her picture in our mouths. He will conquer and kill her brother, and reign in Egypt with Cleopatra for his Queen. And we shall be her guard.

GUARDSMEN O subtlest of all the serpents! O admiration! O wisdom!

BEL AFFRIS He will also have arrived before you have done talking, O word spinner.

BELZANOR That is true. *(An affrighted uproar in the palace interrupts him.)* Quick: the flight has begun: guard the door. *(They rush to the door and form a cordon before it with their spears. A mob of women-servants and nurses surges out. Those in front recoil from the spears, screaming to those behind to keep back.* BELZANOR'S *voice dominates the disturbance as he shouts)* Back there. In again, unprofitable cattle.

THE GUARDSMEN Back, unprofitable cattle.

BELZANOR Send us out Ftatateeta, the Queen's chief nurse.

THE WOMEN *(calling into the palace)* Ftatateeta, Ftatateeta. Come, come. Speak to Belzanor.

A WOMAN Oh, keep back. You are thrusting me on the spearheads.

(A huge grim woman, her face covered with a network of tiny wrinkles, and her eyes old, large, and wise; sinewy handed, very tall, very strong; with the mouth of a bloodhound and the jaws of a bulldog, appears on the threshold. She is dressed like a person of consequence in the palace, and confronts the guardsmen insolently.)

FTATATEETA Make way for the Queen's chief nurse.

BELZANOR *(with solemn arrogance)* Ftatateeta: I am Belzanor, the captain of the Queen's guard, descended from the gods.

FTATATEETA *(retorting his arrogance with interest)* Belzanor: I am Ftatateeta, the Queen's chief nurse; and your divine ancestors were proud to be painted on the wall in the pyramids of the kings whom my fathers served.

(The women laugh triumphantly.)

BELZANOR *(with grim humor)* Ftatateeta: daughter of a long-tongued, swivel-eyed chameleon, the Romans are at hand. *(A cry of terror from the women: they would fly but for the spears.)* Not even the descendants of the gods can resist them; for they have each man seven arms, each carrying seven spears. The blood in their veins is boiling quicksilver; and their wives become mothers in three hours, and are slain and eaten the next day.

(A shudder of horror from the women. FTATATEETA, *despising them and scorning the soldiers, pushes her way through the crowd and confronts the spear points undismayed.)*

FTATATEETA Then fly and save yourselves, O cowardly sons of the cheap clay gods that are sold to fish porters; and leave us to shift for ourselves.

BELZANOR Not until you have first done our bidding, O terror of manhood. Bring out Cleopatra the Queen to us; and then go whither you will.

FTATATEETA *(with a derisive laugh)* Now I know why the gods have taken her out of our hands. *(The guardsmen start and look at one another)* Know, thou foolish soldier, that the Queen has been missing since an hour past sundown.

BELZANOR *(furiously)* Hag: you have hidden her to sell to Cæsar or her brother. *(He grasps her by the left wrist, and drags her, helped by a few of the guard, to the middle of the courtyard, where, as they fling her on her knees, he draws a murderous looking knife.)* Where is she? Where is she? or—*(he threatens to cut her throat.)*

FTATATEETA *(savagely)* Touch me, dog; and the Nile will not rise on your fields for seven times seven years of famine.

BELZANOR *(frightened, but desperate)* I will sacrifice: I will pay. Or stay. *(to the* PERSIAN*)* You, O subtle one: your father's lands lie far from the Nile. Slay her.

PERSIAN *(threatening her with his knife)* Persia has but one god; yet he loves the blood of old women. Where is Cleopatra?

FTATATEETA Persian: as Osiris lives, I do not know. I chid her for bringing evil days upon us by talking to the sacred cats of the priests, and carrying them in her arms. I told her she would be left alone here when the Romans came as a punishment for her disobedience. And now she is gone—run away—hidden. I speak the truth. I call Osiris to witness—

THE WOMEN *(protesting officiously)* She speaks the truth, Belzanor.

BELZANOR You have frightened the child: she is hiding. Search—quick—into the palace—search every corner.

(The guards, led by BELZANOR, *shoulder their way into the palace through the flying crowd of women, who escape through the courtyard gate.)*

FTATATEETA *(screaming)* Sacrilege! Men in the Queen's chambers! Sa—*(her voice dies away as the* PERSIAN *puts his knife to her throat.)*

BEL AFFRIS *(laying a hand on Ftatateeta's left shoulder)* Forbear her yet a moment, Persian. *(to* FTATATEETA, *very significantly)* Mother: your gods are asleep or away hunting; and the sword is at your throat. Bring us to where the Queen is hid, and you shall live.

FTATATEETA *(contemptuously)* Who shall stay the sword in the hand of a fool, if the high gods put it there? Listen to me, ye young men without understanding. Cleopatra fears me; but she fears the Romans more. There is but one power greater in her eyes than the wrath of the Queen's nurse and the cruelty of Cæsar; and that is the power of the Sphinx that sits in the desert watching the way to the sea. What she would have it know, she tells into the ears of the sacred cats; and on her birthday she sacrifices to it and decks it with poppies. Go ye therefore into the desert and seek Cleopatra in the shadow of the Sphinx; and on your heads see to it that no harm comes to her.

BEL AFFRIS *(to the* PERSIAN*)* May we believe this, O subtle one?

PERSIAN Which way come the Romans?

BEL AFFRIS Over the desert, from the sea, by this very Sphinx.

PERSIAN *(to* FTATATEETA*)* O mother of guile! O aspic's tongue! You have made up this tale so that we two may go into the desert and perish on the spears of the Romans. *(lifting his knife)* Taste death.

FTATATEETA Not from thee, baby. *(She snatches his ankle from under him and flies stooping along the palace wall, vanishing in the darkness within its precinct.* BEL AFFRIS *roars with laughter as the* PERSIAN *tumbles. The guardsmen rush out of the palace with* BELZANOR *and a mob of fugitives, mostly carrying bundles.)*

PERSIAN Have you found Cleopatra?

BELZANOR She is gone. We have searched every corner.

THE NUBIAN SENTINEL *(appearing at the door of the palace)* Woe! Alas! Fly, fly!

BELZANOR What is the matter now?

THE NUBIAN SENTINEL The sacred white cat has been stolen.

ALL Woe! woe! *(General panic. They all fly with cries of consternation. The torch is thrown down and extinguished in the rush. The noise of the fugitives dies away. Darkness and dead silence.)*

act I

(The same darkness into which the temple of Ra and the Syrian palace vanished. The same silence. Suspense. Then the blackness and stillness break softly into silver mist and strange airs as the windswept harp of Memnon[1] plays at the dawning of the moon. It rises full over the desert; and a vast horizon comes into relief, broken by a huge shape which soon reveals itself in the spreading radiance as a Sphinx pedestalled on the sands. The light still clears, until the upraised eyes of the image are distinguished looking straight forward and upward in infinite fearless vigil, and a mass of color between its great paws defines itself as a heap of red poppies on which a girl lies motionless, her silken vest heaving gently and regularly with the breathing of a dreamless sleeper, and her braided hair glittering in a shaft of moonlight like a bird's wing.

Suddenly there comes from afar a vaguely fearful sound (it might be the bellow of a Minotaur[2] softened by great distance) and Memnon's music stops. Silence: then a few faint high-ringing trumpet notes. Then

[1]A statue at Thebes named by the Greeks after Memnon, the son of Eos. This statue was said to make a musical sound at daybreak at which time Memnon greeted his mother, the goddess of dawn.

[2]A monster with the head of a bull and the body of a man.

silence again. Then a man comes from the south with stealing steps, ravished by the mystery of the night, all wonder, and halts, lost in contemplation, opposite the left flank of the Sphinx, whose bosom, with its burden, is hidden from him by its massive shoulder.)

THE MAN Hail, Sphinx: salutation from Julius Cæsar! I have wandered in many lands, seeking the lost regions from which my birth into this world exiled me, and the company of creatures such as I myself. I have found flocks and pastures, men and cities, but no other Cæsar, no air native to me, no man kindred to me, none who can do my day's deed, and think my night's thought. In the little world yonder, Sphinx, my place is as high as yours in this great desert; only I wander, and you sit still; I conquer, and you endure; I work and wonder, you watch and wait; I look up and am dazzled, look down and am darkened, look round and am puzzled, whilst your eyes never turn from looking out—out of the world—to the lost region—the home from which we have strayed. Sphinx, you and I, strangers to the race of men, are no strangers to one another: have I not been conscious of you and of this place since I was born? Rome is a madman's dream: this is my Reality. These starry lamps of yours I have seen from afar in Gaul, in Britain, in Spain, in Thessaly, signalling great secrets to some eternal sentinel below, whose post I never could find. And here at last is their sentinel—an image of the constant and immortal part of my life, silent, full of thoughts, alone in the silver desert. Sphinx, Sphinx: I have climbed mountains at night to hear in the distance the stealthy footfall of the winds that chase your sands in forbidden play—our invisible children, O Sphinx, laughing in whispers. My way hither was the way of destiny; for I am he of whose genius you are the symbol: part brute, part woman, and part god—nothing of man in me at all. Have I read your riddle, Sphinx?

THE GIRL *(who has wakened, and peeped cautiously from her nest to see who is speaking)* Old gentleman.

CÆSAR *(starting violently, and clutching his sword)* Immortal gods!

THE GIRL Old gentleman: dont run away.

CÆSAR *(stupefied)* "Old gentleman: dont run away"!!! This! to Julius Cæsar!

THE GIRL *(urgently)* Old gentleman.

CÆSAR Sphinx: you presume on your centuries. I am younger than you, though your voice is but a girl's voice as yet.

THE GIRL Climb up here, quickly; or the Romans will come and eat you.

CÆSAR *(running forward past the Sphinx's shoulder, and seeing her)* A child at its breast! a divine child!

THE GIRL Come up quickly. You must get up at its side and creep round.

CÆSAR *(amazed)* Who are you?

THE GIRL Cleopatra, Queen of Egypt.

CÆSAR Queen of the Gypsies,[3] you mean.

[3]Gypsies are named thus because at one time it was believed that they had come into Europe from Egypt.

CLEOPATRA You must not be disrespectful to me, or the Sphinx will let the Romans eat you. Come up. It is quite cosy here.

CÆSAR *(to himself)* What a dream! What a magnificent dream! Only let me not wake, and I will conquer ten continents to pay for dreaming it out to the end. *(He climbs to the Sphinx's flank, and presently reappears to her on the pedestal, stepping round its right shoulder.)*

CLEOPATRA Take care. That's right. Now sit down: you may have its other paw. *(She seats herself comfortably on its left paw.)* It is very powerful and will protect us; but *(shivering, and with plaintive loneliness)* it would not take any notice of me or keep me company. I am glad you have come: I was very lonely. Did you happen to see a white cat anywhere?

CÆSAR *(sitting slowly down on the right paw in extreme wonderment)* Have you lost one?

CLEOPATRA Yes: the sacred white cat: is it not dreadful? I brought him here to sacrifice him to the Sphinx; but when we got a little way from the city a black cat called him, and he jumped out of my arms and ran away to it. Do you think that the black cat can have been my great-great-great-grandmother?

CÆSAR *(staring at her)* Your great-great-great-grandmother! Well, why not? Nothing would surprise me on this night of nights.

CLEOPATRA I think it must have been. My great-grandmother's great-grandmother was a black kitten of the sacred white cat; and the river Nile made her his seventh wife. That is why my hair is so wavy. And I always want to be let do as I like, no matter whether it is the will of the gods or not: that is because my blood is made with Nile water.

CÆSAR What are you doing here at this time of night? Do you live here?

CLEOPATRA Of course not: I am the Queen; and I shall live in the palace at Alexandria when I have killed my brother, who drove me out of it. When I am old enough I shall do just what I like. I shall be able to poison the slaves and see them wriggle, and pretend to Ftatateeta that she is going to be put into the fiery furnace.

CÆSAR Hm! Meanwhile why are you not at home and in bed?

CLEOPATRA Because the Romans are coming to eat us all. You are not at home and in bed either.

CÆSAR *(with conviction)* Yes I am. I live in a tent; and I am now in that tent, fast asleep and dreaming. Do you suppose that I believe you are real, you impossible little dream witch?

CLEOPATRA *(giggling and leaning trustfully towards him)* You are a funny old gentleman. I like you.

CÆSAR Ah, that spoils the dream. Why dont you dream that I am young?

CLEOPATRA I wish you were; only I think I should be more afraid of you. I like men, especially young men with round strong arms; but I am afraid of them. You are old and rather thin and stringy; but you have a nice voice; and I like to have somebody to talk to, though I think you are a little mad. It is the moon that makes you talk to yourself in that silly way.

CÆSAR What! you heard that, did you? I was saying my prayers to the great Sphinx.

CLEOPATRA But this isnt the great Sphinx.

CÆSAR *(much disappointed, looking up at the statue)* What!

CLEOPATRA This is only a dear little kitten of a Sphinx. Why, the great Sphinx is so big that it has a temple between its paws. This is my pet Sphinx. Tell me: do you think the Romans have any sorcerers who could take us away from the Sphinx by magic?

CÆSAR Why? Are you afraid of the Romans?

CLEOPATRA *(very seriously)* Oh, they would eat us if they caught us. They are barbarians. Their chief is called Julius Cæsar. His father was a tiger and his mother a burning mountain; and his nose is like an elephant's trunk. *(*CÆSAR *involuntarily rubs his nose.)* They all have long noses, and ivory tusks, and little tails, and seven arms with a hundred arrows in each; and they live on human flesh.

CÆSAR Would you like me to shew you a real Roman?

CLEOPATRA *(terrified)* No. You are frightening me.

CÆSAR No matter: this is only a dream—

CLEOPATRA *(excitedly)* It is not a dream: it is not a dream. See, see. *(She plucks a pin from her hair and jabs it repeatedly into his arm.)*

CÆSAR Ffff—Stop. *(wrathfully)* How dare you?

CLEOPATRA *(abashed)* You said you were dreaming. *(whimpering)* I only wanted to shew you—

CÆSAR *(gently)* Come, come: dont cry. A queen mustnt cry. *(He rubs his arm, wondering at the reality of the smart.)* Am I awake? *(He strikes his hand against the Sphinx to test its solidity. It feels so real that he begins to be alarmed, and says perplexedly)* Yes, I—*(quite panicstricken)* no: impossible: madness, madness! *(desperately)* Back to camp—to camp. *(He rises to spring down from the pedestal.)*

CLEOPATRA *(flinging her arms in terror round him)* No: you shant leave me. No, no, no: dont go. I'm afraid—afraid of the Romans.

CÆSAR *(as the conviction that he is really awake forces itself on him)* Cleopatra: can you see my face well?

CLEOPATRA Yes. It is so white in the moonlight.

CÆSAR Are you sure it is the moonlight that makes me look whiter than an Egyptian? *(grimly)* Do you notice that I have a rather long nose?

CLEOPATRA *(recoiling, paralysed by a terrible suspicion)* Oh!

CÆSAR It is a Roman nose, Cleopatra.

CLEOPATRA Ah! *(With a piercing scream she springs up; darts round the left shoulder of the Sphinx; scrambles down to the sand; and falls on her knees in frantic supplication, shrieking)* Bite him in two, Sphinx: bite him in two. I meant to sacrifice the white cat—I did indeed—I *(*CÆSAR, *who has slipped down from the pedestal, touches her on the shoulder)*—Ah! *(She buries her head in her arms.)*

CÆSAR Cleopatra: shall I teach you a way to prevent Cæsar from eating you?

CLEOPATRA *(clinging to him piteously)* Oh do, do, do. I will steal Ftatateeta's jewels and give them to you. I will make the river Nile water your lands twice a year.

CÆSAR Peace, peace, my child. Your gods are afraid of the Romans: you see the Sphinx dare not bite me, nor prevent me carrying you off to Julius Cæsar.

CLEOPATRA *(in pleading murmurings)* You won't, you won't. You said you wouldn't.

CÆSAR Cæsar never eats women.

CLEOPATRA *(springing up full of hope)* What!

CÆSAR *(impressively)* But he eats girls *(she relapses)* and cats. Now you are a silly little girl; and you are descended from the black kitten. You are both a girl and a cat.

CLEOPATRA *(trembling)* And will he eat *me?*

CÆSAR Yes; unless you make him believe that you are a woman.

CLEOPATRA Oh, you must get a sorcerer to make a woman of me. Are you a sorcerer?

CÆSAR Perhaps. But it will take a long time; and this very night you must stand face to face with Cæsar in the palace of your fathers.

CLEOPATRA No, no. I darent.

CÆSAR Whatever dread may be in your soul—however terrible Cæsar may be to you—you must confront him as a brave woman and a great queen; and you must feel no fear. If your hand shakes: if your voice quavers; then—night and death! *(She moans.)* But if he thinks you worthy to rule, he will set you on the throne by his side and make you the real ruler of Egypt.

CLEOPATRA *(despairingly)* No: he will find me out: he will find me out.

CÆSAR *(rather mournfully)* He is easily deceived by women. Their eyes dazzle him; and he sees them not as they are, but as he wishes them to appear to him.

CLEOPATRA *(hopefully)* Then we will cheat him. I will put on Ftatateeta's head-dress; and he will think me quite an old woman.

CÆSAR If you do that he will eat you at one mouthful.

CLEOPATRA But I will give him a cake with my magic opal and seven hairs of the white cat baked in it; and—

CÆSAR *(abruptly)* Pah! you are a little fool. He will eat your cake and you too. *(He turns contemptuously from her.)*

CLEOPATRA *(running after him and clinging to him)* Oh please, *please!* I will do whatever you tell me. I will be good. I will be your slave. *(Again the terrible bellowing note sounds across the desert, now closer at hand. It is the bucina, the Roman war trumpet.)*

CÆSAR Hark!

CLEOPATRA *(trembling)* What was that?

CÆSAR Cæsar's voice.

CLEOPATRA *(pulling at his hand)* Let us run away. Come. Oh, come.

CÆSAR You are safe with me until you stand on your throne to receive Cæsar. Now lead me thither.

CLEOPATRA *(only too glad to get away)* I will, I will. *(Again the bucina)* Oh come, come, come: the gods are angry. Do you feel the earth shaking?

CÆSAR It is the tread of Cæsar's legions.

CLEOPATRA *(drawing him away)* This way, quickly. And let us look for the white cat as we go. It is he that has turned you into a Roman.

CÆSAR Incorrigible, oh, incorrigible! Away! *(He follows her, the bucina sounding louder as they steal across the desert. The moonlight wanes: the horizon again shows black against the sky, broken only by the fantastic silhouette of the Sphinx. The sky itself vanishes in darkness, from which there is no relief until the gleam of a distant torch falls on great Egyptian pillars supporting the roof of a majestic corridor. At the further end of this corridor a* NUBIAN SLAVE *appears carrying the torch.* CÆSAR, *still led by* CLEOPATRA, *follows him. They come down the corridor,* CÆSAR *peering keenly about at the strange architecture, and at the pillar shadows between which, as the passing torch makes them hurry noiselessly backwards, figures of men with wings and hawks' heads, and vast black marble cats, seem to flit in and out of ambush. Further along, the wall turns a corner and makes a spacious transept in which* CÆSAR *sees, on his right, a throne, and behind the throne a door. On each side of the throne is a slender pillar with a lamp on it.)*

CÆSAR What place is this?

CLEOPATRA This is were I sit on the throne when I am allowed to wear my crown and robes. *(The slave holds his torch to shew the throne.)*

CÆSAR Order the slave to light the lamps.

CLEOPATRA *(shyly)* Do you think I may?

CÆSAR Of course. You are the Queen. *(She hesitates.)* Go on.

CLEOPATRA *(timidly, to the slave)* Light all the lamps.

FTATATEETA *(suddenly coming from behind the throne)* Stop. *(The slave stops. She turns sternly to* CLEOPATRA, *who quails like a naughty child.)* Who is this you have with you; and how dare you order the lamps to be lighted without my permission? *(*CLEOPATRA *is dumb with apprehension.)*

CÆSAR Who is she?

CLEOPATRA Ftatateeta.

FTATATEETA *(arrogantly)* Chief nurse to—

CÆSAR *(cutting her short)* I speak to the Queen. Be silent. *(to* CLEOPATRA*)* Is this how your servants know their places? Send her away; and you *(to the slave)* do as the Queen has bidden. *(The slave lights the lamps. Meanwhile* CLEOPATRA *stands hesitating, afraid of* FTATATEETA.*)* You are the Queen: send her away.

CLEOPATRA *(cajoling)* Ftatateeta, dear: you must go away—just for a little.

CÆSAR You are not commanding her to go away: you are begging her. You are no Queen. You will be eaten. Farewell. *(He turns to go.)*

CLEOPATRA *(clutching him)* No, no, no. Dont leave me.

CÆSAR A Roman does not stay with queens who are afraid of their slaves.

CLEOPATRA I am not afraid. Indeed I am not afraid.

FTATATEETA We shall see who is afraid here. *(menacingly)* Cleopatra—

CÆSAR On your knees, woman: am I also a child that you dare trifle with me? *(He points to the floor at* CLEOPATRA'S *feet.* FTATATEETA, *half cowed, half savage, hesitates.* CÆSAR *calls to the Nubian)* Slave. *(The*

NUBIAN *comes to him)* Can you cut off a head? *(The* NUBIAN *nods and grins ecstatically, showing all his teeth.* CÆSAR *takes his sword by the scabbard, ready to offer the hilt to the* NUBIAN, *and turns again to* FTATATEETA, *repeating his gesture.)* Have you remembered yourself, mistress?

*(*FTATATEETA, *crushed, kneels before* CLEOPATRA, *who can hardly believe her eyes.)*

FTATATEETA *(hoarsely)* O Queen, forget not thy servant in the days of thy greatness.

CLEOPATRA *(blazing with excitement)* Go. Begone. Go away. *(*FTATATEETA *rises with stooped head, and moves backwards towards the door.* CLEOPATRA *watches her submission eagerly, almost clapping her hands, which are trembling. Suddenly she cries)* Give me something to beat her with. *(She snatches a snake-skin from the throne and dashes after* FTATATEETA, *whirling it like a scourge in the air.* CÆSAR *makes a bound and manages to catch her and hold her while* FTATATEETA *escapes.)*

CÆSAR You scratch, kitten, do you?

CLEOPATRA *(breaking from him)* I will beat somebody. I will beat him. *(She attacks the slave.)* There, there, there! *(The slave flies for his life up the corridor and vanishes. She throws the snake-skin away and jumps on the step of the throne with her arms waving, crying)* I am a real Queen at last—a real, real Queen! Cleopatra the Queen! *(*CÆSAR *shakes his head dubiously, the advantage of the change seeming open to question from the point of view of the general welfare of Egypt. She turns and looks at him exultantly. Then she jumps down from the steps, runs to him, and flings her arms round him rapturously, crying)* Oh, I love you for making me a Queen.

CÆSAR But queens love only kings.

CLEOPATRA I will make all the men I love kings. I will make you a king. I will have many young kings, with round, strong arms; and when I am tired of them I will whip them to death; but you shall always be my king: my nice, kind, wise, good old king.

CÆSAR Oh, my wrinkles, my wrinkles! And my child's heart! You will be the most dangerous of all Cæsar's conquests.

CLEOPATRA *(appalled)* Cæsar! I forgot Cæsar. *(Anxiously)* You will tell him that I am a Queen, will you not?—a real Queen. Listen! *(stealthily coaxing him):* let us run away and hide until Cæsar is gone.

CÆSAR If you fear Cæsar, you are no true queen; and though you were to hide beneath a pyramid, he would go straight to it and lift it with one hand. And then—! *(he chops his teeth together.)*

CLEOPATRA *(trembling)* Oh!

CÆSAR Be afraid if you dare. *(The note of the bucina resounds again in the distance. She moans with fear.* CÆSAR *exults in it, exclaiming)* Aha! Cæsar approaches the throne of Cleopatra. Come: take your place. *(He takes her hand and leads her to the throne. She is too downcast to speak.)* Ho, there, Teetatota. How do you call your slaves?

CLEOPATRA *(spiritlessly, as she sinks on the throne and cowers there, shaking)* Clap your hands.

(He claps his hands. FTATATEETA *returns.)*

CÆSAR Bring the Queen's robes, and her crown, and her women; and prepare her.

CLEOPATRA *(eagerly—recovering herself a little)* Yes, the crown, Ftatateeta: I shall wear the crown.

FTATATEETA For whom must the Queen put on her state?

CÆSAR For a citizen of Rome. A king of kings, Totateeta.

CLEOPATRA *(stamping at her)* How dare you ask questions? Go and do as you are told. *(*FTATATEETA *goes out with a grim smile.* CLEOPATRA *goes on eagerly, to* CÆSAR*)* Cæsar will know that I am a Queen when he sees my crown and robes, will he not?

CÆSAR No. How shall he know that you are not a slave dressed up in the Queen's ornaments?

CLEOPATRA You must tell him.

CÆSAR He will not ask me. He will know Cleopatra by her pride, her courage, her majesty, and her beauty. *(She looks very doubtful.)* Are you trembling?

CLEOPATRA *(shivering with dread)* No, I—I—*(in a very sickly voice)* No.

*(*FTATATEETA *and three women come in with the regalia.)*

FTATATEETA Of all the Queen's women, these three alone are left. The rest are fled. *(They begin to deck* CLEOPATRA, *who submits, pale and motionless.)*

CÆSAR Good, good. Three are enough. Poor Cæsar generally has to dress himself.

FTATATEETA *(contemptuously)* The queen of Egypt is not a Roman barbarian. *(to* CLEOPATRA*)* Be brave, my nursling. Hold up your head before this stranger.

CÆSAR *(admiring* CLEOPATRA, *and placing the crown on her head)* Is it sweet or bitter to be a Queen, Cleopatra?

CLEOPATRA Bitter.

CÆSAR Cast out fear; and you will conquer Cæsar. Tota: are the Romans at hand?

FTATATEETA They are at hand; and the guard has fled.

THE WOMEN *(wailing subduedly)* Woe to us!

(The NUBIAN *comes running down the hall.)*

NUBIAN The Romans are in the courtyard. *(He bolts through the door. With a shriek, the women fly after him.* FTATATEETA'S *jaw expresses savage resolution: she does not budge.* CLEOPATRA *can hardly restrain herself from following them.* CÆSAR *grips her wrist, and looks steadfastly at her. She stands like a martyr.)*

CÆSAR The Queen must face Cæsar alone. Answer "So be it."

CLEOPATRA *(white)* So be it.

CÆSAR *(releasing her)* Good.

(A tramp and tumult of armed men is heard. CLEOPATRA'S *terror increases. The bucina sounds close at hand, followed by a formidable clangor of trumpets. This is too much for* CLEOPATRA: *she utters a cry and darts towards the door.* FTATATEETA *stops her ruthlessly.)*

FTATATEETA You are my nursling. You have said "So be it"; and if you die for it, you must make the Queen's word good. *(She hands* CLEOPATRA *to* CÆSAR, *who takes her back, almost beside herself with apprehension, to the throne.)*

CÆSAR Now, if you quail—! *(He seats himself on the throne.)*

(She stands on the step, all but unconscious, waiting for death. The Roman soldiers troop in tumultuously through the corridor, headed by their ensign with his eagle, and their bucinator, a burly fellow with his instrument coiled round his body, its brazen bell shaped like the head of a howling wolf. When they reach the transept, they stare in amazement at the throne; dress into ordered rank opposite it; draw their swords and lift them in the air with a shout of Hail, Cæsar, CLEOPATRA *turns and stares wildly at* CÆSAR; *grasps the situation; and, with a great sob of relief, falls into his arms.)*

act II

Alexandria. A hall on the first floor of the Palace, ending in a loggia approached by two steps. Through the arches of the loggia the Mediterranean can be seen, bright in the morning sun. The clean lofty walls, painted with a procession of the Egyptian theocracy, presented in profile as flat ornament, and the absence of mirrors, sham perspectives, stuffy upholstery and textiles, make the place handsome, wholesome, simple and cool, or, as a rich English manufacturer would express it, poor, bare, ridiculous and unhomely. For Tottenham Court Road civilization is to this Egyptain civilization as glass bead and tattoo civilization is to Tottenham Court Road.[4]

The young king PTOLEMY DIONYSUS *(aged ten) is at the top of the steps, on his way in through the loggia, led by his guardian* POTHINUS, *who has him by the hand. The court is assembled to receive him. It is made up of men and women (some of the women being officials) of various complexions and races, mostly Egyptian; some of them, comparatively fair, from lower Egypt, some, much darker, from upper Egypt; with a few Greeks and Jews. Prominent in a group on* PTOLEMY'S *right hand is* THEODOTUS, PTOLEMY'S *tutor. Another group, on* PTOLEMY'S *left, is headed by* ACHILLAS, *the general of Ptolemy's troops.* THEODOTUS *is a little old man, whose features are as cramped and wizened as his limbs, except his tall straight forehead, which occupies more space than all the rest of his face. He maintains an air of magpie keenness and profundity, listening to what the others say with the sarcastic vigilance of a philosopher listening to the exercises of his disciples.* ACHILLAS *is a tall handsome man of thirty-five, with a fine black beard curled like the coat of a poodle. Apparently not a clever man, but distinguished and dignified.* POTHINUS *is a vigorous man of fifty, a eunuch, passionate, energetic and quick witted, but of common mind and character; impatient and unable to control his temper.*

[4]This commercial London street is here used to signify European civilization in Shaw's day.

He has fine tawny hair, like fur. PTOLEMY, *the King, looks much older than an English boy of ten; but he has the childish air, the habit of being in leading strings, the mixture of impotence and petulance, the appearance of being excessively washed, combed and dressed by other hands, which is exhibited by court-bred princes of all ages.*

All receive the king with reverences. He comes down the steps to a chair of state which stands a little to his right, the only seat in the hall. Taking his place before it, he looks nervously for instructions to POTHINUS, *who places himself at his left hand.*

POTHINUS The king of Egypt has a word to speak.

THEODOTUS *(in a squeak which he makes impressive by sheer self-opinionativeness)* Peace for the King's word!

PTOLEMY *(without any vocal inflexions: he is evidently repeating a lesson)* Take notice of this all of you. I am the first-born son of Auletes the Flute Blower who was your King. My sister Berenice drove him from his throne and reigned in his stead but—but—*(he hesitates)*—

POTHINUS *(stealthily prompting)*—but the gods would not suffer—

PTOLEMY Yes—the gods would not suffer—not suffer— *(He stops; then, crestfallen)* I forget what the gods would not suffer.

THEODOTUS Let Pothinus, the King's guardian, speak for the King.

POTHINUS *(suppressing his impatience with difficulty)* The King wished to say that the gods would not suffer the impiety of his sister to go unpunished.

PTOLEMY *(hastily)* Yes: I remember the rest of it. *(He resumes his monotone.)* Therefore the gods sent a stranger one Mark Antony a Roman captain of horsemen across the sands of the desert and he set my father again upon the throne. And my father took Berenice my sister and struck her head off. And now that my father is dead yet another of his daughters my sister Cleopatra would snatch the kingdom from me and reign in my place. But the gods would not suffer—*(*POTHINUS *coughs admonitorily)*—the gods—the gods would not suffer—

POTHINUS *(prompting)*—will not maintain—

PTOLEMY Oh yes—will not maintain such iniquity they will give her head to the axe even as her sister's. But with the help of the witch Ftatateeta she hath cast a spell on the Roman Julius Cæsar to make him uphold her false pretence to rule in Egypt. Take notice then that I will not suffer—that I will not suffer—*(pettishly, to* POTHINUS*)* What is it that I will not suffer?

POTHINUS *(suddenly exploding with all the force and emphasis of political passion)* The King will not suffer a foreigner to take from him the throne of our Egypt. *(A shout of applause)* Tell the King, Achillas, how many soldiers and horsemen follow the Roman?

THEODOTUS Let the King's general speak!

ACHILLAS But two Roman legions, O King. Three thousand soldiers and scarce a thousand horsemen.

(The court breaks into derisive laughter; and a great chattering begins, amid which RUFIO, *a Roman officer, appears in the loggia. He is a*

burly, black-bearded man of middle age, very blunt, prompt and rough, with small clear eyes, and plump nose and cheeks, which, however, like the rest of his flesh, are in ironhard condition.)

RUFIO *(from the steps)* Peace, ho! *(The laughter and chatter cease abruptly.)* Cæsar approaches.

THEODOTUS *(with much presence of mind)* The King permits the Roman commander to enter!

*(*CÆSAR, *plainly dressed, but wearing an oak wreath to conceal his baldness, enters from the loggia, attended by* BRITANNUS, *his secretary, a Briton, about forty, tall, solemn, and already slightly bald, with a heavy, drooping, hazel-colored moustache trained so as to lose its ends in a pair of trim whiskers. He is carefully dressed in blue, with portfolio, inkhorn, and reed pen at his girdle. His serious air and sense of the importance of the business in hand is in marked contrast to the kindly interest of* CÆSAR, *who looks at the scene, which is new to him, with the frank curiosity of a child, and then turns to the king's chair:* BRITANNUS *and* RUFIO *posting themselves near the steps at the other side.)*

CÆSAR *(looking at* POTHINUS *and* PTOLEMY*)* Which is the King? the man or the boy?

POTHINUS I am Pothinus, the guardian of my lord the King.

CÆSAR *(patting* PTOLEMY *kindly on the shoulder)* So you are the King. Dull work at your age, eh? *(to* POTHINUS*)* Your servant, Pothinus. *(He turns away unconcernedly and comes slowly along the middle of the hall, looking from side to side at the courtiers until he reaches* ACHILLAS.*)* And this gentleman?

THEODOTUS Achillas, the King's general.

CÆSAR *(to* ACHILLAS, *very friendly)* A general, eh? I am a general myself. But I began too old, too old. Health and many victories, Achillas!

ACHILLAS As the gods will, Cæsar.

CÆSAR *(turning to* THEODOTUS*)* And you, sir, are—?

THEODOTUS Theodotus, the King's tutor.

CÆSAR You teach men how to be kings, Theodotus. That is very clever of you. *(Looking at the gods on the walls as he turns away from* THEODOTUS *and goes up again to* POTHINUS*)* And this place?

POTHINUS The council chamber of the chancellors of the King's treasury, Cæsar.

CÆSAR Ah! that reminds me. I want some money.

POTHINUS The King's treasury is poor, Cæsar.

CÆSAR Yes: I notice that there is but one chair in it.

RUFIO *(shouting gruffly)* Bring a chair there, some of you, for Cæsar.

PTOLEMY *(rising shyly to offer his chair)* Cæsar—

CÆSAR *(kindly)* No, no, my boy: that is your chair of state. Sit down.

(He makes PTOLEMY *sit down again. Meanwhile* RUFIO, *looking about him, sees in the nearest corner an image of the god Ra, represented as a seated man with the head of a hawk. Before the image is a bronze tripod, about as large as a three-legged stool, with a stick of incense burning on it.* RUFIO, *with Roman resourcefulness and indifference to*

foreign superstitions, promptly seizes the tripod; shakes off the incense; blows away the ash; and dumps it down behind CÆSAR, *nearly in the middle of the hall.*

RUFIO Sit on that, Cæsar.

(A shiver runs through the court, followed by a hissing whisper of Sacrilege!*)*

CÆSAR *(seating himself)* Now, Pothinus, to business. I am badly in want of money.

BRITANNUS *(disapproving of these informal expressions)* My master would say that there is a lawful debt due to Rome by Egypt, contracted by the King's deceased father to the Triumvirate; and that it is Cæsar's duty to his country to require immediate payment.

CÆSAR *(blandly)* Ah, I forgot. I have not made my companions known here. Pothinus: this is Britannus, my secretary. He is an islander from the western end of the world, a day's voyage from Gaul. *(*BRITANNUS *bows stiffly.)* This gentleman is Rufio, my comrade in arms. *(*RUFIO *nods.)* Pothinus: I want 1,600 talents.

(The courtiers, appalled, murmur loudly, and THEODOTUS *and* ACHILLAS *appeal mutely to one another against so monstrous a demand.)*

POTHINUS *(aghast)* Forty million sesterces! Impossible. There is not so much money in the King's treasury.

CÆSAR *(encouragingly)* Only sixteen hundred talents, Pothinus. Why count it in sesterces? A sestertius is only worth a loaf of bread.

POTHINUS And a talent is worth a racehorse. I say it is impossible. We have been at strife here, because the King's sister Cleopatra falsely claims his throne. The King's taxes have not been collected for a whole year.

CÆSAR Yes they have, Pothinus. My officers have been collecting them all morning. *(Renewed whisper and sensation, not without some stifled laughter, among the courtiers.)*

RUFIO *(bluntly)* You must pay, Pothinus. Why waste words? You are getting off cheaply enough.

POTHINUS *(bitterly)* Is it possible that Cæsar, the conqueror of the world, has time to occupy himself with such a trifle as our taxes?

CÆSAR My friend: taxes are the chief business of a conqueror of the world.

POTHINUS Then take warning, Cæsar. This day, the treasures of the temple and the gold of the King's treasury shall be sent to the mint to be melted down for our ransom in the sight of the people. They shall see us sitting under bare walls and drinking from wooden cups. And their wrath be on your head, Cæsar, if you force us to this sacrilege!

CÆSAR Do not fear, Pothinus: the people know how well wine tastes in wooden cups. In return for your bounty, I will settle this dispute about the throne for you, if you will. What say you?

POTHINUS If I say no, will that hinder you?

RUFIO *(defiantly)* No.

CÆSAR You say the matter has been at issue for a year, Pothinus. May I have ten minutes at it?

POTHINUS You will do your pleasure, doubtless.

CÆSAR Good! But first, let us have Cleopatra here.

THEODOTUS She is not in Alexandria: she is fled into Syria.

CÆSAR I think not. *(To* RUFIO*)* Call Totateeta.

RUFIO *(Calling)* Ho there, Teetatota.

*(*FTATATEETA *enters the loggia, and stands arrogantly at the top of the steps.)*

FTATATEETA Who pronounces the name of Ftatateeta, the Queen's chief nurse?

CÆSAR Nobody can pronounce it, Tota, except yourself. Where is your mistress?

*(*CLEOPATRA, *who is hiding behind* FTATATEETA, *peeps out at them laughing.* CÆSAR *rises.)*

CÆSAR Will the Queen favor us with her presence for a moment?

CLEOPATRA *(pushing* FTATATEETA *aside and standing haughtily on the brink of the steps)* Am I to behave like a Queen?

CÆSAR Yes.

*(*CLEOPATRA *immediately comes down to the chair of state; seizes* PTOLEMY; *drags him out of his seat; then takes his place in the chair.* FTATATEETA *seats herself on the step of the loggia, and sits there, watching the scene with sibylline intensity.)*

PTOLEMY *(mortified, and struggling with his tears)* Cæsar: this is how she treats me always. If I am a king why is she allowed to take everything from me?

CLEOPATRA You are not to be King, you little cry-baby. You are to be eaten by the Romans.

CÆSAR *(touched by* PTOLEMY'S *distress)* Come here, my boy, and stand by me.

*(*PTOLEMY *goes over to* CÆSAR, *who, resuming his seat on the tripod, takes the boy's hand to encourage him.* CLEOPATRA, *furiously jealous, rises and glares at them.*

CLEOPATRA *(with flaming cheeks)* Take your throne: I dont want it. *(She flings away from the chair, and approaches* PTOLEMY, *who shrinks from her.)* Go this instant and sit down in your place.

CÆSAR Go, Ptolemy. Always take a throne when it is offered to you.

RUFIO I hope you will have the good sense to follow your own advice when we return to Rome, Cæsar.

*(*PTOLEMY *slowly goes back to the throne, giving* CLEOPATRA *a wide berth, in evident fear of her hands. She takes his place beside* CÆSAR.*)*

CÆSAR Pothinus—

CLEOPATRA *(interrupting him)* Are you not going to speak to me?

CÆSAR Be quiet. Open your mouth again before I give you leave; and you shall be eaten.

CLEOPATRA I am not afraid. A queen must not be afraid. Eat my husband there, if you like: he is afraid.

CÆSAR *(starting)* Your husband! What do you mean?

CLEOPATRA *(pointing to* PTOLEMY*)* That little thing.

(The two Romans and the Briton stare at one another in amazement.)

THEODOTUS Cæsar: you are a stranger here, and not conversant with our laws. The kings and queens of Egypt may not marry except with their own royal blood. Ptolemy and Cleopatra are born king and consort just as they are born brother and sister.

BRITANNUS *(shocked)* Cæsar: this is not proper.

THEODOTUS *(outraged)* How!

CÆSAR *(recovering his self-possession)* Pardon him, Theodotus: he is a barbarian, and thinks that the customs of his tribe and island are the laws of nature.

BRITANNUS On the contrary, Cæsar, it is these Egyptians who are barbarians; and you do wrong to encourage them. I say it is a scandal.

CÆSAR Scandal or not, my friend, it opens the gate of peace. *(He addresses* POTHINUS *seriously.)* Pothinus: hear what I propose.

RUFIO Hear Cæsar there.

CÆSAR Ptolemy and Cleopatra shall reign jointly in Egypt.

ACHILLAS What of the King's younger brother and Cleopatra's younger sister?

RUFIO *(explaining)* There is another little Ptolemy, Cæsar: so they tell me.

CÆSAR Well, the little Ptolemy can marry the other sister; and we will make them both a present of Cyprus.

POTHINUS *(impatiently)* Cyprus is of no use to anybody.

CÆSAR No matter: you shall have it for the sake of peace.

BRITANNUS *(unconsciously anticipating a later statesman)* Peace with honor, Pothinus.

POTHINUS *(mutinously)* Cæsar: be honest. The money you demand is the price of our freedom. Take it; and leave us to settle our own affairs.

THE BOLDER COURTIERS *(encouraged by* POTHINUS'S *tone and* CÆSAR'S *quietness)* Yes, yes. Egypt for the Egyptians!

(The conference now becomes an altercation, the Egyptians becoming more and more heated. CÆSAR *remains unruffled; but* RUFIO *grows fiercer and doggeder, and* BRITANNUS *haughtily indignant.)*

RUFIO *(contemptuously)* Egypt for the Egyptians! Do you forget that there is a Roman army of occupation here, left by Aulus Gabinius[5] when he set up your toy king for you?

ACHILLAS *(suddenly asserting himself)* And now under my command. *I* am the Roman general here, Cæsar.

CÆSAR *(tickled by the humor of the situation)* And also the Egyptian general, eh?

POTHINUS *(triumphantly)* That is so, Cæsar.

CÆSAR *(to* ACHILLAS*)* So you can make war on the Egyptians in the name of Rome, and on the Romans—on me, if necessary—in the name of Egypt?

ACHILLAS That is so, Cæsar.

CÆSAR And which side are you on at present, if I may presume to ask,

[5]Roman general and statesman who restored Ptolemy XI (Cleopatra's father) to the throne of Egypt.

general?

ACHILLAS On the side of the right and of the gods.

CÆSAR Hm! How many men have you?

ACHILLAS That will appear when I take the field.

RUFIO *(truculently)* Are your men Romans? If not, it matters not how many there are, provided you are no stronger than 500 to ten.

POTHINUS It is useless to try to bluff us, Rufio. Cæsar has been defeated before and may be defeated again. A few weeks ago Cæsar was flying for his life before Pompey: a few months hence he may be flying for his life before Cato and Juba of Numidia, the African King.

ACHILLAS *(following up* POTHINUS'S *speech menacingly)* What can you do with 4,000 men?

THEODOTUS *(following up* ACHILLAS'S *speech with a raucous squeak)* And without money? Away with you.

ALL THE COURTIERS *(shouting fiercely and crowding towards* CÆSAR*)* Away with you. Egypt for the Egyptians! Begone.

*(*RUFIO *bites his beard, too angry to speak.* CÆSAR *sits as comfortably as if he were at breakfast, and the cat were clamoring for a piece of Finnan-haddie.)*

CLEOPATRA Why do you let them talk to you like that, Cæsar? Are you afraid?

CÆSAR Why, my dear, what they say is quite true.

CLEOPATRA But if you go away, I shall not be Queen.

CÆSAR I shall not go away until you are Queen.

POTHINUS Achillas: if you are not a fool, you will take that girl whilst she is under your hand.

RUFIO *(daring them)* Why not take Cæsar as well, Achillas?

POTHINUS *(retorting the defiance with interest)* Well said, Rufio. Why not?

RUFIO Try, Achillas. *(Calling)* Guard there.

(The loggia immediately fills with CÆSAR'S *soldiers, who stand, sword in hand, at the top of the steps, waiting the word to charge from their centurion, who carries a cudgel. For a moment the Egyptians face them proudly: then they retire sullenly to their former places.)*

BRITANNUS You are Cæsar's prisoners, all of you.

CÆSAR *(benevolently)* Oh no, no, no. By no means. Cæsar's guests, gentlemen.

CLEOPATRA Won't you cut their heads off?

CÆSAR What! Cut off your brother's head?

CLEOPATRA Why not? He would cut off mine, if he got the chance. Wouldn't you, Ptolemy?

PTOLEMY *(pale and obstinate)* I would. I will, too, when I grow up.

*(*CLEOPATRA *is rent by a struggle between her newly-acquired dignity as a queen, and a strong impulse to put out her tongue at him. She takes no part in the scene which follows, but watches it with curiosity and wonder, fidgeting with the restlessness of a child, and sitting down on* CÆSAR'S *tripod when he rises.*

POTHINUS Cæsar: if you attempt to detain us–

RUFIO He will succeed, Egyptian: make up your mind to that. We hold the palace, the beach, and the eastern harbor. The road to Rome is open; and you shall travel it if Cæsar chooses.

CÆSAR *(courteously)* I could do no less, Pothinus, to secure the retreat of my own soldiers. I am accountable for every life among them. But you are free to go. So are all here, and in the palace.

RUFIO *(aghast at this clemency)* What! Renegades and all?

CÆSAR *(softening the expression)* Roman army of occupation and all, Rufio.

POTHINUS *(bewildered)* But—but—but—

CÆSAR Well, my friend?

POTHINUS You are turning us out of our own palace into the streets; and you tell us with a grand air that we are free to go! It is for you to go.

CÆSAR Your friends are in the street, Pothinus. You will be safer there.

POTHINUS This is a trick. I am the king's guardian: I refuse to stir. I stand on my right here. Where is your right?

CÆSAR It is in Rufio's scabbard, Pothinus. I may not be able to keep it there if you wait too long.
(sensation)

POTHINUS *(bitterly)* And this is Roman justice!

THEODOTUS But not Roman gratitude, I hope.

CÆSAR Gratitude! Am I in your debt for any service, gentlemen?

THEODOTUS Is Cæsar's life of so little account to him that he forgets that we have saved it?

CÆSAR My life! Is that all?

THEODOTUS Your life. Your laurels. Your future.

POTHINUS It is true. I can call a witness to prove that but for us, the Roman army of occupation, led by the greatest soldier in the world, would now have Cæsar at its mercy. *(Calling through the loggia)* Ho, there, Lucius Septimius (CÆSAR *starts, deeply moved)*: if my voice can reach you, come forth and testify before Cæsar.

CÆSAR *(shrinking)* No, no.

THEODOTUS Yes, I say. Let the military tribune bear witness.
(LUCIUS SEPTIMIUS, *a clean shaven, trim athlete of about 40, with symmetrical features, resolute mouth, and handsome, thin Roman nose, in the dress of a Roman officer, comes in through the loggia and confronts* CÆSAR, *who hides his face with his robe for a moment; then, mastering himself, drops it, and confronts the tribune with dignity.)*

POTHINUS Bear witness, Lucius Septimius. Cæsar came hither in pursuit of his foe. Did we shelter his foe?

LUCIUS As Pompey's foot touched the Egyptian shore, his head fell by the stroke of my sword.

THEODOTUS *(with viperish relish)* Under the eyes of his wife and child! Remember that, Cæsar! They saw it from the ship he had just left. We have given you a full and sweet measure of vengeance.

CÆSAR *(with horror)* Vengeance!

POTHINUS Our first gift to you, as your galley came into the roadstead, was the head of your rival for the empire of the world. Bear witness,

Lucius Septimius: is it not so?

LUCIUS It is so. With this hand, that slew Pompey, I placed his head at the feet of Cæsar.

CÆSAR Murderer! So would you have slain Cæsar, had Pompey been victorious at Pharsalia.

LUCIUS Woe to the vanquished, Cæsar! When I served Pompey, I slew as good men as he, only because he conquered them. His turn came at last.

THEODOTUS *(flatteringly)* The deed was not yours, Cæsar, but ours—nay, mine; for it was done by my counsel. Thanks to us, you keep your reputation for clemency, and have your vengeance too.

CÆSAR Vengeance! Vengeance!! Oh, if I could stoop to vengeance, what would I not exact from you as the price of this murdered man's blood? *(They shrink back, appalled and disconcerted.)* Was he not my son-in-law, my ancient friend, for 20 years the master of great Rome, for 30 years the compeller of victory? Did not I, as a Roman, share his glory? Was the Fate that forced us to fight for the mastery of the world, of our making? Am I Julius Cæsar, or am I a wolf, that you fling to me the grey head of the old soldier, the laurelled conqueror, the mighty Roman, treacherously struck down by this callous ruffian, and then claim my gratitude for it! *(to* LUCIUS SEPTIMIUS*)* Begone: you fill me with horror.

LUCIUS *(cold and undaunted)* Pshaw! You have seen severed heads before, Cæsar, and severed right hands too, I think; some thousands of them, in Gaul, after you vanquished Vercingetorix. Did you spare him, with all your clemency? Was that vengeance?

CÆSAR No, by the gods! would that it had been! Vengeance at least is human. No, I say: those severed right hands, and the brave Vercingetorix basely strangled in a vault beneath the Capitol, were *(with shuddering satire)* a wise severity, a necessary protection to the commonwealth, a duty of statesmanship—follies and fictions ten times bloodier than honest vengeance! What a fool was I then! To think that men's lives should be at the mercy of such fools! *(Humbly)* Lucius Septimius, pardon me: why should the slayer of Vercingetorix rebuke the slayer of Pompey? You are free to go with the rest. Or stay if you will: I will find a place for you in my service.

LUCIUS The odds are against you, Cæsar. I go. *(He turns to go out through the loggia.)*

RUFIO *(full of wrath at seeing his prey escaping)* That means that he is a Republican.

LUCIUS *(turning defiantly on the loggia steps)* And what are you?

RUFIO A Cæsarian, like all Cæsar's soldiers.

CÆSAR *(courteously)* Lucius: believe me, Cæsar is no Cæsarian. Were Rome a true republic, then were Cæsar the first of Republicans. But you have made your choice. Farewell.

LUCIUS Farewell. Come, Achillas, whilst there is yet time.

*(*CÆSAR*, seeing that* RUFIO'S *temper threatens to get the worse of him, puts his hand on his shoulder and brings him down the hall out of*

harm's way, BRITANNUS *accompanying them and posting himself on* CÆSAR'S *right hand. This movement brings the three in a little group to the place occupied by* ACHILLAS, *who moves haughtily away and joins* THEODOTUS *on the other side.* LUCIUS SEPTIMIUS *goes out through the soldiers in the loggia.* POTHINUS, THEODOTUS *and* ACHILLAS *follow him with the courtiers, very mistrustful of the soldiers, who close up in their rear and go out after them, keeping them moving without much ceremony. The King is left in his chair, piteous, obstinate, with twitching face and fingers. During these movements* RUFIO *maintains an energetic grumbling, as follows:)*—

RUFIO *(as* LUCIUS *departs)* Do you suppose he would let us go if he had our heads in his hands?

CÆSAR I have no right to suppose that his ways are any baser than mine.

RUFIO Psha!

CÆSAR Rufio: if I take Lucius Septimius for my model, and become exactly like him, ceasing to be Cæsar, will you serve me still?

BRITANNUS Cæsar: this is not good sense. Your duty to Rome demands that her enemies should be prevented from doing further mischief. *(*CÆSAR, *whose delight in the moral eye-to-business of his British secretary is inexhaustible, smiles indulgently.)*

RUFIO It is no use talking to him, Britannus: you may save your breath to cool your porridge. But mark this, Cæsar. Clemency is very well for you; but what is it for your soldiers, who have to fight tomorrow the men you spared yesterday? You may give what orders you please; but I tell you that your next victory will be a massacre, thanks to your clemency. *I*, for one, will take no prisoners. I will kill my enemies in the field; and then you can preach as much clemency as you please: I shall never have to fight them again. And now, with your leave, I will see these gentry off the premises. *(He turns to go.)*

CÆSAR *(turning also and seeing* PTOLEMY*)* What! have they left the boy alone! Oh shame, shame!

RUFIO *(taking* PTOLEMY'S *hand and making him rise)* Come, your majesty!

PTOLEMY *(to* CÆSAR, *drawing away his hand from* RUFIO*)* Is he turning me out of my palace?

RUFIO *(grimly)* You are welcome to stay if you wish.

CÆSAR *(kindly)* Go, my boy. I will not harm you; but you will be safer away, among your friends. Here you are in the lion's mouth.

PTOLEMY *(turning to go)* It is not the lion I fear, but *(looking at* RUFIO*)* the jackal. *(He goes out through the loggia.)*

CÆSAR *(laughing approvingly)* Brave boy!

CLEOPATRA *(jealous of* CÆSAR'S *approbation, calling after* PTOLEMY*)* Little silly. You think that very clever.

CÆSAR Britannus: attend the King. Give him in charge to that Pothinus fellow. *(*BRITANNUS *goes out after* PTOLEMY.*)*

RUFIO *(pointing to* CLEOPATRA*)* And this piece of goods? What is to be done with her? However, I suppose I may leave that to you. *(He goes out through the loggia.)*

CLEOPATRA *(flushing suddenly and turning on* CÆSAR*)* Did you mean me to go with the rest?

CÆSAR *(a little preoccupied, goes with a sigh to* PTOLEMY'S *chair, whilst she waits for his answer with red cheeks and clenched fist)* You are free to do just as you please, Cleopatra.

CLEOPATRA Then you do not care whether I stay or not?

CÆSAR *(smiling)* Of course I had rather you stayed.

CLEOPATRA Much, much rather?

CÆSAR *(nodding)* Much, much rather.

CLEOPATRA Then I consent to stay, because I am asked. But I do not want to, mind.

CÆSAR That is quite understood. *(Calling)* Totateeta.

*(*FTATATEETA, *still seated, turns her eyes on him with a sinister expression, but does not move.)*

CLEOPATRA *(with a splutter of laughter)* Her name is not Totateeta: it is Ftatateeta. *(Calling)* Ftatateeta. *(*FTATATEETA *instantly rises and comes to* CLEOPATRA.*)*

CÆSAR *(stumbling over the name)* Tfatafeeta will forgive the erring tongue of a Roman. Tota: the Queen will hold her state here in Alexandria. Engage women to attend upon her; and do all that is needful.

FTATATEETA Am I then the mistress of the Queen's household?

CLEOPATRA *(sharply)* No: *I* am the mistress of the Queen's household. Go and do as you are told, or I will have you thrown into the Nile this very afternoon, to poison the poor crocodiles.

CÆSAR *(shocked)* Oh no, no.

CLEOPATRA Oh yes, yes. You are very sentimental, Cæsar; but you are clever; and if you do as I tell you, you will soon learn to govern.

*(*CÆSAR, *quite dumbfounded by this impertinence, turns in his chair and stares at her.* FTATATEETA, *smiling grimly, and showing a splendid set of teeth, goes, leaving them alone together.)*

CÆSAR Cleopatra: I really think I must eat you, after all.

CLEOPATRA *(kneeling beside him and looking at him with eager interest, half real, half affected to shew how intelligent she is)* You must not talk to me now as if I were a child.

CÆSAR You have been growing up since the sphinx introduced us the other night; and you think you know more than I do already.

CLEOPATRA *(taken down, and anxious to justify herself)* No: that would be very silly of me: of course I know that. But— *(suddenly)* are you angry with me?

CÆSAR No.

CLEOPATRA *(only half believing him)* Then why are you so thoughtful?

CÆSAR *(rising)* I have work to do, Cleopatra.

CLEOPATRA *(drawing back)* Work! *(Offended)* You are tired of talking to me; and that is your excuse to get away from me.

CÆSAR *(sitting down again to appease her)* Well, well: another minute. But then—work!

CLEOPATRA Work! what nonsense! You must remember that you are a king now: I have made you one. Kings don't work.

CÆSAR Oh! Who told you that, little kitten? Eh?

CLEOPATRA My father was King of Egypt; and he never worked. But he was a great king, and cut off my sister's head because she rebelled against him and took the throne from him.

CÆSAR Well; and how did he get his throne back again?

CLEOPATRA *(eagerly, her eyes lighting up)* I will tell you. A beautiful young man, with strong round arms, came over the desert with many horsemen, and slew my sister's husband and gave my father back his throne. *(Wistfully)* I was only twelve then. Oh, I wish he would come again, now that I am queen. I would make him my husband.

CÆSAR It might be managed, perhaps; for it was I who sent that beautiful young man to help your father.

CLEOPATRA *(enraptured)* You know him!

CÆSAR *(nodding)* I do.

CLEOPATRA Has he come with you? *(*CÆSAR *shakes his head: she is cruelly disappointed.)* Oh, I wish he had, I wish he had. If only I were a little older; so that he might not think me a mere kitten, as you do! But perhaps that is because you are old. He is many many years younger than you, is he not?

CÆSAR *(as if swallowing a pill)* He is somewhat younger.

CLEOPATRA Would he be my husband, do you think, if I asked him?

CÆSAR Very likely.

CLEOPATRA But I should not like to ask him. Could you not persuade him to ask me—without knowing that I wanted him to?

CÆSAR *(touched by her innocence of the beautiful young man's character)* My poor child!

CLEOPATRA Why do you say that as if you were sorry for me? Does he love anyone else?

CÆSAR I am afraid so.

CLEOPATRA *(tearfully)* Then I shall not be his first love.

CÆSAR Not quite the first. He is greatly admired by women.

CLEOPATRA I wish I could be the first. But if he loves me, I will make him kill all the rest. Tell me: is he still beautiful? Do his strong arms shine in the sun like marble?

CÆSAR He is in excellent condition—considering how much he eats and drinks.

CLEOPATRA Oh, you must not say common, earthly things about him; for I love him. He is a god.

CÆSAR He is a great captain of horsemen, and swifter of foot than any other Roman.

CLEOPATRA What is his real name?

CÆSAR *(puzzled)* His real name?

CLEOPATRA Yes. I always call him Horus, because Horus is the most beautiful of our gods. But I want to know his real name.

CÆSAR His name is Mark Antony.

CLEOPATRA *(musically)* Mark Antony, Mark Antony, Mark Antony! What a beautiful name! *(She throws her arms round* CÆSAR'S *neck.)* Oh, how I love you for sending him to help my father! Did you love my father very much?

CÆSAR No, my child; but your father, as you say, never worked. I always work. So when he lost his crown he had to promise me 16,000 talents to get it back for him.

CLEOPATRA Did he ever pay you?

CÆSAR Not in full.

CLEOPATRA He was quite right: it was too dear. The whole world is not worth 16,000 talents.

CÆSAR That is perhaps true, Cleopatra. Those Egyptians who work paid as much of it as he could drag from them. The rest is still due. But as I most likely shall not get it, I must go back to my work. So you must run away for a little and send my secretary to me.

CLEOPATRA *(coaxing)* No: I want to stay and hear you talk about Mark Antony.

CÆSAR But if I do not get to work, Pothinus and the rest of them will cut us off from the harbor; and then the way from Rome will be blocked.

CLEOPATRA No matter: I dont want you to go back to Rome.

CÆSAR But you want Mark Antony to come from it.

CLEOPATRA *(springing up)* Oh yes, yes, yes: I forgot. Go quickly and work, Cæsar; and keep the way over the sea open for my Mark Antony. *(She runs out through the loggia, kissing her hand to Mark Antony across the sea.)*

CÆSAR *(going briskly up the middle of the hall to the loggia steps)* Ho, Britannus. *(He is startled by the entry of a wounded Roman soldier, who confronts him from the upper step.)* What now?

SOLDIER *(pointing to his bandaged head)* This, Cæsar; and two of my comrades killed in the market place.

CÆSAR *(quiet, but attending)* Ay. Why?

SOLDIER There is an army come to Alexandria, calling itself the Roman army.

CÆSAR The Roman army of occupation. Ay?

SOLDIER Commanded by one Achillas.

CÆSAR Well?

SOLDIER The citizens rose against us when the army entered the gates. I was with two others in the market place when the news came. They set upon us. I cut my way out; and here I am.

CÆSAR Good. I am glad to see you alive. *(*RUFIO *enters the loggia hastily, passing behind the soldier to look out through one of the arches at the quay beneath.)* Rufio: we are besieged.

RUFIO What! Already?

CÆSAR Now or tomorrow: what does it matter? We shall be besieged. *(*BRITANNUS *runs in.)*

BRITANNUS Cæsar—

CÆSAR *(anticipating him)* Yes: I know. *(*RUFIO *and* BRITANNUS *come down the hall from the loggia at opposite sides, past* CÆSAR, *who waits for a moment near the step to say to the soldier)* Comrade: give the word to turn out on the beach and stand by the boats. Get your wound attended to. Go. *(The soldier hurries out.* CÆSAR *comes down the hall between* RUFIO *and* BRITANNUS*)* Rufio: we have some ships in the west harbor. Burn them.

RUFIO *(staring)* Burn them!!

CÆSAR Take every boat we have in the east harbor, and seize the Pharos —that island with the lighthouse. Leave half our men behind to hold the beach and the quay outside this palace: that is the way home.

RUFIO *(disapproving strongly)* Are we to give up the city?

CÆSAR We have not got it, Rufio. This palace we have; and—what is that building next door?

RUFIO The theatre.

CÆSAR We will have that too: it commands the strand. For the rest, Egypt for the Egyptians!

RUFIO Well, you know best, I suppose. Is that all?

CÆSAR That is all. Are those ships burnt yet?

RUFIO Be easy: I shall waste no more time. *(He runs out.)*

BRITANNUS Cæsar: Pothinus demands speech of you. In my opinion he needs a lesson. His manner is most insolent.

CÆSAR Where is he?

BRITANNUS He waits without.

CÆSAR Ho there! admit Pothinus.

(Pothinus appears in the loggia, and comes down the hall very haughtily to CÆSAR'S *left hand.)*

CÆSAR Well, Pothinus?

POTHINUS I have brought you our ultimatum, Cæsar.

CÆSAR Ultimatum! The door was open: you should have gone out through it before you declared war. You are my prisoner now. *(He goes to the chair and loosens his toga.)*

POTHINUS *(scornfully)* I *your* prisoner! Do you know that you are in Alexandria, and that King Ptolemy, with an army outnumbering your little troop a hundred to one, is in possession of Alexandria?

CÆSAR *(unconcernedly taking off his toga and throwing it on the chair)* Well, my friend, get out if you can. And tell your friends not to kill any more Romans in the market place. Otherwise my soldiers, who do not share my celebrated clemency, will probably kill you. Britannus: pass the word to the guard; and fetch my armor. (BRITANNUS *runs out.* RUFIO *returns.)* Well?

RUFIO *(pointing from the loggia to a cloud of smoke drifting over the harbor)* See there! (POTHINUS *runs eagerly up the steps to look out.)*

CÆSAR What, ablaze already! Impossible!

RUFIO Yes, five good ships, and a barge laden with oil grappled to each. But it is not my doing: the Egyptians have saved me the trouble. They have captured the west harbor.

CÆSAR *(anxiously)* And the east harbor? The lighthouse, Rufio?

RUFIO *(with a sudden splutter of raging ill usage, coming down to* CÆSAR *and scolding him)* Can I embark a legion in five minutes? The first cohort is already on the beach. We can do no more. If you want faster work, come and do it yourself.

CÆSAR *(soothing him)* Good, good. Patience, Rufio, patience.

RUFIO Patience! Who is impatient here, you or I? Would I be here, if I could not oversee them from that balcony?

CÆSAR Forgive me, Rufio; and *(anxiously)* hurry them as much as— *(He is interrupted by an outcry as of an old man in the extremity of misfortune. It draws near rapidly; and* THEODOTUS *rushes in, tearing his hair, and squeaking the most lamentable exclamations.* RUFIO *steps back to stare at him, amazed at his frantic condition.* POTHINUS *turns to listen.)*

THEODOTUS *(on the steps, with uplifted arms)* Horror unspeakable! Woe, alas! Help!

RUFIO What now?

CÆSAR *(frowning)* Who is slain?

THEODOTUS Slain! Oh, worse than the death of ten thousand men! Loss irreparable to mankind!

RUFIO What has happened, man?

THEODOTUS *(rushing down the hall between them)* The fire has spread from your ships. The first of the seven wonders of the world perishes. The library of Alexandria is in flames.

RUFIO Psha! *(Quite relieved, he goes up to the loggia and watches the preparations of the troops on the beach.)*

CÆSAR Is that all?

THEODOTUS *(unable to believe his senses)* All! Cæsar: will you go down to posterity as a barbarous soldier too ignorant to know the value of books?

CÆSAR Theodotus: I am an author myself; and I tell you it is better that the Egyptians should live their lives than dream them away with the help of books.

THEODOTUS *(kneeling, with genuine literary emotion: the passion of the pedant)* Cæsar: once in ten generations of men, the world gains an immortal book.

CÆSAR *(inflexible)* If it did not flatter mankind, the common executioner would burn it.

THEODOTUS Without history, death will lay you beside your meanest soldier.

CÆSAR Death will do that in any case. I ask no better grave.

THEODOTUS What is burning there is the memory of mankind.

CÆSAR A shameful memory. Let it burn.

THEODOTUS *(wildly)* Will you destroy the past?

CÆSAR Ay, and build the future with its ruins. *(*THEODOTUS, *in despair, strikes himself on the temples with his fists.)* But harken, Theodotus, teacher of kings: you who valued Pompey's head no more than a shepherd values an onion, and who now kneel to me, with tears in your old eyes, to plead for a few sheepskins scrawled with errors. I cannot spare you a man or a bucket of water just now; but you shall pass freely out of the palace. Now, away with you to Achillas; and borrow his legions to put out the fire. *(He hurries him to the steps.)*

POTHINUS *(significantly)* You understand, Theodotus: I remain a prisoner.

THEODOTUS A prisoner!

CÆSAR Will you stay to talk whilst the memory of mankind is burning?

(Calling through the loggia) Ho there! Pass Theodotus out. *(To* THEODOTUS*)* Away with you.

THEODOTUS *(To* POTHINUS*)* I must go to save the library. *(He hurries out.)*

CÆSAR Follow him to the gate, Pothinus. Bid him urge your people to kill no more of my soldiers, for your sake.

POTHINUS My life will cost you dear if you take it, Cæsar. *(He goes out after* THEODOTUS.*)*

*(*RUFIO, *absorbed in watching the embarkation, does not notice the departure of the two Egyptians.)*

RUFIO *(shouting from the loggia to the beach)* All ready, there?

A CENTURION *(from below)* All ready. We wait for Cæsar.

CÆSAR Tell them Cæsar is coming—the rogues! *(Calling)* Britannicus. *(This magniloquent version of his secretary's name is one of* CÆSAR'S *jokes. In later years it would have meant, quite seriously and officially, Conqueror of Britain.)*

RUFIO *(calling down)* Push off, all except the longboat. Stand by it to embark, Cæsar's guard there. *(He leaves the balcony and comes down into the hall.)* Where are those Egyptians? Is this more clemency? Have you let them go?

CÆSAR *(chuckling)* I have let Theodotus go to save the library. We must respect literature, Rufio.

RUFIO *(raging)* Folly on folly's head! I believe if you could bring back all the dead of Spain, Gaul, and Thessaly to life, you would do it that we might have the trouble of fighting them over again.

CÆSAR Might not the gods destroy the world if their only thought were to be at peace next year? *(*RUFIO, *out of all patience, turns away in anger.* CÆSAR *suddenly grips his sleeve, and adds slyly in his ear)* Besides, my friend: every Egyptian we imprison means imprisoning two Roman soldiers to guard him. Eh?

RUFIO Agh! I might have known there was some fox's trick behind your fine talking. *(He gets away from* CÆSAR *with an ill-humored shrug, and goes to the balcony for another look at the preparations; finally goes out.)*

CÆSAR Is Britannus asleep? I sent him for my armor an hour ago. *(Calling)* Britannicus, thou British islander. Britannicus!

*(*CLEOPATRA *runs in through the loggia with* CÆSAR'S *helmet and sword, snatched from* BRITANNUS, *who follows her with a cuirass and greaves. They come down to* CÆSAR, *she to his left hand,* BRITANNUS *to his right.)*

CLEOPATRA I am going to dress you, Cæsar. Sit down. *(He obeys.)* These Roman helmets are so becoming! *(She takes off his wreath.)* Oh! *(She bursts out laughing at him.)*

CÆSAR What are you laughing at?

CLEOPATRA You're bald *(beginning with a big B, and ending with a splutter.)*

CÆSAR *(almost annoyed)* Cleopatra! *(He rises, for the convenience of* BRITANNUS, *who puts the cuirass on him.)*

CLEOPATRA So that is why you wear the wreath—to hide it.

BRITANNUS Peace, Egyptian: they are the bays of the conqueror. *(He buckles the cuirass.)*

CLEOPATRA Peace, thou: islander! *(To* CÆSAR*)* You should rub your head with strong spirits of sugar, Cæsar. That will make it grow.

CÆSAR *(with a wry face)* Cleopatra: do you like to be reminded that you are very young?

CLEOPATRA *(pouting)* No.

CÆSAR *(sitting down again, and setting out his leg for* BRITANNUS, *who kneels to put on his greaves)* Neither do I like to be reminded that I am—middle aged. Let me give you ten of my superfluous years. That will make you 26, and leave me only—no matter. Is it a bargain?

CLEOPATRA Agreed. 26, mind. *(She puts the helmet on him.)* Oh! How nice! You look only about 50 in it!

BRITANNUS *(looking up severely at* CLEOPATRA*)* You must not speak in this manner to Cæsar.

CLEOPATRA Is it true that when Cæsar caught you on that island, you were painted all over blue?

BRITANNUS Blue is the color worn by all Britons of good standing. In war we stain our bodies blue; so that though our enemies may strip us of our clothes and our lives, they cannot strip us of our respectability. *(He rises.)*

CLEOPATRA *(with* CÆSAR'S *sword)* Let me hang this on. Now you look splendid. Have they made any statues of you in Rome?

CÆSAR Yes, many statues.

CLEOPATRA You must send for one and give it to me.

RUFIO *(coming back into the loggia, more impatient than ever)* Now Cæsar: have you done talking? The moment your foot is aboard there will be no holding our men back: the boats will race one another for the lighthouse.

CÆSAR *(drawing his sword and trying the edge)* Is this well set today, Britannicus? At Pharsalia it was as blunt as a barrel-hoop.

BRITANNUS It will split one of the Egyptian's hairs today, Cæsar. I have set it myself.

CLEOPATRA *(suddenly throwing her arms in terror round* CÆSAR*)* Oh, you are not really going into battle to be killed?

CÆSAR No, Cleopatra. No man goes to battle to be killed.

CLEOPATRA But they *do* get killed. My sister's husband was killed in battle. You must not go. Let *him* go *(pointing to* RUFIO. *They all laugh at her.)* Oh please, *please* dont go. What will happen to me if you never come back?

CÆSAR *(gravely)* Are you afraid?

CLEOPATRA *(shrinking)* No.

CÆSAR *(with quiet authority)* Go to the balcony; and you shall see us take the Pharos. You must learn to look on battles. Go. *(She goes, downcast, and looks out from the balcony.)* That is well. Now, Rufio. March.

CLEOPATRA *(suddenly clapping her hands)* Oh, you will not be able to go!

CÆSAR Why? What now?

CLEOPATRA They are drying up the harbor with buckets—a multitude of soldiers—over there *(pointing out across the sea to her left)*—they are dipping up the water.

RUFIO *(hastening to look)* It is true. The Egyptian army! Crawling over the edge of the west harbor like locusts. *(With sudden anger he strides down to* CÆSAR.*)* This is your accursed clemency, Cæsar. Theodotus has brought them.

CÆSAR *(delighted at his own cleverness)* I meant him to, Rufio. They have come to put out the fire. The library will keep them busy whilst we seize the lighthouse. Eh? *(He rushes out buoyantly through the loggia, followed by* BRITANNUS.*)*

RUFIO *(disgustedly)* More foxing! Agh! *(He rushes off. A shout from the soldiers announces the appearance of* CÆSAR *below.)*

CENTURION *(below)* All aboard. Give way there. *(Another shout)*

CLEOPATRA *(waving her scarf through the loggia arch)* Goodbye, goodbye, dear Cæsar. Come back safe. Goodbye!

act III

The edge of the quay in front of the palace, looking out west over the east harbor of Alexandria to Pharos island, just off the end of which, and connected with it by a narrow mole, is the famous lighthouse, a gigantic square tower of white marble diminishing in size storey by storey to the top, on which stands a cresset beacon. The island is joined to the main land by the Heptastadium, a great mole or causeway five miles long bounding the harbor on the south.

In the middle of the quay a Roman sentinel stands on guard, pilum in hand, looking out to the lighthouse with strained attention, his left hand shading his eyes. The pilum is a stout wooden shaft 4 1/2 feet long, with an iron spit about three feet long fixed in it. The sentinel is so absorbed that he does not notice the approach from the north end of the quay of four Egyptian market porters carrying rolls of carpet, preceded by FTATATEETA *and* APOLLODORUS *the Sicilian.* APOLLODORUS *is a dashing young man of about 24, handsome and debonair, dressed with deliberate æstheticism in the most delicate purples and dove greys, with ornaments of bronze, oxydized silver, and stones of jade and agate. His sword, designed as carefully as a medieval cross, has a blued blade showing through an openwork scabbard of purple leather and filagree. The porters, conducted by* FTATATEETA*, pass along the quay behind the sentinel to the steps of the palace, where they put down their bales and squat on the ground.* APOLLODORUS *does not pass along with them: he halts, amused by the preoccupation of the sentinel.*

APOLLODORUS *(calling to the sentinel)* Who goes there, eh?

SENTINEL *(starting violently and turning with his pilum at the charge, revealing himself as a small, wiry, sandy-haired, conscientious young man with an elderly face)* Whats this? Stand. Who are you?

APOLLODORUS I am Apollodorus the Sicilian. Why, man, what are you dreaming of? Since I came through the lines beyond the theatre there, I have brought my caravan past three sentinels, all so busy staring at the lighthouse that not one of them challenged me. Is this Roman discipline?

SENTINEL We are not here to watch the land but the sea. Cæsar has just landed on the Pharos. *(Looking at* FTATATEETA*)* What have you here? Who is this piece of Egyptian crockery?

FTATATEETA Apollodorus: rebuke this Roman dog; and bid him bridle his tongue in the presence of Ftatateeta, the mistress of the Queen's household.

APOLLODORUS My friend: this is a great lady, who stands high with Cæsar.

SENTINEL *(not at all impressed, pointing to the carpets)* And what is all this truck?

APOLLODORUS Carpets for the furnishing of the Queen's apartments in the palace. I have picked them from the best carpets in the world; and the Queen shall choose the best of my choosing.

SENTINEL So you are the carpet merchant?

APOLLODORUS *(hurt)* My friend: I am a patrician.

SENTINEL A patrician! A patrician keeping a shop instead of following arms!

APOLLODORUS I do not keep a shop. Mine is a temple of the arts. I am a worshipper of beauty. My calling is to choose beautiful things for beautiful queens. My motto is Art for Art's sake.

SENTINEL That is not the password.

APOLLODORUS It is a universal password.

SENTINEL I know nothing about universal passwords. Either give me the password for the day or get back to your shop.

*(*FTATATEETA, *roused by his hostile tone, steals towards the edge of the quay with the step of a panther, and gets behind him.)*

APOLLODORUS How if I do neither?

SENTINEL Then I will drive this pilum through you.

APOLLODORUS At your service, my friend. *(He draws his sword, and springs to his guard with unruffled grace.)*

FTATATEETA *(suddenly seizing the sentinel's arms from behind)* Thrust your knife into the dog's throat, Apollodorus. *(The chivalrous* APOLLODORUS *laughingly shakes his head; breaks ground away from the sentinel towards the palace; and lowers his point.)*

SENTINEL *(struggling vainly)* Curse on you! Let me go. Help ho!

FTATATEETA *(lifting him from the ground)* Stab the little Roman reptile. Spit him on your sword.

(A couple of Roman soldiers, with a centurion, come running along the edge of the quay from the north end. They rescue their comrade, and throw off FTATATEETA, *who is sent reeling away on the left hand of the sentinel.)*

CENTURION *(an unattractive man of fifty, short in his speech and manners, with a vinewood cudgel in his hand)* How now? What is all this?

FTATATEETA *(to* APOLLODORUS*)* Why did you not stab him? There was time!

APOLLODORUS Centurion: I am here by order of the Queen to—

CENTURION *(interrupting him)* The Queen! Yes, yes: *(to the sentinel)* pass him in. Pass all these bazaar people into the Queen, with their goods. But mind you pass no one out that you have not passed in—not even the Queen herself.

SENTINEL This old woman is dangerous: she is as strong as three men. She wanted the merchant to stab me.

APOLLODORUS Centurion: I am not a merchant. I am a patrician and a votary of art.

CENTURION Is the woman your wife?

APOLLODORUS *(horrified)* No, no! *(Correcting himself politely)* Not that the lady is not a striking figure in her own way. But *(emphatically)* she is *not* my wife.

FTATATEETA *(to the centurion)* Roman: I am Ftatateeta, the mistress of the Queen's household.

CENTURION Keep your hands off our men, mistress; or I will have you pitched into the harbor, though you were as strong as ten men. *(To his men)* To your posts: march! *(He returns with his men the way they came.)*

FTATATEETA *(looking malignantly after him)* We shall see whom Isis loves best: her servant Ftatateeta or a dog of a Roman.

SENTINEL *(to* APOLLODORUS, *with a wave of his pilum towards the palace)* Pass in there; and keep your distance. *(Turning to* FTATATEETA*)* Come within a yard of me, you old crocodile; and I will give you this *(the pilum)* in your jaws.

CLEOPATRA *(calling from the palace)* Ftatateeta, Ftatateeta.

FTATATEETA *(looking up, scandalized)* Go from the window, go from the window. There are men here.

CLEOPATRA I am coming down.

FTATATEETA *(distracted)* No, no. What are you dreaming of? O ye gods, ye gods! Apollodorus: bid your men pick up your bales; and in with me quickly.

APOLLODORUS Obey the mistress of the Queen's household.

FTATATEETA *(impatiently, as the porters stoop to lift the bales)* Quick, quick: she will be out upon us. *(*CLEOPATRA *comes from the palace and runs across the quay to* FTATATEETA*)* Oh that ever I was born!

CLEOPATRA *(eagerly)* Ftatateeta: I have thought of something. I want a boat—at once.

FTATATEETA A boat! No, no: you cannot. Apollodorus: speak to the Queen.

APOLLODORUS *(gallantly)* Beautiful queen: I am Apollodorus the Sicilian, your servant, from the bazaar. I have brought you the three most beautiful Persian carpets in the world to choose from.

CLEOPATRA I have no time for carpets today. Get me a boat.

FTATATEETA What whim is this? You cannot go on the water except in the royal barge.

APOLLODORUS Royalty, Ftatateeta, lies not in the barge but in the Queen.

(To CLEOPATRA*)* The touch of your majesty's foot on the gunwale of the meanest boat in the harbor will make it royal. *(He turns to the harbor and calls seaward)* Ho there, boatman! Pull in to the steps.

CLEOPATRA Apollodorus: you are my perfect knight; and I will always buy my carpets through you. *(*APOLLODORUS *bows joyously. An oar appears above the quay; and the boatman, a bullet-headed, vivacious, grinning fellow, burnt almost black by the sun, comes up a flight of steps from the water on the sentinel's right, oar in hand, and waits at the top.)* Can you row, Apollodorus?

APOLLODORUS My oars shall be your majesty's wings. Whither shall I row my Queen?

CLEOPATRA To the lighthouse. Come. *(She makes for the steps.)*

SENTINEL *(opposing her with his pilum at the charge)* Stand. You cannot pass.

CLEOPATRA *(flushing angrily)* How dare you? Do you know that I am the Queen?

SENTINEL I have my orders. You cannot pass.

CLEOPATRA I will make Cæsar have you killed if you do not obey me.

SENTINEL He will do worse to me if I disobey my officer. Stand back.

CLEOPATRA Ftatateeta: strangle him.

SENTINEL *(alarmed—looking apprehensively at* FTATATEETA, *and brandishing his pilum)* Keep off, there.

CLEOPATRA *(running to* APOLLODORUS*)* Apollodorus: make your slaves help us.

APOLLODORUS I shall not need their help, lady. *(He draws his sword.)* Now, soldier: choose which weapon you will defend yourself with. Shall it be sword against pilum, or sword against sword?

SENTINEL Roman against Sicilian, curse you. Take that. *(He hurls his pilum at* APOLLODORUS, *who drops expertly on one knee. The pilum passes whizzing over his head and falls harmless.* APOLLODORUS, *with a cry of triumph, springs up and attacks the sentinel, who draws his sword and defends himself, crying)* Ho there, guard. Help!

*(*CLEOPATRA, *half frightened, half delighted, takes refuge near the palace, where the porters are squatting among the bales. The boatman, alarmed, hurries down the steps out of harm's way, but stops, with his head just visible above the edge of the quay, to watch the fight. The sentinel is handicapped by his fear of an attack in the rear from* FTATATEETA. *His swordsmanship, which is of a rough and ready sort, is heavily taxed, as he has occasionally to strike at her to keep her off between a blow and a guard with* APOLLODORUS. *The centurion returns with several soldiers.* APOLLODORUS *springs back towards* CLEOPATRA *as this reinforcement confronts him.)*

CENTURION *(coming to the sentinel's right hand)* What is this? What now?

SENTINEL *(panting)* I could do well enough by myself if it werent for the old woman. Keep her off me: that is all the help I need.

CENTURION Make your report, soldier. What has happened?

FTATATEETA Centurion: he would have slain the Queen.

SENTINEL *(bluntly)* I would, sooner than let her pass. She wanted to take boat, and go—so she said—to the lighthouse. I stopped her, as I was ordered to; and she set this fellow on me. *(He goes to pick up his pilum and returns to his place with it.)*

CENTURION *(turning to* CLEOPATRA*)* Cleopatra: I am loth to offend you; but without Cæsar's express order we dare not let you pass beyond the Roman lines.

APOLLODORUS Well, Centurion; and has not the lighthouse been within the Roman lines since Cæsar landed there?

CLEOPATRA Yes, yes. Answer that, if you can.

CENTURION *(to* APOLLODORUS*)* As for you, Apollodorus, you may thank the gods that you are not nailed to the palace door with a pilum for your meddling.

APOLLODORUS *(urbanely)* My military friend, I was not born to be slain by so ugly a weapon. When I fall, it will be *(holding up his sword)* by this white queen of arms, the only weapon fit for an artist. And now that you are convinced that we do not want to go beyond the lines, let me finish killing your sentinel and depart with the Queen.

CENTURION *(as the sentinel makes an angry demonstration)* Peace there, Cleopatra: I must abide by my orders, and not by the subtleties of this Sicilian. You must withdraw into the palace and examine your carpets there.

CLEOPATRA *(pouting)* I will not: I am the Queen. Cæsar does not speak to me as you do. Have Cæsar's centurions changed manners with his scullions?

CENTURION *(sulkily)* I do my duty. That is enough for me.

APOLLODORUS Majesty: when a stupid man is doing something he is ashamed of, he always declares that it is his duty.

CENTURION *(angry)* Apollodorus—

APOLLODORUS *(interrupting him with defiant elegance)* I will make amends for that insult with my sword at fitting time and place. Who says artist, says duellist. *(To* CLEOPATRA*)* Hear my counsel, star of the east. Until word comes to these soldiers from Cæsar himself, you are a prisoner. Let me go to him with a message from you, and a present; and before the sun has stooped half way to the arms of the sea, I will bring you back Cæsar's order of release.

CENTURION *(sneering at him)* And you will sell the Queen the present, no doubt.

APOLLODORUS Centurion: the Queen shall have from me, without payment, as the unforced tribute of Sicilian taste to Egyptian beauty, the richest of these carpets for her present to Cæsar.

CLEOPATRA *(exultantly, to the centurion)* Now you see what an ignorant common creature you are!

CENTURION *(curtly)* Well, a fool and his wares are soon parted. *(He turns to his men.)* Two more men to this post here; and see that no one leaves the palace but this man and his merchandize. If he draws his sword again inside the lines, kill him. To your posts. March.

(He goes out, leaving two auxiliary sentinels with the other.)

APOLLODORUS *(with polite goodfellowship)* My friends: will you not enter the palace and bury our quarrel in a bowl of wine? *(He takes out his purse, jingling the coins in it.)* The Queen has presents for you all.

SENTINEL *(very sulky)* You heard our orders. Get about your business.

FIRST AUXILIARY Yes: you ought to know better. Off with you.

SECOND AUXILIARY *(looking longingly at the purse—this sentinel is a hooknosed man, unlike his comrade, who is squab faced)* Do not tantalize a poor man.

APOLLODORUS *(to* CLEOPATRA*)* Pearl of Queens: the centurion is at hand; and the Roman soldier is incorruptible when his officer is looking. I must carry your word to Cæsar.

CLEOPATRA *(who has been meditating among the carpets)* Are these carpets very heavy?

APOLLODORUS It matters not how heavy. There are plenty of porters.

CLEOPATRA How do they put the carpets into boats? Do they throw them down?

APOLLODORUS Not into small boats, majesty. It would sink them.

CLEOPATRA Not into that man's boat, for instance? *(pointing to the boatman.)*

APOLLODORUS No. Too small.

CLEOPATRA But you can take a carpet to Cæsar in it if I send one?

APOLLODORUS Assuredly.

CLEOPATRA And you will have it carried gently down the steps and take great care of it?

APOLLODORUS Depend on me.

CLEOPATRA Great, great care?

APOLLODORUS More than of my own body.

CLEOPATRA You will promise me not to let the porters drop it or throw it about?

APOLLODORUS Place the most delicate glass goblet in the palace in the heart of the roll, Queen; and if it be broken, my head shall pay for it.

CLEOPATRA Good. Come, Ftatateeta. *(*FTATATEETA *comes to her.* APOLLODORUS *offers to squire them into the palace.)* No, Apollodorus, you must not come. I will choose a carpet for myself. You must wait here. *(She runs into the palace.)*

APOLLODORUS *(to the porters)* Follow this lady *(indicating* FTATATEETA*)* and obey her.

(The porters rise and take up their bales.)

FTATATEETA *(addressing the porters as if they were vermin)* This way. And take your shoes off before you put your feet on those stairs.

(She goes in, followed by the porters with the carpets. Meanwhile APOLLODORUS *goes to the edge of the quay and looks out over the harbor. The sentinels keep their eyes on him malignantly.)*

APOLLODORUS *(addressing the sentinel)* My friend—

SENTINEL *(rudely)* Silence there.

FIRST AUXILIARY Shut your muzzle, you.

SECOND AUXILIARY *in a half whisper, glancing apprehensively towards the north end of the quay)* Cant you wait a bit?

APOLLODORUS Patience, worthy three-headed donkey. *(They mutter ferociously; but he is not at all intimidated.)* Listen: were you set here to watch me, or to watch the Egyptians?

SENTINEL We know our duty.

APOLLODORUS Then why dont you do it? There is something going on over there *(pointing southwestward to the mole.)*

SENTINEL *(sulkily)* I do not need to be told what to do by the like of you.

APOLLODORUS Blockhead. *(He begins shouting)* Ho there, Centurion. Hoiho!

SENTINEL Curse your meddling. *(Shouting)* Hoiho! Alarm! Alarm!

FIRST AND SECOND AUXILIARIES Alarm! alarm! Hoiho!

(The CENTURION *comes running in with his guard.)*

CENTURION What now? Has the old woman attacked you again? *(Seeing* APOLLODORUS*)* Are *you* here still?

APOLLODORUS *(pointing as before)* See there. The Egyptians are moving. They are going to recapture the Pharos. They will attack by sea and land: by land along the great mole; by sea from the west harbor. Stir yourselves, my military friends: the hunt is up. *(A clangor of trumpets from several points along the quay.)* Aha! I told you so.

CENTURION *(quickly)* The two extra men pass the alarm to the south posts. One man keep guard here. The rest with me—quick.

(The two auxiliary sentinels run off to the south. The centurion and his guard run off northward; and immediately afterwards the bucina sounds. The four porters come from the palace carrying a carpet, followed by FTATATEETA.*)*

SENTINEL *(handling his pilum apprehensively)* You again! *(The porters stop.)*

FTATATEETA Peace, Roman fellow: you are now single-handed. Apollodorus: this carpet is Cleopatra's present to Cæsar. It has rolled up in it ten precious goblets of the thinnest Iberian crystal, and a hundred eggs of the sacred blue pigeon. On your honor, let not one of them be broken.

APOLLODORUS On my head be it! *(To the porters)* Into the boat with them carefully.

(The porters carry the carpet to the steps.)

FIRST PORTER *(looking down at the boat)* Beware what you do, sir. Those eggs of which the lady speaks must weigh more than a pound apiece. This boat is too small for such a load.

BOATMAN *(excitedly rushing up the steps)* Oh thou injurious porter! Oh thou unnatural son of a she-camel! *(To* APPOLLODORUS*)* My boat, sir, hath often carried five men. Shall it not carry your lordship and a bale of pigeon's eggs? *(To the porter)* Thou mangey dromedary, the gods shall punish thee for this envious wickedness.

FIRST PORTER *(stolidly)* I cannot quit this bale now to beat thee; but another day I will lie in wait for thee.

APOLLODORUS *(going between them)* Peace there. If the boat were but a single plank, I would get to Cæsar on it.

FTATATEETA *(anxiously)* In the name of the gods, Apollodorus, run no risks with that bale.

APOLLODORUS Fear not, thou venerable grotesque: I guess its great worth. *(To the porters)* Down with it, I say; and gently; or ye shall eat nothing but stick for ten days.[6]

The boatman goes down the steps, followed by the porters with the bale: FTATATEETA *and* APOLLODORUS *watching from the edge.)*

APOLLODORUS Gently, my sons, my children—*(with sudden alarm)* gently, ye dogs. Lay it level in the stern—so—tis well.

FTATATEETA *(screaming down at one of the porters)* Do not step on it, do not step on it. Oh thou brute beast!

FIRST PORTER *(ascending)* Be not excited, mistress: all is well.

FTATATEETA *(panting)* All well! Oh, thou hast given my heart a turn! *(She clutches her side, gasping.)*

(The four porters have now come up and are waiting at the stairhead to be paid.)

APOLLODORUS Here, ye hungry ones. *(He gives money to the first porter, who holds it in his hand to shew to the others. They crowd greedily to see how much it is, quite prepared, after the Eastern fashion, to protest to heaven against their patron's stinginess. But his liberality overpowers them.)*

FIRST PORTER O bounteous prince!

SECOND PORTER O lord of the bazaar!

THIRD PORTER O favored of the gods!

FOURTH PORTER O father to all the porters of the market!

SENTINEL *(enviously, threatening them fiercely with his pilum)* Hence, dogs: off. Out of this. *(They fly before him northward along the quay.)*

APOLLODORUS Farewell, Ftatateeta. I shall be at the lighthouse before the Egyptians. *(He descends the steps.)*

FTATATEETA The gods speed thee and protect my nursling!

(The sentry returns from chasing the porters and looks down at the boat, standing near the stairhead lest FTATATEETA *should attempt to escape.)*

APOLLODORUS *(from beneath, as the boat moves off)* Farewell, valiant pilum pitcher.

SENTINEL Farewell, shopkeeper.

APOLLODORUS Ha, ha! Pull, thou brave boatman, pull. Soho-o-o-o-o! *(He begins to sing in barcarolle measure to the rhythm of the oars)*

My heart, my heart, spread out thy wings:
Shake off thy heavy load of love—

Give me the oars, O son of a snail.

SENTINEL *(threatening* FTATATEETA*)* Now mistress: back to your henhouse. In with you.

FTATATEETA *(falling on her knees and stretching her hands over the waters)* Gods of the seas, bear her safely to the shore!

SENTINEL Bear who safely? What do you mean?

FTATATEETA *(looking darkly at him)* Gods of Egypt and of Vengeance,

[6]Refers to a form of Eastern punishment, beating the soles of the feet.

let this Roman fool be beaten like a dog by his captain for suffering her to be taken over the waters.

SENTINEL Accursed one: is she then in the boat? *(He calls over the sea)* Hoiho, there, boatman! Hoiho!

APOLLODORUS *(singing in the distance)*

> My heart, my heart, be whole and free:
> Love is thine only enemy.

(Meanwhile RUFIO, *the morning's fighting done, sits munching dates on a faggot of brushwood outside the door of the lighthouse, which towers gigantic to the clouds on his left. His helmet, full of dates, is between his knees; and a leathern bottle of wine is by his side. Behind him the great stone pedestal of the lighthouse is shut in from the open sea by a low stone parapet, with a couple of steps in the middle to the broad coping. A huge chain with a hook hangs down from the lighthouse crane above his head. Faggots like the one he sits on lie beneath it ready to be drawn up to feed the beacon.*

CÆSAR *is standing on the step at the parapet looking out anxiously, evidently ill at ease.* BRITANNUS *comes out of the lighthouse door.)*

RUFIO Well, my British islander. Have you been up to the top?

BRITANNUS I have. I reckon it at 200 feet high.

RUFIO Anybody up there?

BRITANNUS One elderly Tyrian to work the crane; and his son, a well conducted youth of 14.

RUFIO *(looking at the chain)* What! An old man and a boy work that! Twenty men, you mean.

BRITANNUS Two only, I assure you. They have counterweights, and a machine with boiling water in it which I do not understand: it is not of British design. They use it to haul up barrels of oil and faggots to burn in the brazier on the roof.

RUFIO But—

BRITANNUS Excuse me: I came down because there are messengers coming along the mole to us from the island. I must see what their business is. *(He hurries out past the lighthouse.)*

CÆSAR *(coming away from the parapet, shivering and out of sorts)* Rufio: this has been a mad expedition. We shall be beaten. I wish I knew how our men are getting on with that barricade across the great mole.

RUFIO *(angrily)* Must I leave my food and go starving to bring you a report?

CÆSAR *(soothing him nervously)* No, Rufio, no. Eat, my son, eat. *(He takes another turn,* RUFIO *chewing dates meanwhile.)* The Egyptians cannot be such fools as not to storm the barricade and swoop down on us here before it is finished. It is the first time I have ever run an avoidable risk. I should not have come to Egypt.

RUFIO An hour ago you were all for victory.

CÆSAR *(apologetically)* Yes: I was a fool—rash, Rufio—boyish.

RUFIO Boyish! Not a bit of it. Here *(offering him a handful of dates.)*

CÆSAR What are these for?

RUFIO To eat. Thats whats the matter with you. When a man comes to your age, he runs down before his midday meal. Eat and drink; and then have another look at our chances.

CÆSAR *(taking the dates)* My age! *(He shakes his head and bites a date.)* Yes, Rufio: I am an old man—worn out now—true, quite true. *(He gives way to melancholy contemplation, and eats another date.)* Achillas is still in his prime: Ptolemy is a boy. *(He eats another date, and plucks up a little.)* Well, every dog has his day; and I have had mine: I cannot complain. *(With sudden cheerfulness)* These dates are not bad, Rufio. *(*BRITANNUS *returns, greatly excited, with a leathern bag.* CÆSAR *is himself again in a moment.)* What now?

BRITANNUS *(triumphantly)* Our brave Rhodian mariners have captured a treasure. There! *(He throws the bag down at* CÆSAR'S *feet.)* Our enemies are delivered into our hands.

CÆSAR In that bag?

BRITANNUS Wait till you hear, Cæsar. This bag contains all the letters which have passed between Pompey's party and the army of occupation here.

CÆSAR Well?

BRITANNUS *(impatient of* CÆSAR'S *slowness to grasp the situation)* Well, we shall now know who your foes are. The name of every man who has plotted against you since you crossed the Rubicon may be in these papers, for all we know.

CÆSAR Put them in the fire.

BRITANNUS Put them—*(he gasps)*!!!!

CÆSAR In the fire. Would you have me waste the next three years of my life in proscribing and condemning men who will be my friends when I have proved that my friendship is worth more than Pompey's was—than Cato's is. O incorrigible British islander: am I a bull dog, to seek quarrels merely to shew how stubborn my jaws are?

BRITANNUS But your honor—the honor of Rome—

CÆSAR I do not make human sacrifices to my honor, as your Druids[7] do. Since you will not burn these, at least I can drown them. *(He picks up the bag and throws it over the parapet into the sea.)*

BRITANNUS Cæsar: this is mere eccentricity. Are traitors to be allowed to go free for the sake of a paradox?

RUFIO *(rising)* Cæsar: when the islander has finished preaching, call me again. I am going to have a look at the boiling water machine. *(He goes into the lighthouse.)*

BRITANNUS *(with genuine feeling)* O Cæsar, my great master, if I could but persuade you to regard life seriously, as men do in my country!

CÆSAR Do they truly do so, Britannus?

BRITANNUS Have you not been there? Have you not seen them? What Briton speaks as you do in your moments of levity? What Briton neglects to attend the services at the sacred grove? What Briton wears

[7]Priests of Celtic Great Britain and Gaul.

clothes of many colors as you do, instead of plain blue, as all solid, well esteemed men should? These are moral questions with us.

CÆSAR Well, well, my friend: some day I shall settle down and have a blue toga, perhaps. Meanwhile, I must get on as best I can in my flippant Roman way. *(*APOLLODORUS *comes past the lighthouse.)* What now?

BRITANNUS *(turning quickly, and challenging the stranger with official haughtiness)* What is this? Who are you? How did you come here?

APOLLODORUS Calm yourself, my friend: I am not going to eat you. I have come by boat, from Alexandria, with precious gifts for Cæsar.

CÆSAR From Alexandria!

BRITANNUS *(severely)* That is Cæsar, sir.

RUFIO *(appearing at the lighthouse door)* Whats the matter now?

APOLLODORUS Hail, great Cæsar! I am Apollodorus the Sicilian, an artist.

BRITANNUS An artist! Why have they admitted this vagabond?

CÆSAR Peace, man. Apollodorus is a famous patrician amateur.

BRITANNUS *(disconcerted)* I crave the gentleman's pardon. *(To* CÆSAR*)* I understood him to say that he was a professional. *(Somewhat out of countenance, he allows* APOLLODORUS *to approach* CÆSAR, *changing places with him.* RUFIO, *after looking* APOLLODORUS *up and down with marked disparagement, goes to the other side of the platform.)*

CÆSAR You are welcome, Apollodorus. What is your business?

APOLLODORUS First, to deliver to you a present from the Queen of Queens.

CÆSAR Who is that?

APOLLODORUS Cleopatra of Egypt.

CÆSAR *(taking him into his confidence in his most winning manner)* Apollodorus: this is no time for playing with presents. Pray you, go back to the Queen, and tell her that if all goes well I shall return to the palace this evening.

APOLLODORUS Cæsar: I cannot return. As I approached the lighthouse, some fool threw a great leathern bag into the sea. It broke the nose of my boat; and I had hardly time to get myself and my charge to the shore before the poor little cockleshell sank.

CÆSAR I am sorry, Apollodorus. The fool shall be rebuked. Well, well: what have you brought me? The Queen will be hurt if I do not look at it.

RUFIO Have we time to waste on this trumpery? The Queen is only a child.

CÆSAR Just so: that is why we must not disappoint her. What is the present, Apollodorus?

APOLLODORUS Cæsar: it is a Persian carpet—a beauty! And in it are—so I am told—pigeons' eggs and crystal goblets and fragile precious things. I dare not for my head have it carried up that narrow ladder from the causeway.

RUFIO Swing it up by the crane, then. We will send the eggs to the cook; drink our wine from the goblets; and the carpet will make a bed for Cæsar.

APOLLODORUS The crane! Cæsar: I have sworn to tender this bale of carpets as I tender my own life.

CÆSAR *(cheerfully)* Then let them swing you up at the same time; and if the chain breaks, you and the pigeons' eggs will perish together. *(He goes to the chain and looks up along it, examining it curiously.)*

APOLLODORUS *(to* BRITANNUS*)* Is Cæsar serious?

BRITANNUS His manner is frivolous because he is an Italian; but he means what he says.

APOLLODORUS Serious or not, he spake well. Give me a squad of soldiers to work the crane.

BRITANNUS Leave the crane to me. Go and await the descent of the chain.

APOLLODORUS Good. You will presently see me there *(turning to them all and pointing with an eloquent gesture to the sky above the parapet)* rising like the sun with my treasure.

(He goes back the way he came. BRITANNUS *goes into the lighthouse.)*

RUFIO *(ill-humoredly)* Are you really going to wait here for this foolery, Cæsar?

CÆSAR *(backing away from the crane as it gives signs of working)* Why not?

RUFIO The Egyptians will let you know why not if they have the sense to make a rush from the shore end of the mole before our barricade is finished. And here we are waiting like children to see a carpet full of pigeons' eggs.

(The chain rattles, and is drawn up high enough to clear the parapet. It then swings round out of sight behind the lighthouse.)

CÆSAR Fear not, my son Rufio. When the first Egyptian takes his first step along the mole, the alarm will sound; and we two will reach the barricade from our end before the Egyptians reach it from their end —we two, Rufio: I, the old man, and you, his biggest boy. And the old man will be there first. So peace; and give me some more dates.

APOLLODORUS *(from the causeway below)* Soho, haul away. So-ho-o-o-o!

(The chain is drawn up and comes round again from behind the lighthouse. APOLLODORUS *is swinging in the air with his bale of carpet at the end of it. He breaks into song as he soars above the parapet)*

Aloft, aloft, behold the blue
That never shone in woman's eyes—

Easy there: stop her. *(He ceases to rise.)* Further round! *(The chain comes forward above the platform.)*

RUFIO *(calling up)* Lower away there. *(The chain and its load begin to descend.)*

APOLLODORUS *(calling up)* Gently—slowly—mind the eggs.

RUFIO *(calling up)* Easy there—slowly—slowly.

*(*APOLLODORUS *and the bale are deposited safely on the flags in the middle of the platform.* RUFIO *and* CÆSAR *help* APOLLODORUS *to cast off the chain from the bale.)*

RUFIO Haul up.

(The chain rises clear of their heads with a rattle. BRITANNUS *comes from the lighthouse and helps them to uncord the carpet.)*

APOLLODORUS *(when the cords are loose)* Stand off, my friends: let Cæsar see. *(He throws the carpet open.)*

RUFIO Nothing but a heap of shawls. Where are the pigeons' eggs?

APOLLODORUS Approach, Cæsar; and search for them among the shawls.

RUFIO *(drawing his sword)* Ha, treachery! Keep back, Cæsar: I saw the shawl move: there is something alive there.

BRITANNUS *(drawing his sword)* It is a serpent.

APOLLODORUS Dares Cæsar thrust his hand into the sack where the serpent moves?

RUFIO *(turning on him)* Treacherous dog—

CÆSAR Peace. Put up your swords. Apollodorus: your serpent seems to breathe very regularly. *(He thrusts his hand under the shawls and draws out a bare arm.)* This is a pretty little snake.

RUFIO *(drawing out the other arm)* Let us have the rest of you.

(They pull CLEOPATRA *up by the wrists into a sitting position.* BRITANNUS, *scandalized, sheathes his sword with a drive of protest.)*

CLEOPATRA *(gasping)* Oh, I'm smothered. Oh, Cæsar, a man stood on me in the boat; and a great sack of something fell upon me out of the sky; and then the boat sank; and then I was swung up into the air and bumped down.

CÆSAR *(petting her as she rises and takes refuge on his breast)* Well, never mind: here you are safe and sound at last.

RUFIO Ay; and now that she is here, what are we to do with her?

BRITANNUS She cannot stay here, Cæsar, without the companionship of some matron.

CLEOPATRA *(jealously, to* CÆSAR, *who is obviously perplexed)* Aren't you glad to see me?

CÆSAR Yes, yes; *I* am very glad. But Rufio is very angry; and Britannus is shocked.

CLEOPATRA *(contemptuously)* You can have their heads cut off, can you not?

CÆSAR They would not be so useful with their heads cut off as they are now, my sea bird.

RUFIO *(to* CLEOPATRA*)* We shall have to go away presently and cut some of your Egyptians' heads off. How will you like being left here with the chance of being captured by that little brother of yours if we are beaten?

CLEOPATRA But you mustnt leave me alone. Cæsar: you will not leave me alone, will you?

RUFIO What! not when the trumpet sounds and all our lives depend on Cæsar's being at the barricade before the Egyptians reach it? Eh?

CLEOPATRA Let them lose their lives: they are only soldiers.

CÆSAR *(gravely)* Cleopatra: when that trumpet sounds, we must take every man his life in his hand, and throw it in the face of Death. And of my soldiers who have trusted me there is not one whose hand I shall not hold more sacred than your head. *(*CLEOPATRA *is overwhelmed. Her eyes fill with tears.)* Apollodorus: you must take her back to the palace.

APOLLODORUS Am I a dolphin, Cæsar, to cross the seas with young ladies on my back? My boat is sunk: all yours are either at the barricade or have returned to the city. I will hail one if I can: that is all I can do. *(He goes back to the causeway.)*

CLEOPATRA *(struggling with her tears)* It does not matter. I will not go back. Nobody cares for me.

CÆSAR Cleopatra—

CLEOPATRA You want me to be killed.

CÆSAR *(still more gravely)* My poor child: your life matters little here to anyone but yourself. *(She gives way altogether at this, casting herself down on the faggots weeping. Suddenly a great tumult is heard in the distance, bucinas and trumpets sounding through a storm of shouting.* BRITANNUS *rushes to the parapet and looks along the mole.* CÆSAR *and* RUFIO *turn to one another with quick intelligence.)*

CÆSAR Come, Rufio.

CLEOPATRA *(scrambling to her knees and clinging to him)* No no. Do not leave me, Cæsar. *(He snatches his skirt from her clutch.)* Oh!

BRITANNUS *(from the parapet)* Cæsar: we are cut off. The Egyptians have landed from the west harbor between us and the barricade!!!

RUFIO *(running to see)* Curses! It is true. We are caught like rats in a trap.

CÆSAR *(ruthfully)* Rufio, Rufio: my men at the barricade are between the sea party and the shore party. I have murdered them.

RUFIO *(coming back from the parapet to* CÆSAR'S *right hand)* Ay: that comes of fooling with this girl here.

APOLLODORUS *(coming up quickly from the causeway)* Look over the parapet, Cæsar.

CÆSAR We have looked, my friend. We must defend ourselves here.

APOLLODORUS I have thrown the ladder into the sea. They cannot get in without it.

RUFIO Ah; and we cannot get out. Have you thought of that?

APOLLODORUS Not get out! Why not? You have ships in the east harbor.

BRITANNUS *(hopefully, at the parapet)* The Rhodian galleys are standing in towards us already. *(*CÆSAR *quickly joins* BRITANNUS *at the parapet.)*

RUFIO *(to* APOLLODORUS, *impatiently)* And by what road are we to walk to the galleys, pray?

APOLLODORUS *(with gay, defiant rhetoric)* By the road that leads everywhere—the diamond path of the sun and moon. Have you never seen the child's shadow play of The Broken Bridge? "Ducks and geese with ease get over"—eh? *(He throws away his cloak and cap, and binds his sword on his back.)*

RUFIO What are you talking about?

APOLLODORUS I will shew you. *(Calling to* BRITANNUS*)* How far off is the nearest galley?

BRITANNUS Fifty fathom.

CÆSAR No, no: they are further off than they seem in this clear air to your British eyes. Nearly quarter of a mile, Apollodorus.

APOLLODORUS Good. Defend yourselves here until I send you a boat from that galley.

RUFIO Have you wings, perhaps?

APOLLODORUS Water wings, soldier. Behold!
(He runs up the steps between CÆSAR *and* BRITANNUS *to the coping of the parapet; springs into the air; and plunges head foremost into the sea.)*
CÆSAR *(like a schoolboy—wildly excited)* Bravo, bravo! *(Throwing off his cloak)* By Jupiter, I will do that too.
RUFIO *(seizing him)* You are mad. You shall not.
CÆSAR Why not? Can I not swim as well as he?
RUFIO *(frantic)* Can an old fool dive and swim like a young one? He is twenty-five and you are fifty.
CÆSAR *(breaking loose from* RUFIO*)* Old!!!
BRITANNUS *(shocked)* Rufio: you forget yourself.
CÆSAR I will race you to the galley for a week's pay, father Rufio.
CLEOPATRA But me! me!! me!!! what is to become of me?
CÆSAR I will carry you on my back to the galley like a dolphin. Rufio: when you see me rise to the surface, throw her in: I will answer for her. And then in with you after her, both of you.
CLEOPATRA No, no, NO. I shall be drowned.
BRITANNUS Cæsar: I am a man and a Briton, not a fish. I must have a boat. I cannot swim.
CLEOPATRA Neither can I.
CÆSAR *(to* BRITANNUS*)* Stay here, then, alone, until I recapture the lighthouse: I will not forget you. Now, Rufio.
RUFIO You have made up your mind to this folly?
CÆSAR The Egyptians have made it up for me. What else is there to do? And mind where you jump: I do not want to get your fourteen stone in the small of my back as I come up. *(He runs up the steps and stands on the coping.)*
BRITANNUS *(anxiously)* One last word, Cæsar. Do not let yourself be seen in the fashionable part of Alexandria until you have changed your clothes.
CÆSAR *(calling over the sea)* Ho, Apollodorus: *(he points skyward and quotes the barcarolle)*

The white upon the blue above—

APOLLODORUS *(swimming in the distance)*

Is purple on the green below—

CÆSAR *(exultantly)* Aha! *(He plunges into the sea.)*
CLEOPATRA *(running excitedly to the steps)* Oh, let me see. He will be drowned (RUFIO *seizes her)*—Ah—ah—ah—ah! *(He pitches her screaming into the sea.* RUFIO *and* BRITANNUS *roar with laughter.)*
RUFIO *(looking down after her)* He has got her. *(To* BRITANNUS*)* Hold the fort, Briton. Cæsar will not forget you. *(He springs off.)*
BRITANNUS *(running to the steps to watch them as they swim)* All safe, Rufio?

RUFIO *(swimming)* All safe.

CÆSAR *(swimming further off)* Take refuge up there by the beacon; and pile the fuel on the trap door, Britannus.

BRITANNUS *(calling in reply)* I will first do so, and then commend myself to my country's gods. *(A sound of cheering from the sea.* BRITANNUS *gives full vent to his excitement.)* The boat has reached him: Hip, hip, hip, hurrah!

act IV

*(*CLEOPATRA'S *sousing in the east harbor of Alexandria was in October 48* B.C. *In March 47 she is passing the afternoon in her boudoir in the palace, among a bevy of her ladies, listening to a slave girl who is playing the harp in the middle of the room. The harpist's master, an old musician, with a lined face, prominent brows, white beard, moustache and eyebrows twisted and horned at the ends, and a consciously keen and pretentious expression, is squatting on the floor close to her on her right, watching her performance.* FTATATEETA *is in attendance near the door, in front of a group of female slaves. Except the harp player all are seated:* CLEOPATRA *in a chair opposite the door on the other side of the room; the rest on the ground.* CLEOPATRA'S *ladies are all young, the most conspicuous being* CHARMIAN *and* IRAS, *her favorites.* CHARMIAN *is a hatchet faced, terra cotta colored little goblin, swift in her movements, and neatly finished at the hands and feet.* IRAS *is a plump, goodnatured creature, rather fatuous, with a profusion of red hair, and a tendency to giggle on the slightest provocation.)*

CLEOPATRA Can I—

FTATATEETA *(insolently, to the player)* Peace, thou! The Queen speaks. *(The player stops.)*

CLEOPATRA *(to the old* MUSICIAN*)* I want to learn to play the harp with my own hands. Cæsar loves music. Can you teach me?

MUSICIAN Assuredly I and no one else can teach the queen. Have I not discovered the lost method of the ancient Egyptians, who could make a pyramid tremble by touching a bass string? All the other teachers are quacks: I have exposed them repeatedly.

CLEOPATRA Good: you shall teach me. How long will it take?

MUSICIAN Not very long: only four years. Your Majesty must first become proficient in the philosophy of Pythagoras.

CLEOPATRA Has she *(indicating the slave)* become proficient in the philosophy of Pythagoras?

MUSICIAN Oh, she is but a slave. She learns as a dog learns.

CLEOPATRA Well, then, I will learn as a dog learns; for she plays better than you. You shall give me a lesson every day for a fortnight. *(The* MUSICIAN *hastily scrambles to his feet and bows profoundly.)* After that, whenever I strike a false note you shall be flogged; and if I strike so many that there is not time to flog you, you shall be thrown into the Nile to feed the crocodiles. Give the girl a piece of gold; and send them away.

MUSICIAN *(much taken aback)* But true art will not be thus forced.

FTATATEETA *(pushing him out)* What is this? Answering the Queen, forsooth. Out with you.

(He is pushed out by FTATATEETA, *the girl following with her harp, amid the laughter of the ladies and slaves.)*

CLEOPATRA Now, can any of you amuse me? Have you any stories or any news?

IRAS Ftatateeta—

CLEOPATRA Oh, Ftatateeta, Ftatateeta, always Ftatateeta. Some new tale to set me against her.

IRAS No: this time Ftatateeta has been virtuous. *(All the ladies laugh—not the slaves.)* Pothinus has been trying to bribe her to let him speak with you.

CLEOPATRA *(wrathfully)* Ha! you all sell audiences with me, as if I saw whom you please, and not whom I please. I should like to know how much of her gold piece that harp girl will have to give up before she leaves the palace.

IRAS We can easily find out that for you.

(The ladies laugh.)

CLEOPATRA *(frowning)* You laugh; but take care, take care. I will find out some day how to make myself served as Cæsar is served.

CHARMIAN Old hooknose! *(They laugh again.)*

CLEOPATRA *(revolted)* Silence. Charmian: do not you be a silly Egyptian fool. Do you know why I allow you all to chatter impertinently just as you please, instead of treating you as Ftatateeta would treat you if she were Queen?

CHARMIAN Because you try to imitate Cæsar in everything; and he lets everybody say what they please to him.

CLEOPATRA No; but because I asked him one day why he did so; and he said "Let your women talk; and you will learn something from them." What have I to learn from them? I said. "What they are," said he; and oh! you should have seen his eye as he said it. You would have curled up, you shallow things. *(They laugh. She turns fiercely on* IRAS.*)* At whom are you laughing—at me or at Cæsar?

IRAS At Cæsar.

CLEOPATRA If you were not a fool, you would laugh at me; and if you were not a coward you would not be afraid to tell me so. (FTATATEETA *returns.)* Ftatateeta: they tell me that Pothinus has offered you a bribe to admit him to my presence.

FTATATEETA *(protesting)* Now by my father's gods—

CLEOPATRA *(cutting her short despotically)* Have I not told you not to deny things? You would spend the day calling your father's gods to witness to your virtues if I let you. Go take the bribe; and bring in Pothinus. (FTATATEETA *is about to reply.)* Dont answer me. Go.

(FTATATEETA *goes out; and* CLEOPATRA *rises and begins to prowl to and fro between her chair and the door, meditating. All rise and stand.)*

IRAS *(as she reluctantly rises)* Heigho! I wish Cæsar were back in Rome.

CLEOPATRA *(threateningly)* It will be a bad day for you all when he goes. Oh, if I were not ashamed to let him see that I am as cruel at heart as my father, I would make you repent that speech! Why do you wish him away?

CHARMIAN He makes you so terribly prosy and serious and learned and philosophical. It is worse than being religious, at our ages. *(The ladies laugh.)*

CLEOPATRA Cease that endless cackling, will you. Hold your tongues.

CHARMIAN *(with mock resignation)* Well, well: we must try to live up to Cæsar.

(They laugh again. CLEOPATRA *rages silently as she continues to prowl to and fro.* FTATATEETA *comes back with* POTHINUS, *who halts on the threshold.)*

FTATATEETA *(at the door)* Pothinus craves the ear of the—

CLEOPATRA There, there: that will do: let him come in. *(She resumes her seat. All sit down except* POTHINUS, *who advances to the middle of the room.* FTATATEETA *takes her former place.)* Well, Pothinus: what is the latest news from your rebel friends?

POTHINUS *(haughtily)* I am no friend of rebellion. And a prisoner does not receive news.

CLEOPATRA You are no more a prisoner than I am—than Cæsar is. These six months we have been besieged in this palace by my subjects. You are allowed to walk on the beach among the soldiers. Can I go further myself, or can Cæsar?

POTHINUS You are but a child, Cleopatra, and do not understand these matters.

(The ladies laugh. CLEOPATRA *looks inscrutably at him.)*

CHARMIAN I see you do not know the latest news, Pothinus.

POTHINUS What is that?

CHARMIAN That Cleopatra is no longer a child. Shall I tell you how to grow much older, and much, much wiser in one day?

POTHINUS I should prefer to grow wiser without growing older.

CHARMIAN Well, go up to the top of the lighthouse; and get somebody to take you by the hair and throw you into the sea. *(The ladies laugh.)*

CLEOPATRA She is right, Pothinus: you will come to the shore with much conceit washed out of you. *(The ladies laugh.* CLEOPATRA *rises impatiently.)* Begone, all of you. I will speak with Pothinus alone. Drive them out, Ftatateeta. *(They run out laughing.* FTATATEETA *shuts the door on them.)* What are you waiting for?

FTATATEETA It is not meet that the Queen remain alone with—

CLEOPATRA *(interrupting her)* Ftatateeta: must I sacrifice you to your father's gods to teach you that *I* am Queen of Egypt, and not you?

FTATATEETA *(indignantly)* You are like the rest of them. You want to be what these Romans call a New Woman. *(She goes out, banging the door.)*

CLEOPATRA *(sitting down again)* Now, Pothinus: why did you bribe Ftatateeta to bring you hither?

POTHINUS *(studying her gravely)* Cleopatra: what they tell me is true. You are changed.

CLEOPATRA Do you speak with Cæsar every day for six months: and *you* will be changed.

POTHINUS It is the common talk that you are infatuated with this old man?

CLEOPATRA Infatuated? What does that mean? Made foolish, is it not? Oh no: I wish I were.

POTHINUS You wish you were made foolish! How so?

CLEOPATRA When I was foolish, I did what I liked, except when Ftatateeta beat me; and even then I cheated her and did it by stealth. Now that Cæsar has made me wise, it is no use my liking or disliking: I do what must be done, and have no time to attend to myself. That is not happiness; but it is greatness. If Cæsar were gone, I think I could govern the Egyptians; for what Cæsar is to me, I am to the fools around me.

POTHINUS *(looking hard at her)* Cleopatra: this may be the vanity of youth.

CLEOPATRA No, no: it is not that I am so clever, but that the others are so stupid.

POTHINUS *(musingly)* Truly, that is the great secret.

CLEOPATRA Well, now tell me what you came to say?

POTHINUS *(embarrassed)* I! Nothing.

CLEOPATRA Nothing!

POTHINUS At least—to beg for my liberty: that is all.

CLEOPATRA For that you would have knelt to Cæsar. No, Pothinus: you came with some plan that depended on Cleopatra being a little nursery kitten. Now that Cleopatra is a Queen, the plan is upset.

POTHINUS *(bowing his head submissively)* It is so.

CLEOPATRA *(exultant)* Aha!

POTHINUS *(raising his eyes keenly to hers)* Is Cleopatra then indeed a Queen, and no longer Cæsar's prisoner and slave?

CLEOPATRA Pothinus: we are all Cæsar's slaves—all we in this land of Egypt—whether we will or no. And she who is wise enough to know this will reign when Cæsar departs.

POTHINUS You harp on Cæsar's departure.

CLEOPATRA What if I do?

POTHINUS Does he not love you?

CLEOPATRA Love me! Pothinus: Cæsar loves no one. Who are those we love. Only those whom we do not hate: all people are strangers and enemies to us except those we love. But it is not so with Cæsar. He has no hatred in him: he makes friends with everyone as he does with dogs and children. His kindness to me is a wonder: neither mother, father, nor nurse have ever taken so much care for me, or thrown open their thoughts to me so freely.

POTHINUS Well: is not this love?

CLEOPATRA What! when he will do as much for the first girl he meets on his way back to Rome? Ask his slave, Britannus: he has been just as good to him. Nay, ask his very horse! His kindness is not for anything in me: it is in his own nature.

POTHINUS But how can you be sure that he does not love you as men love women?

CLEOPATRA Because I cannot make him jealous. I have tried.

POTHINUS Hm! Perhaps I should have asked, then, do *you* love *him*?

CLEOPATRA Can one love a god? Besides, I love another Roman: one whom I saw long before Cæsar—no god, but a man—one who can love and hate—one whom I can hurt and who would hurt me.

POTHINUS Does Cæsar know this?

CLEOPATRA Yes.

POTHINUS And he is not angry?

CLEOPATRA He promises to send him to Egypt to please me!

POTHINUS I do not understand this man.

CLEOPATRA *(with superb contempt) You* understand Cæsar! How could you? *(Proudly)* I do—by instinct.

POTHINUS *(deferentially, after a moment's thought)* Your Majesty caused me to be admitted today. What message has the Queen for me?

CLEOPATRA This. You think that by making my brother king, you will rule in Egypt, because you are his guardian and he is a little silly.

POTHINUS The Queen is pleased to say so.

CLEOPATRA The Queen is pleased to say this also. That Cæsar will eat you up, and Achillas, and my brother, as a cat eats up mice; and that he will put on this land of Egypt as a shepherd puts on his garment. And when he has done that, he will return to Rome, and leave Cleopatra here as his viceroy.

POTHINUS *(breaking out wrathfully)* That he shall never do. We have a thousand men to his ten; and we will drive him and his beggarly legions into the sea.

CLEOPATRA *(with scorn, getting up to go)* You rant like any common fellow. Go, then, and marshal your thousands; and make haste; for Mithridates of Pergamos[8] is at hand with reinforcements for Cæsar. Cæsar has held you at bay with two legions: we shall see what he will do with twenty.

POTHINUS Cleopatra—

CLEOPATRA Enough, enough: Cæsar has spoiled me for talking to weak things like you. *(She goes out.* POTHINUS, *with a gesture of rage, is following, when* FTATATEETA *enters and stops him.)*

POTHINUS Let me go forth from this hateful place.

FTATATEETA What angers you?

POTHINUS The curse of all the gods of Egypt be upon her! She has sold her country to the Roman, that she may buy it back from him with her kisses.

FTATATEETA Fool: did she not tell you that she would have Cæsar gone?

POTHINUS You listened?

FTATATEETA I took care that some honest woman should be at hand whilst you were with her.

[8]An ancient city in Asia Minor which was under the domination of Rome at the time of the play.

POTHINUS Now by the gods—

FTATATEETA Enough of your gods! Cæsar's gods are all powerful here. It is no use *you* coming to Cleopatra: you are only an Egyptian. She will not listen to any of her own race: she treats us all as children.

POTHINUS May she perish for it!

FTATATEETA *(balefully)* May your tongue wither for that wish! Go! send for Lucius Septimius, the slayer of Pompey. He is a Roman: may be she will listen to him. Begone!

POTHINUS *(darkly)* I know to whom I must go now.

FTATATEETA *(suspiciously)* To whom, then?

POTHINUS To a greater Roman than Lucius. And mark this, mistress. You thought, before Cæsar came, that Egypt should presently be ruled by you and your crew in the name of Cleopatra. I set myself against it—

FTATATEETA *(interrupting him—wrangling)* Ay; that it might be ruled by you and your crew in the name of Ptolemy.

POTHINUS Better me, or even you, than a woman with a Roman heart; and that is what Cleopatra is now become. Whilst I live, she shall never rule. So guide yourself accordingly. *(He goes out.)*

(It is by this time drawing on to dinner time. The table is laid on the roof of the palace; and thither RUFIO *is now climbing, ushered by a majestic palace official, wand of office in hand, and followed by a slave carrying an inlaid stool. After many stairs they emerge at last into a massive colonnade on the roof. Light curtains are drawn between the columns on the north and east to soften the westering sun. The official leads* RUFIO *to one of these shaded sections. A cord for pulling the curtains apart hangs down between the pillars.)*

THE OFFICIAL *(bowing)* The Roman commander will await Cæsar here. *(The slave sets down the stool near the southernmost column, and slips out through the curtains.)*

RUFIO *(sitting down, a little blown)* Pouf! That was a climb. How high have we come?

THE OFFICIAL We are on the palace roof, O Beloved of Victory!

RUFIO Good! the Beloved of Victory has no more stairs to get up.

(A second official enters from the opposite end, walking backwards.)

THE SECOND OFFICIAL Cæsar approaches.

*(*CÆSAR, *fresh from the bath, clad in a new tunic of purple silk, comes in, beaming and festive, followed by two slaves carrying a light couch, which is hardly more than an elaborately designed bench. They place it near the northmost of the two curtained columns. When this is done they slip out through the curtains; and the two officials, formally bowing, follow them.* RUFIO *rises to receive* CÆSAR.*)*

CÆSAR *(coming over to him)* Why, Rufio! *(Surveying his dress with an air of admiring astonishment)* A new baldrick! A new golden pommel to your sword! And you have had your hair cut! But not your beard—? impossible! *(He sniffs at* RUFIO'S *beard.)* Yes, perfumed, by Jupiter Olympus!

RUFIO *(growling)* Well: is it to please myself?

CÆSAR *(affectionately)* No, my son Rufio, but to please me—to celebrate my birthday.

RUFIO *(contemptuously)* Your birthday! You always have a birthday when there is a pretty girl to be flattered or an ambassador to be conciliated. We had seven of them in ten months last year.

CÆSAR *(contritely)* It is true, Rufio! I shall never break myself of these petty deceits.

RUFIO Who is to dine with us—besides Cleopatra?

CÆSAR Apollodorus the Sicilian.

RUFIO That popinjay!

CÆSAR Come! the popinjay is an amusing dog—tells a story; sings a song; and saves us the trouble of flattering the Queen. What does she care for old politicians and camp-fed bears like us? No: Apollodorus is good company, Rufio, good company.

RUFIO Well, he can swim a bit and fence a bit: he might be worse, if he only knew how to hold his tongue.

CÆSAR The gods forbid he should ever learn! Oh, this military life! this tedious, brutal life of action! That is the worst of us Romans: we are mere doers and drudgers: a swarm of bees turned into men. Give me a good talker—one with wit and imagination enough to live without continually doing something!

RUFIO Ay! a nice time he would have of it with you when dinner was over! Have you noticed that I am before my time?

CÆSAR Aha! I thought that meant something. What is it?

RUFIO Can we be overheard here?

CÆSAR Our privacy invites eavesdropping. I can remedy that. *(He claps his hands twice. The curtains are drawn, revealing the roof garden with a banqueting table set across in the middle for four persons, one at each end, and two side by side. The side next* CÆSAR *and* RUFIO *is blocked with golden wine vessels and basins. A gorgeous major-domo is superintending the laying of the table by a staff of slaves. The colonnade goes round the garden at both sides to the further end, where a gap in it, like a great gateway, leaves the view open to the sky beyond the western edge of the roof, except in the middle, where a life size image of Ra, seated on a huge plinth, towers up, with hawk head and crown of asp and disk. His altar, which stands at his feet, is a single white stone.)* Now everybody can see us, nobody will think of listening to us. *(He sits down on the bench left by the two slaves.)*

RUFIO *(sitting down on his stool)* Pothinus wants to speak to you. I advise you to see him: there is some plotting going on here among the women.

CÆSAR Who is Pothinus?

RUFIO The fellow with hair like squirrel's fur—the little King's bear leader, whom you kept prisoner.

CÆSAR *(annoyed)* And has he not escaped?

RUFIO No.

CÆSAR *(rising imperiously)* Why not? You have been guarding this man instead of watching the enemy. Have I not told you always to let prisoners escape unless there are special orders to the contrary? Are there not enough mouths to be fed without him?

RUFIO Yes; and if you would have a little sense and let me cut his throat you would save his rations. Anyhow, he wont escape. Three sentries have told him they would put a pilum through him if they saw him again What more can they do? He prefers to stay and spy on us. So would if I had to do with generals subject to fits of clemency.

CÆSAR *(resuming his seat, argued down)* Hm! And so he wants to see me

RUFIO Ay. I have brought him with me. He is waiting there *(jerking hi thumb over his shoulder)* under guard.

CÆSAR And you want me to see him?

RUFIO *(obstinately)* I dont want anything. I daresay you will do wha you like. Dont put it on to me.

CÆSAR *(with an air of doing it expressly to indulge* RUFIO*)* Well, well let us have him.

RUFIO *(calling)* Ho there, guard! Release your man and send him up *(Beckoning.)* Come along!

*(*POTHINUS *enters and stops mistrustfully between the two, lookin from one to the other.)*

CÆSAR *(graciously)* Ah, Pothinus! You are welcome. And what is th news this afternoon?

POTHINUS Cæsar: I come to warn you of a danger, and to make you a offer.

CÆSAR Never mind the danger. Make the offer.

RUFIO Never mind the offer. Whats the danger?

POTHINUS Cæsar: you think that Cleopatra is devoted to you.

CÆSAR *(gravely)* My friend: I already know what I think. Come to you offer.

POTHINUS I will deal plainly. I know not by what strange gods you hav been enabled to defend a palace and a few yards of beach against a cit and an army. Since we cut you off from Lake Mareotis, and you dug well in the salt sea sand and brought up buckets of fresh water from them we have known that your gods are irresistible, and that you are a worke of miracles. I no longer threaten you–

RUFIO *(sarcastically)* Very handsome of you, indeed.

POTHINUS So be it: you are the master. Our gods sent the north wes winds to keep you in our hands; but you have been too strong for them

CÆSAR *(gently urging him to come to the point)* Yes, yes, my friend. Bu what then?

RUFIO Spit it out, man. What have you to say?

POTHINUS I have to say that you have a traitress in your camp. Cleopatra–

THE MAJOR-DOMO *(at the table, announcing)* The Queen! *(*CÆSAR *an* RUFIO *rise.)*

RUFIO *(aside to* POTHINUS*)* You should have spat it out sooner, you foo Now it is too late.

*(*CLEOPATRA, *in gorgeous raiment, enters in state through the gap i the colonnade, and comes down past the image of Ra and past the tabl to* CÆSAR. *Her retinue, headed by* FTATATEETA, *joins the staff at th table.* CÆSAR *gives* CLEOPATRA *his seat, which she takes.)*

CLEOPATRA *(quickly, seeing* POTHINUS*)* What is *he* doing here?

CÆSAR *(seating himself beside her, in the most amiable of tempers)* Just going to tell me something about you. You shall hear it. Proceed, Pothinus.

POTHINUS *(disconcerted)* Cæsar—*(he stammers.)*

CÆSAR Well, out with it.

POTHINUS What I have to say is for your ear, not for the Queen's.

CLEOPATRA *(with subdued ferocity)* There are means of making you speak. Take care.

POTHINUS *(defiantly)* Cæsar does not employ those means.

CÆSAR My friend; when a man has anything to tell in this world, the difficulty is not to make him tell it, but to prevent him from telling it too often. Let me celebrate my birthday by setting you free. Farewell: we shall not meet again.

CLEOPATRA *(angrily)* Cæsar: this mercy is foolish.

POTHINUS *(to* CÆSAR*)* Will you not give me a private audience? Your life may depend on it. *(*CÆSAR *rises loftily.)*

RUFIO *(aside to* POTHINUS*)* Ass! Now we shall have some heroics.

CÆSAR *(oratorically)* Pothinus—

RUFIO *(interrupting him)* Cæsar: the dinner will spoil if you begin preaching your favorite sermon about life and death.

CLEOPATRA *(priggishly)* Peace, Rufio. I desire to hear Cæsar.

RUFIO *(bluntly)* Your Majesty has heard it before. You repeated it to Apollodorus last week; and he thought it was all your own. *(*CÆSAR'S *dignity collapses. Much tickled, he sits down again and looks roguishly at* CLEOPATRA, *who is furious.* RUFIO *calls as before)* Ho there, guard! Pass the prisoner out. He is released. *(To* POTHINUS*)* Now off with you. You have lost your chance.

POTHINUS *(his temper overcoming his prudence)* I *will* speak.

CÆSAR *(to* CLEOPATRA*)* You see. Torture would not have wrung a word from him.

POTHINUS Cæsar: you have taught Cleopatra the arts by which the Romans govern the world.

CÆSAR Alas! they cannot even govern themselves. What then?

POTHINUS What then? Are you so besotted with her beauty that you do not see that she is impatient to reign in Egypt alone, and that her heart is set on your departure?

CLEOPATRA *(rising)* Liar!

CÆSAR *(shocked)* What! Protestations! Contradictions!

CLEOPATRA *(ashamed, but trembling with suppressed rage)* No. I do not deign to contradict. Let him talk. *(She sits down again.)*

POTHINUS From her own lips I have heard it. You are to be her catspaw: you are to tear the crown from her brother's head and set it on her own, delivering us all into her hand—delivering yourself also. And then Cæsar can return to Rome, or depart through the gate of death, which is nearer and surer.

CÆSAR *(calmly)* Well, my friend; and is not this very natural?

POTHINUS *(astonished)* Natural! Then you do not resent treachery?

CÆSAR Resent! O thou foolish Egyptian, what have I to do with resentment? Do I resent the wind when it chills me, or the night when it makes me stumble in the darkness? Shall I resent youth when it turns from age, and ambition when it turns from servitude? To tell me such a story as this is but to tell me that the sun will rise tomorrow.

CLEOPATRA *(unable to contain herself)* But it is false—false. I swear it.

CÆSAR It is true, though you swore it a thousand times, and believed all you swore. *(She is convulsed with emotion. To screen her, he rises and takes* POTHINUS *to* RUFIO, *saying)* Come, Rufio: let us see Pothinus past the guard. I have a word to say to him. *(Aside to them)* We must give the Queen a moment to recover herself. *(Aloud)* Come. *(He takes* POTHINUS *and* RUFIO *out with him, conversing with them meanwhile.)* Tell your friends, Pothinus, that they must not think I am opposed to a reasonable settlement of the country's affairs—*(They pass out of hearing.)*

CLEOPATRA *(in a stifled whisper)* Ftatateeta, Ftatateeta.

FTATATEETA *(hurrying to her from the table and petting her)* Peace, child: be comforted—

CLEOPATRA *(interrupting her)* Can they hear us?

FTATATEETA No, dear heart, no.

CLEOPATRA Listen to me. If he leaves the Palace alive, never see my face again.

FTATATEETA He? Poth—

CLEOPATRA *(striking her on the mouth)* Strike his life out as I strike his name from your lips. Dash him down from the wall. Break him on the stones. Kill, kill, *kill* him.

FTATATEETA *(shewing all her teeth)* The dog shall perish.

CLEOPATRA Fail in this, and you go out from before me for ever.

FTATATEETA *(resolutely)* So be it. You shall not see my face until his eyes are darkened.

*(*CÆSAR *comes back, with* APOLLODORUS, *exquisitely dressed, and* RUFIO.*)*

CLEOPATRA *(to* FTATATEETA*)* Come soon—soon. *(*FTATATEETA *turns her meaning eyes for a moment on her mistress; then goes grimly away past Ra and out.* CLEOPATRA *runs like a gazelle to* CÆSAR.*)* So you have come back to me, Cæsar. *(Caressingly)* I thought you were angry. Welcome, Apollodorus. *(She gives him her hand to kiss, with her other arm about* CÆSAR.*)*

APOLLODORUS Cleopatra grows more womanly beautiful from week to week.

CLEOPATRA Truth, Apollodorus?

APOLLODORUS Far, far short of the truth! Friend Rufio threw a pearl into the sea: Cæsar fished up a diamond.

CÆSAR Cæsar fished up a touch of rheumatism, my friend. Come: to dinner! to dinner! *(They move towards the table.)*

CLEOPATRA *(skipping like a young fawn)* Yes, to dinner. I have ordered *such* a dinner for you, Cæsar!

CÆSAR Ay? What are we to have?

CLEOPATRA Peacocks' brains.

CÆSAR *(as if his mouth watered)* Peacocks' brains, Apollodorus!

APOLLODORUS Not for me. I prefer nightingales' tongues. *(He goes to one of the two covers set side by side.)*

CLEOPATRA Roast boar, Rufio!

RUFIO *(gluttonously)* Good! *(He goes to the seat next* APOLLODORUS, *on his left.)*

CÆSAR *(looking at his seat, which is at the end of the table, to Ra's left hand)* What has become of my leathern cushion?

CLEOPATRA *(at the opposite end)* I have got new ones for you.

THE MAJOR-DOMO These cushions, Cæsar, are of Maltese gauze, stuffed with rose leaves.

CÆSAR Rose leaves! Am I a caterpillar? *(He throws the cushions away and seats himself on the leather mattress underneath.)*

CLEOPATRA What a shame! My new cushions!

THE MAJOR-DOMO *(at* CÆSAR'S *elbow)* What shall we serve to whet Cæsar's appetite?

CÆSAR What have you got?

THE MAJOR-DOMO Sea hedgehogs, black and white sea acorns, sea nettles, beccaficoes, purple shellfish –

CÆSAR Any oysters?

MAJOR-DOMO Assuredly.

CÆSAR *British* oysters?

MAJOR-DOMO *(assenting)* British oysters, Cæsar.

CÆSAR Oysters, then. *(The* MAJOR-DOMO *signs to a slave at each order; and the slave goes out to execute it.)* I have been in Britain – that western land of romance – the last piece of earth on the edge of the ocean that surrounds the world. I went there in search of its famous pearls. The British pearl was a fable; but in searching for it I found the British oyster.

APOLLODORUS All posterity will bless you for it. *(To the* MAJOR-DOMO*)* Sea hedgehogs for me.

RUFIO Is there nothing solid to begin with?

MAJOR-DOMO Fieldfares with asparagus –

CLEOPATRA *(interrupting)* Fattened fowls! have some fattened fowls, Rufio.

RUFIO Ay, that will do.

CLEOPATRA *(greedily)* Fieldfares for me.

MAJOR-DOMO Cæsar will deign to choose his wine? Sicilian, Lesbian, Chian –

RUFIO *(contemptuously)* All Greek.

APOLLODORUS Who would drink Roman wine when he could get Greek. Try the Lesbian, Cæsar.

CÆSAR Bring me my barley water.

RUFIO *(with intense disgust)* Ugh! Bring me my Falernian.[9] *(The Falernian is presently brought to him.)*

[9]An Italian wine.

CLEOPATRA *(pouting)* It is waste of time giving you dinners, Cæsar. My scullions would not condescend to your diet.

CÆSAR *(relenting)* Well, well: let us try the Lesbian. *(The* MAJOR-DOMO *fills* CÆSAR'S *goblet; then* CLEOPATRA'S *and* APOLLODORUS'S.*)* But when I return to Rome, I will make laws against these extravagances. I will even get the laws carried out.

CLEOPATRA *(coaxingly)* Never mind. Today you are to be like other people: idle, luxurious, and kind. *(She stretches her hand to him along the table.)*

CÆSAR Well, for once I will sacrifice my comfort—*(kissing her hand)* there! *(He takes a draught of wine.)* Now are you satisfied?

CLEOPATRA And you no longer believe that I long for your departure for Rome?

CÆSAR I no longer believe anything. My brains are asleep. Besides, who knows whether I shall return to Rome?

RUFIO *(alarmed)* How? Eh? What?

CÆSAR What has Rome to shew me that I have not seen already? One year of Rome is like another, except that I grow older, whilst the crowd in the Appian Way is always the same age.

APOLLODORUS It is no better here in Egypt. The old men, when they are tired of life, say "We have seen everything except the source of the Nile."

CÆSAR *(his imagination catching fire)* And why not see that? Cleopatra: will you come with me and track the flood to its cradle in the heart of the regions of mystery? Shall we leave Rome behind us—Rome, that has achieved greatness only to learn how greatness destroys nations of men who are not great! Shall I make you a new kingdom, and build you a holy city there in the great unknown?

CLEOPATRA *(rapturously)* Yes, yes. You shall.

RUFIO Ay: now he will conquer Africa with two legions before we come to the roast boar.

APOLLODORUS Come: no scoffing. This is a noble scheme: in it Cæsar is no longer merely the conquering soldier, but the creative poet-artist. Let us name the holy city, and consecrate it with Lesbian wine.

CÆSAR Cleopatra shall name it herself.

CLEOPATRA It shall be called Cæsar's Gift to his Beloved.

APOLLODORUS No, no. Something vaster than that—something universal, like the starry firmament.

CÆSAR *(prosaically)* Why not simply The Cradle of the Nile?

CLEOPATRA No: the Nile is my ancestor; and he is a god. Oh! I have thought of something. The Nile shall name it himself. Let us call upon him. *(To the* MAJOR-DOMO*)* Send for him. *(The three men stare at one another; but the* MAJOR-DOMO *goes out as if he had received the most matter-of-fact order.)* And *(to the retinue)* away with you all.

(The retinue withdraws, making obeisance.)

(A priest enters, carrying a miniature sphinx with a tiny tripod before it. A morsel of incense is smoking in the tripod. The priest comes to the table and places the image in the middle of it. The light begins to

change to the magenta purple of the Egyptian sunset, as if the god had brought a strange colored shadow with him. The three men are determined not to be impressed; but they feel curious in spite of themselves.)

CÆSAR What hocus-pocus is this?

CLEOPATRA You shall see. And it is *not* hocus-pocus. To do it properly, we should kill something to please him; but perhaps he will answer Cæsar without that if we spill some wine to him.

APOLLODORUS *(turning his head to look up over his shoulder at Ra)* Why not appeal to our hawkheaded friend here?

CLEOPATRA *(nervously)* Sh! He will hear you and be angry.

RUFIO *(phlegmatically)* The source of the Nile is out of his district, I expect.

CLEOPATRA No: I will have my city named by nobody but my dear little sphinx, because it was in its arms that Cæsar found me asleep. *(She languishes at* CÆSAR *then turns curtly to the priest.)* Go. I am a priestess, and have power to take your charge from you. *(The priest makes a reverence and goes out.)* Now let us call on the Nile all together. Perhaps he will rap on the table.

CÆSAR What! table rapping! Are such superstitions still believed in this year 707 of the Republic?

CLEOPATRA It is no superstition: our priests learn lots of things from the tables. Is it not so, Apollodorus?

APOLLODORUS Yes: I profess myself a converted man. When Cleopatra is priestess, Apollodorus is devotee. Propose the conjuration.

CLEOPATRA You must say with me "Send us thy voice, Father Nile."

ALL FOUR *(holding their glasses together before the idol)* Send us thy voice, Father Nile.

(The death cry of a man in mortal terror and agony answers them. Appalled, the men set down their glasses, and listen. Silence. The purple deepens in the sky. CÆSAR, *glancing at* CLEOPATRA, *catches her pouring out her wine before the god, with gleaming eyes, and mute assurances of gratitude and worship.* APOLLODORUS *springs up and runs to the edge of the roof to peer down and listen.)*

CÆSAR *(looking piercingly at* CLEOPATRA*)* What was that?

CLEOPATRA *(petulantly)* Nothing. They are beating some slave.

CÆSAR Nothing.

RUFIO A man with a knife in him, I'll swear.

CÆSAR *(rising)* A murder!

APOLLODORUS *(at the back, waving his hand for silence)* S-sh! Silence. Did you hear that?

CÆSAR Another cry?

APOLLODORUS *(returning to the table)* No, a thud. Something fell on the beach, I think.

RUFIO *(grimly, as he rises)* Something with bones in it, eh?

CÆSAR *(shuddering)* Hush, hush, Rufio. *(He leaves the table and returns to the colonnade:* RUFIO *following at his left elbow, and* APOLLODORUS *at the other side.)*

CLEOPATRA *(still in her place at the table)* Will you leave me, Cæsar? Apollodorus: are you going?

APOLLODORUS Faith, dearest Queen, my appetite is gone.

CÆSAR Go down to the courtyard, Apollodorus; and find out what has happened.

*(*APOLLODORUS *nods and goes out, making for the staircase by which* RUFIO *ascended.)*

CLEOPATRA Your soldiers have killed somebody, perhaps. What does it matter?

(The murmur of a crowd rises from the beach below. CÆSAR *and* RUFIO *look at one another.)*

CÆSAR This must be seen to. *(He is about to follow* APOLLODORUS *when* RUFIO *stops him with a hand on his arms as* FTATATEETA *comes back by the far end of the roof, with dragging steps, a drowsy satiety in her eyes and in the corners of the bloodhound lips. For a moment* CÆSAR *suspects that she is drunk with wine. Not so* RUFIO: *he knows well the red vintage that has inebriated her.)*

RUFIO *(in a low tone)* There is some mischief between those two.

FTATATEETA The Queen looks again on the face of her servant.

*(*CLEOPATRA *looks at her for a moment with an exultant reflection of her murderous expression. Then she flings her arms round her; kisses her repeatedly and savagely; and tears off her jewels and heaps them on her. The two men turn from the spectacle to look at one another.* FTATATEETA *drags herself sleepily to the altar; kneels before Ra; and remains there in prayer.* CÆSAR *goes to* CLEOPATRA, *leaving* RUFIO *in the colonnade.)*

CÆSAR *(with searching earnestness)* Cleopatra: what has happened?

CLEOPATRA *(in mortal dread of him, but with her utmost cajolery)* Nothing, dearest Cæsar. *(With sickly sweetness, her voice almost failing)* Nothing. I am innocent. *(She approaches him affectionately.)* Dear Cæsar: are you angry with me? Why do you look at me so? I have been here with you all the time. How can I know what has happened?

CÆSAR *(reflectively)* That is true.

CLEOPATRA *(greatly relieved, trying to caress him)* Of course it is true. *(He does not respond to the caress)* You know it is true, Rufio.

(The murmur without suddenly swells to a roar and subsides.)

RUFIO I shall know presently. *(He makes for the altar in the burly trot that serves him for a stride, and touches* FTATATEETA *on the shoulder.)* Now, mistress: I shall want you. *(He orders her, with a gesture, to go before him.)*

FTATATEETA *(rising and glowering at him)* My place is with the Queen.

CLEOPATRA She has done no harm, Rufio.

CÆSAR *(to* RUFIO*)* Let her stay.

RUFIO *(sitting down on the altar)* Very well. Then my place is here too; and you can see what is the matter for yourself. The city is in a pretty uproar, it seems.

CÆSAR *(with grave displeasure)* Rufio: there is a time for obedience.

RUFIO And there is a time for obstinacy. *(He folds his arms doggedly.)*

CÆSAR *(to* CLEOPATRA*)* Send her away.

CLEOPATRA *(whining in her eagerness to propitiate him)* Yes, I will. I will do whatever you ask me, Cæsar, always, because I love you. Ftatateeta: go away.

FTATATEETA The Queen's word is my will. I shall be at hand for the Queen's call. *(She goes out past Ra, as she came.)*

RUFIO *(following her)* Remember, Cæsar, your bodyguard also is within call. *(He follows her out.)*

*(*CLEOPATRA, *presuming upon* CÆSAR'S *submission to* RUFIO, *leaves the table and sits down on the bench in the colonnade.)*

CLEOPATRA Why do you allow Rufio to treat you so? You should teach him his place.

CÆSAR Teach him to be my enemy, and to hide his thoughts from me as you are now hiding yours.

CLEOPATRA *(her fears returning)* Why do you say that, Cæsar? Indeed, indeed, I am not hiding anything. You are wrong to treat me like this. *(She stifles a sob.)* I am only a child; and you turn into stone because you think some one has been killed. I cannot bear it. *(She purposely breaks down and weeps. He looks at her with profound sadness and complete coldness. She looks up to see what effect she is producing. Seeing that he is unmoved, she sits up, pretending to struggle with her emotion and to put it bravely away.)* But there: I know you hate tears: you shall not be troubled with them. I know you are not angry, but only sad; only I am so silly, I cannot help being hurt when you speak coldly. Of course you are quite right: it is dreadful to think of anyone being killed or even hurt; and I hope nothing really serious has—*(her voice dies away under his contemptuous penetration.)*

CÆSAR What has frightened you into this? What have you done? *(A trumpet sounds on the beach below.)* Aha! that sounds like the answer.

CLEOPATRA *(sinking back trembling on the bench and covering her face with her hands)* I have not betrayed you, Cæsar: I swear it.

CÆSAR I know that. I have not trusted you. *(He turns from her, and is about to go out when* APOLLODORUS *and* BRITANNUS *drag in* LUCIUS SEPTIMIUS *to him.* RUFIO *follows.* CÆSAR *shudders.)* Again, Pompey's murderer!

RUFIO The town has gone mad, I think. They are for tearing the palace down and driving us into the sea straight away. We laid hold of this renegade in clearing them out of the courtyard.

CÆSAR Release him. *(They let go his arms.)* What has offended the citizens, Lucius Septimius?

LUCIUS What did you expect, Cæsar? Pothinus was a favorite of theirs.

CÆSAR What has happened to Pothinus? I set him free, here, not half an hour ago. Did they not pass him out?

LUCIUS Ay, through the gallery arch sixty feet above ground, with three inches of steel in his ribs. He is as dead as Pompey. We are quits now, as to killing—you and I.

CÆSAR *(shocked)* Assassinated!—our prisoner, our guest! *(He turns reproachfully on* RUFIO*)* Rufio—

RUFIO *(emphatically—anticipating the question)* Whoever did it was a wise man and a friend of yours (CLEOPATRA *is greatly emboldened)* but none of *us* had a hand in it. So it is no use to frown at me. (CÆSAR *turns and looks at* CLEOPATRA.)

CLEOPATRA *(violently—rising)* He was slain by order of the Queen of Egypt. I am not Julius Cæsar the dreamer, who allows every slave to insult him. Rufio has said I did well: now the others shall judge me too. *(She turns to the others.)* This Pothinus sought to make me conspire with him to betray Cæsar to Achillas and Ptolemy. I refused; and he cursed me and came privily to Cæsar to accuse me of his own treachery. I caught him in the act; and he insulted me—*me*, the Queen! to my face. Cæsar would not avenge me: he spoke him fair and set him free. Was I right to avenge myself? Speak, Lucius.

LUCIUS I do not gainsay it. But you will get little thanks from Cæsar for it.

CLEOPATRA Speak, Apollodorus. Was I wrong?

APOLLODORUS I have only one word of blame, most beautiful. You should have called upon me, your knight; and in fair duel I should have slain the slanderer.

CLEOPATRA *(passionately)* I will be judged by your very slave, Cæsar. Britannus: speak. Was I wrong?

BRITANNUS Were treachery, falsehood, and disloyalty left unpunished, society must become like an arena full of wild beasts, tearing one another to pieces. Cæsar is in the wrong.

CÆSAR *(with quiet bitterness)* And so the verdict is against me, it seems.

CLEOPATRA *(vehemently)* Listen to me, Cæsar. If one man in all Alexandria can be found to say that I did wrong, I swear to have myself crucified on the door of the palace by my own slaves.

CÆSAR If one man in all the world can be found, now or forever, to *know* that you did wrong, that man will have either to conquer the world as I have, or be crucified by it. *(The uproar in the streets again reaches them.)* Do you hear? These knockers at your gate are also believers in vengeance and in stabbing. You have slain their leader: it is right that they shall slay you. If you doubt it, ask your four counsellors here. And then in the name of that *right (he emphasizes the word with great scorn)* shall I not slay them for murdering their Queen, and be slain in my turn by their countrymen as the invader of their fatherland? Can Rome do less then than slay these slayers, too, to shew the world how Rome avenges her sons and her honor. And so, to the end of history, murder shall breed murder, always in the name of right and honor and peace, until the gods are tired of blood and create a race that can understand. *(Fierce uproar.* CLEOPATRA *becomes white with terror.)* Hearken, you who must not be insulted. Go near enough to catch their words: you will find them bitterer than the tongue of Pothinus. *(loftily, wrapping himself up in an impenetrable dignity)* Let the Queen of Egypt now give her orders for vengeance, and take her measures for defence; for she has renounced Cæsar. *(He turns to go.)*

CLEOPATRA *(terrified, running to him and falling on her knees)* You will not desert me, Cæsar. You will defend the palace.

CÆSAR You have taken the powers of life and death upon you. I am only a dreamer.

CLEOPATRA But they will kill me.

CÆSAR And why not?

CLEOPATRA In pity—

CÆSAR Pity! What! has it come to this so suddenly, that nothing can save you now but pity? Did it save Pothinus?

(She rises, wringing her hands, and goes back to the bench in despair. APOLLODORUS *shews his sympathy with her by quietly posting himself behind the bench. The sky has by this time become the most vivid purple, and soon begins to change to a glowing pale orange, against which the colonnade and the great image shew darklier and darklier.)*

RUFIO Cæsar: enough of preaching. The enemy is at the gate.

CÆSAR *(turning on him and giving way to his wrath)* Ay; and what has held him baffled at the gate all these months? Was it my folly, as you deem it, or your wisdom? In this Egyptian Red Sea of blood, whose hand has held all your heads above the waves? *(turning on* CLEOPATRA*)* And yet, when Cæsar says to such an one, "Friend, go free," you, clinging for your little life to my sword, dare steal out and stab him in the back? And you, soldiers and gentlemen, and honest servants as you forget that you are, applaud this assassination, and say "Cæsar is in the wrong." By the gods, I am tempted to open my hand and let you all sink into the flood.

CLEOPATRA *(with a ray of cunning hope)* But, Cæsar, if you do, you will perish yourself.

*(*CÆSAR'S *eyes blaze.)*

RUFIO *(greatly alarmed)* Now, by great Jove, you filthy little Egyptian rat, that is the very word to make him walk out alone into the city and leave us here to be cut to pieces. *(Desperately, to* CÆSAR*)* Will you desert us because we are a parcel of fools? I mean no harm by killing: I do it as a dog kills a cat, by instinct. We are all dogs at your heels; but we have served you faithfully.

CÆSAR *(relenting)* Alas, Rufio, my son, my son: as dogs we are like to perish now in the streets.

APOLLODORUS *(at his post behind* CLEOPATRA'S *seat)* Cæsar: what you say has an Olympian ring in it: it must be right; for it is fine art. But I am still on the side of Cleopatra. If we must die, she shall not want the devotion of a man's heart nor the strength of a man's arm.

CLEOPATRA *(sobbing)* But I dont want to die.

CÆSAR *(sadly)* Oh, ignoble, ignoble!

LUCIUS *(coming forward between* CÆSAR *and* CLEOPATRA.*)* Hearken to me, Cæsar. It may be ignoble; but I also mean to live as long as I can.

CÆSAR Well, my friend, you are likely to outlive Cæsar. Is it any magic of mine, think you, that has kept your army and this whole city at bay for so long? Yesterday, what quarrel had they with me that they should risk their lives against me? But today we have flung them down their hero, murdered; and now every man of them is set upon clearing out this nest of assassins—for such we are and no more. Take courage then; and sharpen your sword. Pompey's head has fallen; and Cæsar's head is ripe.

APOLLODORUS Does Cæsar despair?

CÆSAR *(with infinite pride)* He who has never hoped can never despair. Cæsar, in good or bad fortune, looks his fate in the face.

LUCIUS Look it in the face, then; and it will smile as it always has on Cæsar.

CÆSAR *(with involuntary haughtiness)* Do you presume to encourage me?

LUCIUS I offer you my services. I will change sides if you will have me.

CÆSAR *(suddenly coming down to earth again, and looking sharply at him, divining that there is something behind the offer)* What! At this point?

LUCIUS *(firmly)* At this point.

RUFIO Do you suppose Cæsar is mad, to trust you?

LUCIUS I do not ask him to trust me until he is victorious. I ask for my life, and for a command in Cæsar's army. And since Cæsar is a fair dealer, I will pay in advance.

CÆSAR Pay! How?

LUCIUS With a piece of good news for you.

*(*CÆSAR *divines the news in a flash.)*

RUFIO What news?

CÆSAR *(with an elate and buoyant energy which makes* CLEOPATRA *sit up and stare)* What news! What news, did you say, my son Rufio? The relief has arrived: what other news remains for us? Is it not so, Lucius Septimius? Mithridates of Pergamos is on the march.

LUCIUS He has taken Pelusium.[10]

CÆSAR *(delighted)* Lucius Septimius: you are henceforth my officer. Rufio: the Egyptians must have sent every soldier from the city to prevent Mithridates crossing the Nile. There is nothing in the streets now but mob—mob!

LUCIUS It is so. Mithridates is marching by the great road to Memphis to cross above the Delta. Achillas will fight him there.

CÆSAR *(all audacity)* Achillas shall fight Cæsar there. See, Rufio. *(He runs to the table; snatches a napkin; and draws a plan on it with his finger dipped in wine, whilst* RUFIO *and* LUCIUS SEPTIMIUS *crowd about him to watch, all looking closely, for the light is now almost gone.)* Here is the palace *(pointing to his plan):* here is the theatre. You *(to* RUFIO*)* take twenty men and pretend to go by that street *(pointing it out);* and whilst they are stoning you, out go the cohorts by this and this. My streets are right, are they, Lucius?

LUCIUS Ay, that is the fig market—

CÆSAR *(too much excited to listen to him)* I saw them the day we arrived. Good! *(He throws the napkin on the table, and comes down again into the colonnade.)* Away, Britannus: tell Petronius that within an hour half our forces must take ship for the western lake. See to my

[10]An important Egyptian citadel.

horse and armor. (BRITANNUS *runs out.)* With the rest, *I* shall march round the lake and up the Nile to meet Mithridates. Away, Lucius; and give the word. *(*LUCIUS *hurries out after* BRITANNUS.*)* Apollodorus: lend me your sword and your right arm for this campaign.

APOLLODORUS Ay, and my heart and life to boot.

CÆSAR *(grasping his hand)* I accept both. *(mighty handshake.)* Are you ready for work?

APOLLODORUS Ready for Art—the Art of War *(he rushes out after* LUCIUS, *totally forgetting* CLEOPATRA.*)*

RUFIO Come! this is something like business.

CÆSAR *(buoyantly)* Is it not, my only son? *(He claps his hands. The slaves hurry in to the table.)* No more of this mawkish revelling: away with all this stuff: shut it out of my sight and be off with you. *(The slaves begin to remove the table; and the curtains are drawn, shutting in the colonnade.)* You understand about the streets, Rufio?

RUFIO Ay, I think I do. I will get through them, at all events.

(The bucina sounds busily in the courtyard beneath.)

CÆSAR Come, then: we must talk to the troops and hearten them. You down to the beach: I to the courtyard. *(He makes for the staircase.)*

CLEOPATRA *(rising from her seat, where she has been quite neglected all this time, and stretching out her hands timidly to him)* Cæsar.

CÆSAR *(turning)* Eh?

CLEOPATRA Have you forgotten me?

CÆSAR *(indulgently)* I am busy now, my child, busy. When I return your affairs shall be settled. Farewell; and be good and patient.

(He goes, preoccupied and quite indifferent. She stands with clenched fists, in speechless rage and humiliation.)

RUFIO That game is played and lost, Cleopatra. The woman always gets the worst of it.

CLEOPATRA *(haughtily)* Go. Follow your master.

RUFIO *(in her ear, with rough familiarity)* A word first. Tell your executioner that if Pothinus had been properly killed—*in the throat*—he would not have called out. Your man bungled his work.

CLEOPATRA *(enigmatically)* How do you know it was a man?

RUFIO *(startled, and puzzled)* It was not you: you were with us when it happened. *(She turns her back scornfully on him. He shakes his head, and draws the curtains to go out. It is now a magnificent moonlit night. The table has been removed.* FTATATEETA *is seen in the light of the moon and stars, again in prayer before the white altar-stone of Ra.* RUFIO *starts; closes the curtains again softly; and says in a low voice to* CLEOPATRA*)* Was it she? with her own hand?

CLEOPATRA *(threateningly)* Whoever it was, let my enemies beware of her. Look to it, Rufio, you who dare make the Queen of Egypt a fool before Cæsar.

RUFIO *(looking grimly at her)* I will look to it, Cleopatra. *(He nods in confirmation of the promise, and slips out through the curtains, loosening his sword in its sheath as he goes.)*

ROMAN SOLDIERS *(in the courtyard below)* Hail, Cæsar! Hail, hail!

(CLEOPATRA *listens. The bucina sounds again, followed by several trumpets.)*

CLEOPATRA *(wringing her hands and calling)* Ftatateeta. Ftatateeta. It is dark; and I am alone. Come to me. *(silence)* Ftatateeta. *(louder)* Ftatateeta. *(Silence. In a panic she snatches the cord and pulls the curtains apart.)*

(FTATATEETA *is lying dead on the altar of Ra, with her throat cut. Her blood deluges the white stone.)*

act V

(High noon. Festival and military pageant on the esplanade before the palace. In the east harbor CÆSAR'S *galley, so gorgeously decorated that it seems to be rigged with flowers, is alongside the quay, close to the steps* APOLLODORUS *descended when he embarked with the carpet. A Roman guard is posted there in charge of a gangway, whence a red floorcloth is laid down the middle of the esplanade, turning off to the north opposite the central gate in the palace front, which shuts in the esplanade on the south side. The broad steps of the gate, crowded with* CLEOPATRA'S *ladies, all in their gayest attire, are like a flower garden. The façade is lined by her guard, officered by the same gallants to whom* BEL AFFRIS *announced the coming of* CÆSAR *six months before in the old palace on the Syrian border. The north side is lined by Roman soldiers, with the townsfolk on tiptoe behind them, peering over their heads at the cleared esplanade, in which the officers stroll about, chatting. Among these are* BELZANOR *and the* PERSIAN; *also the centurion, vinewood cudgel in hand, battle worn, thick-booted, and much outshone, both socially and decoratively, by the Egyptian officers.*

APOLLODORUS *makes his way through the townsfolk and calls to the officers from behind the Roman line.)*

APOLLODORUS Hullo! May I pass?

CENTURION Pass Apollodorus the Sicilian there! *(The soldiers let him through.)*

BELZANOR Is Cæsar at hand?

APOLLODORUS Not yet. He is still in the market place. I could not stand any more of the roaring of the soldiers! After half an hour of the enthusiasm of an army, one feels the need of a little sea air.

PERSIAN Tell us the news. Hath he slain the priests?

APOLLODORUS Not he. They met him in the market place with ashes on their heads and their gods in their hands. They placed the gods at his feet. The only one that was worth looking at was Apis: a miracle of gold and ivory work. By my advice he offered the chief priest two talents for it.

BELZANOR *(appalled)* Apis the all-knowing for two talents! What said the Priest?

APOLLODORUS He invoked the mercy of Apis, and asked for five.

BELZANOR There will be famine and tempest in the land for this.

PERSIAN Pooh! Why did not Apis cause Cæsar to be vanquished by Achillas? Any fresh news from the war, Apollodorus?

APOLLODORUS The little King Ptolemy was drowned.

BELZANOR Drowned! How?

APOLLODORUS With the rest of them. Cæsar attacked them from three sides at once and swept them into the Nile. Ptolemy's barge sank.

BELZANOR A marvellous man, this Cæsar! Will he come soon, think you?

APOLLODORUS He was settling the Jewish question when I left.

(A flourish of trumpets from the north, and commotion among the townsfolk, announces the approach of CÆSAR.*)*

PERSIAN He has made short work of them. Here he comes. *(He hurries to his post in front of the Egyptian lines.)*

BELZANOR *(following him)* Ho there! Cæsar comes.

(The soldiers stand at attention, and dress their lines. APOLLODORUS *goes to the Egyptian line.)*

CENTURION *(hurrying to the gangway guard)* Attention there! Cæsar comes.

*(*CÆSAR *arrives in state with* RUFIO: BRITANNUS *following. The soldiers receive him with enthusiastic shouting.)*

CÆSAR I see my ship awaits me. The hour of Cæsar's farewell to Egypt has arrived. And now, Rufio, what remains to be done before I go?

RUFIO *(at his left hand)* You have not yet appointed a Roman governor for this province.

CÆSAR *(looking whimsically at him, but speaking with perfect gravity)* What say you to Mithridates of Pergamos, my reliever and rescuer, the great son of Eupator?

RUFIO Why, that you will want him elsewhere. Do you forget that you have some three or four armies to conquer on your way home?

CÆSAR Indeed! Well, what say you to yourself?

RUFIO *(incredulously)* I! I a governor! What are you dreaming of? Do you not know that I am only the son of a freedman?

CÆSAR *(affectionately)* Has not Cæsar called you his son? *(Calling to the whole assembly)* Peace awhile there; and hear me.

THE ROMAN SOLDIERS Hear Cæsar.

CÆSAR Hear the service, quality, rank and name of the Roman governor. By service, Cæsar's shield; by quality, Cæsar's friend; by rank, a Roman soldier. *(The Roman soldiers give a triumphant shout.)* By name, Rufio. *(They shout again.)*

RUFIO *(kissing* CÆSAR'S *hand)* Ay: I am Cæsar's shield; but of what use shall I be when I am no longer on Cæsar's arm? Well, no matter—*(He becomes husky and turns away to recover himself.)*

CÆSAR Where is that British Islander of mine?

BRITANNUS *(coming forward on* CÆSAR'S *right hand)* Here, Cæsar.

CÆSAR Who bade you, pray, thrust yourself into the battle of the Delta, uttering the barbarous cries of your native land, and affirming yourself a match for any four of the Egyptians, to whom you applied unseemly epithets?

BRITANNUS Cæsar: I ask you to excuse the language that escaped me in the heat of the moment.

CÆSAR And how did you, who cannot swim, cross the canal with us when we stormed the camp?

BRITANNUS Cæsar: I clung to the tail of your horse.

CÆSAR These are not the deeds of a slave, Britannicus, but of a free man.

BRITANNUS Cæsar: I was born free.

CÆSAR But they call you Cæsar's slave.

BRITANNUS Only as Cæsar's slave have I found real freedom.

CÆSAR *(moved)* Well said. Ungrateful that I am, I was about to set you free; but now I will not part from you for a million talents. *(He claps him friendly on the shoulder.* BRITANNUS, *gratified, but a trifle shamefaced, takes his hand and kisses it sheepishly.)*

BELZANOR *(to the* PERSIAN*)* This Roman knows how to make men serve him.

PERSIAN Ay: men too humble to become dangerous rivals to him.

BELZANOR O subtle one! O cynic!

CÆSAR *(seeing* APOLLODORUS *in the Egyptian corner, and calling to him)* Apollodorus: I leave the art of Egypt in your charge. Remember: Rome loves art and will encourage it ungrudgingly.

APOLLODORUS I understand, Cæsar. Rome will produce no art itself; but it will buy up and take away whatever the other nations produce.

CÆSAR What! Rome produce no art! Is peace not an art? is war not an art? is government not an art? is civilization not an art? All these we give you in exchange for a few ornaments. You will have the best of the bargain. *(turning to* RUFIO*)* And now, what else have I to do before I embark? *(trying to recollect)* There is something I cannot remember: what can it be? Well, well: it must remain undone: we must not waste this favorable wind. Farewell, Rufio.

RUFIO Cæsar: I am loth to let you go to Rome without your shield. There are too many daggers there.

CÆSAR It matters not: I shall finish my life's work on my way back; and then I shall have lived long enough. Besides: I have always disliked the idea of dying: I had rather be killed. Farewell.

RUFIO *(with a sigh, raising his hands and giving* CÆSAR *up as incorrigible)* Farewell. *(They shake hands.)*

CÆSAR *(waving his hand to* APOLLODORUS*)* Farewell, Apollodorus, and my friends, all of you. Aboard!

(The gangway is run out from the quay to the ship. As CÆSAR *moves towards it,* CLEOPATRA, *cold and tragic, cunningly dressed in black, without ornaments or decoration of any kind, and thus making a striking figure among the brilliantly dressed bevy of ladies as she passes through it, comes from the palace and stands on the steps.* CÆSAR *does not see her until she speaks.)*

CLEOPATRA Has Cleopatra no part in this leavetaking?

CÆSAR *(enlightened)* Ah, I knew there was something. *(To* RUFIO*)* How could you let me forget her, Rufio? *(Hastening to her)* Had I gone without seeing you, I should never have forgiven myself. *(He takes her* *hands, and brings her into the middle of the esplanade. She submits stonily.)* Is this mourning for me?

CLEOPATRA No.

CÆSAR *(remorsefully)* Ah, that was thoughtless of me! It is for your brother.

CLEOPATRA No.

CÆSAR For whom, then?

CLEOPATRA Ask the Roman governor whom you have left us.

CÆSAR Rufio?

CLEOPATRA Yes: Rufio. *(She points at him with deadly scorn.)* He who is to rule here in Cæsar's name, in Cæsar's way, according to Cæsar's boasted laws of life.

CÆSAR *(dubiously)* He is to rule as he can, Cleopatra. He has taken the work upon him, and will do it in his own way.

CLEOPATRA Not in your way, then?

CÆSAR *(puzzled)* What do you mean by my way?

CLEOPATRA Without punishment. Without revenge. Without judgment.

CÆSAR *(approvingly)* Ay: that is the right way, the great way, the only possible way in the end. *(To* RUFIO*)* Believe it, Rufio, if you can.

RUFIO Why, I believe it, Cæsar. You have convinced me of it long ago. But look you. You are sailing for Numidia today. Now tell me: if you meet a hungry lion there, you will not punish it for wanting to eat you?

CÆSAR *(wondering what he is driving at)* No.

RUFIO Nor revenge upon it the blood of those it has already eaten.

CÆSAR No.

RUFIO Nor judge it for its guiltiness.

CÆSAR No.

RUFIO What, then, will you do to save your life from it?

CÆSAR *(promptly)* Kill it, man, without malice, just as it would kill me. What does this parable of the lion mean?

RUFIO Why, Cleopatra had a tigress that killed men at her bidding. I thought she might bid it kill you some day. Well, had I not been Cæsar's pupil, what pious things might I not have done to that tigress! I might have punished it. I might have revenged Pothinus on it.

CÆSAR *(interjects)* Pothinus!

RUFIO *(continuing)* I might have judged it. But I put all these follies behind me; and, without malice, only cut its throat. And that is why Cleopatra comes to you in mourning.

CLEOPATRA *(vehemently)* He has shed the blood of my servant Ftatateeta. On your head be it as upon his, Cæsar, if you hold him free of it.

CÆSAR *(energetically)* On my head be it, then; for it was well done. Rufio: had you set yourself in the seat of the judge, and with hateful ceremonies and appeals to the gods handed that woman over to some hired executioner to be slain before the people in the name of justice, never again would I have touched your hand without a shudder. But this was natural slaying: I feel no horror at it.

*(*RUFIO*, satisfied, nods at* CLEOPATRA*, mutely inviting her to mark that.)*

CLEOPATRA *(pettish and childish in her impotence)* No: not when a Roman slays an Egyptian. All the world will now see how unjust and corrupt Cæsar is.

CÆSAR *(taking her hands coaxingly)* Come: do not be angry with me. I am sorry for that poor Totateeta. *(She laughs in spite of herself.)* Aha! you are laughing. Does that mean reconciliation?

CLEOPATRA *(angry with herself for laughing)* No, no, NO!! But it is so ridiculous to hear you call her Totateeta.

CÆSAR What! As much a child as ever, Cleopatra! Have I not made a woman of you after all?

CLEOPATRA Oh, it is you who are a great baby: you make me seem silly because you will not behave seriously. But you have treated me badly; and I do not forgive you.

CÆSAR Bid me farewell.

CLEOPATRA I will not.

CÆSAR *(coaxing)* I will send you a beautiful present from Rome.

CLEOPATRA *(proudly)* Beauty from Rome to Egypt indeed! What can Rome give *me* that Egypt cannot give me?

APOLLODORUS That is true, Cæsar. If the present is to be really beautiful, I shall have to buy it for you in Alexandria.

CÆSAR You are forgetting the treasures for which Rome is most famous, my friend. You cannot buy *them* in Alexandria.

APOLLODORUS What are they, Cæsar?

CÆSAR Her sons. Come, Cleopatra: forgive me and bid me farewell; and I will send you a man, Roman from head to heel and Roman of the noblest; not old and ripe for the knife; not lean in the arms and cold in the heart; not hiding a bald head under his conqueror's laurels; not stooped with the weight of the world on his shoulders; but brisk and fresh, strong and young, hoping in the morning, fighting in the day, and revelling in the evening. Will you take such an one in exchange for Cæsar?

CLEOPATRA *(palpitating)* His name, his name?

CÆSAR Shall it be Mark Antony? *(She throws herself into his arms.)*

RUFIO You are a bad hand at a bargain, mistress, if you will swop Cæsar for Antony.

CÆSAR So now you are satisfied.

CLEOPATRA You will not forget.

CÆSAR I will not forget. Farewell: I do not think we shall meet again. Farewell. *(He kisses her on the forehead. She is much affected and begins to sniff. He embarks.)*

THE ROMAN SOLDIERS *(as he sets his foot on the gangway)* Hail, Cæsar; and farewell!

(He reaches the ship and returns RUFIO'S *wave of the hand.)*

APOLLODORUS *(to* CLEOPATRA*)* No tears, dearest Queen: they stab your servant to the heart. He will return some day.

CLEOPATRA I hope not. But I cant help crying, all the same. *(She waves her handkerchief to* CÆSAR; *and the ship begins to move.)*

THE ROMAN SOLDIERS *(drawing their swords and raising them in the air)* Hail, Cæsar!

ronald peacock

shaw

For the spectator who is interested in poetry and drama and theatre in their interfusion Shaw is embarrassing. "The poet in Shaw was still-born," writes Eliot. We have all felt again and again an extraordinary deflation as soon as the curtain has fallen. The agility and wit of Shaw's social criticism holds his plays together and casts his spell into the auditorium. The plays do not live as plays beyond the fall of the curtain. As they draw to a close they do not give the feeling of a building being completed; the forces which propel them are indeed bent all the other way, towards demolition. These works do not, after their emergence in time, solidify, as the great dramas do, into a shape for the memory; they leave us without the retrospective vision of form achieved. And yet Shaw cannot be thought out of the theatre by a theory of drama and poetry. It is not so much that he has simply conquered the stage and made it serve his own purposes; he has also, in spite of our reservations, served some of *its* purposes; of that there is as little doubt as of the fact that he has not served all its purposes or its greatest, as Jonson and Molière did.

There is a certain quality of calculation in Shaw's approach to comedy. It may be a wonderful calculation, of which the pleasantest thing to say would be that it is the "instinct of his genius." He has never hidden the fact that he is at heart an evangelist; and he has thirsted for more souls than the pamphlet—"his" form if ever there was one—could procure. He tried the novel. But he is essentially a man of ideas, of agile intellectual criticisms, and the novel, with all its apparatus of description and report, is a bore to him. Moreover, the audience of the novel is the individual; and the object of Shaw's criticism is society. In the theatre he catches three large groups who together make up the whole of mankind except its eccentrics: those interested in entertainment, those interested in ideas, and those interested in art. He catches them, moreover, in their social agglomeration and cohesiveness—his address is to society, and there it is assembled before the stage.

Having turned to theatre, it was undoubtedly a stroke of personal genius to choose comedy for his form in the conditions obtaining in the theatre and intellectual life generally at the turn of this century. Comedy carries didacticism with a better grace than other kinds of drama. If there are to be ideas and debate in plays, then they offend the intellectual nature of comedy less than the emotional nature of tragedy or "serious" drama. There are reasons for Shaw's eminence that have less to do with the theatre proper than with his person and his ideas; but here is a reason for his eminence that springs from the very conditions of theatre and drama at that time. In an age of "problem plays" comedy, as a form, even though it does lose something, loses less than other forms. Shaw therefore appears as the culmination of an epoch that was opened by Ibsen (Dumas fils was of course a harbinger). He may dominate in part by qualities that would have given him eminence outside the theatre; but he also dominates on grounds of drama alone, in the age in which he wrote. It is a culmination, viewed broadly, of three things: social thought, its application in the theatre, and Shaw's own conviction, aggressively held, that art should always be parable. His work is the *best* effort of all the drama that was inspired by social criticism. It is even superior to Ibsen's, where Ibsen's implications are social.

The novelty of Shaw's comedy called forth inevitably protagonists and antagonists, and it has been defended mainly as a comedy of ideas in contrast to one of manners or situation. That battle is won. We know now that in Shaw's "pamphlets in dramatic form" we have to watch the drama of ideas, of which persons and events are the diagrammatic illustration.

As an iconographer, he has with consistent conscientiousness always given us both the theory and the example, the thought and the illustration, the preface and the play. And no doubt the only proper way of judging his work finally is one that takes account of the unity of preface and play.

This is the tribute that Shaw wrests from us; compelling us to ask the question that has always been asked since romantic criticism taught us to put it: what unique quality of personal experience is he endeavouring to convey?—before we judge his work. Yet matters do not end with this romantic interest in personal messages, and unique ways of stating them. Shaw claims to be an artist and he works in a well-recognized form; and so it is fitting to recall that art may depend on artists, but artists also depend on art. Artists may revolt; they also submit. Forms—lyric, dramatic, narrative—admit of extensive variation, they are developed and modified. Yet they are not without a certain constancy of character, and impose, sometimes when we are least aware of it, an authority of their own which is above the single worker. Shaw does not escape. One could write a lot about him with the merest reference to comedy as an art with traditions. But he did not create his form out of the void; he selected it from amongst others for his use, and he owes something to it. Again, at the moment he entered the theatre, drama had been given a powerful direction by Ibsen; he owes something to this too. In the relation between what he owes and what he gives criticism discovers something both about drama and about Shaw.

Within the limits of the art of comedy he has displayed a striking originality in two principal directions; first in the point of view he adopts for his critical attack, and secondly in his adaptation of comedy to the naturalist technique.

Regarding the first point, Shaw conforms to tradition in the sense that you must have a fixed point from which to work, to launch your criticism. In Molière, for instance, the established position is generally interpreted as the rule of the golden mean of reason. Shaw is also devoted to reason. But whilst Molière takes his fixed point from the general experience of men as rational and social beings, Shaw takes his from a rational philosophy of his own. Hence he inverts the usual method. Instead of isolating the unreasonable character, he isolates the reasonable one. Molière gives us a series of characters who offend our idea of rational behaviour: Harpagon, Alceste, Arnolphe, Argan, Tartuffe are examples. Shaw, on the other hand, gives us a series that illustrates his own idea of rational behaviour: Dudgeon, Cæsar, Tanner, Dubedat, Undershaft, Shotover, Magnus, Joan, and so on—all characters with a head, with their eye on the point, piercing illusions and grasping reality.

The difference is accounted for by a difference of interest. Molière—and we can say Jonson too—feeding on the thought of the Renaissance, was interested in a conception of man; Shaw, under the influence of the thought of the late nineteenth century, in a conception of society. His main attack being on society, his transformation of traditional comic method is brilliant. Taking an unconventional character, a person with the gift of insight and freedom, he impinges it upon a group of conventional social animals, and the impact reveals at every turn stock notions and reactions, prejudices and dishonesties, in short the illusionary, the unreal, the irrational. Molière exposes one character in turn; Shaw the social herd, all together. And these characters of his are most certainly dramatic conceptions, because they create, by being what they are, startling situations.

It is not necessary to dwell on the remarkable efficacy of this transformation for Shaw's purpose. It shows itself all of a piece with the man, his temperament, his challenge, his message. We accept it as an instrument supremely adapted to its use, and acknowledge the immense talent that could make such an adaptation of a comedic method. But this is the point where, if we cannot detract from the personal genius of Shaw, we can arraign the artist, for the cunning of the method cannot cover the inadequacy of the result, when we apply the standards set by the highest imaginative comedy. Molière's Harpagon and Alceste, Jonson's Volpone and Sir Epicure Mammon, are imaginative creations. You cannot agree or disagree with them; in their simplicity and ideality, they *are*. They have an existence and a permanence that are unassailable; and they are, moreover, centres from which moral energy radiates with an operation that cannot be limited by the fall of a curtain. Shaw's principals are not products of this kind of imaginative power. At the most it can be said that his series has a certain force and solidity because each member of it is a reflection of Shaw's own intelligence, and their effect is cumulative. The core of each one of them lies in their critical penetration, a quality of their creator. It is their only real vitality. They are without the vitality of instinct that makes a total living creature and on which the characters of Molière are based. For this reason we remember less what they are than how they talked; and every time we disagree with their opinions they lose some of their power. Each one of Molière's great creations is an image of a human folly, and he leaves us a whole gallery of them. Shaw gives us but one image: of the critical mind acting as a solvent. There is a point outside the drama where the two authors meet, on the ground of philosophy and practical wisdom, or the effort towards it. It would be difficult to decide which is the greater intellect. But it is easy to judge Molière the greater artist, because he gives us forms, against which Shaw can only put a *perpetuum mobile* of critical comment.

The second point about the mutual relations between Shaw's personal aim and the dramatic form concerns the realist convention in which he works. His comedy flowing from his criticism of society, he needs for his purposes the ordinary social milieu, with the sort of crisis that arises from typical bourgeois circumstances. In this milieu he lets his unconventional characters challenge the creatures of habit by word and action, and the rest follows. His material is that of all bourgeois drama since the middle of the nineteenth century, more particularly since Ibsen. One of the things he admired most in the latter was the way he made his audience feel that what they saw on the stage was what went on in their own homes. The direct attack is of the essence of Shaw's intention. His method in fact is to give us a comic version of Ibsen's principal theme, the rebel against society, the true man against the false. Ibsen being swayed on the whole by the Germanic seriousness, by some deep-seated emotional need for tragic crisis, his subjects and treatments were generally the reverse of comic. Here and there, however, he explores this latter vein, and *An Enemy of the People* appears as the embryo of Shaw's comic method. In developing his work from this position Shaw achieves a remarkable feat. For in the first place comedy and wit introduce a compensating element of imagination into the lamentably prosaic waste of bourgeois realist drama; Shaw avoids the mistake of other imitators of Ibsen. And in the second place he liberates comedy from the cruder forms of its long-accustomed artificialities and tricks—the disguises, the eavesdroppings, the mistaken identities, the stock characters and so on. They have been the properties of comedy since Plautus and were made necessary by the demands for concentration and sustained liveliness of situation in the theatre. Having found another source of vivacious movement in his unflagging raillery, Shaw dispenses with the traditional tricks as the main tools of construction, and uses the "realistic" social scheme. Not that he foregoes altogether the prerogative of comedy in the matter of fantastic incident and improbable dénouement. In fact he gains here another advantage over the "serious" social problem dramatist, because he can treat more cavalierly the difficulty of contriving a probable end as well as a probable situation. He may use far-fetched incidents and dénouements, but they are not the part of his material that really counts. For example, the arrival from the air of Percival and Lina Shchepanowska in *Misalliance* is quite fantastic, and so is Lina herself in the circumstances of the play; but the basic situation had become a commonplace one of contemporary social life. The incident in itself adds superficially to the entertainment; no writer of stage comedy, not even Molière, can afford to neglect any source of amusement, and Shaw has the good sense to be as small on occasion as his greatest predecessor. But even so, the real Shavian comedy is independent of the bit of fantasy; for it follows when we see the impact of Lina, an original character, a free woman and true to herself, on the convention-drenched people around her.

These are the two principal features of Shaw's work which make a mutual relationship between him and his form clear. Our first impulse is to say: this is not comedy as it ought to be. Our second is to justify it as the proper mode for Shaw's idea. With our third impulse we look more closely at work that seems to owe no obligation except to its own law, its own subject-matter, and we discover that it does owe something to its genre, to its predecessors, to pre-existent authorities. It illustrates a continuity, not a break. Shaw adheres first to the principle that comedy must have a fixed vantage-point, though he transforms it to suit his own purpose. He retains, too, the prerogatives and tricks of comedy, without, however, the necessity of being chained to them. He also keeps to stock types for comic purposes, but his new social philosophy gives him a new set of types. Even in incidentals he can follow well-worn grooves of the art; the Straker-Tanner relationship in *Man and Superman* rests on the conventional master-valet set-up, given a completely new vitality from the new social background. And his second great obligation is to the dramatic developments that immediately preceded him and in which he was caught up. He uses the natural probable situation of bourgeois life, public or domestic, that focuses a problem of social behaviour. And he acknowledges the debt by originality of treatment; that is, he gives us what no one else gave and Ibsen had only hinted at, comedy.

anton chekhov 1860–1904

uncle vanya

translated by Constance Garnett

"To judge between good and bad, between successful and unsuccessful, would need the eye of God," Chekhov wrote. But this kindliest of writers was not indifferent to human weakness, vulgarity or idleness. Chekhov, son of a shopkeeper, descended from serfs, early assumed the burden of supporting his bankrupt family as well as financing his own medical studies. He started publishing comic sketches, took his degree, and thereafter practiced both medicine and literature. The successful volume of humorous stories freed him for more serious writing, and there followed his great tales. In 1887 Chekhov wrote his first full-length play, *Ivanov*, which failed. Not until 1896 did he attempt another, *The Sea Gull*, which also failed. But the Moscow Art Theatre, founded by Nemirovitch-Dantchenko and Stanislavsky, successfully revived *The Sea Gull*, and for that theatre Chekhov wrote his remaining masterpieces: *Uncle Vanya* (1897), *The Three Sisters* (1900), and *The Cherry Orchard* (1904). Chekhov wrote of the ignorance which darkened Russia and of the aimless lives of the unproductive classes. His guiding principle for living was purposeful labor. In addition to his writing, he continued to practice medicine, studied peasant life, and investigated prison conditions before his early death from tuberculosis at the age of forty-four.

the characters

ALEXANDER VLADIMIROVITCH SEREBRYAKOV, *a retired professor*
YELENA ANDREYEVNA, *his wife, aged 27*
SOFYA ALEXANDROVNA (SONYA), *his daughter by his first wife*
MARYA VASSILYEVNA VOYNITSKY, *widow of a privy councillor and mother of professor's first wife*
IVAN PETROVITCH VOYNITSKY, *her son*
MIHAIL LVOVITCH ASTROV, *a doctor*
ILYA ILYITCH TELYEGIN, *a landowner reduced to poverty*
MARINA, *an old nurse*
A LABORER

(The setting is SEREBRYAKOV'S *estate.)*

act 1

(Garden. Part of the house can be seen with the verandah. In the avenue under an old poplar there is a table set for tea. Garden seats and chairs;

on one of the seats lies a guitar. Not far from the table there is a swing. Between two and three o'clock on a cloudy afternoon.

MARINA, *a heavy old woman, slow to move, is sitting by the samovar, knitting a stocking, and* ASTROV *is walking up and down near her.)*

MARINA *(pours out a glass of tea)* Here, drink it, my dear.

ASTROV *(reluctantly takes the glass)* I don't feel much like it.

MARINA Perhaps you would have a drop of vodka?

ASTROV No. I don't drink vodka every day. Besides, it's so sultry *(a pause).* Nurse, how many years have we known each other?

MARINA *(pondering)* How many? The Lord help my memory. . . . You came into these parts . . . when? Vera Petrovna, Sonitchka's mother, was living then. You came to see us two winters before she died. . . . Well, that must be eleven years ago. *(after a moment's thought)* Maybe even more. . . .

ASTROV Have I changed much since then?

MARINA Very much. You were young and handsome in those days, and now you have grown older. And you are not as good-looking. There's another thing too—you take a drop of vodka now.

ASTROV Yes. . . . In ten years I have become a different man. And what's the reason of it? I am overworked, nurse. From morning till night I am always on my legs, not a moment of rest, and at night one lies under the bedclothes in continual terror of being dragged out to a patient. All these years that you have known me I have not had one free day. I may well look old! And the life in itself is tedious, stupid, dirty. . . . This life swallows one up completely. There are none but queer people about one—they are a queer lot, all of them—and when one has lived two or three years among them, by degrees one turns queer too, without noticing it. It's inevitable *(twisting his long moustache).* Ough, what a huge moustache I've grown . . . a stupid moustache. . . . I've turned into a queer fish, nurse. I haven't grown stupid yet, thank God! My brains are in their place, but my feelings are somehow blunter. There is nothing I want, nothing I care about, no one I am fond of . . . except you, perhaps—I am fond of you *(kisses her on the head).* I had a nurse like you when I was a child.

MARINA Perhaps you would like something to eat?

ASTROV No. In the third week of Lent I went to Malitskoe, where there was an epidemic . . . spotted typhus . . . in the huts the people were lying about in heaps. There was filth, stench, smoke . . . calves on the ground with the sick . . . little pigs about too. I was hard at work all day, did not sit down for a minute, and hadn't a morsel of food, and when I got home they wouldn't let me rest. They brought me a signalman from the line. I laid him on the table to operate upon him, and he went and died under the chloroform. And just when they weren't wanted, my feelings seemed to wake up again, and I was as conscience-stricken as though I had killed him on purpose. I sat down, shut my eyes like this, and thought: those who will live a hundred or two hundred years after us, for whom we are struggling now to beat out a road, will they remember and say a good word for us? Nurse, they won't, you know!

MARINA Men will not remember, but God will remember.

ASTROV Thank you for that. That's a good saying.

(Enter VOYNITSKY.*)*

VOYNITSKY *(comes out of the house; he has had a nap after lunch and looks rumpled; he sits down on the garden-seat and straightens his fashionable tie)* Yes . . . *(a pause).* Yes. . . .

ASTROV Had a good sleep?

VOYNITSKY Yes . . . very *(yawns).* Ever since the Professor and his wife have been here our life has been turned topsy-turvy. I sleep at the wrong time, at lunch and dinner I eat all sorts of messes, I drink wine – it's not good for one! In old days I never had a free moment. Sonya and I used to work in grand style, but now Sonya works alone, while I sleep and eat and drink. It's bad!

MARINA *(shaking her head)* Such goings-on! The Professor gets up at twelve o'clock, and the samovar is boiling all the morning waiting for him. Before they came we always had dinner about one o'clock, like other people, and now they are here we have it between six and seven. The Professor spends the night reading and writing, and all at once, at two o'clock in the morning, he'll ring his bell. Goodness me! What is it? Tea! People have to be waked out of their sleep to get him the samovar. What goings-on!

ASTROV And will they be here much longer?

VOYNITSKY *(whistles)* A hundred years. The Professor has made up his mind to settle here.

MARINA Look now! The samovar has been on the table for the last two hours, and they've gone for a walk.

VOYNITSKY They are coming. They are coming! Don't worry.

(There is a sound of voices; from the farther part of the garden enter SEREBRYAKOV, YELENA ANDREYEVNA, SONYA *and* TELYEGIN *returning from a walk.)*

SEREBRYAKOV Lovely, lovely! . . . Exquisite views!

TELYEGIN Remarkable, your Excellency.

SONYA We'll go to the plantation tomorrow, father. Shall we?

VOYNITSKY Tea is ready!

SEREBRYAKOV My friends, be so kind as to send my tea into the study for me. I have something more I must do today.

SONYA You will be sure to like the plantation.

(YELENA ANDREYEVNA, SEREBRYAKOV, *and* SONYA *go into the house.* TELYEGIN *goes to the table and sits down beside* MARINA.)

VOYNITSKY It's hot, stifling; but our great man of learning is in his great-coat and goloshes, with an umbrella and gloves too.

ASTROV That shows that he takes care of himself.

VOYNITSKY And how lovely she is! How lovely! I've never seen a more beautiful woman.

TELYEGIN Whether I drive through the fields, Marina Timofeyevna, or walk in the shady garden, or look at this table, I feel unutterably joyful. The weather is enchanting, the birds are singing, we are all living in peace and concord—what more could one wish for? *(taking his glass)* I am truly grateful to you!

VOYNITSKY *(dreamily)* Her eyes . . . an exquisite woman!

ASTROV Tell us something, Ivan Petrovitch.

VOYNITSKY *(listlessly)* What am I to tell you?

ASTROV Is there nothing new?

VOYNITSKY Nothing. Everything is old. I am just as I always was, perhaps worse, for I have grown lazy. I do nothing but just grumble like some old crow. My old magpie *maman* is still babbling about the rights of women. With one foot in the grave, she is still rummaging in her learned books for the dawn of a new life.

ASTROV And the Professor?

VOYNITSKY The Professor, as before, sits in his study writing from morning till dead of night. "With furrowed brow and racking brains, We write and write and write, And ne'er a word of praise we hear, Our labours to requite." Poor paper! He had much better be writing his autobiography. What a superb subject! A retired professor, you know—an old dry-as-dust, a learned fish. Gout, rheumatism, migraine, envy and jealousy have affected his liver. The old fish is living on his first wife's estate, living there against his will because he can't afford to live in the town. He is forever complaining of his misfortunes, though, as a matter of fact, he is exceptionally fortunate. *(nervously)* Just think how fortunate! The son of a humble sacristan, he has risen to university distinctions and the chair of a professor; he has become "your Excellency," the son-in-law of a senator, and so on, and so on. All that is no great matter, though. But just take this. The man has been lecturing and writing about art for twenty-five years, though he knows absolutely nothing about art. For twenty-five years he has been chewing over other men's ideas about realism, naturalism, and all sorts of nonsense; for twenty-five years he has been lecturing and writing on things all intelligent people know about already and stupid ones aren't interested in—so for twenty-five years he has been simply wasting his time. And with all that, what conceit! What pretensions! He has retired, and not a living soul knows anything about him; he is absolutely unknown. So that for twenty-five years all he has done is to keep a better man out of a job! But just look at him: he struts about like a demi-god!

ASTROV Come, I believe you are envious.

VOYNITSKY Yes, I am. And the success he has with women! Don Juan is not in it. His first wife, my sister, a lovely, gentle creature, pure as this blue sky, noble, generous, who had more suitors than he has had pupils, loved him as only pure angels can love beings as pure and beautiful as themselves. My mother adores him to this day, and he still inspires in her a feeling of devout awe. His second wife, beautiful, intelligent—you have just seen her—has married him in his old age, sacrificed her youth, her beauty, her freedom, her brilliance, to him. What for? Why?

ASTROV Is she faithful to the Professor?

VOYNITSKY Unhappily, she is.

ASTROV Why unhappily?

VOYNITSKY Because that fidelity is false from beginning to end. There is plenty of fine sentiment in it, but no logic. To deceive an old husband whom one can't endure is immoral; but to try and stifle her piteous youth and living feeling—that's not immoral.

TELYEGIN *(in a tearful voice)* Vanya, I can't bear to hear you talk like that. Come, really! Anyone who can betray wife or husband is a person who can't be trusted and who might betray his country.

VOYNITSKY *(with vexation)* Dry up, Waffles!

TELYEGIN Excuse me, Vanya. My wife ran away from me with the man she loved the day after our wedding, on the ground of my unprepossessing appearance. But I have never been false to my vows. I love her to this day and am faithful to her. I help her as far as I can, and I gave all I had for the education of her children by the man she loved. I have lost my happiness, but my pride has been left to me. And she? Her youth is over, her beauty, in accordance with the laws of nature, has faded, the man she loved is dead. . . . What has she left?

(Enter SONYA *and* YELENA ANDREYEVNA *and a little later,* MARYA VASSILYEVNA *with a book; she sits down and reads. They hand her tea, and she drinks it without looking at it.)*

SONYA *(hurriedly to the nurse)* Nurse, darling, some peasants have come. Go and speak to them. I'll look after the tea.

(Exit Nurse. YELENA ANDREYEVNA *takes her cup and drinks it sitting in the swing.)*

ASTROV *(to* YELENA ANDREYEVNA*)* I've come to see your husband. You wrote to me that he was very ill—rheumatism and something else—but it appears he is perfectly well.

YELENA Last night he was poorly, complaining of pains in his legs, but today he is all right. . . .

ASTROV And I have galloped twenty miles at break-neck speed! But there, it doesn't matter! it's not the first time. I shall stay with you till tomorrow to make up for it, and anyway I shall sleep *quantum satis.*

SONYA That's splendid! It's not often you stay the night with us. I expect you've not had dinner?

ASTROV No, I haven't.

SONYA Oh, well, you will have some dinner, then! We have dinner now between six and seven *(drinks tea).* The tea is cold!

TELYEGIN The temperature in the samovar has perceptibly dropped.

YELENA Never mind, Ivan Ivanitch; we will drink it cold.

TELYEGIN I beg your pardon, I am not Ivan Ivanitch, but Ilya Ilyitch—Ilya Ilyitch Telyegin, or, as some people call me on account of my pock-marked face, Waffles. I stood godfather to Sonetchka; and his Excellency, your husband, knows me very well. I live here now on your estate. If you've been so kind as to observe it, I have dinner with you every day.

SONYA Ilya Ilyitch is our helper, our right hand. *(tenderly)* Let me give you another cup, godfather.

MARYA Ach!

SONYA What is it, grandmamma?

MARYA I forgot to tell Alexandr—I am losing my memory—I got a letter today from Harkov, from Pavel Alexeyevitch . . . he has sent his new pamphlet.

ASTROV Is it interesting?

MARYA It's interesting, but it's rather queer. He is attacking what he himself maintained seven years ago. It's awful.

VOYNITSKY There's nothing awful in it. Drink your tea, *maman.*

MARYA But I want to talk.

VOYNITSKY But we have been talking and talking for fifty years and reading pamphlets. It's about time to leave off.

MARYA You don't like listening when I speak; I don't know why. Forgive my saying so, Jean, but you have so changed in the course of the last year that I hardly know you. You used to be a man of definite principles, of elevating ideas.

VOYNITSKY Oh, yes! I was a man of elevating ideas which elevated nobody *(a pause).* . . . A man of elevating ideas . . . you could not have made a more malignant joke! Now I am forty-seven. Till last year I tried, like you, to blind myself with all your pedantic rubbish on purpose to avoid seeing life as it is—and thought I was doing the right thing. And now, if only you knew! I can't sleep at night for vexation, for rage that I so stupidly wasted the time when I might have had everything from which my age now shuts me out.

SONYA Uncle Vanya, it's so dreary!

MARYA *(to her son)* You seem to be blaming your former principles. It is not they that are to blame, but yourself. You forget that principles alone are no use—a dead letter. You ought to have been working.

VOYNITSKY Working? It is not everyone who can be a writing machine like your Herr Professor.

MARYA What do you mean by that?

SONYA *(in an imploring voice)* Grandmamma! Uncle Vanya! I entreat you!

VOYNITSKY I'll hold my tongue—hold my tongue and apologise.

(A pause.)

YELENA What a fine day! It's not too hot.

(A pause.)

VOYNITSKY A fine day to hang oneself!

*(*TELYEGIN *tunes the guitar.* MARINA *walks to and fro near the house, calling a hen.)*

MARINA Chook, chook, chook!

SONYA Nurse, darling, what did the peasants come about?

MARINA It's the same thing—about the waste land again. Chook, chook, chook!

SONYA Which is it you are calling?

MARINA Speckly has gone off somewhere with her chickens. . . . The crows might get them *(walks away).*

*(*TELYEGIN *plays a polka; they all listen to him in silence. Enter a labourer.)*

LABORER Is the doctor here? *(to* ASTROV*)* If you please, Mihail Lvovitch, they have sent for you.

ASTROV Where from?

LABORER From the factory.

ASTROV *(with vexation)* Much obliged to you. Well, I suppose I must go *(looks round him for his cap).* What a nuisance, hang it!

SONYA How annoying it is, really! Come back from the factory to dinner.

ASTROV No. It will be too late. "How should I? . . . How could I? . . ." *(to the laborer)* Here, my good man, you might get me a glass of vodka, anyway. *(Laborer goes off.)* "How should I? . . . How could I? . . ." *(Finds his cap.)* In one of Ostrovsky's plays there is a man with a big moustache and little wit—that's like me. Well, I have the honour to wish you all good-bye. *(to* YELENA ANDREYEVNA*)* If you ever care to look in upon me, with Sofya Alexandrovna, I shall be truly delighted. I have a little estate, only ninety acres, but there is a model garden and nursery such as you wouldn't find for hundreds of miles round—if that interests you. Next to me is the government plantation. The forester there is old and always ill, so that I really look after all the work.

YELENA I have been told already that you are very fond of forestry. Of course, it may be of the greatest use, but doesn't it interfere with your real work? You are a doctor.

ASTROV Only God knows what is one's real work.

YELENA And is it interesting?

ASTROV Yes, it is interesting work.

VOYNITSKY *(ironically)* Very much so!

YELENA *(to* ASTROV*)* You are still young—you don't look more than thirty-six or thirty-seven . . . and it cannot be so interesting as you say. Nothing but trees and trees. I should think it must be monotonous.

SONYA No, it's extremely interesting. Mihail Lvovitch plants fresh trees every year, and already they have sent him a bronze medal and a diploma. He tries to prevent the old forests being destroyed. If you listen to him you will agree with him entirely. He says that forests beautify the country, that they teach man to understand what is beautiful and develop a lofty attitude of mind. Forests temper the severity of the climate. In countries where the climate is mild, less energy is wasted on the struggle with nature, and so man is softer and milder. In such countries people are beautiful, supple and sensitive; their language is elegant and their movements are graceful. Art and learning flourish among them, their philosophy is not gloomy, and their attitude to women is full of refined courtesy.

VOYNITSKY *(laughing)* Bravo, bravo! That's all charming but not convincing; so *(to* ASTROV*)* allow me, my friend, to go on heating my stoves with logs and building my barns of wood.

ASTROV You can heat your stoves with peat and build your barns of brick. Well, I am ready to let you cut down wood as you need it, but why destroy the forests? The Russian forests are going down under the axe. Millions of trees are perishing, the homes of wild animals and birds are being laid waste, the rivers are dwindling and drying up, wonderful scenery is disappearing never to return; and all because lazy man has not the sense to stoop down and pick up the fuel from the ground. *(to*

YELENA ANDREYEVNA) Am I not right, madam? One must be an unreflecting savage to burn this beauty in one's stove, to destroy what we cannot create. Man is endowed with reason and creative force to increase what has been given him; but hitherto he has not created but destroyed. There are fewer and fewer forests, the rivers are drying up, the wild creatures are becoming extinct, the climate is ruined, and every day the earth is growing poorer and more hideous. *(to* VOYNITSKY*)* Here you are looking at me with irony, and all I say seems to you not serious and—perhaps I really am a crank. But when I walk by the peasants' woods which I have saved from cutting down, or when I hear the rustling of the young copse planted by my own hands, I realise that the climate is to some extent in my power, and that if in a thousand years man is to be happy I too shall have had some small hand in it. When I plant a birch tree and see it growing green and swaying in the wind my soul is filled with pride, and I . . . *(seeing the laborer, who has brought a glass of vodka on a tray).* However *(drinks)* it's time for me to go. Probably the truth of the matter is that I am a crank. I have the honour to take my leave! *(goes towards the house)*

SONYA *(takes his arm and goes with him)* When are you coming to us?

ASTROV I don't know.

SONYA Not for a month again?

*(*ASTROV *and* SONYA *go into the house;* MARYA VASSILYEVNA *and* TELYEGIN *remain at the table;* YELENA ANDREYEVNA *walks towards the verandah.)*

YELENA You have been behaving impossibly again, Ivan Petrovitch. Why need you have irritated Marya Vassilyevna and talked about a writing machine! And at lunch to-day you quarrelled with Alexandr again. How petty it is!

VOYNITSKY But if I hate him?

YELENA There is no reason to hate Alexandr; he is like everyone else. He is no worse than you are.

VOYNITSKY If you could see your face, your movements! You are too indolent to live! Ah, how indolent!

YELENA Ach! indolent and bored! Everyone abuses my husband; everyone looks at me with compassion, thinking, "Poor thing! she has got an old husband." This sympathy for me, oh, how well I understand it! As Astrov said just now, you all recklessly destroy the forests, and soon there will be nothing left on the earth. In just the same way you recklessly destroy human beings, and soon, thanks to you, there will be no fidelity, no purity, no capacity for sacrifice left on earth! Why is it you can never look with indifference at a woman unless she is yours? Because—that doctor is right—there is a devil of destruction in all of you. You have no feeling for the woods, nor the birds, nor for women, nor for one another!

VOYNITSKY I don't like this moralising.

(A pause.)

YELENA That doctor has a weary, sensitive face. An interesting face. Sonya is evidently attracted by him; she is in love with him, and I understand her feeling. He has come three times since I have been here, but I am shy and have not once had a proper talk with him, or been nice to him. He thinks I am disagreeable. Most likely that's why we are such friends, Ivan Petrovitch, that we are both such tiresome, tedious people. Tiresome! Don't look at me like that, I don't like it.

VOYNITSKY How else can I look at you, since I love you? You are my happiness, my life, my youth! I know the chances of your returning my feeling are nil, non-existent, but I want nothing, only let me look at you, listen to your voice. . . .

YELENA Hush, they may hear you! *(They go into the house.)*

VOYNITSKY *(following her)* Let me speak of my love, don't drive me away—that alone will be the greatest happiness for me. . . .

YELENA This is agonising.

(Both go into the house. TELYEGIN *strikes the strings and plays a polka.* MARYA VASSILYEVNA *makes a note on the margin of a pamphlet.)*

act II

(Dining-room in SEREBRYAKOV'S *house. Night. A watchman can be heard tapping in the garden.*

SEREBRYAKOV, *sitting in an arm-chair before an open window, dozing, and* YELENA ANDREYEVNA *sitting beside him, dozing too.)*

SEREBRYAKOV *(waking)* Who is it? Sonya, is it you?

YELENA It's me.

SEREBRYAKOV You, Lenotchka! . . . I am in unbearable pain.

YELENA Your rug has fallen on the floor *(wrapping it round his legs).* I'll shut the window, Alexandr.

SEREBRYAKOV No, I feel suffocated. . . . I just dropped asleep and I dreamed that my left leg did not belong to me. I was awakened by the agonising pain. No, it's not gout; it's more like rheumatism. What time is it now?

YELENA Twenty minutes past twelve *(a pause).*

SEREBRYAKOV Look for Batyushkov in the library in the morning. I believe we have his works.

YELENA What?

SEREBRYAKOV Look for Batyushkov in the morning. I remember we did have him. But why is it so difficult for me to breathe?

YELENA You are tired. This is the second night you have not slept.

SEREBRYAKOV I have been told that Turgenev got *angina pectoris* from gout. I am afraid I may have it. Hateful, detestable old age. Damnation take it! Since I have grown old I have grown hateful to myself. And you must all hate the sight of me.

YELENA You talk of your age as though we were all responsible for it.

SEREBRYAKOV I am most of all hateful to you.

*(*YELENA ANDREYEVNA *gets up and sits down farther away.)*

SEREBRYAKOV Of course, you are right. I am not a fool, and I understand. You are young and strong and good-looking. You want life and I am an old man, almost a corpse. Do you suppose I don't understand? And, of course, it is stupid of me to go on living. But wait a little, I shall soon set you all free. I shan't have to linger on much longer.

YELENA I am worn out . . . for God's sake be quiet!

SEREBRYAKOV It seems that, thanks to me, everyone is worn out, depressed, wasting their youth, and I am the only one enjoying life and satisfied. Oh, yes, of course!

YELENA Be quiet! You make me miserable!

SEREBRYAKOV I make everyone miserable. Of course.

YELENA *(through tears)* It's insufferable! Say, what is it you want of me?

SEREBRYAKOV Nothing.

YELENA Well, be quiet then. I implore you!

SEREBRYAKOV It's a strange thing, Ivan Petrovitch may speak and that old idiot, Marya Vassilyevna, and there is nothing against it, everyone listens—but if I say a word everyone begins to feel miserable. They dislike the very sound of my voice. Well, suppose I am disagreeable, egoistic and tyrannical—haven't I a right, even in my old age, to think of myself? Haven't I earned it? Haven't I the right, I ask you, to be quiet in my old age, to be cared for by other people?

YELENA No one is disputing your rights. *(The window bangs in the wind.)* The wind has got up; I'll shut the window *(shuts the window)*. There will be rain directly. No one disputes your rights.

(A pause; the watchman in the garden taps and sings.)

SEREBRYAKOV After devoting all one's life to learning, after growing used to one's study, to one's lecture-room, to the society of honourable colleagues—all of a sudden to find oneself here in this vault, every day to see stupid people, to hear foolish conversation. I want life, I like success, I like fame, I like distinction, renown, and here—it's like being an exile. Every moment to be grieving for the past, watching the successes of others, dreading death. I can't bear it! It's too much for me! And then they won't forgive me my age!

YELENA Wait a little, have patience: in five or six years I shall be old too. *(Enter* SONYA.*)*

SONYA Father, you told us to send for Doctor Astrov yourself, and now that he has come you won't see him. It isn't nice. You've troubled him for nothing.

SEREBRYAKOV What good is your Astrov to me? He knows as much about medicine as I do about astronomy.

SONYA We can't send for all the great medical authorities here for your gout.

SEREBRYAKOV I am not going to talk to that crazy crank.

SONYA That's as you please *(sits down)*. It doesn't matter to me.

SEREBRYAKOV What's the time?

YELENA Nearly one o'clock.

SEREBRYAKOV I feel stifled. . . . Sonya, fetch me my drops from the table.

SONYA In a minute *(gives him the drops)*.

SEREBRYAKOV *(irritably)* Oh, not those! It's no use asking for anything!

SONYA Please don't be peevish. Some people may like it, but please spare me! I don't like it. And I haven't the time. I have to get up early in the morning, we are hay-making tomorrow.

(Enter VOYNITSKY *in a dressing-gown with a candle in his hand.)*

VOYNITSKY There's a storm coming on. *(a flash of lightning)* There, look! Hélène and Sonya, go to bed. I have come to take your place.

SEREBRYAKOV *(frightened)* No, no! Don't leave me with him. No! He will be the death of me with his talking!

VOYNITSKY But you must let them have some rest! This is the second night they have had no sleep.

SEREBRYAKOV Let them go to bed, but you go too. Thank you. I entreat you to go. For the sake of our past friendship, don't make any objections! We'll talk some other time.

VOYNITSKY *(mockingly)* Our past friendship. . . . Past . . .

SONYA Be quiet, Uncle Vanya.

SEREBRYAKOV *(to his wife)* My love, don't leave me alone with him! He will be the death of me with his talking!

VOYNITSKY This is really getting laughable.

(Enter MARINA *with a candle.)*

SONYA You ought to be in bed, nurse darling! It's late.

MARINA The samovar has not been cleared. One can't very well go to bed.

SEREBRYAKOV Everyone is kept up, everyone is worn out. I am the only one enjoying myself.

MARINA *(going up to* SEREBRYAKOV *tenderly)* Well, master dear, is the pain so bad? I have a grumbling pain in my legs too, such a pain *(tucks the rug in).* You've had this trouble for years. Vera Petrovna, Sonetchka's mother, used to be up night after night with you, wearing herself out. How fond she was of you! *(a pause)* The old are like little children, they like someone to be sorry for them; but no one feels for the old *(kisses* SEREBRYAKOV *on the shoulder).* Come to bed, dear . . . come, my honey. . . . I'll give you some lime-flower tea and warm your legs . . . and say a prayer for you. . . .

SEREBRYAKOV *(moved)* Let us go, Marina.

MARINA I have such a grumbling pain in my legs myself, such a pain *(together with* SONYA *leads him off).* Vera Petrovna used to be crying, and breaking her heart over you. . . . You were only a mite then, Sonetchka, and had no sense. . . . Come along, come along, sir . . .

*(*SEREBRYAKOV, SONYA *and* MARINA *go out.)*

YELENA I am quite worn out with him. I can hardly stand on my feet.

VOYNITSKY You with him, and I with myself. This is the third night I have had no sleep.

YELENA It's dreadful in this house. Your mother hates everything except her pamphlets and the Professor; the Professor is irritated, he does not trust me, and is afraid of you; Sonya is angry with her father, angry with me and has not spoken to me for a fortnight; you hate my husband and show open contempt for your mother; I am overwrought and have been nearly crying twenty times today. . . . It's dreadful in this house.

VOYNITSKY Let us drop this moralising.

YELENA You are a well-educated and intelligent man, Ivan Petrovitch, and I should have thought you ought to understand that the world is not being destroyed through fire or robbery, but through hatred, enmity and all this petty wrangling. . . . It ought to be your work to reconcile everyone, and not to grumble.

VOYNITSKY Reconcile me to myself first! My precious . . . *(bends down and kisses her hand).*

YELENA Don't! *(draws away her hand)* Go away!

VOYNITSKY The rain will be over directly and everything in nature will be refreshed and sigh with relief. But the storm has brought no relief to me. Day and night the thought that my life has been hopelessly wasted weighs on me like a nightmare. I have no past, it has been stupidly wasted on trifles, and the present is awful in its senselessness. Here you have my life and my love! What use to make of them? What am I to do with them? My passion is wasted in vain like a ray of sunshine that has fallen into a pit, and I am utterly lost, too.

YELENA When you talk to me about your love, I feel stupid and don't know what to say. Forgive me, there is nothing I can say to you *(is about to go out).* Good night.

VOYNITSKY *(barring her way)* And if you knew how wretched I am at the thought that by my side, in this same house, another life is being wasted, too—yours! What are you waiting for? What cursed theory holds you back? Understand, do understand . . .

YELENA *(looks at him intently)* Ivan Petrovitch, you are drunk!

VOYNITSKY I may be, I may be . . .

YELENA Where is the doctor?

VOYNITSKY He is in there . . . he is staying the night with me. It may be, it may be . . . anything may be!

YELENA You have been drinking again today. What's that for?

VOYNITSKY There's a semblance of life in it, anyway. . . . Don't prevent me, Hélène!

YELENA You never used to drink, and you did not talk so much. . . . Go to bed! You bore me.

VOYNITSKY *(kisses her hand)* My precious . . . marvellous one!

YELENA *(with vexation)* Don't. This is really hateful *(goes out).*

VOYNITSKY *(alone)* She is gone . . . *(a pause).* Ten years ago I used to meet her at my sister's. Then she was seventeen and I was thirty-seven. Why didn't I fall in love with her then and make her an offer? It might easily have happened then! And now she would have been my wife. . . . Yes. . . . Now we should both have been awakened by the storm; she would have been frightened by the thunder, I should have held her in my arms and whispered, "Don't be frightened, I am here." Oh, wonderful thoughts, what happiness; it makes me laugh with delight—but, my God, my thoughts are in a tangle. Why am I old? Why doesn't she understand me? Her fine phrases, her lazy morality, her nonsensical lazy theories about the ruin of the world—all that is absolutely hateful to me *(a pause).* Oh, how I have been cheated! I adored that Professor, that pitiful gouty invalid, and worked for him like an ox. Sonya and I squeezed every farthing out of the estate; we haggled over linseed oil, peas, curds, like greedy peasants; we grudged ourselves every morsel to save up halfpence and farthings and send him thousands of roubles. I was proud of him and his learning; he was my life, the breath of my being. All his writings and utterances seemed to me inspired by genius. . . . My God, and now! Here he is retired, and now one can see the sum total of his life. He leaves not one page of work behind him, he is utterly unknown, he is nothing—a soap bubble! And I have been cheated. . . . I see it—stupidly cheated. . . .

(Enter ASTROV *in his coat, but without waistcoat or tie; he is a little drunk; he is followed by* TELYEGIN *with the guitar.)*

ASTROV Play something!

TELYEGIN Everyone is asleep!

ASTROV Play!

*(*TELYEGIN *begins playing softly.)*

ASTROV *(to* VOYNITSKY*)* Are you alone? No ladies here? *(putting his arms akimbo sings)* "Dance my hut and dance my stove, the master has no bed to lie on." The storm woke me. Jolly good rain. What time is it?

VOYNITSKY Goodness knows.

ASTROV I thought I heard Yelena Andreyevna's voice.

VOYNITSKY She was here a minute ago.

ASTROV A fine woman. *(Examines the medicine bottles on the table.)* Medicines! What a lot of prescriptions! From Harkov, from Moscow, from Tula. He has bored every town with his gout. Is he really ill or shamming?

VOYNITSKY He is ill *(a pause).*

ASTROV Why are you so melancholy today? Are you sorry for the Professor, or what?

VOYNITSKY Let me alone.

ASTROV Or perhaps you are in love with the Professor's lady?

VOYNITSKY She is my friend.

ASTROV Already?

VOYNITSKY What do you mean by "already"?

ASTROV A woman can become a man's friend only in the following sequence: first agreeable acquaintance, then mistress, then friend.

VOYNITSKY A vulgar theory.

ASTROV What? Yes . . . I must own I am growing vulgar. You see, I am drunk too. As a rule I get drunk like this once a month. When I am in this condition I become coarse and insolent in the extreme. I don't stick at anything then. I undertake the most difficult operations and do them capitally. I make the most extensive plans for the future; I don't think of myself as a crank at such times, but believe that I am being of immense service to humanity—immense! And I have my own philosophy of life at such times, and all you, my good friends, seem to me such insects . . . microbes! *(to* TELYEGIN.*)* Waffles, play!

TELYEGIN My dear soul, I'd be delighted to do anything for you, but do realise—everyone is asleep!

ASTROV Play!

(TELYEGIN *begins playing softly.)*

ASTROV We must have a drink. Come along, I fancy we have still some brandy left. And as soon as it is daylight, we will go to my place. Right? I have an assistant who never says "right," but "roight." He is an awful scoundrel. So we will go, shall we? *(sees* SONYA *entering)* Excuse me, I have no tie on. *(Goes out hurriedly,* TELYEGIN *following him.)*

SONYA Uncle Vanya, you have been drinking with the doctor again. You are a nice pair! He has always been like that, but why do you do it? It's so unsuitable at your age.

VOYNITSKY Age makes no difference. When one has no real life, one has to live on illusions. It's better than nothing, anyway.

SONYA The hay is all cut, it rains every day, it's all rotting, and you are living in illusions. You have quite given up looking after things. . . . I have to work alone, and am quite done up. . . . *(alarmed)* Uncle, you have tears in your eyes!

VOYNITSKY Tears? Not a bit of it . . . nonsense. . . . You looked at me just now so like your dear mother. My darling . . . *(eagerly kisses her hands and face)* My sister . . . my dear sister . . . where is she now? If she knew! Ah, if she knew!

SONYA What, uncle? Knew what?

VOYNITSKY It's painful, useless. . . . Never mind. . . . Afterwards . . . it's nothing . . . I am going *(goes out).*

SONYA *(knocks at the door)* Mihail Lvovitch, you are not asleep, are you? One minute!

ASTROV *(through the door)* I am coming! *(A minute later he comes out with his waistcoat and tie on.)* What can I do for you?

SONYA Drink yourself, if it does not disgust you, but I implore you, don't let my uncle drink! It's bad for him.

ASTROV Very good. We won't drink any more *(a pause).* I am just going home. That's settled and signed. It will be daylight by the time they have put the horses in.

SONYA It is raining. Wait till morning.

ASTROV The storm is passing over, we shall only come in for the end of it. I'm going. And please don't send for me again to see your father. I tell him it's gout and he tells me it's rheumatism; I ask him to stay in bed and he sits in a chair. And to-day he wouldn't speak to me at all.

SONYA He is spoiled. *(looks into the sideboard)* Won't you have something to eat?

ASTROV Well, perhaps.

SONYA I like eating at night. I believe there is something in the sideboard. They say he's been a great favourite with the ladies, and women have spoiled him. Here, have some cheese. *(Both stand at the sideboard and eat.)*

ASTROV I have had nothing to eat all day, only drink. Your father has a difficult temper. *(takes a bottle from the sideboard)* May I? *(drinks a glass)* There is no one here and one may speak frankly. Do you know, it seems to me that I could not exist in your house for a month, I should be choked by the atmosphere. . . . Your father, who is entirely absorbed in his gout and his books, Uncle Vanya with his melancholy, your grandmother, and your stepmother too. . . .

SONYA What about my stepmother?

ASTROV Everything ought to be beautiful in a human being: face, and dress, and soul, and ideas. She is beautiful, there is no denying that, but . . . You know she does nothing but eat, sleep, walk about, fascinate us all by her beauty—nothing more. She has no duties, other people work for her. . . . That's true, isn't it? And an idle life cannot be pure *(a pause)*. But perhaps I am too severe. I am dissatisfied with life like your Uncle Vanya, and we are both growing peevish.

SONYA Are you dissatisfied with life, then?

ASTROV I love life as such, but our life, our everyday provincial life in Russia, I can't endure. I despise it with every fibre of my being. And as for my own personal life, there is absolutely nothing nice in it, I can assure you. You know when you walk through a forest on a dark night, and a light gleams in the distance, you do not notice your weariness, nor the darkness, nor the sharp twigs that lash you in the face. . . . I work—as you know—harder than anyone in the district, fate is for ever lashing at me; at times I am unbearably miserable, but I have no light in the distance. I expect nothing for myself; I am not fond of my fellow creatures. . . . It's years since I cared for anyone.

SONYA You care for no one at all?

ASTROV No one. I feel a certain affection for your nurse—for the sake of old times. The peasants are too much alike, undeveloped, living in dirt, and it is difficult to get on with the educated people. They are all wearisome. Our good friends are small in their ideas, small in their feelings, and don't see beyond their noses—or, to put it plainly, they are stupid. And those who are bigger and more intelligent are hysterical, morbidly absorbed in introspection and analysis. . . . They are for ever whining; they are insanely given to hatred and slander; they steal up to a man sideways, and look at him askance and decide "Oh, he is a neurotic!" or "he is posing." And when they don't know what label to stick on my forehead, they say "he is a queer fellow, very queer!" I am fond of forestry—that's queer; I don't eat meat—that's queer too. There is no direct, genuine, free attitude to people and to nature left among them. . . . None, none! *(is about to drink)*

SONYA *(prevents him)* No, please, I beg you, don't drink any more!

ASTROV Why not?

SONYA It's so out of keeping with you! You are so refined, you have such a soft voice. . . . More than that even, you are unlike everyone else I know—you are beautiful. Why, then, do you want to be like ordinary people who drink and play cards? Oh, don't do it, I entreat you! You always say that people don't create but only destroy what heaven gives them. Then why do you destroy yourself, why? You mustn't, you mustn't, I beseech you, I implore you!

ASTROV *(holds out his hand to her)* I won't drink any more!

SONYA Give me your word.

ASTROV My word of honour.

SONYA *(presses his hand warmly)* Thank you!

ASTROV Enough! I have come to my senses. You see, I am quite sober now and I will be so to the end of my days *(looks at his watch).* And so, as I was saying, my time is over, it's too late for me. . . . I have grown old, I have worked too hard, I have grown vulgar, all my feelings are blunted, and I believe I am not capable of being fond of anyone. I don't love anyone . . . and I don't believe I ever shall. What still affects me is beauty. That does stir me. I fancy if Yelena Andreyevna, for example, wanted to, she could turn my head in one day. . . . But that's not love, that's not affection . . . *(covers his face with his hands and shudders).*

SONYA What is it?

ASTROV Nothing. . . . In Lent one of my patients died under chloroform.

SONYA You ought to forget that by now *(a pause).* Tell me, Mihail Lvovitch . . . if I had a friend or a younger sister, and if you found out that she . . . well, suppose that she loved you, how would you take that?

ASTROV *(shrugging his shoulders)* I don't know. Nohow, I expect. I should give her to understand that I could not care for her . . . and my mind is taken up with other things. Anyway, if I am going, it is time to start. Goodbye, my dear girl, or we shall not finish till morning *(presses her hand).* I'll go through the drawing-room if I may, or I am afraid your uncle may detain me *(goes out).*

SONYA *(alone)* He has said nothing to me. . . . His soul and his heart are still shut away from me, but why do I feel so happy? *(laughs with happiness)* I said to him, you are refined, noble, you have such a soft voice. . . . Was it inappropriate? His voice trembles and caresses one . . . I still feel it vibrating in the air. And when I spoke to him of a younger sister, he did not understand. . . . *(Wringing her hands)* Oh, how awful it is that I am not beautiful! How awful it is! And I know I am not, I know it, I know it! . . . Last Sunday, as people were coming out of church, I heard them talking about me, and one woman said: "She is a sweet generous nature, but what a pity she is so plain. . . ." Plain. . . . *(Enter* YELENA ANDREYEVNA.*)*

YELENA *(opens the window)* The storm is over. What delicious air! *(a pause)* Where is the doctor?

SONYA He is gone *(a pause).*

YELENA Sophie!

SONYA What is it?

YELENA How long are you going to be sulky with me? We have done each other no harm. Why should we be enemies? Let us make it up. . . .

SONYA I wanted to myself . . . *(embraces her)* Don't let us be cross any more.

YELENA That's right. *(both are agitated.)*

SONYA Has father gone to bed?

YELENA No, he is sitting in the drawing-room. . . . We don't speak to each other for weeks, and goodness knows why. . . . *(Seeing that the sideboard is open)* How is this?

SONYA Mihail Lvovitch has been having some supper.

YELENA And there is wine too. . . . Let us drink to our friendship.

SONYA Yes, let us.

YELENA Out of the same glass . . . *(fills it).* It's better so. So now we are friends?

SONYA Friends. *(They drink and kiss each other.)* I have been wanting to make it up for ever so long, but somehow I felt ashamed . . . *(cries).*

YELENA Why are you crying?

SONYA It's nothing.

YELENA Come, there, there . . . *(weeps).* I am a queer creature, I am crying too . . . *(a pause).* You are angry with me because you think I married your father from interested motives. . . . If that will make you believe me, I will swear it—I married him for love. I was attracted by him as a learned, celebrated man. It was not real love, it was all made up; but I fancied at the time that it was real. It's not my fault. And ever since our marriage you have been punishing me with your clever, suspicious eyes.

SONYA Come, peace! peace! Let us forget.

YELENA You mustn't look like that—it doesn't suit you. You must believe in everyone—there is no living if you don't *(a pause).*

SONYA Tell me honestly, as a friend . . . are you happy?

YELENA No.

SONYA I knew that. One more question. Tell me frankly, wouldn't you have liked your husband to be young?

YELENA What a child you are still! Of course I should! *(Laughs)* Well, ask something else, ask away. . . .

SONYA Do you like the doctor?

YELENA Yes, very much.

SONYA *(laughs)* Do I look silly . . . yes? He has gone away, but I still hear his voice and his footsteps, and when I look at the dark window I can see his face. Do let me tell you. . . . But I can't speak so loud; I feel ashamed. Come into my room, we can talk there. You must think me silly? Own up. . . . Tell me something about him.

YELENA What am I to tell you?

SONYA He is clever. . . . He understands everything, he can do anything. . . . He doctors people, and plants forests too. . . .

YELENA It is not a question of forests and medicine. . . . My dear, you must understand he has a spark of genius! And you know what that means? Boldness, freedom of mind, width of outlook. . . . He plants a tree and is already seeing what will follow from it in a thousand years, already he has visions of the happiness of humanity. Such people are rare, one must love them. . . . He drinks, he is sometimes a little coarse —but what does that matter? A talented man cannot keep spotless in Russia. Only think what sort of life that doctor has! Impassable mud on the roads, frosts, snowstorms, the immense distances, the coarse savage peasants, poverty and disease all around him—it is hard for one who is working and struggling day after day in such surroundings to keep spotless and sober till he is forty *(kisses her).* I wish you happiness with all my heart; you deserve it . . . *(gets up).* But I am a tiresome, secondary character. . . . In music and in my husband's house, and in all the love affairs, everywhere in fact, I have always played a secondary part. As a matter of fact, if you come to think of it, Sonya, I am very, very unhappy! *(Walks up and down the stage in agitation.)* There is no happiness in this world for me, none! Why do you laugh?

SONYA *(laughs, hiding her face)* I am so happy . . . so happy!

YELENA I have a longing for music. I should like to play something.

SONYA Do play something! *(Embraces her.)* I can't sleep. . . . Play something!

YELENA In a minute. Your father is not asleep. Music irritates him when he is ill. Go and ask his leave. If he doesn't object, I'll play. Go!

SONYA Very well *(goes out).*

(Watchman taps in the garden.)

YELENA It's a long time since I have played the piano. I shall play and cry, cry like an idiot. *(In the window)* Is that you tapping, Yefim?

WATCHMAN'S VOICE Yes.

YELENA Don't tap, the master is unwell.

WATCHMAN'S VOICE I am just going *(whistles).* Hey there, good dog! Come, lad! Good dog! *(A pause.)*

SONYA *(returning)* We mustn't!

act III

(The drawing-room in SEREBRYAKOV'S *house. Three doors: on the right, on the left and in the middle. Daytime.*

VOYNITSKY *and* SONYA *seated, and* YELENA ANDREYEVNA *walking about the stage, thinking.)*

VOYNITSKY The Herr Professor has graciously expressed a desire that we should all gather together in this room at one o'clock today *(looks at his watch).* It is a quarter to. He wishes to make some communication to the world.

YELENA Probably some business matter.

VOYNITSKY He has no business. He spends his time writing twaddle, grumbling and being jealous.

SONYA *(in a reproachful tone)* Uncle!

VOYNITSKY Well, well, I am sorry *(motioning towards* YELENA ANDREYEVNA*)* Just look at her! she is so lazy that she almost staggers as she walks. Very charming! Very!

YELENA You keep buzzing and buzzing away all day—aren't you tired of it? *(miserably)* I am bored to death. I don't know what I'm to do.

SONYA *(shrugging her shoulders)* Isn't there plenty to do? If only you cared to do it.

YELENA For instance?

SONYA You could help us with the estate, teach the children or look after the sick. There's plenty to do. When father and you were not here, Uncle Vanya and I used to go to the market ourselves and sell the flour.

YELENA I don't know how to do such things. And they are not interesting. It's only in novels with a purpose that people teach and doctor the peasants. How am I, all of a sudden, *à propos* of nothing, to go and teach them or doctor them?

SONYA Well, I don't see how one can help doing it. Wait a little, and you too will get into the way of it *(puts her arm round her).* Don't be depressed, dear *(laughs).* You are bored and don't know what to do with yourself, and boredom and idleness are catching. Look at Uncle Vanya —he does nothing but follow you about like a shadow. I have left my work and run away to talk to you. I have grown lazy—I can't help it! The doctor, Mihail Lvovitch, used to come and see us very rarely, once a month; it was difficult to persuade him to come, and now he drives over every day. He neglects his forestry and his patients. You must be a witch.

VOYNITSKY Why be miserable? *(eagerly)* Come, my precious, my splendid one, be sensible! You have mermaid blood in your veins—be a mermaid! Let yourself go for once in your life! Make haste and fall head over ears in love with some water-sprite—and plunge headlong into the abyss so that the Herr Professor and all of us may throw up our hands in amazement!

YELENA *(angrily)* Leave me in peace! How cruel it is! *(about to go out)*

VOYNITSKY *(prevents her)* Come, come, my dearest, forgive me. . . . I apologize *(kisses her hand).* Peace!

YELENA You would drive an angel out of patience, you know.

VOYNITSKY As a sign of peace and harmony I'll fetch you a bunch of roses; I gathered them for you this morning. Autumn roses—exquisite, mournful roses . . . *(goes out).*

SONYA Autumn roses—exquisite, mournful roses. . . . *(Both look out of window.)*

YELENA It's September already. However are we to get through the winter here? *(a pause)* Where is the doctor?

SONYA In Uncle Vanya's room. He is writing something. I am glad Uncle Vanya is gone. I want to talk to you.

YELENA What about?

SONYA What about! *(Lays her head on* YELENA'S *bosom.)*

YELENA Come, there, there . . . *(stokes her head).*

SONYA I am not good-looking.

YELENA You have beautiful hair.

SONYA No! *(Looks round so as to see herself in the looking-glass.)* No! When a woman is plain, she is always told "You have beautiful eyes, you have beautiful hair." . . . I have loved him for six years. I love him more than my own mother. Every moment I am conscious of him. I feel the touch of his hand and I watch the door. I wait, expecting him every moment to come in. And here you see I keep coming to you simply to talk of him. Now he is here every day, but he doesn't look at me—doesn't see me. . . . That's such agony! I have no hope at all—none, none! *(In despair)* Oh, my God, give me strength . . . I have been praying all night. . . . I often go up to him, begin talking to him, look into his eyes. I have no pride left, no strength to control myself. I couldn't keep it in and told Uncle Vanya yesterday that I love him. . . . And all the servants know I love him. Everybody knows it.

YELENA And he?

SONYA No. He doesn't notice me.

YELENA *(musing)* He is a strange man. . . . Do you know what? Let me speak to him. . . . I'll do it carefully—hint at it . . . *(a pause).* Yes, really—how much longer are you to remain in uncertainty? Let me!

(SONYA nods her head in consent.)

YELENA That's right. It won't be difficult to find out whether he loves you or not. Don't you be troubled, darling; don't be uneasy. I'll question him so tactfully that he won't notice it. All we want to find out is yes or no *(a pause).* If it's no, he had better not come here, had he?

(SONYA nods in agreement.)

YELENA It's easier to bear when one doesn't see the man. We won't put things off; we will question him straight away. He was meaning to show me some charts. Go and tell him that I want to see him.

SONYA *(in violent agitation)* You will tell me the whole truth?

YELENA Yes, of course. It seems to me that the truth, however dreadful it is, is not so dreadful as uncertainty. Rely on me, dear.

SONYA Yes, yes . . . I shall tell him you want to see his charts *(is going, and stops in the doorway)* . . . No, uncertainty is better. . . . One has hope, at least. . . .

YELENA What do you say?

SONYA Nothing *(goes out).*

YELENA *(alone)* Nothing is worse than knowing somebody else's secret and not being able to help. *(musing)* He is not in love with her—that's evident; but why should he not marry her? She is not good-looking, but she would be a capital wife for a country doctor at his age. She is so sensible, so kind and pure-hearted. . . . No, that's not it . . . *(a pause).* I understand the poor child. In the midst of desperate boredom, with nothing but grey shadows wandering about instead of human beings, with only dull commonplaces to listen to, among people who can do nothing but eat, drink and sleep—he sometimes appears on the scene unlike the rest, handsome, interesting, fascinating, like a bright moon rising in the darkness. . . . To yield to the charm of such a man . . . forget oneself . . . I believe I am a little fascinated myself. Yes, I feel bored when he does not come, and even now I am smiling when I think of him. . . . That Uncle Vanya says I have mermaid's blood in my veins. "Let yourself go for once in your life." Well, perhaps that's what I ought to do. . . . If I could fly, free as a bird, away from all of you—from your sleepy faces, from your talk, forget your existence. . . . But I am cowardly and diffident. . . . My conscience troubles me. . . . He comes here every day. I guess why he comes, and already I have a guilty feeling. I am ready to throw myself on my knees before Sonya, to beg her pardon, to cry. . . .

ASTROV *(comes in with a chart)* Good day! *(Shakes hands.)* You wanted to see my handiwork.

YELENA You promised yesterday to show me. . . . Can you spare the time?

ASTROV Oh, of course! *(spreads the map on a card table and fixes it with drawing pins.)* Where were you born?

YELENA *(helping him)* In Petersburg.

ASTROV And where did you study?

YELENA At the School of Music.

ASTROV I expect this won't be interesting to you.

YELENA Why not? It's true that I don't know the country, but I have read a great deal.

ASTROV I have my own table here, in this house . . . in Ivan Petrovitch's room. When I am so exhausted that I feel completely stupefied, I throw everything up and fly here and amuse myself with this for an hour or two. . . . Ivan Petrovitch and Sofya Alexandrovna click their counting beads, and I sit beside them at my table and daub away—and I feel snug and comfortable, and the cricket churrs. But I don't allow myself that indulgence too often—only once a month. . . . *(Pointing to the map)* Now, look here! It's a picture of our district as it was fifty years ago. The dark and light green stands for forest; half of the whole area was covered with forest. Where there is a network of red over the green, elks and wild goats were common. . . . I show both the flora and the fauna here. On this lake there were swans, geese and ducks, and the old people tell us there were "a power" of birds of all sorts, no end of them; they flew in clouds. Besides the villages and hamlets, you see scattered here and there all sorts of settlements—little farms, monasteries of Old Believers, water-mills. . . . Horned cattle and horses were numerous. That is shown by the blue colour. For instance, the blue colour lies thick on this neighbourhood. Here there were regular droves of horses, and every homestead had three on an average *(a pause)*. Now look lower down. That's how it was twenty-five years ago. Already, you see, only a third of the area is under forest. There are no goats left, but there are elks. Both the green and the blue are paler. And so it goes on and on. Let us pass to the third part—a map of the district as it is at present. There is green here and there, but only in patches; all the elks have vanished, and the swans and the capercailzies too. . . . Of the old settlements and farms and monasteries and mills there is not a trace. In fact, it's a picture of gradual and unmistakable degeneration which will, apparently, in another ten or fifteen years be complete. You will say that it is the influence of civilisation—that the old life must naturally give way to the new. Yes, I understand that. If there were highroads and railways on the site of these ruined forests, if there were works and factories and schools, the peasants would be healthier, better off, more intelligent; but, you see, there is nothing of the sort! There are still the same swamps and mosquitoes, the same lack of roads, and poverty, and typhus and diphtheria and fires in the district. . . . We have here a degeneration that is the result of too severe a struggle for existence. This degeneration is due to inertia, ignorance, to the complete lack of understanding, when a man, cold, hungry and sick, simply to save what is left of life, to keep his children alive, instinctively, unconsciously clutches at anything to satisfy his hunger and warm himself and destroys everything heedless of the morrow. . . . Almost everything has been destroyed already, but nothing as yet has been created to take its place. *(coldly)* I see from your face that it doesn't interest you.

YELENA But I understand so little about all that. . . .

ASTROV There's nothing to understand in it; it simply doesn't interest you.

YELENA To speak frankly, I am thinking of something else. Forgive me. I want to put you through a little examination, and I am troubled and don't know how to begin.

ASTROV An examination?

YELENA Yes, an examination . . . but not a very formidable one. Let us sit down. *(They sit down.)* It concerns a certain young lady. We will talk like honest people, like friends, without beating about the bush. Let us talk and forget all about it afterwards. Yes?

ASTROV Yes.

YELENA It concerns my step-daughter Sonya. You like her, don't you?

ASTROV Yes, I have a respect for her.

YELENA Does she attract you as a woman?

ASTROV *(after a pause)* No.

YELENA A few words more, and I have done. Have you noticed nothing?

ASTROV Nothing.

YELENA *(taking him by the hand)* You do not love her . . . I see it from your eyes. . . . She is unhappy. . . . Understand that and . . . give up coming here.

ASTROV *(gets up)* My day is over. Besides, I have too much to do *(shrugging his shoulders)* What time have I for such things? *(He is confused.)*

YELENA Ough! What an unpleasant conversation! I am trembling as though I'd been carrying a ton weight. Well, thank God, that's over! Let us forget it. Let it be as though we had not spoken at all, and . . . and go away. You are an intelligent man . . . you'll understand *(a pause)*. I feel hot all over.

ASTROV If you had spoken a month or two ago I might, perhaps, have considered it; but now . . . *(he shrugs his shoulders)*. And if she is unhappy, then of course . . . There's only one thing I can't understand: what induced you to go into it? *(looks into her eyes and shakes his finger at her)* You are a sly one!

YELENA What does that mean?

ASTROV *(laughs)* Sly! Suppose Sonya is unhappy—I am quite ready to admit it—but why need you go into it? *(preventing her from speaking, eagerly)* Please don't try to look astonished. You know perfectly well what brings me here every day. . . . Why, and on whose account, I am here, you know perfectly well. You charming bird of prey, don't look at me like that, I am an old sparrow. . . .

YELENA *(perplexed)* Bird of prey! I don't understand.

ASTROV A beautiful, fluffy weasel. . . . You must have a victim! Here I have been doing nothing for a whole month. I have dropped everything. I seek you greedily—and you are awfully pleased at it, awfully. . . . Well, I am conquered; you knew that before your examination *(folding his arms and bowing his head).* I submit. Come and devour me!

YELENA You are mad!

ASTROV *(laughs through his teeth)* You—diffident. . . .

YELENA Oh, I am not so bad and so mean as you think! I swear I'm not *(tries to go out).*

ASTROV *(barring the way)* I am going away today. I won't come here again, but . . . *(takes her hand and looks round)* where shall we see each other? Tell me quickly, where? Someone may come in; tell me quickly. . . . *(passionately)* How wonderful, how magnificent you are! One kiss. . . . If I could only kiss your fragrant hair. . . .

YELENA I assure you . . .

ASTROV *(preventing her from speaking)* Why assure me? There's no need. No need of unnecessary words. . . . Oh, how beautiful you are! What hands! *(Kisses her hands.)*

YELENA That's enough . . . go away . . . *(withdraws her hands).* You are forgetting yourself.

ASTROV Speak, speak! Where shall we meet tomorrow? *(puts his arm round her waist)* You see, it is inevitable; we must meet. *(kisses her; at that instant* VOYNITSKY *comes in with a bunch of roses and stands still in the doorway.)*

YELENA *(not seeing* VOYNITSKY*)* Spare me . . . let me go . . . *(lays her head on* ASTROV'S *chest)* No! *(Tries to go out.)*

ASTROV *(holding her by the waist)* Come to the plantation tomorrow . . . at two o'clock. . . . Yes? Yes? You'll come?

YELENA *(seeing* VOYNITSKY*)* Let me go! *(in extreme confusion goes to the window.)* This is awful!

VOYNITSKY *(lays the roses on a chair; in confusion wipes his face and his neck with his handkerchief)* Never mind . . . no . . . never mind. . . .

ASTROV *(carrying it off with bravado)* The weather is not so bad today, honoured Ivan Petrovitch. It was overcast in the morning, as though we were going to have rain, but now it is sunny. To tell the truth, the autumn has turned out lovely . . . and the winter corn is quite promising *(rolls up the map).* The only thing is the days are getting shorter . . . *(goes out).*

YELENA *(goes quickly up to* VOYNITSKY*)* You will try—you will do your utmost that my husband and I should leave here today! Do you hear? This very day.

VOYNITSKY *(mopping his face)* What? Oh, yes . . . very well . . . I saw it all, Hélène—all. . . .

YELENA *(nervously)* Do you hear? I must get away from here today!

(Enter SEREBRYAKOV, TELYEGIN *and* MARINA.*)*

TELYEGIN I don't feel quite the thing myself, your Excellency. I have been poorly for the last two days. My head is rather queer. . . .

SEREBRYAKOV Where are the others? I don't like this house. It's a perfect labyrinth. Twenty-six huge rooms, people wander in different directions, and there is no finding anyone *(rings).* Ask Marya Vassilyevna and Yelena Andreyevna to come here.

YELENA I am here.

SEREBRYAKOV I beg you to sit down, friends.

SONYA *(going up to* YELENA ANDREYEVNA, *impatiently)* What did he say?

YELENA Presently.

SONYA You are trembling! You are agitated! *(Looking searchingly into her face)* I understand. . . . He said that he won't come here again . . . yes? *(a pause)* Tell me: yes?

*(*YELENA ANDREYEVNA *nods.)*

SEREBRYAKOV *(to* TELYEGIN*)* One can put up with illness, after all; but what I can't endure is the whole manner of life in the country. I feel as though I had been cast off the earth into some other planet. Sit down, friends, I beg! Sonya! *(*SONYA *does not hear him; she stands with her head drooping sorrowfully.)* Sonya! *(a pause)* She does not hear. *(To* MARINA*)* You sit down too, nurse. *(Nurse sits down, knitting a stocking.)* I beg you, my friends, hang your ears on the nail of attention, as the saying is *(laughs)*.

VOYNITSKY *(agitated)* Perhaps I am not wanted? Can I go?

SEREBRYAKOV No; it is you whom we need most.

VOYNITSKY What do you require of me?

SEREBRYAKOV Require of you. . . . Why are you cross? *(a pause)* If I have been to blame in any way, pray excuse me.

VOYNITSKY Drop that tone. Let us come to business. What do you want? *(Enter* MARYA VASSILYEVNA.*)*

SEREBRYAKOV Here is maman. I will begin, friends *(a pause)*. I have invited you, gentlemen, to announce that the Inspector-General is coming. But let us lay aside jesting. It is a serious matter. I have called you together to ask for your advice and help, and, knowing your invariable kindness, I hope to receive it. I am a studious, bookish man, and have never had anything to do with practical life. I cannot dispense with the assistance of those who understand it, and I beg you, Ivan Petrovitch, and you, Ilya Ilyitch, and you, *maman*. . . . The point is that *manet omnes una nox*—that is, that we are all mortal. I am old and ill, and so I think it is high time to settle my worldly affairs so far as they concern my family. My life is over. I am not thinking of myself, but I have a young wife and an unmarried daughter *(a pause)*. It is impossible for me to go on living in the country. We are not made for country life. But to live in town on the income we derive from this estate is impossible. If we sell the forest, for instance, that's an exceptional measure which we cannot repeat every year. We must take some steps which would guarantee us a permanent and more or less definite income. I have thought of such a measure, and have the honour of submitting it to your consideration. Omitting details I will put it before you in rough outline. Our estate yields on an average not more than two per cent. on its capital value. I propose to sell it. If we invest the money in suitable securities, we should get from four to five per cent., and I think we might even have a few thousand roubles to spare for buying a small villa in Finland.

VOYNITSKY Excuse me . . . surely my ears are deceiving me! Repeat what you have said.

SEREBRYAKOV To put the money in some suitable investment and with the remainder purchase a villa in Finland.

VOYNITSKY Not Finland. . . . You said something else.

SEREBRYAKOV I propose to sell the estate.

VOYNITSKY That's it. You will sell the estate; superb, a grand idea. . . . And what do you propose to do with me, and your old mother and Sonya here?

SEREBRYAKOV We will settle all that in due time. One can't go into everything at once.

VOYNITSKY Wait a minute. It's evident that up to now I've never had a grain of common sense. Up to now I have always imagined that the estate belongs to Sonya. My father bought this estate as a dowry for my sister. Till now I have been simple; I did not interpret the law like a Turk, but thought that my sister's estate passed to Sonya.

SEREBRYAKOV Yes, the estate belongs to Sonya. Who disputes it? Without Sonya's consent I shall not venture to sell it. Besides, I am proposing to do it for Sonya's benefit.

VOYNITSKY It's inconceivable, inconceivable! Either I have gone out of my mind, or . . . or . . .

MARYA Jean, don't contradict Alexandr. Believe me, he knows better than we do what is for the best.

VOYNITSKY No; give me some water *(drinks water).* Say what you like—say what you like!

SEREBRYAKOV I don't understand why you are so upset. I don't say that my plan is ideal. If everyone thinks it unsuitable, I will not insist on it. *(A pause.)*

TELYEGIN *(in confusion)* I cherish for learning, your Excellency, not simply a feeling of reverence, but a sort of family feeling. My brother Grigory Ilyitch's wife's brother—perhaps you know him?—Konstantin Trofimitch Lakedemonov, was an M.A. . . .

VOYNITSKY Stop, Waffles; we are talking of business. . . . Wait a little—later. . . . *(to* SEREBRYAKOV*)* Here, ask him. The estate was bought from his uncle.

SEREBRYAKOV Oh! why should I ask him? What for?

VOYNITSKY The estate was bought at the time for ninety-five thousand roubles. My father paid only seventy thousand, and twenty-five thousand remained on mortgage. Now, listen. . . . The estate would never have been bought if I had not renounced my share of the inheritance in favour of my sister, whom I loved dearly. What's more, I worked for ten years like a slave and paid off all the mortgage. . . .

SEREBRYAKOV I regret that I broached the subject.

VOYNITSKY The estate is free from debt and in a good condition only owing to my personal efforts. And now that I am old I am to be kicked out of it!

SEREBRYAKOV I don't understand what you are aiming at.

VOYNITSKY I have been managing this estate for twenty-five years. I have worked and sent you money like the most conscientious steward, and you have never thanked me once in all these years. All that time—

both when I was young and now—you have given me five hundred roubles a year as salary—a beggarly wage!—and it never occurred to you to add a rouble to it.

SEREBRYAKOV Ivan Petrovitch, how could I tell? I am not a practical man, and don't understand these things. You could have added as much to it as you chose.

VOYNITSKY Why didn't I steal? How is it you don't all despise me because I didn't steal? It would have been right and I shouldn't have been a pauper now!

MARYA *(sternly)* Jean!

TELYEGIN *(in agitation)* Vanya, my dear soul, don't, don't . . . I am all of a tremble. . . . Why spoil our good relations? *(kisses him)* You mustn't.

VOYNITSKY For twenty-five years I have been here within these four walls with mother, buried like a mole. . . . All our thoughts and feelings belonged to you alone. By day we talked of you and your labours. We were proud of you; with reverence we uttered your name. We wasted our nights reading books and magazines for which now I have the deepest contempt!

TELYEGIN Don't, Vanya, don't . . . I can't stand it. . . .

SEREBRYAKOV *(wrathfully)* I don't know what it is you want.

VOYNITSKY To us you were a being of a higher order, and we knew your articles by heart. . . . But now my eyes are opened! I see it all! You write of art, but you know nothing about art! All those works of yours I used to love are not worth a brass farthing! You have deceived us!

SEREBRYAKOV Do stop him! I am going!

YELENA Ivan Petrovitch, I insist on your being silent! Do you hear?

VOYNITSKY I won't be silent. *(preventing* SEREBRYAKOV *from passing)* Stay! I have not finished. You have destroyed my life! I have not lived! I have not lived! Thanks to you, I have ruined and wasted the best years of my life. You are my bitterest enemy.

TELYEGIN I can't bear it . . . I can't bear it . . . I must go *(goes out, in violent agitation).*

SEREBRYAKOV What do you want from me? And what right have you to speak to me like this? You nonentity! If the estate is yours, take it. I don't want it!

YELENA I am going away from this hell this very minute *(screams).* I can't put up with it any longer!

VOYNITSKY My life is ruined! I had talent, I had courage, I had intelligence! If I had had a normal life I might have been a Schopenhauer, a Dostoevsky. . . . Oh, I am talking like an idiot! I am going mad. . . . Mother, I am in despair! Mother!

MARYA *(sternly)* Do as Alexandr tells you.

SONYA *(kneeling down before the nurse and huddling up to her)* Nurse, darling! Nurse, darling!

VOYNITSKY Mother! What am I to do? Don't speak; there's no need! I know what I must do! *(to* SEREBRYAKOV*)* You shall remember me! *(Goes out through middle door.)*

(MARYA VASSILYEVNA *follows him.)*

SEREBRYAKOV This is beyond everything! Take that madman away! I cannot live under the same roof with him. He is always there *(points to the middle door)*—almost beside me. . . . Let him move into the village, or into the lodge, or I will move; but remain in the same house with him I cannot. . . .

YELENA *(to her husband)* We will leave this place today! We must pack up this minute!

SEREBRYAKOV An utterly insignificant creature!

SONYA *(on her knees, turns her head towards her father; hysterical through her tears).* You must be merciful, father! Uncle Vanya and I are so unhappy! *(Mastering her despair)* You must be merciful! Remember how, when you were younger, Uncle Vanya and grandmamma sat up all night translating books for you, copying your manuscripts . . . all night . . . all night . . . Uncle Vanya and I worked without resting—we were afraid to spend a farthing on ourselves and sent it all to you. . . . We did not eat the bread of idleness. I am saying it all wrong—all wrong; but you ought to understand us, father. You must be merciful!

YELENA *(in agitation, to her husband)* Alexandr, for God's sake make it up with him. . . . I beseech you!

SEREBRYAKOV Very well, I will talk to him. . . . I am not accusing him of anything, I am not angry with him. But you must admit that his behaviour is strange, to say the least of it. Very well, I'll go to him *(goes out by middle door).*

YELENA Be gentle with him, soothe him . . . *(follows him out).*

SONYA *(hugging Nurse)* Oh, nurse, darling! Nurse, darling!

MARINA Never mind, child. The ganders will cackle a bit and leave off. . . . They will cackle and leave off. . . .

SONYA Nurse, darling!

MARINA *(stroking her head)* You are shivering as though you were frozen! There, there, little orphan, God is merciful! A cup of lime-flower water, or raspberry tea, and it will pass. . . . Don't grieve, little orphan. *(looking towards the middle door wrathfully)* What a to-do they make, the ganders! Plague take them!

(A shot behind the scenes; a shriek from YELENA ANDREYEVNA *is heard;* SONYA *shudders.)*

MARINA Ough! Botheration take them!

SEREBRYAKOV *(runs in, staggering with terror)* Hold him! hold him! He is out of his mind!

*(*YELENA ANDREYEVNA *and* VOYNITSKY *struggle in the doorway.)*

YELENA *(trying to take the revolver from him)* Give it up! Give it up, I tell you!

VOYNITSKY Let me go, Hélène! Let me go! *(Freeing himself from her, he runs in, looking for* SEREBRYAKOV*)* Where is he? Oh, here he is! *(Fires at him) Bang! (a pause)* Missed! Missed again! *(Furiously)* Damnation—damnation take it . . . *(Flings revolver on the floor and sinks on to a chair, exhausted.* SEREBRYAKOV *is overwhelmed;* YELENA *leans against the wall, almost fainting.)*

YELENA Take me away! Take me away! Kill me . . . I can't stay here,

I can't!
VOYNITSKY *(in despair)* Oh, what am I doing! What am I doing!
SONYA *(softly)* Nurse, darling! Nurse, darling!

act IV

*(*VOYNITSKY'S *room: it is his bedroom and also his office. In the window there is a big table covered with account books and papers of all sorts; a bureau, bookcases, scales. A smaller table, for* ASTROV; *on that table there are paints and drawing materials; beside it a big portfolio. A cage with a starling in it. On the wall a map of Africa, obviously of no use to anyone. A big sofa covered with American leather. To the left a door leading to other apartments. On the right a door into the hall; near door, on right, there is a doormat, that the peasants may not muddy the floor. An autumn evening. Stillness.*
TELYEGIN *and* MARINA *sitting opposite each other winding wool.)*

TELYEGIN You must make haste, Marina Timofeyevna, they will soon be calling us to say good-bye. They have already ordered the horses.
MARINA *(tries to wind more rapidly)* There is not much left.
TELYEGIN They are going to Harkov. They'll live there.
MARINA Much better so.
TELYEGIN They've had a fright. . . . Yelena Andreyevna keeps saying, "I won't stay here another hour. Let us get away; let us get away." "We will stay at Harkov," she says; "we will have a look round and then send for our things. . . ." They are not taking much with them. It seems it is not ordained that they should live here, Marina Timofeyevna. It's not ordained. . . . It's the dispensation of Providence.
MARINA It's better so. Look at the quarrelling and shooting this morning —a regular disgrace!
TELYEGIN Yes, a subject worthy of the brush of Aïvazovsky.
MARINA A shocking sight it was *(a pause)*. We shall live again in the old way, as we used to. We shall have breakfast at eight, dinner at one, and sit down to supper in the evening; everything as it should be, like other people . . . like Christians *(with a sigh)*. It's a long while since I have tasted noodles, sinner that I am!
TELYEGIN Yes, it's a long time since they have given us noodles at dinner *(a pause)*. A very long time. . . . As I was walking through the village this morning, Marina Timofeyevna, the man at the shop called after me, "You cadger, living upon other people." And it did hurt me so.
MARINA You shouldn't take any notice of that, my dear. We all live upon God. Whether it's you or Sonya or Ivan Petrovitch, none of you sit idle, we all work hard! All of us. . . . Where is Sonya?
TELYEGIN In the garden. She is still going round with the doctor looking for Ivan Petrovitch. They are afraid he may lay hands on himself.
MARINA And where is his pistol?
TELYEGIN *(in a whisper)* I've hidden it in the cellar!

(*Enter* VOYNITSKY *and* ASTROV *from outside.*)

VOYNITSKY Let me alone. (*to* MARINA *and* TELYEGIN) Go away, leave me alone—if only for an hour! I won't endure being watched.

TELYEGIN Certainly, Vanya (*goes out on tiptoe*).

MARINA The gander says, ga-ga-ga! (*gathers up her wool and goes out*)

VOYNITSKY Let me alone!

ASTROV I should be delighted to. I ought to have gone away ages ago, but I repeat I won't go till you give back what you took from me.

VOYNITSKY I did not take anything from you.

ASTROV I am speaking in earnest, don't detain me. I ought to have gone long ago.

VOYNITSKY I took nothing from you. (*Both sit down.*)

ASTROV Oh! I'll wait a little longer and then, excuse me, I must resort to force. We shall have to tie your hands and search you. I am speaking quite seriously.

VOYNITSKY As you please (*a pause*). To have made such a fool of myself: to have fired twice and missed him! I shall never forgive myself for that.

ASTROV If you wanted to be playing with firearms, you would have done better to take a pop at yourself.

VOYNITSKY (*shrugging his shoulders*) It's queer. I made an attempt to commit murder and I have not been arrested; no one has sent for the police. So I am looked upon as a madman (*with a bitter laugh*). I am mad, but people are not mad who hide their crass stupidity, their flagrant heartlessness under the mask of a professor, a learned sage. People are not mad who marry old men and then deceive them before the eyes of everyone. I saw you kissing her! I saw!

ASTROV Yes, I did kiss her, and that's more than you ever have!

VOYNITSKY (*looking towards the door*) No, the earth is mad to let you go on living on it!

ASTROV Come, that's silly.

VOYNITSKY Well, I am mad. I am not responsible. I have a right to say silly things.

ASTROV That's a stale trick. You are not a madman: you are simply a crank. A silly fool. Once I used to look upon every crank as an invalid—as abnormal; but now I think it is the normal condition of man to be a crank. You are quite normal.

VOYNITSKY (*covers his face with his hands*) I am ashamed! If you only knew how ashamed I am! No pain can be compared with this acute shame (*miserably*). It's unbearable (*bends over the table*). What am I to do? What am I to do?

ASTROV Nothing.

VOYNITSKY Give me something! Oh, my God! I am forty-seven. If I live to be sixty, I have another thirteen years. It's a long time! How am I to get through those thirteen years? What shall I do? How am I to fill them up? Oh, you know . . . (*squeezing* ASTROV'S *hand convulsively*); you know, if only one could live the remnant of one's life in some new way. Wake up on a still sunny morning and feel that one had begun a new life, that all the past was forgotten and had melted away like smoke *(weeps)*. To begin a new life. . . . Tell me how to begin it . . . what to begin. . . .

ASTROV *(with vexation)* Oh, get away with you! New life, indeed! Our position – yours and mine – is hopeless.

VOYNITSKY Yes?

ASTROV I am convinced of it.

VOYNITSKY Give me something. . . . *(Pointing to his heart)* I have a scalding pain here.

ASTROV *(shouts angrily)* Leave off! *(Softening)* Those who will live a hundred or two hundred years after us, and who will despise us for having lived our lives so stupidly and tastelessly – they will, perhaps, find a means of being happy; but we . . . There is only one hope for you and me. The hope that when we are asleep in our graves we may, perhaps, be visited by pleasant visions *(with a sigh)*. Yes, old man, in the whole district there were only two decent, well-educated men: you and I. And in some ten years the common round of the trivial life here has swamped us, and has poisoned our life with its putrid vapours, and made us just as despicable as all the rest. *(eagerly)* But don't try to put me off: give me what you took away from me.

VOYNITSKY I took nothing from you.

ASTROV You took a bottle of morphia out of my travelling medicine-chest *(a pause)*. Look here, if you insist on making an end of yourself, go into the forest and shoot yourself. But give me back the morphia or else there will be talk and conjecture. People will think I have given it you. It will be quite enough for me to have to make your post-mortem. Do you think I shall find it interesting?

(Enter SONYA.*)*

VOYNITSKY Leave me alone.

ASTROV *(to* SONYA*)* Sofya Alexandrovna, your uncle has taken a bottle of morphia out of my medicine-chest, and won't give it back. Tell him that it's . . . really stupid. And I haven't the time to waste. I ought to be going.

SONYA Uncle Vanya, did you take the morphia? *(a pause)*

ASTROV He did. I am certain of it.

SONYA Give it back. Why do you frighten us? *(tenderly)* Give it back, Uncle Vanya! I am just as unhappy, perhaps, as you are; but I am not going to give way to despair. I am bearing it, and will bear it, till my life ends of itself. . . . You must be patient too *(a pause)*. Give it back! *(kisses his hands)* Dear, good uncle, darling! give it back! *(weeps)* You are kind, you will have pity on us and give it back. Be patient, uncle! – be patient!

VOYNITSKY *(takes the bottle out of the table-drawer and gives it to* ASTROV*)* There, take it! *(to* SONYA*)* But we must make haste and work, make haste and do something, or else I can't . . . I can't bear it.

SONYA Yes, yes, work. As soon as we have seen our people off, we'll sit down to work. . . . *(nervously turning over the papers on the table)* We have let everything go.

ASTROV *(puts the bottle into his case and tightens the straps)* Now I can set off.

(Enter YELENA.*)*

YELENA Ivan Petrovitch, are you here? We are just starting. Go to Alexandr, he wants to say something to you.

SONYA Go, Uncle Vanya. *(takes* VOYNITSKY *by the arm)* Let us go. Father and you must be reconciled. That's essential.

(SONYA *and* VOYNITSKY *go out.)*

YELENA I am going away. *(gives* ASTROV *her hand)* Good-bye.

ASTROV Already?

YELENA The carriage is waiting.

ASTROV Good-bye.

YELENA You promised me today that you would go away.

ASTROV I remember. I am just going *(a pause).* You have taken fright? *(taking her hand)* Is it so terrible?

YELENA Yes.

ASTROV You had better stay, after all! What do you say? Tomorrow in the plantation——

YELENA No. It's settled. And I look at you so fearlessly just because it is settled. I have only one favour to ask of you: think better of me. I should like you to have a respect for me.

ASTROV Ugh! *(makes a gesture of impatience)* Do stay, I ask you to. Do recognise, you have nothing to do in this world, you have no object in life, you have nothing to occupy your mind, and sooner or later you will give way to feeling–it's inevitable. And it had better not be at Harkov, or somewhere in Kursk, but here, in the lap of nature. . . . It's poetical, anyway, even the autumn is beautiful. . . . There is the forest plantation here, half-ruined homesteads in the Turgenev style. . . .

YELENA How absurd you are. . . . I am angry with you, but yet . . . I shall think of you with pleasure. You are an interesting, original man. We shall never meet again, and so–why conceal it?–I was really a little bit in love with you. Come, let us shake hands and part friends. Don't remember evil against me.

ASTROV *(pressing her hand)* Yes, you had better go . . . *(musing).* You seem to be a good, warm-hearted creature, and yet there is something strange about your whole personality, as it were. You came here with your husband, and all of us who were at work, toiling and creating something, had to fling aside our work and attend to nothing all the summer but your husband's gout and you. The two of you have infected all of us with your idleness. I was attracted by you and have done nothing for a whole month, and, meanwhile, people have been ill, and the peasants have pastured their cattle in my woods, of young, half-grown trees. . . . And so, wherever you and your husband go, you bring destruction everywhere. . . . I am joking, of course, yet . . . it is strange. And I am convinced that if you had stayed here, the devastation would have been immense. I should have been done for . . . and you wouldn't have fared well either! Well, go away. *Finita la commedia!*

YELENA *(taking a pencil from his table and hurriedly putting it in her pocket)* I shall take this pencil as a keepsake.

ASTROV It is strange. . . . We have been friends and all at once for some reason . . . we shall never meet again. So it is with everything in this world. . . . While there is no one here—before Uncle Vanya comes in with a nosegay—allow me to kiss you at parting. . . . Yes? *(kisses her on the cheek)* That's right.

YELENA I wish you all happiness. *(looks round)* Well, so be it! For once in my life! *(Embraces him impulsively and both simultaneously draw rapidly apart from each other.)* I must go—I must go!

ASTROV Make haste and go. Since the carriage is there, you had better set off.

YELENA There's someone coming, I believe. *(Both listen.)*

ASTROV *Finita!*

(Enter SEREBRYAKOV, VOYNITSKY, MARYA VASSILYEVNA, *with a book;* TELYEGIN *and* SONYA.*)*

SEREBRYAKOV *(to* VOYNITSKY*)* Let bygones be bygones. After what has happened, I have gone through and experienced so much in these few hours, that I believe I could write a whole treatise on the art of living for the benefit of posterity. I gladly accept your apologies and apologize myself. Good-bye! *(He and* VOYNITSKY *kiss each other three times.)*

VOYNITSKY You shall receive regularly the same sum as hitherto. Everything shall be as before.

*(*YELENA ANDREYEVNA *embraces* SONYA.*)*

SEREBRYAKOV *(kisses* MARYA VASSILYEVNA'S *hand) Maman. . . .*

MARYA *(kissing him)* Alexandr, have your photograph taken again and send it to me. You know how dear you are to me.

TELYEGIN Good-bye, your Excellency! Don't forget us!

SEREBRYAKOV *(kissing his daughter)* Good-bye . . . good-bye, everyone. *(Shaking hands with* ASTROV*)* Thanks for your pleasant company. I respect your way of thinking, your enthusiasms, your impulses, but permit an old man to add one observation to his farewell message: you must work, my friends! you must work! *(He bows to them all.)* I wish you all things good!

(Goes out, followed by MARYA VASSILYEVNA *and* SONYA.*)*

VOYNITSKY *(warmly kisses* YELENA ANDREYEVNA'S *hand)* Good-bye. . . . Forgive me. . . . We shall never meet again.

YELENA *(moved)* Good-bye, dear Ivan Petrovitch *(kisses him on the head and goes out).*

ASTROV *(to* TELYEGIN*)* Waffles, tell them, by the way, to bring my carriage round too.

TELYEGIN Certainly, my dear soul *(goes out).*

(Only ASTROV *and* VOYNITSKY *remain.)*

ASTROV *(clearing his paints from the table and putting them away in his portmanteau)* Why don't you go and see them off?

VOYNITSKY Let them go, I . . . I can't. My heart is too heavy. I must make haste and occupy myself with something. . . . Work! Work! *(rummages among his papers on the table.)*

(A pause; there is the sound of bells.)

ASTROV They've gone. The Professor is glad, I'll be bound. Nothing will tempt him back.

MARINA *(enters)* They've gone *(sits down in an easy chair and knits her stocking).*

SONYA *(enters)* They've gone *(wipes her eyes).* Good luck to them. *(to her uncle)* Well, Uncle Vanya, let us do something.

VOYNITSKY Work, work. . . .

SONYA It's ever so long since we sat at this table together *(lights the lamp on the table).* I believe there is no ink *(takes the inkstand, goes to the cupboard, and fills it with ink).* But I feel sad that they have gone.

*(*MARYA VASSILYEVNA *comes in slowly.)*

MARYA They've gone *(sits down and becomes engrossed in reading).*

SONYA *(sits down to the table and turns over the pages of the account book)* First of all, Uncle Vanya, let us make out our accounts. We've neglected it all dreadfully. Someone sent for his account again today. Make it out. If you will do one account, I will do another.

VOYNITSKY *(writes)* "Delivered . . . to Mr. . . ." *(Both write in silence.)*

MARINA *(yawning)* I am ready for bye-bye.

ASTROV How quiet it is! The pens scratch and the cricket churrs. It's warm and snug. I don't want to go. *(There is the sound of bells.)* There are my horses. . . . There is nothing left for me but to say good-bye to you, my friends—to say good-bye to my table—and be off! *(Packs up his maps in the portfolio.)*

MARINA Why are you in such a hurry? You might as well stay.

ASTROV I can't.

VOYNITSKY *(writes)* "Account delivered, two roubles and seventy-five kopeks."

(Enter a LABORER.*)*

LABORER Mihail Lvovitch, the horses are ready.

ASTROV I heard them. *(hands him the medicine-chest, the portmanteau and the portfolio)* Here, take these. Mind you don't crush the portfolio.

LABORER Yes, sir.

ASTROV Well? *(goes to say good-bye)*

SONYA When shall we see you again?

ASTROV Not before next summer, I expect. Hardly in the winter. . . . Of course, if anything happens, you'll let me know, and I'll come *(shakes hands).* Thank you for your hospitality, for your kindness—for everything, in fact. *(goes up to nurse and kisses her on the head)* Good-bye, old woman.

MARINA You are not going without tea?

ASTROV I don't want any, nurse.

MARINA Perhaps you'll have a drop of vodka?

ASTROV *(irresolutely)* Perhaps.

*(*MARINA *goes out.)*

ASTROV *(after a pause)* My trace-horse has gone a little lame. I noticed it yesterday when Petrushka was taking it to water.

VOYNITSKY You must change his shoes.

ASTROV I shall have to call in at the blacksmith's in Rozhdestvennoye. It can't be helped. *(goes up to the map of Africa and looks at it)* I suppose in that Africa there the heat must be something terrific now!

VOYNITSKY Yes, most likely.

MARINA *(comes back with a tray on which there is a glass of vodka and a piece of bread)* There you are.

*(*ASTROV *drinks the vodka.)*

MARINA To your good health, my dear *(makes a low bow).* You should eat some bread with it.

ASTROV No, I like it as it is. And now, good luck to you all. *(to* MARINA*)* Don't come out, nurse, there is no need.

(He goes out; SONYA *follows with a candle, to see him off;* MARINA *sits in her easy chair.)*

VOYNITSKY *(writes)* "February the second, Lenten oil, twenty pounds. February sixteenth, Lenten oil again, twenty pounds. Buckwheat . . ." *(a pause).*

(The sound of bells.)

MARINA He has gone *(a pause).*

SONYA *(comes back and puts the candle on the table)* He has gone.

VOYNITSKY *(counts on the beads and writes down)* "Total . . . fifteen . . . twenty-five . . ."

*(*SONYA *sits down and writes.)*

MARINA *(yawns)* Lord have mercy on us!

*(*TELYEGIN *comes in on tiptoe, sits by the door and softly tunes the guitar.)*

VOYNITSKY *(to* SONYA, *passing his hand over her hair)* My child, how my heart aches! Oh, if only you knew how my heart aches!

SONYA There is nothing for it. We must go on living! *(a pause)* We shall go on living, Uncle Vanya! We shall live through a long, long chain of days and weary evenings; we shall patiently bear the trials which fate sends us; we shall work for others, both now and in our old age, and have no rest; and when our time comes we shall die without a murmur, and there beyond the grave we shall say that we have suffered, that we have wept, that life has been bitter to us, and God will have pity on us, and you and I, uncle, dear uncle, shall see a life that is bright, lovely, beautiful. We shall rejoice and look back at these troubles of ours with tenderness, with a smile—and we shall rest. I have faith, uncle; I have fervent, passionate faith. *(Slips on her knees before him and lays her head on his hands; in a weary voice:)* We shall rest!

*(*TELYEGIN *softly plays on the guitar.)*

SONYA We shall rest! We shall hear the angels; we shall see all Heaven lit with radiance; we shall see all earthly evil, all our sufferings, drowned in mercy which will fill the whole world, and our life will be peaceful, gentle and sweet as a caress. I have faith, I have faith *(wipes away his tears with her handkerchief).* Poor Uncle Vanya, you are crying. *(through her tears)* You have had no joy in your life, but wait, Uncle Vanya, wait. We shall rest *(puts her arms round him).* We shall rest! *(The Watchman taps.)*

(TELYEGIN *plays softly;* MARYA VASSILYEVNA *makes notes on the margin of her pamphlet;* MARINA *knits her stocking.)*
SONYA We shall rest!

maxim gorky

anton chekov

He once invited me to visit him in the village of Kuchuk-koi, where he had a tiny plot of ground and a white, two-storey house. He showed me over his "estate," talking animatedly all the time: "If I had lots of money I would build a sanitorium here for sick village teachers. A building full of light, you know, very light, with big windows and high ceilings. I'd have a splendid library, all sorts of musical instruments, an apiary, a vegetable garden, an orchard. I'd have lectures on agronomy, meteorology, and so on—teachers ought to know everything, old man—everything!"

He broke off suddenly, coughed, cast an oblique glance at me, and smiled his sweet, gentle smile, a smile which had an irresistible charm, forcing one to follow his words with the keenest attention.

"Does it bore you to listen to my dreams? I love talking about this. If you only knew the absolute necessity for the Russian countryside of good, clever, educated teachers! In Russia we have simply got to create exceptional conditions for teachers, and that as soon as possible, since we realize that unless the people get an all-round education the state will collapse like a house built from insufficiently baked bricks. The teacher must be an actor, an artist, passionately in love with his work, and our teachers are *navvies,* half-educated individuals, who go to the village to teach children about as willingly as they would go to exile. They are famished, downtrodden, they live in perpetual fear of losing their livelihood. And the teacher ought to be the first man in the village, able to answer all the questions put to him by the peasants, to instil in the peasants a respect for his power worthy of attention and respect, whom no one will dare to shout at . . . to lower his dignity, as in our country everybody does—the village policeman, the rich shopkeeper, the priest, the school patron, the elder and that official who, though he is called a school inspector, busies himself, not over the improvement of conditions for education, but simply and solely over the carrying out of district circulars to the letter. It's absurd to pay a niggardly pittance to one who is called upon to educate the people—to educate the people, mind! It is intolerable that such a one should go about in rags, shiver in a damp, dilapidated school, be poisoned by fumes from badly ventilated stoves, be always catching cold, and by the age of thirty be a mass of disease—laryngitis, rheumatism, tuberculosis.

It's a disgrace to us! For nine or ten months in the year our teachers live the lives of hermits, without a soul to speak to, they grow stupid from loneliness, without books or amusements. And if they venture to invite friends to come and see them, people think they are disaffected—that idiotic word with which cunning folk terrify fools. . . . All this is disgusting . . . a kind of mockery of human beings doing a great and terribly important work. I tell you, when I meet a teacher I feel quite awkward in front of him—for his timidity, and his shabbiness. I feel as if I myself were somehow to blame for the teacher's wretched state—I do, really!"

Pausing for a moment, he threw out his arm and said softly:

"What an absurd, clumsy country our Russia is!"

A shadow of profound sorrow darkened his fine eyes, and a fine network of wrinkles showed at the corners, deepening his glance. He looked around him and began making fun of himself.

"There you are—I've treated you to a full-length leading article from a liberal newspaper. Come on, I'll give you some tea as a reward for your patience. . . ."

This was often the way with him. One moment he would be talking with warmth, gravity and sincerity, and the next, he would be laughing at himself and his own words. And beneath this gentle, sorrowful laughter could be felt the subtle scepticism of a man who knew the value of words, the value of dreams. There was a shade of his attractive modesty, his intuitive delicacy in this laughter, too.

We walked back to the house in silence. It was a warm, bright day; the sound of waves sparkling in the vivid rays of the sun, could be heard. In the valley, a dog was squealing its delight about something. Chekhov took me by the arm and said slowly, his speech interrupted by coughs:

"It's disgraceful and very sad, but it is true—there are many people who envy dogs. . . ."

And then he added, laughing:

"Everything I say today sounds senile—I must be getting old." . . .

It seems to me that in the presence of Anton Pavlovich everyone felt an unconscious desire to be simpler, more truthful, more himself, and I had many opportunities of observing how people threw off their attire of grand bookish phrases, fashionable expressions, and all the rest of the cheap trifles with which Russians, in their anxiety to appear Europeans, adorn themselves, as savages deck themselves with shells and fishes' teeth. Anton Pavlovich was not fond of fishes' teeth and cocks' feathers; all that is tawdry, tinkling, alien, donned by human beings for the sake of an "imposing appearance," embarrassed him, and I noticed that whenever he met with one of these dressed-up individuals he felt an overmastering impulse to free him from his ponderous and superfluous trappings, distorting the true face and living soul of his interlocutor. All his life Anton Pavlovich lived the life of the soul, was always himself, inwardly free, and took no notice of what some expected, and others—less delicate—demanded of Anton Chekhov. He did not like conversations on "lofty" subjects—conversations which Russians, in the simplicity of their hearts, find so amusing, forgetting that it is absurd, and not in the least witty, to talk about the velvet apparel of the future, while not even possessing in the present a decent pair of trousers.

Of a beautiful simplicity himself, he loved all that was simple, real, sincere, and he had a way of his own of making others simple. . . .

He had the art of exposing vulgarity everywhere, an art which can only be mastered by one whose own demands on life are very high, and which springs from the ardent desire to see simplicity, beauty and harmony in man. He was a severe and merciless judge of vulgarity.

Someone said in his presence that the editor of a popular magazine, a man perpetually talking about the necessity for love and sympathy for others, had insulted a railway guard without the slightest provocation, and was in the habit of treating his subordinates roughly.

"Naturally," said Anton Pavlovich, with a grim chuckle. "He's an aristocrat, a cultivated man . . . he went to a seminary. His father went about in bast shoes, but *he* wears patent leather boots."

And the tone in which these words were spoken at once dismissed the "aristocrat" as a mediocre and ridiculous individual.

"A very gifted person," he said of a certain journalist. "His writing is always so lofty, so humane . . . saccharine. He calls his wife a fool in front of people. His servants sleep in a damp room, and they all develop rheumatism. . . ."

"Do you like So-and-So, Anton Pavlovich?"

"Oh, yes. A nice man," replies Anton Pavlovich, coughing. "He knows everything. He reads a lot. He took three books of mine and never returned them. A bit absent-minded, tells you one day that you're a fine fellow, and the next tells someone else that you stole the black silk socks with blue stripes of your mistress's husband." . . .

A subtle mockery almost always twinkled gently in his grey mournful eyes, but occasionally these eyes would become cold, keen, harsh, and at such moments a hard note would creep into the smooth, cordial tones of his voice, and then I felt that this modest, kindly man could stand up against any hostile force, stand up firmly, without knuckling under to it.

It sometimes seemed to me that there was a shade of hopelessness in his attitude to others, something akin to a cold, still despair.

"The Russian is a strange being," he said once. "He is like a sieve, he can hold nothing for long. In his youth he crams himself eagerly with everything that comes his way, and by the time he is thirty nothing is left of it all but a heap of colourless rubbish. If one wants to lead a good life, a human life, one must work. Work with love and with faith. And we don't know how to do that in our country. An architect, having built two or three decent houses, sits down to play cards for the rest of his life or hangs about the backstage of a theatre. As soon as a doctor acquires a practice he stops keeping up with science, never reads anything but *Novosti Terapii (Therapeutical News)* and by the age of forty is firmly convinced that all diseases come from colds. I have never met a single official who had even the slightest idea of the significance of his work—they usually dig themselves in at the capital, or some provincial town, and invent papers which they dispatch to Zmiyev and Smorgon for fulfilment. And whose freedom of movement is impeded in Zmiyev or Smorgon by these documents; the official no more cares than an atheist does about the torments of hell. Having made a name by a successful defence the barrister ceases to bother about the defence of truth and does nothing but defend the rights of property, put money on horses, eat oysters, and pass himself off as a connoisseur of all the arts. An actor, having performed two or three parts with fair success, no longer learns his parts, but puts on a top hat and considers himself a genius. Russia is a land of greedy idlers. People eat and drink enormously, love to sleep in the daytime, and snore in their sleep. They marry for the sake of order in their homes, and take a mistress for the sake of social prestige. Their psychology is a dog's psychology. Beat them and they squeal meekly and sneak off to their kennels. Caress them, and they lie on their backs with their paws up, wagging their tails."

A cold, sorrowful contempt underlay these words. But while despising, he could pity, and when anyone was abused in his presence, Anton Pavlovich was sure to stick up for him.

"Come now! He's an old man, he's seventy. . . ."

Or:

"He's still young, it's just his stupidity. . . ."

And when he spoke like this I could see no signs of disgust in his face. . . .

When one is young, vulgarity seems to be simply amusing and insignificant, but it gradually surrounds the individual, its grey mist creeping into his brains and blood, like poison or charcoal fumes, till he becomes like an old tavern-sign, eaten up with rust—there seems to be something depicted on it, but what, it is impossible to make out.

From the very first Anton Pavlovich managed to reveal, in the grey ocean of vulgarity, its tragically sombre jokes. One only has to read his "humorous" stories carefully, to realize how much that was cruel was seen and shamefacedly concealed by the author in comic narrative and situations.

He had an almost virginal modesty, he could never bring himself to challenge people loudly and openly: "Be more decent—can't you!" vainly trusting that they would themselves realize the urgent necessity for being more decent. Detesting all that was vulgar and unclean, he described the seamy side of life in the lofty language of the poet, with the gentle smile of the humorist, and the bitter inner reproach beneath the polished surface of his stories is scarcely noticeable. . . .

No one ever understood the tragic nature of life's trifles so clearly and intuitively as Chekhov did, never before has a writer been able to hold up to human beings such a ruthlessly truthful picture of all that was shameful and pitiable in the dingy chaos of middle-class life.

His enemy was vulgarity. All his life he fought against it, held it up to scorn, depicted it with a keen impartial pen, discovering the fungus of vulgarity even where, at first glance, everything seemed to be ordered for the best, the most convenient, and even brilliant. And vulgarity got back on him with an ugly trick when his dead body—the body of a poet—was sent to Moscow in an oyster wagon.

This dingy green wagon strikes me as the broad triumphant grin of vulgarity at its weary foe, and the innumerable "reminiscences" of the yellow press—mere hypocritical grief, behind which I seem to feel the cold, stinking breath of that very vulgarity which secretly rejoiced in the death of its enemy.

Reading the works of Chekhov makes one feel as if it were a sad day in late autumn, when the air is transparent, the bare trees stand out in bold relief against the sky, the houses are huddled together, and people are dim and dreary. Everything is so strange, so lonely, motionless, powerless. The remote distances are blue and void, merging with the pale sky, breathing a dreary cold on the half-frozen mud. But the mind of the author, like the autumn sunshine, lights up the well-trodden roads, the crooked streets, the dirty, cramped houses in which pitiful "little" people gasp out their lives in boredom and idleness, filling their dwellings with a meaningless, drowsy bustle. There goes "the darling," as nervous as a little grey mouse, a sweet, humble woman, who loves so indiscriminately and so slavishly. Strike her a blow on the cheek and she will not even dare, meek slave, to cry out. Beside her stands the melancholy Olga from *The Three Sisters;* she, too, is capable of loving and submits patiently to the whims of the depraved, vulgar wife of her fainéant brother; the lives of her sisters fall in ruins around her and she only cries, incapable of doing anything about it, while not a single living, strong word of protest against vulgarity is formed within her.

And there go the tearful Ranevskaya and the rest of the former owners of *The Cherry Orchard*—selfish as children, and flabby as old people. They, who should have been dead long ago, whine and snivel, blind to what is going on around them, comprehending nothing, parasites unable to fasten their suckers into life again. The worthless student Trofimov holds forth eloquently on the need for working, and fritters away his time, amusing himself by dull-witted taunts at Varya, who works unceasingly for the welfare of the idlers.

Vershinin [the hero of *The Three Sisters*] dreams of the good life to come in three hundred years, and in the meantime does not notice that everything around him is falling to pieces, that before his very eyes Solyony is ready, out of boredom and stupidity, to kill the pitiable Baron Tusenbach.

A long procession of slaves to love, to their own stupidity and laziness, to their greed for earthly blessings passes before the reader's eyes. Here are the slaves to the obscure fear of life, moving in vague anxiety and filling the air with inarticulate ravings about the future, feeling that there is no place for them in the present. . . .

Sometimes the report of a gun is heard from the grey mass—this is Ivanov or Treplev, who, having suddenly discovered the only thing to do, has given up the ghost.

Many of them indulge in beautiful dreams of the glorious life to come in two hundred years, and nobody thinks of asking the simple question: who is to make it glorious, if we do nothing but dream?

And now a great, wise man passes by this dull, dreary crowd of impotent creatures, casting an attentive glance on them all, these dreary inhabitants of his native land, and says, with his sad smile, in tones of gentle but profound reproach, with despairing grief on his face and in his heart, in a voice of exquisite sincerity:

"What a dull life you lead, gentlemen!"

I have never met anyone who felt the importance of work as the basis of culture so profoundly and diversely as A. P. This feeling showed itself in all the trifles of his home life, in the selection of things for the home, in that love for things in themselves, and, while quite untainted by the desire to collect, he never wearied of admiring them as the product of man's creative spirit. He loved building, planting gardens, adorning the earth, he felt the poetry of work. With what touching care he watched the growth of the fruit-trees and shrubs he had himself planted. In the midst of the innumerable cares connected with the building of his house at Autko, he said:

"If everyone in the world did all he was capable of on his own plot of land, what a beautiful world it would be!" . . .

He spoke little and reluctantly about his literary work. I had almost said with the same virginal reserve with which he spoke about Lev Tolstoi. Very occasionally, when in spirits, he would relate the plot of a story, chuckling—it was always a humorous story.

"I say, I'm going to write a story about a schoolmistress, an atheist—she adores Darwin, is convinced of the necessity for fighting the prejudices and superstitions of the people, and herself goes to the bath-house at midnight to scald a black cat to get a wishbone for attracting a man and arousing his love—there is such a bone, you know. . . ."

He always spoke of his plays as "amusing," and really seemed to be sincerely convinced that he wrote "amusing plays." No doubt Savva Morozov was repeating Chekhov's own words when he stubbornly maintained: "Chekhov's plays must be produced as lyrical comedies." . . .

His disease sometimes called into being a hypochondriac, or even a misanthropical, mood. At such times he would be extremely critical, and very hard to get on with.

One day, lying on the sofa, giving dry coughs, and playing with the thermometer, he said:

"To live simply to die is by no means amusing, but to live with the knowledge that you will die before your time, that really is idiotic. . . ."

Another time, seated at the open window and gazing out into the distance, at the sea, he suddenly said peevishly:

"We are accustomed to live in hopes of good weather, a good harvest, a nice love-affair, hopes of becoming rich or getting the office of chief of police, but I've never noticed anyone hoping to get wiser. We say to ourselves: it'll be better under a new tsar, and in two hundred years it'll be still better, and nobody tries to make this good time come tomorrow. On the whole, life gets more and more complex every day and moves on at its own sweet will, and people get more and more stupid, and get isolated from life in ever-increasing numbers."

After a pause he added, wrinkling up his forehead:

"Like crippled beggars in a religious procession."

He was a doctor, and the illness of a doctor is always worse than the illnesses of his patients. The patients only feel, but the doctor, as well as feeling, has a pretty good idea of the destructive effect of the disease on his constitution. This is a case in which knowledge brings death nearer. . . .

I once heard Tolstoi praise a story of Chekhov's—*The Darling*, I think it was.

"It's like lace woven by a virtuous maiden," he said. "There used to be girl lace-makers in the old days, who, their whole lives long, wove their dreams of happiness into the pattern. They wove their fondest dreams, their lace was saturated with vague, pure aspirations of love." Tolstoi spoke with true emotion, with tears in his eyes.

But that day Chekhov had a temperature, and sat with his head bent, vivid spots of colour on his cheeks, carefully wiping his pince-nez. He said nothing for some time, and at last, sighing, said softly and awkwardly: "There are misprints in it."

Much could be written of Chekhov, but this would require close, precise narration, and that is what I'm no good at. He should be written about as he himself wrote *The Steppe*, a fragrant, open-air, very Russian story, pensive and wistful. A story for one's self.

It does one good to remember a man like that, it is like a sudden visitation of cheerfulness, it gives a clear meaning to life again.

Man is the axis of the Universe.

And his vices, you ask, his shortcomings?

We all hunger for the love of our fellow creatures, and when one is hungry, even a half-baked loaf tastes sweet.

luigi pirandello 1867–1936

six characters in search of an author

translated by Edward Storer

A native Sicilian, Pirandello was the son of a wealthy mineowner. At the University of Rome and later at Bonn, he studied philology. After receiving a doctorate and publishing several volumes of verse, he entered the literary life of Rome. In 1894 he married a girl chosen by his father and for several years the couple lived on allowances from their parents. Pirandello continued to write short stories, but in 1904 the family fortunes were bankrupted and he had to begin teaching. His wife's mind began to fail, and for fourteen years Pirandello lived in agony with an insane woman. His writing now shifted from local color to psychological probings and to questions of old age, death, and insanity. His work revealed a morbidly obsessed intellect, a grim humor, and an attraction for the grotesque. A recurrent theme in Pirandello was that of illusion and reality, of the true self behind the social mask, explored in such plays as *Right You Are If You Think You Are* (1916), *Six Characters in Search of an Author* (1921), and *Henry IV* (1922). Pirandello's earlier liberalism was replaced by a cynical view of society's sham respectability. Although his outlook was essentially anarchistic, Pirandello willingly accepted the imposed order of Mussolini. He also attempted to establish a national theater. In 1934, two years before his death, Pirandello received the Nobel Prize.

the characters

SIX CHARACTERS

THE FATHER
THE MOTHER
THE STEPDAUGHTER
THE SON
MADAME PACE
THE BOY } *These two do not speak.*
THE CHILD }

ACTORS

THE MANAGER
LEADING LADY
LEADING MAN
SECOND LADY
L'INGÉNUE
JUVENILE LEAD

OTHER ACTORS *and* ACTRESSES, PROMPTER, MANAGER'S SECRETARY, PROPERTY MAN, MACHINIST, DOORKEEPER, SCENE SHIFTERS

(Daytime: the stage of a theater.)

act I

(N.B. The Comedy is without acts or scenes. The performance is interrupted once, without the curtain being lowered, when THE MANAGER *and the chief characters withdraw to arrange the scenario. A second interruption of the action takes place when, by mistake the stage hands let the curtain down.*

The spectators will find the curtain raised and the stage as it usually is during the daytime. It will be half dark, and empty, so that from the beginning the public may have the impression of an impromptu performance.

PROMPTER'S *box and a small table and chair for* THE MANAGER.

Two other small tables and several chairs scattered about as during rehearsals.

The ACTORS *and* ACTRESSES *of the company enter from the back of the stage:*

First one, then another, then two together: nine or ten in all. They are about to rehearse a Pirandello play: Mixing It Up. *Some of the company move off towards their dressing rooms. The* PROMPTER, *who has the "book" under his arm, is waiting for* THE MANAGER *in order to begin the rehearsal.*

The ACTORS *and* ACTRESSES, *some standing, some sitting, chat and smoke. One perhaps reads a paper; another cons his part.*

Finally, THE MANAGER *enters and goes to the table prepared for him. His* SECRETARY *brings him his mail, through which he glances. The* PROMPTER *takes his seat, turns on a light, and opens the "book.")*

THE MANAGER *(throwing a letter down on the table)* I can't see. *(to* PROPERTY MAN*)* Let's have a little light, please!

PROPERTY MAN Yes sir, yes, at once. *(A light comes down on to the stage.)*

THE MANAGER *(clapping his hands)* Come along! Come along! Second act of *Mixing it Up. (Sits down.)*

(The ACTORS *and* ACTRESSES *go from the front of the stage to the wings, all except the three who are to begin the rehearsal.)*

THE PROMPTER *(reading the "book")* "Leo Gala's house. A curious room serving as dining-room and study."

THE MANAGER *(to* PROPERTY MAN*)* Fix up the old red room.

PROPERTY MAN *(noting it down)* Red set. All right!

THE PROMPTER *(continuing to read from the "book")* "Table already laid and writing desk with books and papers. Bookshelves. Exit rear to Leo's bedroom. Exit left to kitchen. Principal exit to right."

THE MANAGER *(energetically)* Well, you understand: The principal exit over there; here, the kitchen. *(turning to* ACTOR *who is to play the part of Socrates)* You make your entrances and exits here. *(to* PROPERTY MAN*)* The baize doors at the rear, and curtains.

PROPERTY MAN *(noting it down)* Right-o!

PROMPTER *(reading as before)* "When the curtain rises, Leo Gala, dressed in cook's cap and apron is busy beating an egg in a cup. Philip, also dressed as a cook, is beating another egg. Guido Venanzi is seated and listening."

LEADING MAN *(to* MANAGER*)* Excuse me, but must I absolutely wear a cook's cap?

THE MANAGER *(annoyed)* I imagine so. It says so there anyway. *(pointing to the "book")*

LEADING MAN But it's ridiculous!

THE MANAGER Ridiculous? Ridiculous? Is it my fault if France won't send us any more good comedies, and we are reduced to putting on Pirandello's works where nobody understands anything, and where the author plays the fool with us all? *(The* ACTORS *grin.* THE MANAGER *goes to* LEADING MAN *and shouts.)* Yes sir, you put on the cook's cap and beat eggs. Do you suppose that with all this egg-beating business you are on an ordinary stage? Get that out of your head. You represent the shell of the eggs you are beating! *(laughter and comments among the* ACTORS*)* Silence! and listen to my explanations, please! *(to* LEADING MAN*):* "The empty form of reason without the fullness of instinct, which is blind"—You stand for reason, your wife is instinct. It's a mixing up of the parts, according to which you who act your own part become the puppet of yourself. Do you understand?

LEADING MAN I'm hanged if I do.

THE MANAGER Neither do I. But let's get on with it. It's sure to be a glorious failure anyway. *(confidentially):* But I say, please face three-quarters. Otherwise, what with the abstruseness of the dialogue, and the public that won't be able to hear you, the whole thing will go to hell. Come on! come on!

PROMPTER Pardon sir, may I get into my box? There's a bit of a draught.

THE MANAGER Yes, yes, of course!

(At this point, the DOORKEEPER *has entered from the stage door and advances towards* THE MANAGER'S *table, taking off his braided cap. During this manoeuver, the* SIX CHARACTERS *enter, and stop by the door at back of stage, so that when the* DOORKEEPER *is about to announce their coming to* THE MANAGER, *they are already on the stage. A tenuous light surrounds them, almost as if irradiated by them—the faint breath of their fantastic reality.*

This light will disappear when they come forward towards the ACTORS. *They preserve, however, something of the dream lightness in which they seem almost suspended; but this does not detract from the essential reality of their forms and expressions.)*

(He who is known as THE FATHER *is a man of about 50: hair, reddish in color, thin at the temples; he is not bald, however; thick moustaches, falling over his still fresh mouth, which often opens in an empty and uncertain smile. He is fattish, pale; with an especially wide fore-*

head. He has blue, oval-shaped eyes, very clear and piercing. Wears light trousers and a dark jacket. He is alternatively mellifluous and violent in his manner.)

(THE MOTHER *seems crushed and terrified as if by an intolerable weight of shame and abasement. She is dressed in modest black and wears a thick widow's veil of crêpe. When she lifts this, she reveals a wax-like face. She always keeps her eyes downcast.)*

(THE STEPDAUGHTER *is dashing, almost impudent, beautiful. She wears mourning too, but with great elegance. She shows contempt for the timid half-frightened manner of the wretched* BOY [*14 years old, and also dressed in black*]; *on the other hand, she displays a lively tenderness for her little sister,* THE CHILD [*about four*], *who is dressed in white, with a black silk sash at the waist.)*

(THE SON [22] *tall, severe in his attitude of contempt for* THE FATHER, *supercilious and indifferent to* THE MOTHER. *He looks as if he had come on the stage against his will.)*

DOORKEEPER *(cap in hand)* Excuse me, sir. . . .

THE MANAGER *(rudely)* Eh? What is it?

DOORKEEPER *(timidly)* These people are asking for you, sir.

THE MANAGER *(furious)* I am rehearsing, and you know perfectly well no one's allowed to come in during rehearsals! *(turning to the* CHARACTERS*)*: Who are you, please? What do you want?

THE FATHER *(coming forward a little, followed by the others, who seem embarrassed)* As a matter of fact . . . we have come here in search of an author. . . .

THE MANAGER *(half angry, half amazed)* An author? What author?

THE FATHER Any author, sir.

THE MANAGER But there's no author here. We are not rehearsing a new piece.

THE STEPDAUGHTER *(vivaciously)* So much the better, so much the better! We can be your new piece.

AN ACTOR *(coming forward from the others)* Oh, do you hear that?

THE FATHER *(to* STEPDAUGHTER*)* Yes, but if the author isn't here . . . *(to* MANAGER*)* . . . unless you would be willing. . . .

THE MANAGER You are trying to be funny.

THE FATHER No, for Heaven's sake, what are you saying? We bring you a drama, sir.

THE STEPDAUGHTER We may be your fortune.

THE MANAGER Will you oblige me by going away? We haven't time to waste with mad people.

THE FATHER *(mellifluously)* Oh sir, you know well that life is full of infinite absurdities, which, strangely enough, do not even need to appear plausible, since they are true.

THE MANAGER What the devil is he talking about?

THE FATHER I say that to reverse the ordinary process may well be considered a madness: that is, to create credible situations, in order that they may appear true. But permit me to observe that if this be madness, it is the sole *raison d'être* of your profession, gentlemen. *(The* ACTORS *look hurt and perplexed)*

THE MANAGER *(getting up and looking at him)* So our profession seems to you one worthy of madmen then?

THE FATHER Well, to make seem true that which isn't true . . . without any need . . . for a joke as it were . . . Isn't that your mission, gentlemen: to give life to fantastic characters on the stage?

THE MANAGER *(interpreting the rising anger of the* COMPANY*)* But I would beg you to believe, my dear sir, that the profession of the comedian is a noble one. If today, as things go, the playwrights give us stupid comedies to play and puppets to represent instead of men, remember we are proud to have given life to immortal works here on these very boards! *(The* ACTORS, *satisfied, applaud their* MANAGER.*)*

THE FATHER *(interrupting furiously)* Exactly, perfectly, to living beings more alive than those who breathe and wear clothes: being less real perhaps, but truer! I agree with you entirely. *(The* ACTORS *look at one another in amazement.)*

THE MANAGER But what do you mean? Before, you said . . .

THE FATHER No, excuse me, I meant it for you, sir, who were crying out that you had no time to lose with madmen, while no one better than yourself knows that nature uses the instrument of human fantasy in order to pursue her high creative purpose.

THE MANAGER Very well—but where does all this take us?

THE FATHER Nowhere! It is merely to show you that one is born to life in many forms, in many shapes, as tree, or as stone, as water, as butterfly, or as woman. So one may also be born a character in a play.

THE MANAGER *(with feigned comic dismay)* So you and these other friends of yours have been born characters?

THE FATHER Exactly, and alive as you see! (MANAGER *and* ACTORS *burst out laughing)*

THE FATHER *(hurt)* I am sorry you laugh, because we carry in us a drama, as you can guess from this woman here, veiled in black.

THE MANAGER *(losing patience at last and almost indignant)* Oh, chuck it! Get away please! Clear out of here! *(to* PROPERTY MAN*)* For Heaven's sake, turn them out!

THE FATHER *(resisting)* No, no, look here, we. . . .

THE MANAGER *(roaring)* We come here to work, you know.

LEADING ACTOR One cannot let oneself be made such a fool of.

THE FATHER *(determined, coming forward)* I marvel at your incredulity, gentlemen. Are you not accustomed to seeing the characters created by an author spring to life in yourselves and face each other? Just because there is no "book" *(pointing to the* PROMPTER'S *box)* which contains us, you refuse to believe. . . .

THE STEPDAUGHTER *(advances towards* MANAGER, *smiling and coquettish)* Believe me, we are really six most interesting characters, sir; side-tracked however.

THE FATHER Yes, that is the word! *(to* MANAGER *all at once)* In the sense, that is, that the author who created us alive no longer wished, or was no longer able, materially to put us into a work of art. And this was a real crime, sir; because he who has had the luck to be born a character can laugh even at death. He cannot die. The man, the writer, the instrument of the creation will die, but his creation does not die. And to live for ever, it does not need to have extraordinary gifts or to be able to work wonders. Who was Sancho Panza? Who was Don Abbondio? Yet they live eternally because—live germs as they were—they had the fortune to find a fecundating matrix, a fantasy which could raise and nourish them: make them live for ever!

THE MANAGER That is quite all right. But what do you want here, all of you?

THE FATHER We want to live.

THE MANAGER *(ironically)* For Eternity?

THE FATHER No, sir, only for a moment . . . in you.

AN ACTOR Just listen to him!

LEADING LADY They want to live, in us! . . .

JUVENILE LEAD *(pointing to the* STEPDAUGHTER*)* I've no objection, as far as that one is concerned!

THE FATHER Look here! Look here! The comedy has to be made. *(to the* MANAGER*)* But if you and your actors are willing, we can soon concert it among ourselves.

THE MANAGER *(annoyed)* But what do you want to concert? We don't go in for concerts here. Here we play dramas and comedies!

THE FATHER Exactly! That is just why we have come to you.

THE MANAGER And where is the "book"?

THE FATHER It is in us! *(The* ACTORS *laugh.)* The drama is in us, and we are the drama. We are impatient to play it. Our inner passion drives us on to this.

THE STEPDAUGHTER *(disdainful, alluring, treacherous, full of impudence)* My passion, sir! Ah, if you only knew! My passion for him! *(Points to the* FATHER *and makes a pretence of embracing him. Then she breaks out into a loud laugh.)*

THE FATHER *(angrily)* Behave yourself! And please don't laugh in that fashion.

THE STEPDAUGHTER With your permission, gentlemen, I, who am a two months' orphan, will show you how I can dance and sing.
(Sings and then dances Prenez garde à Tchou-Tchin-Tchou*)*

> Les chinois sont un peuple malin,
> De Shanghaî à Pékin,
> Ils ont mis des écriteaux partout:
> Prenez garde à Tchou-Tchin-Tchou.

ACTORS and ACTRESSES Bravo! Well done! Tip-top!

THE MANAGER Silence! This isn't a café concert, you know! *(turning to the* FATHER *in consternation)* Is she mad?

THE FATHER Mad? No, she's worse than mad.

THE STEPDAUGHTER *(to* MANAGER*)* Worse? Worse? Listen! Stage this drama for us at once! Then you will see that at a certain moment I . . .

when this little darling here . . . *(takes the* CHILD *by the hand and leads her to the* MANAGER*)* Isn't she a dear? *(takes her up and kisses her)* Darling! Darling! *(puts her down again and adds feelingly)* Well, when God suddenly takes this dear little child away from that poor mother there; and this imbecile here *(seizing hold of the* BOY *roughly and pushing him forward)* does the stupidest things, like the fool he is, you will see me run away. Yes, gentlemen, I shall be off. But the moment hasn't arrived yet. After what has taken place between him and me *(indicates the* FATHER *with a horrible wink)* I can't remain any longer in this society, to have to witness the anguish of this mother here for that fool . . . *(Indicates the* SON*)* Look at him! Look at him! See how indifferent, how frigid he is, because he is the legitimate son. He despises me, despises him *(pointing to the* BOY*)*, despises this baby here; because . . . we are bastards. *(goes to the* MOTHER *and embraces her)* And he doesn't want to recognize her as his mother—she who is the common mother of us all. He looks down upon her as if she were only the mother of us three bastards. Wretch! *(She says all this very rapidly, excitedly. At the word "bastards" she raises her voice, and almost spits out the final "Wretch!")*

THE MOTHER *(to the* MANAGER, *in anguish)* In the name of these two little children, I beg you . . . *(She grows faint and is about to fall.)* Oh God!

THE FATHER *(coming forward to support her as do some of the* ACTORS*)* Quick, a chair, a chair for this poor widow!

THE ACTORS Is it true? Has she really fainted?

THE MANAGER Quick, a chair! Here!

(One of the ACTORS *brings a chair, the others proffer assistance. The* MOTHER *tries to prevent the* FATHER *from lifting the veil which covers her face.)*

THE FATHER Look at her! Look at her!

THE MOTHER No, stop; stop it please!

THE FATHER *(raising her veil)* Let them see you!

THE MOTHER *(rising and covering her face with her hands, in desperation)* I beg you, sir, to prevent this man from carrying out his plan which is loathsome to me.

THE MANAGER *(dumbfounded)* I don't understand at all. What is the situation? Is this lady your wife? *(to the* FATHER*)*

THE FATHER Yes, gentlemen: my wife!

THE MANAGER But how can she be a widow if you are alive? *(The* ACTORS *find relief for their astonishment in a loud laugh.)*

THE FATHER Don't laugh! Don't laugh like that, for Heaven's sake. Her drama lies just here in this: she has had a lover, a man who ought to be here.

THE MOTHER *(with a cry)* No! No!

THE STEPDAUGHTER Fortunately for her, he is dead. Two months ago as I said. We are mourning, as you see.

THE FATHER He isn't here you see, not because he is dead. He isn't here—look at her a moment and you will understand—because her drama isn't a drama of the love of two men for whom she was incapable of feeling anything except possibly a little gratitude—gratitude not for me but for the other. She isn't a woman, she is a mother, and her drama—powerful, sir, I assure you—lies, as a matter of fact, all in these four children she has had by two men.

THE MOTHER I had them? Have you got the courage to say that I wanted them? *(to the* COMPANY*)* It was his doing. It was he who gave me that other man, who forced me to go away with him.

THE STEPDAUGHTER It isn't true.

THE MOTHER *(startled)* Not true, isn't it?

THE STEPDAUGHTER No, it isn't true, it just isn't true.

THE MOTHER And what can you know about it?

THE STEPDAUGHTER It isn't true. Don't believe it. *(to* MANAGER*)* Do you know why she says so? For that fellow there. *(indicates the* SON*)* She tortures herself, destroys herself on account of the neglect of that son there; and she wants him to believe that if she abandoned him when he was only two years old, it was because he *(indicates the* FATHER*)* made her do so.

THE MOTHER *(vigorously)* He forced me to it, and I call God to witness it. *(to the* MANAGER*)* Ask him *(indicates the* FATHER*)* if it isn't true. Let him speak. You *(to* DAUGHTER*)* are not in a position to know anything about it.

THE STEPDAUGHTER I know you lived in peace and happiness with my father while he lived. Can you deny it?

THE MOTHER No, I don't deny it . . .

THE STEPDAUGHTER He was always full of affection and kindness for you. *(to the* BOY, *angrily)* It's true, isn't it? Tell them! Why don't you speak, you little fool?

THE MOTHER Leave the poor boy alone. Why do you want to make me appear ungrateful, daughter? I don't want to offend your father. I have answered him that I didn't abandon my house and my son through any fault of mine, nor from any wilful passion.

THE FATHER It is true. It was my doing.

LEADING MAN *(to the* COMPANY*)* What a spectacle!

LEADING LADY We are the audience this time.

JUVENILE LEAD For once, in a way.

THE MANAGER *(beginning to get really interested)* Let's hear them out. Listen!

THE SON Oh yes, you're going to hear a fine bit now. He will talk to you of the Demon of Experiment.

THE FATHER You are a cynical imbecile. I've told you so already a hundred times. *(to the* MANAGER*)* He tries to make fun of me on account of this expression which I have found to excuse myself with.

THE SON *(with disgust)* Yes, phrases! phrases!

THE FATHER Phrases! Isn't everyone consoled when faced with a trouble or fact he doesn't understand, by a word, some simple word, which tells us nothing and yet calms us?

THE STEPDAUGHTER Even in the case of remorse. In fact, especially then.

THE FATHER Remorse? No, that isn't true. I've done more than use words to quieten the remorse in me.

THE STEPDAUGHTER Yes, there was a bit of money too. Yes, yes, a bit of money. There were the hundred lire he was about to offer me in payment, gentlemen. . . . *(sensation of horror among the* ACTORS*)*

THE SON *(to the* STEPDAUGHTER*)* This is vile.

THE STEPDAUGHTER Vile? There they were in a pale blue envelope on a little mahogany table in the back of Madame Pace's shop. You know Madam Pace—one of those ladies who attract poor girls of good family into their ateliers, under the pretext of their selling *robes et manteaux*.

THE SON And he thinks he has bought the right to tyrannize over us all with those hundred lire he was going to pay; but which, fortunately—note this, gentlemen—he had no chance of paying.

THE STEPDAUGHTER It was a near thing, though, you know! *(laughs ironically)*

THE MOTHER *(protesting)* Shame, my daughter, shame!

THE STEPDAUGHTER Shame indeed! This is my revenge! I am dying to live that scene. . . . The room . . . I see it . . . Here is the window with the mantels exposed, there the divan, the lookingglass, a screen, there in front of the window the little mahogany table with the blue envelope containing one hundred lire. I see it. I see it. I could take hold of it. . . . But you, gentlemen, you ought to turn your backs now: I am almost nude, you know. But I don't blush: I leave that to him. *(indicating* FATHER*)*

THE MANAGER I don't understand this at all.

THE FATHER Naturally enough. I would ask you, sir, to exercise your authority a little here, and let me speak before you believe all she is trying to blame me with. Let me explain.

THE STEPDAUGHTER Ah yes, explain it in your own way.

THE FATHER But don't you see that the whole trouble lies here. In words, words. Each one of us has within him a whole world of things, each man of us his own special world. And how can we ever come to an understanding if I put in the words I utter the sense and value of things as I see them; while you who listen to me must inevitably translate them according to the conception of things each one of you has within himself. We think we understand each other, but we never really do. Look here! This woman *(indicating the* MOTHER*)* takes all my pity for her as a specially ferocious form of cruelty.

THE MOTHER But you drove me away.

THE FATHER Do you hear her? I drove her away! She believes I really sent her away.

THE MOTHER You know how to talk, and I don't; but, believe me sir *(to* MANAGER*)*, after he had married me . . . who knows why? . . . I was a poor insignificant woman. . . .

THE FATHER But, good Heaven! it was just for your humility that I married you. I loved this simplicity in you. *(He stops when he sees she makes signs to contradict him, opens his arms wide in sign of desperation, seeing how hopeless it is to make himself understood.)* You see she denies it. Her mental deafness, believe me, is phenomenal, the limit *(touches his forehead):* deaf, deaf, mentally deaf! She had plenty of feeling. Oh yes, a good heart for the children; but the brain—deaf, to the point of desperation—!

THE STEPDAUGHTER Yes, but ask him how his intelligence has helped us.

THE FATHER If we could see all the evil that may spring from good, what should we do? *(At this point the* LEADING LADY *who is biting her lips with rage at seeing the* LEADING MAN *flirting with the* STEPDAUGHTER, *comes forward and says to the* MANAGER:*)*

LEADING LADY Excuse me, but are we going to rehearse today?

MANAGER Of course, of course; but let's hear them out.

JUVENILE LEAD This is something quite new.

L'INGÉNUE Most interesting!

LEADING LADY Yes, for the people who like that kind of thing. *(casts a glance at* LEADING MAN*)*

THE MANAGER *(to* FATHER*)* You must please explain yourself quite clearly. *(Sits down)*

THE FATHER Very well then: listen! I had in my service a poor man, a clerk, a secretary of mine, full of devotion, who became friends with her. *(Indicating the* MOTHER*)* They understood one another, were kindred souls in fact, without, however, the least suspicion of any evil existing. They were incapable even of thinking of it.

THE STEPDAUGHTER So he thought of it—for them!

THE FATHER That's not true. I meant to do good to them—and to myself, I confess, at the same time. Things had come to the point that I could not say a word to either of them without their making a mute appeal, one to the other, with their eyes. I could see them silently asking each other how I was to be kept in countenance, how I was to be kept quiet. And this, believe me, was just about enough of itself to keep me in a constant rage, to exasperate me beyond measure.

THE MANAGER And why didn't you send him away then—this secretary of yours?

THE FATHER Precisely what I did, sir. And then I had to watch this poor woman drifting forlornly about the house like an animal without a master, like an animal one has taken in out of pity.

THE MOTHER Ah yes! . . .

THE FATHER *(suddenly turning to the* MOTHER*)* It's true about the son anyway, isn't it?

THE MOTHER He took my son away from me first of all.

THE FATHER But not from cruelty. I did it so that he should grow up healthy and strong by living in the country.

THE STEPDAUGHTER *(pointing to him ironically)* As one can see.

THE FATHER *(quickly)* Is it my fault if he has grown up like this? I sent him to a wet nurse in the country, a peasant, as *she* did not seem to me strong enough, though she is of humble origin. That was, anyway, the reason I married her. Unpleasant all this may be, but how can it be helped? My mistake possibly, but there we are! All my life I have had these confounded aspirations towards a certain moral sanity. *(At this point the* STEPDAUGHTER *bursts out into a noisy laugh.)* Oh, stop it! Stop it! I can't stand it.

THE MANAGER Yes, please stop it, for Heaven's sake.

THE STEPDAUGHTER But imagine moral sanity from him, if you please —the client of certain ateliers like that of Madame Pace!

THE FATHER Fool! That is the proof that I am a man! This seeming contradiction, gentlemen, is the strongest proof that I stand here a live man before you. Why, it is just for this very incongruity in my nature that I have had to suffer what I have. I could not live by the side of that woman *(indicating the* MOTHER*)* any longer; but not so much for the boredom she inspired me with as for the pity I felt for her.

THE MOTHER And so he turned me out—.

THE FATHER —well provided for! Yes, I sent her to that man, gentlemen . . . to let her go free of me.

THE MOTHER And to free himself.

THE FATHER Yes, I admit it. It was also a liberation for me. But great evil has come of it. I meant well when I did it; and I did it more for her sake than mine. I swear it. *(Crosses his arms on his chest; then turns suddenly to the* MOTHER*)* Did I ever lose sight of you until that other man carried you off to another town, like the angry fool he was? And on account of my pure interest in you . . . my pure interest, I repeat, that had no base motive in it . . . I watched with the tenderest concern the new family that grew up around her. She can bear witness to this. *(points to the* STEPDAUGHTER*)*

THE STEPDAUGHTER Oh yes, that's true enough. When I was a kiddie, so so high, you know, with plaits over my shoulders and knickers longer than my skirts, I used to see him waiting outside the school for me to come out. He came to see how I was growing up.

THE FATHER This is infamous, shameful!

THE STEPDAUGHTER No. Why?

THE FATHER Infamous! Infamous! *(then excitedly to* MANAGER, *explaining)* After she *(indicating* MOTHER*)* went away, my house seemed suddenly empty. She was my incubus, but she filled my house. I was like a dazed fly alone in the empty rooms. This boy here *(indicating the* SON*)* was educated away from home, and when he came back, he seemed to me to be no more mine. With no mother to stand between him and me, he grew up entirely for himself, on his own, apart, with no tie of intellect or affection binding him to me. And then—strange but true—I was driven, by curiosity at first and then by some tender sentiment, towards her family, which had come into being through my will. The thought of her began gradually to fill up the emptiness I felt all around me. I wanted to know if she were happy in living out the simple daily duties of life. I wanted to think of her as fortunate and happy because far away from the complicated torments of my spirit. And so, to have proof of this, I used to watch that child coming out of school.

THE STEPDAUGHTER Yes, yes. True. He used to follow me in the street and smiled at me, waved his hand, like this. I would look at him with interest, wondering who he might be. I told my mother, who guessed at once. *(The* MOTHER *agrees with a nod.)* Then she didn't want to send me to school for some days; and when I finally went back, there he was again—looking so ridiculous—with a paper parcel in his hands. He came close to me, caressed me, and drew out a fine straw hat from the parcel, with a bouquet of flowers—all for me!

THE MANAGER A bit discursive this, you know!

THE SON *(contemptuously)* Literature! Literature!

THE FATHER Literature indeed! This is life, this is passion!

THE MANAGER It may be, but it won't act.

THE FATHER I agree. This is only the part leading up. I don't suggest this should be staged. She *(pointing to the* STEPDAUGHTER*)*, as you see, is no longer the flapper with plaits down her back—.

THE STEPDAUGHTER —and the knickers showing below the skirt!

THE FATHER The drama is coming now, sir; something new, complex, most interesting.

THE STEPDAUGHTER As soon as my father died. . . .

THE FATHER —there was absolute misery for them. They came back here, unknown to me. Through her stupidity! *(pointing to the* MOTHER*)* It is true she can barely write her own name; but she could anyhow have got her daughter to write to me that they were in need. . . .

THE MOTHER And how was I to divine all this sentiment in him?

THE FATHER That is exactly your mistake, never to have guessed any of my sentiments.

THE MOTHER After so many years apart, and all that had happened. . . .

THE FATHER Was it my fault if that fellow carried you away? It happened quite suddenly; for after he had obtained some job or other, I could find no trace of them; and so, not unnaturally, my interest in them dwindled. But the drama culminated unforeseen and violent on their return, when I was impelled by my miserable flesh that still lives. . . . Ah! what misery, what wretchedness is that of the man who is alone and disdains debasing *liaisons!* Not old enough to do without women, and not young enough to go and look for one without shame. Misery? It's worse than misery; it's a horror; for no woman can any longer give him love; and when a man feels this. . . . One ought to do without, you say? Yes, yes, I know. Each of us when he appears before his fellows is clothed in a certain dignity. But every man knows what unconfessable things pass within the secrecy of his own heart. One gives way to the temptation, only to rise from it again, afterwards, with a great eagerness to reestablish one's dignity, as if it were a tombstone to place on the grave of one's shame, and a monument to hide and sign the memory of our weaknesses. Everybody's in the same case. Some folks haven't the courage to say certain things, that's all!

THE STEPDAUGHTER All appear to have the courage to do them though.

THE FATHER Yes, but in secret. Therefore, you want more courage to say these things. Let a man but speak these things out, and folks at once label him a cynic. But it isn't true. He is like all the others, better indeed, because he isn't afraid to reveal with the light of the intelligence the red shame of human bestiality on which most men close their eyes so as not to see it. Woman—for example, look at her case! She turns tantalizing inviting glances on you. You seize her. No sooner does she feel herself in your grasp than she closes her eyes. It is the sign of her mission, the sign by which she says to man: "Blind yourself, for I am blind."

THE STEPDAUGHTER Sometimes she can close them no more: when she no longer feels the need of hiding her shame to herself, but dry-eyed and dispassionately, sees only that of the man who has blinded himself without love. Oh, all these intellectual complications make me sick, disgust me—all this philosophy that uncovers the beast in man, and then seeks to save him, excuse him . . . I can't stand it, sir. When a man seeks to "simplify" life bestially, throwing aside every relic of humanity, every chaste aspiration, every pure feeling, all sense of ideality, duty, modesty, shame . . . then nothing is more revolting and nauseous than a certain kind of remorse—crocodiles' tears, that's what it is.

THE MANAGER Let's come to the point. This is only discussion.

THE FATHER Very good, sir! But a fact is like a sack which won't stand up when it is empty. In order that it may stand up, one has to put into it the reason and sentiment which have caused it to exist. I couldn't possibly know that after the death of that man, they had decided to return here, that they were in misery, and that she *(pointing to the* MOTHER*)* had gone to work as a modiste, and at a shop of the type of that of Madame Pace.

THE STEPDAUGHTER A real high-class modiste, you must know, gentlemen. In appearance, she works for the leaders of the best society; but she arranges matters so that these elegant ladies serve her purpose . . . without prejudice to other ladies who are . . . well . . . only so so.

THE MOTHER You will believe me, gentlemen, that it never entered my mind that the old hag offered me work because she had her eye on my daughter.

THE STEPDAUGHTER Poor mamma! Do you know, sir, what that woman did when I brought her back the work my mother had finished? She would point out to me that I had torn one of my frocks, and she would give it back to my mother to mend. It was I who paid for it, always I; while this poor creature here believed she was sacrificing herself for me and these two children here, sitting up at night sewing Madame Pace's robes.

THE MANAGER And one day you met there. . . .

THE STEPDAUGHTER Him, him. Yes, sir, an old client. There's a scene for you to play! Superb!

THE FATHER She, the Mother arrived just then. . . .

THE STEPDAUGHTER *(treacherously)* Almost in time!

THE FATHER *(crying out)* No, in time! in time! Fortunately I recognized her . . . in time. And I took them back home with me to my house. You can imagine now her position and mine: she, as you see her; and I who cannot look her in the face.

THE STEPDAUGHTER Absurd! How can I possibly be expected—after that—to be a modest young miss, a fit person to go with his confounded aspirations for "a solid moral sanity"?

THE FATHER For the drama lies all in this—in the conscience that I have, that each one of us has. We believe this conscience to be a single thing, but it is many-sided. There is one for this person, and another for that. Diverse consciences. So we have this illusion of being one person for all, of having a personality that is unique in all our acts. But it isn't true. We perceive this when, tragically perhaps, in something we do, we are, as it were, suspended, caught up in the air on a kind of hook. Then we perceive that all of us was not in that act, and that it would be an atrocious injustice to judge us by that action alone, as if all our existence were summed up in that one deed. Now do you understand the perfidy of this girl? She surprised me in a place where she ought not to have known me, just as I could not exist for her; and she now seeks to attach to me a reality such as I could never suppose I should have to assume for her in a shameful and fleeting moment of my life. I feel this above all else. And the drama, you will see, acquires a tremendous value from this point. Then there is the position of the others . . . his . . . *(indicating the* SON*)*

THE SON *(shrugging his shoulders scornfully)* Leave me alone! I don't come into this.

THE FATHER What? You don't come into this?

THE SON I've got nothing to do with it, and don't want to have; because you know well enough I wasn't made to be mixed up in all this with the rest of you.

THE STEPDAUGHTER We are only vulgar folk! He is the fine gentleman. You may have noticed, Mr. Manager, that I fix him now and again with a look of scorn while he lowers his eyes—for he knows the evil he has done me.

THE SON *(scarcely looking at her)* I?

THE STEPDAUGHTER You! you! I owe my life on the streets to you. Did you or did you not deny us, with your behavior, I won't say the intimacy of home, but even that mere hospitality which makes guests feel at their ease? We were intruders who had come to disturb the kingdom of your legitimacy. I should like to have you witness, Mr. Manager, certain scenes between him and me. He says I have tyrannized over everyone. But it was just his behavior which made me insist on the reason for which I had come into the house—this reason he calls "vile"—into his house, with my mother, who is his mother too. And I came as mistress of the house.

THE SON It's easy for them to put me always in the wrong. But imagine, gentlemen, the position of a son, whose fate it is to see arrive one day at his home a young woman of impudent bearing, a young woman who inquires for his father, with whom who knows what business she has. This young man has then to witness her return bolder than ever, accompanied by that child there. He is obliged to watch her treat his father in an equivocal and confidential manner. She asks money of him in a way that lets one suppose he must give it her, *must*, do you understand, because he has every obligation to do so.

THE FATHER But I have, as a matter of fact, this obligation. I owe it to your mother.

THE SON How should I know? When had I ever seen or heard of her? One day there arrive with her *(indicating* STEPDAUGHTER*)* that lad and this baby here. I am told: "This is *your* mother too, you know." I divine from her manner *(indicating* STEPDAUGHTER *again)* why it is they have come home. I had rather not say what I feel and think about it. I shouldn't even care to confess to myself. No action can therefore be hoped for from me in this affair. Believe me, Mr. Manager, I am an "unrealized" character, dramatically speaking; and I find myself not at all at ease in your company. Leave me out of it, I beg you.

THE FATHER What? It is just because you are so that . . .

THE SON How do you know what I am like? When did you ever bother your head about me?

THE FATHER I admit it. I admit it. But isn't that a situation in itself? This aloofness of yours which is so cruel to me and to your mother, who returns home and sees you almost for the first time grown up, who doesn't recognize you but knows you are her son . . . *(pointing out the* MOTHER *to the* MANAGER*)* See, she's crying!

THE STEPDAUGHTER *(angrily, stamping her foot)* Like a fool!

THE FATHER *(indicating* STEPDAUGHTER*)* She can't stand him, you know. *(then referring again to the* SON*):* He says he doesn't come into the affair, whereas he is really the hinge of the whole action. Look at that lad who is always clinging to his mother, frightened and humiliated. It is on account of this fellow here. Possibly his situation is the most painful of all. He feels himself a stranger more than the others. The poor little chap feels mortified, humiliated at being brought into a home out of charity as it were. *(in confidence)—:* He is the image of his father. Hardly talks at all. Humble and quiet.

THE MANAGER Oh, we'll cut him out. You've no notion what a nuisance boys are on the stage . . .

THE FATHER He disappears soon, you know. And the baby too. She is the first to vanish from the scene. The drama consists finally in this: when that mother re-enters my house, her family born outside of it, and shall we say superimposed on the original, ends with the death of the little girl, the tragedy of the boy and the flight of the elder daughter. It cannot go on, because it is foreign to its surroundings. So after much torment, we three remain: I, the mother, that son. Then, owing to the disappearance of that extraneous family, we too find ourselves strange to one another. We find we are living in an atmosphere of mortal desolation which is the revenge, as he *(indicating* SON*)* scornfully said of the Demon of Experiment, that unfortunately hides in me. Thus, sir, you see when faith is lacking, it becomes impossible to create certain states of happiness, for we lack the necessary humility. Vaingloriously, we try to substitute ourselves for this faith, creating thus for the rest of the world a reality which we believe after their fashion, while, actually, it doesn't exist. For each one of us has his own reality to be respected before God, even when it is harmful to one's very self.

THE MANAGER There is something in what you say. I assure you all this interests me very much. I begin to think there's the stuff for a drama in all this, and not a bad drama either.

THE STEPDAUGHTER *(coming forward)* When you've got a character like me.

THE FATHER *(shutting her up, all excited to learn the decision of the* MANAGER*)* You be quiet!

THE MANAGER *(reflecting, heedless of interruption)* It's new . . . hem . . . yes . . .

THE FATHER Absolutely new!

THE MANAGER You've got a nerve though, I must say, to come here and fling it at me like this . . .

THE FATHER You will understand, sir, born as we are for the stage . . .

THE MANAGER Are you amateur actors then?

THE FATHER No, I say born for the stage, because . . .

THE MANAGER Oh, nonsense. You're an old hand, you know.

THE FATHER No sir, no. We act that rôle for which we have been cast, that rôle which we are given in life. And in my own case, passion itself, as usually happens, becomes a trifle theatrical when it is exalted.

THE MANAGER Well, well, that will do. But you see, without an author . . . I could give you the address of an author if you like . . .

THE FATHER No, no. Look here! You must be the author.

THE MANAGER I? What are you talking about?

THE FATHER Yes, you, you! Why not?

THE MANAGER Because I have never been an author: that's why.

THE FATHER Then why not turn author now? Everybody does it. You don't want any special qualities. Your task is made much easier by the fact that we are all here alive before you . . .

THE MANAGER It won't do.

THE FATHER What? When you see us live our drama . . .

THE MANAGER Yes, that's all right. But you want someone to write it.

THE FATHER No, no. Someone to take it down, possibly, while we play it, scene by scene! It will be enough to sketch it out at first, and then try it over.

THE MANAGER Well . . . I am almost tempted. It's a bit of an idea. One might have a shot at it.

THE FATHER Of course. You'll see what scenes will come out of it. I can give you one, at once . . .

THE MANAGER By Jove, it tempts me. I'd like to have a go at it. Let's try it out. Come with me to my office. *(turning to the* ACTORS*)* You are at liberty for a bit, but don't stop out of the theater for long. In a quarter of an hour, twenty minutes, all back here again! *(to the* FATHER*)* We'll see what can be done. Who knows if we don't get something really extraordinary out of it?

THE FATHER There's no doubt about it. They *(indicating the* CHARACTERS*)* had better come with us too, hadn't they?

THE MANAGER Yes, yes. Come on! come on! *(moves away and then turning to the* ACTORS*)* Be punctual, please! *(*MANAGER *and the* SIX CHARACTERS *cross the stage and go off. The other* ACTORS *remain, looking* *at one another in astonishment.)*

LEADING MAN Is he serious? What the devil does he want to do?

JUVENILE LEAD This is rank madness.

THIRD ACTOR Does he expect to knock up a drama in five minutes?

JUVENILE LEAD Like the improvisers!

LEADING LADY If he thinks I'm going to take part in a joke like this . . .

JUVENILE LEAD I'm out of it anyway.

FOURTH ACTOR I should like to know who they are. *(alludes to* CHARACTERS*)*

THIRD ACTOR What do you suppose? Madmen or rascals!

JUVENILE LEAD And he takes them seriously!

L'INGÉNUE Vanity! He fancies himself as an author now.

LEADING MAN It's absolutely unheard of. If the stage has come to this . . . well I'm . . .

FIFTH ACTOR It's rather a joke.

THIRD ACTOR Well, we'll see what's going to happen next.

(Thus talking, the ACTORS *leave the stage; some going out by the little door at the back; others retiring to their dressing-rooms.*

The curtain remains up.

The action of the play is suspended for twenty minutes)

act II

(The stage call-bells ring to warn the company that the play is about to begin again.)

THE STEPDAUGHTER *(comes out of the* MANAGER'S *office along with the* CHILD *and the* BOY. *As she comes out of the office, she cries:)* Nonsense! Nonsense! Do it yourselves! I'm not going to mix myself up in this mess. *(turning to the* CHILD *and coming quickly with her on to the stage)* Come on, Rosetta, let's run!

*(*THE BOY *follows them slowly, remaining a little behind and seeming perplexed)*

THE STEPDAUGHTER *(stops, bends over the* CHILD *and takes the latter's face between her hands)* My little darling! You're frightened, aren't you? You don't know where we are, do you? *(pretending to reply to a question of the* CHILD*)* What is the stage? It's a place, baby, you know, where people play at being serious, a place where they act comedies. We've got to act a comedy now, dead serious, you know; and you're in it also, little one. *(embraces her, pressing the little head to her breast, and rocking the* CHILD *for a moment)* Oh darling, darling, what a horrid comedy you've got to play! What a wretched part they've found for you! A garden . . . a fountain . . . look . . . just suppose, kiddie, it's here. Where, you say? Why, right here in the middle. It's all pretence you know. That's the trouble, my pet: it's all make-believe here. It's better to imagine it though, because if they fix it up for you, it'll only be painted cardboard, painted cardboard for the rockery, the water, the plants . . . Ah, but I think a baby like this one would sooner have a make-believe fountain than a real one, so she could play with it. What a joke it'll be for the others! But for you, alas! not quite such a joke: you who are real, baby dear, and really play by a real fountain that is big and green and beautiful, with ever so many bamboos around it that are reflected in the water, and a whole lot of little ducks swimming about . . . No, Rosetta, no, your mother doesn't bother about you on account of that wretch of a son there. I'm in the devil of a temper, and as for that lad . . . *(seizes* BOY *by the arm to force him to take one of his hands out of his pockets)* What have you got there? What are you hiding? *(pulls his hand out of his pocket, looks into it and catches the glint of a revolver)* Ah, where did you get this?

(THE BOY, *very pale in the face, looks at her, but does not answer.)*

Idiot! If I'd been in your place, instead of killing myself, I'd have shot one of those two, or both of them: father and son.

(THE FATHER *enters from the office, all excited from his work.* THE MANAGER *follows him.)*

THE FATHER Come on, come on, dear! Come here for a minute! We've arranged everything. It's all fixed up.

THE MANAGER *(also excited)* If you please, young lady, there are one or two points to settle still. Will you come along?

THE STEPDAUGHTER *(following him towards the office)* Ouff! what's the good, if you've arranged everything.

(THE FATHER, MANAGER *and* STEPDAUGHTER *go back into the office again* [*off*] *for a moment. At the same time,* THE SON, *followed by* THE MOTHER, *comes out.)*

THE SON *(looking at the three entering office)* Oh this is fine, fine! And to think I can't even get away!

(THE MOTHER *attempts to look at him, but lowers her eyes immediately when he turns away from her. She then sits down.* THE BOY *and* THE CHILD *approach her. She casts a glance again at the* SON, *and speaks with humble tones, trying to draw him into conversation.)*

THE MOTHER And isn't my punishment the worst of all? *(Then seeing from the* SON'S *manner that he will not bother himself about her)* My God! Why are you so cruel? Isn't it enough for one person to support all this torment? Must you then insist on others seeing it also?

THE SON *(half to himself, meaning the* MOTHER *to hear, however)* And they want to put it on the stage! If there was at least a reason for it! He thinks he has got at the meaning of it all. Just as if each one of us in every circumstance of life couldn't find his own explanation of it! *(pauses)* He complains he was discovered in a place where he ought not to have been seen, in a moment of his life which ought to have remained hidden and kept out of the reach of that convention which he has to maintain for other people. And what about my case? Haven't I had to reveal what no son ought ever to reveal: how father and mother live and are man and wife for themselves quite apart from that idea of father and mother which we give them? When this idea is revealed, our life is then linked at one point only to that man and that woman; and as such it should shame them, shouldn't it?

(THE MOTHER *hides her face in her hands. From the dressing-rooms and the little door at the back of the stage the* ACTORS *and* STAGE MANAGER *return, followed by the* PROPERTY MAN, *and the* PROMPTER. *At the same moment,* THE MANAGER *comes out of his office, accompanied by the* FATHER *and the* STEPDAUGHTER.)

THE MANAGER Come on, come on, ladies and gentlemen! Heh! you there, machinist!

MACHINIST Yes, sir?

THE MANAGER Fix up the white parlor with the floral decorations. Two wings and a drop with a door will do. Hurry up!

(THE MACHINIST *runs off at once to prepare the scene, and arranges it while* THE MANAGER *talks with the* STAGE MANAGER, *the* PROPERTY MAN, *and the* PROMPTER *on matters of detail*).

THE MANAGER *(to* PROPERTY MAN*)* Just have a look, and see if there isn't a sofa or divan in the wardrobe . . .

PROPERTY MAN There's the green one.

THE STEPDAUGHTER No, no! Green won't do. It was yellow, ornamented with flowers—very large! and most comfortable!

PROPERTY MAN There isn't one like that.

THE MANAGER It doesn't matter. Use the one we've got.

THE STEPDAUGHTER Doesn't matter? It's most important!

THE MANAGER We're only trying it now. Please don't interfere. *(to* PROPERTY MAN*)* See if we've got a shop window—long and narrowish.

THE STEPDAUGHTER And the little table! The little mahogany table for the pale blue envelope!

PROPERTY MAN *(to* MANAGER*)* There's that little gilt one.

THE MANAGER That'll do fine.

THE FATHER A mirror.

THE STEPDAUGHTER And the screen! We must have a screen. Otherwise how can I manage?

PROPERTY MAN That's all right, Miss. We've got any amount of them.

THE MANAGER *(to the* STEPDAUGHTER*)* We want some clothes pegs too, don't we?

THE STEPDAUGHTER Yes, several, several!

THE MANAGER See how many we've got and bring them all.

PROPERTY MAN All right!

(The PROPERTY MAN *hurries off to obey his orders. While he is putting the things in their places, the* MANAGER *talks to the* PROMPTER *and then with the* CHARACTERS *and the* ACTORS.*)*

THE MANAGER *(to* PROMPTER*)* Take your seat. Look here: this is the outline of the scenes, act by act. *(hands him some sheets of paper)* And now I'm going to ask you to do something out of the ordinary.

PROMPTER Take it down in shorthand?

THE MANAGER *(pleasantly surprised)* Exactly! Can you do shorthand?

PROMPTER Yes, a little.

MANAGER Good! *(turning to a stage hand)* Go and get some paper from my office, plenty, as much as you can find.

(The STAGE HAND *goes off, and soon returns with a handful of paper*

which he gives to the PROMPTER.*)*

THE MANAGER *(to* PROMPTER*)* You follow the scenes as we play them, and try and get the points down, at any rate the most important ones. *(then addressing the* ACTORS*)* Clear the stage, ladies and gentlemen! Come over here *(pointing to the Left)* and listen attentively.

LEADING LADY But, excuse me, we . . .

THE MANAGER *(guessing her thought)* Don't worry! You won't have to improvise.

LEADING MAN What have we to do then?

THE MANAGER Nothing. For the moment you just watch and listen. Everybody will get his part written out afterwards. At present we're going to try the thing as best we can. They're going to act now.

THE FATHER *(as if fallen from the clouds into the confusion of the stage)* We? What do you mean, if you please, by a rehearsal?

THE MANAGER A rehearsal for them. *(points to the* ACTORS*)*

THE FATHER But since we are the characters . . .

THE MANAGER All right: "characters" then, if you insist on calling yourselves such. But here, my dear sir, the characters don't act. Here the actors do the acting. The characters are there, in the "book"—*(pointing towards* PROMPTER'S *box)* when there is a "book"!

THE FATHER I won't contradict you; but excuse me, the actors aren't the characters. They want to be, they pretend to be, don't they? Now if these gentlemen here are fortunate enough to have us alive before them . . .

THE MANAGER Oh this is grand! You want to come before the public yourselves then?

THE FATHER As we are . . .

THE MANAGER I can assure you it would be a magnificent spectacle!

LEADING MAN What's the use of us here anyway then?

THE MANAGER You're not going to pretend that you can act? It makes me laugh! *(The* ACTORS *laugh.)* There, you see, they are laughing at the notion. But, by the way, I must cast the parts. That won't be difficult. They cast themselves. *(To the* SECOND LADY LEAD*)* You play the Mother. *(To the* FATHER*)* We must find her a name.

THE FATHER Amalia, sir.

THE MANAGER But that is the real name of your wife. We don't want to call her by her real name.

THE FATHER Why ever not, if it is her name? . . . Still, perhaps, if that lady must . . . *(makes a slight motion of the hand to indicate the* SECOND LADY LEAD*)* I see this woman here *(means the* MOTHER*)* as Amalia. But do as you like. *(gets more and more confused)* I don't know what to say to you. Already, I begin to hear my own words ring false, as if they had another sound . . .

THE MANAGER Don't you worry about it. It'll be our job to find the right tones. And as for her name, if you want her Amalia, Amalia it shall be; and if you don't like it, we'll find another! For the moment though, we'll call the characters in this way: *(to* JUVENILE LEAD*)* You are the Son; *(to the* LEADING LADY*)* You naturally are the Stepdaughter . . .

THE STEPDAUGHTER *(excitedly)* What? what? I, that woman there? *(bursts out laughing)*

THE MANAGER *(angry)* What is there to laugh at?

LEADING LADY *(indignant)* Nobody has ever dared to laugh at me. I insist on being treated with respect; otherwise I go away.

THE STEPDAUGHTER No, no, excuse me . . . I am not laughing at you . . .

THE MANAGER *(to* STEPDAUGHTER*)* You ought to feel honored to be played by . . .

LEADING LADY *(at once, contemptuously)* "That woman there" . . .

THE STEPDAUGHTER But I wasn't speaking of you, you know. I was speaking of myself—whom I can't see at all in you! That is all. I don't know . . . but . . . you . . . aren't in the least like me . . .

THE FATHER True. Here's the point. Look here, sir, our temperaments, our souls . . .

THE MANAGER Temperament, soul, be hanged. Do you suppose the spirit of the piece is in you? Nothing of the kind!

THE FATHER What, haven't we our own temperaments, our own souls?

THE MANAGER Not at all. Your soul or whatever you like to call it takes shape here. The actors give body and form to it, voice and gesture. And my actors—I may tell you—have given expression to much more lofty material than this little drama of yours, which may or may not hold up on the stage. But if it does, the merit of it, believe me, will be due to my actors.

THE FATHER I don't dare contradict you, sir; but, believe me, it is a terrible suffering for us who are as we are, with these bodies of ours, these features to see . . .

THE MANAGER *(cutting him short and out of patience)* Good heavens! The make-up will remedy all that, man, the make-up . . .

THE FATHER Maybe. But the voice, the gestures . . .

THE MANAGER Now, look here! On the stage, you as yourself, cannot exist. The actor here acts you, and that's an end to it!

THE FATHER I understand. And now I think I see why our author who conceived us as we are, all alive, didn't want to put us on the stage after all. I haven't the least desire to offend your actors. Far from it! But when I think that I am to be acted by . . . I don't know by whom . . .

LEADING MAN *(on his dignity)* By me, if you've no objection!

THE FATHER *(humbly, mellifluously)* Honored, I assure you, sir. *(bows)* Still, I must say that try as this gentleman may, with all his good will and wonderful art, to absorb me into himself . . .

LEADING MAN Oh chuck it! "Wonderful art!" Withdraw that, please!

THE FATHER The performance he will give, even doing his best with make-up to look like me . . .

LEADING MAN It will certainly be a bit difficult! *(The* ACTORS *laugh.)*

THE FATHER Exactly! It will be difficult to act me as I really am. The effect will be rather—apart from the make-up—according as to how he supposes I am, as he senses me—if he does sense me—and not as I inside of myself feel myself to be. It seems to me then that account should be taken of this by everyone whose duty it may become to criticize us . . .

THE MANAGER Heavens! The man's starting to think about the critics now! Let them say what they like. It's up to us to put on the play if we can. *(looking around)* Come on! come on! Is the stage set? *(to the* ACTORS *and* CHARACTERS*)* Stand back—stand back! Let me see, and don't let's lose any more time! *(to the* STEPDAUGHTER*)* Is it all right as it is now?

THE STEPDAUGHTER Well, to tell the truth, I don't recognize the scene.

THE MANAGER My dear lady, you can't possibly suppose that we can construct that shop of Madame Pace piece by piece here? *(to the* FATHER*)* You said a white room with flowered wall paper, didn't you?

THE FATHER Yes.

THE MANAGER Well then. We've got the furniture right, more or less. Bring that little table a bit further forward. *(The* STAGE HANDS *obey the order. To* PROPERTY MAN*)* You go and find an envelope, if possible, a pale blue one; and give it to that gentleman. *(indicates* FATHER*)*

PROPERTY MAN An ordinary envelope?

MANAGER *and* FATHER Yes, yes, an ordinary envelope.

PROPERTY MAN At once, sir. *(Exit)*

THE MANAGER Ready, everyone! First scene—the Young Lady. *(The* LEADING LADY *comes forward.)* No, no, you must wait. I meant her. *(indicating the* STEPDAUGHTER*)* You must watch—

THE STEPDAUGHTER *(adding at once)* How I shall play it, how I shall live it! . . .

LEADING LADY *(offended)* I shall live it also, you may be sure, as soon as I begin!

THE MANAGER *(with his hands to his head)* Ladies and gentlemen, if you please! No more useless discussions! Scene I: the young lady with Madame Pace: Oh! *(looks around as if lost)* And this Madame Pace, where is she?

THE FATHER She isn't with us, sir.

THE MANAGER Then what the devil's to be done?

THE FATHER But she is alive too.

THE MANAGER Yes, but where is she?

THE FATHER One minute. Let me speak! *(turning to the* ACTRESSES*)* If these ladies would be so good as to give me their hats for a moment . . .

THE ACTRESSES *(half surprised, half laughing, in chorus)* What?
Why?
Our hats?
What does he say?

THE MANAGER What are you going to do with the ladies' hats? *(The* ACTORS *laugh.)*

THE FATHER Oh nothing. I just want to put them on these pegs for a moment. And one of the ladies will be so kind as to take off her mantle . . .

THE ACTORS Oh, what d'you think of that? Only the mantle?
He must be mad.

SOME ACTRESSES But why? Mantles as well?

THE FATHER To hang them up here for a moment. Please be so kind, will you?

THE ACTRESSES *(taking off their hats, one or two also their cloaks, and going to hang them on the racks)* After all, why not?

There you are?

This is really funny.

We've got to put them on show.

THE FATHER Exactly; just like that, on show.

THE MANAGER May we know why?

THE FATHER I'll tell you. Who knows if, by arranging the stage for her, she does not come here herself, attracted by the very articles of her trade? *(inviting the* ACTORS *to look towards the exit at back of stage)* Look! Look!

(The door at the back of stage opens and MADAME PACE *enters and takes a few steps forward. She is a fat, oldish woman with puffy oxygenated hair. She is rouged and powdered, dressed with a comical elegance in black silk. Round her waist is a long silver chain from which hangs a pair of scissors. The* STEPDAUGHTER *runs over to her at once amid the stupor of the* ACTORS.*)*

THE STEPDAUGHTER *(turning towards her)* There she is! There she is!

THE FATHER *(radiant)* It's she! I said so, didn't I? There she is!

THE MANAGER *(conquering his surprise, and then becoming indignant)* What sort of a trick is this?

LEADING MAN *(almost at the same time)* What's going to happen next?

JUVENILE LEAD Where does *she* come from?

L'INGÉNUE They've been holding her in reserve, I guess.

LEADING LADY A vulgar trick!

THE FATHER *(dominating the protests)* Excuse me, all of you! Why are you so anxious to destroy in the name of a vulgar, commonplace sense of truth, this reality which comes to birth attracted and formed by the magic of the stage itself, which has indeed more right to live here than you, since it is much truer than you—if you don't mind my saying so? Which is the actress among you who is to play Madame Pace? Well, here is Madame Pace herself. And you will allow, I fancy, that the actress who acts her will be less true than this woman here, who is herself in person. You see my daughter recognized her and went over to her at once. Now you're going to witness the scene!

(But the scene between the STEPDAUGHTER *and* MADAME PACE *has already begun despite the protest of the* ACTORS *and the reply of* THE FATHER. *It has begun quietly, naturally, in a manner impossible for the stage. So when the* ACTORS, *called to attention by* THE FATHER, *turn round and see* MADAME PACE, *who has placed one hand under the* STEPDAUGHTER'S *chin to raise her head, they observe her at first with great attention, but hearing her speak in an unintelligible manner their interest begins to wane.)*

THE MANAGER Well? well?

LEADING MAN What does she say?

LEADING LADY One can't hear a word.

JUVENILE LEAD Louder! Louder please!

THE STEPDAUGHTER *(leaving* MADAME PACE, *who smiles a Sphinx-like smile, and advancing towards the* ACTORS*)* Louder? Louder? What are you talking about? These aren't matters which can be shouted at the top of one's voice. If I have spoken them out loud, it was to shame him and have my revenge. *(indicates* FATHER*)* But for Madame it's quite a different matter.

THE MANAGER Indeed? indeed? But here, you know, people have got to make themselves heard, my dear. Even we who are on the stage can't hear you. What will it be when the public's in the theater? And anyway, you can very well speak up now among yourselves, since we shan't be present to listen to you as we are now. You've got to pretend to be alone in a room at the back of a shop where no one can hear you.

*(*THE STEPDAUGHTER *coquettishly and with a touch of malice makes a sign of disagreement two or three times with her finger.)*

THE MANAGER What do you mean by no?

THE STEPDAUGHTER *(sotto voce, mysteriously)* There's someone who will hear us if she *(indicating* MADAME PACE*)* speaks out loud.

THE MANAGER *(in consternation)* What? Have you got someone else to spring on us now? *(The* ACTORS *burst out laughing.)*

THE FATHER No, no sir. She is alluding to me. I've got to be here—there behind that door, in waiting; and Madame Pace knows it. In fact, if you will allow me, I'll go there at once, so I can be quite ready. *(moves away)*

THE MANAGER *(stopping him)* No! wait! wait! We must observe the conventions of the theater. Before you are ready . . .

THE STEPDAUGHTER *(interrupting him)* No, get on with it at once! I'm just dying, I tell you, to act this scene. If he's ready, I'm more than ready.

THE MANAGER *(shouting)* But, my dear young lady, first of all, we must have the scene between you and this lady . . . *(indicates* MADAME PACE*)* Do you understand? . . .

THE STEPDAUGHTER Good Heavens! She's been telling me what you know already: that Mamma's work is badly done again, that the material's ruined; and that if I want her to continue to help us in our misery I must be patient . . .

MADAME PACE *(coming forward with an air of great importance)* Yes indeed, sir, I no wanta take advantage of her, I no wanta be hard . . .

(Note: MADAME PACE *is supposed to talk in a jargon half Italian, half English)*

THE MANAGER *(alarmed)* What? What? she talks like that? *(The* ACTORS *burst out laughing again.)*

THE STEPDAUGHTER *(also laughing)* Yes, yes, that's the way she talks, half English, half Italian! Most comical it is!

MADAME PACE Itta seem not verra polite gentlemen laugha atta me eef I traya best speaka English.

THE MANAGER *Diamine!* Of course! Of course! Let her talk like that! Just what we want. Talk just like that, Madame, if you please! The effect will be certain. Exactly what was wanted to put a little comic relief into the crudity of the situation. Of course she talks like that! Magnificent!

THE STEPDAUGHTER Magnificent? Certainly! When certain suggestions are made to one in language of that kind, the effect is certain, since it seems almost a joke. One feels inclined to laugh when one hears her talk about an "old signore" "who wanta talka nicely with you." Nice old signore, eh, Madame?

MADAME PACE Not so old, my dear, not so old! And even if you no lika him, he won't make any scandal!

THE MOTHER *(Jumping up amid the amazement and consternation of the* ACTORS *who had not been noticing her. They move to restrain her.)* You old devil! Your murderess!

THE STEPDAUGHTER *(running over to calm her* MOTHER*)* Calm yourself, mother, calm yourself! Please don't . . .

THE FATHER *(going to her also at the same time)* Calm yourself! Don't get excited! Sit down now!

THE MOTHER Well then, take that woman away out of my sight!

THE STEPDAUGHTER *(to* MANAGER*)* It is impossible for my mother to remain here.

THE FATHER *(to* MANAGER*)* They can't be here together. And for this reason, you see: that woman there was not with us when we came . . . If they are on together, the whole thing is given away inevitably, as you see.

THE MANAGER It doesn't matter. This is only a first rough sketch—just to get an idea of the various points of the scene, even confusedly . . . *(turning to the* MOTHER *and leading her to her chair)* Come along, my dear lady, sit down now, and let's get on with the scene . . .
(Meanwhile, the STEPDAUGHTER, *coming forward again, turns to* MADAME PACE.*)*

THE STEPDAUGHTER Come on, Madame, come on!

MADAME PACE *(offended)* No, no, *grazie.* I not do anything witha your mother present.

THE STEPDAUGHTER Nonsense! Introduce this "old signore" who wants to talk nicely to me. *(addressing the company imperiously)* We've got to do this scene one way or another, haven't we? Come on! *(to* MADAME PACE*)* You can go!

MADAME PACE Ah yes! I go'way! I go'way! Certainly! *(Exits furious)*

THE STEPDAUGHTER *(to the* FATHER*)* Now you make your entry. No, you needn't go over there. Come here. Let's suppose you've already come in. Like that, yes! I'm here with bowed head, modest-like. Come on! Out with your voice! Say "Good morning, Miss" in that peculiar tone, that special tone . . .

THE MANAGER Excuse me, but are you the Manager, or am I? *(to the* FATHER, *who looks undecided and perplexed)* Get on with it, man! Go down there to the back of the stage. You needn't go off. Then come right forward here.
*(*THE FATHER *does as he is told, looking troubled and perplexed at first. But as soon as he begins to move, the reality of the action affects him, and he begins to smile and to be more natural. The* ACTORS *watch intently.)*

THE MANAGER *(sotto voce, quickly to the* PROMPTER *in his box)* Ready! ready? Get ready to write now.

THE FATHER *(coming forward and speaking in a different tone)* Good afternoon, Miss!

THE STEPDAUGHTER *(head bowed down slightly, with restrained disgust)* Good afternoon!

THE FATHER *(Looks under her hat which partly covers her face. Perceiving she is very young, he makes an exclamation, partly of surprise, partly of fear lest he compromise himself in a risky adventure)* Ah . . . but . . . ah . . . I say . . . this is not the first time that you have come here, is it?

THE STEPDAUGHTER *(modestly)* No sir.

THE FATHER You've been here before, eh? *(then seeing her nod agreement)* More than once? *(waits for her to answer, looks under her hat, smiles, and then says)* Well then, there's no need to be so shy, is there? May I take off your hat?

THE STEPDAUGHTER *(anticipating him and with veiled disgust)* No sir . . . I'll do it myself. *(takes it off quickly)*

*(*THE MOTHER, *who watches the progress of the scene with* THE SON *and the other two* CHILDREN *who cling to her, is on thorns; and follows with varying expressions of sorrow, indignation, anxiety, and horror the words and actions of the other two. From time to time she hides her face in her hands and sobs.)*

THE MOTHER Oh, my God, my God!

THE FATHER *(playing his part with a touch of gallantry)* Give it to me! I'll put it down. *(takes hat from her hands)* But a dear little head like yours ought to have a smarter hat. Come and help me choose one from the stock, won't you?

L'INGÉNUE *(interrupting)* I say . . . those are our hats, you know.

THE MANAGER *(furious)* Silence! silence! Don't try and be funny, if you please . . . We're playing the scene now, I'd have you notice. *(to the* STEPDAUGHTER*)* Begin again, please!

THE STEPDAUGHTER *(continuing)* No thank you, sir.

THE FATHER Oh, come now. Don't talk like that. You must take it. I shall be upset if you don't. There are some lovely little hats here; and then—Madame will be pleased. She expects it, anyway, you know.

THE STEPDAUGHTER No, no! I couldn't wear it!

THE FATHER Oh, you're thinking about what they'd say at home if they saw you come in with a new hat? My dear girl, there's always a way round these little matters, you know.

THE STEPDAUGHTER *(all keyed up)* No, it's not that. I couldn't wear it because I am . . . as you see . . . you might have noticed . . . *(showing her black dress)*

THE FATHER . . . in mourning! Of course: I beg your pardon: I'm frightfully sorry . . .

THE STEPDAUGHTER *(forcing herself to conquer her indignation and nausea)* Stop! Stop! It's I who must thank you. There's no need for you to feel mortified or specially sorry. Don't think any more of what I've said. *(tries to smile)* I must forget that I am dressed so . . .

THE MANAGER *(interrupting and turning to the* PROMPTER*)* Stop a minute! Stop! Don't write that down. Cut out that last bit. *(then to the* FATHER *and* STEPDAUGHTER*)* Fine! it's going fine! *(to the* FATHER *only)* And now you can go on as we arranged. *(to the* ACTORS*)* Pretty good that scene, where he offers her the hat, eh?

THE STEPDAUGHTER The best's coming now. Why can't we go on?

THE MANAGER Have a little patience! *(to the* actors*)* Of course, it must be treated rather lightly.

LEADING MAN Still, with a bit of go in it!

LEADING LADY Of course! It's easy enough! *(to* LEADING MAN*)* Shall you and I try it now?

LEADING MAN Why, yes! I'll prepare my entrance. *(Exit in order to make his entrance)*

THE MANAGER *(to* LEADING LADY*)* See here! The scene between you and Madame Pace is finished. I'll have it written out properly after. You remain here . . . oh, where are you going?

LEADING LADY One minute. I want to put my hat on again. *(goes over to hatrack and puts her hat on her head)*

THE MANAGER Good! You stay here with your head bowed down a bit.

THE STEPDAUGHTER But she isn't dressed in black.

LEADING LADY But I shall be, and much more effectively than you.

THE MANAGER *(to* STEPDAUGHTER*)* Be quiet please, and watch! You'll be able to learn something. *(clapping his hands)* Come on! come on! Entrance, please!

(The door at rear of stage opens, and the LEADING MAN *enters with the lively manner of an old gallant. The rendering of the scene by the* ACTORS *from the very first words is seen to be quite a different thing, though it has not in any way the air of a parody. Naturally, the* STEPDAUGHTER *and the* FATHER, *not being able to recognize themselves in the* LEADING LADY *and the* LEADING MAN, *who deliver their words in different tones and with a different psychology, express, sometimes with smiles, sometimes with gestures, the impression they receive.)*

LEADING MAN Good afternoon, Miss . . .

THE FATHER *(at once unable to contain himself)* No! no!

*(*THE STEPDAUGHTER, *noticing the way the* LEADING MAN *enters, bursts out laughing.)*

THE MANAGER *(furious)* Silence! And you, please, just stop that laughing. If we go on like this, we shall never finish.

THE STEPDAUGHTER Forgive me, sir, but it's natural enough. This lady *(indicating* LEADING LADY*)* stands there still; but if she is supposed to be me, I can assure you that if I heard anyone say "Good afternoon" in that manner and in that tone, I should burst out laughing as I did.

THE FATHER Yes, yes, the manner, the tone . . .

THE MANAGER Nonsense! Rubbish! Stand aside and let me see the action.

LEADING MAN If I've got to represent an old fellow who's coming into a house of an equivocal character . . .

THE MANAGER Don't listen to them, for Heaven's sake! Do it again! It goes fine. *(waiting for the* ACTORS *to begin again)* Well?

LEADING MAN Good afternoon, Miss.

LEADING LADY Good afternoon.

LEADING MAN *(imitating the gesture of the* FATHER *when he looked under the hat, and then expressing quite clearly first satisfaction and then fear)* Ah, but . . . I say . . . this is not the first time that you have come here, is it?

THE MANAGER Good, but not quite so heavily. Like this. *(acts himself)* "This isn't the first time that you have come here" . . . *(to* LEADING LADY*)* And you say: "No, sir."

LEADING LADY No, sir.

LEADING MAN You've been here before, more than once.

THE MANAGER No, no, stop! Let her nod "yes" first. "You've been here before, eh?" *(the* LEADING LADY *lifts up her head slightly and closes her eyes as though in disgust. Then she inclines her head twice.)*

THE STEPDAUGHTER *(unable to contain herself)* Oh my God! *(Puts a hand to her mouth to prevent herself from laughing)*

THE MANAGER *(turning round)* What's the matter?

THE STEPDAUGHTER Nothing, nothing!

THE MANAGER *(to* LEADING MAN*)* Go on!

LEADING MAN You've been here before, eh? Well then, there's no need to be so shy, is there? May I take off your hat?

(The LEADING MAN *says this last speech in such a tone and with such gestures that the* STEPDAUGHTER, *though she has her hand to her mouth, cannot keep from laughing.)*

LEADING LADY *(indignant)* I'm not going to stop here to be made a fool of by that woman there.

LEADING MAN Neither am I! I'm through with it!

THE MANAGER *(shouting to* STEPDAUGHTER*)* Silence! for once and all, I tell you!

THE STEPDAUGHTER Forgive me! forgive me!

THE MANAGER You haven't any manners: that's what it is! You go too far.

THE FATHER *(endeavoring to intervene)* Yes, it's true, but excuse her . . .

THE MANAGER Excuse what? It's absolutely disgusting.

THE FATHER Yes, sir, but believe me, it has such a strange effect when . . .

THE MANAGER Strange? Why strange? Where is it strange?

THE FATHER No, sir; I admire your actors—this gentleman here, this lady; but they are certainly not us!

THE MANAGER I should hope not. Evidently they cannot be you, if they are actors.

THE FATHER Just so: actors! Both of them act our parts exceedingly well. But, believe me, it produces quite a different effect on us. They want to be us, but they aren't, all the same.

THE MANAGER What is it then anyway?

THE FATHER Something that is . . . that is theirs—and no longer ours . . .

THE MANAGER But naturally, inevitably. I've told you so already.

THE FATHER Yes, I understand . . . I understand . . .

THE MANAGER Well then, let's have no more of it! *(turning to the* ACTORS*)*

We'll have the rehearsals by ourselves, afterwards, in the ordinary way. I never could stand rehearsing with the author present. He's never satisfied! *(turning to* FATHER *and* STEPDAUGHTER*)* Come on! Let's get on with it again; and try and see if you can't keep from laughing.

THE STEPDAUGHTER Oh, I shan't laugh any more. There's a nice little bit coming from me now: you'll see.

THE MANAGER Well then: when she says "Don't think any more of what I've said. I must forget, etc.," you *(addressing the* FATHER*)* come in sharp with "I understand, I understand"; and then you ask her . . .

THE STEPDAUGHTER *(interrupting)* What?

THE MANAGER Why she is in mourning.

THE STEPDAUGHTER Not at all! See here: when I told him that it was useless for me to be thinking about my wearing mourning, do you know how he answered me? "Ah well," he said, "then let's take off this little frock."

THE MANAGER Great! Just what we want, to make a riot in the theater!

THE STEPDAUGHTER But it's the truth!

THE MANAGER What does that matter? Acting is our business here. Truth up to a certain point, but no further.

THE STEPDAUGHTER What do you want to do then?

THE MANAGER You'll see, you'll see! Leave it to me.

THE STEPDAUGHTER No sir! What you want to do is to piece together a little romantic sentimental scene out of my disgust, out of all the reasons, each more cruel and viler than the other, why I am what I am. He is to ask me why I'm in mourning; and I'm to answer with tears in my eyes, that it is just two months since papa died. No sir, no! He's got to say to me; as he did say: "Well, let's take off this little dress at once." And I; with my two months' mourning in my heart, went there behind that screen, and with these fingers tingling with shame . . .

THE MANAGER *(running his hands through his hair)* For Heaven's sake! What are you saying?

THE STEPDAUGHTER *(crying out excitedly)* The truth! The truth!

THE MANAGER It may be. I don't deny it, and I can understand all your horror; but you must surely see that you can't have this kind of thing on the stage. It won't go.

THE STEPDAUGHTER Not possible, eh? Very well! I'm much obliged to you—but I'm off!

THE MANAGER Now be reasonable! Don't lose your temper!

THE STEPDAUGHTER I won't stop here! I won't! I can see you've fixed it all up with him in your office. All this talk about what is possible for the stage . . . I understand! He wants to get at his complicated "cerebral drama," to have his famous remorses and torments acted; but I want to act my part, *my part!*

THE MANAGER *(annoyed, shaking his shoulders)* Ah! Just *your* part! But, if you will pardon me, there are other parts than yours: his *(indicating the* FATHER*)* and hers! *(indicating the* MOTHER*)* On the stage you can't have a character becoming too prominent and overshadowing all the others. The thing is to pack them all into a neat little framework and then act what is actable. I am aware of the fact that everyone has his own interior life which he wants very much to put forward. But the difficulty lies in this fact: to set out just so much as is necessary for the stage, taking the other characters into consideration, and at the same time hint at the unrevealed interior life of each. I am willing to admit, my dear young lady, that from your point of view it would be a fine idea if each character could tell the public all his troubles in a nice monologue or a regular one-hour lecture. *(good-humoredly)* You must restrain yourself, my dear, and in your own interest, too; because this fury of yours, this exaggerated disgust you show, may make a bad impression, you know. After you have confessed to me that there were others before him at Madame Pace's and more than once . . .

THE STEPDAUGHTER *(bowing her head, impressed)* It's true. But remember those others mean him for me all the same.

THE MANAGER *(not understanding)* What? The others? What do you mean?

THE STEPDAUGHTER For one who has gone wrong, sir, he who was responsible for the first fault is responsible for all that follow. He is responsible for my faults, was, even before I was born. Look at him, and see if it isn't true!

THE MANAGER Well, well! And does the weight of so much responsibility seem nothing to you? Give him a chance to act it, to get it over!

THE STEPDAUGHTER How? How can he act all his "noble remorses," all his "moral torments," if you want to spare him the horror of being discovered one day—after he had asked her what he did ask her—in the arms of her, that already fallen woman, that child, sir, that child he used to watch come out of school? *(She is moved)*

(THE MOTHER *at this point is overcome with emotion, and breaks out into a fit of crying. All are touched. A long pause)*

THE STEPDAUGHTER *(as soon as the* MOTHER *becomes a little quieter, adds resolutely and gravely)* At present, we are unknown to the public. Tomorrow, you will act us as you wish, treating us in your own manner. But do you really want to see drama, do you want to see it flash out as it really did?

THE MANAGER Of course! That's just what I do want, so I can use as much of it as is possible.

THE STEPDAUGHTER Well then, ask that Mother there to leave us.

THE MOTHER *(changing her low plaint into a sharp cry)* No! No! Don't permit it, sir, don't permit it!

THE MANAGER But it's only to try it.

THE MOTHER I can't bear it. I can't.

THE MANAGER But since it has happened already . . . I don't understand!

THE MOTHER It's taking place now. It happens all the time. My torment isn't a pretended one. I live and feel every minute of my torture. Those two children there—have you heard them speak? They can't speak any more. They cling to me to keep my torment actual and vivid for me. But for themselves, they do not exist, they aren't any more. And she *(indicating* STEPDAUGHTER*)* has run away, she has left me, and is lost. If I now see her here before me, it is only to renew for me the tortures I have suffered for her too.

THE FATHER The eternal moment! She *(indicating the* STEPDAUGHTER*)* is here to catch me, fix me, and hold me eternally in the stocks for that one fleeting and shameful moment of my life. She can't give it up! And you sir, cannot either fairly spare me it.

THE MANAGER I never said I didn't want to act it. It will form, as a matter of fact, the nucleus of the whole first act right up to her surprise. *(indicating the* MOTHER*)*

THE FATHER Just so! This is my punishment: the passion in all of us that must culminate in her final cry.

THE STEPDAUGHTER I can hear it still in my ears. It's driven me mad, that cry—You can put me on as you like; it doesn't matter. Fully dressed, if you like—provided I have at least the arm bare; because, standing like this *(she goes close to the* FATHER *and leans her head on his breast)* with my head so, and my arms round his neck, I saw a vein pulsing in my arm here; and then, as if that live vein had awakened disgust in me, I closed my eyes like this, and let my head sink on his breast. *(turning to the* MOTHER*)* Cry out, mother! Cry out! *(buries head in* FATHER'S *breast, and with her shoulders raised as if to prevent her hearing the cry, adds in tones of intense emotion)* Cry out as you did then!

THE MOTHER *(coming forward to separate them)* No! My daughter, my daughter! *(and after having pulled her away from him)* You brute! you brute! She is my daughter! Don't you see she's my daughter?

THE MANAGER *(walking backwards towards footlights)* Fine! fine! Damned good! And then, of course—curtain!

THE FATHER *(going towards him excitedly)* Yes, of course, because that's the way it really happened.

THE MANAGER *(convinced and pleased)* Oh, yes, no doubt about it. Curtain here, curtain!

(At the reiterated cry of THE MANAGER, THE MACHINIST *lets the curtain down, leaving* THE MANAGER *and* THE FATHER *in front of it before the footlights.)*

THE MANAGER The darned idiot! I said "curtain" to show the act should end there, and he goes and lets it down in earnest. *(To the* FATHER, *while he pulls the curtain back to go onto the stage again)* Yes, yes, it's all right. Effect certain! That's the right ending. I'll guarantee the first act, at any rate.

act III

(When the curtain goes up again, it is seen that the stage hands have shifted the bit of scenery used in the last part, and have rigged up instead at the back of the stage a drop, with some trees, and one or two wings. A portion of a fountain basin is visible. THE MOTHER *is sitting on the* Right *with the two children by her side.* THE SON *is on the same side, but away from the others. He seems bored, angry, and full of shame.* THE FATHER

and THE STEPDAUGHTER *are also seated towards the* Right *front. On the other side* (Left) *are the* ACTORS, *much in the positions they occupied before the curtain was lowered. Only* THE MANAGER *is standing up in the middle of the stage, with his hand closed over his mouth, in the act of meditating.)*

THE MANAGER *(shaking his shoulders after a brief pause)* Ah yes: the second act! Leave it to me, leave it all to me as we arranged, and you'll see! It'll go fine!

THE STEPDAUGHTER Our entry into his house *(indicates* FATHER*)* in spite of him . . . *(indicates the* SON*)*

THE MANAGER *(out of patience)* Leave it to me, I tell you!

THE STEPDAUGHTER Do let it be clear, at any rate, that it is in spite of my wishes.

THE MOTHER *(from her corner, shaking her head)* For all the good that's come of it . . .

THE STEPDAUGHTER *(turning towards her quickly)* It doesn't matter. The more harm done us, the more remorse for him.

THE MANAGER *(impatiently)* I understand! Good Heavens! I understand! I'm taking it into account.

THE MOTHER *(supplicatingly)* I beg you, sir, to let it appear quite plain that for conscience' sake I did try in every way . . .

THE STEPDAUGHTER *(interrupting indignantly and continuing for the* MOTHER*)* . . . to pacify me, to dissuade me from spiting him. *(to* MANAGER*)* Do as she wants: satisfy her, because it is true! I enjoy it immensely. Anyhow, as you can see, the meeker she is, the more she tries to get at his heart, the more distant and aloof does he become.

THE MANAGER Are we going to begin this second act or not?

THE STEPDAUGHTER I'm not going to talk any more now. But I must tell you this: you can't have the whole action take place in the garden, as you suggest. It isn't possible!

THE MANAGER Why not?

THE STEPDAUGHTER Because he *(indicates the* SON *again)* is always shut up alone in his room. And then there's all the part of that poor dazed-looking boy there which takes place indoors.

THE MANAGER Maybe! On the other hand, you will understand—we can't change scenes three or four times in one act.

THE LEADING MAN They used to once.

THE MANAGER Yes, when the public was up to the level of that child there.

THE LEADING LADY It makes the illusion easier.

THE FATHER *(irritated)* The illusion! For Heaven's sake, don't say illusion. Please don't use that word, which is particularly painful for us.

THE MANAGER *(astounded)* And why, if you please?

THE FATHER It's painful, cruel, really cruel; and you ought to understand that.

THE MANAGER But why? What ought we to say then? The illusion, I tell you, sir, which we've got to create for the audience . . .

THE LEADING MAN With our acting.
THE MANAGER The illusion of a reality.
THE FATHER I understand; but you, perhaps, do not understand us. Forgive me! You see . . . here for you and your actors, the thing is only—and rightly so . . . a kind of game . . .
THE LEADING LADY *(interrupting indignantly)* A game! We're not children here, if you please! We are serious actors.
THE FATHER I don't deny it. What I mean is the game, or play, of your art, which has to give, as the gentleman says, a perfect illusion of reality.
THE MANAGER Precisely——!
THE FATHER Now, if you consider the fact that we *(indicates himself and the other five* CHARACTERS*)*, as we are, have no other reality outside of this illusion . . .
THE MANAGER *(astonished, looking at his* ACTORS, *who are also amazed)* And what does that mean?
THE FATHER *(after watching them for a moment with a wan smile)* As I say, sir, that which is a game of art for you is our sole reality. *(Brief pause. He goes a step or two nearer the* MANAGER *and adds)* But not only for us, you know, by the way. Just you think it over well. *(looks him in the eyes)* Can you tell me who you are?
THE MANAGER *(perplexed, half smiling)* What? Who am I? I am myself.
THE FATHER And if I were to tell you that that isn't true, because you are I? . . .
THE MANAGER I should say you were mad——! *(The* ACTORS *laugh.)*
THE FATHER You're quite right to laugh: because we are all making believe here. *(to* MANAGER*)* And you can therefore object that it's only for a joke that that gentleman there *(indicates the* LEADING MAN*)*, who naturally is himself, has to be me, who am on the contrary myself—this thing you see here. You see I've caught you in a trap! *(The* ACTORS *laugh.)*
THE MANAGER *(annoyed)* But we've had all this over once before. Do you want to begin again?
THE FATHER No, no! that wasn't my meaning! In fact, I should like to request you to abandon this game of art *(looking at the* LEADING LADY *as if anticipating her)* which you are accustomed to play here with your actors, and to ask you seriously once again: who are you?
THE MANAGER *(astonished and irritated, turning to his* ACTORS*)* If this fellow here hasn't got a nerve! A man who calls himself a character comes and asks me who I am!
THE FATHER *(with dignity, but not offended)* A character, sir, may always ask a man who he is. Because a character has really a life of his own, marked with his especial characteristics; for which reason he is always "somebody." But a man—I'm not speaking of you now—may very well be "nobody."
THE MANAGER Yes, but you are asking these questions of me, the boss, the manager! Do you understand?
THE FATHER But only in order to know if you, as you really are now, see yourself as you once were with all the illusions that were yours then,

with all the things both inside and outside of you as they seemed to you—as they were then indeed for you. Well, sir, if you think of all those illusions that mean nothing to you now, of all those things which don't even *seem* to you to exist any more, while once they *were* for you, don't you feel that—I won't say these boards—but the very earth under your feet is sinking away from you when you reflect that in the same way this *you* as you feel it today—all this present reality of yours—is fated to seem a mere illusion to you tomorrow?

THE MANAGER *(without having understood much, but astonished by the specious argument)* Well, well! And where does all this take us anyway?

THE FATHER Oh, nowhere! It's only to show you that if we *(indicating the* CHARACTERS*)* have no other reality beyond illusion, you too must not count overmuch on your reality as you feel it today, since, like that of yesterday, it may prove an illusion for you tomorrow.

THE MANAGER *(determining to make fun of him)* Ah, excellent! Then you'll be saying next that you, with this comedy of yours that you brought here to act, are truer and more real than I am.

THE FATHER *(with the greatest seriousness)* But of course; without doubt!

THE MANAGER Ah, really?

THE FATHER Why, I thought you'd understand that from the beginning.

THE MANAGER More real than I?

THE FATHER If your reality can change from one day to another . . .

THE MANAGER But everyone knows it can change. It is always changing, the same as anyone else's.

THE FATHER *(with a cry)* No, sir, not ours! Look here! That is the very difference! Our reality doesn't change: it can't change! It can't be other than what it is, because it is already fixed for ever. It's terrible. Ours is an immutable reality which should make you shudder when you approach us if you are really conscious of the fact that your reality is a mere transitory and fleeting illusion, taking this form today and that tomorrow, according to the conditions, according to your will, your sentiments, which in turn are controlled by an intellect that shows them to you today in one manner and tomorrow . . . who knows how? . . . Illusions of reality represented in this fatuous comedy of life that never ends, nor can ever end! Because if tomorrow it were to end . . . then why, all would be finished.

THE MANAGER Oh for God's sake, will you *at least* finish with this philosophizing and let us try and shape this comedy which you yourself have brought me here? You argue and philosophize a bit too much, my dear sir. You know you seem to me almost, almost . . . *(stops and looks him over from head to foot)* Ah, by the way, I think you introduced yourself to me as a—what shall . . . we say—a "character," created by an author who did not afterwards care to make a drama of his own creations.

THE FATHER It is the simple truth, sir.

THE MANAGER Nonsense! Cut that out, please! None of us believes it, because it isn't a thing, as you must recognize yourself, which one can believe seriously. If you want to know, it seems to me you are trying to imitate the manner of a certain author whom I heartily detest—I warn you—although I have unfortunately bound myself to put on one of his works. As a matter of fact, I was just starting to rehearse it, when you arrived. *(turning to the* ACTORS*)* And this is what we've gained—out of the frying-pan into the fire!

THE FATHER I don't know to what author you may be alluding, but believe me I feel what I think; and I seem to be philosphizing only for those who do not think what they feel, because they blind themselves with their own sentiment. I know that for many people this self-blinding seems much more "human"; but the contrary is really true. For man never reasons so much and becomes so introspective as when he suffers; since he is anxious to get at the cause of his sufferings, to learn who has produced them, and whether it is just or unjust that he should have to bear them. On the other hand, when he is happy, he takes his happiness as it comes and doesn't analyze it, just as if happiness were his right. The animals suffer without reasoning about their sufferings. But take the case of a man who suffers and begins to reason about it. Oh no! it can't be allowed! Let him suffer like an animal, and then—ah yes, he is "human!"

THE MANAGER Look here! Look here! You're off again, philosophizing worse than ever.

THE FATHER Because I suffer, sir! I'm not philosophizing: I'm crying aloud the reason of my sufferings.

THE MANAGER *(makes brusque movement as he is taken with a new idea)* I should like to know if anyone has ever heard of a character who gets right out of his part and perorates and speechifies as you do. Have you ever heard of a case? I haven't.

THE FATHER You have never met such a case, sir, because authors, as a rule, hide the labor of their creations. When the characters are really alive before their author, the latter does nothing but follow them in their action, in their words, in the situations which they suggest to him; and he has to will them the way they will themselves—for there's trouble if he doesn't. When a character is born, he acquires at once such an independence, even of his own author, that he can be imagined by everybody even in many other situations where the author never dreamed of placing him; and so he acquires for himself a meaning which the author never thought of giving him.

THE MANAGER Yes, yes, I know this.

THE FATHER What is there then to marvel at in us? Imagine such a misfortune for characters as I have described to you: to be born of an author's fantasy, and be denied life by him; and then answer me if these characters left alive, and yet without life, weren't right in doing what they did do and are doing now, after they have attempted everything in their power to persuade him to give them their stage life. We've all tried him in turn, I, she *(indicating the* STEPDAUGHTER*)* and she. *(indicating the* MOTHER*)*

THE STEPDAUGHTER It's true. I too have sought to tempt him, many,

many times, when he had been sitting at his writing table, feeling a bit melancholy, at the twilight hour. He would sit in his armchair too lazy to switch on the light, and all the shadows that crept into his room were full of our presence coming to tempt him. *(as if she saw herself still there by the writing table, and was annoyed by the presence of the* ACTORS*)* Oh, if you would only go away, go away and leave us alone—mother here with that son of hers—I with that Child—that Boy there always alone—and then I with him—*(just hints at the* FATHER*)*—and then I alone, alone . . . in those shadows! *(makes a sudden movement as if in the vision she has of herself illuminating those shadows she wanted to seize hold of herself)* Ah! my life! my life! Oh, what scenes we proposed to him—and I tempted him more than any of the others!

THE FATHER Maybe. But perhaps it was your fault that he refused to give us life: because you were too insistent, too troublesome.

THE STEPDAUGHTER Nonsense! Didn't he make me so himself? *(goes close to the* MANAGER *to tell him as if in confidence)* In my opinion he abandoned us in a fit of depression, of disgust for the ordinary theater as the public knows it and likes it.

THE SON Exactly what it was, sir; exactly that!

THE FATHER Not at all! Don't believe it for a minute. Listen to me! You'll be doing quite right to modify, as you suggest, the excesses both of this girl here, who wants to do too much, and of this young man, who won't do anything at all.

THE SON No, nothing!

THE MANAGER You too get over the mark occasionally, my dear sir, if I may say so.

THE FATHER I? When? Where?

THE MANAGER Always! Continuously! Then there's this insistence of yours in trying to make us believe you are a character. And then too, you must really argue and philosophize less, you know, much less.

THE FATHER Well, if you want to take away from me the possibility of representing the torment of my spirit which never gives me peace, you will be suppressing me: that's all. Every true man, sir, who is a little above the level of the beasts and plants does not live for the sake of living, without knowing how to live; but he lives so as to give a meaning and a value of his own to life. For me this is *everything.* I cannot give up this, just to represent a mere fact as she *(indicating the* STEPDAUGHTER*)* wants. It's all very well for her, since her "vendetta" lies in the "fact." I'm not going to do it. It destroys my *raison d'être.*

THE MANAGER Your *raison d'être!* Oh, we're going ahead fine! First she starts off, and then you jump in. At this rate, we'll never finish.

THE FATHER Now, don't be offended! Have it your own way—provided, however, that within the limits of the parts you assign us each one's sacrifice isn't too great.

THE MANAGER You've got to understand that you can't go on arguing at your own pleasure. Drama is action, sir, action and not confounded philosophy.

THE FATHER All right. I'll do just as much arguing and philosophizing as everybody does when he is considering his own torments.

THE MANAGER If the drama permits! But for Heaven's sake, man, let's get along and come to the scene.

THE STEPDAUGHTER It seems to me we've got too much action with our coming into his house. *(indicating* FATHER*)* You said, before, you couldn't change the scene every five minutes.

THE MANAGER Of course not. What we've got to do is to combine and group up all the facts in one simultaneous, close-knit action. We can't have it as you want, with your little brother wandering like a ghost from room to room, hiding behind doors and meditating a project which —what did you say it did to him?

THE STEPDAUGHTER Consumes him, sir, wastes him away!

THE MANAGER Well, it may be. And then at the same time, you want the little girl there to be playing in the garden . . . one in the house, and the other in the garden: isn't that it?

THE STEPDAUGHTER Yes, in the sun, in the sun! That is my only pleasure: to see her happy and careless in the garden after the misery and squalor of the horrible room where we all four slept together. And I had to sleep with her—I, do you understand?—with my vile contaminated body next to hers; with her folding me fast in her loving little arms. In the garden, whenever she spied me, she would run to take me by the hand. She didn't care for the big flowers, only the little ones; and she loved to show me them and pet me.

THE MANAGER Well then, we'll have it in the garden. Everything shall happen in the garden; and we'll group the other scenes there. *(calls a* STAGE HAND*)* Here, a back-cloth with trees and something to do as a fountain basin. *(turning round to look at the back of the stage)* Ah, you've fixed it up. Good! *(to* STEPDAUGHTER*)* This is just to give an idea, of course. The Boy, instead of hiding behind the doors, will wander about here in the garden, hiding behind the trees. But it's going to be rather difficult to find a child to do that scene with you where she shows you the flowers. *(turning to the* YOUTH*)* Come forward a little, will you please? Let's try it now! Come along! come along! *(Then seeing him come shyly forward, full of fear and looking lost)* It's a nice business, this lad here. What's the matter with him? We'll have to give him a word or two to say. *(goes close to him, puts a hand on his shoulders, and leads him behind one of the trees)* Come on! come on! Let me see you a little! Hide here . . . yes, like that. Try and show your head just a little as if you were looking for someone . . . *(goes back to observe the effect, when the* BOY *at once goes through the action)* Excellent! fine! *(turning to* STEPDAUGHTER*)* Suppose the little girl there were to surprise him as he looks round, and run over to him, so we could give him a word or two to say?

THE STEPDAUGHTER It's useless to hope he will speak, as long as that fellow there is here . . . *(indicates the* SON*)* You must send him away first.

THE SON *(jumping up)* Delighted! delighted! I don't ask for anything better. *(begins to move away)*

THE MANAGER *(at once stopping him)* No! No! Where are you going? Wait a bit!

(The MOTHER *gets up, alarmed and terrified at the thought that he is really about to go away. Instinctively she lifts her arms to prevent him, without, however, leaving her seat.)*

THE SON *(to* MANAGER, *who stops him)* I've got nothing to do with this affair. Let me go please! Let me go!

THE MANAGER What do you mean by saying you've got nothing to do with this?

THE STEPDAUGHTER *(calmly, with irony)* Don't bother to stop him: he won't go away.

THE FATHER He has to act the terrible scene in the garden with his mother.

THE SON *(suddenly resolute and with dignity)* I shall act nothing at all. I've said so from the very beginning. *(to the* MANAGER*)* Let me go!

THE STEPDAUGHTER *(going over to the* MANAGER*)* Allow me? *(puts down the* MANAGER'S *arm which is restraining the* SON*)* Well, go away then, if you want to! *(The* SON *looks at her with contempt and hatred. She laughs and says)* You see, he can't, he can't go away! He is obliged to stay here, indissolubly bound to the chain. If I, who fly off when that happens which has to happen, because I can't bear him—if I am still here and support that face and expression of his, you can well imagine that he is unable to move. He has to remain here, has to stop with that nice father of his, and that mother whose only son he is. *(turning to the* MOTHER*)* Come on, mother, come along! *(turning to* MANAGER *to indicate her)* You see, she was getting up to keep him back. *(to the* MOTHER, *beckoning her with her hand)* Come on! come on! *(then to* MANAGER*)* You can imagine how little she wants to show these actors of yours what she really feels; but so eager is she to get near him that . . . There, you see? She is willing to act her part. *(And in fact, the* MOTHER *approaches him; and as soon as the* STEPDAUGHTER *has finished speaking, opens her arms to signify that she consents)*

THE SON *(suddenly)* No! No! If I can't go away, then I'll stop here; but I repeat: I act nothing!

THE FATHER *(to* MANAGER *excitedly)* You can force him, sir.

THE SON Nobody can force me.

THE FATHER I can.

THE STEPDAUGHTER Wait a minute, wait . . . First of all, the baby has to go to the fountain . . . *(runs to take the* CHILD *and leads her to the fountain)*

THE MANAGER Yes, yes of course; that's it. Both at the same time.

(The second LADY LEAD *and the* JUVENILE LEAD *at this point separate themselves from the group of* ACTORS. *One watches the* MOTHER *attentively; the other moves about studying the movements and manner of the* SON *whom he will have to act.)*

THE SON *(to* MANAGER*)* What do you mean by both at the same time? It isn't right. There was no scene between me and her. *(indicates the* MOTHER*)* Ask her how it was!

THE MOTHER Yes, it's true. I had come into his room . . .

THE SON Into my room, do you understand? Nothing to do with the garden.

THE MANAGER It doesn't matter. Haven't I told you we've got to group the action?

THE SON *(observing the* JUVENILE LEAD *studying him)* What do you want?

THE JUVENILE LEAD Nothing! I was just looking at you.

THE SON *(turning towards the* SECOND LADY LEAD*)* Ah! she's at it too: to re-act her part! *(indicating the* MOTHER*)*

THE MANAGER Exactly! And it seems to me that you ought to be grateful to them for their interest.

THE SON Yes, but haven't you yet perceived that it isn't possible to live in front of a mirror which not only freezes us with the image of ourselves, but throws our likeness back at us with a horrible grimace?

THE FATHER That is true, absolutely true. You must see that.

THE MANAGER *(to* SECOND LADY LEAD *and* JUVENILE LEAD*)* He's right! Move away from them!

THE SON Do as you like. I'm out of this!

THE MANAGER Be quiet, you, will you? And let me hear your mother! *(to* MOTHER*)* You were saying you had entered . . .

THE MOTHER Yes, into his room, because I couldn't stand it any longer. I went to empty my heart to him of all the anguish that tortures me . . . But as soon as he saw me come in . . .

THE SON Nothing happened! There was no scene. I went away, that's all! I don't care for scenes!

THE MOTHER It's true, true. That's how it was.

THE MANAGER Well now, we've got to do this bit between you and him. It's indispensable.

THE MOTHER I'm ready . . . when you are ready. If you could only find a chance for me to tell him what I feel here in my heart.

THE FATHER *(going to* SON *in a great rage)* You'll do this for your mother, for your mother, do you understand?

THE SON *(quite determined)* I do nothing!

THE FATHER *(taking hold of him and shaking him)* For God's sake, do as I tell you! Don't you hear your mother asking you for a favor? Haven't you even got the guts to be a son?

THE SON *(taking hold of the* FATHER*)* No! No! And for God's sake stop it, or else . . . *(General agitation. The* MOTHER, *frightened, tries to separate them)*

THE MOTHER *(pleading)* Please! please!

THE FATHER *(not leaving hold of the* SON*)* You've got to obey, do you hear?

THE SON *(almost crying from rage)* What does it mean, this madness you've got? *(They separate.)* Have you no decency, that you insist on showing everyone our shame? I won't do it! I won't! And I stand for the will of our author in this. He didn't want to put us on the stage, after all!

THE MANAGER Man alive! You came here . . .

THE SON *(indicating* FATHER*) He* did! I didn't!

THE MANAGER Aren't you here now?

THE SON It was his wish, and he dragged us along with him. He's told you not only the things that did happen, but also things that have never happened at all.

THE MANAGER Well, tell me then what did happen. You went out of your room without saying a word?

THE SON Without a word, so as to avoid a scene!

THE MANAGER And then what did you do?

THE SON Nothing . . . walking in the garden . . . *(hesitates for a moment with expression of gloom)*

THE MANAGER *(coming closer to him, interested by his extraordinary reserve)* Well, well . . . walking in the garden . . .

THE SON *(exasperated)* Why on earth do you insist? It's horrible! *(The* MOTHER *trembles, sobs, and looks towards the fountain.)*

THE MANAGER *(slowly observing the glance and turning towards the* SON *with increasing apprehension)* The baby?

THE SON There in the fountain . . .

THE FATHER *(pointing with tender pity to the* MOTHER*)* She was following him at the moment . . .

THE MANAGER *(to the* SON*, anxiously)* And then you . . .

THE SON I ran over to her; I was jumping in to drag her out when I saw something that froze my blood . . . the boy there, standing stock still, with eyes like a madman's, watching his little drowned sister, in the fountain! *(The* STEPDAUGHTER *bends over the fountain to hide the* CHILD. *She sobs.)* Then . . . *(A revolver shot rings out behind the trees where the* BOY *is hidden.)*

THE MOTHER *(With a cry of terror runs over in that direction together with several of the* ACTORS *amid general confusion)* My son! My son! *(Then amid the cries and exclamations one hears her voice)* Help! Help!

THE MANAGER *(pushing the* ACTORS *aside while they lift up the* BOY *and carry him off)* Is he really wounded?

SOME ACTORS He's dead! dead!

OTHER ACTORS No, no, it's only make believe, it's only pretence!

THE FATHER *(with a terrible cry)* Pretence? Reality, sir, reality!

THE MANAGER Pretence? Reality? To hell with it all! Never in my life has such a thing happened to me. I've lost a whole day over these people, a whole day!

luigi pirandello

six characters in search of an author

It seems like yesterday but is actually many years ago that a nimble little maidservant entered the service of my art. However, she always comes fresh to the job. She is called Fantasy.

A little puckish and malicious, if she likes to dress in black no one will wish to deny that she is often positively bizarre and no one will wish to believe that she always does everything in the same way and in earnest. She sticks her hand in her pocket, pulls out a cap and bells, sets it on her head, red as a cock's comb, and dashes away. Here today, there tomorrow. And she amuses herself by bringing to my house—since I derive stories and novels and plays from them—the most disgruntled tribe in the world, men, women, children, involved in strange adventures which they can find no way out of; thwarted in their plans; cheated in their hopes; with whom, in short, it is often torture to deal.

Well, this little maidservant of mine, Fantasy, several years ago, had the bad inspiration or ill-omened caprice to bring a family into my house. I wouldn't know where she fished them up or how, but, according to her, I could find in them the subject for a magnificent novel.

I found before me a man about fifty years old, in a dark jacket and light trousers, with a frowning air and ill-natured, mortified eyes; a poor woman in widow's weeds leading by one hand a little girl of four and by the other a boy of rather more than ten; a cheeky and "sexy" girl, also clad in black but with an equivocal and brazen pomp, all attremble with a lively, biting contempt for the mortified old man and for a young fellow of twenty who stood on one side closed in on himself as if he despised them all. In short, the six characters who are seen coming on stage at the beginning of the play. Now one of them and now another—often beating down one another—embarked on the sad story of their adventures, each shouting his own reasons, and projecting in my face his disordered passions, more or less as they do in the play to the unhappy Manager.

What author will be able to say how and why a character was born in his fantasy? The mystery of artistic creation is the same as that of birth. A woman who loves may desire to become a mother; but the desire by itself, however intense, cannot suffice. One fine day she will find herself a mother without having any precise intimation when it began. In the same way an artist imbibes very many germs of life and can never say how and why, at a certain moment, one of these vital germs inserts itself into his fantasy, there to become a living creature on a plane of life superior to the changeable existence of every day.

I can only say that, without having made any effort to seek them out, I found before me, alive—you could touch them and even hear them breathe—the six characters now seen on the stage. And they stayed there in my presence, each with his secret torment and all bound together by the one common origin and mutual entanglement of their affairs, while I had them enter the world of art, constructing from their persons, their passions, and their adventures a novel, a drama, or at least a story.

Born alive, they wished to live.

To me it was never enough to present a man or a woman and what is special and characteristic about them simply for the pleasure of presenting them; to narrate a particular affair, lively or sad, simply for the pleasure of narrating it; to describe a landscape simply for the pleasure of describing it.

There are some writers (and not a few) who do feel this pleasure and, satisfied, ask no more. They are, to speak more precisely, historical writers.

But there are others who, beyond such pleasure, feel a more profound spiritual need on whose account they admit only figures, affairs, landscapes which have been soaked, so to speak, in a particular sense of life and acquire from it a universal value. These are, more precisely, philosophical writers.

I have the misfortune to belong to these last.

I hate symbolic art in which the presentation loses all spontaneous movement in order to become a machine, an allegory—a vain and misconceived effort because the very fact of giving an allegorical sense to a presentation clearly shows that we have to do with a fable which by itself has no truth either fantastic or direct; it was made for the demonstration of some moral truth. The spiritual need I speak of cannot be satisfied—or seldom, and that to the end of a superior irony, as for example in Ariosto—by such allegorical symbolism. This latter starts from a concept, and from a concept which creates or tries to create for itself an image. The former, on the other hand, seeks in the image—which must remain alive and free throughout—a meaning to give it value.

Now, however much I sought, I did not succeed in uncovering this meaning in the six characters. And I concluded therefore that it was no use making them live.

I thought to myself: "I have already afflicted my readers with hundreds and hundreds of stories. Why should I afflict them now by narrating the sad entanglements of these six unfortunates?"

And, thinking thus, I put them away from me. Or rather I did all I could to put them away.

But one doesn't give life to a character for nothing.

Creatures of my spirit, these six were already living a life which was their own and not mine any more, a life which it was not in my power any more to deny them.

Thus it is that while I persisted in desiring to drive them out of my spirit, they, as if completely detached from every narrative support, characters from a novel miraculously emerging from the pages of the book that contained them, went on living on their own, choosing certain moments of the day to reappear before me in the solitude of my study and coming—now one, now the other, now two together—to tempt me, to propose that I present or describe this scene or that, to explain the effects that could be secured with them, the new interest which a certain unusual situation could provide, and so forth.

For a moment I let myself be won over. And this condescension of mine, thus letting myself go for a while, was enough, because they drew from it a new increment of life, a greater degree of clarity and addition, consequently a greater degree of persuasive power over me. And thus as it became gradually harder and harder for me to go back and free myself from them, it became easier and easier for them to come back and tempt me. At a certain point I actually became obsessed with them. Until, all of a sudden, a way out of the difficulty flashed upon me.

"Why not," I said to myself, "present this highly strange fact of an author who refuses to let some of his characters live though they have been born in his fantasy, and the fact that these characters, having by now life in their veins, do not resign themselves to remaining excluded from the world of art? They are detached from me; live on their own; have acquired voice and movement; have by themselves—in this struggle for existence that they have had to wage with me—become dramatic characters, characters that can move and talk on their own initiative; already see themselves as such; have learned to defend themselves against me; will even know how to defend themselves against others. And so let them go where dramatic characters do go to have life: on a stage. And let us see what will happen."

That's what I did. And, naturally, the result was what it had to be: a mixture of tragic and comic, fantastic and realistic, in a humorous situation that was quite new and infinitely complex, a drama which is conveyed by means of the characters, who carry it within them and suffer it, a drama, breathing, speaking, self-propelled, which seeks at all costs to find the means of its own presentation; and the comedy of the vain attempt at an improvised realization of the drama on stage. First, the surprise of the poor actors in a theatrical company rehearsing a play by day on a bare stage (no scenery, no flats). Surprise and incredulity at the sight of the six characters announcing themselves as such in search of an author. Then, immediately afterward, through that sudden fainting fit of the Mother veiled in black, their instinctive interest in the drama of which they catch a glimpse in her and in the other members of the strange family, an obscure, ambiguous drama, coming about so unexpectedly on a stage that is empty and unprepared to receive it. And gradually the growth of this interest to the bursting forth of the contrasting passions of Father, of Stepdaughter, of Son, of that poor Mother, passions seeking, as I said, to overwhelm each other with a tragic, lacerating fury.

And here is the universal meaning at first vainly sought in the six characters, now that, going on stage of their own accord, they succeed in finding it within themselves in the excitement of the desperate struggle which each wages against the other and all wage against the Manager and the actors, who do not understand them.

Without wanting to, without knowing it, in the strife of their bedeviled souls, each of them, defending himself against the accusations of the others, expresses as his own living passion and torment the passion and torment which for so many years have been the pangs of my spirit: the deceit of mutual understanding irremediably founded on the empty abstraction of the words, the multiple personality of everyone corresponding to the possibilities of being to be found in each of us, and finally the inherent tragic conflict between life (which is always moving and changing) and form (which fixes it, immutable).

Two above all among the six characters, the Father and the Stepdaughter, speak of that outrageous, unalterable fixity of their form in which he and she see their essential nature expressed permanently and immutably, a nature that for one means punishment and for the other revenge; and they defend it against the factitious affectations and unaware volatility of the actors, and they try to impose it on the vulgar Manager who would like to change it and adapt it to the so-called exigencies of the theatre.

If the six characters don't all seem to exist on the same plane, it is not because some are figures of first rank and others of the second, that is, some are main characters and others minor ones—the elementary perspective necessary to all scenic or narrative art—nor is it that any are not completely created—for their purpose. They are all six at the same point of artistic realization and on the same level of reality, which is the fantastic level of the whole play. Except that the Father, the Stepdaughter, and also the Son are realized as mind; the Mother as nature; the Boy as a presence watching and performing a gesture and the Baby unaware of it all. This fact creates among them a perspective of a new sort. Unconsciously I had had the impression that some of them needed to be fully realized (artistically speaking), others less so, and others merely sketched in as elements in a narrative or presentational sequence: the most alive, the most completely created, are the Father and the Stepdaughter who naturally stand out more and lead the way, dragging themselves along beside the almost dead weight of the others—first, the Son, holding back; second, the Mother, like a victim resigned to her fate, between the two children who have hardly any substance beyond their appearance and who need to be led by the hand.

And actually! actually they had each to appear in that stage of creation which they had attained in the author's fantasy at the moment when he wished to drive them away.

If I now think about these things, about having intuited that necessity, having unconsciously found the way to resolve it by means of a new perspective, and about the way in which I actually obtained it, they seem like miracles. The fact is that the play was really conceived in one of those spontaneous illuminations of the fantasy when by a miracle all the elements of the mind answer to each other's call and work in divine accord. No human brain, working "in the cold," however stirred up it might be, could ever have succeeded in penetrating far enough, could ever have been in a position to satisfy all the exigencies of the play's form. Therefore the reasons which I will give to clarify the values of the play must not be thought of as intentions that I conceived beforehand when I prepared myself for the job and which I now undertake to defend, but only as discoveries which I have been able to make afterward in tranquillity.

I wanted to present six characters seeking an author. Their play does not manage to get presented—precisely because the author whom they seek is missing. Instead is presented the comedy of their vain attempt with all that it contains of tragedy by virtue of the fact that the six characters have been rejected.

But can one present a character while rejecting him? Obviously, to present him one needs, on the contrary, to receive him into one's fantasy before one can express him. And I have actually accepted and realized the six characters: I have, however, accepted and realized them as rejected: in search of *another* author.

What have I rejected of them? Not themselves, obviously, but their drama, which doubtless is what interests them above all but which did not interest me—for the reasons already indicated.

And what is it, for a character—his drama?

Every creature of fantasy and art, in order to exist, must have his drama, that is, a drama in which he may be a character and for which he *is* a character. This drama is the characters *raison d'être,* his vital function, necessary for his existence.

In these six, then, I have accepted the "being" without the reason for being. I have taken the organism and entrusted to it, not its own proper function, but another more complex function into which its own function entered, if at all, only as a datum. A terrible and desperate situation especially for the two—Father and Stepdaughter—who more than the others crave life and more than the others feel themselves to be characters, that is, absolutely need a drama and therefore their own drama—the only one which they can envisage for themselves yet which meantime they see rejected: an "impossible" situation from which they feel they must escape at whatever cost; it is a matter of life and death. True, I have given them another *raison d'être,* another function: precisely that "impossible" situation, the drama of being in search of an author and rejected. But that this should be a *raison d'être*, that it should have become their real function, that it should be necessary, that it should suffice, they can hardly suppose; for they have a life of their own. If someone were to tell them, they wouldn't believe him. It is not possible to believe that the sole reason for our living should lie in a torment that seems to us unjust and inexplicable.

I cannot imagine, therefore, why the charge was brought against me that the character of the Father was not what it should have been because it stepped out of its quality and position as a character and invaded at times the author's province and took it over. I who understand those who don't quite understand me see that the charge derives from the fact that the character expresses and makes his own a torment of spirit which is recognized as mine. Which is entirely natural and of absolutely no significance. Aside from the fact that this torment of spirit in the character of the Father derives from causes, and is suffered and lived for reasons that have nothing to do with the drama of my personal experience, a fact which alone removes all substance from the criticism, I want to make it clear that the inherent torment of my spirit is one thing, a torment which I can legitimately—provided that it be organic—reflect in a character, and that the activity of my spirit as revealed in the realized work, the activity that succeeds in forming a drama out of the six characters in search of an author is another thing. If the Father participated in this latter activity, if he competed in forming the drama of the six characters without an author, then and only then would it by all means be justified to say that he was at times the author himself and therefore not the man he should be. But the Father suffers and does not create his existence as a character in search of an author. He suffers it as an inexplicable fatality and as a situation which he tries with all his powers to rebel against, which he tries to remedy; hence it is that he is a character in search of an author and nothing more, even if he expresses as his own the torment of my spirit. If he, so to speak, assumed some of the author's responsibilities, the fatality would be completely explained. He would, that is to say, see himself accepted, if only as a rejected character, accepted in the poet's heart of hearts, and he would no longer have any reason to suffer the despair of not finding someone to construct and affirm his life as a character. I mean that he would quite willingly accept the *raison d'être* which the author gives him and without regrets would forgo his own, throwing over the Manager and the actors to whom in fact he runs as his only recourse.

There is one character, that of the Mother, who on the other hand does not care about being alive (considering being alive as an end in itself). She hasn't the least suspicion that she is *not* alive. It has never occurred to ask how and why and in what manner she lives. In short, she is not aware of being a character inasmuch as she is never, even for a moment, detached from her role. She doesn't know she has a role.

This makes her perfectly organic. Indeed, her role of Mother does not of itself, in its natural essence, embrace mental activity. And she does not exist as a mind. She lives in an endless continuum of feeling, and therefore she cannot acquire existence as a character. But with all this, even she, in her own way and for her own ends, seeks an author, and at a certain stage seems happy to have been brought before the Manager. Because she hopes to take life from him, perhaps? No: because she hopes the Manager will have her present a scene with the Son in which she would put so much of her own life. But it is a scene which does not exist, which never has and never could take place. So unaware is she of being a character, that is, of the life that is possible to her, all fixed and determined, moment by moment, in every action, every phrase.

She appears on stage with the other characters but without understanding what the others make her do. Obviously, she imagines that the itch for life with which the husband and the daughter are afflicted and for which she herself is to be found on stage is no more than one of the usual incomprehensible extravagances of this man who is both tortured and torturer and—horrible, most horrible—a new equivocal rebellion on the part of that poor erring girl. The Mother is completely passive. The events of her own life and the values they assume in her eyes, her very character, are all things which are "said" by the others and which she only once contradicts, and that because the maternal instinct rises up and rebels within her to make it clear that she didn't at all wish to abandon either the son or the husband: the Son was taken from her and the husband forced her to abandon him. She is only correcting data; she explains and knows nothing.

In short, she is nature. Nature fixed in the figure of a mother.

This character gave me a satisfaction of a new sort, not to be ignored. Nearly all my critics, instead of defining her, after their habit, as "unhuman"—which seems to be the peculiar and incorrigible characteristic of all my creatures without exception—had the goodness to note "with real pleasure" that at last a *very human* figure had emerged from my fantasy. I explain this praise to myself in the following way: since my poor Mother is entirely limited to the natural attitude of a Mother with no possibility of free mental activity, being, that is, little more than a lump of flesh completely alive in all its functions—procreation, lactation, caring for and loving its young—without any need therefore of exercising her brain, she realizes in her person the true and complete "human type." That must be how it is, since in a human organism nothing seems more superfluous than the mind.

But the critics have tried to get rid of the Mother with this praise without bothering to penetrate the nucleus of poetic values which the character in the play represents. A very human figure, certainly, because mindless, that is, unaware of being what she is or not caring to explain it to herself. But now knowing that she is a character doesn't prevent her from being one. That is her drama in my play. And the most living expression of it comes spurting out in her cry to the Manager, who wants her to think all these things have happened already and therefore cannot now be a reason for renewed lamentations: "No, it's happening now, it's happening always! My torture is not a pretense, signore! I am alive and present, always, in every moment of my torture: it is renewed, alive, and present always!" This she *feels*, without being conscious of it, and feels it therefore as something inexplicable: but she feels it so terribly that she doesn't think it *can* be something to explain either to herself or to others. She feels it and that is that. She feels it as pain and this pain is immediate; she cries it out. Thus she reflects the growing fixity of life in a form—the same thing, which in another way, tortures the Father and the Stepdaughter. In them, mind. In her, nature. The mind rebels and, as best it may, seeks an advantage; nature, if not aroused by sensory stimuli, weeps.

Conflict between life-in-movement and form is the inexorable condition not only of the mental but also of the physical order. The life which in order to exist has become fixed in our corporeal form little by little kills that form. The tears of a nature thus fixed lament the irreparable, continuous aging of our bodies. Hence the tears of the Mother are passive and perpetual. Revealed in three faces, made significant in three distinct and simultaneous dramas, this inherent conflict finds in the play its most complete expression. More: the Mother declares also the particular value of artistic form—a form which does not delimit or destroy its own life and which life does not consume—in her cry to the Manager. If the Father and Stepdaughter began their scene a hundred thousand times in succession, always, at the appointed moment, at the instant when the life of the work of art must be expressed with that cry, it would always be heard, unaltered and unalterable in its form, not as a mechanical repetition, not as a return determined by external necessities, but, on the contrary, alive every time and as new, suddenly born *thus forever!* embalmed alive in its incorruptible form. Hence, always, as we open the book, we shall find Francesca alive and confessing to Dante her sweet sin, and if we turn to the passage a hundred thousand times in succession, Francesca will speak her words, never repeating them mechanically, but saying them as though each time were the first time with such living and sudden passion that Dante every time will turn faint. All that lives, by the fact of living, has a form, and by the same token must die—except the work of art which lives forever in so far as it *is* form.

The birth of a creature of human fantasy, a birth which is a step across the threshold between nothing and eternity, can also happen suddenly, occasioned by some necessity. An imagined drama needs a character who does or says a certain necessary thing; accordingly this character is born and is precisely what he had to be. In this way Madame Pace is born among the six characters and seems a miracle, even a trick, realistically portrayed on the stage. It is no trick. The birth is real. The new character is alive not because she was alive already but because she is now happily born as is required by the fact of her being a character—she is obliged to be as she is. There is a break here, a sudden change in the level of reality of the scene, because a character can be born in this way only in the poet's fancy and not on the boards of a stage. Without anyone's noticing it, I have all of a sudden changed the scene: I have gathered it up again into my own fantasy without removing it from the spectator's eyes. That is, I have shown them, instead of the stage, my own fantasy in the act of creating—my own fantasy in the form of this same stage. The sudden and uncontrollable changing of a visual phenomenon from one level of reality to another is a miracle comparable to those of the saint who sets his own statue in motion: it is neither wood nor stone at such a moment. But the miracle is not arbitrary. The stage—a stage which accepts the fantastic reality of the six characters—is no fixed, immutable datum. Nothing in this play exists as given and preconceived. Everything is in the making, is in motion, is a sudden experiment: even the place in which this unformed life, reaching after its own form, changes and changes again, contrives to shift position organically. The level of reality changes. When I had the idea of bringing Madame Pace to birth right there on the stage, I felt I could do it and I did it. Had I noticed that this birth was unhinging and silently, unnoticed, in a second, giving another shape, another reality to my scene, I certainly wouldn't have brought it about. I would have been afraid of the apparent lack of logic. And I would have committed an ill-omened assault on the beauty of my work. The fervor of my mind saved me from doing so. For, despite appearances, with their specious logic, this fantastic birth is sustained by a real necessity in mysterious, organic relation with the whole life of the work.

That someone now tells me it hasn't all the value it could have because its expression is not constructed but chaotic, because it smacks of romanticism, makes me smile.

I understand why this observation was made to me: because in this work of mine the presentation of the drama in which the six characters are involved appears tumultuous and never proceeds in an orderly manner. There is no logical development, no concatenation of the events. Very true. Had I hunted it with a lamp I couldn't have found a more disordered, crazy, arbitrary, complicated, in short, romantic way of presenting "the drama in which the six characters are involved." Very true. But I have not presented that drama. I have presented another—and I won't undertake to say again what!—in which, among the many fine things that everyone, according to his tastes, can find, there is a discreet satire on romantic procedures: in the six characters thus excited to the point where they stifle themselves in the roles which each of them plays in a certain drama while I present them as characters in another play which they don't know and don't suspect the existence of, so that this inflammation of their passions—which belongs to the realm of romantic procedures—is humorously "placed," located in the void. And the drama of the six characters presented not as it would have been organized by my fantasy had it been accepted but in this way, as a rejected drama, could not exist in the work except as a "situation," with some little development, and could not come out except in indications, stormily, disorderedly, in violent foreshortenings, in a chaotic manner: continually interrupted, sidetracked, contradicted (by one of its characters), denied, and (by two others) not even seen.

There is a character indeed—he who denies the drama which makes him a character, the Son—who draws all his importance and value from being a character not of the comedy in the making—which as such hardly appears—but from the presentation that I made of it. In short, he is the only one who lives solely as "a character in search of an author"—inasmuch as the author he seeks is not a dramatic author. Even this could not be otherwise. The character's attitude is an organic product of my conception, and it is logical that in the situation it should produce greater confusion and disorder and another element of romantic contrast.

But I had precisely to *present* this organic and natural chaos. And to present a chaos is not at all to present chaotically, that is, romantically. That my presentation is the reverse of confused, that it is quite simple, clear, and orderly, is proved by the clarity which the intrigue, the characters, the fantastic and realistic, dramatic and comic levels of the work have had for every public in the world and by the way in which, for those with more searching vision, the unusual values enclosed within it come out.

Great is the confusion of tongues among men if criticisms thus made find words for their expression. No less great than this confusion is the intimate law of order which, obeyed in all points, makes this work of mine classical and typical and at its catastrophic close forbids the use of words. Though the audience eventually understands that one does not create life by artifice and that the drama of the six characters cannot be presented without an author to give them value with his spirit, the Manager remains vulgarly anxious to know how the thing turned out, and the "ending" is remembered by the Son in its sequence of actual moments, but without any sense and therefore not needing a human voice for its expression. It happens stupidly, uselessly, with the going off of a mechanical weapon on stage. It breaks up and disperses the sterile experiment of the characters and the actors, which has apparently been made without the assistance of the poet.

The poet, unknown to them, as if looking on at a distance during the whole period of the experiment, was at the same time busy creating—with it and of it—his own play.

bertolt brecht 1898–1956

the caucasian chalk circle

translated by Eric Bentley and Maja Apelman

Brecht was born in Augsburg, Germany, the son of a factory manager. At Berlin and Munich he studied natural science and medicine, but Brecht's true interest lay in literature and theater. Early in adult life he developed antipathy for militarism; he joined radical groups and earned the enmity of the military and Fascist elements in Germany. For a while Brecht supported himself by singing in cabarets, but in 1922 he succeeded in the theater with his play *Drums in the Night.* He soon formed one of the outstanding acting troupes in Europe and developed his theory of "epic theatre." Brecht's use of naked staging, narrators, pantomime, songs, film projections, captions, etc., was intended to keep the audience aware that they were in a theater, not participating in real life, and so compel them to a critical rather than a blindly emotional response. In 1928 Brecht triumphed with *The Three Penny Opera,* with music by Kurt Weill. Other plays with a radical Marxist view followed. With Hitler's rise to power, Brecht was forced into exile; he lived in France, Norway, the Soviet Union, and the United States. During this period Brecht wrote some of his best plays: *Mother Courage* (1939), *Galileo* (1939), *The Good Woman of Setzuan* (1940), and *Herr Puntila and His Servant Matti* (1941). To the end, Brecht was anti-bourgeois and revolutionary. He settled in East Berlin after the war and directed his famous Berliner Ensemble. His last major play was *The Caucasian Chalk Circle* (1945), a parable of justice and true belonging.

the characters

OLD MAN *on the right*
PEASANT WOMAN *on the right*
YOUNG PEASANT
A VERY YOUNG WORKER
OLD MAN *on the left*
PEASANT WOMAN *on the left*
AGRICULTURALIST KATO
GIRL TRACTORIST
WOUNDED SOLDIER
THE DELEGATE *from the capital*
THE STORY TELLER
GEORGI ABASHWILI, *the* GOVERNOR
NATELLA, *the* GOVERNOR'S WIFE

MICHAEL, *their son*
SHALVA, *an Adjutant*
ARSEN KAZBEKI, *a fat prince*
MESSENGER, *from the capital*
NIKO MIKADZE *and* MIKA LOLADZE, *doctors*
SIMON SHASHAVA, *a soldier*
GRUSHA VASHNADZE, *a kitchen maid*
OLD PEASANT *with the milk*
CORPORAL *and* PRIVATE
PEASANT *and* HIS WIFE
LAVRENTI VASHNADZE, GRUSHA'S *brother*
ANIKO, *his wife*
PEASANT WOMAN, *for a while* GRUSHA'S *mother-in-law*
JUSSUP, *her son*
MONK
AZDAK, *village recorder*
SHAUWA, *a policeman*
GRAND DUKE
DOCTOR
INVALID
LIMPING MAN
BLACKMAILER
LUDOVICA
INNKEEPER, *her father-in-law*
STABLEBOY
POOR OLD PEASANT WOMAN
IRAKLI, *her brother-in-law, a bandit*
THREE WEALTHY FARMERS
ILLO SHUBOLADZE *and* SANDRO OBOLADZE, *lawyers*
OLD MARRIED COUPLE

SOLDIERS, SERVANTS, PEASANTS, BEGGARS, MUSICIANS, MERCHANTS, NOBLES, ARCHITECTS

THE JUDGE Officer, fetch a piece of chalk. You will trace below the bench a circle, in the center of which you will place the young child. Then you will order the two women to wait, each of them at opposite sides of the circle. When the real mother takes hold of him, it will be easy for the child to come outside the circle. But the pretended mother cannot lead him out.
(The officer traces a circle with the chalk and motions the child to stand in the center of it. MRS. MA *takes the child's hand and leads him out of the circle.* HAI-TANG *fails to contend with her.)*

THE JUDGE It is evident that Hai-Tang is not the mother of the child, since she did not come forward to draw him out of the circle.

HAI-TANG I supplicate you, Honored Sir, to calm your wrath. If I cannot obtain my son without dislocating his arm or bruising his baby flesh, I would rather perish under the blows than make the least effort to take him out of the circle.

THE JUDGE A sage of old once said: What man can hide what he really is? Behold the power of the Chalk Circle! In order to seize an inheritance, Mrs. Ma has raised a young child that is not her own. But the Chalk Circle augustly brought out the truth and the falsehood. Mrs. Ma has an engaging exterior but her heart is corrupt. The true mother—Hai-Tang—is at last recognized.

From *The Chalk Circle,* an anonymous Chinese play of about 1300 A.D.

prologue

(Among the ruins of a shattered Caucasian village the members of two Kolkhoz villages, mostly women and older men, are sitting in a circle, smoking and drinking wine. With them is a delegate of the State Reconstruction Commission from the capital.)

PEASANT WOMAN, *left (pointing)* In those hills over there we stopped three Nazi tanks, but the apple orchard was already destroyed.

OLD MAN, *right* Our beautiful dairy farm, too: all in ruins.

GIRL TRACTORIST I laid the fire, Comrade.
(pause)

THE DELEGATE Now listen to the Report. Delegates of the goatbreeding Kolkhoz "Galinsk" have been to Nuka. When Hitler's armies approached, the Kolkhoz moved its goat-herds on orders from the authorities, further east. They are now thinking of returning. Their delegates have investigated the village and grounds and found a lot of it destroyed. *(Delegates on right nod.)* The neighboring fruit-culture Kolkhoz *(to the left)* "Rosa Luxemburg" brings forward a motion to use the former grazing land of Kolkhoz "Galinsk," a valley with scanty growth of grass, for orchards and vineyards. As a delegate of the Reconstruction Commission, I request the two Kolkhoz villages to decide between themselves whether Kolkhoz "Galinsk" shall return here or not.

OLD MAN, *right* First of all, I want to protest against the restriction of time for discussion. We of Kolkhoz "Galinsk" have spent three days and three nights getting here. And now discussion is limited to half a day.

WOUNDED SOLDIER, *left* Comrade, we haven't as many villages as we used to have. We haven't as many hands. We haven't as much time.

GIRL TRACTORIST All pleasures have to be rationed. Tobacco is rationed, and wine: and now discussion should be.

OLD MAN, *right (sighing)* Death to the fascists! But I will come to the point and explain to you why we want to have our valley back. There are a great many reasons, but I want to begin with one of the simplest. Makinä Abakidze, unpack the goat cheese. *(A peasant woman from right takes from a basket an enormous cheese wrapped in a cloth. Applause and laughter.)* Help yourselves, Comrades, start in!

OLD MAN, *left (suspiciously)* Is this a way of influencing us?

OLD MAN, *right (amid laughter)* How could it be a way of influencing you,

Surab, you valley-thief? Everyone knows that you will take the cheese and the valley, too. *(laughter)* All I expect from you is an honest answer: Do you like the cheese?

OLD MAN, *left* The answer is: yes.

OLD MAN, *right* Really. *(bitterly)* I ought to have known you know nothing about cheese.

OLD MAN, *left* Why not? When I tell you I like it.

OLD MAN, *right* Because you can't like it. Because it's not what it was in the old days. And why not? Because our goats don't like the new grass as they used to like the old. Cheese is not cheese because grass is not grass, that's the thing. Please put that in your report.

OLD MAN, *left* But your cheese is excellent.

OLD MAN, *right* It isn't excellent. It's just passable. The new grazing land is no good, whatever the young people may say. One can't live there. It doesn't even smell of morning in the morning. *(Several people laugh.)*

THE DELEGATE Don't mind their laughing: they understand you. Comrades, why does one love one's country? Because the bread tastes better there, the air smells better, voices sound stronger, the sky is higher, the ground is easier to walk on. Isn't that so?

OLD MAN, *right* The valley has belonged to us from all eternity.

SOLDIER, *left* What's that mean—from all eternity? Nothing belongs to anyone from all eternity. When you were young you didn't even belong to yourself, but to the Kazbeki princes.

OLD MAN, *right* Doesn't it make a difference maybe what kind of trees stand next to the house you are born in? Or what kind of neighbor you have? Doesn't that make a difference? We want to go back just to have you near our Kolkhoz, you valley-thief. Now you can all laugh again.

OLD MAN, *left (laughing)* Then why don't you listen to what your neighbor, Kato Wachtang, our agriculturist, has to say about the valley?

PEASANT WOMAN, *right* We've by no means said everything there is to be said about our valley. Not all the houses are destroyed. As for the dairy farm, at least the foundation wall is still standing.

DELEGATE You can claim State support—here and there—you know that. I have suggestions here in my pocket.

PEASANT WOMAN, *right* Comrade Specialist, we haven't come here to bargain. I can't take your cap and hand you another, and say: "This one's better." The other one might be better, but you like yours better.

GIRL TRACTORIST A piece of land is not like a cap—not in our country, Comrade.

DELEGATE Don't get angry. It's true that we have to consider a piece of land as a tool to produce something useful with, but it's also true that we must recognize the love for a particular piece of land. As far as I'm concerned, I'd like to find out more exactly what you *(to those on the left)* want to do with the valley.

OTHERS Yes, let Kato speak.

DELEGATE Comrade Agriculturist!

KATO *(rising; she's in military uniform)* Comrades, last winter, while we were fighting in these hills here as Partisans, we discussed how, after the expulsion of the Germans, we could build up our fruit culture to ten times it original size. I've prepared a plan for an irrigation project. By means of a cofferdam on our mountain lake, 300 hectares of unfertile land can be irrigated. Our Kolkhoz could then not only cultivate more fruit, but also have vineyards. The project, however, would pay only if the disputed valley of Kolkhoz "Galinsk" were also included. Here are the calculations. *(She hands the delegate a briefcase.)*

OLD MAN, *right* Write into the report that our Kolkhoz plans to start a new stud farm.

GIRL TRACTORIST Comrades, the project was conceived during days and nights when we had to take cover in the mountains and were often without ammunition for our half-dozen rifles. Even to get a pencil was difficult. *(Applause from both sides.)*

OLD MAN, *right* Our thanks to the Comrades of Kolkhoz "Rosa Luxemburg" and to all who have defended our country! *(They shake hands and embrace.)*

PEASANT WOMAN, *left* In doing this our thought was that our soldiers—both your men and our men—should return to a still more productive homeland.

GIRL TRACTORIST As the poet Mayakovski said: "The home of the Soviet people shall also be the home of Reason"! *(The delegates including the* OLD MAN *on right have got up, and with the delegate specified, proceed to study the agriculturist's drawings. Exclamations such as: "Why is the altitude of fall 22 meters?"—"This rock here must be blown up"—"Actually, all they need is cement and dynamite"—"They force the water to come down here, that's clever!")*

A VERY YOUNG WORKER, *right (to* OLD MAN, *right)* They're going to irrigate all the fields between the hills, look at that, Aleko!

OLD MAN, *right* I'm not going to look. I knew the project would be good. I won't have a revolver pointed at my chest.

DELEGATE But they only want to point a pencil at your chest. *(laughter)*

OLD MAN, *right (gets up gloomily, and walks over to look at the drawings)* These valley-thieves know only too well that we can't resist machines and projects in this country.

PEASANT WOMAN, *right* Aleko Bereshwili, you yourself are the worst one with new projects. That's well known.

DELEGATE What about my report? May I write that you will support at your Kolkhoz the cession of your old valley for this project?

PEASANT WOMAN, *right* I will support it. What about you, Aleko?

OLD MAN, *right (bent over drawings)* I suggest that you give us copies of the drawings to take along.

PEASANT WOMAN, *right* Then we can sit down to eat. Once he has the drawings and is ready to discuss them, the affair is settled. I know him. And it will be the same with the rest of us.
(Delegates laughingly embrace again.)

OLD MAN, *left* Comrades, in honor of the visit of the delegates from Kolkhoz "Galinsk," and of the Specialist, we have arranged, with the collaboration of the Story Teller Arkadi Tscheidse, to produce a play which has a bearing on our problem. *(Applause.* GIRL TRACTORIST *has gone off to bring* THE STORY TELLER.*)*

PEASANT WOMAN, *right* Comrades, your play had better be good. We're going to pay for it with a valley.

PEASANT WOMAN, *left* Arkadi Tscheidse knows 21,000 verses.

OLD MAN, *left* It's very difficult to get him. You and the Planning Commission should see to it that you get him to come North more often, Comrade.

DELEGATE We are more interested in economics.

OLD MAN, *left (smiling)* You arrange the redistribution of vines and tractors, why not of songs?

(Enter THE STORY TELLER *Arkadi Tscheidse, led by* GIRL TRACTORIST. *He is a well-built man of simple manners, accompanied by four musicians with their instruments. The artists are greeted with applause.)*

GIRL TRACTORIST This is the Comrade Specialist, Arkadi.

*(*THE STORY TELLER *greets them all.)*

DELEGATE I'm honored to make your acquaintance. I heard about your songs when I was a boy at school.

THE STORY TELLER This time it's a play with songs, and nearly the whole Kolkhoz takes part. We've brought the old masks along.

DELEGATE Will it be one of the old legends?

THE STORY TELLER A very old one. It's called the "Circle of Chalk" and comes from the Chinese. But we'll do it, of course, in a changed version. Jura, show them the masks.

OLD PEASANT, *right (recognizing one of the masks)* Ah! Prince Kazbeki!

THE STORY TELLER Comrades, it's an honor for me to entertain you after a difficult debate. We hope you will find that the voice of the old poet also sounds well in the shadow of Soviet tractors. It may be a mistake to mix different wines, but old and new wisdom mix admirably. Now I hope we'll get something to eat before the performance begins. That surely helps.

VOICES Certainly! Everyone into the Club House!

(While everyone begins to move, the DELEGATE *turns to the* GIRL TRACTORIST.*)*

DELEGATE How long will the story take, Arkadi? I've got to get back to Tiflis tonight.

THE STORY TELLER *(casually)* It's actually two stories. A few hours.

GIRL TRACTORIST *(confidentially)* Couldn't you make it shorter?

THE STORY TELLER No.

(And they all go happily to eat.)

part I

scene 1

THE NOBLE CHILD

(As the lights go up, THE STORY TELLER *is seen sitting on the floor, a black sheepskin cloak round his shoulders, and a little, well-thumbed notebook*

in his hand. A small group of listeners—the chorus—sits with him. The manner of his recitation makes it clear that he has told this story over and over again. He mechanically fingers the pages, seldom looking at them. With appropriate gestures, he gives the signal for each scene to begin.)

THE STORY TELLER
In olden times, in a bloody time,
There ruled in a Caucasian city—
Men called it the City of the Damned—
A governor.
His name was Georgi Abashwili.
He was rich as Croesus
He had a beautiful wife
He had a healthy child.
No other governor in Grusinia
Had so many horses in his stable
So many beggars on his doorstep
So many soldiers in his service
So many petitioners in his courtyard.
Georgi Abashwili—how shall I describe him?
He enjoyed his life.
On the morning of Easter Sunday
The Governor and his family went to church.
(At the left a large doorway, at the right an even larger gateway. Beggars and petitioners pour from the gateway, holding up thin children, crutches, and petitions. They are followed by two IRONSHIRTS, *and then, expensively dressed,* THE GOVERNOR'S *family.)*

BEGGARS AND PETITIONERS Mercy! Mercy, Your Grace! The taxes are way up, we can't pay!
—I lost my leg in the Persian War, where can I get . . .
—My brother is innocent, Your Grace, there's been a misunderstanding . . .
—The child is starving in my arms!
—Our petition is for our son's discharge from the army, our last remaining son!
—Please, Your Grace, the water inspector takes bribes.
(One servant collects the petitions, another distributes coins from a purse. Soldiers push the crowd back, lashing at them with thick leather whips.)

THE SOLDIER Get back! Clear the church door!
(Behind THE GOVERNOR, *his* WIFE, *and* THE ADJUTANT, THE GOVERNOR'S CHILD *is brought through the gateway in an ornate carriage.)*

THE CROWD The child!
—I can't see it, don't shove so hard!
—God bless the child, Your Grace!

THE STORY TELLER *(while the crowd is driven back with whips)*
For the first time on that Easter Sunday, the people saw the Governor's

heir.
Two doctors never moved from the noble child, apple of the Governor's eye.
Even the mighty Prince Kazbeki bows before it at the church door.
(A FAT PRINCE *steps forward and greets the family.)*

THE FAT PRINCE Happy Easter, Natella Abashwili! A magnificent day! When it was raining in the night, I thought to myself: gloomy holidays! But this morning I said to myself: the sky is gay! I love a gay sky, a simple heart, Natella Abashwili. And little Michael is a governor from head to foot! Tititi! *(He tickles the child.)*

THE GOVERNOR'S WIFE What do you think of this, Arsen? At last Georgi has decided to start building the wing on the east side. All those wretched slums are to be torn down to make room for a garden.

THE FAT PRINCE That's good news after so much bad! What's the latest about the war, Brother Georgi? *(*THE GOVERNOR *indicates a lack of interest.)* A strategical retreat, I hear. Well, minor reverses are to be expected. Sometimes things go well, sometimes not. Such is war! What difference does it make?

THE GOVERNOR'S WIFE He's coughing. Georgi, did you hear? *(She speaks sharply to the* DOCTORS, *two dignified men standing close to the little carriage.)* He's coughing!

THE FIRST DOCTOR *(to the second)* May I remind you, Niko Mikadze, that I was against the lukewarm bath? *(To* THE GOVERNOR'S WIFE*)* There's been a little error over warming the bath water, Your Grace.

THE SECOND DOCTOR *(equally polite)* Mika Loladze, I can't possibly agree with you. The temperature of the bath water was the one prescribed by our great, beloved Mishiko Oboladze. It was more likely a slight draft during the night, Your Grace.

THE GOVERNOR'S WIFE But do pay more attention to him. He looks feverish, Georgi.

THE FIRST DOCTOR *(bending over the child)* No cause for alarm, Your Grace. The bath water will be warmer. It won't occur again.

THE SECOND DOCTOR *(with a venomous glance at the first)* I won't forget that, my dear Mika Loladze. No cause for concern, Your Grace.

THE FAT PRINCE Well, well, well! I always say: One pain in my liver and the doctor get fifty strokes on the soles of his feet. That's because we are living in a decadent age. In the old days one simply said: Off with his head!

THE GOVERNOR'S WIFE Let's go into the church. Very likely it's the draft here. *(The procession of family and servants turns into the doorway.* THE FAT PRINCE *follows, but* THE GOVERNOR *is kept back by* THE ADJUTANT, *a handsome young man. When the crowd of petitioners has been driven off, a young dust-stained rider, his arm in a sling, remains behind.)*

THE ADJUTANT *(pointing at the rider, who steps forward)* Won't you listen to the messenger from the capital, Your Excellency? He arrived this morning. With confidential papers.

THE GOVERNOR Not before Service, Shalva. But did you hear Brother

Kazbeki bid me a happy Easter? That's all very well, but so far as I know, it didn't rain here last night.

THE ADJUTANT *(nodding)* That will have to be gone into.

THE GOVERNOR Yes, at once. Tomorrow.

*(They pass through the doorway. The rider, who has waited in vain for an audience, turns sharply round and, muttering a curse, goes off. Only one of the Palace Guards—*SIMON SHASHAVA*—remains at the door.)*

THE STORY TELLER

On the church square, pigeons are strutting.
The city is still.
A soldier of the Palace Guard
Is joking with a kitchen maid
As she comes up from the river with a bundle.

*(A girl—*GRUSHA VASHNADZE*—comes through the gateway with a bundle made of large green leaves under her arm.)*

SIMON What, the young lady is not in church? Shirking?

GRUSHA I was dressed to go. But they needed another goose for the banquet. And they asked me to go and get it. I know a thing or two about geese.

SIMON A goose? *(He feigns suspicion.)* I'd like to see that goose. (GRUSHA *does not understand.)* One has to be on one's guard with women. "I only went for a fish," they tell you, and then it turns out to be something else.

GRUSHA *(walking resolutely toward him and showing him the goose)* There! And if it isn't a fifteen-pound goose stuffed full of corn, I'll eat the feathers.

SIMON A queen of a goose. The Governor himself will eat it. So the young lady has been down to the river again?

GRUSHA Yes, at the poultry farm.

SIMON Really? At the poultry farm, down by the river . . . not higher up maybe? Near those willows?

GRUSHA I only go to the willows to wash the linen.

SIMON *(insinuatingly)* Exactly.

GRUSHA Exactly what?

SIMON *(winking)* Exactly that.

GRUSHA Why shouldn't I wash the linen by the willows?

SIMON *(with exaggerated laughter)* Why shouldn't I wash the linen by the willows! That's good, really good!

GRUSHA I don't understand the soldier. What's so good about it?

SIMON *(slyly)* "If something *I* know someone learns, she'll grow hot and cold by turns!"

GRUSHA I don't know what I *could* learn about those willows.

SIMON Not even if there were a bush opposite? And everything could be seen from it? Everything that goes on there when a certain person is—er—"washing linen"?

GRUSHA What *is* it that goes on? Won't the soldier say what he means and have done with it?

SIMON Something goes on. And something can be seen.

GRUSHA Could the soldier mean I put my toes in the water? When it was hot once in a while? There was nothing else.

SIMON There were the toes. And more.

GRUSHA More what? At most the foot?

SIMON The foot. And a little more. *(He laughs heartily.)*

GRUSHA *(angrily)* Simon Shashava, you ought to be ashamed of yourself! To sit in a bush on a hot day and wait till someone comes and dips her foot in the river! And I bet you bring a friend along too! *(She runs off.)*

SIMON *(shouting after her)* I didn't bring any friend along!

(As THE STORY TELLER *resumes his tale, the soldier steps into the doorway as though to listen to the service.)*

THE STORY TELLER

The city lies still,
But why are there armed men?
The Governor's palace is at peace.
But why is it a fortress?
And the Governor returned to his palace
And the fortress was a trap
And the goose was plucked and roasted
But the goose was not eaten this time
And noon was no longer the time to eat
Noon was the time to die.

(From the doorway at the left THE FAT PRINCE *quickly appears, stands still, looks around. Before the gateway at the right two* IRONSHIRTS *are squatting and playing dice.* THE FAT PRINCE *sees them, walks slowly past, making a sign to them. They rise: one goes through the gateway, the other goes off at the right. Muffled voices are heard from various directions in the rear:* "To your posts!" *The palace is surrounded.* THE FAT PRINCE *quickly goes off. Church bells in the distance. Enter, through the doorway,* THE GOVERNOR'S *family and procession, returning from church.)*

THE GOVERNOR'S WIFE *(passing* THE ADJUTANT*)* It's impossible to live in this slum. But Georgi, of course, builds only for his little Michael. Never for me. Michael is all! All for Michael!

(The procession turns into the gateway. Again THE ADJUTANT *lingers behind. He waits. Enter the wounded rider from the doorway. Two* IRONSHIRTS *of the Palace Guard have taken up positions by the gateway.)*

THE ADJUTANT *(to the rider)* The Governor doesn't wish to receive military reports before dinner—particularly if they are of a depressing nature, as I assume. In the afternoon His Excellency will devote himself to conferences with prominent architects who are also invited to dinner. Here they are already. *(Enter three gentlemen through the doorway.)* Go to the kitchen and get yourself something to eat, friend. *(As the rider goes,* THE ADJUTANT *greets* THE ARCHITECTS.*)* Gentlemen, His Excellency expects you at dinner. All his time will be devoted to you. To your great new plans! Come, quickly!

ONE OF THE ARCHITECTS We marvel that His Excellency intends to build. There are disquieting rumors abroad that the war in Persia has taken a bad turn.

THE ADJUTANT All the more reason to build! That's nothing, you know. Persia is a long way off. The garrison here would let itself be hacked to bits for its Governor. *(Noise from the palace. The shrill scream of a woman. Someone is shouting orders. Dumbfounded,* THE ADJUTANT *moves toward the gateway. An* IRONSHIRT *steps out, points his lance at him.)* What's going on here? Put down that lance, you dog!

ONE OF THE ARCHITECTS The Princes! Don't you realize that the Princes met last night in the capital? And that they are against the Grand Duke and his Governors? Gentlemen, we'd better make ourselves scarce. *(They rush off.* THE ADJUTANT *remains helplessly behind.)*

THE ADJUTANT *(furiously to the Palace Guard)* Lay down your arms. Don't you realize an attempt is being made on the Governor's life? *(The* IRONSHIRTS *of the Palace Guard refuse to obey. They stare coldly and indifferently at* THE ADJUTANT *and follow the next events without interest.)*

THE STORY TELLER

O blindness of great ones!
They wander like gods,
Great over bent backs,
Sure of hired fists,
Trusting in the power
Which has lasted so long.
But long is not forever.
O change from age to age!
Thou hope of the people!

(Enter THE GOVERNOR, *through the gateway, between two soldiers fully armed. He is in chains. His face is gray.)*

Up, great sir, deign to walk upright!
From your palace the eyes of many foes follow you!
You no longer need an architect, a carpenter will do!
You will not move into a new palace
But into a little hole in the ground.
Look about you once more, blind man!
(The arrested man looks round.)
Does all you had please you?
Between the Easter mass and the Easter meal
You are walking to the place whence no one returns.
*(*THE GOVERNOR *is led off. A horn sounds an alarm. Noise behind the gateway.)*
When the house of a great one collapses
Many little ones are slain.
Those who had no share in the *good* fortunes of the mighty
Often have a share in their *mis*fortunes.
The plunging wagon
Drags the sweating beasts with it
Into the abyss.
*(*THE SERVANTS *come rushing through the gateway in panic.)*

THE SERVANTS *(among themselves)* The baskets!
–Take them all into the third courtyard! Food for five days!
–The mistress has fainted! Someone must carry her down. She must get away.
–What about us? We'll be slaughtered like chickens, that's how it always is.
–Goodness gracious, what'll happen? There's bloodshed already in the city, they say.
–Nonsense, the Governor has just been politely asked to appear at a Princes' meeting. Everything'll be ironed out. I heard this on the best authority . . .
*(*THE TWO DOCTORS *rush into the courtyard.)*

THE FIRST DOCTOR *(trying to restrain the other)* Niko Mikadze, it is your duty as a doctor to attend Natella Abashwili.

THE SECOND DOCTOR My duty! It's yours!

THE FIRST DOCTOR Whose turn is it to look after the child today, Niko Mikadze, yours or mine?

THE SECOND DOCTOR Do you really think, Mika Loladze, I'm going to stay a minute longer in this blasted house on that little brat's account? *(They start fighting. All one hears is:* "You neglect your duty!" *and* "Duty here, duty there!" *Then* THE SECOND DOCTOR *knocks* THE FIRST *down.)* Oh, go to hell! *(Exit.)*
(Enter the soldier, SIMON SHASHAVA. *He searches in the crowd for* GRUSHA.*)*

THE SERVANTS There's still time before tonight. The soldiers won't be drunk till then.
–Does anyone know if the mutiny has begun?
–The Palace Guard rode off.
–Doesn't anybody know what's happened?

GRUSHA Meliva the fisherman says a comet with a red tail has been seen in the sky over the capital. That means bad luck.

THE SERVANTS Yesterday they were saying in the capital that the Persian War is lost.
–The Princes have staged a big uprising.
–There's a rumor that the Grand Duke has fled already.
–All his governors are to be executed.
–The little people will be left alone.
–I have a brother with the Ironshirts.

THE ADJUTANT *(appearing in the doorway)* Everyone get into the third courtyard! Everyone help with the packing!
(He drives THE SERVANTS *away. At last* SIMON *finds* GRUSHA.*)*

SIMON Grusha! There you are at last! What are you going to do?

GRUSHA Nothing. If the worst comes to the worst, I've a brother in the mountains. What about you?

SIMON There is nothing to say about me. *(Formally again)* Grusha Vashnadze, your desire to know my plans fills me with satisfactions. I have been ordered to accompany Madam Natella Abashwili as her guard.

GRUSHA But hasn't the Palace Guard mutinied?

SIMON *(seriously)* That's a fact.

GRUSHA But isn't it dangerous to accompany her?

SIMON In Tiflis, they say: Is not the stabbing dangerous for the knife?

GRUSHA You're not a knife. You're a man, Simon Shashava. What has that woman to do with you?

SIMON That woman has nothing to do with me. I have my orders, and I go.

GRUSHA The soldier is pigheaded: he gets himself into danger for nothing —nothing at all. Now I must go into the third courtyard. I'm in a hurry.

SIMON Since we're in a hurry we shouldn't quarrel. You need time for a good quarrel. May I ask if the young lady still has parents?

GRUSHA No, only a brother.

SIMON As time is short—the second question is this: Is the young lady as healthy as a fish in water?

GRUSHA Maybe once in a while I have a pain in the right shoulder. Otherwise I'm strong enough for my job. No one has complained. So far.

SIMON Everyone knows that. Even if it's Easter Sunday, and there's a question who should run for the goose, she's the one. The third question is this: Is the young lady impatient? Does she want apples in winter?

GRUSHA Impatient? No. But if a man goes to war without any reason and no message arrives—that's bad.

SIMON A message will come. And now the final question . . .

GRUSHA Simon Shashava, I must go to the third courtyard and quick. My answer is yes.

SIMON *(very embarrassed)* Haste, they say, is the name of the wind that blows down the scaffolding. But they also say: The rich don't know what haste is. I'm from . . .

GRUSHA Kutsk . . .

SIMON So the young lady has already inquired about me? I'm healthy, have no dependents, make ten piasters a month, as a paymaster twenty piasters and I'm asking—very sincerely—for your hand.

GRUSHA Simon Shashava, it suits me well.

SIMON *(taking from his neck a thin chain with a little cross on it)* My mother gave me this cross, Grusha Vashnadze. The chain is silver. Please wear it.

GRUSHA Many thanks, Simon. *(He hangs it round her neck.)*

SIMON It would be better for the young lady to go to the third courtyard now. Or there will be difficulties. Anyway, I have to harness the horses. The young lady will understand.

GRUSHA Yes, Simon.

(They stand undecided.)

SIMON I'll only take the mistress to the troops that have remained loyal. When the war's over, I'll be back. In two weeks. Or three. I hope my intended won't get tired, waiting my return.

GRUSHA Simon Shashava, I shall wait for you.

Go calmly into battle, soldier
The bloody battle, the bitter battle
From which not everyone returns:
When you return I shall be there.

I shall be waiting for you under the green elm
I shall be waiting for you under the bare elm
I shall wait until the last soldier has returned
And longer.
When you come back from the battle
No boots will lie before the door
The pillow beside mine will be empty
And my mouth will be unkissed.
When you return, when you return
You will be able to say: All is as it was.

SIMON I thank you, Grusha Vashnadze. And goodbye!
(He bows low before her. She does the same before him. Then she runs quickly off without looking round. Enter THE ADJUTANT *from the gateway.)*

THE ADJUTANT *(harshly)* Harness the horses to the carriage! Don't stand there doing nothing, louse!
*(*SIMON SHASHAVA *stands to attention and goes off. Two servants crawl from the gateway, bent low under huge trunks. Behind them, supported by her women, stumbles* NATELLA ABASHWILI. *She is followed by a woman carrying the child.)*

THE GOVERNOR'S WIFE I hardly know if my head's still on. Where's Michael? Don't hold him so clumsily. Pile the trunks onto the carriage. Shalva, is there any news from the city?

THE ADJUTANT No. So far, all is quiet. But there's not a minute to lose. There's not enough room for the trunks in the carriage. Pick out what you need. *(Exit quickly.)*

THE GOVERNOR'S WIFE Only essentials! Quick, open the trunks. I'll tell you what I've got to have. *(The trunks are lowered and opened. She points at some brocade dresses.)* The green one! And of course the one with the fur trimming. Where are Niko Mikadze and Mika Loladze? I've suddenly got the most terrible migraine again. It always starts in the temples. *(Enter* GRUSHA.*)* You're taking your time, eh? Go at once and get the hot water bottles. *(*GRUSHA *runs off, returns later with hot water bottles.* THE GOVERNOR'S WIFE *orders her about by signs.)* Don't tear the sleeves.

A YOUNG WOMAN Pardon, madam, no harm has come to the dress.

THE GOVERNOR'S WIFE Because I stopped you. I've been watching you for a long time. Nothing in your head but making eyes at Shalva Tzereteli. I'll kill you, you bitch! *(She beats the woman.)*

THE ADJUTANT *(appearing in the gateway)* Please make haste, Natella Abashwili. Firing has broken out in the city. *(Exit.)*

THE GOVERNOR'S WIFE *(letting go of the young woman)* Oh, dear, do you think they'll do something to us? Why should they? Why? *(She herself begins to rummage in the trunks.)* How's Michael? Asleep?

THE WOMAN WITH THE CHILD Yes, madam.

THE GOVERNOR'S WIFE Then put him down a moment and get my little saffron-colored boots from the bedchamber. I need them for the green dress. *(The woman puts down the child and goes off.)* Just look how these things have been packed! No love! No understanding! If you don't give them every order yourself . . . At such moments you realize what kind of servants you have! They gorge themselves, and never a word of gratitude! I'll remember this.

THE ADJUTANT *(entering, very excited)* Natella, you must leave at once!

THE GOVERNOR'S WIFE Why? I've got to take this silver dress—it cost a thousand piasters. And that one there, and where's the wine-colored one?

THE ADJUTANT *(trying to pull her away)* Riots have broken out! We must leave at once. Where's the child?

THE GOVERNOR'S WIFE *(calling to the young woman who was holding the child)* Maro, get the child ready! Where on earth are you?

THE ADJUTANT *(leaving)* We'll probably have to leave the carriage and go on horseback.

*(*THE GOVERNOR'S WIFE *rummages again among her dresses, throws some onto the heap of chosen clothes, then takes them off again. Noises, drums are heard. The young woman who was beaten creeps away. The sky begins to grow red.)*

THE GOVERNOR'S WIFE *(rummaging desperately)* I simply cannot find the wine-colored dress. Take the whole pile and carry it as it is to the carriage. Where's Asja? And why hasn't Maro come back? Have you all gone crazy?

THE ADJUTANT *(returning)* Quick! Quick!

THE GOVERNOR'S WIFE *(to the first woman)* Run! Just throw them into the carriage!

THE ADJUTANT We are not going by carriage. Come on or I'll ride off on my own!

THE GOVERNOR'S WIFE *(as the first woman can't carry everything)* Where's that bitch Asja? *(*THE ADJUTANT *pulls her away.)* Maro, bring the child! *(To the first woman)* Go and look for Masha. No, first take the dresses to the carriage. Such nonsense, I wouldn't dream of going on horseback!

(Turning round, she sees the red sky, and starts back rigid. The fire burns. She is pulled out by THE ADJUTANT. *Shaking, the first woman follows with the dresses.)*

MARO *(from the doorway with the boots)* Madam! *(She sees the trunks and dresses and runs toward the child, picks it up, and holds it a moment.)* They left it behind, the beasts. *(She hands it to* GRUSHA.*)* Hold it a moment. *(She runs off, following* THE GOVERNOR'S WIFE. *Enter servants from the gateway.)*

THE COOK Well, they've actually gone. Without the food wagons, and not a minute too early. Now it's time to get out!

A GROOM This'll be an unhealthy house for a while. *(To one of the women)* Suliko, take a few blankets and wait for me in the foal stables.

GRUSHA What have they done to the Governor?

THE GROOM *(gesturing throat cutting)* Ffffft.

A FAT WOMAN *(seeing the gesture and becoming hysterical)* Oh dear, oh dear, oh dear, oh dear! Our master Georgi Abashwili! A picture of health he was, at the Morning Mass—and now! Oh, take me away, we're all lost! We must die in sin! Like our master, Georgi Abashwili!

THE OTHER WOMAN *(soothing her)* Calm down, Nina! You'll be taken to safety. You've never done anyone any harm.

THE FAT WOMAN *(being led out)* Oh dear, oh dear, oh dear! Quick! Let's all get out before they come. Before they come!

A YOUNG WOMAN Nina takes it more to heart than the mistress, that's a fact. *They* even have to have their weeping done for them.

THE COOK We'd better get out, all of us.

ANOTHER WOMAN *(glancing back)* That must be the East Gate burning.

THE YOUNG WOMAN *(seeing the child in* GRUSHA'S *arms)* The child! What are *you* doing with it?

GRUSHA It got left behind.

THE YOUNG WOMAN She simply left it! Michael, who was kept out of all the drafts! *(The servants gather round the child.)*

GRUSHA He's waking up.

THE GROOM Better put him down, I tell you. I'd rather not think what'd happen to anybody who's seen with that child.

THE COOK That's right. Once they start, they'll kill each other off, whole families at a time. Let's go.

(Exeunt all but GRUSHA, *with the child on her arm, and* TWO WOMEN.*)*

THE TWO WOMEN Didn't you hear? Better put him down.

GRUSHA The nurse asked me to hold him a moment.

THE OLDER WOMAN She'll never come back, you simpleton.

THE YOUNGER WOMAN Keep your hands off it.

THE OLDER WOMAN *(amiably)* Grusha, you're a good soul, but you're not very bright and you know it. I tell you, if he had the plague it couldn't be worse.

GRUSHA *(stubbornly)* He hasn't got the plague. He looks at me! He's human!

THE OLDER WOMAN Don't look at *him*. You are a fool—just the kind that always gets put upon. Someone says to you "Run for the salad, you have the longest legs," and you run. My husband has an ox cart—you can come with us if you hurry! Lord, by now the whole neighborhood must be in flames.

(Both women leave, sighing. After some hesitation, GRUSHA *puts the sleeping child down, looks at it for a moment, then takes a brocade blanket from the heap of clothes and covers it. Then both women return, dragging bundles.* GRUSHA *starts guiltily away from the child and walks a few steps to one side.)*

THE YOUNGER WOMAN Haven't you packed anything yet? There isn't much time, you know. The Ironshirts will be here from the barracks.

GRUSHA Coming.

(She runs through the doorway. Both women go to the gateway and wait. The sound of horses is heard. They flee, screaming.)

(Enter THE FAT PRINCE *with drunken* IRONSHIRTS. *One of them carries* THE GOVERNOR'S *head on a lance.)*

THE FAT PRINCE Here! In the middle! *(One soldier climbs onto the other's back, takes the head, holds it tentatively over the door.)* That's not the middle. Farther to the right. That's it. What I do, my friends, I do well. *(while, with hammer and nail, the soldier fastens the head to the wall by its hair)* This morning at the church door I said to Georgi Abashwili: "I love a clear sky." Actually I prefer the lightning that comes out of a clear sky. Yes indeed. It's a pity they took the brat along, though, I need him. Urgently.

(Exit with IRONSHIRTS *through the gateway. Trampling of horses again. Enter* GRUSHA *through the doorway looking cautiously about her. Clearly she has waited for the* IRONSHIRTS *to go. Carrying a bundle, she walks toward the gateway. At the last moment, she turns to see if the child is still there. Catching sight of the head over the doorway, she screams. Horrified, she picks up her bundle again, and is about to leave when* THE STORY TELLER *starts to speak. She stands rooted to the spot.)*

THE STORY TELLER

As she was standing between courtyard and gate,
She heard or she thought she heard a low voice calling;
The child called to her,
Not whining, but calling quite sensibly,
At least so it seemed to her.
"Woman," it said, "help me."
And it went on, not whining, but saying quite sensibly:
"Know, woman, he who hears not a cry for help
But passes by with troubled ears will never hear
The gentle call of a lover nor the blackbird at dawn
Nor the happy sigh of the exhausted grape-picker as the Angelus rings."
(She walks a few steps toward the child and bends over it.)
Hearing this she went back for one more look at the child.
Only to sit with him for a moment or two,
Only till someone should come,
Its mother, perhaps, or anyone else.
(Leaning on a trunk, she sits facing the child.)
Only till she would have to leave, for the danger was too great,
The city was full of flame and crying.
(The light grows dimmer, as though evening and night were coming on.)
Terrible is the seductive power of goodness!
*(*GRUSHA *now settles down to watch over the child through the night. Once, she lights a small lamp to look at it. Once, she tucks it in with a coat. From time to time she listens and looks to see whether someone is coming.)*
A long time she sat with the child
Till evening came, till night came, till dawn came.
Too long she sat, too long she saw
The soft breathing, the little fists,
Till toward morning the temptation grew too strong
And she rose, and bent down and, sighing, took the child
And carried it off.

(She does what THE STORY TELLER *says as he describes it.)*
Like plunder she took it to herself
Like a thief she crept away.

scene 2

THE FLIGHT INTO THE NORTHERN MOUNTAINS

THE STORY TELLER
As Grusha Vashnadze left the city
On the Grusinian highway
On the way to the Northern Mountains
She sang a song, she bought some milk.
THE CHORUS
How will this human child escape
The bloodhounds, the trap-setters?
Into the deserted mountains she journeyed
Along the Grusinian highway she journeyed
She sang a song, she bought some milk.
(GRUSHA VASHNADZE *walks on. On her back she carries the child in a sack, in one hand is a large stick, in the other a bundle. She sings.)*

THE SONG OF THE FOUR GENERALS

Four generals
Set out for Baku.
The first no war had ever begun
The second fought but never won
For the third no weather was ever right
For the fourth the men would never fight
Four generals
And none got through.

Sosso Robakidse
Marched to Iran
A mighty war he'd soon begun
A mighty battle he'd soon won
For him the weather was always right
For him the men would always fight
Sosso Robakidse
Is our man!
(A peasant's cottage appears.)

GRUSHA *(to the child)* Noontime is eating time. Now we'll sit hopefully in the grass, while the good Grusha goes and buys a little pitcher of milk. *(She lays the child down and knocks at the cottage door. An* OLD MAN *opens it.)* Grandfather, could I have a little pitcher of milk? And a corn cake, maybe?

THE OLD MAN Milk? We haven't any milk. The soldiers from the city have our goats. Go to the soldiers if you want milk.

GRUSHA But grandfather, you must have a little pitcher of milk for a child?

THE OLD MAN And for a God-bless-you, eh?

GRUSHA Who said anything about a God-bless-you? *(She shows her purse.)* We're going to pay like princes. "Head in the clouds, backside in the water." *(The peasant goes off, grumbling, for milk.)* How much for this little pitcher?

THE OLD MAN Three piasters. Milk has gone up.

GRUSHA Three piasters for that little drop? *(Without a word* THE OLD MAN *shuts the door in her face.)* Michael, did you hear that? Three piasters! We can't afford it! *(She goes back, sits down again, and gives the child her breast.)* Suck. Think of the three piasters. There's nothing there, but you *think* you're drinking, and that's something. *(Shaking her head, she sees that the child isn't sucking any more. She gets up, walks back to the door, and knocks again.)* Open, grandfather, we'll pay. *(Softly)* May lightning strike you! *(when* THE OLD MAN *appears)* I thought it would be half a piaster. But the child must have something. What about one piaster for that little drop?

THE OLD MAN Two.

GRUSHA Don't shut the door again. *(She fishes a long time in her bag.)* Here are two piasters. But the milk better be good. I still have two days' journey ahead of me. This is a murderous business and a sin too!

THE OLD MAN Kill the soldiers if you want milk.

GRUSHA *(giving the child some milk)* This is an expensive joke. Take a sip, Michael, it's a week's pay. The people here think we earned our money just sitting around. Michael, Michael, you're a nice little load for anyone to take on! *(Uneasy, she gets up, puts the child on her back, and walks on.* THE OLD MAN, *grumbling, picks up the pitcher and looks after her unmoved.)*

THE STORY TELLER

As Grusha Vashnadze went northward
The Princes' Ironshirts went after her.

THE CHORUS

How will the barefoot girl escape the Ironshirts,
The bloodhounds, the trap-setters?
They are hunting even by night.
Pursuers never get tired.
Butchers sleep little.

*(*TWO IRONSHIRTS *are trudging along the highway.)*

THE CORPORAL You'll never amount to anything, blockhead! Your heart's not in it. Your senior officer sees it in little things. Yesterday, when I made the fat gal, I admit you grabbed her husband as I commanded, and you *did* kick him in the stomach, but did you enjoy doing it like a loyal Private? Or were you just doing your duty? I've kept my eyes on you, blockhead. You're a hollow reed and a tinkling cymbal. You won't get promoted. *(They walk a while in silence.)* Don't imagine I don't remember how insubordinate you are in everything. I forbid you to limp! You only do it because I sold the horses, and I sold 'em because I couldn't have got that price again. You limp just to show me you don't like marching. I know you. It won't help. You wait. Sing!

THE TWO IRONSHIRTS *(singing)*

Off to the wars I went my way
Leaving my loved one at her door
My friends will keep her honor safe
Till from the wars I'm back once more.

THE CORPORAL Louder!

THE TWO IRONSHIRTS *(singing)*

And when my heavenly rest is won
My love will at my grave declare:
"Here rest the feet that once to me would run
And here the hands that once caressed my hair!"

(They begin to walk again in silence.)

THE CORPORAL A good soldier has his heart and soul in it. When he receives an order, he gets a hard on, and when he sends his lance into the enemy's guts, he comes. *(He shouts for joy.)* He lets himself be torn to pieces for his superior officer, and as he lies dying he takes note that his corporal is nodding approval. That's reward enough for him. That's all he wants. But *you* won't get a nod. Yet you'll croak all the same. Christ, how am I to get my hands on the Governor's bastard with a fool like you! *(They stay on stage behind.)*

THE STORY TELLER

When Grusha Vashnadze came to the River Sirra
The flight grew too much for her, the helpless child too heavy.
In the cornfields the rosy dawn
Is cold to the sleepless one, only cold.
The gay clatter of the milk cans in the farmyard where the smoke rises
Is only a threat to the fugitive.
She who carries the child feels its weight and little more.

*(*GRUSHA *stops in front of a farm. A fat* PEASANT WOMAN *is carrying a milk can through the door.* GRUSHA *waits until she has gone in, then approaches the house cautiously.)*

GRUSHA *(to the child)* Now you've wet yourself again, and you know I've no linen. Michael, this is where we part company. This is far enough from the city. They wouldn't want you so much, little good-for-nothing, that they'd follow you all this way. The peasant woman is kind, and can't you just smell the milk? *(She bends down to lay the child on the threshold.)* So farewell, Michael, I will forget how you kicked me in the back all night to make me go faster. And you, forget the meager fare—it was meant well. I would like to have kept you—your nose is so tiny—but it cannot be. I would have shown you your first rabbit and how not to wet yourself, but I must turn back. My sweetheart the soldier might soon return. And suppose he didn't find me? You can't ask that.

(She creeps up to the door and lays the child on the threshold. Then, hiding behind a tree, she waits until THE PEASANT WOMAN *opens the door and sees the bundle.)*

THE PEASANT WOMAN Good heavens, what's that? Husband!

THE PEASANT *(coming)* What's up? Let me get on with my soup.

THE PEASANT WOMAN *(to the child)* Where's your mother then? Haven't you got one? It's a boy. Fine linen—and a child. From a good family, you can see that. And they just leave him on our doorstep. Oh, these are times!

THE PEASANT If they think we're going to feed it, they're mistaken. You can take it to the priest in the village. That's the best we can do.

THE PEASANT WOMAN What will the priest do with it? It needs a mother. There, it's waking up. Don't you think we could keep it though?

THE PEASANT *(shouting)* No!

THE PEASANT WOMAN I could lay it in the corner next to the armchair. I only need a crib for it. And I can take it into the fields with me. See how it's laughing? Husband, we have a roof over our heads and we can do it. Not another word! *(She carries the child into the house.* THE PEASANT *follows, protesting.* GRUSHA *steps out from behind the tree, laughs, and hurries off in the opposite direction.)*

THE STORY TELLER Why so cheerful, making for home?

THE CHORUS

Because the child has won new parents with a laugh,
Because I'm rid of the little one, I'm cheerful.

THE STORY TELLER And why so sad?

THE CHORUS

Because I'm single and free, I'm sad.
Like one robbed, one newly poor.

(She walks for a short while, then meets the TWO IRONSHIRTS, *who point their lances at her.)*

THE CORPORAL Lady, you are running into the Armed Forces. Where are you coming from? And when? Are you having illicit relations with the enemy? Where is he hiding? What sort of movements is he making in your rear? What about the hills? What about the valley? How are your stockings fastened? *(*GRUSHA *stands there frightened.)* Don't be scared, we always stage a retreat, if necessary . . . what, blockhead? I always stage a retreat. In that respect, I can be relied on. Why are you staring like that at the lance? In the field no soldier ever drops his lance, that's a rule. Learn it by heart, blockhead. Now then, lady, where are you heading for?

GRUSHA To meet my intended, one Simon Shashava, of the Palace Guard in Nuka.

THE CORPORAL Simon Shashava? Sure, I know *him.* He gave me the key so I could look you up once in a while. Blockhead, we are getting to be unpopular. We must make her realize we have honorable intentions. Lady, behind apparent frivolity I conceal a serious nature. And so let me tell you officially: I want a child from you. *(*GRUSHA *utters a little scream.)* Blockhead, she understood. Uh-huh, isn't it a sweet shock? "Then first I must take the noodles out of the oven, Officer. Then first I must change my torn shirt, Colonel." But away with jokes, away with the lance! We are looking for a child in these parts. A child from a good family. Have you heard of such a child, from the city, dressed in fine linen, and suddenly turning up here?

GRUSHA No, I haven't heard a thing. *(Suddenly she turns round and runs back, panic-stricken.* THE IRONSHIRTS *glance at each other, then follow her, cursing.)*

THE STORY TELLER

Run, kind girl! The killers are coming!
Help the helpless child, helpless girl!
And so she runs!

THE CHORUS

In the bloodiest times
There are kind people.

(As GRUSHA *rushes into the cottage,* THE PEASANT WOMAN *is bending over the child's crib.)*

GRUSHA Hide it! Quick! The Ironshirts are coming! It was I who laid it on your doorstep. But it isn't mine. It's from a good family.

THE PEASANT WOMAN Who's coming? What sort of Ironshirts?

GRUSHA Don't ask questions. The Ironshirts that are looking for it.

THE PEASANT WOMAN They've no business in my house. But I must have a little talk with *you*, it seems.

GRUSHA Take off the fine linen. That will give us away.

THE PEASANT WOMAN Linen here, linen there. In this house *I* make the decisions. *You* can't vomit in *my* room! But why did you abandon it? That's a sin.

GRUSHA *(looking out of the window)* There, they're coming from behind the trees. I shouldn't have run away. That made them angry. Oh, what shall I do?

THE PEASANT WOMAN *(looking out of the window and suddenly starting with fear)* Good gracious! Ironshirts!

GRUSHA They're after the child!

THE PEASANT WOMAN But suppose they come in!

GRUSHA You mustn't give it to them. Say it's yours.

THE PEASANT WOMAN Yes.

GRUSHA They'll run it through if you hand it over.

THE PEASANT WOMAN But suppose they ask for it? The silver for the harvest is in the house.

GRUSHA If you let them have it, they'll run it through, here in your room! You've got to say it's yours!

THE PEASANT WOMAN Yes. But what if they don't believe me?

GRUSHA You must speak firmly.

THE PEASANT WOMAN They'll burn the roof over our heads.

GRUSHA That's why you've got to say it's yours. His name's Michael. I shouldn't have told you that. (THE PEASANT WOMAN *nods.)* Don't nod like that. And don't tremble—they'll notice.

THE PEASANT WOMAN Yes.

GRUSHA Stop saying yes, I can't stand it. *(She shakes the woman.)* Haven't *you* got a child?

THE PEASANT WOMAN *(muttering)* In the war.

GRUSHA Then maybe he's an Ironshirt too? Do you want him to run children through with his lance? You'd bawl him out. "No fooling with a lance in *my* house!" you'd shout, "is that what I've reared you for? Wash your neck before you speak to your mother!"

THE PEASANT WOMAN That's true, he couldn't get away with that around here!

GRUSHA Promise me you'll say it's yours.

THE PEASANT WOMAN Yes.

GRUSHA There! They're coming now!

(There is a knocking at the door. The women don't answer. Enter IRONSHIRTS. THE PEASANT WOMAN *bows low.)*

THE CORPORAL Well, there she is. What did I tell you? What a nose I have! I smell her. Lady, I have a question to ask you. Why did you run away? What did you think I would do to you? I'll bet it was something dirty. Confess!

GRUSHA *(while* THE PEASANT WOMAN *bows again and again)* I'd left some milk on the stove, and I suddenly remembered.

THE CORPORAL Or maybe you imagined I'd looked at you in a dirty way? Like there could be something between us? A lewd look, know what I mean?

GRUSHA I didn't see it.

THE CORPORAL But it's possible, huh? You admit that. After all, I might be a swine. I'll be frank with you: I could think of all sorts of things if we were alone. *(to* THE PEASANT WOMAN*)* Shouldn't you be busy in the yard? Feeding the hens?

THE PEASANT WOMAN *(falling suddenly to her knees)* Soldier, I didn't know a thing about it. Please don't burn the roof over our heads.

THE CORPORAL What are you talking about?

THE PEASANT WOMAN I had nothing to do with it. She left it on my doorstep, I swear!

THE CORPORAL *(suddenly seeing the child and whistling)* Ah, there's a little something in the crib! Blockhead, I smell a thousand piasters. Take the old girl out and hold on to her. It looks like I have a little cross-examining to do. (THE PEASANT WOMAN *lets herself be led out by the Private, without a word.)* Well, you've got that child I wanted from you. *(He walks toward the crib.)*

GRUSHA Officer, it's mine. It's not the one you're after.

THE CORPORAL I'll just take a look. *(He bends over the crib.* GRUSHA *looks round in despair.)*

GRUSHA It's mine! It's mine!

THE CORPORAL Fine linen!

(GRUSHA *dashes at him to pull him away. He throws her off and again bends over the crib. Again looking round in despair, she sees a log of wood, seizes it, and hits* THE CORPORAL *over the head from behind.* THE CORPORAL *collapses. She quickly picks up the child and rushes off.)*

THE STORY TELLER

And in her flight from the Ironshirts
After twenty-two days of journeying
At the foot of the Janga-Tu glacier
Grusha Vashnadze decided to adopt the child.

THE CHORUS
The helpless girl adopted the helpless child.
*(*GRUSHA *squats over a half-frozen stream to get the child water in the hollow of her hand.)*

GRUSHA
Since no one else will take you, son,
I must take you now.
Since no one else will take you, son,
(O black day in a lean, lean year!)
You must take me.
I have carried you too long
My feet are tired and sore
And the milk cost much too much
I've grown fond of you:
I wouldn't be without you any more
I'll throw away your silken shirt
And wrap you in rags.
I'll wash you, son, and christen you
In glacier water.
You must see it through.
(She has taken off the child's fine linen and wrapped it in a rag.)

THE STORY TELLER
When Grusha Vashnadze
Pursued by the Ironshirts
Came to the bridge on the glacier
Leading to the villages of the Eastern Slope
She sang the Song of the Rotten Bridge
And risked two lives.
(A wind has risen. The bridge on the glacier is visible in the dark. One rope is broken and half the bridge is hanging down the abyss. Merchants, two men and a woman, stand undecided before the bridge as GRUSHA *and the child arrive. One man is trying to catch the hanging rope with a stick.)*

THE FIRST MAN Take your time, young woman. You won't get over that pass anyway.

GRUSHA But I simply have to get the little one over to the east side. To my brother.

THE MERCHANT WOMAN Have to? What d'you mean by "have to"? I have to get there, too—because I have to buy two carpets in Atum—carpets a woman had to sell because her husband had to die. But can I do what I have to? Can she? For hours Andréi has been fishing for that rope. And I ask you, how are we to fasten it, even if he gets it up?

THE FIRST MAN *(listening)* Hush, I think I hear something.

GRUSHA The bridge is not quite rotten. I think I'll try and make it.

THE MERCHANT WOMAN I wouldn't try that if the devil himself were after me. Why, it's suicide.

THE FIRST MAN *(shouting)* Hi!

GRUSHA Don't call! *(to* THE MERCHANT WOMAN*)* Tell him not to call.

THE FIRST MAN But there's someone down there calling. Maybe they've lost their way.

THE MERCHANT WOMAN Why shouldn't he call? Is there something wrong about you? Are they after you?

GRUSHA All right, I'll tell you. The Ironshirts are after me. I knocked one down.

THE SECOND MAN Hide our merchandise!

(The WOMAN *hides a sack behind a rock.)*

THE FIRST MAN Why didn't you tell us right away? *(to the others)* If they catch her they'll make mincemeat out of her!

GRUSHA Get out of my way. I've got to cross that bridge.

THE SECOND MAN You can't. The precipice is two thousand feet deep.

THE FIRST MAN Even with the rope it'd be no use. We could hold it with our hands, but then the Ironshirts could cross the same way.

GRUSHA Go away.

(There are calls from the distance) "Hi, up there!"

THE MERCHANT WOMAN They're getting near. But you can't take the child across that bridge. It's sure to break. Just look down. *(*GRUSHA *looks down into the abyss. The* IRONSHIRTS *are heard calling again from below.)*

THE SECOND MAN Two thousand feet!

GRUSHA But those men are worse.

THE FIRST MAN You can't do it. There's the child. Risk *your* life but not the child's.

THE SECOND MAN With the child she's all the heavier!

THE MERCHANT WOMAN Maybe she's really got to get across. Give me the child. I'll hide it. You cross the bridge alone.

GRUSHA I won't. We belong together. *(to the child)* "Live together, die together." *(She sings.)*

THE SONG OF THE ROTTEN BRIDGE

Deep is the abyss, son,
I see the weak bridge sway
But it's not for us, son,
To choose the way.

The way I know
Is the one you must tread,
And all you will eat
Is my bit of bread.

Of every four pieces
You shall have three.
Would that I knew
How big they will be!
Get out of my way, I'll try it without the rope.

THE MERCHANT WOMAN That's tempting God!

(There are shouts from below.)

GRUSHA Please, throw that stick away, or they'll get the rope and follow me. *(Pressing the child to her, she steps onto the swaying bridge.* THE MERCHANT WOMAN *screams when it looks as though the bridge is about to collapse. But* GRUSHA *walks on and reaches the far side.)*

THE FIRST MAN She's done it!

THE MERCHANT WOMAN *(who has fallen on her knees and begun to pray, angrily)* I still think it was a sin.

(The IRONSHIRTS *appear;* THE CORPORAL'S *head is bandaged.)*

THE CORPORAL Seen a woman with a child?

THE FIRST MAN *(while* THE SECOND MAN *throws the stick into the abyss)* Yes, there! But the bridge won't carry *you!*

THE CORPORAL You'll pay for this, blockhead!

*(*GRUSHA, *from the far bank, laughs and shows the child to the* IRONSHIRTS. *She walks on. The wind blows.)*

GRUSHA *(turning to the child)* You mustn't fear the wind. He's just a poor thing too. He has to push the clouds along and he gets cold doing it. *(Snow starts falling.)* And the snow is not so bad, either, Michael. It covers the little fir trees so they won't die in winter. And now I'll sing you a little song. Listen! *(She sings.)*

THE SONG OF THE CHILD

Your father is a thief,
Your mother is a whore,
And all good people
Will kneel at your door.

The sons of the tiger
Are the horse's brothers,
The child of the snake
Brings milk to the mothers.

scene 3

IN THE NORTHERN MOUNTAINS

THE STORY TELLER

Seven days the sister, Grusha Vashnadze,
Journeyed across the glacier
And down the slopes she journeyed.
"When I enter my brother's house," she thought
"He will rise and embrace me."
"Is that you, sister?" he will say,
"I have been expecting you so long.
This is my dear wife.
And this is my farm, come to me by marriage,
With eleven horses and thirty-one cows. Sit down.
Sit down with your child at our table and eat."

The brother's house was in a lovely valley.
When the sister came to the brother,
She was ill from walking.
The brother rose from the table.
(A fat peasant couple rise from the table. LAVRENTI VASHNADZE *still has a napkin round his neck, as* GRUSHA, *pale and supported by a servant, enters with the child.)*

LAVRENTI Where do you come from, Grusha?

GRUSHA *(feebly)* I've walked across the Janga-Tu Pass, Lavrenti.

THE SERVANT I found her in front of the hay barn. She has a child with her.

THE SISTER-IN-LAW Go and groom the mare. *(Exit* THE SERVANT.*)*

LAVRENTI This is my wife. Aniko.

THE SISTER-IN-LAW I thought you were in service in Nuka.

GRUSHA *(barely able to stand)* Yes, I was.

THE SISTER-IN-LAW Wasn't it a good job? We were told it was.

GRUSHA The Governor got killed.

LAVRENTI Yes, we heard there were riots. Your aunt told us about it. Remember, Aniko?

THE SISTER-IN-LAW Here, with us, it's very quiet. City people always want something going on. *(She walks toward the door, calling)* Sosso, Sosso, don't take the cake out of the oven yet, d'you hear? Where on earth are you? *(Exit, calling.)*

LAVRENTI *(quietly, quickly)* Is there a father? *(As she shakes her head:)* I thought not. We must think up something. She's religious.

THE SISTER-IN-LAW *(returning)* Those servants! *(to* GRUSHA*)* You have a child.

GRUSHA It's mine. *(She collapses.* LAVRENTI *rushes to her assistance.)*

THE SISTER-IN-LAW Good heavens, she's ill—what are we to do?

LAVRENTI *(escorting her to a bench near the stove)* Sit down, sit down. I think it's just weakness, Aniko.

THE SISTER-IN-LAW As long as it's not scarlet fever!

LAVRENTI Then she'd have spots. It's only weakness. Don't worry, Aniko. *(to* GRUSHA*)* It's better sitting down?

THE SISTER-IN-LAW Is the child hers?

GRUSHA It's mine.

LAVRENTI She's on her way to her husband.

THE SISTER-IN-LAW I see. Your meat's getting cold. *(*LAVRENTI *sits down and begins to eat.)* Cold food's not good for you, the fat mustn't get cold, you know your stomach's your weak spot. *(to* GRUSHA*)* If your husband's not in the city, where is he?

LAVRENTI She got married on the other side of the mountain, she says.

THE SISTER-IN-LAW Oh, on the other side. *(She also sits down to eat.)*

GRUSHA I think I should lie down somewhere, Lavrenti.

THE SISTER-IN-LAW If it's consumption we'll all get it. *(She goes on cross-examining her.)* Has your husband got a farm?

GRUSHA He's a soldier.

LAVRENTI But he's coming into a farm—a small one from his father.

THE SISTER-IN-LAW Isn't he in the war? Why not?
GRUSHA *(with effort)* Yes, he's in the war.
THE SISTER-IN-LAW Then why d'you want to go to the farm?
LAVRENTI When he comes back from the war, he'll return to his farm.
THE SISTER-IN-LAW But you're going there now?
LAVRENTI Yes, to wait for him.
THE SISTER-IN-LAW *(calling shrilly)* Sosso, the cake!
GRUSHA *(murmuring feverishly)* A farm—a soldier—waiting—sit down, eat.
THE SISTER-IN-LAW It's scarlet fever.
GRUSHA *(starting up)* Yes, he's got a farm!
LAVRENTI I think it's just weakness, Aniko. Wouldn't you like to go look after the cake yourself, dear?
THE SISTER-IN-LAW But when will he come back if war's broken out again as people say? *(She waddles off, shouting:)* Sosso! Where on earth are you? Sosso!
LAVRENTI *(getting up quickly and going to* GRUSHA*)* You'll get a bed in a minute. She has a good heart. But wait till after supper.
GRUSHA *(holding out the child to him)* Take him.
LAVRENTI *(taking it and looking around)* But you can't stay here long with the child. She's religious, you see. *(*GRUSHA *collapses.* LAVRENTI *catches her.)*
THE STORY TELLER
The sister was so ill,
The cowardly brother had to give her shelter.
Summer departed, winter came.
The winter was long, the winter was short:
People mustn't know anything,
The rats mustn't bite,
The spring mustn't come.
*(*GRUSHA *sits over the weaving loom in a workroom. She and the child, who is squatting on the floor, are wrapped in blankets. She sings.)*

THE SONG OF THE CENTER

And the lover started to leave
And his betrothed ran pleading after him
Pleading and weeping, weeping and teaching:
"Dearest mine, Dearest mine
When you go to war as now you do
When you fight the foe as soon you will
Don't lead with the front line
And don't push with the rear line
At the front is red fire
In the rear is red smoke
Stay in the war's center
Stay near the standard bearer
The first always die

The last are also hit
Those in the center come home."

Michael, we must be clever. If we make ourselves as small as cockroaches, the sister-in-law will forget we are in the house. Then we can stay till the snow melts.

(Enter LAVRENTI. *He sits down beside his sister.)*

LAVRENTI Why are you two sitting there muffled up like coachmen? Is it too cold in the room?

GRUSHA *(hastily removing one shawl)* It's not too cold, Lavrenti.

LAVRENTI If it's too cold, you oughtn't to sit here with the child. Aniko would think herself to blame. *(pause)* I hope our priest didn't question you about the child?

GRUSHA He did, but I didn't tell him anything.

LAVRENTI That's good. I wanted to talk to you about Aniko. She has a good heart but she's very very sensitive. People have only to mention our farm and she's worried. She takes everything so hard, you see. One time our milkmaid went to church with a hole in her stocking. Ever since that day my Aniko has worn two pairs of stockings at church. It may seem hard to believe, but it's the old family in her. *(He listens.)* Are you sure there are no rats around? If there are, you couldn't live here. *(There are sounds as of dripping from the roof.)* What's that dripping?

GRUSHA It must be a barrel leaking.

LAVRENTI Yes, it must be a barrel. You've been here half a year now, haven't you? Was I talking about Aniko? *(They listen again to the snow melting.)* You can't imagine how worried she is about your soldier-husband. "Supposing he comes back and doesn't find her!" she says and lies awake. "He can't come before the spring," I tell her. The dear woman! *(The drops begin to fall faster.)* When d'you think he'll come? What do *you* think? *(*GRUSHA *is silent.)* Not before the spring, you think that too? *(*GRUSHA *is silent.)* So now you don't believe he'll come at all? *(*GRUSHA *is silent.)* But when the spring comes and the snow is melting here and on the passes, you can't stay any longer. They may come and look for you. People are already beginning to talk about an illegitimate child. *(The "glockenspiel" of the falling drops has grown faster and steadier.)* Grusha, the snow is melting on the roof. And spring is here.

GRUSHA Yes.

LAVRENTI *(eagerly)* Let me tell you what we'll do. You need a place to go, and because of the child *(he sighs)* you have to have a husband so people won't talk. Now I've made cautious inquiries to see if we can get a husband for you. Grusha, I've found one. I talked to a woman who has a son. Just the other side of the mountain, a small farm. She's willing.

GRUSHA But I can't marry anyone! I must wait for Simon Shashava.

LAVRENTI Of course. That's all been taken care of. You don't need a man in bed—you need a man on paper. And I've found you one. The son of this peasant woman is just going to die. Isn't it wonderful? He's at the last gasp. And everything's as we said it was. A husband from the other side the mountain. When you met him he was at the last gasp. And so you're a widow. What do you say?

GRUSHA I could do with a document with stamps on it for Michael.

LAVRENTI The stamps make all the difference. Without something in writing the Shah of Persia couldn't prove he's it. And you'll have a place to live.

GRUSHA How much does the woman want?

LAVRENTI Four hundred piasters.

GRUSHA Where will you find the money?

LAVRENTI *(guiltily)* Aniko's milk money.

GRUSHA No one would know us there. I'll do it.

LAVRENTI *(getting up)* I'll let the peasant woman know right away. *(Quick exit.)*

GRUSHA Michael, you cause a lot of fuss. I came to you as the pear tree comes to the sparrows. And because a Christian bends down and picks up a crust of bread so nothing will go to waste. Michael, it would have been better had I walked quickly away on that Easter Sunday in Nuka in the second courtyard. Now I *am* a fool.

THE STORY TELLER

The bridegroom was lying on his deathbed when the bride arrived.
The bridegroom's mother was waiting at the door, telling her to hurry.
The bride brought a child along.
The witness hid it during the wedding.

(On one side the bed. Under the mosquito net lies a very sick man. GRUSHA *is pulled in at a run by her future mother-in-law. They are followed by* LAVRENTI *and the child.)*

THE MOTHER-IN-LAW Quick! Quick! Or he'll die on us before the wedding. *(to* LAVRENTI*)* I was never told she had a child already.

LAVRENTI What difference does it make? *(pointing toward the dying man:)* It can't matter to him—in his condition.

THE MOTHER-IN-LAW To him? But I'll never survive the shame. We are honest people. *(she begins to weep.)* My Jussup doesn't have to marry a girl with a child!

LAVRENTI All right, I'll give you another two hundred piasters. You have it in writing that the farm will go to you. But she has the right to live here for two years.

THE MOTHER-IN-LAW *(drying her tears)* It'll hardly cover the funeral expenses. I hope she'll really lend me a hand with the work. And now what's happened to the monk? He must have crept out through the kitchen window. We'll have the whole village round our necks when they get wind that Jussup's end has come! Oh dear! I'll run and bring the monk. But he mustn't see the child.

LAVRENTI I'll take care he doesn't see it. But why only a monk? Why not a priest?

THE MOTHER-IN-LAW Oh, he's just as good. I only made one mistake: I paid half his fee in advance. Enough to go to the tavern with. I only hope . . . *(She runs off.)*

LAVRENTI She saved on the priest, the wretch! Hired a cheap monk.

GRUSHA Send Simon Shashava over to see me if he turns up after all.

LAVRENTI Yes. *(pointing at the sick man)* Won't you have a look at him? *(*GRUSHA, *taking* MICHAEL *to her, shakes her head.)* He's not moving an eyelid. I hope we aren't too late.

(The listen. On the opposite side enter neighbors who look around and take up positions against the walls, thus forming another wall near the bed, yet leaving an opening so that the bed can be seen. They start murmuring prayers. Enter THE MOTHER-IN-LAW *with a* MONK. *Showing some annoyance and surprise, she bows to the guests.)*

THE MOTHER-IN-LAW If you don't mind, please wait a few moments. My son's bride has just arrived from the city and an emergency wedding is about to take place. *(to the* MONK *in the bedroom)* I might have known you couldn't keep your mouth shut. *(to* GRUSHA*)* The wedding can take place immediately. Here's the license. I and the bride's brother (LAVRENTI *tries to hide in the background, after having quietly taken* MICHAEL *back from* GRUSHA. THE MOTHER-IN-LAW *waves him away)* who will appear at once, are the witnesses.

*(*GRUSHA *has bowed to* THE MONK. *They go to the bed.* THE MOTHER-IN-LAW *lifts the mosquito net.* THE MONK *starts reeling off the marriage ceremony in Latin. Meanwhile,* THE MOTHER-IN-LAW *beckons to* LAVRENTI *to get rid of the child, but fearing that it will cry he draws its attention to the ceremony.* GRUSHA *glances once at the child, and* LAVRENTI *waves the child's hand in a greeting.)*

THE MONK Are you prepared to be a faithful, obedient, and good wife to this man, and to cleave to him until death you do part?

GRUSHA *(looking at the child)* I am.

THE MONK *(to the sick peasant)* And are you prepared to be a good and loving husband to your wife until death you do part? *(As the sick peasant does not answer,* THE MONK *looks inquiringly around.)*

THE MOTHER-IN-LAW Of course he is! Didn't you hear him say yes?

THE MONK All right. We declare the marriage contracted! Now what about extreme unction?

THE MOTHER-IN-LAW Nothing doing! The wedding was quite expensive enough. Now I must take care of the mourners. *(to* LAVRENTI*)* Did we say seven hundred?

LAVRENTI Six hundred. *(He pays.)* Now I don't want to sit with the guests and get to know people. So farewell, Grusha. And if my widowed sister comes to visit me one day, she'll get a welcome from my wife, or I'll show my teeth. (LAVRENTI *nods, gives the child to* GRUSHA, *and leaves. The mourners glance after him without interest.)*

THE MONK And may one ask where this child comes from?

THE MOTHER-IN-LAW Is there a child? I don't see a child. And you don't see one either—you understand? Or else, I shall have seen all kinds of things in the tavern! Now come on. *(After* GRUSHA *has put the child down and told him to be quiet, they move over left.* GRUSHA *is introduced to the neighbors.)* This is my daughter-in-law. She arrived just in time to find dear Jussup still alive.

ONE WOMAN He's been ill now a whole year, hasn't he? When our Vassili was drafted he was there to say goodbye.

ANOTHER WOMAN Such things are terrible for a farm. The corn all ripe and the farmer in bed! It'll really be a blessing if he doesn't suffer too long, I say.

THE FIRST WOMAN *(confidentially)* At first we thought it was because of the draft he'd taken to his bed, you know. And now his end is coming!

THE MOTHER-IN-LAW Sit yourselves down, please, and have some cakes. *(She beckons to* GRUSHA *and both women go into the bedroom, where they pick up the cake pans off the floor. The guests, among them* THE MONK, *sit on the floor and begin conversing in subdued voices.)*

ONE PEASANT *(to whom* THE MONK *has handed the bottle which he has taken from his soutane)* There's a child, you say! How can that have happened to Jussup?

A WOMAN She was certainly lucky to get herself hitched, with him so sick.

THE MOTHER-IN-LAW They're gossiping already. And gorging on the funeral cakes at the same time! If he doesn't die today, I'll have to bake fresh ones tomorrow.

GRUSHA I'll bake them.

THE MOTHER-IN-LAW Yesterday some horsemen rode by, and I went out to see who it was. When I came in again he was lying there like a corpse! That's why I sent for you. It can't take much longer. *(She listens.)*

THE MONK My dear wedding and funeral guests! Deeply touched, we stand before a bed of death and marriage. The bride gets the veil; the groom, a shroud: how varied, my children, are the fates of men! Alas! One man dies and has a roof over his head, and the other is married and the flesh turns to dust, from which it was made. Amen.

THE MOTHER-IN-LAW He's taking his revenge. I shouldn't have hired such a cheap one. It's what you'd expect. A more expensive one would behave himself. In Sura there's one with a real air of sanctity about him, but of course he charges a fortune. A fifty-piaster monk like that has no dignity. And as for piety, just fifty piasters' worth and no more! When I came to get him in the tavern he had just made a speech and was shouting: "The war is over, beware of the peace!" We must go in.

GRUSHA *(giving* MICHAEL *a cake)* Eat this cake, and keep nice and still, Michael.

(The two women offer cakes to THE GUESTS. *The dying man sits up in bed. He puts his head out from under the mosquito net, stares at the two women, then sinks back again.* THE MONK *takes two bottles from his soutane and offers them to* THE PEASANT *beside him. Enter* THREE MUSICIANS *who are greeted with a sly wink by* THE MONK.*)*

THE MOTHER-IN-LAW *(to the* MUSICIANS*)* What are you doing here? With instruments?

ONE MUSICIAN Brother Anastasius here *(pointing at* THE MONK*)* told us there was a wedding on.

THE MOTHER-IN-LAW What? *You* brought them? Three more on my neck! Don't you know there's a dying man in the next room?

THE MONK A very tempting assignment for a musician: something that could be either a subdued Wedding March or a spirited Funeral Dance!

THE MOTHER-IN-LAW Well, you might as well play. Nobody can stop you eating in any case.

(The musicians play a potpourri. The women serve cakes.)

THE MONK The trumpet sounds like a whining baby. And you, little drum, what have you got to tell the world?

THE DRUNKEN PEASANT *(beside* THE MONK, *sings)*

Miss Roundass took the old old man
And said that marriage was the thing
To everyone who met 'er.
She later withdrew from the contract because
Candles are better.

(THE MOTHER-IN-LAW *throws* THE DRUNKEN PEASANT *out. The music stops.* THE GUESTS *are embarrassed.)*

THE GUESTS *(loudly)* Have you heard? The Grand Duke is back! But the Princes are against him.

—Oh, the Shah of Persia, they say, has lent him a great army, to restore order in Grusinia. How is this possible? After all, the Shah of Persia is the enemy . . .

—Only the enemy of Grusinia, you donkey, not of the Grand Duke!

—In any case, the war's over, our soldiers are coming back.

(GRUSHA *drops a cake pan.* GUESTS *help her pick up the cake.)*

AN OLD WOMAN *(to* GRUSHA*)* Are you feeling bad? That's just excitement about dear Jussup. Sit down and rest awhile, my dear. *(*GRUSHA *staggers.)*

THE GUESTS Now everything will be the way it was. Only the taxes'll go up because we'll have to pay for the war.

GRUSHA *(weakly)* Did someone say the soldiers are back?

A MAN I did.

GRUSHA It can't be true.

THE FIRST MAN *(to a woman)* Show her the shawl. We bought it from a soldier. It's from Persia.

GRUSHA *(looking at the shawl)* They are here. *(She gets up, takes a step, kneels down in prayer, takes the silver cross and chain out of her blouse, and kisses it.)*

THE MOTHER-IN-LAW *(while the guests silently watch* GRUSHA*)* What's the matter with you? Won't you look after our guests? What's all this nonsense from the city got to do with us?

THE GUESTS *(resuming conversation while* GRUSHA *remains in prayer)* You can buy Persian saddles from the soldiers too. Though some exchange them for crutches.

—The big shots on one side can win a war, but the soldiers on both sides lose it.

—Anyway, the war's over now. It's something that they can't draft you any more. *(The dying man sits bolt upright in bed. He listens.)* What we need is two weeks of good weather.

—Our pear trees are hardly bearing a thing this year.

THE MOTHER-IN-LAW *(offering cakes)* Have some more cake and enjoy it. There are more. *(*THE MOTHER-IN-LAW *goes to the bedroom with the* *empty cake pans. Unaware of the dying man, she is bending down to pick up another tray when he begins to talk in a hoarse voice.)*

THE PEASANT How many more cakes are you going to stuff down their throats? Does money grow on trees? *(*THE MOTHER-IN-LAW *starts, stares at him aghast, while he climbs out from behind the mosquito net.)*

THE FIRST WOMAN *(talking kindly to* GRUSHA *in the next room)* Has the young wife someone at the front?

A MAN That's good news, they're on their way home, huh?

THE PEASANT Don't stare like that! Where's this wife you've hung round my neck?

(Receiving no answer, he climbs out of bed and in his nightshirt staggers into the other room. Trembling, she follows him with the cake pan.)

THE GUESTS *(seeing him and shrieking)* Good God! Jussup!

(Everyone leaps up in alarm. The women rush to the door. GRUSHA, *still on her knees, turns round and stares at the man.)*

THE PEASANT The funeral supper! *That's* what you would like! Get out before I throw you out! *(As the guests stampede from the house, gloomily to* GRUSHA*)* I've upset the apple cart, huh? *(Receiving no answer, he turns round and takes a cake from the pan which his mother is holding.)*

THE STORY TELLER

O confusion! The wife discovers she has a husband.
By day there's the child, by night there's the husband.
The lover is on his way both day and night.
Husband and wife look at each other.
The bedroom is small.

(Near the bed THE PEASANT *is sitting in a high wooden bathtub, naked.* THE MOTHER-IN-LAW *is pouring water from a pitcher. Opposite,* GRUSHA *cowers with* MICHAEL, *who is playing at mending straw mats.)*

THE PEASANT *(to his* MOTHER*)* That's *her* work, not yours. Where's she hiding out now?

THE MOTHER-IN-LAW *(calling)* Grusha! The peasant wants you!

GRUSHA *(to* MICHAEL*)* There are still two holes to mend.

THE PEASANT *(when* GRUSHA *approaches)* Scrub my back!

GRUSHA Can't the peasant do it himself?

THE PEASANT "Can't the peasant do it himself?" Get the brush! To hell with you! Are you the wife here? Or are you a visitor? *(to* THE MOTHER-IN-LAW*)* It's too cold!

THE MOTHER-IN-LAW I'll run for hot water.

GRUSHA Let me go.

THE PEASANT You stay here. *(*THE MOTHER-IN-LAW *runs.)* Rub harder. And no finagling. You've seen a naked fellow before. That child didn't come out of thin air.

GRUSHA The child was not conceived in joy, if that's what the peasant means.

THE PEASANT *(turning and grinning)* You don't look the type. *(*GRUSHA *stops scrubbing him, starts back. Enter* THE MOTHER-IN-LAW.*)* A nice thing you've hung around my neck! A simpleton for a wife!

THE MOTHER-IN-LAW She just isn't cooperative.

THE PEASANT Pour—but go easy! Ow! Go easy, I said. *(to* GRUSHA*)* Maybe you did something wrong in the city . . . I wouldn't be surprised. Why else should you be here? But I won't talk about that. I've not said a word about the illegitimate object you brought into my house either. But my patience has limits! It's against nature. *(to* THE MOTHER-IN-LAW*)* More! *(to* GRUSHA*)* And even if your soldier does come back, you're married.

GRUSHA Yes.

THE PEASANT But your soldier won't return now. Don't you believe it.

GRUSHA No.

THE PEASANT You're cheating me. You're my wife and you're not my wife. Where you lie, nothing lies, and yet no other woman can lie there. When I go to work in the mornings I'm dead tired—when I lie down at night I'm awake as the devil. God has given you sex—and what d'you do? I don't have ten piasters to buy myself a woman in the city! Besides, it's a long way. Woman weeds the fields and opens up her legs, that's what our calendar says. D'you hear?

GRUSHA *(quietly)* Yes. I didn't mean to cheat you out of it.

THE PEASANT She didn't mean to cheat me out of it! Pour some more water! *(*THE MOTHER-IN-LAW *pours.)* Ow!

THE STORY TELLER

As she sat by the stream to wash the linen
She saw his image in the water
And his face grew dimmer with the passing moons.
As she raised herself to wring the linen
She heard his voice from the murmuring maple
And his voice grew fainter with the passing moons.
Evasions and sighs grew more numerous,
Tears and sweat flowed.
With the passing moons the child grew up.

*(*GRUSHA *sits by a stream, dipping linen into the water. In the rear, a few children are standing.)*

GRUSHA *(to* MICHAEL*)* You can play with them, Michael, but don't let them order you about just because you're the smallest. *(*MICHAEL *nods and joins the children. They start playing.)*

THE BIGGEST BOY Today we're going to play Heads-Off. *(to a* FAT BOY*)* You're the Prince and you must laugh. *(to* MICHAEL*)* You're the Governor, and you laugh. *(to a* GIRL*)* You're the Governor's wife and you cry when his head's chopped off. And I do the chopping. *(He shows his wooden sword.)* With this. First, the Governor is led into the yard. The Prince walks ahead. The Governor's wife comes last. *(They form a procession.* THE FAT BOY *goes ahead and laughs. Then comes* MICHAEL, *then* THE BIGGEST BOY, *and then* THE GIRL, *who weeps.)*

MICHAEL *(standing still)* Me too chop head off.

THE BIGGEST BOY That's my job. You're the smallest. The Governor's part is the easiest. All you have to do is kneel down and have your head chopped off—very simple.

MICHAEL Me too have sword.

THE BIGGEST BOY That's mine. *(He gives him a kick.)*

THE GIRL *(shouting to* GRUSHA*)* He doesn't want to play.

GRUSHA *(laughing)* Even the *little* duck can swim, they say.

THE BIGGEST BOY You can play the Prince if you know how to laugh. *(*MICHAEL *shakes his head.)*

THE FAT BOY I laugh best. Let him chop off a head just once. Then you do it, then me.

(Reluctantly, THE BIGGEST BOY *hands* MICHAEL *the wooden sword and kneels down.* THE FAT BOY *sits down, beats his thigh, and laughs with all his might.* THE GIRL *weeps loudly.* MICHAEL *swings the big sword and "cuts off" the head. In doing so, he topples over.)*

THE BIGGEST BOY Ow! I'll show you how to hit the *right* way!

*(*MICHAEL *runs away. The children run after him.* GRUSHA *laughs, following them with her eyes. On looking back, she sees* SIMON SHASHAVA *standing on the opposite bank. He wears a shabby uniform.)*

GRUSHA Simon!

SIMON Is that Grusha Vashnadze?

GRUSHA Simon!

SIMON *(formally)* A good morning to the young lady. I hope she is well.

GRUSHA *(getting up gaily and bowing low)* A good morning to the soldier. God be thanked he has returned in good health.

SIMON They found better fish, so they didn't eat me, said the haddock.

GRUSHA Courage, said the kitchen boy. Good luck, said the hero.

SIMON And how are things here? Was the winter bearable? The neighbor considerate?

GRUSHA The winter was a trifle rough, the neighbor as usual, Simon.

SIMON May one ask if a certain person still dips her foot in the water when rinsing the linen?

GRUSHA The answer is no. Because of the eyes in the bushes.

SIMON The young lady is speaking of soldiers. Here stands a paymaster.

GRUSHA A job worth twenty piasters?

SIMON And lodgings.

GRUSHA *(with tears in her eyes)* Behind the barracks under the date trees.

SIMON Yes, there. A certain person has kept her eyes open.

GRUSHA She has, Simon.

SIMON And has not forgotten? *(*GRUSHA *shakes her head.)* So the door is still on its hinges as they say? *(*GRUSHA *looks at him in silence and shakes her head again.)* What's this? Is something not as it should be?

GRUSHA Simon Shashava, I can never return to Nuka. Something has happened.

SIMON What can have happened?

GRUSHA For one thing, I knocked an Ironshirt down.

SIMON Grusha Vashnadze must have had her reasons for that.

GRUSHA Simon Shashava, I am no longer called what I used to be called.

SIMON *(after a pause)* I do not understand.

GRUSHA When do women change their names, Simon? Let me explain. Nothing stands between us. Everything is just as it was. You must believe me.

SIMON Nothing stands between us and yet there *is* something?

GRUSHA How can I explain it so fast and with the stream between us? Couldn't you cross the bridge there?

SIMON Perhaps it's no longer necessary.

GRUSHA It is very necessary. Come over on this side, Simon. Quick!

SIMON Does the young lady wish to say that someone has come too late? *(*GRUSHA *looks up at him in despair, her face streaming with tears.* SIMON *stares before him. He picks up a piece of wood and starts cutting it.)*

THE STORY TELLER

So many words are said, so many left unsaid.
The soldier has come.
Where he comes from, he does not say.
Hear what he thought and did not say:
"The battle began gray at dawn, grew bloody at noon
The first fell before me, the second behind, the third at my side
On the first I stepped, the second I left, the third was run through by the captain
One of my brothers died by steel, the other by smoke
My neck was set aflame, my hands froze in my gloves, my toes in my socks
I fed on aspen buds, I drank maple juice, I slept on stone, in water."

SIMON I see a cap in the grass. Is there a little one already?

GRUSHA There is, Simon. How could I hide it? But please don't worry, it is not mine.

SIMON When the wind once begins to blow, they say, it blows through every cranny. The wife need say no more.
*(*GRUSHA *looks into her lap and is silent.)*

THE STORY TELLER

There was yearning, but there was no waiting.
The oath is broken. No one could say why.
Hear what she thought but did not say:
"While you fought in the battle, soldier,
The bloody battle, the bitter battle
I found a child who was helpless
I had not the heart to destroy it
I had to care for what had gone astray
I had to bend down for bread crumbs on the floor
I had to rend myself for that which was not mine
That which was strange.
Someone must help.
For the little tree needs water
The lamb loses its way when the shepherd is asleep
And its cry is unheard!"

SIMON Give me back the cross I gave you. Better still, throw it into the stream. *(He turns to go.)*

GRUSHA *(getting up)* Simon Shashava, don't go away! It isn't mine! It isn't mine! *(She hears the children calling.)* What is the matter, children?

VOICES Soldiers have come! They are taking Michael away!

*(*GRUSHA *stands aghast as two* IRONSHIRTS, *with* MICHAEL *between them, come toward her.)*

ONE OF THE IRONSHIRTS Are you Grusha? *(She nods.)* Is this your child?

GRUSHA Yes. (SIMON *goes.)* Simon!

THE IRONSHIRT We have orders, in the name of the law, to take this child, found in your custody, back to the city. It is suspected that the child is Michael Abashwili, son and heir of the late Governor Georgi Abashwili, and his wife, Natella Abashwili. Here is the document and the seal. *(They lead the child away.)*

GRUSHA *(running after them, shouting)* Leave it here. Please! It's mine!

THE STORY TELLER

The Ironshirts took the child, the beloved child.
The unhappy girl followed them to the city, the dreaded city.
She who had borne him demanded the child.
She who had raised him faced trial.
Who will decide the case?
To whom will the child be assigned?
Who will the judge be? A good judge? A bad?
The city was in flames.
In the judge's seat sat Azdak.

part II

scene 1

THE STORY OF THE JUDGE

THE STORY TELLER

Hear the story of the judge
How he turned judge, how he passed judgment, what kind of judge he was.
On that Easter Sunday of the great revolt, when the Grand Duke was overthrown
And his Governor Abashwili, father of our child, lost his head
The Village Recorder Azdak found in the woods a fugitive and hid him in his hut.

*(*AZDAK, *in rags and slightly drunk, is helping an old beggar into his cottage.)*

AZDAK Stop snorting, you're not a horse. And it won't do you any good with the police if you run like a snotty nose in April. Stand still, I say. *(He catches* THE OLD MAN, *who has marched into the cottage as if he'd like to go through the walls.)* Sit down and feed. Here's a hunk of cheese. *(From under some rags, in a chest, he fishes out some cheese, and* THE OLD MAN *greedily begins to eat.)* Haven't eaten in a long time, huh? *(*THE OLD MAN *growls.)* Why did you run like that, asshole? The cop wouldn't even have seen you.

THE OLD MAN I had to.

AZDAK Blue funk? (THE OLD MAN *stares, uncomprehending.)* Cold feet? Panic? Don't lick your chops like a Grand Duke. Or an old sow. I can't stand it. We have to take respectable stinkers as God made them, but not you! I once heard of a senior judge who farted at a public dinner just to show an independent spirit! Watching you eat like that gives me the most awful ideas. Why don't you say something? *(sharply)* Show me your hand. Can't you hear? (THE OLD MAN *slowly puts out his hand.)* White! So you're not a beggar at all! A fraud, a walking swindle! And I'm hiding you from the cops as though you were a honest man! Why were you running like that if you're a landowner? For that's what you are. Don't deny it, I see it in your guilty face. *(He gets up.)* Get out! (THE OLD MAN *looks at him uncertainly.)* What are you waiting for, pleasant-flogger?

THE OLD MAN Pursued. Need undivided attention. Make proposition . . .

AZDAK Make what? A proposition? Well, if that isn't the height of insolence. He's making me a proposition! The bitten man scratches his fingers bloody, and the leech that's biting him makes him a proposition! Get out, I tell you!

THE OLD MAN Understand point of view. Persuasion! Pay hundred thousand piasters one night. Yes?

AZDAK What, you think you can buy me? For a hundred thousand piasters? Let's say a hundred and fifty thousand. Where are they?

THE OLD MAN Have not them here. Of course. Will be sent. Hope do not doubt.

AZDAK Doubt very much. Get out!

(THE OLD MAN *gets up, waddles to the door. A voice is heard off stage.)*

A VOICE Azdak!

(THE OLD MAN *turns, waddles to the opposite corner, stands still.)*

AZDAK *(calling out)* I'm not in! *(He walks to door.)* So you're sniffing around here again, Shauwa?

POLICEMAN SHAUWA *(reproachfully)* You've caught another rabbit, Azdak. You promised me it wouldn't happen again.

AZDAK *(severely)* Shauwa, don't talk about things you don't understand. The rabbit is a dangerous and destructive beast. It gorges itself on plants, especially on that species of plants known as weeds. It must therefore be exterminated.

SHAUWA Azdak, don't be so hard on me. I'll lose my job if I don't arrest you. I know you have a good heart.

AZDAK I do *not* have a good heart! How often must I tell you I'm a man of intellect?

SHAUWA *(slyly)* I know, Azdak. You're a superior person. You say so yourself. I'm just a Christian and an ignoramus. And so I ask you: When a rabbit of the Prince's is stolen and I'm a policeman, what am I to do with the offending party?

AZDAK Shauwa, Shauwa, shame on you. There you stand asking me a question! What could be more tempting? Suppose you were a woman —let's say Nunowna, that bad girl—and you show me your thigh—

Nunowna's thigh, that is—and ask me: What shall I do with my thigh, it itches? Is she as innocent as she pretends? No. I catch a rabbit, but you catch a man. Man is made in God's image. Not so a rabbit, you know that. I'm a rabbit-eater, but you're a man-eater, Shauwa. And God will pass judgment on you. Shauwa, go home and repent. No, stop, there's something . . . *(He looks at* THE OLD MAN *who stands trembling in the corner.)* No, it's nothing. Go home and repent. *(He slams the door behind* SHAUWA.*)* Now you're surprised, huh? Surprised I didn't hand you over? I couldn't bring myself to hand over a bedbug to that beast! It goes against the grain with me. Don't tremble because of a cop. So old and still so scared? Finish your cheese, but eat it like a poor man, or else they'll still catch you. Must I even tell you how a poor man behaves? *(He pushes him down, and then gives him back the cheese.)* The box is the table. Lay your elbows on the table. Now encircle the cheese on the plate as if it might be snatched away from you at any moment—what right have *you* to be safe, huh? Now hold the knife like an undersized sickle, and give your cheese a troubled look because, like all beautiful things, it's already fading away. *(*AZDAK *watches him.)* They're after you. That speaks in your favor. But how can we be sure they're not mistaken about you? In Tiflis one time they hanged a landowner, a Turk, who could prove he quartered his peasants instead of merely cutting them in half, as is the custom. And he squeezed twice the usual amount of taxes out of them. His zeal was above suspicion. And yet they hanged him like a common criminal—because he was a Turk—a thing he couldn't do much about. An injustice! He got onto the gallows by a sheer fluke. In short, I don't trust you.

THE STORY TELLER

Thus Azdak gave the old beggar a bed,
And learned that old beggar was the old butcher, the Grand Duke himself,
And was ashamed.
He accused himself and ordered the policeman to take him to Nuka, to court, to be judged.

(In the court of justice three IRONSHIRTS *sit drinking. From a beam hangs a man in judge's robes. Enter* AZDAK, *in chains, dragging* SHAUWA *behind him.)*

AZDAK *(shouting)* I have helped the Grand Duke, the Grand Thief, the Grand Butcher, to escape! In the name of justice I ask to be severely judged in public trial!

THE FIRST IRONSHIRT Who's this queer bird?

SHAUWA That's our Recorder, Azdak.

AZDAK I am despicable! treacherous! branded! Tell them, flatfoot, how I insisted on being put in chains and brought to the capital. Because I sheltered the Grand Duke, the Grand Swindler by mistake. And how afterward I found out. Look, a marked man is denouncing himself! Tell them how I forced you to walk with me half the night to clear the whole thing up.

SHAUWA And all by threats. That wasn't nice of you, Azdak.

AZDAK Shut your mouth, Shauwa. You don't understand. A new age has come. It'll go thundering over you. You're finished. The police will be wiped out—pouf! Everything will be gone into, everything brought into the open. A man will give himself up, and why?—because he couldn't escape the people in any case. *(to* SHAUWA*)* Tell them how I have been shouting all along Shoemaker Street. *(with big gestures, looking at the* IRONSHIRTS*)* "In ignorance I let the Grand Swindler escape! Tear me to pieces, brothers!" To get it in first.

THE FIRST IRONSHIRT And what was their answer?

SHAUWA They comforted him in Butcher Street, and they laughed themselves sick in Shoemaker Street. That's all.

AZDAK But here with you it's different, I know you're like iron. Brothers, where's the judge? I must be tried.

THE FIRST IRONSHIRT *(pointing at the hanged man)* Here's the judge. And please stop "brothering" us. That's rather a sore spot this evening.

AZDAK "Here's the judge." That's an answer never heard in Grusinia before. Townsman, where's His Excellency the Governor? *(pointing to the floor)* Here's His Excellency, stranger. Where's the Chief Tax Collector? Where's the official Recruiting Officer? The Patriarch? The Chief of Police? Here, here, here—all here. Brothers, that's what I expected of you.

THE SECOND IRONSHIRT Stop. What did you expect, funny man?

AZDAK What happened in Persia, brother, what happened there?

THE SECOND IRONSHIRT And what did happen in Persia?

AZDAK Forty years ago. Everybody was hanged. Viziers, tax collectors. Everybody. My grandfather, a remarkable man by the way, saw it all. For three whole days. Everywhere.

THE SECOND IRONSHIRT And who ruled when the Vizier was hanged?

AZDAK A peasant.

THE SECOND IRONSHIRT And who commanded the army?

AZDAK A soldier, soldier.

THE SECOND IRONSHIRT And who paid the wages?

AZDAK A dyer. A dyer paid the wages.

THE SECOND IRONSHIRT Wasn't it a weaver, maybe?

THE FIRST IRONSHIRT And why did all this happen, Persian?

AZDAK "Why did all this happen?" Must there be a special reason? Why do you scratch yourself, brother? War! Too long a war! And no justice! My grandfather brought back a song that tells how it was. I and my friend the policeman will sing it for you. *(to* SHAUWA*)* And hold the rope tight. It's very suitable! *(He sings, with* SHAUWA *holding the rope tight around him.)*

THE SONG OF INJUSTICE IN PERSIA

Why don't our sons bleed any more? Why don't our daughters weep?
Why do only the slaughter-house calves have blood in their veins?
Why do only the willows shed tears on Lake Urmi?
The king must have a new province, the peasant must give up his sav-

ings.
That the roof of the world might be conquered, the roof of the cottage is torn down.
Our men are carried to the ends of the earth, so that great ones can eat at home.
The soldiers kill each other, the marshals salute each other.
They bite the widow's tax money to see if it's good, their swords break.
The battle was lost, the helmets were paid for.
(refrain) Is it so? Is it so?

SHAUWA *(refrain)* Yes, yes, yes, yes, yes it's so.

AZDAK Do you want to hear the rest of it?

*(*THE FIRST IRONSHIRT *nods.)*

THE SECOND IRONSHIRT *(to* SHAUWA*)* Did he teach you that song?

SHAUWA Yes, only my voice isn't very good.

THE SECOND IRONSHIRT No. *(to* AZDAK*)* Go on singing.

AZDAK The second verse is about the peace. *(He sings.)*
The offices are packed, the streets overflow with officials.
The rivers jump their banks and ravage the fields.
Those who cannot let down their own trousers rule countries.
They can't count up to four, but they devour eight courses.
The corn farmers, looking round for buyers, see only the starving.
The weavers go home from their looms in rags.
(refrain) Is it so? Is it so?

SHAUWA *(refrain)* Yes, yes, yes, yes, yes it's so.

AZDAK
That's why our sons don't bleed any more, that's why our daughters don't weep.
That's why only the slaughter-house calves have blood in their veins,
And only the willows shed tears by Lake Urmi toward morning.

THE FIRST IRONSHIRT Are you going to sing that song here in town?

AZDAK Sure. What's wrong with it?

THE FIRST IRONSHIRT Do you see how the sky's getting red? *(Turning round,* AZDAK *sees the sky red with fire.)* That's in the suburbs. The carpet weavers have also caught the "Persian Sickness," and have asked if Prince Kazbeki isn't eating too many courses. And this morning they strung up the city judge. We have beaten them to pulp for one hundred piasters a man, you understand?

AZDAK *(after a pause)* I understand. *(He glances shyly round and, creeping away, sits down in a corner, his head in his hands.)*

THE IRONSHIRTS *(to each other)* If there ever was a trouble-maker it's him.
—He must've come to the capital to fish in the troubled waters.

SHAUWA I don't think he's a really bad character, gentlemen. Steals a few chickens here and there. And maybe a rabbit.

THE SECOND IRONSHIRT *(approaching* AZDAK*)* Came to fish in the troubled waters, huh?

AZDAK *(looking up)* I don't know why I came.

THE SECOND IRONSHIRT Are you maybe in with the carpet weavers?

(AZDAK *shakes his head.)*

THE SECOND IRONSHIRT And what about that song?

AZDAK From my grandfather. A silly and ignorant man.

THE SECOND IRONSHIRT Right. And what about the dyer who paid the wages?

AZDAK *(muttering)* That was in Persia.

THE FIRST IRONSHIRT And your denouncing yourself? For not having hanged the Grand Duke with your own hands?

AZDAK Didn't I tell you I let him run? *(He creeps farther away and sits on the floor.)*

SHAUWA I swear to that. He let him run.

(THE IRONSHIRTS *burst out laughing and slap* SHAUWA *on the back.* AZDAK *laughs loudest. They slap* AZDAK *too, and unchain him. They all start drinking as* THE FAT PRINCE *enters with a young man.)*

THE FIRST IRONSHIRT *(to* AZDAK, *pointing at* THE FAT PRINCE*)* There you have your new age! *(more laughter)*

THE FAT PRINCE Well, my friends, what have you got to laugh about? Permit me a serious word. Yesterday morning the Princes of Grusinia overthrew the war-mongering government of the Grand Duke and did away with his Governors. Unfortunately the Grand Duke himself escaped. In this fateful hour our carpet weavers, those eternal troublemakers, had the effrontery to stir up a rebellion and hang the universally loved city judge, our dear Illo Orbeliani. Ts—ts—ts. My friends, we need peace, peace, peace in Grusinia! And justice! Here I bring you my dear nephew, Bizergan Kazbeki. He's to be the new judge. A very gifted fellow. What do you say? I want your opinion. I say: Let the people decide.

THE SECOND IRONSHIRT Does this mean we elect the judge?

THE FAT PRINCE Precisely. The people propose a very gifted fellow. Confer among yourselves, my friends. (THE IRONSHIRTS *confer.)* Don't worry, foxy. The job's yours. And the moment we catch the Grand Duke we'll not have to kiss this rabble's ass any more.

THE IRONSHIRTS *(between themselves)* That'll be fun.

—They have their pants full because they haven't caught the Grand Duke.

—When the outlook isn't so bright, they say: "My friends!" and "Let the people decide!"—Now he even wants justice for Grusinia! But fun is fun as long as it lasts! *(pointing at* AZDAK*)* He knows all about justice. Hey, rascal, would you like to have the nephew be judge?

AZDAK Are you asking me?

THE FIRST IRONSHIRT Why not? Anything for a laugh!

AZDAK I understand you want to test him to the marrow. Correct? Have you a criminal ready? An old hand? So the candidiate can show what he knows?

THE SECOND IRONSHIRT Let me see, we've a couple of doctors downstairs. Let's use them.

AZDAK Stop! That's no good. You can't take real criminals till we're sure of the judge being appointed. He may be dumb, but he must be appointed or else the law is violated. The law is a very sensitive creature. Like the spleen, it must never be assaulted or—it's all over. You can hang those two. Why not? You won't have violated the law, because the judge wasn't there. Judgment must always be pronounced with absolute gravity—why? Because it's such nonsense. Suppose, for instance, a judge jails a woman that's stolen a corncake for her child, and the judge isn't wearing his robes. Maybe he's scratching himself while passing sentence and nearly half his body is uncovered—a man must scratch his thigh once in a while—then the sentence he passes is a disgrace and the law is violated. It would be easier for a judge's robe and a judge's hat to pass judgment than for a mere man with no robe and no hat! If you don't watch out, the law just goes to pot. You don't try out a bottle of wine by offering it to a dog, and why not? Because you'd lose your wine.

THE FIRST IRONSHIRT Then what do you suggest, hair-splitter?

AZDAK I'll be the accused.

THE FIRST IRONSHIRT You! *(He bursts out laughing.)*

THE FAT PRINCE What have you decided?

THE FIRST IRONSHIRT We've decided to have a tryout. Our friend will be the accused, and here's the judge's seat for the candidate.

THE FAT PRINCE It isn't customary, but why not? *(to* THE NEPHEW*)* A mere formality, foxy. What have you learned? Who got there first? The slow runner or the fast?

THE NEPHEW The silent runner, Uncle Arsen.

*(*THE NEPHEW *takes the chair.* THE IRONSHIRTS *and* THE FAT PRINCE *sit on the steps. Enter* AZDAK, *mimicking the gait of* THE GRAND DUKE.*)*

AZDAK Is any here knows me? I am Grand Duke.

THE IRONSHIRTS What is he?

—The Grand Duke. He really knows him.

—That's fine. Get on with the proceedings.

AZDAK Listen! Am accused instigating war. Ridiculous! Am saying ridiculous! That enough? If not, have brought lawyers. Believe five hundred. *(He points behind him, pretending to be surrounded by lawyers.)* Requisition all available seats for lawyers!

*(*THE IRONSHIRTS *laugh;* THE FAT PRINCE *joins in.)*

THE NEPHEW *(to* THE IRONSHIRTS*)* Do you want me to try this case? I must admit I find it rather unusual. From the taste angle, I mean.

THE FIRST IRONSHIRT Let's go!

THE FAT PRINCE *(smiling)* Let him have it, foxy!

THE NEPHEW All right. People of Grusinia versus Grand Duke. Defendant, what have you to say!

AZDAK Plenty. Naturally, have read war lost. Only started on the advice of patriots. Like Uncle Arsen Kazbeki. Demand Uncle Arsen as witness.

THE FAT PRINCE *(to* THE IRONSHIRTS, *delightedly)* What a screwball!

THE NEPHEW Motion rejected. You cannot be accused of declaring a war, which every ruler has to do once in a while, but only of conducting it badly.

AZDAK Rubbish! Did not conduct it at all! Had it conducted! Had it conducted by Princes! Naturally they messed it up.

THE NEPHEW Do you by any chance deny having been commander-in-chief?

AZDAK Not at all! Always was commander-in-chief. At birth shouted at wet nurse. Was trained to drop turds in toilet. Grew accustomed to command. Always commanded officials rob my cash box. Officers flog soldiers only on command. Landowners sleep with peasants' wives only on strictest command. Uncle Arsen here gew his belly only by my command!

THE IRONSHIRTS *(clapping)* He's good! Long live the Grand Duke!

THE FAT PRINCE Answer him, foxy! I'm with you.

THE NEPHEW I shall answer him according to the dignity of the law. Defendant, preserve the dignity of the law!

AZDAK Agreed. I command you to proceed with the trial!

THE NEPHEW It's not your place to command me. So you claim that the Princes forced you to declare war. How can you claim then that they—er—"messed it up"?

AZDAK Did not send enough people. Embezzled funds. Sent sick horses. During attack, drinking in whore house. Propose Uncle Arsen as witness.

THE NEPHEW Are you trying to make the outrageous claim that the Princes of this country did not fight?

AZDAK No. Princes fought. Fought for war contracts.

THE FAT PRINCE *(jumping up)* That's too much! This man talks like a carpet weaver!

AZDAK Really? Nothing but the truth!

THE FAT PRINCE Hang him! Hang him!

THE FIRST IRONSHIRT *(pulling the* PRINCE *down)* Keep quiet! Go on, Excellency!

THE NEPHEW Quiet! I now render a verdict: You must be hanged! By the neck! Having lost war!

AZDAK Young man, seriously advise not to fall publicly into jerky and clipped manner of speech. Cannot be employed as watchdog if howl like wolf. Got it? If people realize Princes talk same language as Grand Duke, may hang Grand Duke *and* Princes, huh? By the way, must overrule verdict. Reason? War lost, but not for Princes. Princes have won *their* war. Got themselves paid 3,863,000 piasters for horses not delivered, 8,240,000 piasters for food supplies not produced. Are therefore victors. War lost only for Grusinia, which is not present in this court.

THE FAT PRINCE I think that's enough, my friends. *(to* AZDAK*)* You can withdraw, funny man. *(to the* IRONSHIRTS*)* I think you can now ratify the new judge's appointment, my friends.

THE FIRST IRONSHIRT Yes, we can. Take down the judge's gown. *(One* IRONSHIRT *climbs on the back of the other, pulls the gown off the hanged man.)* And now *(to* THE NEPHEW*)* you be off so the right ass can get on the right chair! *(to* AZDAK*)* Step forward! Go to the judge's seat and sit up there, man. *(*AZDAK *steps up, bows, and sits down.)* The judge was always a rascal! Now the rascal shall be a judge! *(The judge's gown is placed round his shoulders, the hat on his head.)* And what a judge!

THE STORY TELLER

And there was civil war in the land.
The ruler was unsafe.
And Azdak was made a judge by the Ironshirts.
And Azdak remained a judge for two years.

THE STORY TELLER AND CHORUS

Conflagration's heat, and blood in every street,
And cockroach and bug in every town.
In the castle, fánatics. At the altar, heretics.
And Azdak wearing a judge's gown.

*(*AZDAK *sits in the judge's chair, peeling an apple.* SHAUWA *is sweeping out the hall. On one side an* INVALID *in a wheelchair. Opposite, a young man accused of blackmail. An* IRONSHIRT *stands on guard, holding the Ironshirt's banner.)*

AZDAK In consideration of the large number of cases, the Court today will hear two cases at a time. Before I open the proceedings, a short announcement—I accept—*(He stretches out his hand.* THE BLACKMAILER *is the only one to produce any money. He hands it to* AZDAK.*)*—I reserve for myself the right to punish one of the parties here for contempt of court. *(He glances at* THE INVALID.*)* You *(to* THE DOCTOR*)* are a doctor, and you *(to* THE INVALID*)* are bringing a complaint against him. Is the doctor responsible for your condition?

THE INVALID Yes. I had a stroke because of him.

AZDAK That would be professional negligence.

THE INVALID More than negligence. I gave this man money for his studies. So far, he hasn't paid me back a cent. And when I heard he was treating a patient free, I had a stroke.

AZDAK Rightly. *(to a* LIMPING MAN*)* And what do you want here?

THE LIMPING MAN I'm the patient, your honor.

AZDAK He treated your leg for nothing?

THE LIMPING MAN The wrong leg! My rheumatism was in the left leg, and he operated on the right. That's why I limp now.

AZDAK And you got it free?

THE INVALID A five-hundred-piaster operation free! For nothing! For a God-bless-you! And I paid for this man's studies! *(to* THE DOCTOR:*)* Did they teach you to operate free?

THE DOCTOR Your Honor, it is actually the custom to demand the fee before the operation, as the patient is more willing to pay before an operation than after. Which is only human. In the case in question I was convinced, when I started the operation, that my servant had already received the fee. In this I was mistaken.

THE INVALID He was mistaken! A good doctor doesn't make mistakes! He examines before he operates.

AZDAK That's right. *(to* SHAUWA*)* Public Prosecutor, what's the other case about?

SHAUWA *(busily sweeping)* Blackmail.

THE BLACKMAILER High Court of Justice, I'm innocent. I only wanted to find out from the landowner concerned if he really had raped his niece. He informed me very politely that this was not the case, and gave me the money only so I could pay for my uncle's studies.

AZDAK Hm. *(to* THE DOCTOR*)* You, on the other hand, can cite no extenuating circumstances for your offense, huh?

THE DOCTOR Except that to err is human.

AZDAK And you are perfectly well aware that in money matters a good doctor is conscious of his responsibility? I once heard of a doctor who made a thousand piasters out of one sprained finger: he discovered it had something to do with blood circulation, which a less good doctor might have overlooked. On another occasion he made a real gold mine out of the careful treatment of a somewhat disordered gall bladder. You have no excuse, Doctor. The corn merchant, Uxu, had his son study medicine to get some knowledge of trade, our medical schools are so good. *(to the* BLACKMAILER*)* What's the name of the landowner?

SHAUWA He doesn't want it mentioned.

AZDAK In that case I will pass judgment. The Court considers the blackmail proved. And you *(to* THE INVALID*)* are sentenced to a fine of one thousand piasters. If you have a second stroke, the doctor will have to treat you free. Even if he has to amputate. *(to* THE LIMPING MAN*)* As compensation, you will receive a bottle of rubbing alcohol. *(to* THE BLACKMAILER*)* You are sentenced to hand over half the proceeds of your deal to the Public Prosecutor to keep the landowner's name secret. You are advised, moreover, to study medicine—you seem well suited to that calling. *(to* THE DOCTOR*)* You have perpetrated an unpardonable error in the practice of your profession: you are acquitted. Next cases!

THE STORY TELLER AND CHORUS

With a pound you're on firm ground (no one is willing for a shilling)
And the law is a cat in a sack.
But one whelp brings help to the many for a penny.
The name of this rascal? Azdak.

(Enter AZDAK *from the caravansary on the highroad, followed by an old bearded innkeeper. The judge's chair is carried by a stableman and* SHAUWA. *An* IRONSHIRT, *with a banner, takes up his position.)*

AZDAK Put it here. Then we'll get some air and maybe a good breeze from the lemon grove over there. It does justice good to be administered in the open: the wind blows her skirts up and you can see what she's got underneath. Shauwa, we've eaten too much. These official journeys are very exhausting. *(to* THE INNKEEPER*)* It's a question of your daughter-in-law?

THE INNKEEPER Your Worship, it's a question of the family honor. I wish to bring an action on behalf of my son, who's on business on the other side of the mountain. This is the offending stableman, and here's my daughter-in-law.

(Enter THE DAUGHTER-IN-LAW, *a voluptuous wench. She is veiled.)*

AZDAK *(sitting down)* I accept . . . *(Sighing,* THE INNKEEPER *hands him some money.)* Good. Now the formalities are disposed of. This is a case of rape?

THE INNKEEPER Your Honor, I caught the fellow in the act. Ludovica was already in the straw on the stable floor.

AZDAK Quite right, the stable. Beautiful horses! I particularly liked the little roan.

THE INNKEEPER The first thing I did, of course, was question Ludovica. On my son's behalf.

AZDAK *(seriously)* I said I particularly liked it.

THE INNKEEPER *(coldly)* Really? Ludovica confessed the stableman took her against her will.

AZDAK Take your veil off, Ludovica. *(She does so.)* Ludovica, you please the Court. Tell us how it happened.

LUDOVICA *(well-schooled)* When I entered the stable to see the new foal the stableman said to me on his own accord: "It's hot today!" and laid his hand on my left breast. I said to him: "Don't do that!" But he continued to handle me indecently, which provoked my anger. Before I realized his sinful intentions, he had got much closer. It had already taken place when my father-in-law entered and accidentally trod on me.

THE INNKEEPER *(explaining)* On my son's behalf.

AZDAK *(to* THE STABLEMAN*)* Do you admit you started it?

THE STABLEMAN Yes.

AZDAK Ludovica, do you like to eat sweet things?

LUDOVICA Yes, sunflower seeds!

AZDAK Do you like to lie a long time in the bathtub?

LUDOVICA Half an hour or so.

AZDAK Public Prosecutor, drop your knife—there—on the floor. *(*SHAUWA *does so.)* Ludovica, go and pick up the knife. *(*LUDOVICA, *swaying her hips, does so.)* See that? *(He points at her.)* The way it moves? The rape is now proven. By eating too much—sweet things, especially—by lying too long in warm water, by laziness and too soft a skin, you have raped that unfortunate man. Do you imagine you can run around with a behind like that and get away with it in court? This is a case of intentional assault with a dangerous weapon! You are sentenced to hand over to the Court the little roan which your father liked to ride "on his son's behalf." And now, come with me to the stables, so the Court may inspect the scene of the crime, Ludovica.

THE STORY TELLER AND CHORUS

When visiting your neighbor sharpen up your ax,
For Bible texts and sermons are trivial knickknacks.
What miracles past believing the ax's edge can do!
Sometimes Azdak believed in miracles too.

*(*AZDAK'S *judge's chair is in a tavern. Three rich farmers stand before* AZDAK. SHAUWA *brings him wine. In a corner stands an old peasant woman. In the open doorway, and outside, stand villagers looking on. An* IRONSHIRT *stands guard with a banner.)*

AZDAK The Public Prosecutor has the floor.

SHAUWA It concerns a cow. For five weeks the defendant has had a cow in her stable, the property of the farmer Suru. She was also found to be in possession of a stolen ham, and a number of cows belonging to Shutoff were killed after he had asked the defendant to pay the rent on a piece of land.

THE FARMERS It's a matter of my ham, Your Honor.
—It's a matter of my cow, Your Honor.
—It's a matter of my land, Your Honor.

AZDAK Well, Granny, what have you got to say to all this?

THE OLD WOMAN Your Honor, one night toward morning, five weeks ago, there was a knock at my door, and outside stood a bearded man with a cow, and said: "My dear woman, I am the miracle-working Saint Banditus and because your son has been killed in the war, I bring you this cow as a souvenir. Take good care of it."

THE FARMERS The robber, Irakli, Your Honor!
—Her brother-in-law, Your Honor!
—The cow-thief!
—The incendiary!
—He must be beheaded!

(Outside, a woman screams. The crowd grows restless, retreats. Enter THE BANDIT IRAKLI *with a huge ax.)*

THE BANDIT A very good evening, dear friends! A glass of vodka!

THE FARMERS *(crossing themselves)* Irakli!

AZDAK Public Prosecutor, a glass of vodka for our guest. And who are you?

THE BANDIT I'm a wandering hermit, Your Honor. And thank you for the gracious gift. *(He empties the glass which* SHAUWA *has brought.)* Another!

AZDAK I am Azdak. *(He gets up and bows.* THE BANDIT *also bows.)* The Court welcomes the foreign hermit. Go on with your story, Granny.

THE OLD WOMAN Your Honor, that first night I didn't yet know that Saint Banditus could work miracles, it was only the cow. But one night, a few days later, the farmer's servants came to take the cow away again. Then they turned round in front of my door and went off without the cow. And on their heads sprouted bumps big as a fist. Then I knew that Saint Banditus had changed their hearts and turned them into friendly people. *(*THE BANDIT *roars with laughter.)*

THE FIRST FARMER I know what changed them.

AZDAK That's fine. You can tell us later. Continue.

THE OLD WOMAN Your Honor, the next one to become a good man was the farmer Shutoff—a devil, as everyone knows. But Saint Banditus has arranged it so that he let me off the rent on the little piece of land.

THE SECOND FARMER Because my cows were killed in the field. *(*THE BANDIT *laughs.)*

THE OLD WOMAN *(answering* AZDAK'S *sign to continue)* And then one morning the ham came flying in at my window. It hit me in the small of the back. I'm still lame from it, see, Your Honor. *(She limps a few steps.* THE BANDIT *laughs.)* I ask Your Honor, was there ever a time when a poor old woman could get a ham without a miracle? *(*THE BANDIT *starts sobbing.)*

AZDAK *(rising from his chair)* Granny, that's a question that strikes straight at the Court's heart. Be so kind as to sit down here. *(Hesitating,* THE OLD WOMAN *sits in the judge's chair.* AZDAK *sits on the floor, glass in hand, reciting.)*

Granny, I almost called you Mother Grusinia the Woebegone,
The bereaved one, whose sons are at the war.
She is beaten with fists, but full of hope.
She weeps when she receives a cow.
She is surprised when she is *not* beaten.
May you render a merciful verdict on Us the Damned!

(bellowing at THE FARMERS*)* Admit that you don't believe in miracles, you atheists! Each of you is sentenced to pay five hundred piasters! For your godlessness! Get out! *(*THE FARMERS *slink out.)* And you Granny, and you *(to* THE BANDIT*)* pious man, empty a pitcher of wine with the Public Prosecutor and Azdak!

THE STORY TELLER AND CHORUS

Statute and rule he broke like a loaf to feed the folk.
On the wreck of the law he brought them to the shore,
Granted their shrill demands, took bribes from the empty hands
Of the simple and the poor.
Two years and more Azdak was a wolf to the wolf pack
And weighed with a false scale.
In the judge's seat he'd stay—the gallows not far away—
The law had a sting in its tail.

THE STORY TELLER

But the era of disorder came to an end.
The Grand Duke returned.
The Governor's wife returned.
A trial was held.
Many people died.
The suburbs burned anew,
And fear seized Azdak.

*(*AZDAK'S *judge's chair stands again in the court of justice.* AZDAK *sits on the floor, shaving and talking to* SHAUWA. *Noises outside. In the rear* THE FAT PRINCE'S *head is carried by on a lance.)*

AZDAK Shauwa, the days of your slavery are numbered, maybe even the minutes. For a long time I have held you in the iron curb of reason, and it has torn your mouth till it bleeds. I have lashed you with reasonable arguments and manhandled you with logic. You are by nature a weak man, and if one slyly throws an argument in your path, you have to snap it up. You can't resist. By nature, you have to lick the hand of a superior being, but superior beings can be of very different kinds. And now with your liberation, you will soon be able to follow your inclinations, which are low. You will be able to follow your infallible instinct, which teaches you to plant your fat heel on the faces of men. Gone is the era of confusion and disorder, which I find described in the Song of Chaos. Let us now sing that song together in memory of those terrible days. Sit down and don't do violence to the music. Don't be afraid. It sounds all right.

And it has a fine refrain. *(He sings.)*

THE SONG OF CHAOS

Sister, hide your face! Brother, take your knife!
The times are out of joint!
Big men are full of complaints
And small men full of joy.
The city says:
"Let us drive the strong ones from our midst!"
Offices are raided. Lists of serfs are destroyed.
They have set Master's nose to the grindstone.
They who lived in the dark have seen the light.
The ebony poor box is broken.
Sesnem wood is sawed up for beds.
Who had no bread have barns full.
Who begged for alms of corn now mete it out.

SHAUWA *(refrain)* Oh, oh, oh, oh.

AZDAK *(refrain)*
Where are you, General, where are you?
Please, please, please, restore order!

The nobleman's son can no longer be recognized;
The lady's child becomes the son of her slave.
The councilors meet in a shed.
Once, this man was barely allowed to sleep on the wall;
Now, he stretches his limbs in a bed.
Once, this man rowed a boat; now, he owns ships.
Their owner looks for them, but they're his no longer.
Five men are sent on a journey by their master.
"Go yourself," they say, "we have arrived."

SHAUWA *(refrain)* Oh, oh, oh, oh.

AZDAK *(refrain)*
Where are you, General, where are you?
Please, please, please, restore order!

Yes. So it might have been, had order been neglected much longer. But now the Grand Duke has returned to the capital, and the Persians have lent him an army to restore order with. The suburbs are already aflame. Go and get me the big book I always sit on. *(SHAUWA brings the big book from the judge's chair. AZDAK opens it.)* This is the Statute Book and I've always used it, as you can testify. Now I'd better look and see what they can do to me. I've let the down-and-outs get away with murder, and I'll have to pay for it. I helped poverty onto its skinny legs, so they'll hang me for drunkenness. I peeped into the rich man's pocket, which is bad taste. And I can't hide anywhere—everybody knows me because I have helped everybody.

SHAUWA Someone's coming!

AZDAK *(in panic, he walks trembling to the chair)* The end! And now they'd enjoy seeing what a Great Man I am. I'll deprive them of that pleasure. I'll beg on my knees for mercy. Spittle will slobber down my chin. The fear of death is in me. *(Enter* NATELLA ABASHWILI, THE GOVERNOR'S WIFE, *followed by* THE ADJUTANT *and an* IRONSHIRT.*)*

THE GOVERNOR'S WIFE What sort of a creature is that, Shalva?

AZDAK A willing one, Your Highness, a man ready to oblige.

THE ADJUTANT Natella Abashwili, wife of the late Governor, has just returned and is looking for her two-year-old son, Michael. She has been informed that the child was carried off to the mountains by a former servant.

AZDAK It will be brought back, Your Highness, at your service.

THE ADJUTANT They say that the person in question is passing it off as her own child.

AZDAK She will be beheaded, Your Highness, at your service.

THE ADJUTANT That is all.

THE GOVERNOR'S WIFE *(leaving)* I don't like that man.

AZDAK *(following her to door, bowing)* At your service, Your Highness, it will all be arranged.

scene 2

THE CHALK CIRCLE

THE STORY TELLER

Hear now the story of the trial
Concerning Governor Abashwili's child
And the establishing of the true mother
By the famous test of the Chalk Circle.

(The court of justice in Nuka. IRONSHIRTS *lead* MICHAEL *across stage and out at the back.* IRONSHIRTS *hold* GRUSHA *back with their lances under the gateway until the child has been led through. Then she is admitted. She is accompanied by the former Governor's* COOK. *Distant noises and a fire-red sky.)*

GRUSHA *(trying to hide)* He's brave, he can wash himself already.

THE COOK You're lucky. It's not a real judge. It's Azdak. Just a drunk who doesn't understand a thing. The biggest thieves have got by through him. Because he mixes everything up and the rich never offer him big enough bribes, the likes of us sometimes get off pretty well.

GRUSHA Today I *need* luck.

THE COOK Touch wood. *(She crosses herself.)* I'd better offer up another prayer that the judge may be drunk. *(She prays with motionless lips, while* GRUSHA *looks around, in vain, for the child.)*

THE COOK What I can't understand is why you must hold on to it at any price if it isn't yours. In days like these.

GRUSHA He's mine. I brought him up.

THE COOK But have you never thought what'd happen when she came back?

GRUSHA At first I thought I'd give him back to her. Then I thought she *wouldn't* come back.

THE COOK And even a borrowed coat keeps a man warm, hm? *(*GRUSHA *nods.)* I'll swear to anything for you. You're a decent girl. *(She sees the soldier* SIMON SHASHAVA *approaching.)* You have done a great wrong by Simon. I've talked with him. He can't understand it.

GRUSHA *(unaware of* SIMON'S *presence)* Just now I can't be bothered with him if he can't understand.

THE COOK He has understood the child is not yours, but you married and not free until death you do part—he can't understand that.

*(*GRUSHA *sees* SIMON *and greets him.)*

SIMON *(gloomily)* I wanted to inform the lady I am ready to swear I am the father of the child.

GRUSHA *(low)* Thank you, Simon.

SIMON At the same time I would like to inform the lady that I am not hereby bound to anything—nor she either.

THE COOK That's unnecessary. She's married. You know that.

SIMON That's her business and needs no rubbing in.

(Enter an IRONSHIRT.*)*

THE IRONSHIRT Where's the judge? Has anyone seen the judge?

ANOTHER IRONSHIRT *(stepping forward)* The judge isn't here. There's nothing but a bed and a pitcher in the whole house. *(Exeunt* IRONSHIRTS.*)*

THE COOK I hope nothing has happened to him. With any other judge you'd have about as much chance as a chicken has teeth.

GRUSHA *(who has turned away and covered her face)* Stand in front of me. I shouldn't have come to Nuka. If I run into the Ironshirt, the one I hit over the head . . .

(She screams. An IRONSHIRT *had stopped and, turning his back, had been listening to her. He now wheels around. It is* THE CORPORAL, *and he has a huge scar across his face.)*

THE IRONSHIRT *(in the gateway)* What's the matter, Shotta? Do you know her?

THE CORPORAL *(after staring for some time)* No.

THE IRONSHIRT She's the one who's supposed to have stolen the Abashwili child. If you know anything about it you can make a pile of money, Shotta. *(Exit* THE CORPORAL, *cursing.)*

THE COOK Was it him? *(*GRUSHA *nods.)* I think he'll keep his mouth shut, or he'd be admitting he was after the child.

GRUSHA I'd almost forgotten I saved the child from them.

(Enter THE GOVERNOR'S WIFE, *followed by* THE ADJUTANT *and two* LAWYERS.*)*

THE GOVERNOR'S WIFE At least there are no *common* people here, thank God. I can't stand their smell. It always gives me migraine.

THE FIRST LAWYER Madam, I must ask you to be careful what you say until we have another judge.

THE GOVERNOR'S WIFE But I didn't say anything, Illo Shuboladze. I *love* the people with their simple straightforward minds! It's only that their smell brings on my migraine.

THE SECOND LAWYER There won't be many spectators. The population is sitting at home behind locked doors because of the riots in the suburbs.

THE GOVERNOR'S WIFE *(looking at* GRUSHA*)* Is that the creature?

THE FIRST LAWYER Please, most gracious Natella Abashwili, I must ask you to abstain from all invective until it is absolutely certain that the Grand Duke has appointed a new judge, and we've got rid of the present one who is about the lowest fellow ever seen in a judge's gown. Things seem all set to move, you see.

(Enter IRONSHIRTS *from the courtyard.)*

THE COOK Her Grace would pull your hair out on the spot if she didn't know Azdak is for the poor. He goes by the face.

*(*IRONSHIRTS *begin fastening a rope to a beam.* AZDAK, *in chains, is led in, followed by* SHAUWA, *also in chains. The three farmers bring up the rear.)*

AN IRONSHIRT You were trying to run away, it seems. *(He strikes* AZDAK.*)*

ONE FARMER Off with the judge's gown before we string him up. *(*IRONSHIRTS *and farmers tear off* AZDAK'S *gown. His torn underwear is visible. Then someone kicks him.)*

AN IRONSHIRT *(pushing him into someone else)* If you want a heap of justice, here it is! *(Accompanied by shouts of* "You take it!" *and* "Let me have him, brother!" *they throw* AZDAK *back and forth until he collapses. Then he is lifted up and dragged under the noose.)*

THE GOVERNOR'S WIFE *(who, during this "ball-game," has clapped her hands hysterically)* I disliked that man from the moment I first saw him.

AZDAK *(covered with blood, panting)* I can't see. Give me a rag.

AN IRONSHIRT What is it you want to see?

AZDAK You, you dogs! *(He wipes the blood out of his eyes with his shirt.)* Good morning, dogs! How goes it, dogs! How's the dog world? Does it smell good? Got another boot for me to lick? Are you back at each other's throats, dogs?

(Accompanied by a CORPORAL, *a dust-covered* RIDER *enters. He takes some documents from a leather case, looks at them, then interrupts.)*

THE RIDER Stop! I bring a dispatch from the Grand Duke, containing the latest appointments.

THE CORPORAL *(bellowing)* Atten–shun!

THE RIDER Of the new judge it says: "We appoint a man whom we have to thank for saving a life indispensable to the country's welfare–a certain Azdak of Nuka." Which is he?

SHAUWA *(pointing)* That's him, Your Excellency.

THE CORPORAL *(bellowing)* What's going on here?

AN IRONSHIRT I beg to report that His Honor Azdak was already His Honor Azdak, but on these farmers' denunciation was pronounced the Grand Duke's enemy.

THE CORPORAL *(pointing at the farmers)* March them off! *(They are marched off. They bow all the time.)* See to it that His Honor Azdak is exposed to no more violence. *(Exeunt* RIDER *and* CORPORAL.*)*

THE COOK *(to* SHAUWA*)* She clapped her hands! I hope he saw it!
THE FIRST LAWYER It's a catastrophe.

*(*AZDAK *has fainted. Coming to, he is dressed again in judge's robes. He walks, swaying, toward the* IRONSHIRTS.*)*

AN IRONSHIRT What does Your Honor desire?

AZDAK Nothing, fellow dogs, An occasional boot to lick. *(To* SHAUWA*)* I pardon you. *(He is unchained.)* Get me some red wine, the sweet kind. *(*SHAUWA *stumbles off.)* Get out of here, I've got to judge a case. *(Exeunt* IRONSHIRTS. SHAUWA *returns with a pitcher of wine.* AZDAK *gulps it down.)* Something for my backside! *(*SHAUWA *brings the Statute Book, puts it on the judge's chair.* AZDAK *sits on it.)* I accept . . .

(The prosecutors, among whom a worried council has been held, smile with relief. They whisper.)

THE COOK Oh dear!

SIMON A well can't be filled with dew! They say.

THE LAWYERS *(approaching* AZDAK, *who stands up, expectantly)* A quite ridiculous case, Your Honor. The accused has abducted a child and refuses to hand it over.

AZDAK *(stretching out his hand, glancing at* GRUSHA*)* A most attractive person. *(He fingers the money, then sits down, satisfied.)* I open the proceedings and demand the absolute truth. *(to* GRUSHA*)* Especially from you.

THE FIRST LAWYER High Court of Justice! Blood, as the popular saying goes, is thicker than water. This old adage . . .

AZDAK *(interrupting)* The Court wants to know the lawyers' fee.

THE FIRST LAWYER *(surprised)* I beg your pardon? *(*AZDAK, *smiling, rubs his thumb and index finger.)* Oh, I see. Five hundred piasters, Your Honor, to answer the Court's somewhat unusual question.

AZDAK Did you hear? The question is unusual. I ask it because I listen to you in quite a different way when I know you are good.

THE FIRST LAWYER *(bowing)* Thank you, Your Honor. High Court of Justice, of all ties the ties of blood are strongest. Mother and child—is there a more intimate relationship? Can one tear a child from its mother? High Court of Justice, she has conceived it in the holy ecstasies of love. She has carried it in her womb. She has fed it with her blood. She has borne it with pain. High Court of Justice, it has been observed that even the wild tigress, robbed of her young, roams restless through the mountains, shrunk to a shadow. Nature herself . . .

AZDAK *(interrupting, to* GRUSHA*)* What's your answer to all this and anything else the lawyer might have to say?

GRUSHA He's mine.

AZDAK Is that all? I hope you can prove it. In any case, I wonder why you think I should assign the child to you.

GRUSHA I brought him up like the priest says "according to my best knowledge and conscience." I always found him something to eat. Most of the time he had a roof over his head. And I went to such trouble for him. I had expenses too. I didn't look out for my own comfort. I brought the child up to be friendly with everyone, and from the beginning taught him to work as well as he could. He's still a very little thing.

THE FIRST LAWYER Your Honor, it is significant that the girl herself doesn't claim any tie of blood between her and the child.

AZDAK The Court takes note.

THE FIRST LAWYER Thank you, Your Honor. Please permit a woman bowed in sorrow—who has already lost her husband and now has also to fear the loss of her child—to address a few words to you. The gracious Natella Abashwili is . . .

THE GOVERNOR'S WIFE *(quietly)* A most cruel fate, Sir, forces me to ask you to return my beloved child. It is not for me to describe to you the tortures of a bereaved mother's soul, the anxiety, the sleepless nights, the . . .

THE SECOND LAWYER *(bursting out)* It's outrageous the way this woman is being treated. She is not allowed to enter her husband's palace. The revenue of her estates is blocked. She is cold-bloodedly told that it's tied to the heir. She can't do anything without the child. She can't even pay her lawyers! *(to* THE FIRST LAWYER *who, desperate about this outburst, makes frantic gestures to keep him from speaking)* Dear Illo Shuboladze, why shouldn't it be divulged now that it's the Abashwili estates that are at stake?

THE FIRST LAWYER Please, Honored Sandro Oboladze! We had agreed . . . *(to* AZDAK*)* Of course it is correct that the trial will also decide whether our noble client will obtain the right to dispose of the extensive Abashwili estates. I say "also" advisedly, for in the foreground stands the human tragedy of a mother, as Natella Abashwili rightly explained in the first words of her moving statement. Even if Michael Abashwili were *not* the heir of the estates, he would still be the dearly beloved child of my client.

AZDAK Stop! The Court is touched by the mention of the estates. It's a proof of human feeling.

THE SECOND LAWYER Thanks, Your Honor. Dear Illo Shuboladze, we can prove in any case that the woman who took the child is not the child's mother. Permit me to lay before the Court the bare facts. High Court of Justice, by an unfortunate chain of circumstances, the child Michael Abashwili was left behind while his mother was making her escape. Grusha, a palace kitchen maid, who was present on that Easter Sunday, was observed to be busy with the child . . .

THE COOK All her mistress was thinking of was what kind of dresses she'd take along!

THE SECOND LAWYER *(unmoved)* Nearly a year later Grusha turned up in a mountain village with a child and there entered into the state of matrimony with . . .

AZDAK How did you get to that mountain village?

GRUSHA On foot, Your Honor. And he was mine.

SIMON I am the father, Your Honor.

THE COOK The child was in my care, Your Honor, for five piasters.

THE SECOND LAWYER This man is engaged to Grusha, High Court of

Justice, so his testimony is not trustworthy.

AZDAK Are you the man she married in the mountain village?

SIMON No, Your Honor, she married a peasant.

AZDAK *(to* GRUSHA*)* Why? *(pointing at* SIMON:*)* Is he no good in bed? Tell the truth.

GRUSHA We didn't get that far. I married because of the child. So he'd have a roof over his head. *(pointing at* SIMON*)* He was in the war, Your Honor.

AZDAK And now he wants you again, huh?

SIMON I wish to state in evidence . . .

GRUSHA *(angrily)* I am no longer free, Your Honor.

AZDAK And the child, you claim, comes from whoring? *(*GRUSHA *doesn't answer.)* I'm going to ask you a question: What kind of a child is it? Is it a ragged little bastard or a child from a well-to-do family?

GRUSHA *(angrily)* He's just an ordinary child.

AZDAK I mean—did he have refined features from the beginning?

GRUSHA He had a nose on his face.

AZDAK I consider that answer of yours important. It was said of me that once, before rendering a verdict, I went out and sniffed at a rosebush—tricks like that are needed nowadays. Well, I'll make it short, and not listen to any more lies. *(to* GRUSHA*)* Especially not yours. *(To all the accused)* I can imagine what you've cooked up to cheat me! I know you! You're swindlers.

GRUSHA *(suddenly)* I can quite understand your wanting to cut it short, now I've seen what you accepted!

AZDAK Shut up! Did I accept anything from you?

GRUSHA *(while* THE COOK *tries to restrain her)* I haven't got anything.

AZDAK That's true. Quite true. From starvelings I never get a thing. I might just as well starve, myself. You want justice, but do you want to pay for it? When you go to a butcher you know you have to pay, but you go to a judge as if you were off to a funeral supper.

SIMON *(loudly)* When the horse was shod, the horse-fly held out its leg, as the saying is.

AZDAK *(eagerly accepting the challenge)* Better a treasuer in manure than a stone in a mountain stream.

SIMON A fine day. Let's go fishing, said the angler to the worm.

AZDAK I'm my own master, said the servant, and cut off his foot.

SIMON I love you as a father, said the Czar to the peasants, and had the Czarevitch's head chopped off.

AZDAK A fool's worst enemy is himself.

SIMON However, a fart has no nose.

AZDAK Fined ten piasters for indecent language in court! That'll teach you what justice is.

GRUSHA *(furiously)* A fine kind of justice! You play fast and loose with us because we don't talk as refined as that crowd with their lawyers!

AZDAK That's so. You people are too dumb. It's only right you should get it in the neck.

GRUSHA You want to hand the child over to her, and she wouldn't even know how to keep it dry, she's so "refined"! You know about as much about justice as I do!

AZDAK There's something in that. I'm an ignorant man. I haven't even a decent pair of pants under my gown. See for yourself! With me, everything goes for food and drink – I was educated at a convent. Incidentally, I'll fine you ten piasters for contempt of court. And moreover you're a very silly girl, to turn me against you, instead of making eyes at me and wiggling your backside a little to keep me in a good temper. Twenty piasters!

GRUSHA Even if it were thirty, I would tell you what I think of your justice, you drunken onion! *(Incoherently)* How dare you talk to me like the cracked Isaiah on the church window? As if you *were* somebody? For you weren't born to this. You weren't born to rap your own mother on the knuckles if she snitches her little bowl of salt. Aren't you ashamed of yourself when you see how I tremble before you? You have made yourself their servant so no one will take their houses away, and they'd stolen them! Since when have houses belonged to the bedbugs? But you're on the watch, or they couldn't drag our men into their wars! You bribe-taker! *(*AZDAK *half gets up, starts beaming. With his little hammer he half-heartedly knocks on the table as if to get silence. As* GRUSHA'S *scolding continues, he only beats time with his hammer.)* I've no respect for you. No more than for a thief or a robber with a knife! You can do what you want. You can take the child away from me, a hundred against one, but I tell you one thing: only extortioners should be chosen for a profession like yours, and men who rape children! As punishment! They should sit in judgment on their fellow creatures. Which is worse than to hang from gallows.

AZDAK *(sitting down)* Now it'll be thirty! And I won't go on squabbling with you as though we were in a tavern. What'd happen to my dignity as a judge? Anyway, I've lost interest in your case. Where's the couple who wanted a divorce? *(to* SHAUWA:*)* Bring 'em in. This case is adjourned for fifteen minutes.

THE FIRST LAWYER *(to* THE GOVERNOR'S WIFE*)* Even without using the rest of the evidence, Madam, we have the verdict in the bag.

THE COOK *(to* GRUSHA*)* You've gone and spoiled your chances with him. You won't get the child now.

THE GOVERNOR'S WIFE Shalva, my smelling salts!

(Enter a very old couple.)

AZDAK I accept . . . *(The old couple don't understand.)* I hear you want to be divorced. How long have you been living together?

THE OLD WOMAN Forty years, Your Honor.

AZDAK And why do you want a divorce?

THE OLD MAN We don't like each other, Your Honor.

AZDAK Since when?

THE OLD WOMAN Oh, from the very beginning, Your Honor.

AZDAK I'll think about your request and render my verdict when I'm through with the other case. *(*SHAUWA *leads them back.)* I need the child. *(He beckons* GRUSHA *to him, and bends not unkindly toward her.)* I've noticed you have a soft spot for justice. I don't believe he's your child, but if he were yours, woman, wouldn't you want him to be rich? You'd only have to say he isn't yours, and he'd have a palace and many horses in his stable and many beggars on his doorstep and many soldiers in his service and many petitioners in his courtyard, wouldn't he? What do you say—don't you want him to be rich?

(GRUSHA is silent.)

THE STORY TELLER Hear now what the angry girl thought but did not say:

Had he golden shoes to wear
He'd be cruel as a bear.
Evil would his life disgrace.
He'd laugh in my face.
Carrying a heart of flint
Is too troublesome a stint.
Being powerful and bad
Is hard for a lad.
Then let hunger be his foe!
Hungry men and women, no.
Let him fear the darksome night
But not daylight!

AZDAK I think I understand you, woman.

GRUSHA *(suddenly and loudly)* I won't give him up. I've raised him, and he knows me.

(Enter SHAUWA with the child.)

THE GOVERNOR'S WIFE It's in rags!

GRUSHA That's not true. I wasn't given time to put his good shirt on.

THE GOVERNOR'S WIFE It must have been in a pigsty.

GRUSHA *(furiously)* I'm not a pig, but there are some who are! Where did you leave your child?

THE GOVERNOR'S WIFE I'll show you, you vulgar creature! *(She is about to throw herself on GRUSHA, but is restrained by her LAWYERS.)* She's a criminal, she must be whipped. Immediately!

THE SECOND LAWYER *(holding his hand over her mouth)* Gracious Natella Abashwili, you promised . . . Your Honor, the plaintiff's nerves . . .

AZDAK Plaintiff and defendant! The Court has listened to your case, and has come to no decision as to who the real mother is. I, as a judge, am obliged to choose a mother for the child. I'll make a test. Shauwa, get a piece of chalk and draw a circle on the floor. *(SHAUWA does so.)* Now place the child in the center. *(SHAUWA puts MICHAEL, who smiles at GRUSHA, in the center of the circle.)* Stand near the circle, both of you. *(THE GOVERNOR'S WIFE and GRUSHA step up to the circle.)* Now each of you take the child by one hand. *(They do so.)* The true mother is she who can pull the child out of the circle toward herself.

THE SECOND LAWYER *(quickly)* High Court of Justice, I object! The fate of the great Abashwili estates, which are bound to the child, as the heir, should not be made dependent on such a doubtful duel. In addition, my client does not command the strength of this person, who is accustomed to physical work.

AZDAK She looks pretty well fed to me. Pull! *(*THE GOVERNOR'S WIFE *pulls the child out of the circle on her side.* GRUSHA *has let go and stands aghast.)* What's the matter with you? You didn't pull!

GRUSHA I didn't hold on to him.

THE FIRST LAWYER *(congratulating* THE GOVERNOR'S WIFE*)* What did I say! The ties of blood!

GRUSHA *(running to* AZDAK*)* Your Honor, I take back everything I said against you. I ask your forgiveness. If only I could keep him till he can speak all the words. He knows a few.

AZDAK Don't influence the Court. I bet you only know twenty yourself. All right, I'll do the test once more, to make certain. *(The two women take up their positions again.)* Pull! *(Again* GRUSHA *lets go of the child.)*

GRUSHA *(in despair)* I brought him up! Shall I tear him to pieces? I can't do it!

AZDAK *(rising)* And in this manner the Court has established the true mother. *(to* GRUSHA*)* Take your child and be off. I advise you not to stay in the city with him. *(to* THE GOVERNOR'S WIFE*)* And you disappear before I fine you for fraud. Your estates fall to the city. They'll be converted into a playground for the children. They need one, and I've decided it shall be called after me: Azdak's Garden. *(*THE GOVERNOR'S WIFE *has fainted and is carried out by the* LAWYERS *and* THE ADJUTANT. GRUSHA *stands motionless.* SHAUWA *leads the child toward her.)* Now I'll take off this judge's gown—it has grown too hot for me. I'm not cut out for a hero. In token of farewell I invite you all to a little dance outside on the meadow. Oh, I had almost forgotten something in my excitement . . . to sign the divorce decree.

(Using the judge's chair as a table, he writes something on a piece of paper, and prepares to leave. Dance music has started.)

SHAUWA *(having read what is on the paper)* But that's not right. You've not divorced the old people. You've divorced Grusha!

AZDAK Have I divorced the wrong couple? What a pity! And I never retract! If I did, how could we keep order in our state? *(to the old couple)* I'll invite you to my party instead. You don't mind dancing with each other, do you? *(to* GRUSHA *and* SIMON:*)* I've got forty piasters coming from *you.*

SIMON *(pulling out his purse)* Cheap at the price, Your Honor. And many thanks.

AZDAK *(pocketing the cash)* I'll need this.

GRUSHA *(to* MICHAEL*)* So we'd better leave the city tonight, Michael? *(to* SIMON:*)* You like him?

SIMON With my respects, I like him.

GRUSHA And now I'll tell you: I took him because on that Easter Sunday, I got engaged to you. And so he's a child of love. Michael, let's dance. *(She dances with* MICHAEL, SIMON *dances with* THE COOK, *the old couple with each other.* AZDAK *stands lost in thought. The dancers soon hide him from view. Occasionally he is seen, but less and less as more couples join the dance.)*

THE STORY TELLER

And after that evening Azdak disappeared and was not seen again.
The people of Grusinia did not forget him but long remembered
The period of his judging as a brief golden age
Almost an age of justice.
(All the couples dance off. AZDAK *has disappeared.)*
But you, you who have listened to the Story of the Chalk Circle,
Take note what men of old concluded:
That what there is shall go to those who are good for it,
Thus: the children to the motherly, that they prosper
The carts to good drivers, that they are driven well
And the valley to the waterers, that it bring forth fruit.

bertolt brecht

theater for learning

When anyone spoke of modern theatre a few years ago, he mentioned the Moscow, the New York or the Berlin theatre. He may also have spoken of a particular production of Jouvet's in Paris, of Cochran's in London, or the Habima performance of *The Dybbuk*, which, in fact, belonged to Russian theatre since it was directed by Vakhtangov; but by and large, there were only three capitals so far as modern theatre was concerned.

The Russian, the American and the German theatres were very different from one another, but they were alike in being modern, i.e., in introducing technical and artistic innovations. In a certain sense they even developed stylistic similarities, probably because technique is international (not only the technique directly required for the stage, but also that which exerts an influence on it, the film, for example) and because the cities in question were great progressive cities in great industrial countries. Most recently, the Berlin theatre seemed to have taken the lead among the most advanced capitalist countries. What was common to modern theatre found there its strongest and, for the moment, most mature expression.

The last phase of the Berlin theatre, which as I said only revealed in its purest form the direction in which modern theatre was developing, was the so-called *epic theatre*. What was known as the *Zeitstueck*[1] or Piscator theatre or the didactic play all belonged to epic theatre.

EPIC THEATRE

The expression "epic theatre" seemed self-contradictory to many

[1]Play dealing with current problems.

people, since according to the teachings of Aristotle the epic and the dramatic forms of presenting a story were considered basically different from one another. The difference between the two forms was by no means merely seen in the fact that one was performed by living people while the other made use of a book—epic works like those of Homer and the *minnesingers* of the Middle Ages were likewise theatrical performances, and dramas like Goethe's *Faust* or Byron's *Manfred* admittedly achieved their greatest effect as books. Aristotle's teachings themselves distinguished the dramatic from the epic form as a difference in construction, whose laws were dealt with under two different branches of aesthetics. This construction depended on the different way in which the works were presented to the public, either on the stage or through a book, but nevertheless, apart from that, "the dramatic" could also be found in epic works and "the epic" in dramatic works. The bourgeois novel in the last century considerably developed "the dramatic," which meant the strong centralization of plot and an organic interdependence of the separate parts. The dramatic is characterized by a certain passion in the tone of the exposition and a working out of the collision of forces. The epic writer, Döblin,[2] gave an excellent description when he said that the epic, in contrast to the dramatic, could practically be cut up with a scissors into single pieces, each of which could stand alone.

I do not wish to discuss here in what way the contrasts between epic and dramatic, long regarded as irreconcilable, lost their rigidity, but simply to point out that (other causes aside) technical achievements enabled the stage to include narrative elements in dramatic presentations. The potentialities of projection, the film, the greater facility in changing sets through machinery, completed the equipment of the stage and did so at a moment when the most important human events could no longer be so simply portrayed as through personification of the driving forces or through subordinating the characters to invisible, metaphysical powers. To make the events understandable, it had become necessary to play up the "bearing" of the *environment* upon the people living in it.

Of course this environment had been shown in plays before, not, however, as an independent element but only from the viewpoint of the main figure of the drama. It rose out of the hero's reaction to it. It was seen as a storm may be "seen" if you observe on the sea a ship spreading its sails and the sails bellying. But in the epic theatre it was now to appear as an independent element.

The stage began to narrate. The narrator no longer vanished with the fourth wall. Not only did the background make its own comment on stage happenings through large screens which evoked other events occurring at the same time in other places, documenting or contradicting statements by characters through quotations projected onto a screen, lending tangible, concrete statistics to abstract discussions, providing facts and figures for happenings which were plastic but unclear in their meaning; the actors

[2]Alfred Döblin (1878–1957), German novelist and essayist, author of *Berlin Alexanderplatz*, etc.

no longer threw themselves completely into their roles but maintained a certain distance from the character performed by them, even distinctly inviting criticism.

Nothing permitted the audience any more to lose itself through simple empathy, uncritically (and practically without any consequences) in the experiences of the characters on the stage. The presentation exposed the subject matter and the happenings to a process of de-familiarization.[3] De-familiarization was required to make things understood. When things are "self-evident," understanding is cimply dispensed with. The "natural" had to be given an element of the *conspicuous*. Only in this way could the laws of cause and effect become plain. Characters had to behave as they *did* behave, and at the same time be capable of behaving otherwise.

These were great changes.

TWO OUTLINES

The following little outlines may indicate in what respect the function of the epic is distinguished from that of the dramatic theatre:

1

dramatic form	*epic form*
The stage "incarnates" an event.	It relates it.
Involves the audience in an action, uses up its activity.	Makes the audience an observer, but arouses its activity.
Helps it to feel.	Compels it to make decisions.
Communicates experiences.	Communicates insights.
The audience is projected into an event.	Is confronted with it.
Suggestion is used.	Arguments are used.
Sensations are preserved.	Impelled to the level of perceptions.
The character is a known quantity.	The character is subjected to investigation.
Man unchangeable.	Man who can change and make changes.
His drives.	His motives.
Events move in a straight line.	In "irregular" curves.
Natura non facit saltus.	Facit saltus.
The world as it is.	The world as it is becoming.

2

the audience in the dramatic theatre says:

Yes, I have felt that too.—That's how I am.—That is only natural.—That will always be so.—This person's suffering shocks me because he has no way out.—This is great art: everything in it is self-evident.—I weep with the weeping, I laugh with the laughing.

the audience in the epic theatre says:

[3]*Entfremdung*—alienation.

I wouldn't have thought that.—People shouldn't do things like that.—That's extremely odd, almost unbelievable.—This has to stop.—This person's suffering shocks me, because there might be a way out for him.—This is great art: nothing in it is self-evident.—I laugh over the weeping, I weep over the laughing.

DIDACTIC THEATRE

The stage began to instruct.

Oil, inflation, war, social struggles, the family, religion, wheat, the meat-packing industry, became subjects for theatrical portrayal. Choruses informed the audience about facts it did not know. In montage form, films showed events all over the world. Projections provided statistical data. As the "background" came to the fore, the actions of the characters became exposed to criticism. Wrong and right actions were exhibited. People were shown who knew what they were doing, and other people were shown who did not know. The theatre entered the province of the philosophers—at any rate, the sort of philosophers who wanted not only to explain the world but also to change it. Hence the theatre philosophized; hence it instructed. And what became of entertainment? Were the audience put back in school, treated as illiterates? Were they to take examinations and be given marks?

It is the general opinion that a very decided difference exists between learning and being entertained. The former may be useful, but only the latter is pleasant. Thus we have to defend the epic theatre against a suspicion that it must be an extremely unpleasant, a joyless, indeed a wearying business.

Well, we can only say that the contrast between learning and being entertained does not necessarily exist in nature; it has not always existed and it need not always exist.

Undoubtedly, the kind of learning we experienced in school, in training for a profession, etc., is a laborious business. But consider under what circumstances and for what purpose it is done. It is, in fact, a purchase. Knowledge is simply a commodity. It is acquired for the purpose of being resold. All those who have grown too old for school have to pursue knowledge on the Q.T., so to speak, because anybody who admits he still has to study depreciates himself as one who knows too little. Apart from that, the utility of learning is very much limited by factors over which the student has no control. There is unemployment, against which no knowledge protects. There is the division of labor, which makes comprehensive knowledge unnecessary and impossible. Often, those who study do it only when they see no other possibility of getting ahead. There is not much knowledge that procures power, but much knowledge is only procured through power.

Learning means something very different to people in different strata of society. There are people who cannot conceive of any improvement in conditions; conditions seem good enough to them. Whatever may happen to petroleum, they make a profit out of it. And they feel, after all, that they are getting rather old. They can scarcely expect many more years of life. So why continue to learn? They have already spoken their "Ugh!"[4] But there are also people who have not yet "had their turn," who are discontented with the way things are, who have an immense practical interest in learning, who want orientation badly, who know they are lost without learning—these are the best and most ambitious learners. Such differences also exist among nations and peoples. Thus the lust for learning is dependent on various things; in short, there *is* thrilling learning, joyous and militant learning.

If learning could not be delightful, then the theatre, by its very nature, would not be in a position to instruct.

Theatre remains theatre, even when it is didactic theatre; and if it is good theatre it will entertain.

THEATRE AND SCIENCE

"But what has science to do with art? We know very well that science can be diverting, but not everything that diverts belongs in the theatre."

I have often been told when I pointed out the inestimable services that modern science, properly utilized, could render to art (especially to the theatre), that art and science were two admirable but completely different fields of human activity. This is a dreadful platitude, of course, and the best thing to do is admit at once that it is quite right, like most platitudes. Art and science operate in very different ways—agreed. Still, I must admit—bad as this may sound—that I cannot manage as an artist without making use of certain sciences. This may make many people seriously doubt my artistic ability. They are accustomed to regarding poets as unique, almost unnatural beings who unerringly, almost like gods, perceive things that others can only perceive through the greatest efforts and hard work. Naturally, it is unpleasant to have to admit not being one of those so endowed. But it must be admitted. It must also be denied that this application to science has anything to do with some pardonable avocation indulged in the evening after work is done. Everyone knows that Goethe also went in for natural science, Schiller for history, presumably —this is the charitable assumption—as a sort of hobby. I would not simply accuse these two of having needed the science for their poetic labors, nor would I use them to excuse myself, but I must say I need the sciences. And I must even admit that I regard suspiciously all sorts of people who I know do not keep abreast of science, who, in other words, sing as the birds sing, or as they imagine the birds sing. This does not mean that I would reject a nice poem about the taste of a flounder or the pleasure of a boating party just because the author had not studied gastronomy or navi-

[4]Reference to popular German literature about Red Indians, by the author Karl May, in which, after a chieftain had given his opinion at a pow-wow he would conclude, "I have spoken. Ugh!"

gation. But I think that unless every resource is employed towards understanding the great, complicated events in the world of man, they cannot be seen adequately for what they are.

Let us assume that we want to portray great passions or events which influence the fates of peoples. Such a passion today might be the drive for power. Supposing that a poet "felt" this drive and wanted to show someone striving for power—how could he absorb into his own experience the extremely complicated mechanism within which the struggle for power today takes place? If his hero is a political man, what are the workings of politics? If he is a business man, what are the workings of business? And then there are poets who are much less passionately interested in any individual's drive for power than in business affairs and politics as such! How are they to acquire the necessary knowledge? They will scarcely find out enough by going around and keeping their eyes open, although that is at least better than rolling their eyes in a fine frenzy. The establishment of a newspaper like the *Völkische Beobachter* or a business like Standard Oil is a rather complicated matter, and these things are not simply absorbed through the pores. Psychology is an important field for the dramatist. It is supposed that while an ordinary person may not be in a position to discover, without special instruction, what makes a man commit murder, certainly a writer ought to have the "inner resources" to be able to give a picture of a murderer's mental state. The assumption is that you only need look into yourself in such a case; after all, there is such a thing as imagination. . . . For a number of reasons I can no longer abandon myself to this amiable hope of managing so comfortably. I cannot find in myself alone all the motives which, as we learn from newspapers and scientific reports, are discovered in human beings. No more than any judge passing sentence am I able to imagine adequately, unaided, the mental state of a murderer. Modern psychology, from psychoanalysis to behaviorism, provides me with insights which help me to form a quite different judgment of the case, especially when I take into consideration the findings of sociology, and do not ignore economics or history. You may say: This is getting complicated. I must answer, it *is* complicated. Perhaps I can talk you into agreeing with me that a lot of literature is extremely primitive; yet you will ask in grave concern: Wouldn't such an evening in the theatre be a pretty alarming business? The answer to that is: No.

Whatever knowledge may be contained in a poetic work, it must be completely converted into poetry. In its transmuted form, it gives the same type of satisfaction as any poetic work. And although it does not provide that satisfaction found in science as such, a certain inclination to penetrate more deeply into the nature of things, a desire to make the world controllable, are necessary to ensure enjoyment of poetic works generated by this era of great discoveries and inventions.

IS THE EPIC THEATRE A SORT OF "MORAL INSTITUTION"?

According to Friedrich Schiller the theatre should be a moral institution. When Shiller posed this demand it scarcely occurred to him that by moralizing from the stage he might drive the audience out of the theatre. In his day the audience had no objection to moralizing. Only later on did Friedrich Nietzsche abuse him as the moral trumpeter of Säckingen.[5] To Nietzsche a concern with morality seemed a dismal affair; to Schiller it seemed completely gratifying. He knew of nothing more entertaining and satisfying than to propagate ideals. The bourgeoisie was just establishing the concept of the nation. To furnish your house, show off your new hat, present your bills for paymant is highly gratifying. But to speak of the decay of your house, to have to sell your old hat and pay the bills yourself is a truly dismal affair, and that was how Nietzsche saw it a century later. It was no use talking to him about morality or, in consequence, about the other Friedrich. Many people also attacked the epic theatre, claiming it was too moralistic. Yet moral utterances were secondary in the epic theatre. Its intention was less to moralize than to study. And it did study; but then came the rub: the moral of the story. Naturally, we cannot claim that we began making studies just because studying was so much fun and not for any concrete reason, or that the results of our studies then took us completely by surprise. Undoubtedly there were painful discrepancies in the world around us, conditions that were hard to bear, conditions of a kind not only hard to bear for moral reasons. Hunger, cold and hardship are not only burdensome for moral reasons. And the purpose of our investigation was not merely to arouse moral misgivings about certain conditions (although such misgivings might easily be felt, if not by every member of the audience; such misgivings, for example, were seldom felt by those who profited by the conditions in question). The purpose of our investigation was to make visible the means by which those onerous conditions could be done away with. We were not speaking on behalf of morality but on behalf of the wronged. These are really two different things, for moral allusions are often used in telling the wronged that they must put up with their situation. For such moralists, people exist for morality, not morality for people.

Nevertheless it can be deduced from these remarks to what extent and in what sense the epic theatre is a moral institution.

CAN EPIC THEATRE BE PERFORMED ANYWHERE?

From the standpoint of style, the epic theatre is nothing especially new. In its character of show, of demonstration, and its emphasis on the artistic, it is related to the ancient Asian theatre. The medieval mystery play, and also the classical Spanish and Jesuit theatres, showed an instructive tendency.

Those theatre forms corresponded to certain tendencies of their time and disappeared with them. The modern epic theatre is also linked with definite tendencies. It can by no means be performed anywhere. Few of

[5]Nietzsche's quip referred to a banal verse tale by Viktor Scheffel, *Der Trompeter von Sâckingen,* a standard favorite in Germany's "plush sofa kultur"—a parallel of Victorianism—in the second half of the nineteenth century.

the great nations today are inclined to discuss their problems in the theatre. London, Paris, Tokyo and Rome maintain their theatres for quite different purposes. Only in a few places, and not for long, have circumstances been favorable to an epic, instructive theatre. In Berlin, fascism put a violent end to the development of such a theatre.[6]

Besides a certain technical standard, it presupposes a powerful social movement which has an interest in the free discussion of vital problems, the better to solve them, and can defend this interest against all opposing tendencies.

The epic theatre is the broadest and most far-reaching experiment in great modern theatre, and it has to overcome all the enormous difficulties that all vital forces in the area of politics, philosophy, science and art have to overcome.

[6]After the defeat of the Nazis in 1945, the German administrators of the then Soviet-occupied zone – now the German Democratic Republic – invited Brecht to establish his own theatre in East Berlin. This theatre, the "Berliner Ensemble," is recognized today all over the world as a classical type of epic theatre.

tennessee williams 1914–

the glass menagerie

Nobody, not even the rain, has such small hands.
e. e. cummings

Born in Mississippi, Thomas Lanier Williams (he later adopted the name Tennessee) moved with his family to the slums of St. Louis when he was eight. Adapting to the city amid poverty, illness, and taunting schoolmates, he turned to private dreams and to writing. He found understanding with his sister Rose, a shy, fragile girl, who was the model for Laura in *The Glass Menagerie.* The economic depression ended Williams' stay at the University of Missouri, and for two painful years he worked in a warehouse. He suffered a nervous collapse and went South to his grandparents. He then returned to school and in 1938 graduated from the University of Iowa. For a while he drifted about, working at odd jobs and writing poems, stories, and plays. An award for playwriting brought him the attention of a New York agent, Audrey Wood, who helped launch his career with *Battle of Angels* (1940). The play failed. With *The Glass Menagerie* (1944) Williams scored a success, confirmed by *A Streetcar Named Desire* (1947), one of several plays projecting a world of violent passions and action, sex-obsessed and destructive of delicacy and sensitiveness. Other Williams plays include: *Summer and Smoke* (1948), *Camino Real* (1953), *Cat on a Hot Tin Roof* (1955), *Orpheus Descending* (1957), *Suddenly Last Summer* (1957). At their best, Williams' plays are poetic theatre, with radiant language, humor, vivid characterization, and a humane sympathy with weakness and failure.

the characters

AMANDA WINGFIELD *the mother, A little woman of great but confused vitality clinging frantically to another time and place. Her characterization must be carefully created, not copied from type. She is not paranoiac, but her life is paranoia. There is much to admire in Amanda, and as much to love and pity as there is to laugh at. Certainly she has endurance and a kind of heroism, and though her foolishness makes her unwittingly cruel at times, there is tenderness in her slight person.*

LAURA WINGFIELD *her daughter, Amanda, having failed to establish contact with reality, continues to live vitally in her illusions, but Laura's situation is even graver. A childhood illness has left her crippled, one leg slightly shorter than the other, and held in a brace. This defect need not be more than suggested on the stage. Stemming from this,*

Laura's separation increases till she is like a piece of her own glass collection, too exquisitely fragile to move from the shelf.

TOM WINGFIELD *her son, And the narrator of the play. A poet with a job in a warehouse. His nature is not remorseless, but to escape from a trap he has to act without pity.*

JIM O'CONNOR *the gentleman caller, A nice ordinary, young man.*

Scene—an alley in St. Louis.
Part 1—preparation for a Gentleman Caller.
Part 2—the Gentleman calls.
Time—Now and the Past.

production notes

Being a "memory play," *The Glass Menagerie* can be presented with unusual freedom of convention. Because of its considerably delicate or tenuous material, atmospheric touches and subtleties of direction play a particularly important part. Expressionism and all other unconventional techniques in drama have only one valid aim, and that is a closer approach to truth. When a play employs unconventional techniques, it is not, or certainly shouldn't be, trying to escape its responsibility of dealing with reality, or interpreting experience, but is actually or should be attempting to find a closer approach, a more penetrating and vivid expression of things as they are. The straight realistic play with its genuine frigidaire and authentic ice-cubes, its characters that speak exactly as its audience speaks, corresponds to the academic landscape and has the same virtue of a photographic likeness. Everyone should know nowadays the unimportance of the photographic in art: that truth, life, or reality is an organic thing which the poetic imagination can represent or suggest, in essence, only through transformation, through changing into other forms than those which were merely present in appearance.

These remarks are not meant as a preface only to this particular play. They have to do with a conception of a new, plastic theatre which must take the place of the exhausted theatre of realistic conventions if the theatre is to resume vitality as a part of our culture.

THE SCREEN DEVICE

There is *only one important difference between the original and acting version of the play* and that is the *omission* in the latter of the device which I tentatively included in my *original* script. This device was the use of a screen on which were projected magic-lantern slides bearing images or titles. I do not regret the omission of this device from the present Broadway production. The extraordinary power of Miss Taylor's performance made it suitable to have the utmost simplicity in the physical production. But I think it may be interesting to some readers to see how this device was conceived. So I am putting it into the published manuscript. These images and legends, projected from behind, were cast on a section of wall between the front-room and dining-room areas, which should be indistinguishable from the rest when not in use.

The purpose of this will probably be apparent. It is to give accent to certain values in each scene. Each scene contains a particular point (or several) which is structurally the most important. In an episodic play, such as this, the basic structure or narrative line may be obscured from the audience; the effect may seem fragmentary rather than architectural. This may not be the fault of the play so much as a lack of attention in the audience. The legend or image upon the screen will strengthen the effect of what is merely allusion in the writing and allow the primary point to be made more simply and lightly than if the entire responsibility were on the spoken lines. Aside from this structural value, I think the screen will have a definite emotional appeal, less definable but just as important. An imaginative producer or director may invent many other uses for this device than those indicated in the present script. In fact the possibilities of the device seem much larger to me than the instance of this play can possibly utilize.

THE MUSIC

Another extra-literary accent in this play is provided by the use of music. A single recurring tune, "The Glass Menagerie," is used to give emotional emphasis to suitable passages. This tune is like circus music, not when you are on the grounds or in the immediate vicinity of the parade, but when you are at some distance and very likely thinking of something else. It seems under those circumstances to continue almost interminably and it weaves in and out of your preoccupied consciousness; then it is the lightest, most delicate music in the world and perhaps the saddest. It expresses the surface vivacity of life with the underlying strain of immutable and inexpressible sorrow. When you look at a piece of delicately spun glass you think of two things: how beautiful it is and how easily it can be broken. Both of those ideas should be woven into the recurring tune, which dips in and out of the play as if it were carried on a wind that changes. It serves as a thread of connection and allusion between the narrator with his separate point in time and space and the subject of his story. Between each episode it returns as reference to the emotion, nostalgia, which is the first condition of the play. It is primarily LAURA'S music and therefore comes out most clearly when the play focuses upon her and the lovely fragility of glass which is her image.

THE LIGHTING

The lighting in the play is not realistic. In keeping with the atmosphere of memory, the stage is dim. Shafts of light are focused on selected areas or actors, sometimes in contradistinction to what is the apparent center. For instance, in the quarrel scene between TOM and AMANDA, in which LAURA has no active part, the clearest pool of light is on her figure. This is also true of the supper scene, when her silent figure on the sofa should remain the visual center. The light upon LAURA should be distinct from the others, having a peculiar pristine clarity such as light used in early religious portraits of female saints or madonnas. A certain correspondence to light in religious paintings, such as El Greco's, where the figures are radiant in atmosphere that is relatively dusky, could be effectively used throughout the play. [It will also permit a more effective use of the screen.] A free, imaginative use of light can be of enormous value in giving a mobile, plastic quality to plays of a more or less static nature.

T. W.

scene 1

(The Wingfield apartment is in the rear of the building, one of those vast hive-like conglomerations of cellular living-units that flower as warty growths of overcrowded urban centers of lower middle-class population and are symptomatic of the impulse of this largest and fundamentally enslaved section of American society to avoid fluidity and differentiation and to exist and function as one interfused mass of automatism.

The apartment faces an alley and is entered by a fire-escape, a structure whose name is a touch of accidental poetic truth, for all of these huge buildings are always burning with the slow and implacable fires of human desperation. The fire-escape is included in the set—that is, the landing of it and steps descending from it.

The scene is memory and is therefore nonrealistic. Memory takes a lot of poetic license. It omits some details; others are exaggerated, according to the emotional value of the articles it touches, for memory is seated predominantly in the heart. The interior is therefore rather dim and poetic.

At the rise of the curtain, the audience is faced with the dark, grim rear wall of the Wingfield tenement. This building, which runs parallel to the footlights, is flanked on both sides by dark, narrow alleys which run into murky canyons of tangled clotheslines, garbage cans and the sinister latticework of neighboring fire-escapes. It is up and down these side alleys that exterior entrances and exits are made, during the play. At the end of TOM'S *opening commentary, the dark tenement wall slowly reveals [by means of a transparency] the interior of the ground floor Wingfield apartment.*

Downstage is the living room, which also serves as a sleeping room for LAURA, *the sofa unfolding to make her bed. Upstage, center, and divided by a wide arch or second proscenium with transparent faded portieres [or second curtain], is the dining room. In an old-fashioned what-not in the living room are seen scores of transparent glass animals. A blown-up photograph of the father hangs on the wall of the living room, facing the audience, to the left of the archway. It is the face of a very handsome young man in a doughboy's First World War cap. He is gallantly smiling, ineluctably smiling, as if to say, "I will be smiling forever."*

The audience hears and sees the opening scene in the dining room through both the transparent fourth wall of the building and the transparent gauze portieres of the dining-room arch. It is during this revealing scene that the fourth wall slowly ascends, out of sight. This transparent exterior wall is not brought down again until the very end of the play, during TOM'S *final speech.*

The narrator is an undisguised convention of the play. He takes whatever license with dramatic convention as is convenient to his purposes.

TOM *enters dressed as a merchant sailor from alley, stage left, and strolls across the front of the stage to the fire-escape. There he stops and lights a cigarette. He addresses the audience.)*

TOM Yes, I have tricks in my pocket, I have things up my sleeve. But I am the opposite of a stage magician. He gives you illusion that has the appearance of truth. I give you truth in the pleasant disguise of illusion.

To begin with, I turn back time. I reverse it to that quaint period, the thirties, when the huge middle class of America was matriculating in a school for the blind. Their eyes had failed them, or they had failed their eyes, and so they were having their fingers pressed forcibly down on the fiery Braille alphabet of a dissolving economy.

In Spain there was revolution. Here there was only shouting and confusion.

In Spain there was Guernica. Here there were disturbances of labor, sometimes pretty violent, in otherwise peaceful cities such as Chicago, Cleveland, Saint Louis . . .

This is the social background of the play.

*(*MUSIC*)*

The play is memory.

Being a memory play, it is dimly lighted, it is sentimental, it is not realistic.

In memory everything seems to happen to music. That explains the fiddle in the wings.

I am the narrator of the play, and also a character in it.

The other characters are my mother, Amanda, my sister, Laura, and a gentlemen caller who appears in the final scenes.

He is the most realistic character in the play, being an emissary from a world of reality that we were somehow set apart from.

But since I have a poet's weakness for symbols, I am using this character also as a symbol; he is the long delayed but always expected something that we live for.

There is a fifth character in the play who doesn't appear except in this larger-than-life-size photograph over the mantel.

This is our father who left us a long time ago.

He was a telephone man who fell in love with long distances; he gave up his job with the telephone company and skipped the light fantastic out of town . . .

The last we heard of him was a picture post-card from Mazatlan, on the Pacific coast of Mexico, containing a message of two words—"Hello—Good-bye!" and no address.

I think the rest of the play will explain itself. . . .

(AMANDA'S *voice becomes audible through the portieres.)*

(LEGEND ON SCREEN: *"Ou sont les Neiges."*)
(He divides the portieres and enters the upstage area.)
(AMANDA *and* LAURA *are seated at a drop-leaf table. Eating is indicated by gestures without food or utensils.* AMANDA *faces the audience.* TOM *and* LAURA *are seated in profile.)*
(The interior has lit up softly and through the scrim we see AMANDA *and* LAURA *seated at the table in the upstage area.)*

AMANDA *(calling)* Tom?

TOM Yes, Mother.

AMANDA We can't say grace until you come to the table!

TOM Coming, Mother. *(He bows slightly and withdraws, reappearing a few moments later in his place at the table.)*

AMANDA *(to her son)* Honey, don't *push* with your *fingers.* If you have to push with something, the thing to push with is a crust of bread. And chew—chew! Animals have sections in their stomachs which enable them to digest food without mastication, but human beings are supposed to chew their food before they swallow it down. Eat food leisurely, son, and really enjoy it. A well-cooked meal has lots of delicate flavors that have to be held in the mouth for appreciation. So chew your food and give your salivary glands a chance to function!

TOM *(deliberately lays his imaginary fork down and pushes his chair back from the table.)* I haven't enjoyed one bite of this dinner because of your constant directions on how to eat it. It's you that make me rush through meals with your hawk-like attention to every bite I take. Sickening—spoils my appetite—all this discussion of—animals' secretion—salivary glands—mastication!

AMANDA *(lightly)* Temperament like a Metropolitan star! *(He rises and crosses downstage.)* You're not excused from the table.

TOM I'm getting a cigarette.

AMANDA You smoke too much.

LAURA *(rises)* I'll bring in the blanc mange.
(He remains standing with his cigarette by the portieres during the following.)

AMANDA *(rising)* No, sister, no, sister—you be the lady this time and I'll be the darky.

LAURA I'm already up.

AMANDA Resume your seat, little sister— I want you to stay fresh and pretty—for gentlemen callers!

LAURA I'm not expecting any gentlemen callers.

AMANDA *(Crossing out to kitchenette. Airily)* Sometimes they come when they are least expected! Why, I remember one Sunday afternoon in Blue Mountain— *(Enters kitchenette.)*

TOM I know what's coming!

LAURA Yes. But let her tell it.

TOM Again?

LAURA She loves to tell it.
(AMANDA *returns with bowl of dessert.)*

AMANDA One Sunday afternoon in Blue Mountain—your mother received

—*seventeen!*—gentlemen callers! Why, sometimes there weren't chairs enough to accommodate them all. We had to send the nigger over to bring in folding chairs from the parish house.

TOM *(remaining at portieres)* How did you entertain those gentlemen callers?

AMANDA I understood the art of conversation!

TOM I bet you could talk.

AMANDA Girls in those days *knew* how to talk, I can tell you.

TOM Yes?

(IMAGE: AMANDA *as a girl on a porch, greeting callers.)*

AMANDA They knew how to entertain their gentlemen callers. It wasn't enough for a girl to be possessed of a pretty face and a graceful figure—although I wasn't slighted in either respect. She also needed to have a nimble wit and a tongue to meet all occasions.

TOM What did you talk about?

AMANDA Things of importance going on in the world! Never anything coarse or common or vulgar. *(She addresses* TOM *as though he were seated in the vacant chair at the table though he remains by portieres. He plays this scene as though he held the book.)* My callers were gentlemen—all! Among my callers were some of the most prominent young planters of the Mississippi Delta—planters and sons of planters! (TOM *motions for music and a spot of light on* AMANDA. *Her eyes lift, her face glows, her voice becomes rich and elegiac.)*

(SCREEN LEGEND: *"Ou sont les Neiges."*

There was young Champ Laughlin who later became vice-president of the Delta Planters Bank.

Hadley Stevenson who was drowned in Moon Lake and left his widow one hundred and fifty thousand in Government bonds.

There were the Cutrere brothers, Wesley and Bates. Bates was one of my bright particular beaux! He got in a quarrel with that wild Wainwright boy. They shot it out on the floor of Moon Lake Casino. Bates was shot through the stomach. Died in the ambulance on his way to Memphis. His widow was well-provided for, came into eight or ten thousand acres, that's all. She married him on the rebound—never loved her—carried my picture on him the night he died!

And there was that boy that every girl in the Delta had set her cap for! That beautiful, brilliant young Fitzhugh boy from Greene County!

TOM What did he leave his widow?

AMANDA He never married! Gracious, you talk as though all of my old admirers had turned up their toes to the daisies!

TOM Isn't this the first you've mentioned that still survives?

AMANDA That Fitzhugh boy went North and made a fortune—came to be known as the Wolf of Wall Street! He had the Midas touch, whatever he touched turned to gold!

And I could have been Mrs. Duncan J. Fitzhugh, mind you! But—I picked your *father!*

LAURA *(rising)* Mother, let me clear the table.

AMANDA No, dear, you go in front and study your typewriter chart. Or

practice your shorthand a little. Stay fresh and pretty!—It's almost time for our gentlemen callers to start arriving. *(She flounces girlishly toward the kitchenette.)* How many do you suppose we're going to entertain this afternoon?
(TOM throws down the paper and jumps up with a groan.)

LAURA *(Alone in the dining room)* I don't believe we're going to receive any, Mother.

AMANDA *(reappearing, airily)* What? No one—not one? You must be joking! *(LAURA nervously echoes her laugh. She slips in a fugitive manner through the half-open portieres and draws them gently behind her. A shaft of very clear light is thrown on her face against the faded tapestry of the curtains. MUSIC: "The Glass Menagerie" under faintly. Lightly.)* Not one gentleman caller? It can't be true! There must be a flood, there must have been a tornado!

LAURA It isn't a flood, it's not a tornado, Mother. I'm just not popular like you were in Blue Mountain. . . . *(TOM utters another groan. LAURA glances at him with a faint, apologetic smile. Her voice catching a little.)* Mother's afraid I'm going to be an old maid.
(The scene dims out with "Glass Menagerie" music)

scene 2

"Laura, Haven't You Ever Liked Some Boy?"

On the dark stage the screen is lighted with the image of blue roses. Gradually LAURA'S figure becomes apparent and the screen goes out. The music subsides.

LAURA is seated in the delicate ivory chair at the small claw-foot table. She wears a dress of soft violet material for a kimono—her hair tied back from her forehead with a ribbon. She is washing and polishing her collection of glass.

AMANDA appears on the fire-escape steps. At the sound of her ascent, LAURA catches her breath, thrusts the bowl of ornaments away and seats herself stiffly before the diagram of the typewriter keyboard as though it held her spellbound. Something has happened to AMANDA. It is written in her face as she climbs to the landing: a look that is grim and hopeless and a little absurd. She has on one of those cheap or imitation velvety-looking cloth coats with imitation fur collar. Her hat is five or six years old, one of those dreadful cloche hats that were worn in the late twenties and she is clasping an enormous black patent-leather pocketbook with nickel clasps and initials This is her full-dress outfit, the one she usually wears to the D.A.R. Before entering she looks through the door. She purses her lips, opens her eyes very wide, rolls them upward and shakes her head. Then she slowly lets herself in the door. Seeing her mother's expression LAURA touches her lips with a nervous gesture.

LAURA Hello, Mother, I was—*(She makes a nervous gesture toward the chart on the wall. AMANDA leans against the shut door and stares at LAURA with a martyred look.)*

AMANDA Deception? Deception? *(She slowly removes her hat and gloves, continuing the sweet suffering stare. She lets the hat and gloves fall on the floor—a bit of acting.)*

LAURA *(shakily)* How was the D.A.R. meeting? *(*AMANDA *slowly opens her purse and removes a dainty white handkerchief which she shakes out delicately and delicately touches to her lips and nostrils.)* Didn't you go to the D.A.R. meeting, Mother?

AMANDA *(Faintly, almost inaudibly)* —No.—No. *(Then more forcibly.)* I did not have the strength—to go to the D.A.R. In fact, I did not have the courage! I wanted to find a hole in the ground and hide myself in it forever! *(She crosses slowly to the wall and removes the diagram of the typewriter keyboard. She holds it in front of her for a second, staring at it sweetly and sorrowfully—then bites her lip and tears it in two pieces.)*

LAURA *(faintly)* Why did you do that, Mother? *(*AMANDA *repeats the same procedure with the chart of the Gregg Alphabet.)* Why are you—

AMANDA Why? Why? How old are you, Laura?

LAURA Mother, you know my age.

AMANDA I thought that you were an adult; it seems that I was mistaken. *(She crosses slowly to the sofa and sinks down and stares at* LAURA.*)*

LAURA Please don't stare at me, Mother.

*(*AMANDA *closes her eyes and lowers her head. Count ten.)*

AMANDA What are we going to do, what is going to become of us, what is the future?

(Count ten.)

LAURA Has something happened, Mother? *(*AMANDA *draws a long breath and takes out the handkerchief again. Dabbing process.)* Mother, has—something happened?

AMANDA I'll be all right in a minute, I'm just bewildered—*(Count five.)*—by life. . . .

LAURA Mother, I wish that you would tell me what's happened!

AMANDA As you know, I was supposed to be inducted into my office at the D.A.R. this afternoon. (IMAGE: *a swarm of typewriters.)* But I stopped off at Rubicam's business college to speak to your teachers about your having a cold and ask them what progress they thought you were making down there.

LAURA Oh. . . .

AMANDA I went to the typing instructor and introduced myself as your mother. She didn't know who you were. Wingfield, she said. We don't have any such student enrolled at the school!

I assured her she did, that you had been going to classes since early in January.

"I wonder," she said, "if you could be talking about that terribly shy little girl who dropped out of school after only a few days' attendance?"

"No," I said, "Laura, my daughter, has been going to school every day for the past six weeks!"

"Excuse me," she said. She took the attendance book out and there was your name, unmistakably printed, and all the dates you were absent until they decided that you had dropped out of school.

I still said, "No, there must have been some mistake! There must have been some mix-up in the records!"

And she said, "No—I remember her perfectly now. Her hands shook so that she couldn't hit the right keys! The first time we gave a speed-test, she broke down completely—was sick at the stomach and almost had to be carried into the wash-room! After that morning she never showed up any more. We phoned the house but never got any answer—while I was working at Famous and Barr, I suppose, demonstrating those—Oh!"

I felt so weak I could barely keep on my feet!

I had to sit down while they got me a glass of water!

Fifty dollars' tuition, all of our plans—my hopes and ambitions for you—just gone up the spout, just gone up the spout like that. *(*LAURA *draws a long breath and gets awkwardly to her feet. She crosses to the victrola and winds it up.)* What are you doing?

LAURA Oh! *(She releases the handle and returns to her seat.)*

AMANDA Laura, where have you been going when you've gone out pretending that you were going to business college?

LAURA I've just been going out walking.

AMANDA That's not true.

LAURA It is. I just went walking.

AMANDA Walking? Walking? In winter? Deliberately courting pneumonia in that light coat? Where did you walk to, Laura?

LAURA All sorts of places—mostly in the park.

AMANDA Even after you'd started catching that cold?

LAURA It was the lesser of two evils, Mother. (IMAGE: *winter scene in park.)* I couldn't go back up. I—threw up—on the floor!

AMANDA From half past seven till after five every day you mean to tell me you walked around in the park, because you wanted to make me think that you were still going to Rubicam's Business College?

LAURA It wasn't as bad as it sounds. I went inside places to get warmed up.

AMANDA Inside where?

LAURA I went in the art museum and the bird-houses at the Zoo. I visited the penguins every day! Sometimes I did without lunch and went to the movies. Lately I've been spending most of my afternoons in the Jewel-box, that big glass house where they raise the tropical flowers.

AMANDA You did all this to deceive me, just for deception? *(*LAURA *looks down.)* Why?

LAURA Mother, when you're disappointed, you get that awful suffering look on your face, like the picture of Jesus' mother in the museum!

AMANDA Hush!

LAURA I couldn't face it.

(Pause. A whisper of strings.)

(LEGEND: *"The Crust of Humility."*)

AMANDA *(hopelessly fingering the huge pocketbook)* So what are we going to do the rest of our lives? Stay home and watch the parades go by? Amuse ourselves with the glass menagerie, darling? Eternally play those worn-out phonograph records your father left as a painful reminder of him?

We won't have a business career—we've given that up because it gave us nervous indigestion! *(laughs wearily)* What is there left but dependency all our lives? I know so well what becomes of unmarried women who aren't prepared to occupy a position. I've seen such pitiful cases in the South—barely tolerated spinsters living upon the grudging patronage of sister's husband or brother's wife!—stuck away in some little mousetrap of a room—encouraged by one in-law to visit another—little birdlike women without any nest—eating the crust of humility all their life!

Is that the future that we've mapped out for ourselves?

I swear it's the only alternative I can think of!

It isn't a very pleasant alternative, is it?

Of course—some girls *do marry.*

(LAURA *twists her hands nervously.)*

Haven't you ever liked some boy?

LAURA Yes. I liked one once. *(rises.)* I came across his picture a while ago.

AMANDA *(with some interest)* He gave you his picture?

LAURA No, it's in the year-book.

AMANDA *(disappointed)* Oh—a high-school boy.

(SCREEN IMAGE: JIM *as high-school hero bearing a silver cup.)*

LAURA Yes. His name was Jim. (LAURA *lifts the heavy annual from the claw-foot table.)* Here he is in *The Pirates of Penzance.*

AMANDA *(absently)* The what?

LAURA The operetta the senior class put on. He had a wonderful voice and we sat across the aisle from each other Mondays, Wednesdays and Fridays in the Aud. Here he is with the silver cup for debating! See his grin?

AMANDA *(absently)* He must have had a jolly disposition.

LAURA He used to call me—Blue Roses.

(IMAGE: *Blue roses.)*

AMANDA Why did he call you such a name as that?

LAURA When I had that attack of pleurosis—he asked me what was the matter when I came back. I said pleurosis—he thought that I said Blue Roses! So that's what he always called me after that. Whenever he saw me, he'd holler, "Hello, Blue Roses!" I didn't care for the girl that he went out with. Emily Meisenbach. Emily was the best-dressed girl at Soldan. She never struck me, though, as being sincere . . . It says in the Personal Section—they're engaged. That's—six years ago! They must be married by now.

AMANDA Girls that aren't cut out for business careers usually wind up married to some nice man. *(gets up with a spark of revival)* Sister, that's what you'll do!

(LAURA *utters a startled, doubtful laugh. She reaches quickly for a piece of glass.)*

LAURA But, Mother—

AMANDA Yes? *(Crossing to photograph.)*

LAURA *(in a tone of frightened apology)* I'm—crippled!

(IMAGE: *screen.)*

AMANDA Nonsense! Laura, I've told you never, never to use that word. Why, you're not crippled, you just have a little defect—hardly noticeable, even! When people have some slight disadvantage like that, they cultivate other things to make up for it—develop charm—and vivacity—and—*charm!* That's all you have to do! *(She turns again to the photograph.)* One thing your father had *plenty of*—was *charm!*

(TOM *motions to the fiddle in the wings.)*

(The scene fades out with music)

scene 3

(LEGEND ON SCREEN: *"After the Fiasco—")*

(TOM *speaks from the fire-escape landing.)*

TOM After the fiasco at Rubicam's Business College, the idea of getting a gentleman caller for Laura began to play a more and more important part in Mother's calculations.

It became an obsession. Like some archetype of the universal unconscious, the image of the gentleman caller haunted our small apartment. . . .

(IMAGE: *Young man at door with flowers.)*

An evening at home rarely passed without some allusion to this image, this spectre, this hope. . . .

Even when he wasn't mentioned, his presence hung in Mother's preoccupied look and in my sister's frightened, apologetic manner—hung like a sentence passed upon the Wingfields!

Mother was a woman of action as well as words.

She began to take logical steps in the planned direction.

Late that winter and in the early spring—realizing that extra money would be needed to properly feather the nest and plume the bird—she conducted a vigorous campaign on the telephone, roping in subscribers to one of those magazines for matrons called *The Homemaker's Companion*, the type of journal that features the serialized sublimations of ladies of letters who think in terms of delicate cup-like breasts, slim, tapering waists, rich, creamy thighs, eyes like wood-smoke in autumn, fingers that soothe and caress like strains of music, bodies as powerful as Etruscan sculpture.

(SCREEN IMAGE: *Glamor Magazine Cover.)*

(AMANDA *enters with phone on long extension cord. She is spotted in the dim stage.)*

AMANDA Ida Scott? This is Amanda Wingfield!

We *missed* you at the D.A.R. last Monday!

I said to myself: She's probably suffering with that sinus condition! How is that sinus condition?

Horrors! Heaven have mercy!—You're a Christian martyr, yes, that's what you are, a Christian martyr!

Well, I just now happened to notice that your subscription to the *Companion's* about to expire! Yes, it expires with the next issue, honey!—

just when that wonderful new serial by Bessie Mae Hopper is getting off to such an exciting start. Oh, honey, it's something that you can't miss! You remember how *Gone With the Wind* took everybody by storm? You simply couldn't go out if you hadn't read it. All everybody *talked* was Scarlett O'Hara. Well, this is a book that critics already compare to *Gone With the Wind.* It's the *Gone With the Wind* of the post-World War generation!—What?—Burning?—Oh, honey, don't let them burn, go take a look in the oven and I'll hold the wire! Heavens—I think she's hung up!

(Dim Out.)

(LEGEND ON SCREEN: *"You think I'm in love with continental shoemakers?")*

(Before the stage is lighted, the violent voices of TOM *and* AMANDA *are heard. They are quarreling behind the portieres. In front of them stands* LAURA *with clenched hands and panicky expression. A clear pool of light on her figure throughout this scene.)*

TOM What in Christ's name am I—

AMANDA *(shrilly)* Don't you use that—

TOM Supposed to do!

AMANDA Expression! Not in my—

TOM Ohhh!

AMANDA Presence! Have you gone out of your senses?

TOM I have, that's true, *driven* out!

AMANDA What is the matter with you, you—big—big—idiot!

TOM Look!—I've got *no thing,* no single thing—

AMANDA Lower your voice!

TOM In my life here that I can call my own! Everything is—

AMANDA Stop that shouting!

TOM Yesterday you confiscated my books! You had the nerve to—

AMANDA I took that horrible novel back to the library—yes! That hideous book by that insane Mr. Lawrence. *(*TOM *laughs wildly.)* I cannot control the output of diseased minds or people who cater to them—*(*TOM *laughs still more wildly.)* But I won't allow such filth brought into my house! No, no, no, no, no!

TOM House, house! Who pays rent on it, who makes a slave of himself to—

AMANDA *(fairly screeching)* Don't you DARE to—

TOM No, no, *I* mustn't say things! *I've* got to just—

AMANDA Let me tell you—

TOM I don't want to hear any more! *(He tears the portieres open. The upstage area is lit with a turgid smoky red glow.)*

*(*AMANDA'S *hair is in metal curlers and she wears a very old bathrobe, much too large for her slight figure, a relic of the faithless Mr. Wingfield.)*

(An upright typewriter and a wild disarray of manuscripts are on the drop-leaf table. The quarrel was probably precipitated by AMANDA'S *interruption of his creative labor. A chair lying overthrown on the floor.)*

(Their gesticulating shadows are cast on the ceiling by the fiery glow.)

AMANDA You *will* hear more, you—

TOM No, I won't hear more, I'm going out!
AMANDA You come right back in—
TOM Out, out, out! Because I'm—
AMANDA Come back here, Tom Wingfield! I'm not through talking to you!
TOM Oh, go—
LAURA *(desperately)* —Tom!
AMANDA You're going to listen, and no more insolence from you! I'm at the end of my patience!
(He comes back toward her.)
TOM What do you think I'm at? Aren't I supposed to have any patience to reach the end of, Mother? I know, I know. It seems unimportant to you, what I'm *doing*—what I *want* to do—having a little *difference* between them! You don't think that—
AMANDA I think you've been doing things that you're ashamed of. That's why you act like this. I don't believe that you go every night to the movies. Nobody goes to the movies night after night. Nobody in their right minds goes to the movies as often as you pretend to. People don't go to the movies at nearly midnight, and movies don't let out at two A.M. Come in stumbling. Muttering to yourself like a maniac! You get three hours' sleep and then go to work. Oh, I can picture the way you're doing down there. Moping, doping, because you're in no condition.
TOM *(wildly)* No, I'm in no condition!
AMANDA What right have you got to jeopardize your job? Jeopardize the security of us all? How do you think we'd manage if you were—
TOM Listen! You think I'm crazy *about* the *warehouse? (He bends fiercely toward her slight figure.)* You think I'm in love with the Continental Shoemakers? You think I want to spend fifty-five *years* down there in that—*celotex interior!* with—*fluorescent—tubes!* Look! I'd rather somebody picked up a crowbar and battered out my brains—than go back mornings! I *go!* Every time you come in yelling that God damn *"Rise and Shine!" "Rise and Shine!"* I say to myself, "How *lucky dead* people are!" But I get up. I *go!* For sixty-five dollars a month I give up all that I dream of doing and being *ever!* And you say self—*self's* all I ever think of. Why, listen, if self is what I thought of, Mother, I'd be where he is—*gone! (pointing to father's picture)* As far as the system of transportation reaches! *(He starts past her. She grabs his arm.)* Don't grab at me, Mother!
AMANDA Where are you going?
TOM I'm going to the *movies!*
AMANDA I don't believe that lie!
TOM *(crouching toward her, overtowering her tiny figure. She backs away, gasping)* I'm going to opium dens! Yes, opium dens, dens of vice and criminals' hang-outs, Mother. I've joined the Hogan gang, I'm a hired assassin, I carry a tommy-gun in a violin case! I run a string of cat-houses in the Valley! They call me Killer, Killer Wingfield, I'm leading a double-life, a simple, honest warehouse worker by day, by night a dynamic *czar* of the *underworld, Mother.* I go to gambling casinos, I spin

away fortunes on the roulette table! I wear a patch over one eye and a false mustache, sometimes I put on green whiskers. On those occasions they call me—*El Diablo!* Oh, I could tell you things to make you sleepless! My enemies plan to dynamite this place. They're going to blow us all sky-high some night! I'll be glad, very happy, and so will you! You'll go up, up on a broomstick, over Blue Mountain with seventeen gentlemen callers! You ugly—babbling old—*witch. . . . (He goes through a series of violent, clumsy movements, seizing his overcoat, lunging to the door, pulling it fiercely open. The women watch him, aghast. His arm catches in the sleeve of the coat as he struggles to pull it on. For a moment he is pinioned by the bulky garment. With an outraged groan he tears the coat off again, splitting the shoulder of it, and hurls it across the room. It strikes against the shelf of* LAURA'S *glass collection, there is a tinkle of shattering glass.* LAURA *cries out as if wounded.)*

*(*MUSIC. LEGEND: *"The Glass Menagerie.")*

LAURA *(shrilly) My glass!*—menagerie. . . . *(She covers her face and turns away.)*

(But AMANDA *is still stunned and stupefied by the "ugly witch" so that she barely notices this occurrence. Now she recovers her speech.)*

AMANDA *(in an awful voice)* I won't speak to you—until you apologize! *(She crosses through portieres and draws them together behind her.* TOM *is left with* LAURA. LAURA *clings weakly to the mantel with her face averted.* TOM *stares at her stupidly for a moment. Then he crosses to shelf. Drops awkwardly on his knees to collect the fallen glass, glancing at* LAURA *as if he would speak but couldn't.)*

("The Glass Menagerie" steals in as the scene dims out.)

scene 4

(The interior is dark. Faint light in the alley. A deep-voiced bell in a church is tolling the hour of five as the scene commences.

TOM *appears at the top of the alley. After each solemn boom of the bell in the tower, he shakes a little noise-maker or rattle as if to express the tiny spasm of man in contrast to the sustained power and dignity of the Almighty. This and the unsteadiness of his advance make it evident that he has been drinking.*

As he climbs the few steps to the fire-escape landing light steals up inside. LAURA *appears in night-dress, observing* TOM'S *empty bed in the front room.* TOM *fishes in his pockets for door-key, removing a motley assortment of articles in the search, including a perfect shower of movie-ticket stubs and an empty bottle. At last he finds the key, but just as he is about to insert it, it slips from his fingers. He strikes a match and crouches below the door.*

TOM *(bitterly)* One crack—and it falls through!

*(*LAURA *opens the door.)*

LAURA Tom! Tom, what are you doing?

TOM Looking for a door-key.

LAURA Where have you been all this time?
TOM I have been to the movies.
LAURA All this time at the movies?
TOM There was a very long program. There was a Garbo picture and a Mickey Mouse and a travelogue and a newsreel and a preview of coming attractions. And there was an organ solo and a collection for the milk-fund—simultaneously—which ended up in a terrible fight between a fat lady and an usher!
LAURA *(innocently)* Did you have to stay through everything?
TOM Of course! And, oh, I forgot! There was a big stage show! The headliner on this stage show was Malvolio the Magician. He performed wonderful tricks, many of them, such as pouring water back and forth between pitchers. First it turned to wine and then it turned to beer and then it turned to whiskey. I know it was whiskey it finally turned into because he needed somebody to come up out of the audience to help him, and I came up—both shows! It was Kentucky Straight Bourbon. A very generous fellow, he gave souvenirs. *(He pulls from his back pocket a shimmering rainbow-colored scarf.)* He gave me this. This is his magic scarf. You can have it, Laura. You wave it over a canary cage and you get a bowl of gold-fish. You wave it over the gold-fish bowl and they fly away canaries. . . . But the wonderfullest trick of all was the coffin trick. We nailed him into a coffin and he got out of the coffin without removing one nail. *(He has come inside.)* There is a trick that would come in handy for me—get me out of this 2 by 4 situation! *(Flops onto bed and starts removing shoes.)*
LAURA Tom—Shhh!
TOM What're you shushing me for?
LAURA You'll wake up Mother.
TOM Goody, goody! Pay 'er back for all those "Rise an' Shines." *(Lies down, groaning.)* You know it don't take much intelligence to get yourself into a nailed-up coffin, Laura. But who in hell ever got himself out of one without removing one nail?
(As if in answer, the father's grinning photograph lights up.)
(Scene dims out.)
(Immediately following: The church bell is heard striking six. At the sixth stroke the alarm clock goes off in AMANDA'S *room, and after a few moments we hear her calling: "Rise and Shine! Rise and Shine! Laura, go tell your brother to rise and shine!")*
TOM *(sitting up slowly)* I'll rise—but I won't shine.
(The light increases.)
AMANDA Laura, tell your brother his coffee is ready.
*(*LAURA *sips into front room.)*
LAURA Tom!—It's nearly seven. Don't make Mother nervous. *(He stares at her stupidly. Beseechingly.)* Tom, speak to Mother this morning. Make up with her, apologize, speak to her!
TOM She won't to me. It's her that started not speaking.
LAURA If you just say you're sorry she'll start speaking.
TOM Her not speaking—is that such a tragedy?

LAURA Please—please!

AMANDA *(calling from kitchenette)* Laura, are you going to do what I asked you to do, or do I have to get dressed and go out myself?

LAURA Going, going—soon as I get on my coat! *(She pulls on a shapeless felt hat with nervous, jerky movement, pleadingly glancing at* TOM. *Rushes awkwardly for coat. The coat is one of* AMANDA'S, *inaccurately made-over, the sleeves too short for* LAURA.*)* Butter and what else?

AMANDA *(Entering upstage)* Just butter. Tell them to charge it.

LAURA Mother, they make such faces when I do that.

AMANDA Sticks and stones can break our bones, but the expression on Mr. Garfinkel's face won't harm us! Tell your brother his coffee is getting cold.

LAURA *(at door)* Do what I asked you, will you, will you, Tom?

(He looks sullenly away.)

AMANDA Laura, go now or just don't go at all!

LAURA *(rushing out)* Going—going! *(A second later she cries out.* TOM *springs up and crosses to door.* AMANDA *rushes anxiously in.* TOM *opens the door.)*

TOM Laura?

LAURA I'm all right. I slipped, but I'm all right.

AMANDA *(Peering anxiously after her)* If anyone breaks a leg on those fire-escape steps, the landlord ought to be sued for every cent he possesses! *(She shuts door. Remembers she isn't speaking and returns to other room.)*

(As TOM *enters listlessly for his coffee, she turns her back to him and stands rigidly facing the window on the gloomy gray vault of the areaway. Its light on her face with its aged but childish features is cruelly sharp, satirical as a Daumier print.)*

*(*MUSIC UNDER: *"Ave Maria.")*

*(*TOM *glances sheepishly but sullenly at her averted figure and slumps at the table. The coffee is scalding hot; he sips it and gasps and spits it back in the cup. At his gasp,* AMANDA *catches her breath and half turns. Then catches herself and turns back to window.)*

*(*TOM *blows on his coffee, glancing sidewise at his mother. She clears her throat.* TOM *clears his. He starts to rise. Sinks back down again, scratches his head, clears his throat again.* AMANDA *coughs.* TOM *raises his cup in both hands to blow on it, his eyes staring over the rim of it at his mother for several moments. Then he slowly sets the cup down and awkwardly and hesitantly rises from the chair.)*

TOM *(hoarsely)* Mother. I—I apologize, Mother. *(*AMANDA *draws a quick, shuddering breath. Her face works grotesquely. She breaks into childlike tears.)* I'm sorry for what I said, for everything that I said, I didn't mean it.

AMANDA *(sobbingly)* My devotion has made me a witch and so I make myself hateful to my children!

TOM *No,* you *don't.*

AMANDA I worry so much, don't sleep, it makes me nervous!

TOM *(gently)* I understand that.

AMANDA I've had to put up a solitary battle all these years. But you're my right-hand bower! Don't fall down, don't fail!

TOM *(gently)* I try, Mother.

AMANDA *(with great enthusiasm)* Try and you will SUCCEED! *(The notion makes her breathless.)* Why, you—you're just *full* of natural endowments! Both of my children—they're *unusual* children! Don't you think I know it? I'm so—*proud!* Happy and—feel I've—so much to be thankful for but— Promise me one thing, Son!

TOM What, Mother?

AMANDA Promise, son, you'll—never be a drunkard!

TOM *(turns to her grinning)* I will never be a drunkard, Mother.

AMANDA That's what frightened me so, that you'd be drinking! Eat a bowl of Purina!

TOM Just coffee, Mother.

AMANDA Shredded wheat biscuit?

TOM No. No, Mother, just coffee.

AMANDA You can't put in a day's work on an empty stomach. You've got ten minutes—don't gulp! Drinking too-hot liquids makes cancer of the stomach. . . . Put cream in.

TOM No, thank you.

AMANDA To cool it.

TOM No! No, thank you, I want it black.

AMANDA I know, but it's not good for you. We have to do all that we can to build ourselves up. In these trying times we live in, all that we have to cling to is—each other. . . . That's why it's so important to— Tom, I— I sent out your sister so I could discuss something with you. If you hadn't spoken I would have spoken to you. *(Sits down.)*

TOM *(gently)* What is it, Mother, that you want to discuss?

AMANDA *Laura!*

(TOM *puts his cup down slowly.)*

(LEGEND ON SCREEN: *"Laura."*)

(MUSIC: *"The Glass Menagerie."*)

TOM —Oh.—Laura . . .

AMANDA *(Touching his sleeve)* You know how Laura is. So quiet but— still water runs deep! She notices things and I think she—broods about them. (TOM *looks up.)* A few days ago I came in and she was crying.

TOM What about?

AMANDA You.

TOM Me?

AMANDA She has an idea that you're not happy here.

TOM What gave her that idea?

AMANDA What gives her any idea? However, you do act strangely. I—I'm not criticizing, understand *that!* I know your ambitions do not lie in the warehouse, that like everybody in the whole wide world—you've had to—make sacrifices, but—Tom—Tom—life's not easy, it calls for— Spartan endurance! There's so many things in my heart that I cannot describe to you! I've never told you but I—*loved* your father. . . .

TOM *(gently)* I know that, Mother.

AMANDA And you—when I see you taking after his ways! Staying out late—and—well, you *had* been drinking the night you were in that—terrifying condition! Laura says that you hate the apartment and that you go out nights to get away from it! Is that true, Tom?

TOM No. You say there's so much in your heart that you can't describe to me. That's true of me, too. There's so much in my heart that I can't describe to *you!* So let's respect each other's—

AMANDA But, why—*why*, Tom—are you always so *restless?* Where do you *go* to, nights?

TOM I—go to the movies.

AMANDA Why do you go to the movies so much, Tom?

TOM I go to the movies because—I like adventure. Adventure is something I don't have much of at work, so I go to the movies.

AMANDA But, Tom, you go to the movies *entirely* too *much!*

TOM I like a lot of adventure.

(AMANDA *looks baffled, then hurt. As the familiar inquisition resumes he becomes hard and impatient again.* AMANDA *slips back into her querulous attitude toward him.)*

(IMAGE ON SCREEN: *Sailing Vessel with Jolly Roger.)*

AMANDA Most young men find adventure in their careers.

TOM Then most young men are not employed in a warehouse.

AMANDA The world is full of young men employed in warehouses and offices and factories.

TOM Do all of them find adventure in their careers?

AMANDA They do or they do without it! Not everybody has a craze for adventure.

TOM Man is by instinct a lover, a hunter, a fighter, and none of those instincts are given much play at the warehouse!

AMANDA Man is by instinct! Don't quote instinct to me! Instinct is something that people have got away from! It belongs to animals! Christian adults don't want it!

TOM What do Christian adults want, then, Mother?

AMANDA Superior things! Things of the mind and the spirit! Only animals have to satisfy instincts! Surely your aims are somewhat higher than theirs! Than monkeys—pigs—

TOM I reckon they're not.

AMANDA You're joking. However, that isn't what I wanted to discuss.

TOM *(rising)* I haven't much time.

AMANDA *(pushing his shoulders)* Sit down.

TOM You want me to punch in red at the warehouse, Mother?

AMANDA You have five minutes. I want to talk about Laura.

(LEGEND: *"Plans and Provisions.")*

TOM All right! What about Laura?

AMANDA We have to be making some plans and provisions for her. She's older than you, two years, and nothing has happened. She just drifts along doing nothing. It frightens me terribly how she just drifts along.

TOM I guess she's the type that people call home girls.

AMANDA There's no such type, and if there is, it's a pity! That is unless the home is hers, with a husband!

TOM What?

AMANDA Oh, I can see the handwriting on the wall as plain as I see the nose in front of my face! It's terrifying!

More and more you remind me of your father! He was out all hours without explanation!—Then *left! Good-bye!*

And me with the bag to hold. I saw that letter you got from the Merchant Marine. I know what you're dreaming of. I'm not standing here blindfolded.

Very well, then. Then *do* it!

But not till there's somebody to take your place.

TOM What do you mean?

AMANDA I mean that as soon as Laura has got somebody to take care of her, married, a home of her own, independent—why, then you'll be free to go wherever you please, on land, on sea, whichever way the wind blows you!

But until that time you've got to look out for your sister. I don't say me because I'm old and don't matter! I say for your sister because she's young and dependent.

I put her in business college—a dismal failure! Frightened her so it made her sick at the stomach.

I took her over to the Young People's League at the church. Another fiasco. She spoke to nobody, nobody spoke to her. Now all she does is fool with those pieces of glass and play those worn-out records. What kind of a life is that for a girl to lead?

TOM What can I do about it?

AMANDA Overcome selfishness!

Self, self, self is all that you ever think of!

*(*TOM *springs up and crosses to get his coat. It is ugly and bulky. He pulls on a cap with earmuffs.)*

Where is your muffler? Put your wool muffler on! *(He snatches it angrily from the closet and tosses it around his neck and pulls both ends tight.)*

Tom! I haven't said what I had in mind to ask you.

TOM I'm too late to—

AMANDA *(Catching his arm—very importunately. Then shyly)* Down at the warehouse, aren't there some—nice young men?

TOM No!

AMANDA There *must* be—*some* . . .

TOM Mother—

(gesture)

AMANDA Find out one that's clean-living—doesn't drink and—ask him out for sister!

TOM What?

AMANDA For *sister!* To *meet!* Get *acquainted!*

TOM *(stamping to door)* Oh, my *go-osh!*

AMANDA Will you? *(He opens door. Imploringly.)* Will you? *(He starts down.)* Will you? *Will* you, dear?

TOM *(Calling back)* Yes!

(AMANDA *closes the door hesitantly and with a troubled but faintly hopeful expression.)*
(SCREEN IMAGE: *Glamor Magazine Cover.)*
(Spot AMANDA *at phone.)*
AMANDA Ella Cartwright? This is Amanda Wingfield!
How are you, honey?
How is that kidney condition?
(Count five.)
Horrors!
(Count five.)
You're a Christian martyr, yes, honey, that's what you are, a Christian martyr!
Well, I just now happened to notice in my little red book that your subscription to the *Companion* has just run out! I knew that you wouldn't want to miss out on the wonderful serial starting in this new issue. It's by Bessie Mae Hopper. the first thing she's written since *Honeymoon for Three.*
Wasn't that a strange and interesting story? Well, this one is even lovelier, I believe. It has a sophisticated, society background. It's all about the horsey set on Long Island!
(fade out)

scene 5

(LEGEND ON SCREEN: *"Annunciation." Fade with music. It is early dusk of a spring evening. Supper has just been finished in the Wingfield apartment.* AMANDA *and* LAURA *in light-colored dresses are removing dishes from the table, in the upstage area, which is shadowy, their movements formalized almost as a dance or ritual, their moving forms as pale and silent as moths.*
TOM, *in white shirt and trousers, rises from the table and crosses toward the fire-escape.)*
AMANDA *(as he passes her)* Son, will you do me a favor?
TOM What?
AMANDA Comb your hair! You look so pretty when your hair is combed! (TOM *slouches on sofa with evening paper. Enormous caption "Franco Triumphs.")* There is only one respect in which I would like you to emulate your father.
TOM What respect is that?
AMANDA The care he always took of his appearance. He never allowed himself to look untidy. *(He throws down the paper and crosses to fire-escape.)* Where are you going?
TOM I'm going out to smoke.
AMANDA You smoke too much. A pack a day at fifteen cents a pack. How much would that amount to in a month? Thirty times fifteen is how much, Tom? Figure it out and you will be astounded at what you could save. Enough to give you a night-school course in accounting at Washington U! Just think what a wonderful thing that would be for you, Son! (TOM *is unmoved by the thought.)*

TOM I'd rather smoke. *(He steps out on landing, letting the screen door slam.)*

AMANDA *(sharply)* I know! That's the tragedy of it. . . . *(Alone, she turns to look at her husband's picture.)*

(DANCE MUSIC: *"All the World is Waiting for the Sunrise!"*)

TOM *(To the audience)* Across the alley from us was the Paradise Dance Hall. On evenings in spring the windows and doors were open and the music came outdoors. Sometimes the lights were turned out except for a large glass sphere that hung from the ceiling. It would turn slowly about and filter the dusk with delicate rainbow colors. Then the orchestra played a waltz or a tango, something that had a slow and sensuous rhythm. Couples would come outside, to the relative privacy of the alley. You could see them kissing behind ash-pits and telephone poles.

This was the compensation for lives that passed like mine, without any change or adventure.

Adventure and change were imminent in this year. They were waiting around the corner for all these kids.

Suspended in the mist over Berchtesgaden, caught in the folds of Chamberlain's umbrella—

In Spain there was Guernica!

But here there was only hot swing music and liquor, dance halls, bars, and movies, and sex that hung in the gloom like a chandelier and flooded the world with brief, deceptive rainbows. . . .

All the world was waiting for bombardments!

(AMANDA *turns from the picture and comes outside.)*

AMANDA *(sighing)* A fire-escape landing's a poor excuse for a porch. *(She spreads a newspaper on a step and sits down, gracefully and demurely as if she were settling into a swing on a Mississippi veranda.)* What are you looking at?

TOM The moon.

AMANDA Is there a moon this evening?

TOM It's rising over Garfinkel's Delicatessen.

AMANDA So it is! A little silver slipper of a moon. Have you made a wish on it yet?

TOM Um-hum.

AMANDA What did you wish for?

TOM That's a secret.

AMANDA A secret, huh? Well, I won't tell mine either. I will be just as mysterious as you.

TOM I bet I can guess what yours is.

AMANDA Is my head so transparent?

TOM You're not a sphinx.

AMANDA No, I don't have secrets. I'll tell you what I wished for on the moon. Success and happiness for my precious children! I wish for that whenever there's a moon, and when there isn't a moon, I wish for it, too.

TOM I thought perhaps you wished for a gentleman caller.

AMANDA Why do you say that?

TOM Don't you remember asking me to fetch one?

AMANDA I remember suggesting that it would be nice for your sister if you brought home some nice young man from the warehouse. I think that I've made that suggestion more than once.

TOM Yes, you have made it repeatedly.

AMANDA Well?

TOM We are going to have one.

AMANDA *What?*

TOM A gentleman caller!

(The annunciation is celebrated with music.)

*(*AMANDA *rises.)*

*(*IMAGE ON SCREEN: *Caller with Bouquet.)*

AMANDA You mean you have asked some nice young man to come over?

TOM Yep. I've asked him to dinner.

AMANDA You really did?

TOM I did!

AMANDA You did, and did he—*accept?*

TOM He did!

AMANDA Well, well—well, well! That's—lovely!

TOM I thought that you would be pleased.

AMANDA It's definite, then?

TOM Very definite.

AMANDA Soon?

TOM Very soon.

AMANDA For heaven's sake, stop putting on and tell me some things, will you?

TOM What things do you want me to tell you?

AMANDA *Naturally* I would like to know when he's *coming!*

TOM He's coming tomorrow.

AMANDA *Tomorrow?*

TOM Yep. Tomorrow.

AMANDA But, Tom!

TOM Yes, Mother?

AMANDA Tomorrow gives me no time!

TOM Time for what?

AMANDA Preparations! Why didn't you phone me at once, as soon as you asked him, the minute that he accepted? Then, don't you see, I could have been getting ready!

TOM You don't have to make any fuss.

AMANDA Oh, Tom, Tom, Tom, of course I have to make a fuss! I want things nice, not sloppy! Not thrown together. I'll certainly have to do some fast thinking, won't I?

TOM I don't see why you have to think at all.

AMANDA You just don't know. We can't have a gentleman caller in a pig-sty! All my wedding silver has to be polished, the monogrammed table linen ought to be laundered! The windows have to be washed and fresh curtains put up. And how about clothes? We have to *wear* something, don't we?

TOM Mother, this boy is no one to make a fuss over!

AMANDA Do you realize he's the first young man we've introduced to your sister?

It's terrible, dreadful, disgraceful that poor little sister has never recived a single gentleman caller! Tom, come inside! *(She opens the screen door.)*

TOM What for?

AMANDA I want to ask you some things.

TOM If you're going to make such a fuss, I'll call it off, I'll tell him not to come!

AMANDA You certainly won't do anything of the kind. Nothing offends people worse than broken engagements. It simply means I'll have to work like a Turk! We won't be brilliant, but we will pass inspection. Come on inside. *(TOM follows, groaning.)* Sit down.

TOM Any particular place you would like me to sit?

AMANDA Thank heavens I've got that new sofa! I'm also making payments on a floor lamp I'll have sent out! And put the chintz covers on, they'll brighten things up! Of course I'd hoped to have these walls repapered. . . . What is the young man's name?

TOM His name is O'Connor.

AMANDA That, of course, means fish—tomorrow is Friday! I'll have that salmon loaf—with Durkee's dressing! What does he do? He works at the warehouse?

TOM Of course! How else would I—

AMANDA Tom, he—doesn't drink?

TOM Why do you ask me that?

AMANDA Your father *did!*

TOM Don't get started on that!

AMANDA He *does* drink, then?

TOM Not that I know of!

AMANDA Make sure, be certain! The last thing I want for my daughter's a boy who drinks!

TOM Aren't you being a little bit premature? Mr. O'Connor has not yet appeared on the scene!

AMANDA But will tomorrow. To meet your sister, and what do I know about his character? Nothing! Old maids are better off than wives of drunkards!

TOM Oh, my God!

AMANDA Be still!

TOM *(Leaning forward to whisper)* Lots of fellows meet girls whom they don't marry!

AMANDA Oh, talk sensibly, Tom—and don't be sarcastic! *(She has gotten a hairbrush.)*

TOM What are you doing?

AMANDA I'm brushing that cow-lick down!

What is this young man's position at the warehouse?

TOM *(Submitting grimly to the brush and the interrogation)* This young man's position is that of a shipping clerk, Mother.

AMANDA Sounds to me like a fairly responsible job, the sort of a job *you* would be in if you just had more *get-up*.

What is his salary? Have you any idea?

TOM I would judge it to be approximately eighty-five dollars a month.

AMANDA Well—not princely, but—

TOM Twenty more than I make.

AMANDA Yes, how well I know! But for a family man, eighty-five dollars a month is not much more than you can just get by on. . . .

TOM Yes, but Mr. O'Connor is not a family man.

AMANDA He might be, mightn't he? Some time in the future?

TOM I see. Plans and provisions.

AMANDA You are the only young man that I know of who ignores the fact that the future becomes the present, the present the past, and the past turns into everlasting regret if you don't plan for it!

TOM I will think that over and see what I can make of it.

AMANDA Don't be supercilious with your mother! Tell me some more about this—what do you call him?

TOM James D. O'Connor. The D. is for Delaney.

AMANDA Irish on *both* sides! *Gracious!* And doesn't drink?

TOM Shall I call him up and ask him right this minute?

AMANDA The only way to find out about those things is to make discreet inquiries at the proper moment. When I was a girl in Blue Mountain and it was suspected that a young man drank, the girl whose attentions he had been receiving, if any girl *was*, would sometimes speak to the minister of his church, or rather her father would if her father was living, and sort of feel him out on the young man's character. That is the way such things are discreetly handled to keep a young woman from making a tragic mistake!

TOM Then how did you happen to make a tragic mistake?

AMANDA That innocent look of your father's had everyone fooled!

He *smiled*—the world was *enchanted!*

No girl can do worse than put herself at the mercy of a handsome appearance!

I hope that Mr. O'Connor is not too good-looking.

TOM No, he's not too good-looking. He's covered with freckles and hasn't too much of a nose.

AMANDA He's not right-down homely, though?

TOM Not right-down homely. Just medium homely, I'd say.

AMANDA Character's what to look for in a man.

TOM That's what I've always said, Mother.

AMANDA You've never said anything of the kind and I suspect you would never give it a thought.

TOM Don't be so suspicious of me.

AMANDA At least I hope he's the type that's up and coming.

TOM I think he really goes in for self-improvement.

AMANDA What reason have you to think so?

TOM He goes to night school.

AMANDA *(beaming)* Splendid! What does he do, I mean study?

TOM Radio engineering and public speaking!

AMANDA Then he has visions of being advanced in the world!

Any young man who studies public speaking is aiming to have an executive job some day!

And radio engineering? A thing for the future!

Both of these facts are very illuminating. Those are the sort of things that a mother should know concerning any young man who comes to call on her daughter. Seriously or—not.

TOM One little warning. He doesn't know about Laura. I didn't let on that we had dark ulterior motives. I just said, why don't you come and have dinner with us? He said okay and that was the whole conversation.

AMANDA I bet it was! You're eloquent as an oyster.

However, he'll know about Laura when he gets here. When he sees how lovely and sweet and pretty she is, he'll thank his lucky stars he was asked to dinner.

TOM Mother, you mustn't expect too much of Laura.

AMANDA What do you mean?

TOM Laura seems all those things to you and me because she's ours and we love her. We don't even notice she's crippled any more.

AMANDA Don't say crippled! You know that I never allow that word to be used!

TOM But face facts, Mother. She is and—that's not all—

AMANDA What do you mean "not all"?

TOM Laura is very different from other girls.

AMANDA I think the difference is all to her advantage.

TOM Not quite all—in the eyes of others—strangers—she's terribly shy and lives in a world of her own and those things make her seem a little peculiar to people outside the house.

AMANDA Don't say peculiar.

TOM Face the facts. She is.

(The dance-hall music changes to a tango that has a minor and somewhat ominous tone.)

AMANDA In what way is she peculiar—may I ask?

TOM *(gently)* She lives in a world of her own—a world of—little glass ornaments, Mother. . . . *(Gets up.* AMANDA *remains holding brush, looking at him, troubled.)* She plays old phonograph records and—that's about all— *(He glances at himself in the mirror and crosses to door.)*

AMANDA *(sharply)* Where are you going?

TOM I'm going to the movies. *(out screen door)*

AMANDA Not to the movies, every night to the movies! *(follows quickly to screen door.)* I don't believe you always go to the movies! *(He is gone.* AMANDA *looks worriedly after him for a moment. Then vitality and optimism return and she turns from the door. Crossing to portieres.)* Laura! Laura! *(*LAURA *answers from kitchenette.)*

LAURA Yes, Mother.

AMANDA Let those dishes go and come in front! *(*LAURA *appears with dish towel. Gaily.)* Laura, come here and make a wish on the moon! (SCREEN IMAGE: *moon.)*

LAURA *(entering)* Moon—moon?

AMANDA A little silver slipper of a moon.
Look over your left shoulder, Laura, and make a wish!
*(*LAURA *looks faintly puzzled as if called out of sleep.* AMANDA *seizes her shoulders and turns her at an angle by the door.)*
Now!
Now, darling, *wish!*

LAURA What shall I wish for, Mother?

AMANDA *(Her voice trembling and her eyes suddenly filling with tears)*
Happiness! Good fortune!
(The violin rises and the stage dims out.)

scene 6

(IMAGE: *high school hero.)*

TOM And so the following evening I brought Jim home to dinner. I had known Jim slightly in high school. In high school Jim was a hero. He had tremendous Irish good nature and vitality with the scrubbed and polished look of white chinaware. He seemed to move in a continual spotlight. He was a star in basketball, captain of the debating club, president of the senior class and the glee club and he sang the male lead in the annual light operas. He was always running or bounding, never just walking. He seemed always at the point of defeating the law of gravity. He was shooting with such velocity through his adolescence that you would logically expect him to arrive at nothing short of the White House by the time he was thirty. But Jim apparently ran into more interference after his graduation from Soldan. His speed had definitely slowed. Six years after he left high school he was holding a job that wasn't much better than mine.
(IMAGE: *Clerk.)*
He was the only one at the warehouse with whom I was on friendly terms. I was valuable to him as soneone who could remember his former glory, who had seen him win basketball games and the silver cup in debating. He knew of my secret practice of retiring to a cabinet of the wash-room to work on poems when business was slack in the warehouse. He called me Shakespeare. And while the other boys in the warehouse regarded me with suspicious hostility, Jim took a humorous attitude toward me. Gradually his attitude affected the others, their hostility wore off and they also began to smile at me as people smile at an oddly fashioned dog who trots across their path at some distance.

I knew that Jim and Laura had known each other at Soldan, and I had heard Laura speak admiringly of his voice. I didn't know if Jim remembered her or not. In high school Laura had been as unobtrusive as Jim had been astonishing. If he did remember Laura, it was not as my sister, for when I asked him to dinner, he grinned and said, "You know, Shakespeare, I never thought of you as having folks!"

He was about to discover that I did. . . .
(LIGHT UPSTAGE.*)*
(LEGEND ON SCREEN: *"The accent of a coming foot.")*
(Friday evening. It is about five o'clock of a late spring evening which

comes "scattering poems in the sky.")

(A delicate lemony light is in the Wingfield apartment.)

*(*AMANDA *has worked like a Turk in preparation for the gentleman caller. The results are astonishing. The new floor lamp with its rose-silk shade is in place, a colored paper lantern conceals the broken light fixture in the ceiling, new billowing white curtains are at the windows, chintz covers are on chairs and sofa, a pair of new sofa pillows make their initial appearance.)*

(Open boxes and tissue paper are scattered on the floor.)

*(*LAURA *stands in the middle with lifted arms while* AMANDA *crouches before her, adjusting the hem of the new dress, devout and ritualistic. The dress is colored and designed by memory. The arrangement of* LAURA'S *hair is changed; it is softer and more becoming. A fragile, unearthly prettiness has come out in* LAURA: *she is like a piece of translucent glass touched by light, given a momentary radiance, not actual, not lasting.)*

AMANDA *(Impatiently)* Why are you trembling?

LAURA Mother, you've made me so nervous!

AMANDA How have I made you nervous?

LAURA By all this fuss! You make it seem so important!

AMANDA I don't understand you, Laura. You couldn't be satisfied with just sitting home, and yet whenever I try to arrange something for you, you seem to resist it. *(She gets up.)*

Now take a look at yourself.

No, wait! Wait just a moment—I have an idea!

LAURA What is it now?

*(*AMANDA *produces two powder puffs which she wraps in handkerchiefs and stuffs in* LAURA'S *bosom.)*

LAURA Mother, what are you doing?

AMANDA They call them "Gay Deceivers"!

LAURA I won't wear them!

AMANDA You will!

LAURA Why should I?

AMANDA Because, to be painfully honest, your chest is flat.

LAURA You make it seem like we were setting a trap.

AMANDA All pretty girls are a trap, a pretty trap, and men expect them to be.

(LEGEND: *"a pretty trap."*)

Now look at yourself, young lady. This is the prettiest you will ever be!

I've got to fix myself now! You're going to be surprised by your mother's appearance! *(She crosses through portieres, humming gaily.)*

*(*LAURA *moves slowly to the long mirror and stares solemnly at herself.)*

(A wind blows the white curtains inward in a slow, graceful motion and with a faint, sorrowful sighing.)

AMANDA *(Off stage)* It isn't dark enough yet. (LAURA *turns slowly before the mirror with a troubled look.)*

(LEGEND ON SCREEN: *"This is my sister: celebrate her with strings!"*

music.)

AMANDA *(laughing, off)* I'm going to show you something. I'm going to make a spectacular appearance!

LAURA What is it, Mother?

AMANDA Possess your soul in patience—you will see!

Something I've resurrected from that old trunk! Styles haven't changed so terribly much after all. . . .

(She parts the portieres.)

Now just look at your mother!

(She wears a girlish frock of yellowed voile with a blue silk sash. She carries a bunch of jonquils—the legend of her youth is nearly revived. Feverishly.)

This is the dress in which I led the cotillion. Won the cakewalk twice at Sunset Hill, wore one spring to the Governor's ball in Jackson!

See how I sashayed around the ballroom, Laura?

(She raises her skirt and does a mincing step around the room.)

I wore it on Sundays for my gentlemen callers! I had it on the day I met your father—

I had malaria fever all that spring. The change of climate from East Tennessee to the Delta—weakened resistance—I had a little temperature all the time—not enough to be serious—just enough to make me restless and giddy!—Invitations poured in—parties all over the Delta!—"Stay in bed," said Mother, "you have fever!"—but I just wouldn't.—I took quinine but kept on going, going!—Evenings, dances!—Afternoons, long, long rides! Picnics—lovely!—So lovely, that country in May.—All lacy with dogwood, literally flooded with jonquils!—That was the spring I had the craze for jonquils. Jonquils became an absolute obsession. Mother said, "Honey, there's no more room for jonquils." And still I kept on bringing in more jonquils. Whenever, wherever I saw them, I'd say, "Stop! Stop! I see jonquils!" I made the young men help me gather the jonquils! It was a joke, Amanda and her jonquils! Finally there were no more vases to hold them, every available space was filled with jonquils. No vases to hold them? All right, I'll hold them myself! And then I—*(She stops in front of the picture.* MUSIC.*)* met your father!

Malaria fever and jonquils and then—this—boy. . . .

(She switches on the rose-colored lamp.)

I hope they get here before it starts to rain.

(She crosses upstage and places the jonquils in bowl on table.)

I gave your brother a little extra change so he and Mr. O'Connor could take the service car home.

LAURA *(With altered look)* What did you say his name was?

AMANDA O'Connor.

LAURA What is his first name?

AMANDA I don't remember. Oh, yes, I do. It was—Jim!

(LAURA *sways slightly and catches hold of a chair.)*

(LEGEND ON SCREEN: *"Not Jim!")*

LAURA *(faintly)* Not—Jim!

AMANDA Yes, that was it, it was Jim! I've never known a Jim that wasn't nice!

*(*MUSIC: *ominous.)*

LAURA Are you sure his name is Jim O'Connor?

AMANDA Yes. Why?

LAURA Is he the one that Tom used to know in high school?

AMANDA He didn't say so. I think he just got to know him at the warehouse.

LAURA There was a Jim O'Connor we both knew in high school—*(Then, with effort.)* If that is the one that Tom is bringing to dinner—you'll have to excuse me, I won't come to the table.

AMANDA What sort of nonsense is this?

LAURA You asked me once if I'd ever liked a boy. Don't you remember I showed you this boy's picture?

AMANDA You mean the boy you showed me in the year book?

LAURA Yes, that boy.

AMANDA Laura, Laura, were you in love with that boy?

LAURA I don't know, Mother. All I know is I couldn't sit at the table if it was him!

AMANDA It won't be him! It isn't the least bit likely. But whether it is or not, you will come to the table. You will not be excused.

LAURA I'll have to be, Mother.

AMANDA I don't intend to humor your silliness, Laura. I've had too much from you and your brother, both!

So just sit down and compose yourself till they come. Tom has forgotten his key so you'll have to let them in, when they arrive.

LAURA *(panicky)* Oh, Mother—*you* answer the door!

AMANDA *(lightly)* I'll be in the kitchen—busy!

LAURA Oh, Mother, please answer the door, don't make me do it!

AMANDA *(crossing into kitchenette)* I've got to fix the dressing for the salmon. Fuss, fuss—silliness!—over a gentleman caller!

(Door swings shut. LAURA *is left alone.)*

*(*LEGEND: *"terror!")*

(She utters a low moan and turns off the lamp—sits stiffly on the edge of the sofa, knotting her fingers together.)

*(*LEGEND ON SCREEN: *"the opening of a door!")*

*(*TOM *and* JIM *appear on the fire-escape steps and climb to landing. Hearing their approach,* LAURA *rises with a panicky gesture. She retreats to the portieres.)*

(The doorbell. LAURA *catches her breath and touches her throat. Low drums.)*

AMANDA *(calling)* Laura, sweetheart! The door!

*(*LAURA *stares at it without moving.)*

JIM I think we just beat the rain.

TOM Uh-huh. *(He rings again, nervously.* JIM *whistles and fishes for a cigarette.)*

AMANDA *(Very, very gaily)* Laura, that is your brother and Mr. O'Connor! Will you let them in, darling?

(LAURA *crosses toward kitchenette door.)*

LAURA *(breathlessly)* Mother—you go to the door!

*(*AMANDA *steps out of kitchenette and stares furiously at* LAURA. *She points imperiously at the door.)*

LAURA Please, please!

AMANDA *(in a fierce whisper)* What is the matter with you, you silly thing?

LAURA *(desperately)* Please, you answer it, *please!*

AMANDA I told you I wasn't going to humor you, Laura. Why have you chosen this moment to lose your mind?

LAURA Please, please, please, you go!

AMANDA You'll have to go to the door because I can't!

LAURA *(despairingly)* I can't either!

AMANDA *Why?*

LAURA I'm *sick!*

AMANDA I'm sick, too—of your nonsense! Why can't you and your brother be normal people? Fantastic whims and behavior!

*(*TOM *gives a long ring.)*

Preposterous goings on! Can you give me one reason—*(Calls out lyrically.)* Coming! Just one second!—why you should be afraid to open a door? Now you answer it, Laura!

LAURA Oh, oh, oh . . . *(She returns through the portieres. Darts to the victrola and winds it frantically and turns it on.)*

AMANDA Laura Wingfield, you march right to that door!

LAURA Yes—yes, Mother!

(A faraway, scratchy rendition of "Dardanella" softens the air and gives her strength to move through it. She slips to the door and draws it cautiously open.)

*(*TOM *enters with the caller,* JIM O'CONNOR.*)*

TOM Laura, this is Jim. Jim, this is my sister, Laura.

JIM *(stepping inside)* I didn't know that Shakespeare had a sister!

LAURA *(retreating stiff and trembling from the door)* How—how do you do?

JIM *(heartily extending his hand)* Okay!

*(*LAURA *touches it hesitantly with hers.)*

JIM Your hand's *cold,* Laura!

LAURA Yes, well—I've been playing the victrola. . . .

JIM Must have been playing classical music on it! You ought to play a little hot swing music to warm you up!

LAURA Excuse me—I haven't finished playing the victrola. . . . *(She turns awkwardly and hurries into the front room. She pauses a second by the victrola. Then catches her breath and darts through the portieres like a frightened deer.)*

JIM *(grinning)* What was the matter?

TOM Oh—with Laura? Laura is—terribly shy.

JIM Shy, huh? It's unusual to meet a shy girl nowadays. I don't believe you ever mentioned you had a sister.

TOM Well, now you know. I have one. Here is the *Post Dispatch.* You want a piece of it?

JIM Uh-huh.
TOM What piece? The comics?
JIM Sports! *(glances at it)* Ole Dizzy Dean is on his bad behavior.
TOM *(disinterest)* Yeah? *(Lights cigarette and crosses back to fire-escape door.)*
JIM Where are *you* going?
TOM I'm going out on the terrace.
JIM *(goes after him)* You know, Shakespeare—I'm going to sell you a bill of goods!
TOM What goods?
JIM A course I'm taking.
TOM Huh?
JIM In public speaking! You and me, we're not the warehouse type.
TOM Thanks—that's good news.
But what has public speaking got to do with it?
JIM It fits you for—executive positions!
TOM Awww.
JIM I tell you it's done a helluva lot for me.
(IMAGE: *executive at desk.)*
TOM In what respect?
JIM In every! Ask yourself what is the difference between you an' me and men in the office down front? Brains?—No!—Ability?—No! Then what? Just one little thing—
TOM What is that one little thing?
JIM Primarily it amounts to—social poise! Being able to square up to people and hold your own on any social level!
AMANDA *(off stage)* Tom?
TOM Yes, Mother?
AMANDA Is that you and Mr. O'Connor?
TOM Yes, Mother.
AMANDA Well, you just make yourselves comfortable in there.
TOM Yes, Mother.
AMANDA Ask Mr. O'Connor if he would like to wash his hands.
JIM Aw, no—no—thank you—I took care of that at the warehouse. Tom—
TOM Yes?
JIM Mr. Mendoza was speaking to me about you.
TOM Favorably?
JIM What do you think?
TOM Well—
JIM You're going to be out of a job if you don't wake up.
TOM I am waking up—
JIM You show no signs.
TOM The signs are interior.
(IMAGE ON SCREEN: *The sailing vessel with Jolly Roger again.)*
TOM I'm planning to change. *(He leans over the rail speaking with quiet exhilaration. The incandescent marquees and signs of the first-run movie houses light his face from across the alley. He looks like a voyager.)* I'm right at the point of committing myself to a future that doesn't

include the warehouse and Mr. Mendoza or even a night-school course in public speaking.

JIM What are you gassing about?

TOM I'm tired of the movies.

JIM Movies!

TOM Yes, movies! Look at them– *(A wave toward the marvels of Grand Avenue.)* All of those glamorous people–having adventures–hogging it all, gobbling the whole thing up! You know what happens? People go to the *movies* instead of *moving!* Hollywood characters are supposed to have all the adventures for everybody in America, while everybody in America sits in a dark room and watches them have them! Yes, until there's a war. That's when adventure becomes available to the masses! *Everyone's* dish, not only Gable's! Then the people in the dark room come out of the dark room to have some adventures themselves–Goody, goody!–It's our turn now, to go the South Sea Islands–to make a safari –to be exotic, far-off!–But I'm not patient. I don't want to wait till then. I'm tired of the *movies* and I am *about* to *move!*

JIM *(Incredulously)* Move?

TOM Yes.

JIM When?

TOM Soon!

JIM Where? Where?

(Theme three music seems to answer the question, while Tom thinks it over. He searches among his pockets.)

TOM I'm starting to boil inside. I know I seem dreamy, but inside–well, I'm boiling!–Whenever I pick up a shoe, I shudder a little thinking how short life is and what I am doing!–Whatever that means, I know it doesn't mean shoes–except as something to wear on a traveler's feet! *(Finds paper.)* Look–

JIM What?

TOM I'm a member.

JIM *(reading)* The Union of Merchant Seamen.

TOM I paid my dues this month, instead of the light bill.

JIM You will regret it when they turn the lights off.

TOM I won't be here.

JIM How about your mother?

TOM I'm like my father. The bastard son of a bastard! See how he grins? And he's been absent going on sixteen years!

JIM You're just talking, you drip. How does your mother feel about it?

TOM Shhh!–Here comes Mother! Mother is not acquainted with my plans!

AMANDA *(Enters portieres)* Where are you all?

TOM On the terrace, Mother.

(They start inside. She advances to them. TOM *is distinctly shocked at her appearance. Even* JIM *blinks a little. He is making his first contact with girlish Southern vivacity and in spite of the night-school course in public speaking is somewhat thrown off the beam by the unexpected outlay of social charm.)*

(Certain responses are attempted by JIM *but are swept aside by* AMANDA'S *gay laughter and chatter.* TOM *is embarrassed but after the first shock* JIM *reacts very warmly. Grins and chuckles, is altogether won over.)*

(IMAGE: AMANDA *as a girl.)*

AMANDA *(Coyly smiling, shaking her girlish ringlets)* Well, well, well, so this is Mr. O'Connor. Introductions entirely unnecessary. I've heard so much about you from my boy. I finally said to him, Tom – good gracious! – why don't you bring this paragon to supper? I'd like to meet this nice young man at the warehouse! – Instead of just hearing you sing his praises so much!

I don't know why my son is so stand-offish – that's not Southern behavior!

Let's sit down and – I think we could stand a little more air in here! Tom, leave the door open. I felt a nice fresh breeze a moment ago. Where has it gone to?

Mmm, so warm already! And not quite summer, even. We're going to burn up when summer really gets started.

However, we're having – we're having a very light supper.

I think light things are better fo' this time of year. The same as light clothes are. Light clothes an' light food are what warm weather calls fo'. You know our blood gets so thick during th' winter – it takes a while fo' us to *adjust* ou'selves! – when the season changes . . .

It's come so quick this year. I wasn't prepared. All of a sudden – heavens! Already summer! – I ran to the trunk an' pulled out this light dress – Terribly old! Historical almost! But feels so good – so good an' co-ol, y' know. . . .

TOM Mother –

AMANDA Yes, honey?

TOM How about – supper?

AMANDA Honey, you go ask Sister if supper is ready! You know that Sister is in full charge of supper!

Tell her you hungry boys are waiting for it.

(To JIM.*)*

Have you met Laura?

JIM She –

AMANDA Let you in? Oh, good, you've met already! It's rare for a girl as sweet an' pretty as Laura to be domestic! But Laura is, thank heavens, not only pretty but also very domestic. I'm not at all. I never was a bit. I never could make a thing but angel-food cake. Well, in the South we had so many servants. Gone, gone, gone. All vestige of gracious living! Gone completely! I wasn't prepared for what the future brought me. All of my gentlemen callers were sons of planters and so of course I assumed that I would be married to one and raise my family on a large piece of land with plenty of servants. But man proposes – and woman accepts the proposal! – To vary that old, old saying a little bit – I married no planter! I married a man who worked for the telephone company! – That gallantly smiling gentleman over there! *(Points to the picture.)* A telephone man who—fell in love with long distance!—Now he travels and I don't even know where!—But what am I going on for about my—tribulations?

Tell me yours—I hope you don't have any!

Tom?

TOM *(returning)* Yes, Mother?

AMANDA Is supper nearly ready?

TOM It looks to me like supper is on the table.

AMANDA Let me look— *(She rises prettily and looks through portieres.)* Oh, lovely!—But where is Sister?

TOM Laura is not feeling well and she says that she thinks she'd better not come to the table.

AMANDA What?—Nonsense!—Laura? Oh, Laura!

LAURA *(Off stage, faintly)* Yes, Mother.

AMANDA You really must come to the table. We won't be seated until you come to the table!

Come in, Mr. O'Connor. You sit over there, and I'll—

Laura? Laura Wingfield!

You're keeping us waiting, honey! We can't say grace until you come to the table!

(The back door is pushed weakly open and LAURA *comes in. She is obviously quite faint, her lips trembling, her eyes wide and staring. She moves unsteadily toward the table.)*

(LEGEND: *"terror!")*

(Outside a summer storm is coming abruptly. The white curtains billow inward at the swindows and there is a sorrowful murmur and deep blue dusk.)

*(*LAURA *suddenly stumbles—she catches at a chair with a faint moan.)*

TOM Laura!

AMANDA Laura!

(There is a clap of thunder.)

(LEGEND: *"ah!")*

(Despairingly.)

Why, Laura, you *are* sick, darling! Tom, help your sister into the living room, dear!

Sit in the living room, Laura—rest on the sofa.

Well!

(To the gentleman caller.)

Standing over the hot stove made her ill!—I told her that it was just too warm this evening, but—

*(*TOM *comes back in.* LAURA *is on the sofa.)*

Is Laura all right now?

TOM Yes.

AMANDA What *is* that? Rain? A nice cool rain has come up *(She gives the gentleman caller a frightened look.)*

I think we may—have grace—now . . .

*(*TOM *looks at her stupidly.)*

Tom, honey—you say grace!

TOM Oh . . .

"For these and all thy mercies—"
(They bow their heads, AMANDA *stealing a nervous glance at* JIM. *In the living room* LAURA, *stretched on the sofa, clenches her hand to her lips, to hold back a shuddering sob.)*
God's Holy Name be praised—
(The scene dims out.)

scene 7

A SOUVENIR.
Half an hour later. Dinner is just being finished in the upstage area which is concealed by the drawn portieres.

As the curtain rises LAURA *is still huddled upon the sofa, her feet drawn under her, her head resting on a pale blue pillow, her eyes wide and mysteriously watchful. The new floor lamp with its shade of rose-colored silk gives a soft, becoming light to her face, bringing out the fragile, unearthly prettiness which usually escapes attention. There is a steady murmur of rain, but it is slackening and stops soon after the scene begins; the air outside becomes pale and luminous as the moon breaks out.*

A moment after the curtain rises, the lights in both rooms flicker and go out.)

JIM Hey, there, Mr. Light Bulb!
*(*AMANDA *laughs nervously.)*
*(*LEGEND: *"suspension of a public service.")*
AMANDA Where was Moses when the lights went out? Ha-ha. Do you know the answer to that one, Mr. O'Connor?
JIM No, Ma'am, what's the answer?
AMANDA In the dark!
*(*JIM *laughs appreciatively.)*
Everybody sit still. I'll light the candles. Isn't it lucky we have them on the table? Where's a match? Which of you gentlemen can provide a match?
JIM Here.
AMANDA Thank you, sir.
JIM Not at all, Ma'am!
AMANDA I guess the fuse has burnt out. Mr. O'Connor, can you tell a burnt-out fuse? I know I can't and Tom is a total loss when it comes to mechanics.
*(*SOUND: *Getting up: voices recede A little to kitchenette.)*
Oh, be careful you don't bump into something. We don't want our gentleman caller to break his neck. Now wouldn't that be a fine howdy-do?
JIM Ha-ha!
Where is the fuse-box?
AMANDA Right here next to the stove. Can you see anything?
JIM Just a minute.
AMANDA Isn't electricity a mysterious thing?
Wasn't it Benjamin Franklin who tied a key to a kite?

We live in such a mysterious universe, don't we? Some people say that science clears up all the mysteries for us. In my opinion it only creates more!

Have you found it yet?

JIM No, Ma'am. All these fuses look okay to me.

AMANDA Tom!

TOM Yes, Mother?

AMANDA That light bill I gave you several days ago. The one I told you we got the notices about?

*(*LEGEND: *"ha!")*

TOM Oh.—Yeah.

AMANDA Didn't! I might have known it!

JIM Shakespeare probably wrote a poem on that light bill, Mrs. Wingfield.

AMANDA I might have known better than to trust him with it! There's such a high price for negligence in this world!

JIM Maybe the poem will win a ten-dollar prize.

AMANDA We'll just have to spend the remainder of the evening in the nineteenth century, before Mr. Edison made the Mazda lamp!

JIM Candlelight is my favorite kind of light.

AMANDA That shows you're romantic! But that's no excuse for Tom.

Well, we got through dinner. Very considerate of them to let us get through dinner before they plunged us into everlasting darkness, wasn't it, Mr. O'Connor?

JIM Ha-ha!

AMANDA Tom, as a penalty for your carelessness you can help me with the dishes.

JIM Let me give you a hand.

AMANDA Indeed you will not!

JIM I ought to be good for something.

AMANDA Good for something? *(Her tone is rhapsodic.)*

You? Why, Mr. O'Connor, nobody, *nobody's* given me this much entertainment in years—as you have!

JIM Aw, now, Mrs. Wingfield!

AMANDA I'm not exaggerating, not one bit! But Sister is all by her lonesome. You go keep her company in the parlor!

I'll give you this lovely old candelabrum that used to be on the altar at the church of the Heavenly Rest. It was melted a little out of shape when the church burnt down. Lightning struck it one spring. Gypsy Jones was holding a revival at the time and he intimated that the church was destroyed because the Episcopalians gave card parties.

JIM Ha-ha.

AMANDA And how about you coaxing Sister to drink a little wine? I think it would be good for her! Can you carry both at once?

JIM Sure. I'm Superman!

AMANDA Now, Thomas, get into this apron!

(The door of kitchenette swings closed on AMANDA'S *gay laughter; the flickering light approaches the portieres.)*

*(*LAURA *sits up nervously as he enters. Her speech at first is low and*

breathless from the almost intolerable strain of being alone with a stranger.)

(THE LEGEND: *"I don't suppose you remember me at all!")*

(In her first speeches in this scene, before JIM'S *warmth overcomes her paralyzing shyness,* LAURA'S *voice is thin and breathless as though she has just ran up a steep flight of stairs.)*

*(*JIM'S *attitude is gently humorous. In playing this scene it should be stressed that while the incident is apparently unimportant, it is to* LAURA *the climax of her secret life.)*

JIM Hello, there, Laura.

LAURA *(Faintly)* Hello. *(She clears her throat.)*

JIM How are you feeling now? Better?

LAURA Yes. Yes, thank you.

JIM This is for you. A little dandelion wine. *(He extends it toward her with extravagant gallantry.)*

LAURA Thank you.

JIM Drink it—but don't get drunk!
(He laughs heartily. LAURA *takes the glass uncertainly; laughs shyly.)* Where shall I set the candles?

LAURA Oh—oh, anywhere . . .

JIM How about here on the floor? Any objections?

LAURA No.

JIM I'll spread a newspaper under to catch the drippings. I like to sit on the floor. Mind if I do?

LAURA Oh, no.

JIM Give me a pillow?

LAURA What?

JIM A pillow!

LAURA Oh . . . *(Hands him one quickly.)*

JIM How about you? Don't you like to sit on the floor?

LAURA Oh—yes.

JIM Why don't you, then?

LAURA I—will.

JIM Take a pillow! *(*LAURA *does. Sits on the other side of the candelabrum.* JIM *crosses his legs and smiles engagingly at her.)* I can't hardly see you sitting way over there.

LAURA I can—see you.

JIM I know, but that's not fair, I'm in the limelight. *(*LAURA *moves her pillow closer.)* Good! Now I can see you! Confortable?

LAURA Yes.

JIM So am I. Comfortable as a cow! Will you have some gum?

LAURA No, thank you.

JIM I think that I will indulge, with your permission. *(musingly unwraps it and holds it up.)* Think of the fortune made by the guy that invented the first piece of chewing gum. Amazing, huh? The Wrigley Building is one of the sights of Chicago.—I saw it summer before last when I went up to the Century of Progress. Did you take in the Century of Progress?

LAURA No, I didn't.

JIM Well, it was quite a wonderful exposition. What impressed me most was the Hall of Science. Gives you an idea of what the future will be in America, even more wonderful than the present time is! *(Pause. Smiling at her.)* Your brother tells me you're shy. Is that right, Laura?

LAURA I—don't know.

JIM I judge you to be an old-fashioned type of girl. Well, I think that's a pretty good type to be. Hope you don't think I'm being too personal—do you?

LAURA *(hastily, out of embarrassment)* I believe I *will* take a piece of gum, if you—don't mind. *(clearing her throat)* Mr. O'Connor, have you—kept up with your singing?

JIM Singing? Me?

LAURA Yes. I remember what a beautiful voice you had.

JIM When did you hear me sing?

(VOICE OFF STAGE IN THE PAUSE.)

VOICE *(Off stage)*

O blow, ye winds, heigh-ho,
A-roving I will go!
I'm off to my love
With a boxing glove—
Ten thousand miles away!

JIM You say you've heard me sing?

LAURA Oh, yes! Yes, very often . . . I don't suppose—you remember me—at all?

JIM *(Smiling doubtfully)* You know I have an idea I've seen you before. I had that idea soon as you opened the door. It seemed almost like I was about to remember your name. But the name that I started to call you—wasn't a name! And so I stopped myself before I said it.

LAURA Wasn't it—Blue Roses?

JIM *(springs up, grinning)* Blue Roses!—My gosh, yes—Blue Roses! That's what I had on my tongue when you opened the door!

Isn't it funny what tricks your memory plays! I din't connect you with high school somehow or other.

But that's where it was; it was high school. I didn't even know you were Shakespeare's sister!

Gosh, I'm sorry.

LAURA I didn't expect you to. You—barely knew me!

JIM But we did have a speaking acquaintance, huh?

LAURA Yes, we—spoke to each other.

JIM When did you recognize me?

LAURA Oh, right away!

JIM Soon as I came in the door?

LAURA When I heard your name I thought it was probably you. I knew that Tom used to know you a little in high school. So when you came in the door—

Well, then I was—sure.

JIM Why didn't you *say* something, then?

LAURA *(breathlessly)* I didn't know what to say, I was—too surprised!

JIM For goodness' sakes! You know, this sure is funny!
LAURA Yes! Yes, isn't it, though . . .
JIM Didn't we have a class in something together!
LAURA Yes, we did.
JIM What class was that?
LAURA It was—singing—Chorus!
JIM Aw!
LAURA Mondays, Wednesdays and Fridays.
JIM Now I remember—you always came in late.
LAURA Yes, it was so hard for me, getting upstairs. I had that brace on my leg—it clumped so loud!
JIM I never heard any clumping.
LAURA *(Wincing at the recollection)* To me it sounded like—thunder!
JIM Well, well, well, I never even noticed.
LAURA And everybody was seated before I came in I had to walk in front of all those people. My seat was in the back row. I had to go clumping all the way up the aisle with everyone watching!
JIM You shouldn't have been self-conscious.
LAURA I know, but I was. It was always such a relief when the singing started.
JIM Aw, yes, I've placed you now! I used to call you Blue Roses. How was it that I got started calling you that?
LAURA I was out of school a little while with pleurosis. When I came back you asked me what was the matter. I said I had pleurosis—you thought I said Blue Roses. That's what you always called me after that!
JIM I hope you didn't mind.
LAURA Oh, no—I liked it. You see, I wasn't acquainted with many—people. . . .
JIM As I remember you sort of stuck by yourself.
LAURA I—I—never have had much luck at—making friends.
JIM I don't see why you wouldn't.
LAURA Well, I—started out badly.
JIM You mean being—
LAURA Yes, it sort of—stood between me—
JIM You shouldn't have let it!
LAURA I know, but it did, and—
JIM You were shy with people!
LAURA I tried not to be but never could—
JIM Overcome it?
LAURA No, I—I never could!
JIM I guess being shy is something you have to work out of kind of gradually.
LAURA *(sorrowfully)* Yes—I guess it—
JIM Takes time!
LAURA Yes—
JIM People are not so dreadful when you know them. That's what you have to remember! And everybody has problems, not just you, but practically everybody has got some problems.

You think of yourself as having the only problems, as being the only one who is disappointed. But just look around you and you will see lots of people as disappointed as you are. For instance, I hoped when I was going to high school that I would be further along at this time, six years later, than I am now—You remember that wonderful write-up I had in *The Torch?*

LAURA Yes! *(She rises and crosses to table.)*

JIM It said I was bound to succeed in anything I went into!

*(*LAURA *returns with the annual.)* Holy Jeez! *The Torch! (He accepts it reverently. They smile across it with mutual wonder.* LAURA *crouches beside him and they begin to turn through it.* LAURA'S *shyness is dissolving in his warmth.)*

LAURA Here you are in *The Pirates of Penzance!*

JIM *(wistfully)* I sang the baritone lead in that operetta.

LAURA *(raptly)* So—*beautifully!*

JIM *(protesting)* Aw—

LAURA Yes, yes—beautifully—beautifully!

JIM You heard me?

LAURA All three times!

JIM No!

LAURA Yes!

JIM All three performances?

LAURA *(looking down)* Yes.

JIM Why?

LAURA I—wanted to ask you to—autograph my program.

JIM Why didn't you ask me to?

LAURA You were always surrounded by your own friends so much that I never had a chance to.

JIM You should have just—

LAURA Well, I—thought you might think I was—

JIM Thought I might think you was—what?

LAURA Oh—

JIM *(with reflective relish)* I was beleaguered by females in those days.

LAURA You were terribly popular!

JIM Yeah—

LAURA You had such a—friendly way—

JIM I was spoiled in high school.

LAURA Everybody—liked you!

JIM Including you?

LAURA I—yes, I—I did, too— *(She gently closes the book in her lap.)*

JIM Well, well, well!—Give me that program, Laura. *(She hands it to him. He signs it with a flourish.)* There you are—better late than never!

LAURA Oh, I—what a—surprise!

JIM My signature isn't worth very much right now.

But some day—maybe—it will increase in value!

Being disappointed is one thing and being discouraged is something else. I am disappointed but I am not discouraged.

I'm twenty-three years old.

How old are you?

LAURA I'll be twenty-four in June.

JIM That's not old age!

LAURA No, but—

JIM You finished high school?

LAURA *(with difficulty)* I didn't go back.

JIM You mean you dropped out?

LAURA I made bad grades in my final examinations. *(She rises and replaces the book and the program. Her voice strained.)* How is—Emily Meisenbach getting along?

JIM Oh, that kraut-head!

LAURA Why do you call her that?

JIM That's what she was.

LAURA You're not still—going with her?

JIM I never see her.

LAURA It said in the Personal Section that you were—engaged!

JIM I know, but I wasn't impressed by that—propaganda!

LAURA It wasn't—the truth?

JIM Only in Emily's optimistic opinion!

LAURA Oh—

(LEGEND: *"What have you done since high school?"*)

(JIM *lights a cigarette and leans indolently back on his elbows smiling at* LAURA *with a warmth and charm which lights her inwardly with altar candles. She remains by the table and turns in her hands a piece of glass to cover her tumult.)*

JIM *(After several reflective puffs on a cigarette)* What have you done since high school? *(She seems not to hear him.)* Huh? (LAURA *looks up.)* I said what have you done since high school, Laura?

LAURA Nothing much.

JIM You must have been doing something these six long years.

LAURA Yes.

JIM Well, then, such as what?

LAURA I took a business course at business college—

JIM How did that work out?

LAURA Well, not very—well—I had to drop out, it gave me—indigestion— (JIM *laughs gently.)*

JIM What are you doing now?

LAURA I don't do anything—much. Oh, please don't think I sit around doing nothing! My glass collection takes up a good deal of time. Glass is something you have to take good care of.

JIM What did you say—about glass?

LAURA Collection I said—I have one— *(She clears her throat and turns away again, acutely shy.)*

JIM *(abruptly)* You know what I judge to be the trouble with you?

Inferiority complex! Know what that is? That's what they call it when someone low-rates himself!

I understand it because I had it, too. Although my case was not so aggravated as yours seems to be. I had it until I took up public speaking, developed my voice, and learned that I had an aptitude for science. Before that time I never thought of myself as being outstanding in any way whatsoever!

Now I've never made a regular study of it, but I have a friend who says I can analyze people better than doctors that make a profession of it. I don't claim that to be necessarily true, but I can sure guess a person's psychology, Laura! *(takes out his gum)* Excuse me, Laura. I always take it out when the flavor is gone. I'll use this scrap of paper to wrap it in. I know how it is to get it stuck on a shoe.

Yep—that's what I judge to be your principal trouble. A lack of confidence in yourself as a person. You don't have the proper amount of faith in yourself. I'm basing that fact on a number of your remarks and also on certain observations I've made. For instance that clumping you thought was so awful in high school. You say that you even dreaded to walk into class. You see what you did? You dropped out of school, you gave up an education because of a clump, which as far as I know was practically non-existent! A little physical defect is what you have. Hardly noticeable even! Magnified thousands of times by imagination!

You know what my strong advice to you is? Think of yourself as *superior* in some way!

LAURA In what way would I think?

JIM Why, man alive, Laura! Just look about you a little. What do you see? A world full of common people! All of 'em born and all of 'em going to die!
Which of them has one-tenth of your good points! Or mine! Or anyone else's, as far as that goes—Gosh!
Everybody excels in some one thing. Some in many!
(Unconsciously glances at himself in the mirror.)
All you've got to do is discover in *what!*
Take me, for instance.
(He adjusts his tie at the mirror.)
My interest happens to lie in electro-dynamics. I'm taking a course in radio engineering at night school, Laura, on top of a fairly responsible job at the warehouse. I'm taking that course and studying public speaking.

LAURA Ohhhh.

JIM Because I believe in the future of television!
(Turning back to her.)
I wish to be ready to go up right along with it. Therefore I'm planning to get in on the ground floor. In fact I've already made the right connections and all that remains is for the industry itself to get under way! Full steam—
(His eyes are starry.)
Knowledge—Zzzzzp! Money—Zzzzzzp!—Power!
That's the cycle democracy is built on!
(His attitude is convincingly dynamic. LAURA *stares at him, even her shyness eclipsed in her absolute wonder. He suddenly grins.)*
I guess you think I think a lot of myself!

LAURA No—o-o-o, I—

JIM Now how about you? Isn't there something you take more interest in than anything else?

LAURA Well, I do—as I said—have my—glass collection— *(A peal of girlish laughter from the kitchen.)*

JIM I'm not right sure I know what you're talking about.
What kind of glass is it?

LAURA Little articles of it, they're ornaments mostly!
Most of them are little animals made out of glass, the tiniest little animals in the world. Mother calls them a glass menagerie!
Here's an example of one, if you'd like to see it!
This one is one of the oldest. It's nearly thirteen.
(MUSIC: "The Glass Menagerie.")
(He stretches out his hand.)
Oh, be careful—if you breathe, it breaks!

JIM I'd better not take it. I'm pretty clumsy with things.

LAURA Go on, I trust you with him!
(places it in his palm)
There now—you're holding him gently!
Hold him over the light, he loves the light! You see how the light shines through him?

JIM It sure does shine!

LAURA I shouldn't be partial, but he is my favorite one.

JIM What kind of a thing is this one supposed to be?

LAURA Haven't you noticed the single horn on his forehead?

JIM A unicorn, huh?

LAURA Mmm-hmmm!

JIM Unicorns, aren't they extinct in the modern world?

LAURA I know!

JIM Poor little fellow, he must feel sort of lonesome.

LAURA *(smiling)* Well, if he does he doesn't complain about it. He stays on a shelf with some horses that don't have horns and all of them seem to get along nicely together.

JIM How do you know?

LAURA *(lightly)* I haven't heard any arguments among them!

JIM *(grinning)* No arguments, huh? Well, that's a pretty good sign!
Where shall I set him?

LAURA Put him on the table. They all like a change of scenery once in a while!

JIM *(stretching)* Well, well, well, well—
Look how big my shadow is when I stretch!

LAURA Oh, oh, yes—it stretches across the ceiling!

JIM *(crossing to door)* I think it's stopped raining. *(opens fire-escape door)* Where does the music come from?

LAURA From the Paradise Dance Hall across the alley.

JIM How about cutting the rug a little, Miss Wingfield?

LAURA Oh, I—

JIM Or is your program filled up? Let me have a look at it. *(grasps imagi-*

nary card) Why, every dance is taken! I'll just have to scratch some out. *(*WALTZ MUSIC: *"La Golondrina.")* Ahhh, a waltz! *(He executes some sweeping turns by himself then holds his arms toward* LAURA.*)*

LAURA *(breathlessly)* I—can't dance!

JIM There you go, that inferiority stuff!

LAURA I've never danced in my life!

JIM Come on, try!

LAURA Oh, but I'd step on you!

JIM I'm not made out of glass.

LAURA How—how—how do we start?

JIM Just leave it to me. You hold your arms out a little.

LAURA Like this?

JIM A little bit higher. Right. Now don't tighten up, that's the main thing about it—relax.

LAURA *(laughing breathlessly)* It's hard not to.

JIM Okay.

LAURA I'm afraid you can't budge me.

JIM What do you bet I can't? *(He swings her into motion.)*

LAURA Goodness, yes, you can!

JIM Let yourself go, now, Laura, just let yourself go.

LAURA I'm—

JIM Come on!

LAURA Trying!

JIM Not so stiff—Easy does it!

LAURA I know but I'm—

JIM Loosen th' backbone! There now, that's a lot better.

LAURA Am I?

JIM Lots, lots better! *(He moves her about the room in a clumsy waltz.)*

LAURA Oh, my!

JIM Ha-ha!

LAURA Oh, my goodness!

JIM Ha-ha-ha! *(They suddenly bump into the table.* JIM *stops.)* What did we hit on?

LAURA Table.

JIM Did something fall off it? I think—

LAURA Yes.

JIM I hope that it wasn't the little glass horse with the horn!

LAURA Yes.

JIM Aw, aw, aw. Is it broken?

LAURA Now it is just like all the other horses.

JIM It's lost its—

LAURA Horn!

It doesn't matter. Maybe it's a blessing in disguise.

JIM You'll never forgive me. I bet that that was your favorite piece of glass.

LAURA I don't have favorites much. It's no tragedy, Freckles. Glass breaks so easily. No matter how careful you are. The traffic jars the shelves and things fall off them.

JIM Still I'm awfully sorry that I was the cause.

LAURA *(smiling)* I'll just imagine he had an operation.
The horn was removed to make him feel less—freakish!
(They both laugh.)
Now he will feel more at home with the other horses, the ones that don't have horns. . . .

JIM Ha-ha, that's very funny!
(suddenly serious)
I'm glad to see that you have a sense of humor.
You know—you're—well—very different!
Surprisingly different from anyone else I know!
(His voice becomes soft and hesitant with a genuine feeling.)
Do you mind me telling you that?
(LAURA is abashed beyond speech.)
I mean it in a nice way . . .
(LAURA nods shyly, looking away.)
You make me feel sort of—I don't know how to put it!
I'm usually pretty good at expressing things, but—
This is something that I don't know how to say!
(LAURA touches her throat and clears it—turns the broken unicorn in her hands.)
(even softer)
Has anyone ever told you that you were pretty?
(Pause: music.)
(LAURA looks up slowly, with wonder, and shakes her head.)
Well, you are! In a very different way from anyone else.
And all the nicer because of the difference, too.
(His voice becomes low and husky. LAURA turns away, nearly faint with the novelty of her emotions.)
I wish that you were my sister. I'd teach you to have some confidence in yourself. The different people are not like other people, but being different is nothing to be ashamed of. Because other people are not such wonderful people. They're one hundred times one thousand. You're one times one! They walk all over the earth. You just stay here. They're common as—weeds, but—you—well, you're—*Blue Roses!*
(IMAGE ON SCREEN: *Blue Roses.)*
(music changes.)

LAURA But blue is wrong for—roses . . .

JIM It's right for you!—You're—pretty!

LAURA In what respect am I pretty?

JIM In all respects—believe me! Your eyes—your hair—are pretty! Your hands are pretty!
(He catches hold of her hand.)
You think I'm making this up because I'm invited to dinner and have to be nice. Oh, I could do that! I could put on an act for you, Laura, and say lots of things without being very sincere. But this time I am. I'm talking to you sincerely. I happened to notice you had this inferiority complex that keeps you from feeling comfortable with people. Some-

body needs to build your confidence up and make you proud instead of shy and turning away and—blushing—

Somebody—ought to—

Ought to—*kiss* you, Laura!

(His hand slips slowly up her arm to her shoulder.)

(music swells tumultuously.)

(He suddenly turns her about and kisses her on the lips.)

(When he releases her, LAURA *sinks on the sofa with a bright, dazed look.)*

*(*JIM *backs away and fishes in his pocket for a cigarette.)*

(LEGEND ON SCREEN: *"souvenir."*)

Stumble-john!

(He lights the cigarette, avoiding her look.)

(There is a peal of girlish laughter from AMANDA *in the kitchen.)*

*(*LAURA *slowly raises and opens her hand. It still contains the little broken glass animal. She looks at it with a tender, bewildered expression.)*

Stumble-john!

I shouldn't have done that— That was way off the beam.

You don't smoke, do you?

(She looks up, smiling, not hearing the question.)

(He sits beside her a little gingerly. She looks at him speechlessly—waiting.)

(He coughs decorously and moves a little farther aside as he considers the situation and senses her feelings, dimly, with perturbation.)

(gently.)

Would you—care for a—mint?

(She doesn't seem to hear him but her look grows brighter even.)

Peppermint—Life-Saver?

My pocket's a regular drug store—wherever I go . . .

(He pops a mint in his mouth. Then gulps and decides to make a clean breast of it. He speaks slowly and gingerly.)

Laura, you know, if I had a sister like you, I'd do the same thing as Tom. I'd bring out fellows and—introduce her to them. The right type of boys of a type to—appreciate her.

Only—well—he made a mistake about me.

Maybe I've got no call to be saying this. That may not have been the idea in having me over. But what if it was?

There's nothing wrong about that. The only trouble is that in my case —I'm not in a situation to—do the right thing.

I can't take down your number and say I'll phone.

I can't call up next week and—ask for a date.

I thought I had better explain the situation in case you—misunderstood it and—hurt your feelings. . . .

(pause)

(Slowly, very slowly, LAURA'S *look changes, her eyes returning slowly from his to the ornament in her palm.*

*(*AMANDA *utters another gay laugh in the kitchen.)*

LAURA *(Faintly)* You—won't—call again?
JIM No, Laura, I can't.
(He rises from the sofa.)
As I was just explaining, I've—got strings on me.
Laura, I've—been going steady!
I go out all of the time with a girl named Betty. She's a home-girl like you, and Catholic, and Irish, and in a great many ways we—get along fine.
I met her last summer on a moonlight boat trip up the river to Alton, on the *Majestic.*
Well—right away from the start it was—love!
(LEGEND: *Love!)*
(LAURA *sways slightly forward and grips the arm of the sofa. He fails to notice, now enrapt in his own comfortable being.)*
Being in love has made a new man of me!
(Leaning stiffly forward, clutching the arm of the sofa, LAURA *struggles visibly with her storm. But* JIM *is oblivious, she is a long way off.)*
The power of love is really pretty tremendous!
Love is something that—changes the whole world, Laura!
(The storm abates a little and LAURA *leans back. He notices her again.)*
It happened that Betty's aunt took sick, she got a wire and had to go to Centralia. So Tom—when he asked me to dinner—I naturally just accepted the invitation, not knowing that you—that he—that I—
(He stops awkwardly.)
Huh—I'm a stumble-john!
(He flops back on the sofa.)
(The holy candles in the altar of LAURA'S *face have been snuffed out. There is a look of almost infinite desolation.)*
(JIM *glances at her uneasily.)*
I wish that you would—say something. *(She bites her lip which was trembling and then bravely smiles. She opens her hand again on the broken glass ornament. Then she gently takes his hand and raises it level with her own. She carefully places the unicorn in the palm of his hand, then pushes his fingers closed upon it.)* What are you—doing that for? You want me to have him?—Laura? *(She nods.)* What for?
LAURA A—souvenir . . .
(She rises unsteadily and crouches beside the victrola to wind it up.)
(LEGEND ON SCREEN: *"Things have a way of turning out so badly!")*
(OR IMAGE: *"Gentleman Caller waving good-bye!—gaily.")*
(At this moment AMANDA *rushes brightly back in the front room. She bears a pitcher of fruit punch in an old-fashioned cut-glass pitcher and a plate of macaroons. The plate has a gold border and poppies painted on it.)*
AMANDA Well, well, well! Isn't the air delightful after the shower? I've made you children a little liquid refreshment. *(Turns gaily to the gentleman caller.)* Jim, do you know that song about lemonade?
"Lemonade, lemonade
Made in the shade and stirred with a spade—

Good enough for any old maid!"
JIM *(uneasily)* Ha-ha! No—I never heard it.
AMANDA Why, Laura! You look so serious!
JIM We were having a serious conversation.
AMANDA Good! Now you're better acquainted!
JIM *(uncertainly)* Ha-ha! Yes.
AMANDA You modern young people are much more serious-minded than my generation. I was so gay as a girl!
JIM You haven't changed, Mrs. Wingfield.
AMANDA Tonight I'm rejuvenated! The gaiety of the occasion, Mr. O'Connor!
(She tosses her head with a peal of laughter. Spills lemonade.)
Oooo! I'm baptizing myself!
JIM Here—let me—
AMANDA *(setting the pitcher down)* There now. I discovered we had some maraschino cherries. I dumped them in, juice and all!
JIM You shouldn't have gone to that trouble, Mrs. Wingfield.
AMANDA Trouble, trouble? Why, it was loads of fun!
Didn't you hear me cutting up in the kitchen? I bet your ears were burning! I told Tom how outdone with him I was for keeping you to himself so long a time! He should have brought you over much, much sooner! Well, now that you've found your way, I want you to be a very frequent caller! Not just occasional but all the time.
Oh, we're going to have a lot of gay times together! I see them coming!
Mmmm, just breathe that air! So fresh, and the moon's so pretty!
I'll skip back out—I know where my place is when young folks are having a—serious conversation!
JIM Oh, don't go out, Mrs. Wingfield. The fact of the matter is I've got to be going.
AMANDA Going, now? You're joking! Why, it's only the shank of the evening, Mr. O'Connor!
JIM Well, you know how it is.
AMANDA You mean you're a young workingman and have to keep workingmen's hours. We'll let you off early tonight. But only on the condition that next time you stay later.
What's the best night for you? Isn't Saturday night the best night for you workingmen?
JIM I have a couple of time-clocks to punch, Mrs. Wingfield. One at morning, another one at night!
AMANDA My, but you *are* ambitious! You work at night, too?
JIM No, Ma'am, not work but—Betty! *(He crosses deliberately to pick up his hat. The band at the Paradise Dance Hall goes into a tender waltz.)*
AMANDA Betty? Betty? Who's—Betty!
(There is an ominous cracking sound in the sky.)
JIM Oh, just a girl. The girl I go steady with! *(He smiles charmingly. The sky falls.)*
(LEGEND: *"The sky falls."*)
AMANDA *(A long-drawn exhalation)* Ohhhh . . . Is it a serious romance,

Mr. O'Connor?

JIM We're going to be married the second Sunday in June.

AMANDA Ohhhh—how nice!

Tom didn't mention that you were engaged to be married.

JIM The cat's not out of the bag at the warehouse yet.

You know how they are. They call you Romeo and stuff like that.

(He stops at the oval mirror to put on his hat. He carefully shapes the brim and the crown to give a discreetly dashing effect.)

It's been a wonderful evening, Mrs. Wingfield. I guess this is what they mean by Southern hospitality.

AMANDA It really wasn't anything at all.

JIM I hope it don't seem like I'm rushing off. But I promised Betty I'd pick her up at the Wabash depot, an' by the time I get my jalopy down there her train'll be in. Some women are pretty upset if you keep 'em waiting.

AMANDA Yes, I know— The tyranny of women!

(Extends her hand.)

Good-bye, Mr. O'Connor.

I wish you luck—and happiness—and success! All three of them, and so does Laura!—Don't you, Laura?

LAURA Yes!

JIM *(Taking her hand)* Good-bye, Laura. I'm certainly going to treasure that souvenir. And don't you forget the good advice I gave you.

(Raises his voice to a cheery shout.)

So long, Shakespeare!

Thanks again, ladies— Good night!

(He grins and ducks jauntily out.)

(Still bravely grimacing, AMANDA *closes the door on the gentleman caller. Then she turns back to the room with a puzzled expression. She and* LAURA *don't dare to face each other.* LAURA *crouches beside the victrola to wind it.)*

AMANDA *(faintly)* Things have a way of turning out so badly.

I don't believe that I would play the victrola.

Well, well—well—

Our gentleman caller was engaged to be married!

Tom!

TOM *(from back)* Yes, Mother?

AMANDA Come in here a minute. I want to tell you something awfully funny.

TOM *(enters with macaroon and a glass of lemonade)* Has the gentleman caller gotten away already?

AMANDA The gentleman caller has made an early departure.

What a wonderful joke you played on us!

TOM How do you mean?

AMANDA You didn't mention that he was engaged to be married.

TOM Jim? Engaged?

AMANDA That's what he just informed us.

TOM I'll be jiggered! I didn't know about that.

AMANDA That seems very peculiar.
TOM What's peculiar about it?
AMANDA Didn't you call him your best friend down at the warehouse?
TOM He is, but how did I know?
AMANDA It seems extremely peculiar that you wouldn't know your best friend was going to be married!
TOM The warehouse is where I work, not where I know things about people!
AMANDA You don't know things anywhere! You live in a dream; you manufacture illusions!
(He crosses to door.)
Where are you going?
TOM I'm going to the movies.
AMANDA That's right, now that you've had us make such fools of ourselves. The effort, the preparations, all the expense! The new floor lamp, the rug, the clothes for Laura! All for what? To entertain some other girl's fiancé!

Go to the movies, go! Don't think about us, a mother deserted, an unmarried sister who's crippled and has no job! Don't let anything interfere with your selfish pleasure!

Just go, go, go—to the movies!
TOM All right, I will! The more you shout about my selfishness to me the quicker I'll go, and I won't go to the movies!
AMANDA Go, then! Then go to the moon—you selfish dreamer!
*(*TOM *smashes his glass on the floor. He plunges out on the fire-escape, slamming the door.* LAURA *screams—cut by door.)*
(Dance-hall music up. TOM *goes to the rail and grips it desperately, lifting his face in the chill white moonlight penetrating the narrow abyss of the alley.)*
(LEGEND ON SCREEN: *"and so good-bye . . ."*)
*(*TOM'S *closing speech is timed with the interior pantomime. The interior scene is played as though viewed through soundproof glass.* AMANDA *appears to be making a comforting speech to* LAURA *who is huddled upon the sofa. Now that we cannot hear the mother's speech, her silliness is gone and she has dignity and tragic beauty.* LAURA'S *dark hair hides her face until at the end of the speech she lifts it to smile at her mother.* AMANDA'S *gestures are slow and graceful, almost dancelike, as she comforts the daughter. At the end of her speech she glances a moment at the father's picture—then withdraws through the portieres. At the close of* TOM'S *speech,* LAURA *blows out the candles, ending the play.)*
TOM I didn't go to the moon, I went much further—for time is the longest distance between two places—

Not long after that I was fired for writing a poem on the lid of a shoebox.

I left Saint Louis. I descended the steps of this fire-escape for a last time and followed, from then on, in my father's footsteps, attempting to find in motion what was lost in space—

I traveled around a great deal. The cities swept about me like dead leaves, leaves that were brightly colored but torn away from the branches.

I would have stopped, but I was pursued by something.

It always came upon me unawares, taking me altogether by surprise. Perhaps it was a familiar bit of music. Perhaps it was only a piece of transparent glass—

Perhaps I am walking along a street at night, in some strange city, before I have found companions. I pass the lighted window of a shop where perfume is sold. The window is filled with pieces of colored glass, tiny transparent bottles in delicate colors, like bits of a shattered rainbow.

Then all at once my sister touches my shoulder. I turn around and look into her eyes . . .

Oh, Laura, Laura, I tried to leave you behind me, but I am more faithful than I intended to be!

I reach for a cigarette, I cross the street, I run into the movies or a bar, I buy a drink, I speak to the nearest stranger—anything that can blow your candles out!

(LAURA *bends over the candles.)*

—for nowadays the world is lit by lightning! Blow out your candles, Laura—and so good-bye. . . .

(She blows the candles out.)

(The scene dissolves.)

aristotle

the poetics

. . . The making of epics and of tragedies, and also comedy, and the art of the dithyramb, and most flute and lyre art, all have this in common, that they are imitations. . . . When the imitators imitate the doings of people, the people in the imitation must be either be high or low; the characters almost always follow this line exclusively, for all men differ in character according to their degree of goodness or badness. They must therefore be either above our norm, or below it, or normal . . . This is the difference that marks tragedy out from comedy; comedy is inclined to imitate persons below the level of our world, tragedy persons above it.

There seem to be two causes that gave rise to poetry in general, and they are natural. The impulse to imitate is inherent in man from his childhood;

he is distinguished among the animals by being the most imitative of them, and he takes the first steps of his education by imitating. Everyone's enjoyment of imitation is also inborn. What happens with works of art demonstrates this: though a thing itself is disagreeable to look at, we enjoy contemplating the most accurate representations of it—for instance, figures of the most despicable animals, or of human corpses. The reason for this lies in another fact: learning is a great pleasure, not only to philosophers but likewise to everyone else, however limited his gift for it may be. He enjoys looking at these representations, because in the act of studying them he is learning. . . .

And just as imitation is natural to us, so also are music and rhythm (metres, clearly, are constituent parts of rhythms). Thus, from spontaneous beginnings, mankind developed poetry by a series of mostly minute changes out of these improvisations. . . .

Comedy is, as I have said, an imitation of lower types; though it does not include the full range of badness, nevertheless to be ridiculous is a kind of deformity. The causes of laughter are errors and disgraces not accompanied by pain or injury; the comic mask, for instance, is deformed and distorted, but not painfully so. We know something of the stages through which tragedy passed and the men to whom they were due, but there are no early records of comedy, because it was not highly valued. . . .

Let us now discuss tragedy, having first picked up from what has been said the definition of its essence that has so far emerged. Tragedy, then, is an imitation of an action of high importance, complete and of some amplitude; in language enhanced by distinct and varying beauties; acted not narrated; by means of pity and fear effecting its purgation of these emotions. By the beauties enhancing the language I mean rhythm and melody; by "distinct and varying" I mean that some are produced by metre alone, and others at another time by melody.

Now since the imitating is done by actors, it would follow of necessity that one element in a tragedy must be the *Mise en scène.* Others are Melody and Language, for these are the media in which the imitating is done. By Language, I mean the component parts of the verse, whereas Melody has an entirely sensuous effect. Again, since the object imitated is an action, and doings are done by persons, whose individuality will be determined by their Character and their Thought (for these are the factors we have in mind when we define the quality of their doings), it follows that there are two natural causes of these doings, Thought and Character; and these causes determine the good or ill fortune of everyone. But the Fable is the imitation of the action; and by the Fable I mean the whole structure of the incidents. By Character I mean the factor that enables us to define the particular quality of the people involved in the doings; and Thought is shown in everything they say when they are demonstrating a fact or disclosing an opinion. There are therefore necessarily six elements in every tragedy, which give it its quality; and they are the Fable, Character, Language, Thought, the *Mise en scène*, and Melody. . . .

The chief of these is the plotting of the incidents; for tragedy is an imitation not of men but of doings, life, happiness; unhappiness is located in doings, and our end is a certain kind of doing, not a personal quality; it is their characters that give men their quality, but their doings that make them happy or the opposite. So it is not the purpose of the actors to imitate character, but they include character as a factor in the doings. Thus it is the incidents (that is to say the Fable) that are the end for which tragedy exists; and the end is more important than anything else. Also, without an action there could not be a tragedy, but without Character there could. . . . Further, the chief means by which tragedy moves us, Irony of events and Disclosure, are elements in the Fable. . . .

So much for analysis. Now let us discuss in what sort of way the incidents should be plotted, since that is the first and chief consideration in tragedy. Our data are that tragedy is an imitation of a whole and complete action of some amplitude (a thing can be whole and yet quite lacking in amplitude). Now a whole is that which has a beginning, a middle, and an end. A beginning is that which does not itself necessarily follow anything else, but which leads naturally to another event or development; an end is the opposite, that which itself naturally (either of necessity or most commonly) follows something else, but nothing else comes after it; and a middle is that which itself follows something else and is followed by another thing. So, well-plotted fables must not begin or end casually, but must follow the pattern here described.

But, besides this, a picture, or any other composite object, if it is to be beautiful, must not only have its parts properly arranged, but be of an appropriate size; for beauty depends on size and structure. Accordingly, a minute picture cannot be beautiful (for when our vision has almost lost its sense of time it becomes confused); nor can an immense one (for we cannot take it all in together, and so our vision loses its unity and wholeness)—imagine a picture a thousand miles long! So, just as there is a proper size for bodies and pictures (a size that can be well surveyed), there is also a proper amplitude for fables (what can be kept well in one's mind). But as to amplitude, the invariable rule dictated by the nature of the action is the fuller the more beautiful so long as the outline remains clear; and for a simple rule of size, the number of happenings that will make a chain of probability (or necessity) to change a given situation from misfortune to good fortune or from good fortune to misfortune is the minimum.

Unity in a fable does not mean, as some think, that it has one man for its subject. To any one man many things happen—an infinite number—and some of them do not make any sort of unity; and in the same way one man has many doings which cannot be made into a unit of action. . . . so, since the fable is an imitation of an action, that action must be a complete unit, and the events of which it is made up must be so plotted that if any of these elements is moved or removed the whole is altered and upset. For when a thing can be included or not included without making any noticeable difference, that thing is no part of the whole.

From what has been said it is also clear that it is not the poet's business to tell what has happened, but the kind of things that would happen—what is possible according to probability or necessity. The difference between the historian and the poet is not the difference between writing in verse or prose; the work of Herodotus could be put into verse, and it would be just as much a history in verse as it is in prose. The difference is that the one tells what has happened, and the other the kind of things that would happen. It follows therefore that poetry is more philosophical and of higher value than history; for poetry universalizes more, whereas history particularizes . . .

. . . The action imitated must contain incidents that evoke fear and pity, besides being a complete action; but this effect is accentuated when these incidents occur logically as well as unexpectedly, which will be more sensational than if they happen arbitrarily, by chance. . . .

Some fables are simple, others complex: for the obvious reason that the original actions imitated by the fables are the one or the other. By a simple action I mean one that leads to the catastrophe in the way we have laid down, directly and singly, without Irony of events or Disclosure.

An action is complex when the catastrophe involves Disclosure, or Irony, or both. But these complications should develop out of the very structure of the fable, so that they fit what has gone before, either necessarily or probably. To happen after something is by no means the same as to happen because of it.

Irony is a reversal in the course of events, of the kind specified, and, as I say, in accordance with probability or necessity. Thus in the *Oedipus* the arrival of the messenger, which was expected to cheer Oedipus up by releasing him from his fear about his mother, did the opposite by showing him who he was. . . .

A Disclosure, as the term indicates, is a change from ignorance to knowledge; if the people are marked out for good fortune it leads to affection, if for misfortune, to enmity. Disclosure produces its finest effect when it is connected with Irony, as the disclosure in the *Oedipus* is. . . .

Following the proper order, the next subject to discuss after this would be: What one should aim at and beware of in plotting fables; that is to say, What will produce the tragic effect. Since, then, tragedy, to be at its finest, requires a complex, not a simple, structure, and its structure should also imitate fearful and pitiful events (for that is the peculiarity of this sort of imitation), it is clear: first, that decent people must not be shown passing from good furtune to misfortune (for that is not fearful or pitiful but disgusting); again, vicious people must not be shown passing from misfortune to good fortune (for that is the most untragic situation possible—it has none of the requisites, it is neither humane, nor pitiful, nor fearful); nor again should an utterly evil man fall from good fortune into misfortune (for though a plot of that kind would be humane, it would not induce pity or fear—pity is induced by undeserved misfortune, and fear by the misfortunes of normal people, so that this situation will be neither pitiful nor fearful). So we are left with the man between these extremes: that is to say, the kind of man who neither is distinguished for excellence and virtue, nor comes to grief on account of baseness and vice, but on account of some error; a man of great reputation and prosperity, like Oedipus and Thyestes and conspicuous people of such families as theirs. So, to be well informed, a fable must be single rather than (as some say) double—there must be no change from misfortune to good fortune, but only the opposite, from good fortune to misfortune; the cause must not be vice, but a great error; and the man must be either of the type specified or better, rather than worse. . . .

This is the plot that will produce the technically finest tragedy. Those critics are therefore wrong who censure Euripides on this very ground—because he does this in his tragedies, and many of them end in misfortune; for it is, as I have said, the right thing to do. This is clearly demonstrated on the stage in the competitions, where such plays, if they succeed, are the most tragic, and Euripides, even if he is inefficient in every other respect, still shows himself the most tragic of our poets. . . .

The pity and fear can be brought about by the *Mise en scène;* but they can also come from the mere plotting of the incidents, which is preferable, and better poetry. For, without seeing anything, the fable ought to have been so plotted that if one heard the bare facts, the chain of circumstances would make one shudder and pity. That would happen to anyone who heard the fable of the *Oedipus*. . . .

Let us, then, take next the kind of circumstances that seem terrible or lamentable. Now, doings of that kind must be between friends, or enemies, or neither. If an enemy injures an enemy, there is no pity either beforehand or at the time, except on account of the bare fact; nor is there if they are neutral; but when sufferings are engendered among the affections—for example, if murder is done or planned, or some similar outrage is committed, by brother on brother, or son on father, or mother on son, or son on mother—that is the thing to aim at. . . .

And in the characterization, as in the plotting of the incidents, the aim should always be either necessity or probability: so that they say or do such things as it is necessary or probable that they would, being what they are; and that for this to follow that is either necessary or probable. . . . (Thus it is clear that the untying of the fable should follow on the circumstances of the fable itself, and not be done *ex machina*, as it is in the *Medea*, or in Book 2 of the *Iliad*. But the *deus ex machina* should be used for matters outside the drama—either things that happened before and that man could not know, or future events that need to be announced prophetically; for we allow the gods to see everything. As for extravagant incidents, there should be none in the story, or if there are they should be kept outside the tragedy, as is the one in the *Oedipus* of Sophocles.). . .

Treat the chorus as though it were one of the actors; it should be an organic part of the play and reinforce it, not as it is in Euripides, but as in Sophocles.

émile faguet

on the nature of dramatic emotions

What is the fundamental nature of the dramatic emotion?

The question is not new; Saint-Marc-Girardin long ago placed it, with many others, at the head of his *Cours de Littérature Dramatique;* and now the excellent M. Herckenrath is asking it again in his *Problèmes d'Esthétique et de Morale.* M. Herckenrath is a professor at the Lycée de Groningue and a man of original ideas. He asks, as you may have asked yourselves: "Does not the pleasure which we find in the performance of a tragedy seem at first sight a barbarous enjoyment? We are looking at suffering eagerly, instead of turning away our eyes. Is this pleasure, then, of the same nature as that which certain persons experience in seeing an animal slaughtered, or in witnessing a bloody fight? . . . In short, how can one who is moved by it and who weeps over it, enjoy that sensation?"

These are exactly the questions that Saint-Marc-Girardin answered by saying: "The base of the dramatic emotion is the sympathy of man for man." We go to the theatre to be moved by the misfortunes of our fellowmen because we love them; we share their griefs, their pains, their sorrows and their despair, etc.

This is ingenious, but it has never quite convinced me. To *seek out*—note this point, for here's the rub—to seek out the spectacle of human suffering in order to be moved by it, does not seem to me characteristic of an extremely sympathetic and eminently humane soul.

To encounter human misery and to pity it, and particularly to relieve it, and "to relieve it to the point of sharing it" (to recall Mérimée's charming phrase in regard to Nodier), yes, that is to be kind-hearted. But to seek out human suffering with the intention of being moved by it, and with the consoling knowledge that one will not be called upon to relieve it, I don't see wherein that reveals a sympathy of man for man; and I can see, I fear I do see, wherein that indicates the instinct of ferocity, pure and simple, softened, no doubt, by civilization.

And I have a tendency not to be very much irritated by our good Mr. Herckenrath, who says to us gently:

This real pleasure which we take in seeing suffering, seems to me to be the result of the cruel predispositions engendered in the race by war, formerly a necessary and frequently an habitual condition of tribes and communities. The necessity of inflicting injuries in self-defense has given rise to the pleasure of inflicting them. . . . In most individuals, the ferocious instinct has become weakened; but we must seek vestiges of it in the taste for bloody spectacles, bull-fights, dog-fights, cock-fights, the chase, or recitals of scenes of horror. It finds nourishment daily in the sensational serials, and in the newspaper reports of crimes.

It seems to me that there is some justice in M. Herckenrath's argument, whence it would follow that the base of the dramatic emotion is not exactly the sympathy of man for man, but rather the ferocity of man toward his fellows.

For, after all, we must observe that Saint-Marc-Girardin neglected half the problem in order to simplify it. He based his argument on tragedy, admitting, in the pleasure caused by it, only the pleasure of weeping over great misfortunes; and he left comedy completely out of account.

Now, no one will claim that the pleasure which one experiences at a comedy is founded on the sympathy of man for man. It is too clearly founded on malignity. What we enjoy at a comedy, is laughing at the foibles of beings like ourselves. This is evidently a pleasure founded on ferocity. The gossip, the slanderer, the practical joker, the malicious man, and the man who enjoys comedy, are and must be placed in the same ethical category. They are vicious brutes. I know that very well for I am one of them. They are at bottom, and with differences of degree, vicious brutes.

Well, there is half the drama based on human malignity. Do you believe that the other half is in contrast with it, and is based upon a contrary sentiment?

It might be so, surely; and if someone has made the profound observation that the world is a comedy for the man who thinks, and a tragedy for the man who feels, it may be that the world is also a comedy for the malicious, and a tragedy for the altruistic. However, let us investigate.

In the first place, is there any essential difference between comedy and tragedy? Not at all. There is a difference of degree. The same subjects are comic or tragic. They are comic so long as the passions placed in action and on view before us seem to involve only consequences of small importance; they become tragic when we begin to perceive that they involve and foreshadow consequences which may be terrible.

There is no other difference between comedy and tragedy than the greater or smaller range of the consequences which the passions they depict are supposed to produce.

"Well! but then they are both founded on the same sentiment. At comedy as well as at tragedy we come to see suffering."

"But at comedy we come to see slight suffering, and to laugh at it; at tragedy we come to see horrible suffering, and to weep over it."

"Granted; but in either case, the seeking of this pleasure is not the act of a highly philanthropic soul; and if laughing at human sorrows proves that we come to the comedy from cruelty, weeping over these sorrows does not justify us entirely for having come to the tragedy to enjoy them as a spectacle. You can't get away from this; to happen upon misfortune without having sought it, and then to be moved by it—that is to be tenderhearted; to seek the spectacle of misfortune, even though this be in order to weep over it, evidences depraved liking; it is a dilettantism founded in barbarism."

"I have seen *Phédre.* It is very sad. I wept copiously."

"Did you know what it was?"

"No."

"Did you know what a tragedy is?"

"No."

"*Absolvo te.* You are only to be pitied.

"I have seen *Phèdre.* It is very sad. I wept."

"Did you know what it was?"

"I knew that it was a play in which a woman kills herself from disappointment in love, and where a father kills his son from jealousy."

"And you went to see that? You are not tender-hearted."

"But I wept!"

"That is no excuse for going out and hunting up such a spectacle out of mere curiosity, and paying money for it."

"But I wept!"

"And you found pleasure in weeping."

"Yes."

"That pleasure wipes out even what justification there might have been in your having wept. You went to seek pleasure in the misfortune of others, and you found it. That is all that remains at the bottom of the crucible. You are vicious. Taine would tell you that you are partly cruel gorilla. He claimed, you know, that man is a descendant, only slightly modified, of the cruel and lecherous gorilla. The lecherous gorilla for comedy, and cruel gorilla, for serious drama."

"You are at least cruel yourself, sir."

"I exaggerate a little, that's all. Man is an exaggerating gorilla."

Exaggeration apart, I am within the truth. Man goes to tragedy to seek a pleasure which is derived from the misfortune of man.

Besides, do you ever see on the stage, on any stage, a picture of happiness? Never! Neither in comedy nor in tragedy. Comedy: picture of ludicrous misfortunes. Tragedy: picture of terrifying misfortunes. Picture of happiness, where? Nowhere.

If man, "fond of spectacles" as Bossuet says, "and who makes a spectacle of the depicting of his own errors," enjoyed the spectacle of human happiness, he would have created a dramatic species devoted to the depicting of happiness. But this dramatic species does not exist. The conclusion is obvious.

Some wit once remarked: "Why do all the comedies end with a marriage? Because after that, the tragedy begins."

That is not bad; but it is not complete. We should say that comedy itself is a picture of misfortune. It consists, even when it is not satirical, even when it is sentimental, of the petty troubles of two young people who would like to get married and can't. As soon as they can, it is all over. Oh! drop the curtain! They are going to be happy now; I am going. That has no interest for me any more.

Never has a playwright depicted a honeymoon, except at the moment when it commences to be embittered.

No; the spectacle of happiness does not appeal to us at all, and the lines of Destouches may be applied to any one of us:

> Another's happiness gives us chagrin;
> Your neighbor's plumpness makes you grow more thin.

And on the other hand the spectacle of misfortune contains for us inexhaustible delights. The theatre, as I have shown, is merely the picture of misfortune, great or small. The novel is the same thing, of course. Women —whom we should always consult to find out what man is, because they are more permanent than we, because their evolution is less, and less rapid, because they are nearer to primitive man, because they constitute an almost unchanging element in the human race—women who go to the circulating library to ask for a book, if they do not know what they want, nearly always ask in the end for "something sad." They like to weep. They meet for that purpose. They come to it very quickly. . . .

> For let a woman start to weep, another will begin,
> And all the rest who come along will eagerly join in.

The drama, literature, poetry, the conversation of sentimental men and women, all these things are simply the depicting of the misfortunes of humanity.

That explains certain constantly recurring tendencies in literature and drama, and conversely, is explained by these tendencies. Periodically the theatre makes an attempt to the point of horror to depict human ills, in obedience to the law of increasing intensity which prevails in the whole field of spectacle. Recently in France the Théâtre-Libre, wishing at the start to make a strong impression on the public imagination with something quite novel, devoted itself to representations of sickness, of violence, and of death. If Saint-Sorlin had been alive, he would have repeated:

> *Les uns sont pulmoniques,*
> *Les autres catharreux, les autres hydropiques.*

That sort of thing does not succeed very long. But what does this indicate? That we do not want the emotion caused in us by the misfortune of others to reach the point of shuddering horror. Do you see? We like to contemplate misfortune so long as it does not affect us. In a word, we like to see suffering without suffering ourselves. And it seems to me that is not the sympathy of man for man.

An interesting example, cited by M. Herckenrath: "In a little town of Dutch Brabant, a sanguinary drama was being presented. Several murders were committed, one after the other. After viewing two or three in silence, the peaceable townspeople could contain themselves no longer. They crowded on the stage and stopped the performance, crying: 'Enough of this bloodshed!' The incident was related to me by an eyewitness."

These townspeople were, in the first place, very good people; in the second place, people of little learning, that is to say, unversed in the pleasure which it is the function of literature to extract from human suffering; and finally unaccustomed to the theatre and consequently capable, like children, of the dramatic illusion, and believing (almost) that the murders committed on the stage were real.

Therefore, it was too much for them. For man enjoys human suffering up to a certain point. He is not a savage. He is only partly savage. The amount of savagery which remains in the heart of man, the exact amount—that is precisely what the theatre, comic as well as tragic, must know in each generation, and that is also what it registers. We find Molière's comedy somewhat cruel, in *Georges Dandin*, or in the fifth act of the *Misanthrope*. This means that our cruelty is a little less violent than that of our forefathers of the seventheenth century. The melodrama played before the citizens of the little town in Brabant passed the bounds of their bloodthirstiness, as the pathological exhibitions of the early days of the Théâtre-Libre passed the bounds of ours.

But the fundamental fact remains: this is, that the theatre exploits the tendency we have to find pleasure, in one way or another, either with laughter or with tears, in the misfortune of others, without ourselves suffering.

But is this all? This is the principal thing. I maintain that. I withdraw nothing of what precedes. However, this is not all. There is something more, something a little more noble, a little more elevated, that enters in, or rather is added to all that I have set forth thus far; something which in some persons is non-existent, in many is more or less developed and which in a few is almost the principal thing, without ever, I think, prevailing entirely.

The misfortune of others makes us laugh, the misfortune of others makes us weep, and in both cases it gives pleasure. To be sure; but also, but furthermore, but at the same time, if you like, it makes us think. Then, along with the cruel pleasure which comedy gives, along with the sad pleasure that tragedy gives, along with these *mala gaudia mentis*, there is mingled or added the pleasure of reflecting on the ills of humanity, of seeing them, not as *res fruenda oculis*, but as matter for thought and meditation; and this is a new point of view. The pleasure which man finds in the theatre, comic as well as tragic, in the representation of the misfortune of others, is in the first place malignity; it is also a desire for truth—and it is furthermore a desire to consider human affairs in a serious manner.

It is a desire for truth. Schopenhauer maintained all his life that there is nothing real in the world except misfortune, for the sufficient reason that pain is incontestably real and that pleasure is never anything but the satisfaction of a want, which is suffering, whence it follows that pleasure is negative and that suffering alone is positive.

I am aware of the objections to this view, and I myself consider it incomplete. But there is a good deal of truth in it. It is true in general; it is almost a platitude. Do you realize that after all it leaves out, it misses, only the aesthetic pleasures, which are not the satisfaction of a want, which are a joy that needs no suffering to create, which are pleasures not born of pain, and which consequently are not only pure pleasures, but positive pleasures.

As for all the other pleasures, Schopenhauer's theory applies to them perfectly. And if this is the case, this theory may be considered true, in a very general sense.

Now I believe that men, after the age of fifteen and a half, are aware of it. They feel that the one thing which is real in the world is pain; and that the rest is sometimes an illusion and sometimes only a desire satisfied, that is to say a very brief reprieve from suffering. And accordingly, in the domain of art, they do not exactly refuse the representation of happiness, since they know that happiness is still true, in a relative and, so to speak, accidental fashion; they do not refuse the representation of happiness; they are willing to read, and not without pleasure, Lamartine's *Chant d'amour*; they are willing, at the theatre, to listen, and not without pleasure, to an idyllic love episode; but they don't want these things to last too long. These things seem false, or they seem insufficiently true.

Why is it that one need only speak ill of men—perhaps even of women—to have the appearance of knowing them? In the first place that comes of human malignity—and I shall return to this. In the second place, it is because man knows that if it is true that he is good, it is even truer that he is not, and that if unselfishness is true, selfishness is even truer. In the same way, to paint humanity "happy" irritates the reader a little, the same as to paint it "beautiful." He does not say: "No!" He does not revolt. He does not enter a categorical denial. But he says: "Let us not exaggerate." To dwell on it provokes a slight suspicion of ingenuousness or of charlatanism.

We must be careful here, because there are many distinctions. Man is irritated also by those who paint misfortune too exclusively and too persistently. He finds that also more or less false, and he is right. And besides, he suspects that this arises from malice, and not merely from the desire for truth: "In God's name, sir, that we are miserable or despicable seems to cause you a good deal of satisfaction!" And again, he likes a little deception, in the direction of optimism, for consolation. "You flatter me; but go on" is a very human attitude; and humanity has always said to its entertainers: "Gild the truth a little, to console me—but not too much."

But in spite of all these reservations, which were necessary, mankind loves truth in art, and that is why it likes art sad—sad in the true sense of the word; and I have shown that comedy is even sadder than tragedy. It likes in art reality forcefully presented; and the most idealistic art is nothing more than a certain reality presented with all the force of a powerful genius.

For these reasons, since mankind comes to the theatre to seek above all a picture of life, an optimistic drama would seem to it false or childish, and we would promptly call it a Sunday school.

Notice that I say "optimistic" and not "noble." Every audience in the world has always been very susceptible to the appeal to admiration. That is another matter. To admire a hero, that is to say a fine specimen of humanity, will always be to readers of novels, to readers of epic poems, to theatergoers, a keen delight. For it isn't there that he finds the unreal. Nothing, though it be rare, is truer. Man knows that he has good instincts. Man knows that he is capable of courage and magnanimity. For example, man knows that he can conquer himself, and that he then experiences an indescribable pleasure, the greatest pleasure that it is granted him to feel here below.

And do you know why? After all, I don't know myself, but I can imagine. Man is a combative animal. It is only by fearful struggles that he has attained, first, his place on the earth, and then civilization. Now that he no longer has such terrible battles to fight (by "now" I mean the historical period), the instinct remains: man still needs to fight. Therefore he fights against himself, against his passions. He experiences infinite pleasure in conquering them, in taming them; and it is still the old tamer of wild beasts who then survives. This pleasure is so keen that sometimes he fights for nothing, without a prize, "for fun," precisely because it is a pleasure. The mania of Corneille in his old age was to show us men exercising their will against themselves, without utility, without any duty to accomplish, and for the mere joy of exercising it; this is an exaggeration, but it is not an absurdity. Such men exist still and are not superhuman; they are still quite within human nature. The ascetics, for example.

Men accept, then, the noble in drama, but not the optimistic, not the drama which paints humanity as happy, because such a drama is not true. And a good proof, both that this drama would not be true and that men do not desire it, is that it does not exist.

In conclusion I will add that if men accept only a relatively sad drama, it is because that is the only kind that makes them think. Even if it were true, the optimistic drama would be hollow.

Let us suppose that mankind is happy, and that the stage depicts it as it is—but in that case, why depict it? In this world, the thing to think about, and to remedy if possible, is presumably the thing we lack. You have noticed the popular phrase, very French: "There's nothing to say to that." That means: "All goes well." And the fact is there is really "nothing to say" when all goes well. Happy nations have no history. That is why all nations have one. Happiness never needs to be narrated, nor described, nor painted, nor explained. It furnishes no material for the chronicler or dramatist. It is, and it is quite content with merely existing.

Happy people—and there are such and I have seen them—are very interesting to study, and somewhat surprising. They rarely concern themselves with literature, philosophy, ethics, history, or sociology; and they are somehwat surprised that any one else should do so. This is because all those things, at bottom you may be sure, are only different forms of the search for happiness. Now as they possess this, they are somewhat puzzled that others should be obliged to seek it. Can you imagine literature undertaking to describe and analyze those people?

In the first place we should discover that it would be undertaking a study of the unusual; secondly we should wonder, vaguely, unconsciously, what is the use of depicting those who have found, instead of those who seek, those who have arrived instead of those who are on the way.

—"To show the goal!"

—To be sure, but it is not the goal that needs to be shown; that does no good. It is the way that leads to it which is useful; and the obstacles in the way, which are the most important. The obstacles in the way: our passions, our mistakes, our follies, our illusions, our vices—that is tragedy; our pettinesses, our faults, our absurdities—that is comedy. These are precisely what interest us: these are precisely what give food for reflection; these are precisely what make us think a little; and these are precisely what furnish material for literature and particularly for drama.

We are not clearly aware of it, because we go to the theatre for entertainment. We go only for that. So much is undeniable. But we should make a grave mistake if we thought that on entering the theatre we leave behind the part of us that thinks, which reflects, which is concerned and anxious about the great problems of humanity, and that we have in the orchestra chair only the part of us that wants to be amused. We may think that we have only the latter, but we have at the same time all the companion parts that exist in us.

It is our whole personality that we bring with us; and without our suspecting it, without our intending it, it is our whole personality that the author who is behind the curtain has undertaken to entertain. He will succeed only on condition that he captivate and hold it almost as a whole; and while we laugh at merry jests, or while we weep at pathos, we shall be truly captivated—unconsciously, of course—but we shall be truly captivated only if we are touched deeply, almost entirely, only if we have a vague consciousness that something very serious is in the background of the little story.

It is for no other reason that we are not merely interested, but moved and enthralled when we see *Polyeucte*, *Athalie*, *King Lear*, *Othello*, *Misanthrope*, *Maitre Guérin*, the *Visite de Noces*, the *Ami des Femmes;* and for my part, if I place the *Mariage de Figaro* below all these, it is doubtless because in this case I am amused, but I do not feel stirring in me as a spectator the whole man that is myself, or at least the man in me who is interested in the destinies, the happiness or the misfortune, the trials and the hopes and efforts of my fellow man.

Since there is nothing, then, more important in this world than pain, since there is nothing which makes us reflect more deeply than the sight of the things which prevent us from being happy, and of those which cause us to be unhappy, is it surprising that the drama should consist on the one hand of the delineation of our faults, on the other of the representation of our misfortunes, and that thus it is all sad, even when it is apparently gay, sadder still when it is sad because it intends to be?

In a word, it is sad whenever it is not superficial, for the excellent reason given by Mme. de Staël: "Have you never gone to the bottom of everything—that is, to sorrow?"

A little cruelty or malice—a little love of truth—a concern, invincible even when we try to conquer it, with serious things: that is what the spectator always brings to the drama, and that is what forces the drama as a whole, except for brief exceptions, to be the picture of human ills.

It is so in order to be solid, it is so in order to be permanent, it is so in order to exist. Petrarch said:

Null' altro che pianto al mondo dura.
(Nothing endures in the world but sorrow.)

benjamin lehmann

comedy and laughter

The student of literature, reviewing what has been written about comedy, may well be dismayed. For what has been written about the subject is, except for incidental insights, not about comedy. It is about satire. There are indeed studies of individual comedies, of comic devices, of a single writer's practices, and of comedy in a period or in a tradition. But these also more or less involve themselves, without due distinction of terms, with satire. And with an incidental exception or two when a general view of comedy is undertaken, attention is fixed upon the ludicrous, the absurd, the ridiculous. Laughter is said to be provoked by these human manifestations. The laughter, it is said, is corrective; we are invited to believe that the chief end of comedy is to reform manners and dispositions. Laughter itself has been inquired into; its bases in physiology, in psychology, and in group reaction have been explored, not without illumination. The illumination falls, however, not on comedy; it is shed on satire and on the comic, those fragments of action and utterance which beget the flash laugh. It does not fall on the work of literary art all consent to call comedy, whether for audiences in a theater or for readers by a fireside.

Yet the literary mode called comedy is an ancient one, and in our time of remarkable vitality. Epic, we often hear, is no longer possible; lyric, we are told, is now for a special audience; of tragedy, it is said, the essentials no longer exist in our world view. Comedy prospers. We may set aside as childish the notion that the age seeks merely to be amused; it seeks recreation, an honorable seeking which the arts are intended to foster. In design and color, in tone and implication, comedy seems now even more than in other times to meet a need, to correspond to a primary and universal intuition of life and the world. Is it not possible to examine the comedies, to discover that intuition of life and the world which so persistently captivates the human spirit? The incongruities and all the rest of which the critics speak are in the service of a vision of reality the average man takes daily for granted and delights to see illustrated and affirmed. In the service of that vision are also the mistaken identities, disguises, the eavesdropping, the non-sequiturs, the famous mechanical incrustation of vitality; even the wisecrack and the pratfall, for which the average man invented words.

At the outset, we must observe that though we laugh at actions and utterances in comedy, we do not laugh at the comedy as a whole. For the comedy as a whole is a serious work, making an affirmation about life that chimes with our intuitive sense of how things are and with our deep human desire to have the necessary and agreeable prevail and our even deeper human desire to arrest before our minds a condition of things pleasant in itself and completely free from the threat of time and of disruption. For time brings the aftermath, in which the seeds of disruptive forces will sprout, in which decay will set in, and the whole process of making the necessary and agreeable secure will have to start over. That golden lads and girls must like chimney sweepers come to dust is not the stuff of comedy; it is a comment from beyond comedy's world on that world, and so appalling that its truth must be obscured by a pun. Never in comedy are we without love, and almost never without lovers. Comedy fixes the lads and girls forever in their brilliant moment; it usually contrives to close our minds to what lies ahead. This is not from any desire to deny life all its stages. We know it would be no true bliss that was bliss always, and that this enchanting hour is itself possible because of the not entirely comfortable growth that preceded it. Ambivalently perhaps, but certainly, though we desire for these lovers and for ourselves all the stages of life, it is yet pleasant, it agrees with the feeling we have of valuable things, to put a period here where the mates are free of all save their own inner commitment. That commitment is of course one in which we have a vicarious refreshment of old innocence, or, if we are very young, a veiled prevision of an hour when innocence will be lost. But it is more than that. It reassures us about life and its continuation—the more so, that these lovers are so young, so beautiful or so charming, if also so compelled. We do not laugh at all this. We are delighted; we are content. The folk have a phrase for it: all the world loves a lover, they say.

But the folk have another phrase: the course of true love never runs smooth, they also say. If this saying is large enough to include postmarital trials, that is as it should be, for comedy, in putting a period at mating, does not deny the aftermath; it simply ignores it for these lovers. The course of true love that does not run smooth is in comedy the preceding course. In that phase, there are difficulties. They arise at many points and from many causes in human nature and human circumstance: social prejudice, finances, an older generation that has forgotten its youth, even conflicts within the lovers that for a while thwart their profound instinctive sense that they can, in the mysterious way of things, complete one another.

Against that prevision of completeness nothing can prevail: not poverty, not social barriers, not advice, not even upon occasion a glimpsing foresight that life may be one long bickering. The elements, within and around lovers, which stand in the way of their fulfilling themselves and their biological function, are in comedy usually treated with sympathetic derision. It is folly to oppose this compulsion to mate, and what opposes properly falls under a derisive light.

The forces that oppose lovers, however, are themselves constituted in the nature of things. All these exasperating parents, these crotchety uncles and spinster aunts with lapdogs and money, these competing lovers, jealous, irresponsible, full of devious plans, these group attitudes regarding social status, race, religion, culture—these too have come into existence as inevitably as the lovers' promptings. The manners and the morals of the group, and the members of the group themselves, are manifestations of the freedom of all things to be what they are, to improve such opportunities as exist for realizing the never ceasing activity of becoming what further they may become. Consequently in the world of comedy the greatest diversity of being and of morals is deployed, and it is granted that those who seek to frustrate our lovers have a right to be what they are. Yet since not all possibilities of being can happily exist together, some must be sacrificed, some must be defeated. Social homogeneity, or true unity, cannot be always maintained; there is bound to be schism. But the sacrificed will be gently discarded, after being duly wrapped in derision, away from our complete sympathy; and the mutually opposed parties will fuse once more in a firm social unity.

The vision of comedy, then, keeps its eye on lovers, its foresight upon their prosperous mating and on implied procreation. And it consents heartily that the world they live in shall be populated by a richly diverse humanity, some for and some against the desired consummation, provided only all these illustrate the variety of the possibilities of being, generous or crabbed, fulfilled or thwarted, and provided further that the crabbed and the thwarted exhibit to us within their limits the best realization of their meager possibilities and, when necessary, yield duly to clear the way for fuller, better-natured possibilities. The vision of comedy fixes its eye on separateness, on diversity, even on oppositions, but it insists at last on togetherness for lovers and on the restored social fabric, on solidarity for the group. From its world are excluded insurmountable barriers, unassimilable evils, and suffering that strikes at the core or is irremediable. In that world all is tipped toward life, abundance, health, energy, companionship, respect, and admiration. Song, music, dance, feasting belong in it. Whatever within the range of vision is otherwise will be minimized by laughter, though it is understood it cannot be abolished from the world, and that all will end happily for human beings, not merely for human minds.

Historically, what is called comedy grew out of carnival, and the secrets of carnival are masquerade, fellow feeling, and such immersion in being that the sense of impermanence vanishes. Originally the carnival was dedicated to the continuity of life; in its beginnings comedy was involved with the fertility of the species, and with that animality which puritans might condemn but could only advertise. That nothing lasts, that we may as well be ourselves, that when we are ourselves the mask is thrown off and primal forces emerge in us, these ancient intuitions in the circumstances of carnival call out gaiety and joyousness. The sense of human isolation is dissolved by the communal activity and the sense of impermanence is annihilated by the promised projection of life. The participants seem to say, we are not only solidly here in this company, but in time to come there will also be others. Birth, maturity, mating—though these are not the ecclesiastical sacraments, for life they are sacramental, and they are ceremonially so recognized in all religions. Comedy, from this point of view, is seen, once again, to deal with mating and marriage, with maturity which is their condition, and birth which is their consequence.

Seeing things as they are, however, involves more than a clear gaze at the agents of the life-stream. Though these agents are rarely left out of the picture, and though they are sometimes exhibited in a more advanced phase, shown for example as married and readjusting with the passing years and the changing natures, often they constitute a contrapuntal design in a picture of the diversely populated world, or a reassuring frame for the picture of that world. If from Menander to our own day we can follow the tradition the folk has summarized in the sayings that all the world loves a lover and that the course of true love never runs smooth, we can also from Aristophanes to Shaw follow another tradition. In it derision, verging on half-affectionate raillery, is played upon human instances and patterns of behavior that appear to prevent free fulfillment of any kind whatsoever. Long ago Wilamovitz made clear that Aristophanic comedy was not intended to improve the morals of the audience, and Werner Jaeger has in recent years and in a larger context taken the same position. What an unbiased reading of the comedies of Aristophanes shows us is that, except when—as in his invective against Cleon—he is a bitter satirist, he stands for freedom. The freedom he stands for is sometimes the freedom of the immediate past, but it is always the freedom of man to be and to become what it lies in him to be and to become, unhampered by the community, by the mob, by law, by too much or too little money, by the newfangled and the restricting old-fashioned. "Freedom to *be*" is the motto, freedom from disorder, lust, cruelty, war. The image is Cloud-Cuckoo-Land where all the hampering forces are abolished, where not only lovers but every man is free and winged, subject only to those self-deceptions which are harmless because they are in the nature of things and laughable because they are harmless. Cloud-Cuckoo-Land comes through into our day in such plays as *Harvey*, *Arsenic and Old Lace*, and in the Wonderland of Alice. It is not love of lovers but love of humanity's best and most various possibilities which is the spirit of this comedy. Such comedy realizes the insight of certain Pythagoreans and of Plato that civilization should foster the fulfillment of the real individual both in himself and in his natural affiliations. The freedom desired is beyond any conceived in political and economic utopias and would of course be impossible under political or economic despotism. Under despotism, deviation from the prescribed would be the object of unmitigated ridicule and invective, what we call satire. It is in democracy that comedy particularly prospers, for true democracy and true comedy are of an immense hospitality and have respect for all men. That Molière, for example, lived under a sort of despotism does not alter the case. An era is not despotic about everything: about the forms Molière chiefly explored and exhibited, his era was not despotic; it assumes the absolute validity of the satirist's values and is intolerant; it judges without misgiving; it does more than condemn, it excludes. Aristophanes and Molière, thus, show themselves despotic in behalf of freedom when they are primarily satirists.

At its truest, comedy of the Aristophanic kind is devoted to the free maturing of diverse and even of eccentric possibilities. Like the comedy of lovers, this is a serious affirmation of life, delightedly asserted, joyously accepted, and oftenest with laughter. The fullest comedy, at all events, intuitively rendering unity in diversity, now and in time to come, views the world simultaneously in both the Aristophanic and the Menanderian modes. When it does not, the boy-gets-girl fable will seem trite and perhaps trivial, for it will lack reference, relation, affiliation. It will be what we call romance. In romance life has ceased to be a forest; it has become a park. The underbrush has been cleaned out, the windfalls and the deadfalls have been cleaned up, and nature's way of enriching herself by her own decay is lost to us. On the other hand, without the lovers the satiric practice which derides the old-established morals in the hope of destroying them will seen, if not heartless, at least without a sufficient symbol of dedication; and all observations of human nature will seem too intellectual not because there is too much intellect in the observation but because it is observation without love of life. Phenomenal mental energy expressed in notable wit, may conceal this truth, as it sometimes does in Aristophanes and in Shaw and in Ben Jonson.

By glancing now at individual works, we can perhaps at once test the validity of the general position here set forth and take note of some of the special ways in which comedy employs congenial attitudes and convenient devices, of what may be called the practice of comedy, as distinguished from comic vision. We can also by proceeding in this way suggest the complexity which is characteristic of a wholly achieved work of literary art in this genre, the more readily if we include among our instances some works which though deficient as works of art have proved persuasive for large audiences. . . .

Comic practice, we said, views with half-affectionate derision the unfruitful, the incomplete, and the contrived, when they seek to frustrate vitality and fulfillment, and, when they merely exist in the neighborhood, presents such to us as examples of the rich variety in the human scene. Though comic vision is devoted to spontaneous and fulfilling expression, it knows that fulfillment is not always possible. Then comic practice shows us how the wise keep their heads down. . . .

Reason is a function much spoken of in connection with comedy. Sometimes it is made the heart of the matter. In that case we observe a snobbery of the self-valuing intelligence; more often we are in the presence of a failure to understand the role reason plays in human affairs. Reason, when it shows to a degree at which it may be separately designated, sees the many diverse claims made upon our imagination, our loyalties, our sympathies, our energy, or our time. It may sometimes appear to make a choice among these diverse claims. But reason is not really free. Were it not tied to the needs of the body and the demand of events, it would still be the creature of the nervous system, at the very least enslaved by accustomed ways of being reasonable. To be natural, which we are by virtue of being alive, and to be rational is to be confronted from hour to hour not so much by choice, as by the necessity for adapting, for making the best of it, as we say, even perhaps for throwing reason out. Reason is not the instrument of comic vision. It is part of the material upon which comic vision gazes.

Here we have the overarching incongruity, which all other incongruities are lighted by. There are many others. Under the most fortunate circumstances it is incongruous that mind should see clearly and sometimes soar but the body should feed and sleep; that the human spirit should feel perennial and the matter of which spirit is a function should be changing always; that the state of being whose nature it is to pledge itself eternally should be so fragilely grounded, so briefly possible; and it is incongruous that the freedom lovers find to commit themselves should at once deprive them of their freedoms. Since nothing remains as it is, it is inconsistent to take satisfaction in an arrived-at solidarity, for it too will be destroyed and succeeded by another, different, whether better or worse. The freedom Aristophanes desired would be procured at the cost of freedom to other entities to be themselves. All other incongruities arise from these, and illustrate these, actually or typically or symbolically.

Comedy did not invent incongruity, it discovered it. Long before psychiatry formulated analogous concepts, comedy discovered the masque, the disguise, mistaken identity. Comedy found them what we call laughable, but on the deeper level felt them as symbolic expression. It recognized in non-sequiturs the verbal symbol of those minor derangements in the sequence of events which are always present when we view reality with preconceptions. It found in wit—the surprising juxtaposition, implied or expressed and happily phrased—the verbal suggestion of the infinite possibilities of being and of connection. In those unillusioned judgments made with love, what we call humor, it found the manner of consent to all possible being and all possible connection. In puns, which begin with one meaning and end with another, it found the verbal means of rendering those random collisions of phenomena which both do, and do not, make sense. And each of these, perceived, may make us laugh; but their doing so is incidental to another effect which is a delight too deep for laughter, a joy too pervasive for laughter. That effect is a felt affirmation about life which chimes with our intuitive sense of how things are and with our deep human desire to be re-created by seeing true humanness prevail, against the frightening altitudes of aspiration, against the set mechanism of the habitual and conventional, against the threat of corruption and of time.

SELECTIVE BIBLIOGRAPHY

PERIODICALS

The following are the major periodicals of drama criticism: *Drama Survey; Educational Theatre Journal; Plays and Players; Tulane Drama Review; World Theatre*

GENERAL WORKS: THEORY

Bentley, Eric, *The Life of the Drama*, New York, 1964.
Drew, Elizabeth, *Discovering Drama*, New York, 1937.
Freud, Sigmund, *Wit and Its Relation to the Unconscious*, in *Basic Writings of Sigmund Freud*, New York, 1938.
Guthke, Karl, *Modern Tragicomedy*, New York, 1966.
Lesser, Simon, *Fiction and the Unconscious*, New York, 1962.
McCollom, William, *Tragedy*, New York, 1957.
Meyers, Henry, *Tragedy, A View of Life*, Ithaca, 1956.
Nicoll, Allardyce, *The Theory of Drama*, London, 1937.
Peacock, Ronald, *The Art of the Drama*, London, 1957.
Potts, L., *Comedy*, London, 1949.
Sewall, Richard, *The Vision of Tragedy*, New Haven, 1959.
Sypher, Wylie, ed., *Comedy: An Essay on Comedy*, by G. Meredith, *Laughter* by H. Bergson, *The Meaning of Comedy*, by W. Sypher, Garden City, New York, 1956.

GENERAL WORKS: HISTORY AND CRITICISM

Bentley, Eric, *The Playwright as Thinker*, New York, 1946.
Brustein, Robert, *The Theatre of Revolt*, Boston, 1964.
Esslin, Martin, *The Theatre of the Absurd*, Garden City, New York, 1961.
Fergusson, Francis, *The Idea of a Theater*, Princeton, 1949.
Gassner, John, *Masters of the Drama*, New York, 1954.
———, *Form and Idea in Modern Drama*, New York, 1956.
Muller, Herbert, *The Spirit of Tragedy*, New York, 1956.
Peacock, Ronald, *The Poet in the Theatre*, New York, 1960.
Steiner, George, *The Death of Tragedy*, New York, 1961.
Thompson, Alan, *The Dry Mock, a Study of Irony in Drama*, Berkeley, 1948.

THEATRE

Gaster, T., *Thespis*, New York, 1950.
Gorelik, M., *New Theatres for Old*, New York, 1940.
Hartnoll, P., *The Oxford Companion to the Theatre*, New York, 1951.
Hunningher, B., *The Origin of the Theatre*, New York, 1961.
Macgowan, K. and W. Melnitz, *The Living Stage*, New York, 1955.
Nagler, A. M., *A Source Book in Theatrical History*, New York, 1959.

COLLECTIONS OF ESSAYS

Abel, Lionel, ed., *Moderns on Tragedy*, Greenwich, Conn., 1967.
Clark, Barrett, ed., *European Theories of the Drama*, New York, 1965.
Cole, Toby, ed., *Playwrights on Playwriting*, New York, 1961.
Corrigan, Robert, ed., *Comedy: Meaning and Form*, San Francisco, 1965.
———, ed., *Tragedy: Vision and Form*, San Francisco, 1965.

AUTHORS

aristophanes: Lever, K., *The Art of Greek Comedy*, London, 1956.
Norwood, G., *Greek Comedy*, Boston, 1930.
Whitman, C. H., *Aristophanes and the Comic Hero*, Cambridge, Mass., 1964.
brecht: Brecht, Bertolt, *Brecht on Theatre*, ed. John Willet, New York, 1964.
Brustein, Robert, *The Theatre of Revolt*, Boston, 1964.
Demetz, Peter, ed., *Brecht*, Englewood Cliffs, N.J., 1962.
Esslin, Martin, *Brecht: The Man and His Work*, Garden City, 1960.
Sartre, Jean-Paul, "Beyond Bourgeois Theatre," in *Theatre in the Twentieth Century*, ed. R. Corrigan, New York, 1963.
Willet, John, *The Theatre of Bertolt Brecht*, London, 1959.
chekhov: Bruford, W., *Chekhov and His Russia*, New Haven, 1947.
Brustein, R., *The Theatre of Revolt*, Boston, 1964.
Chekhov, Anton, *Selected Letters*, ed. L. Hellman, New York, 1955.
Margarshak, D., *Chekhov the Dramatist*, New York, 1952.
Valency, Maurice, *The Breaking String; the Plays of Anton Chekhov*, New York, 1966.
ibsen: Bradbrook, Muriel, *Ibsen, the Norwegian*, London, 1946.
Brustein, R., *The Theatre of Revolt*, Boston, 1964.
Fjelde, Rolf, ed., *Ibsen*, Englewood Cliffs, N.J., 1965.
Northam, John, *Ibsen's Dramatic Method*, London, 1953.
Shaw, G. B., *The Quintessence of Ibsenism*, New York, 1957.
Weigand, H., *The Modern Ibsen*, New York, 1960.
molière: Guicharnaud, J., ed., *Molière*, Englewood Cliffs, N.J., 1964.
Moore, W. G., *Molière, a New Criticism*, New York, 1950.
Thompson, Alan, *The Dry Mock*, Berkeley, 1948.
Turnell, M., *The Classical Moment*, New York, 1948.
pirandello: Brustein, R., *The Theatre of Revolt*, Boston, 1964.
Cambon, G., ed., *Pirandello*, Englewood Cliffs, N.J., 1967.
Starkie, Walter, *Luigi Pirandello*, London, 1926; Berkeley, 1965.
Vittorini, D., *The Drama of Luigi Pirandello*, Philadelphia, 1935.
shaw: Bentley, Eric, *Bernard Shaw*, New York, 1957.
Chesterton, G. K., *George Bernard Shaw*, London, 1909; New York, 1956.
Henderson, Archibald, *George Bernard Shaw: Man of the Century*, New York, 1956.
Irvine, W., *The Universe of G. B. S.*, New York, 1949.
Kaufmann, R. J., ed., *Shaw*, Englewood Cliffs, N.J., 1965.
Kronenberger, L., ed., *George Bernard Shaw, A Critical Survey*, Cleveland and New York, 1953.
Nethercot, A., *Men and Supermen*, Cambridge, Mass., 1954.
Winsten, S., ed., *G. B. S. 90*, New York, 1946.
sophocles: Bowra, C. M., *Sophoclean Tragedy*, Oxford, 1944.
Kitto, H. D., *Greek Tragedy*, New York, 1950.
Knox, Bernard, *The Heroic Temper, Studies in Sophoclean Tragedy*, Berkeley, 1964.
Whitman, C. H., *Sophocles*, Cambridge, Mass., 1951.
Woodard, Thomas, ed., *Sophocles*, Englewood Cliffs, N.J., 1966.
williams: Nelson, Benjamin, *Tennessee Williams*, New York, 1961.
Popkin, H., "The Plays of Tennessee Williams," *Tulane Drama Review*, IV (Spring 1960), 45-64.
Rogoff, G., "The Restless Intelligence of Tennessee Williams," *Tulane Drama Review*, X (Summer 1966), 78-92.
Tischler, Nancy, *Tennessee Williams, Rebellious Puritan*, New York, 1961.

ACKNOWLEDGEMENTS

Sophocles, *Oedipus the King*. From *Oedipus the King* by Sophocles, translated by Kenneth Cavander, published by Chandler Publishing Company, San Francisco. Copyright © 1961 by Chandler Publishing Company. Reprinted by permission.

Fergusson, "Oedipus, Myth and Play." Reprinted by permission of Princeton University Press, from *The Idea of a Theater* by Fergusson, 1949.

Aristophanes, *Lysistrata*. Translated by Jack Lindsay and reprinted with his permission.

Whitman, "War Between the Sexes." Reprinted by permission of the publishers from Cedric H. Whitman, *Aristophanes and the Comic Hero*, Cambridge, Mass.: Harvard University Press, Copyright, 1964, by the Board of Trustees of Oberlin College.

Molière, *The Misanthrope*. Molière's *The Misanthrope*, translated by Richard Wilbur. Copyright © 1954, 1955, by Richard Wilbur. Reprinted by permission of Harcourt, Brace & World, Inc. and Faber & Faber, Ltd.
CAUTION: Professionals and amateurs are hereby warned that this translation, being fully protected under the copyright laws of the United States of America, the British Empire, including the Dominion of Canada, and all other countries which are signatories to the Universal Copyright Convention and the International Copyright Union, is subject to royalty. All rights, including professional, amateur, motion picture, recitation, lecturing, public reading, radio broadcasting, and television, are strictly reserved. Particular emphasis is laid on the question of readings, permission for which must be secured from the author's agent in writing. Inquiries on profession rights should be addressed to Mr. Gilbert Parker, Savan-Parker, Inc., 59 East 54th Street, New York, New York 10019; inquiries on translation rights should be addressed to Harcourt, Brace & World, Inc.; 757 Third Avenue, New York, New York 10017.
The amateur acting rights in *The Misanthrope* are controlled exclusively by the Dramatist's Play Service, Inc., 440 Park Avenue South, New York, New York. No amateur performance of the play may be given without obtaining in advance the written permission of the Dramatists Play Service, Inc. and paying the requisite fee.

Nelson, "The Unreconstructed Heroes of Molière." By Robert Nelson. First published in the *Tulane Drama Review*, Vol. 4, No. 3, (LT7, Spring 1960) and reprinted by permission of the publisher. Copyright *Tulane Drama Review*, 1960.

Ibsen, *Ghosts*. From *Ghosts; An Enemy of the People; The Warriors at Helgeland* by Henrik Ibsen. Translated by R. Farquarson Sharp. Everyman's Library Edition. Reprinted by permission of E. P. Dutton & Co., Inc. and J. M. Dent & Sons, Ltd.

Bentley, "Ibsen—A Personal Statement." This selection is the second part of an essay originally published in EDDA, 1956, but appearing in its present form in Columbia University *Forum*, Winter, 1957, copyright © 1957 by Columbia University, copyright transferred to Eric Bentley 1958. Reprinted by permission of Eric Bentley here.

Shaw, *Caesar and Cleopatra*. Reprinted by permission of the Public Trustee and The Society of Authors.

Peacock, "Shaw." From *The Poet in the Theatre* by Ronald Peacock. Copyright 1946, copyright © 1960 by Ronald Peacock. Reprinted by permission of Hill & Wang, Inc., and Routledge & Kegan Paul Ltd.

Gorky, "Chekhov." From "Literary Portraits" in *On Literature* by Maxim Gorky. Moscow: Foreign Languages Publishing House. n.d.

Pirandello, *Six Characters in Search of an Author*. From the book *Naked Masks: Five Plays* by Luigi Pirandello. Edited by Eric Bentley. Copyright, 1922, 1952 by E. P. Dutton & Company, Inc. Renewal, 1950, in the names of Stefano, Fausto, and Lietta Pirandello. Dutton Paperback Series. Reprinted by permission of the publishers and International Copyright Bureau Ltd.

Brecht, *The Caucasian Chalk Circle*. © Copyright 1947, 1948, 1961, 1963 by Eric Bentley; prologue © copyright 1959 by Eric Bentley. Introduction © copyright 1965 by Eric Bentley. Originally published in the volume *Parables for the Theatre: Two Plays by Bertolt Brecht* by the University of Minnesota Press. Reprinted by permission.

Brecht, "Theatre for Learning." This essay first appeared in the *Tulane Drama Review*, Vol. VI, No. 1. Copyright 1961, by the *Tulane Drama Review*. Reprinted by permission of the publisher.

Williams, *The Grass Menagerie*. Copyright 1945 by Tennessee Williams and Edwina D. Williams. Reprinted from *Six Modern American Plays* by permission of Random House, Inc. and Elaine Greene, Ltd.

Faguet, "On the Nature of Dramatic Emotion." This essay first appeared in the *Tulane Drama Review*, Vol. III, No. 2. Copyright, 1958, by the *Tulane Drama Review*. Reprinted by permission of the publisher.

Lehmann, "Comedy and Laughter." From *English Studies*, Vol. 10. Reprinted by permission of the University of California Press.